CONCEPTS
and CONTROVERSY
in ORGANIZATIONAL
BEHAVIOR

edited by WALTER R. NORD
Washington University

GOODYEAR PUBLISHING COMPANY, INC.
Pacific Palisades, California

Current printing (last digit):
10 9 8 7 6 5 4 3 2 1

ISBN: 0-87620-198-2

Library of Congress Catalogue Card Number: 75-156865

Y-1982-1

Printed in the United States of America

DEDICATED TO

Ann Nord
Arthur Nord
Elizabeth Nord

Contents

Acknowledgments

Many people have contributed substantially to this book. Some have influenced my thinking, others have contributed specifically to the text as it appears, and many have helped with clerical and administrative problems.

I am most grateful to several people who have shaped my thinking about organizational behavior. Ned Rosen and Lawrence Williams first stimulated my interest in psychology and exposed me to the knowledge and methods of organizational behavior. In addition, Jack Glidewell, Richard Willis, and Robert Hamblin are a few of my many teachers who contributed greatly to my ideas. More recently, my wife, Ann has been a valued source of learning. Her questioning and creative approaches to human behavior have widened my horizons.

A second group of people has made contributions directly to the book itself. Of special importance are Karl Jackson, Marshall Rosenberg, Dennis Shea, and Arthur Schulman who prepared papers specifically to help me cover topics which otherwise could not have been included. Sterling Schoen and Raymond Hilgert introduced me to several readings which appear in the compendium. Joseph Towle, Dick Beatty, Fred Russell, Jim Rhea, Pete Skoglund and Ken Runyon all helped in a variety of ways. I especially wish to express my gratitude to Ken Runyon who was a valued and constructive critic of my work. In addition I am extremely grateful to Jane Warren whose efforts and editing skills have enabled me to express what I want to say.

Several people were extremely helpful in the compiling, clerical details, and related problems in producing a book of this kind. Those who contributed here include Virginia Reed, Joan Aach, and Ruth Scheetz. The efforts of Ruth Scheetz, whose typing translated several revisions of barely legible drafts into a readable manuscript, are most gratefully appreciated. Also, I wish to acknowledge the help of Roger Mac Quarrie who was my first contact with my publisher.

The help of the reference department of Olin Library and the supporting services of the Graduate School of Business at Washington University are gratefully acknowledged.

As always, the errors in the book are the responsibility of the author. My hope is that those who find the errors will give their best efforts to seeing that these mistakes are corrected in the literature and in the management of social organizations.

Introduction

The growth of knowledge in the behavioral sciences, accelerating since World War II, has been paralleled by an increasing recognition of the potential contributions of behavioral science to organizational effectiveness. One result has been an expanding role for psychologists and sociologists as teachers in schools of administration and as consultants to managers of organizations. The new field of organizational behavior is a product of these trends.

Although we cannot separate it completely from its foundation disciplines, we can identify certain ideas shared by those who have established organizational behavior as a field of study. First, they believe that knowledge from a wide variety of disciplines is necessary for the effective study and management of organizations. Second, knowledge from these disciplines can be and should be applied to problems of the management of people. Third, the application of knowledge can result in simultaneous increases in organizational effectiveness and the psychological health and growth of organizational particpants. Although there is disagreement as to the extent to which these two goals can be pursued concurrently, most of the work in organizational behavior is oriented to such an accommodation. Finally, the potential of organizational behavior for solving organizational problems is only beginning to be realized.

The infant field of organizational behavior is rife with problems. One set of problems is substantive. First, the findings in the foundation disciplines are often unreliable. Second, even when reliable findings exist, they usually account for only a small part of the phenomena they are attempting to explain. Third, the problems studied are complex, and relevant findings are scattered throughout several academic disciplines.

An additional set of problems is more social-psychological in nature. Even when the subject matter is not humanity, all science is confounded by the influence of values about what can be studied, what can be changed or manipulated, and what will be accepted. Ethical issues are central in the study and practice of organizational behavior. Second, "conventional wisdom" (Galbraith, 1958) often inhibits progress. Practitioners and students often have inaccurate and incomplete understanding of how organizations really work and therefore hold tenaciously to erroneous prescriptions for effective management of people. As a result, frequently the organizational behaviorist must change and/or remove existing beliefs and feelings before progress can be made. A third social-psychological problem stems from the disparity between the needs of the client population and the existing state of knowledge. Action-oriented practitioners demand answers or solutions to complex problems with a degree of precision and authority beyond what existing knowledge permits. Organizational behavior is only beginning to face these substantive and social-psychological problems.

IS ORGANIZATIONAL BEHAVIOR A USEFUL CONCEPT?

One controversial issue in organizational behavior is the name of the field itself, particularly the utility of the modifier "organizational." While arguing about names is often fruitless and unexciting, some attention to this question may help the reader develop a "feel" for the area.

Weick (1969) argued that the word "organizational" adds no meaning to "behavior" and therefore serves no useful guiding function. Behavior is behavior whether it occurs in organizations or not, and "organizational" often influences people to look for non-existent differences or discontinuities between behavior in general and behavior which occurs in organizations. Weick concluded that "organizational" has a net negative utility.

Weick is correct in stressing the continuity of behavior but errs in suggesting that "organizational" necessarily implies a lack of continuity. In fact, most people who use the term stress the continuity and do not find that the modifier "organizational" is a barrier to such a view. More importantly, "organizational" may prove to be an asset.

A term must be evaluated according to its worth in the relevant verbal community. "Organizational behavior" is useful in three ways. First, it suggests that problems in modern organizations must be approached at both the sociological and psychological levels.[1] Very often one finds psychologists attempting to apply their knowledge without an understanding of the requirements and forces existing in a formal organization. Similarly, sociologists have written about human organizations with only a limited understanding of individual behavior. "Organizational behavior," composed of a central word from each of the two major foundation disciplines, fosters the required interdisciplinary approach. "Organizational" reminds one of the important fact that organizations are social systems which have powerful effects on the behavior of participants.

Second, even though behavior is behavior whether it occurs inside or outside organizations, some determinants are more important in organizational settings than in other situations. For example, formal authority has more important consequences on behavior inside organizations than it does outside. The modifier "organizational" may well direct our attention to such variables and thus provide a useful guiding function.

[1] This is, of course a minimum requirement. Many other disciplines and fields—including political science, economics, anthropology, management, personnel, industrial engineering, and information systems—have much to contribute.

A third advantage of the term, although potentially a disadvantage too, is the utilitarian connotation that it tends to have in current usage. Organizational behavior courses are more likely to be offered by business and professional schools than by departments of psychology or sociology. The term directs attention to knowledge about behavior which can be used in the short run. In comparison with the foundation disciplines the emphasis of the area is more clinical and practical than theoretical. However, this practical tendency does not mean that theory is not important in organizational behavior. It is. Rather it means that a course or instructor in organizational behavior often asks questions of a theory in addition to those asked by an organizational sociologist or a research psychologist. The organizational behaviorist is apt to ask how and under what conditions the knowledge can be used to produce practical consequences, in addition to examining its uniqueness, its scientific merit, and its explanatory value. The applied scientist, who is interested in improving action and decisions, may find a model or a theory useful, even if it has not been "proven" or thoroughly tested. While "applied" science and "pure" science are not really separable, they emphasize different criteria of knowledge because they use that knowledge in different ways.

In summary, organizational behavior appears to be a useful term. First, it suggests the need for an interdisciplinary approach. Second, while not being inconsistent with the view that human behavior is continuous between different contexts, it also directs attention to certain classes of variables which may be relatively more important in organizational settings than elsewhere. Finally, it may describe an orientation toward action on the basis of existing (albeit limited) knowledge. In the sense that the term has a utilitarian connotation for the people in the field, it is useful.

ORGANIZATIONAL BEHAVIOR AND THE TRAINING OF MANAGERS

Managers of organizations every day are called on to make decisions and take actions concerning human behavior for which current knowledge provides no convenient guide. Courses in organizational behavior need to teach students *about* behavior, but they also need to teach students how to behave, how to learn about their own and others' behavior, and how to react to behavior and influence it by managerial action.

The emphasis on facilitating action does not indicate a non-theoretical approach. Most of the readings in this book could quite well be included in academic courses in psychology, sociology, and social psychology. In fact, many of them have been. Nevertheless, the aim of this book is to provide readings and theories which are academically sound and have a high probability of aiding the management of human resources. The existing concepts of psychology and sociology are essential tools for management action but extreme care must be exercised in moving to general principles. It is for this reason that controversy has been selected as the orienting principle of this book.

While the concepts are useful, existing knowledge does not permit certainty as to exactly what is useful exactly when and where. The literature reveals conflict among competent scholars on almost every topic. The controversy does not indicate that there is no creditable knowledge in the field. Rather, it is indicative of the complexity of human behavior in organizations, a complexity characterized by the interaction of factors varying from organization to organization and indeed from division to division and from time to time within the same organization. The best way to orient someone who must act in such systems is to increase his sensitivity to the variables, their interaction, and the variety of alternative actions which have a high probability of success under a given set of conditions. It is hoped that the emphasis on controversy will help the student to develop a "feel" for the complexity of the social systems we call organizations.

In this book the reader will not find a "best" answer; rather he will find ideas to improve his exploration in poorly mapped areas. Gouldner (1965) distinguished between "clinical" and "engineering" applications; organizational behavior, at present, is more of a clinical field. In other words, it is oriented to the needs of a particular client in a particular situation. Campbell, Dunnette, Lawler, and Weick (1970) pointed out that the management of people must be individualized in terms of the job, the person, and the organization.

Controversy as a guiding theme has important advantages for exploring organizational behavior as it now exists. Controversy should, first of all, end the prospective manager's hope that he is going to find a canned program for "instant human relations" and insulate him from those who will attempt to sell him such a program. Once students shed this expectation, they are more apt to be receptive to the ambiguity which characterizes knowledge in this field. Second, the existing controversy, rooted as it is in contradictory findings, seems to suggest that some things do "work," but only under some conditions. Thus, while extreme optimism is discouraged, all is not chaos. Controversy encourages a search for valid concepts as well as the parameters which limit their validity.

Controversy is also an important theme for developing theoretical knowledge. Boring (1929) observed that scientific truths come about through controversy. He noted that the history of science is a dialectical process, in which advances result from a long series of theses and antitheses. Often new movements are negative, overthrowing the " . . . progress of the past." The new movements must gain attention in order to overcome the "perseverative" tendency in scientific thought which, according to Boring, exists because the drive which motivates a man to do research and to publicize it also drives him to preserve his findings against criticism. New findings must fight the "establishment." Thus, science progresses by controversy of ideas but also progresses through "promoters." Ideas must be, in a sense, sold to the academic community. An important part of scientific progress is social-psychological.

The same social-psychological process characterizes organizational behavior. Interesting and valuable ideas and findings have been vigorously promoted.

Evidence of promotion can be discovered in the common practice of publishing one or a few ideas repeatedly in a variety of books and journals. In organizational behavior, the perseverative tendency may be especially strong, since the established ideas are profitable economically as well as scientifically. In applied areas, the perseverative tendency is perhaps even stronger in the uses made of the knowledge. For example, there may be strong forces which reduce the incentive to make radical changes in training programs once they have been developed and marketed. Furthermore, to the degree that a "scientist" becomes a "practitioner," he has less time to keep up with the new findings.[2] As a result, the perseverative tendency in an applied science, such as organizational behavior, may be stronger than in other types of scientific endeavor. An emphasis on controversy may help to increase the rate at which antitheses will be promoted to develop fruitful syntheses.

A further advantage to considering organizational behavior from the perspective of controversy has to do with the nature of organizations themselves. The controversies highlighted in this book, with its source in a multitude of interacting variables, should demonstrate the need for regarding organizations and management as systems. Both old and new ideas and practices must be viewed in the context of the unique state of interdependent social forces operating at a given time in the organization. In addition, this type of controversy should convey the feeling of a continuing need for evaluation and adjustment of practices in light of changes at any point in the system. Finally, the focus on controversy may stimulate comparison, which is likely to reveal areas of at least partial agreement. Furthermore, controversy has stimulus value as a source of excitement and encouragement of future exploration.

One remaining advantage of controversy may be the most important one. Controversy may have the important advantage of developing a feeling—or what some might wish to call an intuitive ability—about systems. Cognitive awareness that organizations are complex systems is only part of the battle. We have known this for a long time. The real application of organizational behavior may require us to do more than to "think systems". Rather, it may require affective or emotional characteristics, thought patterns, and information-processing abilities which have yet to be developed.[3] Organizational participants need an ability to search out the systems variables, to "feel" the complexity and diversity of human systems. It is hoped that the focus on controversy will convey not only the current concepts but also help the students to develop a better "feel" for appreciating and dealing with organizations as systems.

A caution about controversy. While the organization around controversy helps to convey the state of knowledge in organizational behavior in a realistic, comprehensive, and exciting way, it has possible disadvantages. One point of caution is especially important. The apparent lack of agreement among "the experts" can lead a beginning student to feel that organizational behavior is a chaotic field and therefore of little practical importance. Such discouragement can be a real barrier to learning unless the student is helped to search for areas of

[2] This problem is perhaps most clearly recognized in medicine.
[3] The need to train people to respond in systems terms will be more fully treated in the concluding note at the end of the work.

accord. The introductory sections throughout the book stress commonality and agreement as well as controversy. The concluding chapter is also designed to aid the integration process.

To be sure, teaching beginning students about the controversy in the field runs the risk of losing them through discouragement. However, failing to give them the controversy may lead them to a false sense of security and acceptance of current "knowledge." Both of these are serious errors. Given the current state of knowledge in the area, the second error would seem to be more dangerous than the first. In such a rapidly changing, relatively immature field, questioning and analysis would seem more likely to have utility for future managers and academicians than would premature acceptance. At the present time we must develop diagnosticians. Controversy acts to stimulate creative thought and search. If nothing else, even if the student becomes discouraged by looking at the controversy, he is apt to learn something about how to learn in this field, which may well be the most important skill that can be transmitted.

ORGANIZATION OF THE BOOK

The readings demonstrate the major concepts in organizational behavior as well as the controversies at both the applied and conceptual levels. In some cases the controversy is contained within one selection, while in others it is between consecutive selections. The readings are organized in four parts. The first three view organizations in terms of variables commonly considered by psychologists, sociologists, and social psychologists. The final part focuses on several behaviorally-based management strategies and future possibilities. Generally, the introductory sections and the early readings attempt to develop the conceptual basis of the field. Many of the other readings are concerned with application. Finally, in several sections, short integrating selections appear after the readings since certain points seemed most relevant if they followed the readings rather than introduced them.

Focus On The Individual

Part I introduces basic concepts about human behavior. The section begins with the nature-nurture controversy, moves into consideration of perception and motivation, and finally explores personal development in terms of learning and culture. The coverage of these topics, while of limited depth, does include many basic psychological issues.

The first topic, the nature and nurture question, provides a basis for evaluating assumptions which managers and students often make about human nature. The literature in this area is replete with explicit and implicit assumptions about man's nature but offers very little supporting evidence. The study of organizational behavior must begin with some understanding of the properties of man and the limits of his modifiability. The next two sections in part I include some of the more standard readings on perception and motivation, although especially the section on motivation, a focus on controversy encourages evaluation of the "conventional wisdom" in the field. Many books in this area limit their treatment of motivation to the work of Maslow, McGregor, and Herzberg. However, recent work dealing with motivation, in both the theoretical and applied sense, suggests just how tentative the widely accepted beliefs really are. The final selections in part I deal with personality, learning, culture, and some ethical issues about the control of behavior. The focus on environment in this section helps to set the stage for part II.

Organizations As Systems

Part II introduces the student to the properties of formal organizations—those complex social systems which are distinguished from other social groups primarily by their being deliberately structured for the achievement of stated goals. Understanding formal organizations requires knowledge about the interaction between their deliberately created structure and their human resources. From the point of view of organizational planners, often the human beings appear to be "villains" rather than resources. Part II attempts to clarify the reasons for human problems in organizations. It begins with a brief overview of the study and theory of formal organizations. Then it attempts to help the student to see how unanticipated outcomes develop in organizations and how both anticipated and unanticipated outcomes affect organizational and personal goals.

Social Processes

Successful management requires the integration of organizational and personal goals. Part III introduces some of the basic social-psychological variables which are related to this integration. The concept of influence is central to this section. The readings deal with how influence is exerted through communication, power, attitudes, and group behavior.

In general, part III attempts to provide the student with some basic social-psychological concepts which are central in behavioral approaches to management.

Some Answers To Management Problems

The final part of this book deals with some common approaches that behavioral scientists have been instrumental in introducing into organizational management. The two topics dealt with extensively are participative management—or democratic leadership, and management by objectives. Although both of these topics are dealt with earlier in the book, in the final part they are treated as strategies in themselves. A third paper in this section demonstrates a newer contingency approach. A concluding note, prepared by the editor, attempts to provide some possible directions in which the field organizational behavior may develop.

OVERVIEW

Materials which are basic to successful management are presented in a manner which may aid the understanding and application of what we know and the exploration of what we need to know. In addition to the basic concepts, a variety of points of view are highlighted throughout this entire book. The student of organizational behavior will find selections from many "old friends," such as Maslow, McGregor, Herzberg, Argyris, and Homans. However, he will find some powerful challenges to their ideas. While the "human-relations tradition" is seriously considered, so are a number of counter-arguments. Many of these new ideas, rather than rejecting the human-relations view, have qualified and limited it. While human relations is still an important force in the nucleus of organizational behavior, the field itself has grown well beyond its core.

The book is intended primarily for future practitioners and beginning academicians. Many competing anthologies already exist. Some are heavily oriented toward sociology or psychology, and some are well balanced. All attempt to overcome common problems. First, how can an immature and imprecise body of knowledge about complex, interacting variables be translated into action in such complex social systems as organizations? Second, in an interdisciplinary field how can one be all things to all men? This book faces the same problems and limitations but deals with them a little differently. The attempt to highlight both the concepts and controversy should promote learning, inquiry, and a realistic approach (both cognitively and emotionally) to application.

part 1

INDIVIDUAL BEHAVIOR

All decisions and actions by a person are influenced by implicit and/or explicit assumptions about the nature of reality. This fact is especially important in social interaction; my assumptions influence my behavior toward others and hence affect their behavior toward me. For example, if I treat someone as if he were hostile, he often will become hostile. Faulty assumptions about "human nature" are dangerous because they may generate undesired consequences; and because they are often self-fulfilling, they may lead to problems which cannot be easily diagnosed or corrected. It is the purpose of this first section to explore what is known about the properties of a human being and to develop some implications of this knowledge for the behavior of people in organizations.

This section may be most meaningful if the reader engages in a personal exercise before continuing. Record your answers to the following questions: What is man basically like?—i.e., what is his basic nature, and how malleable is he? How do people interact with their social and physical environment?—i.e., how do they view their environment and learn about it? What causes men to act or behave?—i.e., what motivates man? Finally, in view of your answers to the first three questions, how could you design a society or a social system which could change man in any direction in which you would like to change him? What problems would you face in developing such a system? How would you apply these principles to the design of work organizations? These are the questions that organizational psychology seeks to answer.

After reading part 1, the reader should repeat this exercise and measure his learning by comparing the two sets of answers. Hopefully, his assumptions will be both clearer to himself and more complex; that is, he will have gained a greater awareness of the variables which need to be considered in the management of human resources. The frustrating "nature-nurture" question underlies all issues in human behavior.

chapter 1

The Nature-Nurture Question

The question of the relative influence of heredity and environment on human behavior is at the root of all psychology and management of human behavior. The issue is frustrating because it is difficult to investigate. The major research problem is that most human traits are a product of both nature and nurture.

Research on the nature-nurture issue has been hampered by the difficulty of doing precise work with human subjects. First, the only pairs of people with the same genetic compositions are identical twins, and almost never is there enough information about their environments to allow conclusive research. Our attitude toward the use of humans for research do not permit the appropriate experiments to be conducted. Second, research dealing with human beings is influenced by other value questions. For example, much research on the nature-nurture issue has been designed to prove or disprove the hypothesis that racial differences in such factors as intelligence are innate. Jensen (1969) demonstrated how complex such issues really are and how certain value judgments of psychologists have perhaps influenced the nature of inquiry. Jensen's thorough and scholarly work sent shock waves throughout the liberal community of academic psychologists by documenting the case that racial differences in intelligence are largely genetic. Many of the reactions to Jensen's work have reflected value dimensions. However, many of them involved important substantive matters. For example, a group of experts (Kagan, Hunt, Crow, Bereiter, Elkind, Cronbach, and Brazziel, 1969), in reacting to Jensen's article demonstrated the controversy and complexity of the problem by disagreeing sharply both with Jensen and among themselves. A useful way of dealing with these difficulties for purposes of this book is to assume an "interactionist" position.

One of the major contributors to current understanding of an "interactionist" view has been the geneticist Dobzhansky (1964). He has argued that, to deal with the nature-nurture question adequately, we must ask it in an appropriate manner. Dobzhansky maintained that almost all traits are a product of the interaction of both genetic and environmental forces. Therefore, the question is not whether a given trait is a result of nature or nurture but rather to what extent different traits are influenced by genes and by environment. Of course, establishing the relative contribution of each is a difficult task. The selection by Dobzhansky in this section gives his argument in more detail.

The nature-nurture issue is further complicated by the conditions which are experienced between conception and birth. McCurdy (1961) argued convincingly that variations in the prenatal environment play a vital role in an individual's development. Thus, even a complete understanding of genetics and comprehensive knowledge of post-birth environments would not be enough to account for all the variation in human behavior.

Nevertheless, recent research has provided some interesting insights. Three sets of studies, in addition to the work cited in following selections, deserve brief mention.

First is the exploratory work of Rosenzweig (1966). He found that he could induce physical and chemical changes in the brains of rodents by varying the complexity of the environment. Animals reared in "enriched" environments (i.e., environments offering many stimuli) were better at solving problems than animals reared in deprived (i.e., relatively unstimulating environments). Remarkably, certain portions of the brains of the "enriched" animals were larger than those of the deprived. Of course, it is difficult to generalize about human behavior from such experiments, but the results do suggest the possibility that environmental experience may be encoded via physiological changes, which in turn may influence the ability to learn. Again, the question with respect to intelligence is not nature or nurture but degree of nature and nurture.

A second line of inquiry, by Bell (1968), questioned the model of socialization which takes into account only the effects of parental behavior on children. Bell cited considerable evidence that certain congenital factors contribute to types of child behavior, which in turn influence parental behavior. Infants differ in assertiveness, activity, and desire for such stimuli as social reinforcement. As a result, the same parents respond differently to different children. Compare, for example, the probable adult actions toward a sickly, delicate child with those toward a healthy, robust one. Thus, while environmental experience may be encoded via physiological changes, which in behaves, the action of a child himself may be an independent variable which partially determines the environment. The interaction of nature and nurture is thus more complex than assumed, since nature to some degree determines nurture.

The third set of studies has been provided by ethologists, zoologists who study animal behavior. According to Tinbergen (1968), the ethological approach applies the method of biology to behavior to study the relationship of behavior to the survival of the animal, the causes of the behavior at a given moment, the development of the behavioral machinery through individual growth, and the evolution of behavioral systems within a particular species. Tinbergen argued that this approach should be applied to the study of man himself. Such an application suggests some interesting ideas about the nature-nurture question and the very survival of social organization as we know it.

Tinbergen argued that there are "innate" patterns which depend on interaction with the environment for their development.[1] For example, certain parts of the eye of a tadpole do not function properly unless they have been exposed to light. Also, evidence exists that birds acquire their songs in part through exposure to the full song of an adult male of the same species. Furthermore, while behavior is influenced by rewards which follow it, the particular rewards which have effects vary from one species, stage of development, or occasion to another. Thus, development of behavior is a product of "programmed instructions" given by one's genetic membership in a species and their interaction with the environment. Language learning is a prime example. A human infant can make many sounds. However, the particular sounds he comes to make will be only the ones his environment supports. Again, the notion of complete interrelatedness of nature and nurture in development is clear.

Consideration of innate predispositions and mechanisms provides an important new dimension to the nature-nurture question which may have profound implications for organizational behavior. Many theories of psychology and management have failed to consider the species-specific nature of behavior. The interactionist view of behavior as determined jointly by species characteristics, inherited individual differences, and behavioral modifications of individuals may provide a useful model for understanding organizational behavior. Many theories of psychology and management have failed to consider the species-specific nature of behavior. Many approaches to organizational behavior tend to focus on certain variables which highlight the similarity of all men. Other theories focus on variables which highlight individual differences among men. The approach here suggests that men are more homogeneous on some dimensions than in others. Where greater homogeneity exists, it is expected that the characteristic may be common to the species rather than peculiar to some individuals. The search should be directed to distinguishing these dimensions from each other. The practical approach to each set of dimensions is different. Along some dimensions, on which most men are relatively homogeneous, the design of social systems may best take certain characteristics as given. On other variables, there are important individual differences between many people. Where such heterogeneity exists there are two practical choices: selection of people with the desired characteristics and training of those without them. In part this choice is determined by the relative contributions of heredity and environment. Obviously, training is apt to be more useful when environment contributes substantial variance. However, the species questions must still be considered. For example, even though some responses may be largely environmentally determined, often they are easier to learn at certain stages of development. Improper assumptions about the nature-nurture issue can lead to an excess of either optimism or pessimism about the potential of man. Both consequences are costly, since they misdirect resources allocated to treatment of human problems.

---

1. While it is not directly relevant here, it should be noted that Tinbergen also maintained that learning at various developmental stages is limited by "internally imposed restrictions."

By way of summary, the nature-nurture question is very difficult to answer, even when it is appropriately phrased. The evidence suggests that species factors, individual genetics, and environment are all important factors. The readings which follow support this contention. Dobzhansky suggests just how complex the interaction is. Hebb, in the second article, deals indirectly with the nature-nurture question by suggesting that all behavior must be viewed in the context of the environment in which it occurs. In other words, a person is highly dependent on the state of his environment and, at least to some degree, is a different individual in every context. Changes in the protective cocoon in which the individual functions, produce change in the individual's behavior.

This argument is extremely important for managers of organizations. Changes in the organizational and social climate produce changes in the organizational participant. Each individual is a unique human being. In addition to being different from other people in many ways, an individual constantly exhibits changes in himself as he experiences new or different environments. Inappropriate assumptions about the nature-nurture issue often lead into systematic overestimation of the stability of individual characteristics, consequently underestimating [2] the influences of environmental factors in organizational performance. Some assumptions about the nature-nurture question, either explicit or implicit, underlie all approaches to management and organizational behavior. The following readings attempt to improve the quality of these assumptions.

REFERENCES

Bell, Richard Q. "A Reinterpretation of the Direction of Effects of Studies of Socialization." *Psychological Review* 75 (1968): 81-95.

Dobzhansky, Theodosius. *Heredity and the Nature of Man.* New York: New American Library, 1964.

Jensen, Arthur J. "How Much Can We Boost IQ and Scholastic Achievement?" *Harvard Educational Review* 39, no. 1 (1969): 1-123.

Kagan, J. S., Hunt J. Mc., Crow, J. F., Bereiter, C., Elkind, D., Cronbach, L. J., and Brazziel, W. F. "How Much Can We Boost IQ and Scholastic Achievement?" A discussion. *Harvard Educational Review* 39, no. 1 (1969): 273-356.

McCurdy, Harold Grier. *The Personal World.* New York: Harcourt Brace Jovanovich, Inc., 1961.

Rosenzweig, Mark R. "Environmental Complexity, Cerebral Change, and Behavior." *American Psychologist* 21 (1966): 321-32.

Tinbergen, N. "On War and Peace in Animals and Man." *Science* 160 (1968): 1411-18.

---

2. Inappropriate assumptions about the nature-nurture issue can also lead to an overestimation of the role of environmental factors with equally costly consequences. At present, most managers I have met seem to make the error described in the text above.

Theodosius Dobzhansky

HEREDITY

GENOTYPE AND PHENOTYPE

The biological inheritance of every person consists of genes received from his parents. The totality of the genes is the "genotype." The concept of the genotype framed by Johannsen (1909, 1911) is now extended beyond its initial usage: the genotype subsumes all self-reproducing bodily constituents regardless of their localization — the genes in the chromosomes as well as the plasmogenes in the cell cytoplasm.

The function of the genotype, or at least one of its functions, is to make more of itself: genes induce synthesis of their own copies. Some of the shorthand language used by biologists is grossly misleading if its metaphorical character is not understood. For example, what is the meaning of the often made statement that the genotype of a person does not change in his lifetime? Since the amount of deoxyribonucleic acids in the cell nucleus is doubled between the end of one cell division and the beginning of the next, I obviously no longer have the genes which I had as an infant or as a fertilized egg cell; what I do have, instead, are true copies of these genes. It is even less accurate to say that I carry the genes of my remote ancestors, because I possess copies of only some of their genes. My genes do not change, but solely in the sense that they make new genes just like themselves.

It is an interesting speculation, but nothing more, that the development of the body is a by-product of the self-copying of the genes. The genes reproduce themselves by converting the materials taken up from their surroundings in the cell into their replicas. But cells and organisms, any organisms whatever, grow and reproduce by assimilation of food, in other words by intake of suitable materials from the environment. However, not all cell components give rise to their replicas, as genes do; for example, muscle and nerve fibers and various secretions are not present in the sex cells but are formed by, or from, other cell constituents, ultimately by or from genes.

A long, complex, and little known sequence of processes intervene between the genotype which was present in the egg cell at fertilization and the organism as we observe it. These processes are subsumed under the name "development." Development is neither completed in the womb nor concluded at birth. Although the embryonic, or fetal, development is the period when changes are rapid and spectacular, development goes on throughout life—infancy, childhood,

From Theodosius Dobzhansky, *Mankind Evolving: the Evolution of the Human Species,* pp. 40-46. Reprinted by Permission of Yale University Press, © 1962 by Yale University.

adolescence, maturity, senility, and inevitable dissolution. Life is unceasing development, although some organisms, such as seeds and spores of plants, may remain quiescent for more or less long periods. However that may be, the organism can be observed and studied at any stage of the eternally recurrent metamorphosis of life. To designate the sum total of the observable characteristics of the organism, Johannsen has proposed the term "phenotype."

The phenotype changes throughout time. The changes in the phenotype of a person may be shown by, for example, a series of photographs taken at different ages, but it should be stressed that the phenotype includes more than the external appearance of a person: his physiology, metabolism, gross and microscopic anatomy, bodily chemical processes, even the appearance of the chromosomes in his cells—all are aspects of the phenotype, as are his behavior, thinking processes, and adjustment or maladjustment to society. In short, the phenotype is the total of everything that can be observed or inferred about an individual, excepting only his genes. The phenotype obviously cannot be inherited; it can only develop as life goes on. As stated above, only the genes are inherited or, more precisely still, only the genes in the sex cells, of which the genes that an individual possesses are true copies.

The genes interact with the environment, and the outcome is the process of development, or aging. Development results in an orderly succession of phenotypes. The genotype determines the reactions and responses of the developing, or aging, organism to the environment: it determines the norm of reaction. My phenotype at this moment has been determined by the norm of reaction of my genotype to the succession of environments that I have met in my lifetime; my phenotype tomorrow, or a year hence, will be determined by its present state, as modified by my responses to the environments that I shall have encountered in the meantime.

All the traits, characters, or features of the phenotype are, of necessity, determined by the genotype and by the sequence of environments with which the genotype interacts. There is no organism without a genotype and no genotype can exist outside a spatio-temporal continuum, an environment.

WHICH CHARACTERISTICS ARE HEREDITARY AND WHICH ENVIRONMENTAL?

The man in the street believes that some traits are herditary and others environmental. Belief in a sharp dichotomy between hereditary and environmental traits almost invariably goes hand in hand with a misunderstanding of the roles of social conditions and medicine and education: an hereditary disease is supposedly incurable, a disease contracted by exposure to some noxious environment may perhaps be cured; if the IQ of a child depends on his schooling, then it cannot be hereditary.

The dichotomy of hereditary and environmental traits is, however, untenable: in principle any trait is modifiable by changes in the genes and by manipulation of the environment. Contrary to the . . . opinion of Adler [1927] recognition of the genotypic component in human personality need not hinder the educator nor deprive him of confidence. Education is a form of management of the human environment, and except for a pathological minority, all human genotypes respond to some extent to this management. But the educator had better recognize that not all genotypes respond uniformly and different genotypes may profit most by different forms of management.

At this point, illustrations of what is meant by the statement that all characters or traits are both genotypic and environmental are in order. It is generally agreed that at least some forms of the disease known as diabetes mellitus are genetically conditioned, although it is still uncertain whether the disease behaves as a Mendelian recessive or dominant or whether there are several varieties of the disease with different genetic causations . . . . Physiologically, the disease is due to a failure of certain cells in the pancreas to secrete enough of the hormone insulin, needed for normal utilization of blood sugars. This leads to the excretion of sugar in the urine, accumulation of fatty acids in the blood stream and blood vessels, and susceptibility to infections and other complications which may result in death. When diabetes is discovered, a reduction of sugars and starches in the diet is prescribed and in mild cases this treatment may suffice to remove the symptoms. In more severe cases regular injections of insulin are necessary to maintain health. Thus, diabetes can be "cured" by manipulation of the environment.

Most certainly neither the dietary rules nor the insulin injections change the "diabetic genes" and make the pancreas manufacture its own insulin, although they do relieve the morbid symptoms of the disease: health or disease is surely a condition of the phenotype, i.e., the well-being of person with a certain genotype requires a sugar-free but insulin-rich environment. One may even speculate that a mankind consisting entirely of persons with diabetic genotypes could be reasonably well off in in an environment where factories maintained a regular supply of synthetic insulin. Diabetes would then be an environmental disease caused by insulin deficiency, like the once-dreaded but now fortunately preventable scurvy, which is caused by a deficiency of vitamin C.

Conversely, malaria, syphilis, and influenza are environmental diseases: they arise because of infection with specific microorganisms, and persons who live in environments free of the infecting agents are free of the diseases. And yet the microorganisms infect only possessors of certain genotypes − particularly human genotypes. (Very few other animals that can be infected with the human forms of these diseases are known, and it is surely not accidental that susceptibility to syphilis, for example, is restricted to man's closest relatives among the primates.) Furthermore, not all human beings are easily infected with malaria or influenza, and there are good reasons to think that a part of the variation in susceptibility is genetic. It has long been believed people of European origin are more likely to contract malaria and to have a severe form of the disease than natives of many tropical lands. Swellengrebel (1940) found such a situation in parts of Guiana: the human population and the malarial parasite had reached a sort of mutual accommodation, with most of the potential hosts infected but the disease rarely lethal. The discovery of Allison (1945a,b, 1955) that persons heterozygous for the sickle-cell gene are relatively immune to infection with quartan malaria is an even better example. Although this situation will be discussed in more detail later, we should here consider a population in which some persons carry the gene for sickle cells and others do not. If such a population lived in a tropical lowland where quartan malaria was pandemic, the infection or noninfection with malaria might conceivably be a matter of heredity rather than environment.

HEREDITARY AND ENVIRONMENTAL DIFFERENCES

I certainly do not maintain that the nature-nurture problem is meaningless and that all human variation is always due as much to heredity as to environment. But to make the distinction between genetic and environmental effects on the phenotype meaningful, the problem must be stated with greater care than it often is.

It is easy to observe that some people have dark and others light skins; some enjoy robust health and others are handicapped in various ways; some are bright and others dull; some have kindly and others irascible dispositions. Skin pigmentation, health, intelligence, and temperament are all, like life itself, necessarily determined by the interaction of the genotypes with their environments. A question may, however, be validly posed: To what extent are the differences observed between persons due to genotypic or to environmental causes (Fig.1)? Or to put it another way: What part of the observed variance in a given trait in a given population is due to the diversity of the genotypes and what part to the diversity of the environments?

With the problem so stated, two things become apparent. First, the contribution of the genetic and environmental variables may be quite different for different characteristics: to which blood group a person belongs is decided, as far as is known, entirely by the genotype and not at all by the environment; which language a person speaks is decided entirely by environment and not at all by genotype, except that some low-grade mental defectives may be unable to learn any language and the defect may be genetic. Second, the relative weights of the genetic and the environmental variables are not constant: they change in space and time.

Take human stature as an example. It has been known for a long time that children of tall parents are on the average taller than those of short parents, but by itself this proves nothing, since a parent-offspring correlation may be due to common genes or common environments. Studies of twins have shown, however, that monozygotic twins, when reared together or apart, resemble each other in stature more than do dizygotic twins. There is, then, a strong genetic component in the determination of stature. (The statures of the twins described in the classical work of Newman, Freeman, and Holzinger, 1937, were correlated rather more closely than in the newer study of Osborn and DeGeorge, 1959. . . .) On the other hand, children of Japanese immigrants born in the United States are taller than their parents born in Japan. The environment is clearly responsible for a part of the variance in stature. If environment becomes homogeneous, owing to more uniform diet and child care, people will differ in stature mostly

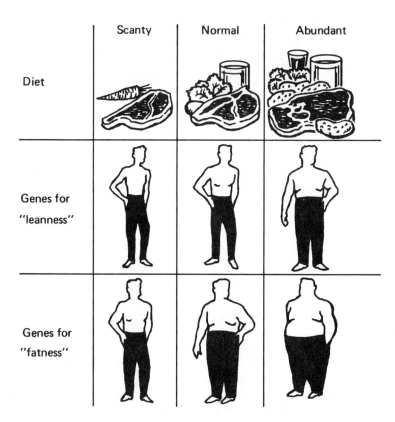

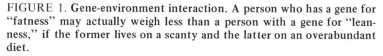

FIGURE 1. Gene-environment interaction. A person who has a gene for "fatness" may actually weigh less than a person with a gene for "leanness," if the former lives on a scanty and the latter on an overabundant diet.

because of the differences in their genes and, conversely, in genetically homogeneous populations the environmental differences will account for a relatively greater part of the variance in stature than in genetically heterogeneous ones. There is clearly no single solution to the nature-nurture problem, and the matter must be studied separately for each character. Even then the results may have validity only for a population studied at a certain time and place

*   *   *

REFERENCES

Adler A. *Understanding Human Nature.* New York: Premier Books, (Fawcett), 1957.

Allison, A.C. Protection Afforded by Sickle Cell Trait Against Subtertian Malarial Infection, *Brit. Med. J.* 1: 290-92.

—— "Notes on Sickle-Cell Polymorphism." *Ann. Human Genetics* 19: 39-57.

—— "Aspects of Polymorphism in Man." *Cold Spring Harbor Symp. Quant. Biol.* 20: 239-55.

Johannsen, W. *Elemente der exakten Erbichkeitslehre.* Jean: Fischer, 1909.

—— *The Genotype Conception of Heredity. Am. Nat.* 45 (1911): 129-59.

Osborn, R.H., and F.V. DeGeorge. *Genetic Basis of Morphological Variation.* Cambridge: Harvard University Press, 1959.

Swellengrebel, N.H. "The Efficient Parasite." *Proceedings of the 3rd International Congress on Microbiology* 1940, 119-27.

D. O. Hebb

THE MAMMAL
AND HIS ENVIRONMENT

The original intention in this paper was to discuss the significance of neuro-physiological theory for psychiatry and psychology, and to show, by citing the work done by some of my colleagues, that the attempt to get at the neural mechanisms of behavior can stimulate and clarify purely behavioral—that is, psychiatric and psychological—thinking. The research to be described has, I think, a clear relevance to clinical problems; but its origin lay in efforts to learn how the functioning of individual neurons and synapses relates to the functions of the whole brain, and to understand the physiological nature of learning, emotion, thinking, or intelligence.

In the end, however, my paper has simply become a review of the research referred to, dealing with the relation of the mammal to his environment. The question concerns the normal variability of the sensory environment and this has been studied from two points of view. First, one may ask what the significance of perceptual activity is during growth; for this purpose one can rear an animal with a considerable degree of restriction, and see what effects there are upon mental development. Secondly, in normal animals whose development is complete, one can remove a good deal of the supporting action of the normal environment, to discover how far the animal continues to be dependent on it even after maturity.

THE ROLE OF THE ENVIRONMENT
DURING GROWTH

The immediate background of our present research on the intelligence and

From D. O. Hebb, "The Mammal and His Environment," *American Journal of Psychiatry,* 111 (1955): 826-31. Copyright 1955, the American Psychiatric Association.

personality of the dog is the work of Hymovitch (6) on the intelligence of rats. He reared laboratory rats in 2 ways: (1) in a psychologically restricted environment, a small cage, with food and water always at hand and plenty of opportunity for exercise (in an activity wheel), but with no problems to solve, no need of getting on with others, no pain; and (2) in a "free" environment, a large box with obstacles to pass, blind alleys to avoid, other rats to get on with, and thus ample opportunity for problem-solving and great need for learning during growth. Result: the rats brought up in a psychologically restricted (but biologically adequate) environment have a lasting inferiority in problem-solving. This does not mean, of course, the environment is everything, heredity nothing: here heredity was held constant, which prevents it from affecting the results. When the reverse experiment is done we find problem solving varying with heredity instead. The same capacity for problem-solving is fully dependent on both variables for its development.

To take this further, Thompson and others have been applying similar methods to dogs (9). The same intellectual effect of an impoverished environment is found again, perhaps more marked in the higher species. But another kind of effect can be seen in dogs, which have clearly marked personalities. Personality—by which I mean complex individual differences of emotion and motivation—is again strongly affected by the infant environment. These effects, however, are hard to analyze, and I cannot at present give any rounded picture of them.

First, observations during the rearing itself are significant. A Scottish terrier is reared in a small cage, in isolation from other Scotties and from the human staff. Our animal man, William Ponman, is a dog lover and undertook the experiment with misgivings, which quickly disappeared. In a cage 30 by 30 inches, the dogs are "happy as larks," eat more than normally reared dogs, grow well, are physically vigorous: as Ponman says, "I never saw such healthy dogs—they're like bulls." If you put a normally reared dog into such a cage, shut off from everything, his misery is unmistakable, and we have not been able to bring ourselves to continue such experiments. Not so the dog that has known nothing else. Ponman showed some of these at a dog show of national standing, winning first-prize ribbons with them.

Observations by Dr. Ronald Melzack on pain are extremely interesting. He reared two dogs, after early weaning, in complete isolation, taking care that there was little opportunity for experience of pain (unless the dog bit himself). At maturity, when the dogs were first taken out for study, they were extraordinarily excited, with random, rapid movement. As a result they got their tails or paws stepped on repeatedly—but paid no attention to an event that would elicit howls from a normally reared dog. After a few days, when their movements were calmer, they were tested with an object that gave electric shock, and paid little attention to it. Through five testing periods, the dog repeatedly thrust his nose into a lighted match; and months later, did the same thing several times with a lighted cigar.

A year and a half after coming out of restriction they are still hyperactive. Clipping and trimming one of them is a two man job; if the normal dog does not stand still, a cuff on the ear will remind him of his duty; but cuffing the experimental dog "has as much effect as if you patted him—except he pays no attention to it." It seems certain, especially in view of the related results reported by Nissen, Chow, and Semmes (7) for a chimpanzee, that the adult's perception of pain is essentially a function of pain experience during growth—and that what we call pain is not a single sensory quale but a complex mixture of a particular kind of synthesis with past learning and emotional disturbance.

Nothing bores the dogs reared in restriction. At an "open house," we put two restricted dogs in one enclosure, two normal ones in another, and asked the public to tell us which were the normal. Without exception, they picked out the two alert, lively, interested animals—not the lackadaisical pair lying in the corner, paying no attention to the visitors. The alert pair, actually, were the restricted; the normal dogs had seen all they wanted to see of the crowd in the first two minutes, and then went to sleep, thoroughly bored. The restricted dogs, so to speak, haven't the brains to be bored.

Emotionally, the dogs are "immature," but not in the human or clinical sense. They are little bothered by imaginative fears. Dogs suffer from irrational fears, like horses, porpoises, elephants, chimpanzees, and man; but it appears that this is a product of intellectual development, characteristic of the brighter, not the duller animal. Our dogs in restriction are not smart enough to fear strange objects. Things that cause fear in normal dogs produce only a generalized, undirected excitement in the restricted. If both normal and restricted dogs are exposed to the same noninjurious but exciting stimulus repeatedly, fear gradually develops in the restricted; but the normals, at first afraid, have by this time gone on to show a playful aggression instead. On the street, the restricted dogs "lead well," not bothered by what goes on around them, while those reared normally vary greatly in this respect. Analysis has a long way to go in these cases, but we can say now that dogs reared in isolation are not like ordinary dogs. They are both stupid and peculiar.

Such results clearly support the clinical evidence, and the animal experiments of others (1), showing that early environment has a lasting effect on the form of adjustment at maturity. We do not have a great body of evidence yet, and before we generalize too much it will be particularly important to repeat these observations with animals of different heredity. But I have been very surprised, personally, by the lack of evidence of emotional instability, neurotic tendency, or the like, when the dogs are suddenly plunged into a normal world. There is, in fact, just the opposite effect. This suggests caution in interpreting data with human children, such as those of Spitz (8) or Bowlby (3). Perceptual restriction in infancy certainly produces a low level of intelligence, but it may not, by itself, produce emotional disorder. The observed results seem to mean, not that the stimulus of another attentive organism (the mother) is necessary from the first but that it may become necessary only as psychological *dependence* on the mother develops. However, our limited data certainly cannot prove anything for man, though they may suggest other interpretations besides those that have been made.

THE ENVIRONMENT AT MATURITY

Another approach to the relation between the mammal and his environment is possible: that is, one can take the normally reared mammal and cut him off at maturity from his usual contact with the world. It seems clear that thought and personality characteristics develop as a function of the environment. Once developed, are they independent of it? This experiment is too cruel to do with animals, but not with college students. The first stage of the work was done by Bexton, Heron, and Scott(2). It follows up some work by Mackworth on the effects of monotony, in which he found extraordinary lapses of attention. Heron and his co-workers set out to make the monotony more prolonged and more complete.

The subject is paid to do nothing 24 hours a day. He lies on a comfortable bed in a small closed cubicle, is fed on request, goes to the toilet on request. Otherwise he does nothing. He wears frosted glass goggles that admit light but do not allow pattern vision. His ears are covered by a sponge rubber pillow in which are embedded small speakers by which he can be communicated with, and a microphone hangs near to enable him to answer. His hands are covered with gloves, and cardboard cuffs extend from the upper forearm beyond his fingertips, permitting free joint movement but with little tactual perception.

The results are dramatic. During the stay in the cubicle, the experimental subject shows extensive loss, statistically significant, in solving simple problems. He complains subjectively that he cannot concentrate; his boredom is such that he looks forward eagerly to the next problem, but when it is presented he finds himself unwilling to make the effort to solve it.

On emergence from the cubicle the subject is given the same kind of intelligence tests as before entering, and shows significant loss. There is disturbance of motor control. Visual perception is changed in a way difficult to describe; it is as if the object looked at was exceptionally vivid, but impaired in its relation to other objects and the background — a disturbance perhaps of the larger organization of perception. This condition may last up to 12 or 24 hours.

Subjects reported some remarkable hallucinatory activity, some which resembled the effects of mescal, or the results produced by Grey Walter with flickering light. These hallucinations were primarily visual, perhaps only because the experimenters were able to control visual perception most effectively; however, some auditory and somesthetic hallucinations have been observed as well.

The nature of these phenomena is best conveyed by quoting one subject who reported over the microphone that he had just been asleep and had a very vivid dream and although he was awake, the dream was continuing. The study of dreams has a long history, and is clearly important theoretically, but is hampered by the impossibility of knowing how much the subject's report is distorted by memory. In many ways the hallucinatory activity of the present experiments is indistinguishable from what we know about dreams; if it is in essence the same process, but going on while the subject can describe it (not merely hot but still on the griddle), we have a new source of information, a means of direct attack, on the nature of the dream.

In its early stages the activity as it occurs in the experiment is probably not dream like. The course of development is fairly consistent. First, when the eyes are closed the visual field is light rather than dark. Next there are reports of dots of light, lines, or simple geometrical patterns, so vivid that they are described as being a new experience. Nearly all experimental subjects reported such activity. (Many of course could not tolerate the experimental conditions very long, and left before the full course of development was seen.) The next stage is the occurrence of repetitive patterns, like a wallpaper design, reported by three-quarters of the subjects; next, the appearance of isolated objects, without background, seen by half the subjects; and finally, integrated scenes, involving action, usually containing dreamlike distortions, and apparently with all the vividness of an animated cartoon, seen by about a quarter of the subjects. In general, these amused the subject, relieving his boredom, as he watched to see what the movie program would produce next. The subjects reported that the scenes seemed to be out in front of them. A few could, apparently, "look at" different parts of the scene in central vision, as one could with a movie; and up to a point could change its content by "trying." It was not, however, well under control. Usually, it would disappear if the subject were given an interesting task, but not when the subject described it, nor if he did physical exercises. Its persistence and vividness interfered with sleep for some subjects, and at this stage was irritating.

In their later stages the hallucinations were elaborated into everything from a peaceful rural scene to naked women diving and swimming in a woodland pool to prehistoric animals plunging through tropical forests. One man saw a pair of spectacles, which were then joined by a dozen more, without wearers, fixed intently on him; faces sometimes appeared behind the glasses, but with no eyes visible. The glasses sometimes moved in unison, as if marching in procession. Another man saw a field onto which a bathtub rolled: it moved slowly on rubber-tired wheels, with chrome hub caps. In it was seated an old man wearing a battle helmet. Another subject was highly entertained at seeing a row of squirrels marching single file across a snowy field, wearing snowshoes and carying little bags over their shoulders.

Some of the scenes were in three dimensions, most in two (that is, as if projected on a screen). A most interesting feature was that some of the images were persistently tilted from the vertical, and a few reports were given of inverted scenes, completely upside down.

There were a few reports of auditory phenomena—one subject heard the people in his hallucination talking. There are also some esthetic imagery, as when one saw a doorknob before him, and as he touched it felt an electric shock; or when another saw a miniature rocket ship maneuvering around him, and discharging pellets that he felt hitting his arm. But the most interesting of these phenomena the subject, apparently, lacked words to describe adequately. There were references to a feeling of "otherness," to bodily "strangeness." One said that his mind was like a ball of cottonwool floating in the air above him.

Two independently reported that they perceived a second body, or second person, in the cubicle. One subject reported that he could not tell which of the two bodies was his own, and described the two bodies as overlapping in space—not like Siamese twins, but two complete bodies with an arm, shoulder, and side of each occupying the same space.

THEORETICAL SIGNIFICANCE

The theoretical interest of these results for us extends in two directions. On the one hand, they interlock with work using more physiological methods, of brain stimulation and recording, and especially much of the recent work on the relation of the brain stem to cortical "arousal." Points of correspondence between behavioral theory and knowledge of neural function are increasing, and each new point of correspondence provides both a corrective for theory and a stimulation for further research. A theory of thought and of consciousness in physiologically intelligible terms need no longer be completely fantastic.

On the other hand, the psychological data cast new light on the relation of man to his environment, including his social environment, and it is this that I should like to discuss a little further. To do so I must go back for a moment to some earlier experiments on chimpanzee emotion. They indicate that the higher mammal may be psychologically at the mercy of his environment to a much greater degree than we have been accustomed to think.

Studies in our laboratory of the role of the environment during infancy and a large body of work reviewed recently by Beach and Jaynes(1) make it clear that psychological development is fully dependent on stimulation from the environment. Without it, intelligence does not develop normally, and the personality is grossly atypical. The experiment with college students shows that a short period—even a day or so—of deprivation of a normal sensory input produces personality changes and a clear loss of capacity to solve problems. Even at maturity, then, the organism is still essentially dependent on a normal sensory environment for the maintenance of its psychological integrity.

The following data show yet another way in which the organism appears psychologically vulnerable. It has long been known that the chimpanzee may be frightened by representation of animals, such as a small toy donkey. An accidental observation of my own extended this to include representations of the chimpanzee himself, of man, and of parts of the chimpanzee or human body. A model of a chimpanzee head, in clay, produced terror in the colony of the Yerkes Laboratories, as did a lifelike representation of a human head, and a number of related objects such as an actual chimpanzee head, preserved in formalin, or a colored representation of a human eye and eyebrow. A deeply anesthetized chimpanzee, "dead" as far as the others were concerned, aroused fear in some animals and vicious attacks by others(4).

I shall not deal with this theoretically. What matters for our present purposes is the conclusion, rather well supported by the animal evidence, that the greater the development of intelligence the greater the vulnerability to emotional breakdown. The price of high intelligence is susceptibility to imaginative fears and unreasoning suspicion and other emotional weaknesses. The conclusion is not only supported by the animal data, but also agrees with the course of development in children, growing intelligence being accompanied by increased frequency and strength of emotional problems—up to the age of five years.

Then, apparently, the trend is reversed. Adult man, more intelligent than chimpanzee or five-year-old child, seems not more subject to emotional disturbances but less. Does this then disprove the conclusion? It seemed a pity to abandon a principle that made sense of so many data that had not made sense before, and the kind of theory I was working with—neurophysiologically oriented—also pointed in the same direction. The question then was, is it possible that something is concealing the adult human being's emotional weaknesses?

From this point of view it became evident that the concealing agency is man's culture, which acts as a protective cocoon. There are many indications that our emotional stability depends more on our successful avoidance of emotional provocation than on our essential characteristics: that urbanity depends on an urbane social and physical environment. Dr. Thompson and I(5) reviewed the evidence, and came to the conclusion that the development of what is called "civilization" is the progressive elimination of sources of acute fear, disgust, and anger; and that civilized man may not be less, but more, susceptible to such disturbance because of his success in protecting himself from disturbing situations so much of the time.

We may fool ourselves thoroughly in this matter. We are surprised that children are afraid of the dark, or afraid of being left alone, and congratulate ourselves on having got over such weakness. Ask anyone you know whether he is afraid of the dark, and he will either laugh at you or be insulted. This attitude is easy to maintain in a well-lighted, well-behaved suburb. But try being alone in complete darkness in the streets of a strange city, or alone at night in the deep woods, and see if you still feel the same way.

We read incredulously of the taboo rules of primitive societies; we laugh at the superstitious fear of the dead in primitive people. What is there about a dead body to produce disturbance? Sensible, educated people are not so affected. One can easily show that they are, however, and that we have developed an extraordinarily complete taboo system—not just moral prohibition, but full-fledged ambivalent taboo—to deal with the dead body. I took a poll of an undergraduate class of 198 persons, including some nurses and veterans, to see how many had encountered a dead body. Thirty-seven had never seen a dead body in any circumstances, and 91 had seen one only after an undertaker had prepared it for burial; making a total of 65 percent who had never seen a dead body in, so to speak, its natural state. It is quite clear that for some reason we protect society against sight of, contact with, the dead body. Why?

Again, the effect of moral education, and training in the rules of courtesy, and the compulsion to dress, talk and act as others do, adds up to ensuring that the individual member of society will not act in a way that is a provocation to others—will not, that is, be a source of strong emotional disturbance, except in highly ritualized circumstances approved by society. The social behavior of a group of civilized persons, then, makes up that protective cocoon which allows us to think of ourselves as being less emotional than the explosive four-year-old or the equally explosive chimpanzee.

The well-adjusted adult therefore is not intrinsically less subject to emotional disturbance: he is well-adjusted, relatively unemotional, as long as he is in his cocoon. The problem of moral education, from this point of view, is not simply to produce a stable individual, but to produce an individual that will (1) be stable in the existing social environment, and (2) contribute to its protective uniformity. We think of some persons as being emotionally dependent, others not; but it looks as though we are all completely dependent on the environment in a way and to a degree that we have not suspected.

BIBLIOGRAPHY

1. Beach, F. A., and Jaynes, J. *Psychol. Bull.* 51 (1954): 239.
2. Bexton, W. H., Heron, W., and Scott, T. H. *Canad. J. Psychol.* 8 (1954): 70.
3. Bowlby, J. *Maternal Care and Mental Health.* Geneva: WHO Monogr. No. 2, 1951.
4. Hebb, D. O. *Psychol. Rev.* 53 (1946): 259.
5. Hebb, D. O., and Thompson, W. R. In Lindzey, G. (Ed.), *Handbook of Social Psychology.* Cambridge: Addison-Wesley, 1954.
6. Hymovitch, B. J. *Comp. Physiol. Psychol.* 45 (1952): 313.
7. Nissen, H. W., Chow, R. L., and Semmes, Josephine. *Am. J. Psychol.* 64 (1951): 485.
8. Spitz, R. A. *Psychoanalytic Study of the Child,* 2 (1946): 113.
9. Thompson, W. R., and Heron, W. *Canad. J. Psychol.* 8 (1954): 17.

chapter 2

Perception

Perception is the process by which an individual gives meaning to his environment. While there are many definitions of the term, most of them include, at least implicitly, all of the following elements; some external stimulus, some process by which the external stimulus is transmitted into psychological experience, and some interpretation or meaning of that psychological experience given by the individual. Because they take an active part in giving meaning to stimuli, different individuals will see the same thing in different ways. Further, it is how a person "sees" that will determine his behavior. Therefore, it is the way a person "sees" the situation, not the situation per se, that has important practical implications for organizational behavior. Recognition of the active role of the perceiver is important for the student and practitioner of organizational behavior.

Because it is central to our understanding of human behavior, the perceptual process has been the subject of a tremendous volume of research. In a book of this sort, only the issues which have the most clear implications for human social behavior can be dealt with. The following readings discuss some of the basic concepts of perception and their relationships to interpersonal behavior and organizational functioning. This introductory section covers some of the more general issues in the field of perception, giving particular emphasis to social perception.[1]

The "mind-body" problem which underlies perception has never been fully resolved. It concerns the relationship between the "physical world" and the "experienced world" of the individual. Laymen have generally assumed that an individual's senses receive and transmit valid information about the external world into the individual. As the history of psychology and philosophy demonstrates, however, many scholars have raised serious questions about the relationship of the internal and external worlds. Some have doubted the existence of mind, while others have doubted the existence of body.

Recognizing that this issue has not been settled, for present purposes we will make several assumptions consistent with the laymen's view mentioned above.

1. For further reading, Allport (1955), Gibson (1969), Secord and Backman (1964), and Taguiri (1969) are suggested.

First, we will assume that some material world exists, and through the senses people absorb forms of energy which are experienced as a representation of the material world. In addition, there is transmission of internally generated energy which may also be reported as experience. The exact relationship between the source of the energy and the reported experiences is not known, although some relationship is presumed to exist. Attempts to understand the relationship between the source and the experience are the basis of a variety of theories of perception.

Most theories agree that the psychological meaning given to an energy source is determined by the interaction of previous experiences, current states of the organism, the context in which the perceived object exists, and the unique sensing system of an individual. Variations in all these factors mean that there may be considerable intraindividual and interindividual variability in how a given object is experienced. For example, oftentimes perception is determined by particular needs and values as well as by the stimulus itself. Furthermore, perception is "selective," in that people attend to only part of the stimulus situation. The expectations of an individual and his particular current interests also influence what he sees. In addition, the way needs have been satisfied in the past influence perception.

Bruner (1958) coined the phrase "perceptual readiness" to reflect the requirements that what is seen will be influenced not only by needs and goals but by the efficiency of means of goal attainment. In other words, perception is influenced by the way a person has learned to deal with his needs, as well as by the factors noted above. As a consequence of variations in all these factors, there is room for considerable disagreement among people as to what is "seen." Fortunately, people seem to share enough experience concerning a sufficiently large number of objects to permit social organization to exist. An adequate perceptual theory must be able to explain not only variability and uniqueness but also the stability and commonality in the relationship between object or source and experience.

The complexity of the perceptual process has caused considerable controversy about competing theories of object perception. The controversy becomes even more difficult to resolve when the perceived objects are people. In interpersonal perception the relationship between the source and the perceiver is more complex, because the source varies as the process evolves. Furthermore, the behavior of the perceiver influences the source, and the perceiver is also a source himself. In object perception the state of the source is at least more stable. However, many of the problems in organizations involve interpersonal perception, and therefore the process must be understood.

A MODEL OF INTERPERSONAL PERCEPTION

Figure 2 summarizes the interaction of variables in interpersonal perception by describing an interaction between two individuals, named "Person" and "Other." The two lower circles in the diagram represent the inner worlds of each party, and the upper portion of the figure represents the context and interaction as they "really are."[2] Consider the lower portion first, particularly Person's inner world.

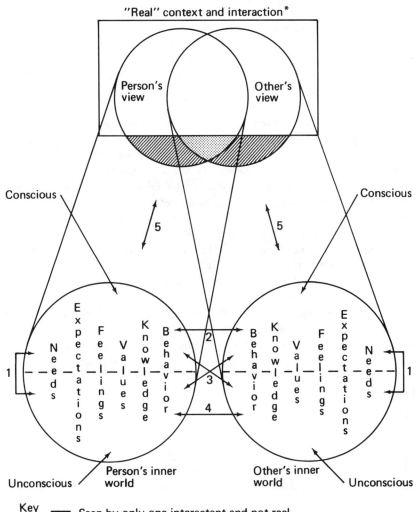

FIGURE 2. Model of Interpersonal Perception *Note that the behavior of Person and Other are part of the "real" situation that can be observed. The behavior was not shown as part of the "real situation" only so that the figure could focus more clearly.

2. When I say refer to things "as they really are," I am making a simplifying assumption that there is an objective reality. If the reader prefers, he may call this a consensual reality—i.e., the situation as seen by several people.

Person's inner world is composed of such factors as needs, expectations, feelings, values, and knowledge. These are communicated to Other through Person's behavior, as the arrows between Person and Other show. A major reason for interpersonal problems is that Person's behavior, for a variety of reasons, does not represent his inner world accurately. Some portions of Person's behavior may be interpreted as representing internal states which are not present in Person, while other states may be present but not represented behaviorally. While Person is aware of some of these discrepancies, he is unaware of many others. However, the nonconscious factors play an important role in influencing behavior and conscious experience.

Arrows numbered 1 represent the influence of conscious and nonconscious elements on each other. However, as arrows numbered 3 and 4 indicate, often the unconscious portion may be communicated by Person's behavior without his awareness.

All of the elements within Person are dynamic. Person's actual inner state may change instantaneously as a result of his own behavior. For example if Person is angry with Other, as soon as he expresses it his anger may subside. In general, both the unconscious nature of much of Person's inner world and the dynamic nature of his internal being are sources of problems in interpersonal relationships. In addition, the internal states of Person and Other are constantly changed as a result of the interaction itself.

Arrows 2, 3, and 4 show the different levels of interaction on which the behavior and internal states of one party may be changed by the behavior of the other. Arrow 2 represents exchanges which occur between Person and Other on the conscious level. In other words, these exchanges involve elements which Person sends consciously and Other receives consciously and vice versa. Such exchanges are relatively clear to both parties, although they can be a source of difficulty. For example, Person may "put up a front" by consciously sending false data to manipulate Other's perception. Error can also result from Other's misperception in the same manner that error occurs in object perception.

Arrows numbered 3 are exchanges between the conscious level of one party and the nonconscious level of the other; they suggest two more ways in which the two parties may come to operate on different information. One possibility is that Person may be consciously sending information to Other which Other is not aware of receiving. For example, Person may be aware of telling Other to do something, but Other may never be aware of Person's behavior. A second possible source of error along arrow 3 is the chance that Person may receive information from Other that Other is not aware of sending. For example, Other may consciously state, "I am not angry." However, the tone of Other's voice, which Other is not aware of, may lead Person to believe that Other is very angry. Both types of error are apt to lead to tension and conflict.

Arrow 4 represents exchanges between nonconscious levels. The inner-personal world of Person is affected by actions of Other which neither Person nor Other recognize. For example, the body movements of Person may influence Other's nonconscious world without either party being aware of how. An interesting corollary is that nonverbal behavior is an important channel of communication.[3] Nevertheless, problems can occur on this level as a result of normal perceptual errors and conflicts between what is sent on this level with what is sent on the conscious levels.

The "Real" Interaction and Its Context

In addition to the errors represented in the lower portion of Figure 2, interpersonal perception is affected by the "real situation." The upper portion of Figure 2 represents the context in which Person and Other are interacting and the actual interaction itself.[4] Person's view of the context is influenced by things of which he is aware and unaware. Arrows numbered 5 are "two-way" because, while the context influences Person and his perception, his inner world also helps shape his view of the context. The errors here are similar to those of object perception.

There are several additional, important considerations about the context itself. First, the large rectangle represents the "objective" or "real" context. Person's view of the situation coincides only partially with the "real situation." Similarly, Other's view coincides only partially with reality. Furthermore, Other's and Person's views overlap only to a limited extent, allowing only partial agreement between the two individuals. Thus Person and Other agree on only a part of reality, and both miss part of reality. It is also important to note that both Person and Other may "see" some things that are not part of reality. This possibility is represented by the cross—hatched areas extending beyond the real context. Finally, the dark area where the cross—hatched areas overlap represents the possibility that Person and Other could agree on things that do not really exist. For example, two employees may agree that their job is in danger when in fact it is not.

This model is an attempt to summarize interpersonal perception. While object and interpersonal perception are similar, the latter is more complex because of the different levels of awareness, the possibility of deliberate distortion, unrepresentative behavior, the dynamic changes which occur within both parties, and contextual factors. The probability that interpersonal and organizational problems will be rooted in perception is so great that in many ways perception is the most central concern for managers.

PERCEPTION AND MANAGEMENT: THE READINGS

The readings in this section focus on the basic process of perception and its implications for interpersonal and organizational behavior. The problem of perception is important to managers above and beyond the problems of interpersonal perception. It is not only important that people agree enough about what they "see" to be able to coordinate their efforts; it is also important

3. See Schulman's paper in Part III.
4. It is important to emphasize the footnote to Fig. 1, which states that the behavior of the participants is part of the "real situation."

that people see the "real" world "accurately enough to be able to deal with it in a functional manner." In other words, it is important for people to be able to see the world with a minimum of distortion. Often, under certain conditions, people find it useful to defend themselves perceptually by distorting or overlooking information which threatens their view of the world or themselves. For example, a person questioning a grade given him by a professor may misinterpret the professor's statements. The teacher may be attempting to say "You missed the point." The student may tell himself—"I just misunderstood the meaning of a word or two." The problem is compounded by the professor's own defensiveness. The student may be saying "I don't understand your question." The teacher may be "seeing" a hostile, disrespectful, immature individual. Such a view allows the professor to defend his own self-view from the threat he perceives to his favorite exam question.

Similar perceptual defenses operate in all organizations. It is commonly believed that types of distortion are systematically related to particular needs and that distortion is often increased under conditions of psychological threat. Further, previous training and experience predisposes people to "see" certain things and not others. Effective management of people requires an awareness of the possibility of distortion, a recognition of its probable sources, and a means to prevent and alleviate it.

The readings in this section begin with a selection by Cantril describing the nature of perception and its implications for interpersonal behavior. The Dearborn and Simon reading which follows points to the interaction between organizational and perceptual factors. Their study suggests the consequences that performance of organizational roles can have for one's ability to see the world. Their findings are supported by many other studies. For example, Toch and Schulte (1961) found that the training that policemen receive increases the probability that they will see themes of violence in ambiguous pictures. A final reading explores the work of Marshall McLuhan, who introduced the view that the way in which stimuli are communicated has important consequences for perception. The implications of McLuhan's stress on the process of communication for organizational behavior have not been fully realized. An example of the implications of process for organizations was provided by Postman and Weingartner (1969) who pointed out that what is learned in schools may be more a consequence of *how* things are taught than of *what* is taught. In this sense, process becomes the central variable in perception and the attainment of organizational goals.

These selections represent only a small sampling of relevant material on perception. However, many of the issues which are not fully treated here reappear in the sections on motivation, learning, personality, communication and group behavior. Many of the unanticipated consequences discussed in part II also have their roots in perception.

REFERENCES

Allport, F.H. *Theories of Perception and the Concept of Structure.* New York: John Wiley, 1955.

Bruner, J. "Social Psychology and Perception." In E. Maccoby, T. Newcomb, & E. Hartley (eds.), *Readings in Social Psychology.* (3rd ed.) New York: Holt, Rinehart and Winston, 1958, 85-94.

Gibson, E.J. *Principles of Perceptual Learning and Development.* New York: Appleton-Century-Crofts, 1969.

Postman, N., & Weingartner, C. *Teaching as a Subversive Activity.* New York: Delacorte, 1969.

Secord, P.F., & Backman, C.W. *Social Psychology.* New York: McGraw-Hill Book Company, 1964.

Taguiri, R. "Person Perception." In G. Lindzey, & E. Aronson (eds.) *The Handbook of Social Psychology.* 2nd ed. vol. 3. Reading, Mass.: Addison-Wesley, 1969, 395-449.

Toch, H., & Schulte, R. "Readiness to Perceive Violence as a Result of Police Training." *British Journal of Psychology* 52, 1961: 389-93.

Hadley Cantril

PERCEPTION AND
INTERPERSONAL RELATIONS

It is with a very profound feeling of humility that I, as a psychologist, offer any comments for the consideration of psychiatrists on the subject of perception and interpersonal relations. For the more one studies perception, the more one sees that what we label "perception" is essentially a process which man utilizes to make his purposive behavior more effective and satisfying, and that this behavior always stems from and is rooted in a personal behavioral center. Thus perception involves numerous aspects of behavior which we rather artificially and necessarily differentiate in order to get a toe-hold for understanding, but which, in the on-going process of living, orchestrate together in a most interdependent way.

This means, then, that the nature of perception can only be understood if somehow we manage to start off with what some of us call a "first person point of view" as contrasted to the "third person point of view" represented by the traditional psychological investigator. And so my very genuine feeling of humility in accepting an invitation of psychiatrists derives from the fact that the psychiatrist, perhaps more than any other specialist concerned with the study of human beings, is primarily concerned with the first-person point of view, is skilled in the art of uncovering what this may be for his patient, and knows from his own experience the wide gap that exists between this first-person experience and the abstractions we have created as scientists in order to analyze, conceptualize, and communicate. A very nice expression of this last state of affairs was, incidentally, recently made by Aldous Huxley in his book *The Genius and the Goddess:*

> "What a gulf between *im*pression and *ex*pression! That's our ironic fate—to have Shakespearian feelings and (unless by billion-to-one chance we happen to *be* Shakespeare) to talk about them like automobile salesmen or teen-agers or college professors.
>
> We practice alchemy in reverse — touch gold and it turns to lead; touch the pure lyrics of experience, and they turn into the verbal equivalents of tripe and hogwash.

Abridged from Hadley Cantril, "Perception and Interpersonal Relations," *American Journal of Psychiatry* 114 (1957):119-26. Copyright 1957, the American Psychiatric Association. Reprinted by permission.

BACKGROUND

Most of you are probably familiar to some extent with a point of view that has developed rather recently in psychology and has been dubbed "transactional psychology." While I do not want to spend time here repeating what has been published in a variety of sources, I might at least very briefly note some of the major emphases of transactional psychology before discussing certain aspects and some experimental results which may be of particular interest to psychiatrists[1, 2, 3, 4].

Here, then, are some of the emphases of transactional psychology which may give us a take-off for discussion:

Our perception depends in large part on the assumptions we bring to any particular occasion. It is, as Dewey and Bentley long ago pointed out, not a "reaction to" stimuli in the environment but may be more accurately described as a "transaction with" an environment.

This implies that the meanings and significances we assign to things, to symbols, to people, and to events are the meanings and significances we have built up through our past experience, and are not inherent or intrinsic in the "stimulus" itself.

Since our experience is concerned with purposive behavior, our perceptions are learned in terms of our purposes and in terms of what is important and useful to us.

Since the situations we are in seldom repeat themselves exactly and since change seems to be the rule of nature and of life, our perception is largely a matter of weighing probabilities, of guessing, of making hunches concerning the probable significance or meaning of "what is out there" and of what our reaction should be toward it, in order to protect or preserve ourselves and our satisfactions, or to enchance our satisfactions. This process of weighing the innumerable cues involved in nearly any perception is, of course, a process that we are generally not aware of.

CREATING CONSTANCIES

Since things in the world outside us—the physical world and more especially the social world—are by no means static, are not entirely determined and predictable, experience for most of us often carries at least some mild overtone of "concern" which we can label "curiosity," "doubt" or "anxiety" depending on the circumstances involved.

* * *

Thus we seldom can count on complete 100 percent surety in terms of a perfect correspondence between our assumptions concerning the exact experience we may have if we do a certain thing and the experience we actually do have as the consequence of the action we undertake.

In an attempt to try to minimize our potential lack of surety concerning any single occasion and thereby maximize our sense of surety concerning the effectiveness of our action in achieving our intent, we build up "constancies" and begin to count on them. While a great deal of experimental work has been done on "constancies" in the psychological laboratory, we still have much more to learn. And above all, we have a great deal to learn about constancy as we extend this concept into the field of our interpersonal relations.

Parenthetically, one of the most important things we have to learn is that the "constancy" we create and that we describe usually by means of some word, symbol, or abstract concept *is* man's creation, the validity of which can only be tested and the meaning of which can only be experienced in terms of some behavior which has consequences to us and signals to us what the concept refers to.

We create these constancies by attributing certain *consistent* and *repeatable* characteristics to what they refer to, so that we can guess with a fair degree of accuracy what the significances and meanings are of the various sensory cues that impinge upon us. We do this so that we will not have to make fresh guesses at every turn.

These significances we build up about objects, people, symbols, and events, or about ideas all orchestrate together to give us what we might call our own unique *"reality world."* This "reality world" as we experience it includes, of course, our own fears and hopes, frustrations and aspirations, our own anxiety and our own faith. For these psychological characteristics of life—as the psychiatrist knows better than anyone else—are just as real for us in determining our behavior as are chairs, stones or mountains or automobiles. It seems to me that anything that takes on significance for us in terms of our own personal behavioral center *is* "real" in the psychological sense.

ASSIGNING SIGNIFICANCES

Let me illustrate with reference to a few recent experiments the way in which the significance we attach to others "out there" seems to be affected by what we bring to the situation. Incidentally but important: I do want to underscore that the experiments mentioned here are only exploratory; are only, I believe, opening up interesting vistas ahead. I am in no sense attempting to indicate what their full theoretical implications may be. But I mention them to show how experiments designed to get at the first person point of view may suggest to the experienced psychiatrist ways of using experimental procedures in his diagnosis and possibly even in therapy. And I also mention them because of my deep conviction that psychology can be both humanistic and methodologically rigorous.

A whole series of most promising experiments now seems possible with the use of a modern adaptation of an old-fashioned piece of psychological equipment, the stereoscope. Dr. Edward Engel who devised the apparatus has already published a description of it and reported some of his first findings(5). As you know, the stereoscope in a psychological laboratory has been used to study binocular rivalry and fusion but the material viewed almost always consisted of dots and lines or geometrical patterns. Engel was curious to see what would happen if meaningful figures were used instead of the traditional material.

The results are really most exciting. In Engel's experiments he prepares what he calls "stereograms" consisting of photographs 2 x 2 inches, one of which is seen with the left eye, the other with the right. The photographs he used first were those of members of the Princeton football team just as they appeared in the football program. Although there were slight differences in the size and position of the heads and in the characteristics of light and shadow, still there was sufficient superimposition to get binocular fusion. And what happens? A person looks into the stereoscope and sees one face. He describes this face. And it almost invariably turns out that he is describing neither the face of the man seen with the left eye nor the face of the man seen with the right eye. He is describing a new and different face, a face that he has created out of the features of the two he is looking at. Generally the face seen in this particular case is made up of the dominant features of the two individuals. And generally the face created by the observer in this situation is more attractive and appealing than either of those seen separately. When the observer is shown the trick of the experiment by asking him to close first one eye and then the other and to compare the face he originally saw with the other two, he himself characterizes the face he created as more handsome, more pleasant, a fellow he'd like better, etc.

I hasten to add, however, that we should by no means jump to the conclusion that an individual picks out the "best" or "most attractive" features of figures presented to him in a situation of binocular fusion. For example, Professor Gordon Allport recently took one of Engel's stereoscopes with him to South Africa and initiated some experimental work there, using photographs of members of the different racial groups which make up that complex community.

While the experiments in South Africa have only just begun and no conclusion should be drawn, it is significant to note that in recent letters communicating the early results, Allport reported that when the stereograms consist of a European paired with an Indian, a colored person compared with an Indian, etc. the Zulus see an overwhelming preponderance of Indians. For the Zulu is most strongly prejudiced against the Indian who represents a real threat to him. Allport also reports that when Europeans in South Africa view the stereogram they tend to see more colored faces than white. It would seem, then, that a person sees what is "significant," with significance defined in terms of his relationship to what he is looking at.

One pair of slides we use in demonstrating this piece of equipment consists of two stereograms, each a photograph of a statue in the Louvre. One of the statues is that of a Madonna with Child, the other a lovely young female nude. While I am unable so far to predict what any given individual will "see," no doubt such a prediction might be made after some good psychiatric interviewing. But let me describe what happened in a typical viewing of these stereograms. The viewers happened to be two distinguished psychologists who were visiting me one morning, one from Harvard, the other from Yale. The first looked into the stereoscope and reported that he saw a Madonna with Child. A few seconds later he exclaimed, "But my God, she is undressing." What had happened so far was that somehow she had lost the baby she was holding and her robe had slipped down from her shoulders and stopped just above the breast line. Then in a few more seconds she lost her robe completely and became the young nude. For this particular professor, the nude never did get dressed again. Then my second friend took his turn. For a few seconds he could see nothing but the nude and then he exclaimed, "But now a robe is wrapping itself around her." And very soon he ended up with the Madonna with Child and as far as I know still remains with that vision. Some people will never see the nude; others will never see the Madonna if they keep the intensity of light the same on both stereograms.

In the situation described above, we do not have conditions for genuine fusion, but rather a condition which introduces conflict and choice in the possible meaning of the content represented. In order to learn whether or not there might be differences in choice that would be culturally determined, a cross cultural comparison was made by Dr. James Bagby (6). He constructed pairs of stereograms that would create binocular rivalry: in one stereogram of each pair he had a picture of some individual, object or symbol that would be of particular interest to Mexicans; in the other stereogram he had a picture that would be of particular significance to Americans. For example, one pair of slides consisted of a picture of a bull fighter matched with a stereogram picturing a baseball player. When these pairs were shown to a sample of Mexican school teachers, an overwhelming proportion of them "saw" the Mexican symbol; when the same slides were presented to a group of American school teachers, the overwhelming proportion "saw" the American symbol.

Incidentally, the Engel stereoscope is so constructed that one can get some idea of the relative "strength" of each of the stereograms by adjusting the intensity of the lighting on each. Hence, if the lighting is equivalent on two stereograms in a rivalry situation, one can reduce the amount of lighting on the one that originally predominates, increase the amount of light on the one that was not "seen" and find the point where the first one disappears and the second one "comes in."

A modification of the stereoscope has just been completed by Mr. Adlerstein in the Princeton laboratory. Our thought was that it might be extremely useful both in the clinical and social areas, if instead of having to use photographs of objects or people, a person could view the real thing—that is, the faces of real, live individuals or pairs of actual objects. So by means of prisms and mirrors this device was constructed and I have only very recently had the opportunity of experiencing the resulting phenomena. I must say it is strange and wonderful. For example, when I viewed Mr. Adlerstein and Mrs. Pauline Smith, Curator of our Demonstration Center, I seemed to be looking at a very effeminate Mr. Adlerstein who was wearing Mrs. Smith's glasses. Though weird, he was extremely "real." At one point while I was observing them Mrs. Smith began to talk yet it was Adlerstein's lips that were moving! Tingling with excitement and with a certain amount of anxiety, I drove home and asked my wife and daughter to come down to the laboratory so that I could take a look at them. I was, of course, fearful that I might see only one or the other. But fortunately, again I got an amazing fusion—a quite real and lovely head composed of a blending of my daughter's hair and chin and my wife's eyes and mouth—an harmonious composition that would do justice to any artist and which I created almost instantaneously and without any awareness of what was going on. These pieces of apparatus seem to me to have enormous potential usefulness for studying the way in which we create the world around us. I am hoping, for example, that before long someone in a position to do so may use this sort of equipment in a study of disturbed children. The child—having two eyes and two parents—might in some situations and in a very few seconds reveal a good bit about his inner life and his interpersonal family relations.

An interesting series of experiments on perception and interpersonal relations began systematically a few years ago after an observation I made one Sunday morning in our laboratory. An old friend of mine, who was a distinguished lawyer in New York and has since died, called me at home to say that he and his wife had been in town for the weekend and would I be willing to show them some of the Ames' demonstrations about which he had heard. It is important for this story to emphasize the fact that the gentleman in question was really a most unusual man in terms of his ability, charm, accomplishments, and his devotion to his family and friends.

Many of you are familiar, I am sure, with the "distorted room" designed by Adelbert Ames, Jr. which produces the same image on the retina as a regular square room if it is viewed monocularly from a certain point. Since the room is seen as square, persons or objects within the room or people looking through the windows become distorted. I had shown this room to hundreds of individuals and among other phenomena had demonstrated that when two people look through the back windows, the head of one individual appeared to be very large, the head of the other to be very small. When the individuals reversed the windows they were looking through, the size of their heads appeared to the observer to change. But on this Sunday morning when my friend's wife was observing him and me, she said, "Well, Louis, your head is the same size as ever, but Hadley, your head is very small." Then we changed the windows we were looking through and she said, "Louis, you're still the same, but Hadley you've become awfully large." Needless to say this remark made a shiver go up my spine and I asked her how she saw the room. It turned out that for her — unlike any other observer until then—the room had become somewhat distorted. In other words, she was using her husband—to whom she was particularly devoted—as her standard. She would not let him go. His nickname for her was "Honi" and we have dubbed this the "Honi phenomenon."

This observation was followed systematically in a series of experiments on married couples by Dr. Warren Wittreich. He found that if couples had been married less than a year there was a very definite tendency not to let the new marital partner distort as quickly or as much as was allowed by people who had been married for a considerable time (7). But, again, I hasten to add that it is not a simple matter of how long one has been married that determines how willing one is to distort the size or shape of one's marital partner! The original observation was made on a couple who were already grandparents. Preliminary investigation also seems to show that parents of young children will not allow their children to distort as readily as will parents of older children.

We could continue at some length reporting experiments which seem to show that what we "perceive" is, as already emphasized, in large part our own creation and depends on the assumptions we bring to the particular occasion. We seem to give meaning and order to sensory impingements in terms of our own needs and purposes and this process of selection is actively creative.

SOCIAL CONSTANCIES
AND SELF-CONSTANCY

It is clear that when we look for constancies in other people either as individuals or as members of a group a variety of complications is introduced. For when people are involved, as contrasted to inorganic objects or most other forms of life, we are dealing with purposes, with motives, with intentions which we have to take into account in our perceptual process—the purposes, motives and intentions of other people often difficult to understand. The purposes and intentions of these other people will, of course, change as conditions change; and they will change as behavior progresses from one goal to another. Other people's purposes will be affected by our purposes, just as our purposes will be affected by theirs.

It is by no means a quick and easy process, then, to endow the people with whom we participate in our interpersonal relations with constancies and repeatabilities that we can always rely on. And yet we must, of course, continue the attempt to do so, so that our own purposeful action will have a greater chance of bringing about the satisfying consequences we intended. So we try to pigeonhole people according to some role, status, or position. We create constancies concerning people and social situations. These provide us with certain consistent characteristics that will ease our interpretation and make our actions more effective so long as there is some correspondence between the attribution we make and the consequence we experience from it in our own action.

The "social constancies" we learn obviously involve the relationships between ourselves and others. So if any social constancy is to be operational, there must also be a sense of "self-constancy." The two are interdependent. Since the human being necessarily derives so much of his value satisfaction from association with other human beings, his conception of his "self," his own "self-constancy" and "self-significance" is determined to a large extent by the significance he has to other people and the way they behave toward him. This point is, of course, a familiar one to the psychiatrist and has been eloquently illustrated in literature as, for example, in Shaw's *Pygmalion.*

But it seems to me of paramount importance in any discussion of perception and interpersonal relations that we should not slip into the error of positing an abstract "self" or "ego" that can somehow be isolated, pointed to, analyzed, or experienced apart from any social context. It is only through the life setting and the process of participation with others that meaning and continuity are given to the "self." If the constancy of "self" is upset, it becomes difficult for us to assess changes in our interpersonal relations and accommodate to them. We lose the compass that keeps us going in a direction. "We" are lost.

This does not mean in any sense that for self-constancy to be maintained there can be no development or growth. On the contrary, self-development and growth are themselves aspects of social constancy. But this development must, as the psychiatrist knows better than anyone, flow from form if it is to be recognized, if there is to be continuity, and if there is to be a standard for comparison. Obviously, each of us surrounds himself with anchoring points of one kind or another which help to maintain this self-constancy in the process of ceaseless change around us. In this connection I think, for example, of Konrad Lorenz' interpretation of why people like dogs. In his book *King Solomon's Ring,* he writes that we should "not lie to ourselves that we need the dog as a protection for our house. We *do* need him, but not as a watch-dog. I, at least in dreary foreign towns, have certainly stood in need of my dog's company and I have derived, from the mere fact of his existence, a great sense of inward security, such as one finds in a childhood memory or in the prospect of the scenery of one's own home country, for me the Blue Danube, for you the White Cliffs of Dover. In the almost film-like flitting-by of modern life, a man needs something to tell him, from time to time, that he is still himself, and nothing can give him this assurance in so comforting a manner as the 'four feet trotting behind.'"

This interdependent problem of social constancy and self-constancy has been submitted to some preliminary investigation. For example, when a person is wearing a pair of aniseikonic spectacles, which greatly distort the shape of the environment when familiar monocular cues are ruled out, he will generally see another person as distorted if that person is standing in an environment which has itself already become distorted. With a certain pair of these spectacles, for example, an individual will be seen as leaning forward with the upper and lower half of his body distorted in length. Dr. Wittreich set up such a situation at the Naval Training Center at Bainbridge, Maryland to see what might happen when the relationship of the person who was doing the viewing and the person being viewed was altered. His subjects were 24 white male Navy recruits. They first observed an authority figure dressed up as a first class petty officer and, second, a nonauthority figure dressed up in a white enlisted uniform with the marks of a recruit. Wittreich found that the authority figure did not distort nearly as much as the nonauthority figure. In other words, the disciplinary training imposed in an organization that depends for effective functioning on the rigid acceptance of roles had produced a "constancy" which overpowered physiological changes in the optical system.

Another finding using the aniseikonic spectacles may be of interest to psychiatrists: namely, that a person tends to report much less distortion of his own image when he looks at himself in a full-length mirror while wearing aniseikonic spectacles than he reports when he is looking at a stranger. When one looks at one's self, the changes that appear seem to be minor and detailed—for example, slight distortions in the hands or feet; when one looks at a stranger, there is the more general bodily distortion plus the leaning one way or another, depending on the kind of spectacles used.

A subsequent study by Wittreich and one which I emphasize is only suggestive, was made comparing 21 subjects obtained from the patient roster of the neuropsychiatric unit at the Bethesda Naval Hospital. When these disturbed individuals were wearing aniseikonic spectacles and saw their own image in the mirror, they tended to see the gross distortions that the "normal" population attributed to others; and, conversely, when the disturbed clinic population looked at others, they tended to see the more detailed and minor distortions which the "normal" population had seen in themselves. All I should like to conclude about this particular experiment so far is that there seems to be some difference between the normal individual and the clinical patient in the functional importance assigned to his bodily image; the patient may conceivably be operating in terms of a relatively fixed and homogeneous image of himself which does not alter readily with the demands of the environment.

PERCEPTUAL CHANGE

Laboratory experimentation as well as research in the field of opinion and attitude change seems to demonstrate beyond a shadow of a doubt that the major condition for a change in our perception, our attitudes or opinions is a frustration experienced in carrying out our purposes effectively because we are acting on the basis of assumptions that prove "wrong." For example, Dr. Kilpatrick has demonstrated that apparently the only way in which we can "learn" to see our distorted room distorted is to become frustrated with the assumption that the room is "square" in the process of trying to carry out some action in the room(8). It is clear that an "intellectual," "rational," or "logical" understanding of a situation is by no means sufficient to alter perception. The psychotherapist has taught us how successful reconditioning requires a therapy which simplifies goals so that their accomplishment can be assured through an individual's action as he experiences the successful consequences of his own behavior and thereby rebuilds his confidence in himself.

In this connection I recall a conversation I had in 1948 in Paris with an extremely intelligent woman who was at that time a staff member of the Soviet Embassy in Paris. We were at some social gathering and she began to ask me about American elections and the two-party system. She just couldn't understand it. She wasn't trying to be "smart" or supercilious. She was simply baffled. She couldn't "see" why we had to have two parties. For, obviously, one man was better than another and why wasn't he made President and kept as President as long as he proved to be the best man? It was a difficult argument for me to understand, just as my argument was impossible for her to understand. It was much more than a matter of opinion, stereotype or prejudice on either side. We were simply living in different reality worlds, actually experiencing entirely different significances in happenings which might appear to "an objective" "outside" observer to be the same for both of us.

Parenthetically, while one of the outstanding characteristics of man is often said to be his amazing capacity to learn, it seems to me that an equally outstanding characteristic is man's amazing capacity to "unlearn" which is, I think, not the exact opposite. Because man is not entirely a creature of habit, he has the fortunate ability to slough off what is no longer of use to him.

THE REALITY OF ABSTRACTIONS AND THE COMMONNESS OF PURPOSES

In order to ease our interpersonal relations and to increase the commonness of the significances we may attribute to the happenings around us, man has created abstractions in his attempt to bring order into disorder and to find more universal guides for living no matter what the unique and individual purposes and circumstances of an individual may be. Such abstractions are represented by our scientific formulations, our ethical, political, legal and religious systems. The abstractions can be recalled and repeated at will. They can be communicated. They are repeatable because they are static and have fixed characteristics.

The value of these abstractions for us in our interpersonal relations seems to be that when the tangibles of our personal reality world break down, we can turn to the intangible—to the abstractions we have learned that have been created by others and have presumably proved useful to them. We can begin to check our own particular situation, possibly a frustrating one, against the abstraction and thereby, perhaps experience for ourselves what the abstraction is referring to. Only then will the abstraction become real for us. For when it does become functional for us in our own individual lives, it *is* real as a determinant of our experience and behavior.

I will close this discussion of perception and interpersonal relations with a story which seems to sum a good deal of what I have been talking about. The story concerns three baseball umpires who were discussing the problems of their profession. The first umpire said, "Some's balls and some's strikes and I calls 'em as they is." The second umpire said, "Some's balls and some's strikes and I calls 'em as I sees 'em." While the third umpire said, "Some's balls and some's strikes but they ain't nothin' till I calls 'em."

BIBLIOGRAPHY

1. Cantril, Hadley. *The "Why" of Man's Experience.* New York: The Macmillan Company, 1950.
2. Kilpatrick, F.P. (ed.). Human Behavior from the Transactional Point of View. Hanover, N. H.: Institute for Associated Research, 1952.
3. Kilpatrick, F.P. Recent Transactional Perceptual Research, a summary. Final Report, Navy Contract N6onr 27014, Princeton University, May, 1955.
4. Cantril, Hadley. ETC: A Review of General Semantics, 12: No.4, 278, 1955.
5. Engel, Edward. *Amer. J. Psychol.,* 69: No. I, 87, 1956.
6. Bagby, James. A Cross Cultural Study of Perceptual Predominance in Binocular Rivalry. 1956 (to be published).

7. Wittreich, Warren. *J. Abnorm. Soc. Psychol.*, 47:705, 1952.

8. Kilpatrick, F. P. *J. Exp. Psychol.*, 47: No. 5, 362, 1954.

DeWitt C. Dearborn
Herbert A. Simon

SELECTIVE PERCEPTION: A NOTE ON THE DEPARTMENTAL IDENTIFICATIONS OF EXECUTIVES

An important proposition in organization theory asserts that each executive will perceive those aspects of the situation that relate specifically to the activities and goals of his department (2, Ch. 5, 10). The proposition is frequently supported by anecdotes of executives and observers in organizations, but little evidence of a systematic kind is available to test it. It is the purpose of this note to supply some such evidence.

The proposition we are considering is not peculiarly organizational. It is simply an application to organizational phenomena of a generalization that is central to any explanation of selective perception: Presented with a complex stimulus, the subject perceives in it what he is "ready" to perceive; the more complex or ambiguous the stimulus, the more the perception is determined by what is already "in" the subject and the less by what is in the stimulus (1,pp. 132-133).

Cognitive and motivational mechanisms mingle in the selective process, and it may be of some use to assess their relative contributions. We might suppose either: (1) selective attention to a part of a stimulus reflects a deliberate ignoring of the remainder as irrelevant to the subject's goals and motives, or (2) selective attention is a learned response stemming from some past history of reinforcement. In the latter case we might still be at some pains to determine the nature of the reinforcement, but by creating a situation from which any immediate motivation for selectivity is removed, we should be able to separate the second mechanism from the first. The situation in which we obtained our data meets this condition, and hence our data provide evidence for internalization of the selective processes.

Abridged from DeWitt C. Dearborn and Herbert A. Simon, "Selective Perception: A Note on the Departmental Identifications of Executives," *Sociometry* 21 (1958):140-44. Reprinted by permission.

METHOD OF THE STUDY

A group of 23 executives, all employed by a single large manufacturing concern and enrolled in a company sponsored executive training program, was asked to read a standard case that is widely used in instruction in business policy in business schools. The case, Castengo Steel Company, described the organization and activities of a company of moderate size specializing in the manufacture of seamless steel tubes, as of the end of World War II. The case, which is about 10,000 words in length, contains a wealth of descriptive material about the company and its industry and the recent history of both (up to 1945), but little evaluation. It is deliberately written to hold closely to concrete facts and to leave as much as possible of the burden of interpretation to the reader.

When the executives appeared at a class session to discuss the case, but before they had discussed it, they were asked by the instructor to write a brief statement of what they considered to be the most important problem facing the Castengo Steel Company—the problem a new company president should deal with first. Prior to this session, the group had discussed other cases, being reminded from time to time by the instructor that they were to assume the role of the top executive of the company in considering its problems.

The executives were a relatively homogeneous group in terms of status, being drawn from perhaps three levels of the company organization. They were in the range usually called "middle management," representing such positions as superintendent of a department in a large factory, product manager responsible for profitability of one of the ten product groups manufactured by the company, and works physician for a large factory. In terms of departmental affiliation, they fell in four groups:

Sales (6): Sales product managers or assistant product managers, and one field sales supervisor.

Production (5): Three department superintendents, one assistant factory manager, and one construction engineer.

Accounting (4): An assistant chief accountant, and three accounting supervisors—for a budget division and two factory departments.

Miscellaneous (8): Two members of the legal department, two in research and development, and one each from public relations, industrial relations, medical and purchasing.

THE DATA

We tested our hypothesis by determining whether there was a significant relation between the "most important problem" mentioned and the departmental affiliation of the mentioner. In the cases of executives who mentioned more than one problem, we counted all those they mentioned. We compared (1) the executives who mentioned "sales," "marketing," or "distribution" with those who did not; (2) the executives who mentioned "clarifying the organization" or some equivalent with those who did not; (3) the executives who mentioned "human relations," "employee relations" or "teamwork" with those who did not. The findings are summarized in the Table.

The difference between the percentages of sales executives (83 percent) and other executives (29 percent) who mentioned sales as the most important problem is significant at the 5 percent level. Three of the five nonsales executives, moreover, who mentioned sales were in the accounting department, and all of these were in positions that involved analysis of product profitability. This accounting activity was, in fact, receiving considerable emphasis in the company at the time of the case discussion and the accounting executives had frequent and close contacts with the product managers in the sales department. If we combine sales and accounting executives, we find that 8 out of 10 of these mentioned sales as the most important problem; while only 2 of the remaining 13 executives did.

Department	Total number of executives	Sales	Number who mentioned "Clarify organization"	Human relations
Sales	6	5	1	0
Production	5	1	4	0
Accounting	4	3	0	0
Miscellaneous	8	1	3	3
Totals	23	10	8	3

Organization problems (other than marketing organization) were mentioned by four out of five production executives, the two executives in research and development, and the factory physician, but by only one sales executive and no accounting executives. The difference between the percentage for production executives (80 percent) and other executives (22 percent) is also significant at the 5 percent level. Examination of the Castengo case shows that the main issue discussed in the case that relates to manufacturing is the problem of poorly defined relations among the factory manager, the metallurgist, and the company president. The presence of the metallurgist in the situation may help to explain the sensitivity of the two research and development executives (both of whom were concerned with metallurgy) to this particular problem area.

It is easy to conjecture why the public relations, industrial relations, and medical executives should all have mentioned some aspect of human relations, and why one of the two legal department executives should have mentioned the board of directors.

CONCLUSION

We have presented data on the selective perceptions of industrial executives exposed to case material that support the hypothesis that each executive will perceive those aspects of a situation that relate specifically to the activities and goals of his department. Since the situation is one in which the executives were motivated to look at the problem from a company-wide rather than a departmental viewpoint, the data indicate further that the criteria of selection have become internalized. Finally, the method for obtaining data that we have used holds considerable promise as a projective device for eliciting the attitudes and perceptions of executives.

REFERENCES

1. Bruner, J. S. "On Perceptual Readiness." *Psychological Review* 64 (1957): 123-52.
2. Simon, H. A. *Administrative Behavior.* New York: Macmillan, 1947.

*   *   *

Marshall McLuhan

UNDERSTANDING MEDIA: THE EXTENSIONS OF MAN

PREFACE TO THE THIRD PRINTING

Jack Paar mentioned that he once had said to a young friend, "Why do you kids use 'cool' to mean 'hot'?" The friend replied, "Because you folks used up the word 'hot' before we came along." It is true that "cool" is often used nowadays to mean what used to be conveyed by "hot." Formerly a "hot argument" meant one in which people were deeply involved. On the other hand, a "cool attitude" used to mean one of detached objectivity and disinterestedness. In those days the word "disinterested" meant a noble quality of fairmindedness. Suddenly it got to mean "couldn't care less." The word "hot" has fallen into similar disuse as these deep changes of outlook have developed. But the slang term "cool" conveys a good deal besides the old idea of "hot." It indicates a kind of commitment and participation in situations that involves all of one's faculties. In that sense, one can say that automation is cool, whereas the older mechanical kinds of specialist or fragmented "jobs" are "square." The "square" person and situation are not "cool" because they manifest little of the habit of depth involvement of our faculties. The young now say, "Humor is not cool." Their favorite jokes bear this out. They ask, "What is purple and hums?" Answer, "An electric grape." "Why does it hum?" Answer, "Because it doesn't know the words." Humor is presumably not "cool" because it inclines us to laugh *at* something, instead of getting us emphatically involved in something. The story line is dropped from "cool" jokes and "cool" movies alike. The Bergman and Fellini movies demand far more involvement than do narrative shows. A story line encompasses a set of events much like a melodic line in music. Melody, the *melos modos,* "the road round," is a continuous, connected, and repetitive structure that is not used in the "cool" art of the Orient. The art and poetry of Zen create involvement by means of the *interval,* not by the *connection* used in the visually organized Western world. Spectator becomes artist in oriental art because he must supply all the connections.

The section on "media hot and cool" confused many reviewers of *Understanding Media* who were unable to recognize the very large structural changes in human outlook that are occurring today. [Slang offers an immediate index to changing perception.] Slang is based not on theories but on immediate experience. The student of media will not only value slang as a guide to changing perception, but he will also study media as bringing about new perceptual habits.

The section on "the medium is the message" can, perhaps, be clarified by pointing out that any technology gradually creates a totally new human environment. Environments are not passive wrappings but active processes. In his splendid work *Preface to Plato* (Harvard University Press, 1963), Eric Havelock contrasts the oral and written cultures of the Greeks. By Plato's time the written word had created a new environment that had grown up by benefit of the process of the *tribal encyclopedia.* They had memorized the poets. The poets provided specific operational wisdom for all the contingencies of life—Ann Landers in verse. With the advent of individual detribalized man, a new education was needed. Plato devised such a new program for literate men. It was based on the Ideas. With the phonetic alphabet, classified wisdom took over from the operational wisdom of Homer and Hesiod and the tribal encyclopedia. Education by classified data has been the Western program ever since.

Now, however, in the electronic age, data classification yields to pattern recognition, the key phrase at IBM. When data move instantly, classification is too fragmentary. In order to cope with data at electric speed in typical situations of "information overload," men resort to the study of configurations, like the sailor in Edgar Allan Poe's *Maelstrom.* The drop-out situation in our schools at present has only begun to develop. The young student today grows up in an electrically configured world. It is a world not of wheels but of circuits, not of fragments but of integral patterns. The student today *lives* mythically and in depth. At school, however, he encounters a situation organized by means of classified information. The subjects are unrelated. They are visually conceived in terms of a blueprint. The student can find no possible means of involvement for himself, nor can he discover how the educational scene relates to the "mythic" world of electronically processed data and experience that he takes for granted. As one IBM executive puts it, "My children had lived several lifetimes compared to their grandparents when they began grade one."

"The medium is the message" means, in terms of the electronic age, that a totally new environment has been created. The "content" of this new environment is the old mechanized environment of the industrial age. The new environment reprocesses the old one as radically as TV is reprocessing the film. For the "content" of TV is the movie. TV is environmental and imperceptible, like all environments. We are aware only of the "content" or the old environment. When machine production was new, it gradually created an environment whose content was the old environment of agrarian life and the arts and crafts. This older environment was elevated to an art form by the new mechanical environment. The machine turned Nature into an art form. For the first time men began to regard Nature as a source of aesthetic and spiritual values. They began to marvel that earlier ages had been so unaware of the world of Nature as Art. Each new technology creates an environment that is itself regarded as corrupt and degrading. Yet the new one turns its predecessor into an art form. When writing was new, Plato transformed the old oral dialogue into an art form. When printing was new the Middle Ages became an art form. "The Elizabethan world view" was a view of the Middle Ages. And the industrial age turned the Renaissance into an art form as seen in the work of Jacob Burckhardt. Siegfried Giedion, in turn, has in the electric age taught us how to see the entire process of mechanization as an art process. *(Mechanization Takes Command)*

As our proliferating technologies have created a whole series of new environments, men have become aware of the arts as "anti-environments" or "counter-environments" that provide us with the means of perceiving the environment itself. For, as Edward T. Hall has explained in *The Silent Language*, men are never aware of the ground rules of their environmental systems of cultures. Today technologies and their consequent environments succeed each other so rapidly that one environment makes us aware of the next. Technologies begin to perform the function of art in making us aware of the psychic and social consequences of technology.

Art as anti-environment becomes more than ever a means of training perception and judgment. Art offered as a consumer commodity rather than as a means of training perception is as ludicrous and snobbish as always. Media study at once opens the doors of perception. And here it is that the young can do top-level research work. The teacher has only to invite the student to do as complete an inventory as possible. Any child can list the effects of the telephone or the radio or the motor car in shaping the life and work of his friends and his society. An inclusive list of media effects opens many unexpected avenues of awareness and investigation.

Edmund Bacon, of the Philadelphia town-planning commission, discovered that school children could be invaluable researchers and colleagues in the task of remaking the image of the city. We are entering the new age of education that is programmed for discovery rather than instruction. As the means of input increase, so does the need for insight or pattern recognition. The famous Hawthorne experiment, at the General Electric plant near Chicago, revealed a mysterious effect years ago. No matter how the conditions of the workers were altered, the workers did more and better work. Whether the heat and light and leisure were arranged adversely or pleasantly, the quantity and quality of output improved. The testers gloomily concluded that testing distorted the evidence. They missed the all-important fact that when the workers are permitted to join their energies to a process of learning and discovery, the increased efficiency is phenomenal.

Earlier it was mentioned how the school drop-out situation will get very much worse because of the frustration of the student need for participation in the learning process. This situation concerns also the problem of "the culturally disadvantaged child." This child exists not only in the slums but increasingly in the suburbs of the upper-income homes. The culturally disadvantaged child is the TV child. For TV has provided a new environment of low visual orientation and high involvement that makes accommodation to our older educational establishment quite difficult. One strategy of cultural response would be to raise the visual level of the TV image to enable the young student to gain access to the old visual world of the classroom and the curriculum. This would be worth trying as a temporary expedient. But TV is only one component of the electric environment of instant circuitry that has succeeded the old world of the wheel and nuts and bolts. We would be foolish not to ease our transition from the fragmented visual world of the existing educational establishment by every possible means.

The existential philosophy, as well as the Theater of the Absurd, represents anti-environments that point to the critical pressures of the new electric environment. Jean-Paul Sartre, as much as Samuel Beckett and Arthur Miller, has declared the futility of blueprints and classified data and "jobs" as a way out. Even the words "escape" and "vicarious living" have dwindled from the new scene of electronic involvement. TV engineers have begun to explore the braille-like character of the TV image as a means of enabling the blind to see by having this image projected directly onto their skins. We need to use all media in this wise, to enable us to see our situation.

On page 27 there are some lines from *Romeo and Juliet* whimsically modified to make an allusion to TV. Some reviewers have imagined that this was an involuntary misquotation.

The power of the arts to anticipate future social and technological developments, by a generation and more, has long been recognized. In this century Ezra Pound called the artist "the antennae of the race." Art as radar acts as "an early alarm system," as it were, enabling us to discover social and psychic targets in lots of time to prepare to cope with them. This concept of the arts as prophetic, contrasts with the popular idea of them as mere self-expression. If art is an "early warning system," to use the phrase from World War II, when radar was new, art has the utmost relevance not only to media study but to the development of media controls.

When radar was new it was found necessary to eliminate the balloon system for city protection that had preceded radar. The balloons got in the way of the electric feedback of the new radar information. Such may well prove to be the case with much of our existing school curriculum, to say nothing of the generality of the arts. We can afford to use only those portions of them that enhance the perception of our technologies, and their psychic and social consequences. Art as a radar environment takes on the function of indispensable perceptual training rather than the role of a privileged diet for the elite. While the arts as radar feedback provide a dynamic and changing corporate image, their purpose may be not to enable us to change but rather to maintain an even course toward permanent goals, even amidst the most disrupting innovations. We have already discovered the futility of changing our goals as often as we change our technologies.

chapter 3

Motivation

For ages, people charged with managing others have sought an elixir for motivating people. Still today, if one is writing a book for managers, he is well-advised to put "motivation" in the title, even if that is not the subject of the book. The reasons are obvious. The concept of motivation encompasses the variables responsible for the initiation, direction, and intensity of behavior. If these variables are known, they can be more easily manipulated to affect the maximum contribution of people toward organizational goals. With a better understanding of human motivation, we can reduce the energy expended on undesired behavior and increase the energy spent on desired behavior by effecting changes in individual characteristics and situational variables. Unfortunately, or perhaps fortunately, the problem of motivating people has proven to be too complex to permit a simple answer.

A full understanding of motivation requires answers to many of the unresolved issues of the nature-nurture question and of perception. First, any attempt to deal with causes of behavior almost inevitably gravitates to either implicit or explicit concern with the degree to which characteristics of the individual are inherited and acquired. Second, perception and motivation are treated separately here only for purposes of exposition. In reality, they are highly interdependent. Furthermore, as with perception, discussions of motivation often involve inferences about the inner world of another person.

My ability to make accurate inferences about your inner world is influenced by both my own inner world and your behavior. For example, what could I say about your motivation at the present time? Descriptively, your eyes are running across the words on this page, and your body is in some position relative to the book. I infer that you are reading. But why? Are you reading for knowledge? to gain power over people? for fun? to improve your grades? or for some other reason? If you are doing any one or some combination[1] of these things, are you doing it out of a fear of failure, or are you doing it for some more positive reason? Often, I both raise and answer such questions about you to myself, without either of us being aware of it while, only infrequently do I even think of

1. The term "combination" is important. Most behavior probably is multidetermined or overdetermined—that is to say, it occurs for many reasons.

testing the accuracy of my inferences with you. Rather, I often infer that you are reading this book for the same reasons for which I might read it under similar conditions. Even when attempting to test my inferences, I still impute my own inner world to you on the basis of my prior experience with you and other people. Thus, when I say something about what motivates you, I am often saying more about what motivates me. Interpreting another's inner world is a risky business.

TYPES OF MOTIVES

The complexity of motivation has not prevented man's mind from attempting to impose order on the cause of behavior. These attempts are reflected in a wide variety of theories, experiments, and other communications, ranging from poems and sermons to manuals for raising children and managing people. Bindra (1959) suggested that many efforts to explain what motivates behavior do not really explain the causes but rather only verbally relate the activity to conditions or events which are considered to be goals in the culture. In other words, what are often called motives are merely classifications of acts rather than causes of acts. While Bindra's point is well taken, these "descriptions" are helpful ways of discussing behavior. The types of motivation can be grouped into four classes, according to the major inferred source. Since the major inferred source is often the only source of motivation treated in each of the classes, any one approach taken alone is only partially adequate at best.

Instincts

While today instincts are infrequently used to explain human behavior, the concept dominated much early psychological thinking about human behavior. Generally instincts are viewed as complex patterns of unlearned behavior which have and/or had survival value for a species. Beach (1955) suggested that instinct gained an important position in scientific thought from the Darwinian approach, which assumed that behavior must be governed by either instinct or reason. Attempts to unseat the concept of instinct were unsuccessful, because those who attempted the change tended to assume that behavior was either acquired or inherited. Beach concluded that, as our knowledge of instinct and behavior advance, the idea of instinctive behavior will be replaced by more useful scientific explanations. The operation of instincts should not be seen as an entirely internal process. Recently the ethologists (Hess, 1962) have shown that some complex, instinctive behavior patterns may require certain environmental cues for their initiation. For example, a bundle of red feathers will produce fighting behavior in a male robin, whereas a dummy male robin without a red breast will not. Further, physical concentration of animals can produce radical changes in individual and social action, as demonstrated by the changes in parental behavior. Severe increases in population density will reduce fertility and/or increase the eating of young by mothers. This recent ethological research has revived interest in research on instincts.

Much of the work on territorial behavior and animal communication has direct parallels in the current attention being given to the role of personal space and nonverbal communication in humans. While animals, including humans, act to define and defend territories, the characteristics of the territories and their defense may be modified by environmental factors.

Drives

A second general approach to motivation relies on such forces as drive reduction, equilibrium creation, or homeostatic processes to account for behavior. Generally, these approaches parallel biological explanations of body functioning, which postulate that environmental changes induce physiological adjustments by the body to reduce tension or produce quiescence. For example, sensed environmental changes produce variations in the concentration of certain substances in the blood. These trigger other physiological changes, such as glandular reactions, which then produce changes in body processes to bring the body back to its initial state prior to the environmental changes.

The analogy of the thermostat provides a useful illustration of such homeostatic processes. As the temperature in the room changes, the shape of a small bar in the thermostat changes, because the two metals of which it is composed contract at different rates as the temperature falls. At a certain point, the bar has changed enough so that it closes a circuit, resulting in the activation at a heat-producing mechanism. The heat mechanism operates until the temperature of the room changes sufficiently to return the bar to its initial position. The desired state is maintained by repetitions of this cycle.

In the same way that the bar helps to maintain the desired internal state, physiological responses enable the body to maintain equilibrium with its environment. For example, changes in the concentration of blood sugar initiate a release of glycogen from the liver, which influences the receptors of the body to be more sensitive to signs of food. Similar mechanisms seem to operate for thirst (Hunt, 1965). While the reduction of many drives is accomplished through motor activity by the animal rather than by an automatic adjustment, the general model of producing and maintaining an equilibrium holds.

These equilibriating mechanisms are primary, in the sense that they occur without any prior learning. The body reacts automatically to reduce the state of disequilibrium. However, the means of drive reduction, such as effective techniques for obtaining food, are learned. Drive theorists have been concerned not only with learned behavior to satisfy the primary drives but also with secondary drives derived from the primary ones. For example, money, which can be used to satisfy many primary drives, may itself become the object of a drive. The drive theorists assume that deficit states of both primary and secondary drives are responsible for the motivation of behavior.

Hunt (1965) has described the drive-reduction approach well, by summarizing how a typical drive theorist treats the eight basic motivational issues: instigation of activity, intensity of behavior, direction of activity, feelings about objects, choices among responses and among goals, source of behavioral change and learning, and the persistence of behavior. Generally, drive theorists maintain that strong and painful external stimuii, homeostatic mechanisms, sex, and acquired drives cause the instigation of activity, with the intensity of the behavior being a function of the degree of need, the intensity of the stimuli, and the intensity of the evoked emotional responses. Behavior is directed toward the reduction of drive levels or away from drive increments. Those objects, responses, and goals which have been associated with successful drive reduction in the past tend to be favored, and the more often a response succeeds the more persistently it will. be chosen in the future. Conversely, unsuccessful responses, which lead to frustration, are chosen with decreasing frequency. Learning is then said to take place.

Drive-reduction models have been and still are at the center of assumptions about motivation in American psychology. They are likely to stay there, since a primary or higher-order drive can usually be inferred to "explain" almost any behavior.[2] Thus, besides its power in generating research, and the dedication and ingenuity of its proponents, the drive-reduction view has been preferred because it is able to deal with a wide variety of behavior and is very difficult to disprove. In spite of all this, drive-reduction theory in its pure form is increasingly being challenged.

Growth, competence, and self-actualization.

The strongest challenge has come from theories and evidence supporting the existence of drive-seeking, self-actualization, or competence and growth motivation. This body of thought springs from diverse sources and has been, at least in part, a polemic against the drive-reduction assumptions. Support for this position has been marshalled from the work of experimental psychologists and the writings of humanistic psychologists such as Maslow and Rogers.

Many of the current theories of management, such as McGregor's and Likert's, share important commonalities with the humanistic or growth-oriented view. In fact, the humanistic assumptions about human motivation have become the dominant ones in organizational behavior. Although recent evidence suggests that growth models are not the sole answer to the problems of management of human behavior, it is nevertheless important to view them in some detail.

Growth models challenge the assumption that human beings (and other animals) are merely drive-reducing mechanisms and propose an alternative view that people seek novel stimuli, mastery over their environment, and growth in order to come closer to their "true essence." Growth theorists argue that, rather than attempting to reduce tension, man often acts to seek stimulation. A growing body of evidence supports this contention. Olds and Olds (1965)

2. The drive-reduction model has played an important role in modern thinking about cognitive functioning as well as about simple behavioral events. Festinger's (1957) theory of cognitive dissonance has been one of the most important foundations for empirical research in recent social psychology. This theory is based on the assumption that organisms respond to a conflict of ideas and attitudes by attempting to bring the conflicting elements into balance. In other words, cognitive conflict, like any other drive, induces organisms to reduce tension.

Festinger's work is treated in more detail in the selection by Secord and Backman in Part III of this book.

reported that animals will work to receive stimulation of certain areas of the brain. For example, rats will press a bar vigorously, until physically fatigued, for reinforcement by electrical stimulation to the septal area of the brain. Other work by Bexton, Heron, and Scott (1954) and Lilly (1956) demonstrated that human beings find it very difficult to tolerate a homogeneous environment.[3] White (1959) wrote of a competence motive, which stimulates men to seek and conquer challenges posed by their environment. White maintained that a persistence of behavior directed towards learning to interact effectively with the environment exists at times when the organism is not dominated by other drives. White called this need for effectiveness, not included in most instinct or drive theories, competence motivation.[4] Hunt (1965) postulated a standard of optimal incongruity, arguing that organisms perfer some tension to no tension. Berlyne's (1960) work has given strong support for an exploratory drive in animals and humans, which supports Hunt's view. Other work by Butler (1953) found that opportunities for visual exploration were rewarding to monkeys. This evidence cannot be explained by drive-reduction theory, at least in its pure form.

Considerable support for the growth model exists among personality theorists. Abraham Maslow has pioneered in proposing a need for self-actualization and growth. He and other theorists supporting this view contend that people seek "higher" goals in addition to the physiological and psychological reduction of drives, that they seek to reach their full potential as people. Maslow (1969) argued that biologists and psychologists, in accepting a normative model, have paid insufficient attention to the conditions which produce the "best" human specimens.

It should be noted that one can accept the evidence which has been collected without necessarily accepting some of the conclusions for which it has been used or the assumptions on which the theory is based. For example, it is possible to translate the concept of exploration needs into drive-reduction terms. All we need do is postulate a drive for an optimal level of stimulation. The data can be reconciled with any of several models of motivation. It may be premature for organizational behaviorists to get "locked into" any one set of assumptions about human nature and human motivation. By contrast, it is very profitable to be familiar with and draw evidence and information from a variety of approaches.

Environment as source of motivation.

The fourth general approach to motivation is perhaps the least well developed of all, since it basically seeks to skirt what most people mean by motivation. This approach focuses on the environment as a source of behavioral change; it does not attempt to investigate the internal processes of the organism but rather treats them as givens. This approach is perhaps best exemplified by the work of B. F. Skinner.[5] Basically this approach stresses the role of factors

3. Hebb's article earlier in this part dealt with this research in further detail.
4. Morse and Lorsch in Part IV rely heavily on White's concept.
5. Although his recent work (Skinner, 1969) draws heavily on ethological thinking and stresses the role of phylogenetic factors, he still places strong reliance on external factors.

external to the organism in influencing behavior. For example, rather than talk about hunger, these investigators refer to the number of hours an animal has been deprived of food. No inferences are made about changes in internal states. Only changes in behavior are dealt with. This approach to motivation is viewed by many as not dealing with motivation. Nevertheless, it does direct attention to the important role of external stimuli in the initiation, direction, and intensity of behavior.

A complete view of motivation must certainly deal with external as well as internal variables. For example, some of the work of the ethologists has shown that the sex drive does not operate in a vacuum. In fact, external stimuli, such as a distinguishing characteristic of a member of the opposite sex of the same species, are necessary for triggering the sexual behavior of many animals. Similarly, Ervin (1964) measured the aggressiveness of responses to the Thematic Apperception Test (TAT) and found that bilingual subjects expressed more aggression when responding in French than when responding in English. Since the language one speaks in is apt to be influenced by the language of the person he is talking with, Ervin's finding suggests that aggression, thought by many to be a personality trait, may be at least in part a function of external factors, such as the language addressed to one.

Berkowitz (1969) has summarized some ways in which situational factors influence motivation and behavior. He noted that traits, attitudes, and personality needs can be viewed as habitual responses to a particular set of stimuli. The stimulus factors may act as both inhibiting and disinhibiting factors. Furthermore, environmental factors may elicit behavior which would not occur in their absence. Taken together, the foregoing arguments demonstrate the importance of situational factors to motivation.

Summary

We have viewed four classes of approaches to motivation. Each approach has much to offer, and each is better in dealing with some topics than with others. At present the issue is not so much choosing the "correct" model as developing an integrated understanding of the knowledge embodied in the varied approaches. Motivation is both innate and acquired, both internal and external, and perhaps both drive-reducing and tension-producing. Vinacke's (1962) model, discussed below, is a useful tool for integrating existing knowledge. While it is unlikely to provide definitive answers it does demonstrate the multi-factor approach that seems essential for an adequate treatment of motivation.

AN INTEGRATIVE APPROACH TO MOTIVATION

Vinacke's drive-modification theory focuses on both extrinsic and intrinsic factors as determinants of motivation. Motivation, according to Vinacke, ". . . concerns the conditions responsible for variation in the intensity, quality, and direction of ongoing behavior (p. 3)." The conditions constitute an organized system of factors which determine responses at any given time. The different components of these conditions are all significantly interrelated.

Vinacke grouped the components into three intrinsic and two extrinsic classes. The first intrinsic class, instigation, corresponds to the activity of the bodily tissues. Instigation includes the components which determine" . . . the forms and degrees of fundamental energy-expenditure of the organism (p.4)." Vinacke's description of the components of instigation parallels more traditional theories in explaining the intensity and direction of energy expenditure. However, drive-modification theory maintains that the tissues and hence the basic drives themselves are modified by learning and experience with the environment. The second intrinsic class regulation includes mechanisms and processes which perform the "steering" function. These include what other writers have called values, sentiments, tastes, defense mechanisms, habits and other regulative processes; they determine the direction and pattern of acts which follow instigation. Vinacke uses "attitude" as a summary term for these processes. The third intrinsic class is adjustment, which includes temporary and specific determinants of responses following instigation and regulation. Adjustment summarizes cognitive processes which ". . . focus behavior by selecting the particular act or series of acts that occurs in a given situation (p. 9)." In the same way that the attitudes or regulative processes determine the expression of energy, the adjustment process determines the expression of the attitudes. In sum, intrinsic motivation involves energy potential which is first generated, then steered in a general manner, and finally focused in terms of a given situation.

The intrinsic levels interact with two extrinsic levels, induction and situation. Induction includes conditions which influence performance by evoking changes in intrinsic variables. These are events which occur before performance can operate at any of the three intrinsic levels. For example, food deprivation acts as an induction factor to produce tissue changes. Finally, motivation is influenced by situational variables involved in task performance itself. Included in situation are such factors as a person's perceptions of the goal, his relation to the goal, his performance, and the properties of the task itself.

All of these variables operate simultaneously to determine motivation. This approach to motivation can be a useful guide to thought in organizational behavior, because it integrates the essential factors which produce motivation. The drive-modification model suggests that motivation is better described as sets of conditions which affect behavior rather than as a personality trait, because it does not take external factors into account. In sum, motivated behavior is the product of environmental conditions, physiological states, and cognitive processes. The direction, quality, and intensity of behavior are determined by a variety of factors operating simultaneously. The effects of extrinsic factors will vary as a result of individual differences in intrinsic factors, and vice versa.

SOME ORIENTING CONCLUSIONS

The readings that follow were selected to provide an orientation and evaluation of contemporary thought about motivation. The ideas of some writers, such as Herzberg and McGregor, have been widely accepted by practicing managers. The generality of these approaches, with their rather sweeping assumptions about the motivation of men, are questioned by other writers. In fact, McGregor, as we will see, based his ideas on the work of Maslow. In the selection by Maslow, we see him questioning the utility of some of his own ideas. Hulin and Blood, in their paper, also question the generality of current models of motivation. The final paper, by Jackson and Shea, expands the work on achievement motivation into an organizational framework.

The reader may find it helpful to search out the assumptions and the implications of these assumptions in each of the selections. However, it is unwise to reject at present any of the recommendations purely on the basis of the particular assumptions about motivation. A host of approaches to this complex problem seems to be required. Open-minded research may facilitate the discovery of various situations and personal conditions which may be critical in the motivation of different people under different circumstances. At the present time, the manager facing motivational problems in his organization will probably find the most useful approach an eclectic one. Thus armed, he will be encouraged to search out and manipulate the significant variables and will not be limited to a few techniques which may be of small value in his particular situation.

REFERENCES

Beach, F. A. "The Descent of Instinct." *Psychological Review* 62 (1955):401-10.

Berkowitz, L. "Social Motivation." In G. Lindzey & E. Aronson, eds., *The Handbook of Social Psychology,* 2nd ed., vol. 3. Reading, Mass.: Addison-Wesley, 1969. pp. 50-135.

Berlyne, D. E. *Conflict, Arousal, and Curiosity.* New York: McGraw-Hill Book Company, 1960.

Bexton, W. H.; Heron, W.; and Scott, T. H. "Effects of Decreased Variation in the Environment." *Canadian Journal of Psychology* 8 (1954):70-76.

Bindra, D. *Motivation: A Systematic Reinterpretation.* New York: Ronald Press, 1959.

Butler, R. A. "The Effect of Deprivation of Visual Incentives on Visual Exploration Motivation in Monkeys." *Journal of Comparative and Physiological Psychology* 46 (1953): 95-98.

Ervin, S. M. "Language and TAT Content in Bilinguals." *Journal of Abnormal and Social Psychology* 68 (1964):500-507.

Festinger, L. *A Theory of Cognitive Dissonance.* Evanston, Ill.: Row, Peterson, 1957.

Hess, Eckhard H. "Ethology." In R. Brown, E. Galanter, E. Hess, and G. Mandley, eds., *New Directions in Psychology.* New York: Holt, Rinehart & Winston, 1962. pp. 157-266.

Hunt, J. McV. "Intrinsic Motivation and its Role in Psychological Development." In S. Levine, ed., *Nebraska Symposium on Motivation* 8:189-282. Lincoln, Neb.: University of Nebraska Press, 1965.

Lilly, J. C. "Mental Effects of Reduction of Ordinary Levels of Physical Stimuli on Intact, Healthy Persons." *Psychiatric Research Reports* no. 5, (1956): 1-9.

Maslow, A. H. "Toward a Humanistic Biology." *American Psychologist* 24 (1969):724-35.

Olds, J., and Olds, M. "Drives, Rewards, and the Brain." In *New Directions in Psychology II,* New York: Holt, Rinehart & Winston, 1965, 327-410.

Skinner, B. F. *Contingencies of Reinforcement.* New York: Appleton-Century-Crofts, 1969.

Vinacke, W. E. "Motivation as a Complex Problem." *Nebraska Symposium on Motivation* 10:1-49. Lincoln, Neb.: University of Nebraska Press, 1962.

Douglas Murray McGregor

THE HUMAN SIDE OF ENTERPRISE

It has become trite to say that industry has the fundamental know-how to utilize physical science and technology for the material benefit of mankind, and that we must now learn how to utilize the social sciences to make our human organizations truly effective.

To a degree, the social sciences today are in a position like that of the physical sciences with respect to atomic energy in the thirties. We know that past conceptions of the nature of man are inadequate and, in many ways, incorrect. We are becoming quite certain that, under proper conditions, unimagined resources of creative human energy could become available within the organizational setting.

We cannot tell industrial management how to apply this new knowledge in simple, economic ways. We know it will require years of exploration, much costly development research, and a substantial amount of creative imagination on the part of management to discover how to apply this growing knowledge to the organization of human effort in industry.

MANAGEMENT'S TASK: THE CONVENTIONAL VIEW

The conventional conception of management's task in harnessing human energy to organizational requirements can be stated broadly in terms of three

Reprinted by permission of the publisher from *Management Review*, November 1957. © 1957 by the American Management Association, Inc. Reprinted by permission of the publisher.

propositions. In order to avoid the complications introduced by a label, let us call this set of propositions "Theory X":

1. Management is responsible for organizing the elements of productive enterprise—money, materials, equipment, people—in the interest of economic ends.
2. With respect to people, this is a process of directing their efforts, motivating them, controlling their actions, modifying their behavior to fit the needs of the organization.
3. Without this active intervention by management, people would be passive—even resistant—to organizational needs. They must therefore be persuaded, rewarded, punished, controlled—their activities must be directed. This is management's task. We often sum it up by saying that management consists of getting things done through other people.

Behind this conventional theory there are several additional beliefs—less explicit, but widespread:

4. The average man is by nature indolent—he works as little as possible.
5. He lacks ambition, dislikes responsibility, prefers to be led.
6. He is inherently self-centered, indifferent to organizational needs.
7. He is by nature resistant to change.
8. He is gullible, not very bright, the ready dupe of the charlatan and the demagogue.

The human side of economic enterprise today is fashioned from propositions and beliefs such as these. Conventional organization structures and managerial policies, practices, and programs reflect these assumptions:

In accomplishing its task—with these assumptions as guides—management has conceived of a range of possibilities.

At one extreme, management can be "hard" or "strong". The methods for directing behavior involve coercion and threat (usually disguised), close supervision, tight controls over behavior. At the other extreme, management can be "soft" or "weak". The methods for directing behavior involve being permissive, satisfying people's demands, achieving harmony. Then they will be tractable, accept direction.

This range has been fairly completely explored during the past half century, and management has learned some things from the exploration. There are difficulties in the "hard" approach. Force breeds counter-forces: restriction of output, antagonism, militant unionism, subtle but effective sabotage of management objectives. This "hard" approach is especially difficult during times of full employment.

There are also difficulties in the "soft" approach. It leads frequently to the abdication of management—to harmony, perhaps, but to indifferent performance. People take advantage of the soft approach. They continually expect more, but they give less and less.

Currently, the popular theme is "firm but fair". This is an attempt to gain the advantages of both the hard and the soft approaches. It is reminiscent of Teddy Roosevelt's "speak softly and carry a big stick".

IS THE CONVENTIONAL VIEW CORRECT?

The findings which are beginning to emerge from the social sciences challenge this whole set of beliefs about man and human nature and about the task of management. The evidence is far from conclusive, certainly, but it is suggestive. It comes from the laboratory, the clinic, the schoolroom, the home, and even to a limited extent from industry itself.

The social scientist does not deny that human behavior in industrial organization today is approximately what management perceives it to be. He has, in fact, observed it and studied it fairly extensively. But he is pretty sure that this behavior is *not* a consequence of man's inherent nature. It is a consequence rather of the nature of industrial organizations, of management philosophy, policy, and practice. The conventional approach of Theory X is based on mistaken notions of what is cause and what is effect.

Perhaps the best way to indicate why the conventional approach of management is inadequate is to consider the subject of motivation.

PHYSIOLOGICAL NEEDS

Man is a wanting animal—as soon as one of his needs is satisfied, another appears in its place. This process is unending. It continues from birth to death.

Man's needs are organized in a series of levels—a hierarchy of importance. At the lowest level, but pre-eminent in importance when they are thwarted, are his *physiological needs*. Man lives for bread alone, when there is no bread. Unless the circumstances are unusual, his needs for love, for status, for recognition are inoperative when his stomach has been empty for a while. But when he eats regularly and adequately, hunger ceases to be an important motivation. The same is true of the other physiological needs of man—for rest, exercise, shelter, protection from the elements.

A satisfied need is not a motivator of behavior! This is a fact of profound significance that is regularly ignored in the conventional approach to the management of people. Consider your own need for air: Except as you are deprived of it, it has no appreciable motivating effect upon your behavior.

SAFETY NEEDS

When the physiological needs are reasonably satisfied, needs at the next higher level begin to dominate man's behavior—to motivate him. These are called *safety needs.* They are needs for protection against danger, threat, deprivation. Some people mistakenly refer to these as needs for security. However, unless man is in a dependent relationship where he fears arbitrary deprivation, he does not demand security. The need is for the "fairest possible break." When he is confident of this, he is more than willing to take risks. But when he feels threatened or dependent, his greatest need is for guarantees, for protection, for security.

The fact needs little emphasis that, since every industrial employee is in a dependent relationship, safety needs may assume considerable importance. Arbitrary management actions, behavior which arouses uncertainty with respect to continued employment or which reflects favoritism or discrimination, unpredictable administration of policy—these can be powerful motivators of the safety needs in the employment relationship *at every level,* from worker to vice president.

SOCIAL NEEDS

When man's physiological needs are satisfied and he is no longer fearful about his physical welfare, his *social needs* become important motivators of his behavior—needs for belonging, for association, for acceptance by his fellows, for giving and receiving friendship and love.

Management knows today of the existence of these needs, but it often assumes quite wrongly that they represent a threat to the organization. Many studies have demonstrated that the tightly knit, cohesive work group may, under proper conditions, be far more effective than an equal number of separate individuals in achieving organizational goals.

Yet management, fearing group hostility to its own objectives, often goes to considerable lengths to control and direct human efforts in ways that are inimical to the natural "groupiness" of human beings. When man's social needs—and perhaps his safety needs, too—are thus thwarted, he behaves in ways which tend to defeat organizational objectives. He becomes resistant, antagonistic, uncooperative. But this behavior is a consequence, not a cause.

EGO NEEDS

Above the social needs—in the sense that they do not become motivators until lower needs are reasonably satisfied—are the needs of greatest significance to management and to man himself. They are the *egoistic needs,* and they are of two kinds:

1. Those needs that relate to one's self-esteem—needs for self-confidence, for independence, for achievement, for competence, for knowledge.
2. Those needs that relate to one's reputation—needs for status, for recognition, for appreciation, for the deserved respect of one's fellows.

Unlike the lower needs, these are rarely satisfied; man seeks indefinitely for more satisfaction of these needs once they have become important to him. But they do not appear in any significant way until physiological, safety, and social needs are all reasonably satisfied.

The typical industrial organization offers few opportunities for the satisfaction of these egoistic needs to people at lower levels in the hierarchy. The conventional methods of organizing work, particularly in mass-production industries, give little heed to these aspects of human motivation. If the practices of scientific management were deliberately calculated to thwart these needs, they could hardly accomplish this purpose better than they do.

SELF-FULFILLMENT NEEDS

Finally—a capstone, as it were, on the hierarchy of man's needs—there are what we may call the *needs for self-fulfillment*. These are the needs for realizing one's own potentialities, for continued self-development, for being creative in the broadest sense of that term.

It is clear that the conditions of modern life give only limited opportunity for these relatively weak needs to obtain expression. The deprivation most people experience with respect to other lower-level needs diverts their energies into the struggle to satisfy *those* needs, and the needs for self-fulfillment remain dormant.

MANAGEMENT AND MOTIVATION

We recognize readily enough that a man suffering from a severe dietary deficiency is sick. The deprivation of physiological needs has behavioral consequences. The same is true—although less well recognized—of deprivation of higher-level needs. The man whose needs for safety, association, independence, or status are thwarted is sick just as surely as the man who has rickets. And his sickness will have behavioral consequences. We will be mistaken if we attribute his resultant passivity, his hostility, his refusal to accept responsibility to his inherent "human nature." These forms of behavior are *symptoms* of illness—of deprivation of his social and egoistic needs.

The man whose lower-level needs are satisfied is not motivated to satisfy those needs any longer. For practical purposes they exist no longer. Management often asks, "Why aren't people more productive? We pay good wages, provide good working conditions, have excellent fringe benefits and steady employment. Yet people do not seem to be willing to put forth more than minimum effort."

The fact that management has provided for these physiological and safety needs has shifted the motivational emphasis to the social and perhaps to the egoistic needs. Unless there are opportunities *at work* to satisfy these higher-level needs, people will be deprived; and their behavior will reflect this deprivation. Under such conditions, if management continues to focus its attention on physiological needs, its efforts are bound to be ineffective.

People *will* make insistent demands for more money under these conditions. It becomes more important than ever to buy the material goods and services which can provide limited satisfaction of the thwarted needs. Although money has only limited value in satisfying many higher-level needs, it can become the focus of interest if it is the *only* means available.

THE CARROT-AND-STICK APPROACH

The carrot-and-stick theory of motivation (like Newtonian physical theory) works reasonably well under certain circumstances. The *means* for satisfying man's physiological and (within limits) his safety needs can be provided or withheld by management. Employment itself is such a means, and so are wages, working conditions, and benefits. By these means the individual can be controlled so long as he is struggling for subsistence.

But the carrot-and-stick theory does not work at all once man has reached an adequate subsistence level and is motivated primarily by higher needs. Management cannot provide a man with self-respect, or with the respect of his fellows, or with the satisfaction of needs for self-fulfillment. It can create such conditions that he is encouraged and enabled to seek such satisfactions for *himself*, or it can thwart him by failing to create those conditions.

But this creation of conditions is not "control." It is not a good device for directing behavior. And so management finds itself in an odd position. The high standard of living created by our modern technological know-how provides quite adequately for the satisfaction of physiological and safety needs. The only significant exception is where management practices have not created confidence in a "fair break"—and thus where safety needs are thwarted. But by making possible the satisfaction of low-level needs, management has deprived itself of the ability to use as motivators the devices on which conventional theory has taught it to rely—rewards, promises, incentives, or threats and other coercive devices.

The philosophy of management by direction and control—*regardless of whether it is hard or soft*—is inadequate to motivate because the human needs on which this approach relies are today unimportant motivators of behavior. Direction and control are essentially useless in motivating people whose important needs are social and egoistic. Both the hard and the soft approach fail today because they are simply irrelevant to the situation.

People, deprived of opportunities to satisfy at work the needs which are now important to them, behave exactly as we might predict—with indolence, passivity, resistance to change, lack of responsibility, willingness to follow the demagogue, unreasonable demands for economic benefits. It would seem that we are caught in a web of our own weaving.

A NEW THEORY OF MANAGEMENT

For these and many other reasons, we require a different theory of the task of managing people based on more adequate assumptions about human nature and human motivation. I am going to be so bold as to suggest the broad dimensions of such a theory. Call it "Theory Y," if you will.

1. Management is responsible for organizing the elements of productive enterprise—money, materials, equipment, people—in the interest of economic ends.
2. People are *not* by nature passive or resistant to organizational needs. They have become so as a result of experience in organizations.
3. The motivation, the potential for development, the capacity for assuming responsibility, the readiness to direct behavior toward organizational goals are all present in people. Management does not put them there. It is a responsibility of management to make it possible for people to recognize and develop these human characteristics for themselves.

4. The essential task of management is to arrange organizational conditions and methods of operation so that people can achieve their own goals *best* by directing *their own* efforts toward organizational objectives.

This is a process primarily of creating opportunities, releasing potential, removing obstacles, encouraging growth, providing guidance. It is what Peter Drucker has called "management by objectives" in contrast to "management by control." It does *not* involve the abdication of management, the absence of leadership, the lowering of standards, or the other characteristics usually associated with the "soft" approach under Theory X.

SOME DIFFICULTIES

It is no more possible to create an organization today which will be a full, effective application of this theory than it was to build an atomic power plant in 1945. There are many formidable obstacles to overcome.

The conditions imposed by conventional organization theory and by the approach of scientific management for the past half century have tied men to limited jobs which do not utilize their capabilities, have discouraged the acceptance of responsibility, have encouraged passivity, have eliminated meaning from work. Man's habits, attitudes, expectations—his whole conception of membership in an industrial organization—have been conditioned by his experience under these circumstances.

People today are accustomed to being directed, manipulated, controlled in industrial organizations and to finding satisfaction for their social, egoistic, and self-fulfillment needs away from the job. This is true of much of management as well as of workers. Genuine "industrial citizenship"—to borrow again a term from Drucker—is a remote and unrealistic idea, the meaning of which has not even been considered by most members of industrial organizations.

Another way of saying this is that Theory X places exclusive reliance upon external control of human behavior, while Theory Y relies heavily on self-control and self-direction. It is worth noting that this difference is the difference between treating people as children and treating them as mature adults. After generations of the former, we cannot expect to shift to the latter overnight.

STEPS IN THE RIGHT DIRECTION

Before we are overwhelmed by the obstacles, let us remember that the application of theory is always slow. Progress is usually achieved in small steps. Some innovative ideas which are entirely consistent with Theory Y are today being applied with some success.

Decentralization and Delegation

These are ways of freeing people from the too-close control of conventional organization, giving them a degree of freedom to direct their own activities, to assume responsibility, and, importantly, to satisfy their egoistic needs. In this connection, the flat organization of Sears, Roebuck and Company provides an interesting example. It forces "management by objectives," since it enlarges the number of people reporting to a manager until he cannot direct and control them in the conventional manner.

Job Enlargement

This concept, pioneered by I.B.M. and Detroit Edison, is quite consistent with Theory Y. It encourages the acceptance of responsibility at the bottom of the organization; it provides opportunities for satisfying social and egoistic needs. In fact, the reorganization of work at the factory level offers one of the more challenging opportunities for innovation consistent with Theory Y.

Participation and Consultative Management

Under proper conditions, participation and consultative management provide encouragement to people to direct their creative energies toward organizational objectives, give them some voice in decisions that affect them, provide significant opportunities for the satisfaction of social and egoistic needs. The Scanlon Plan is the outstanding embodiment of these ideas in practice.

Performance Appraisal

Even a cursory examination of conventional programs of performance appraisal within the ranks of management will reveal how completely consistent they are with Theory X. In fact, most such programs tend to treat the individual as though he were a product under inspection on the assembly line.

A few companies—among them General Mills, Ansul Chemical, and General Electric—have been experimenting with approaches which involve the individual in setting "targets" or objectives *for himself* and in a *self-* evaluation of performance semiannually or annually. Of course, the superior plays an important leadership role in this process—one, in fact, which demands substantially more competence than the conventional approach. The role is, however, considerably more congenial to many managers than the role of "judge" or "inspector" which is usually forced upon them. Above all, the individual is encouraged to take a greater responsibility for planning and appraising his own contribution to organizational objectives; and the accompanying effects on egoistic and self-fulfillment needs are substantial.

APPLYING THE IDEAS

The not infrequent failure of such ideas as these to work as well as expected is often attributable to the fact that a management has "bought the idea" but applied it within the framework of Theory X and its assumptions.

Delegation is not an effective way of exercising management by control. Participation becomes a farce when it is applied as a sales gimmick or a device for kidding people into thinking they are important. Only the management that has confidence in human capacities and is itself directed toward organizational objectives rather than toward the preservation of personal power can grasp the implications of this emerging theory. Such management will find and apply successfully other innovative ideas as we move slowly toward the full implementation of a theory like Y.

THE HUMAN SIDE OF ENTERPRISE

It is quite possible for us to realize substantial improvements in the effectiveness of industrial organizations during the next decade or two. The social sciences can contribute much to such developments; we are only beginning to grasp the implications of the growing body of knowledge in these fields. But if this conviction is to become a reality instead of a pious hope, we will need to view the process much as we view the process of releasing the energy of the atom for constructive human ends—as a slow, costly, sometimes discouraging approach toward a goal which would seem to many to be quite unrealistic.

The ingenuity and the perseverance of industrial management in the pursuit of economic ends have changed many scientific and technological dreams into commonplace realities. It is now becoming clear that the application of these same talents to the human side of enterprise will not only enhance substantially these materialistic achievements, but will bring us one step closer to "the good society."

*   *   *

Abraham H. Maslow

MANAGEMENT AS A PSYCHOLOGICAL EXPERIMENT

There are enough data available, and enough industrial experiences, and also enough clinical-psychological data on human motivations, to warrant taking a chance on the experiment of Theory Y type of management. And yet it is well to keep in mind always that this will be a kind of a pilot experiment for the simple reason that the data which justify this experiment are definitely not final data, not clearly convincing beyond a shadow of a doubt. There is still plenty of room for doubt, as is evidenced by the fact that many academic people and many managers still do, in fact, doubt the validity of the whole line of thinking involved, and this is not entirely arbitrary. They do bring up evidence, experience, data against the new kind of management. We must certainly agree

Abridged from Abraham H. Maslow, *Eupsychian Management,* pp. 53-60. Reprinted by permission of Richard D. Irwin, Inc. © 1965.

that there is plenty of doubt, and that the whole business is an experiment, and we must also be very aware of the fact that we need lots of data, lots of answers to a lot of questions yet to come.

For instance, the whole philosophy of this new kind of management may be taken as an expression of faith in the goodness of human beings, in trustworthiness, in enjoyment of efficiency, of knowledge, of respect, etc. But the truth is that we don't really have exact and quantitative information on the proportion of the human population which does in fact have some kind of feeling for workmanship, some kind of desire for all the facts and all the truth, some sort of desire for efficiency over against inefficiency, etc. We know certainly that some individual human beings have these needs, and we know a little about the conditions under which these needs will appear, but we don't have any mass surveys of large populations that would give us some quantitative indication of just how many people prefer to have somebody else do their thinking for them, for instance. We don't know the answers to the question: What proportion of the population is irreversibly authoritarian? We don't even know what proportion of the population are psychopaths or paranoiac characters or overdependent or safety-motivated, etc., etc.

These are all crucial kinds of information that we would need in order to be absolutely certain about enlightened management policy. We don't know how many people or what proportion of the working population would actually prefer to participate in management decisions, and how many would prefer not to have anything to do with them. What proportion of the population take a job as simply any old kind of a job which they must do in order to earn a living, while their interests are very definitely centered elsewhere outside of the job.

An example is the woman who works only because she has to support her children. It's perfectly true that she'll prefer a nice and pleasant job to a rotten job, but just how does she define rotten job? How much involvement does she really want in the enterprise if the center of her life is definitely in her children rather than in her job? What proportion of the population prefer authoritarian bosses, prefer to be told what to do, don't want to bother thinking, etc? What proportion of the population is reduced to the concrete and so finds planning for the future totally incomprehensible and boring? How many people prefer honesty and how strongly do they prefer it to dishonesty, how strong a tendency is there in people against being thieves? We know very little about physical inertia or psychic inertia. How lazy are people and under what circumstances and what makes them not lazy? We just don't know.

All of this then is an experiment (because of inadequate final data) in just about the same way that political democracy is an experiment which is based upon a scientifically unproven assumption: namely that human beings like to participate in their own fate, that given sufficient information they will make wise decisions about their own lives, and that they prefer freedom to being bossed, that they prefer to have a say in everything which affects their future, etc. None of these assumptions has been adequately enough proven so that we would call it scientific fact in about the same way that we would label biological fact scientific. We have to know more about these psychological factors then we do. Because this is so, we ought to again be very aware, very conscious, of the fact that these are articles of faith rather than articles of final knowledge, or perhaps better said that they are articles of faith with some grounding in fact though not yet enough to convince people who are characterologically against these articles of faith.

I suppose that the ultimate test of scientific fact is that those people who are by temperament and character unsympathetic to the conclusion must accept it as a fact anyway. We will know that our knowledge of the authoritarian character structure is truly scientific final fact when an average authoritarian character will be able to read the information on the subject and then regard his own authoritarian character as undesirable or sick or pathological and will go about trying to get rid of it. Just so long as an authoritarian character can wave aside all the evidence which indicates that he is sick, just so long are those facts not sufficient, not final enough.

After all, if we take the whole thing from McGregor's point of view of a contrast between a Theory X view of human nature, a good deal of the evidence upon which he bases his conclusions comes from my researches and my papers on motivations, self-actualization, etc. But I of all people should know just how shaky this foundation is as a final foundation. My work on motivations came from the clinic, from a study of neurotic people. The carry-over of this theory to the industrial situation has some support from industrial studies, but certainly I would like to see a lot more studies of this kind before feeling finally convinced that this carry-over from the study of neurosis to the study of labor in factories is legitimate.

The same thing is true of my studies of self-actualizing people—there is only this one study of mine available (1). There were many things wrong with the sampling, so many in fact that it must be considered to be, in the classical sense anyway, a bad or poor or inadequate experiment. I am quite willing to concede this—as a matter of fact, I am eager to concede it—because I'm a little worried about this stuff which I consider to be tentative being swallowed whole by all sorts of enthusiastic people, who really should be a little more tentative, in the way that I am. The experiment needs repeating and checking—it needs working over in other societies—it needs a lot of things which it doesn't yet have. The main support for this theory—and, of course, there's plenty of this support—has come mostly from psychotherapists like Rogers and Fromm.

This, of course, leaves the problem of carry-over from the therapeutic situation to the industrial situation still open to testing. It needs to be validated as a legitimate carry-over. I may say also that my paper on the need for knowledge (2), on curiosity in the human being, is also practically the only thing of its kind, and while I trust it and believe my own conclusions, I am still willing to admit like a cautious scientist that it ought to be checked by other people before being taken as final. As we become aware of the probable errors of the data, we must underscore the necessity for more research. Smugness and certainty tend to stop research rather than to stimulate it.

On the other hand, of course, I should make clear that the evidence upon which Theory X management is based is practically nil; that there is even less evidence for Theory X than there is for Theory Y. It rests entirely on habit and tradition. It's no use saying that it rests on long experience, as most of its proponents would say, because this experience is a kind of self, or at least *can* be a kind of self-fulfilling prophecy. That is to say that the people who support Theory X on nonscientific grounds then proceed to use it as a management philosophy, which brings about just that behavior in the workers which Theory X would predict. But with this kind of Theory X treatment of workers, no other kind of behavior would be possible as a result.

To sum this up I would say that there is insufficient grounding for a firm and final trust in Theory Y management philosophy; but then I would hastily add that there is even less firm evidence for Theory X. If one adds up all the researches that have actually been done under scientific auspices and in the industrial situation itself, practically all of them come out on the side of one or another version of Theory Y; practically none of them come out in favor of Theory X philosophy except in small and detailed and specific special circumstances.

The same is true for the studies of the authoritarian personality. These also come out generally in favor of the democratic personality. And yet there are a few specific special instances in which it is better to have an authoritarian personality, in which the authoritarian will get better results. For instance, an authoritarian personality will get better results for a transitional period as a teacher with authoritarian students than will a democratic and permissive Theory Y kind of teacher. This is the same order of evidence which indicates that practically *any* human being, however sick, can be used some place in a complex industrial civilization. I think, for instance, of Bob Holt's demonstration of the adaptive value even of the paranoid character; he showed that such people tend to make better detectives than do normal people — or at least that they do as well.

Another point here comes from my reading of the chapter by Scoutten in the book edited by Mason Haire called *Organization Theory in Industrial Practice.* Scoutten brings to mind that as soon as we take into account such factors as the long-range health of the business (instead of a merely short-range health), the duties to a demoncratic society, the need in an individualized situation for pretty highly developed human beings as workers and managers, etc., etc., *then* the necessity for Theory Y management becomes greater and greater. He speaks of production and sales as the only functions, the only goals, of the company with which he is connected, the Maytag Company. Everything else he considers unnecessary or subsidiary to these two functions. But it should be pointed out that this is a kind of isolated or encapsulated view of the situation, i.e., as if this company had no relationship with the community, the environment, or the society, nor any debt to it. He takes an awful lot for granted in a situation like this, including a democratic society with high levels of education, with great respect for law and property, etc., etc. He leaves these things out entirely. If you include them, then it becomes obvious also that the company or the enterprise has to give certain things to the society as well as receive certain things from the society, and this makes a different picture altogether. The picture that Scoutten gives of an enterprise might work perfectly well in a fascist economy, but it would not work at all if it were taken seriously in our democratic society, where any enterprise – as a matter of fact, any individual – has also its obligations to the whole society.

(At this point there should be a reference to my memorandum on the patriot, and on the enlightened industrialist as a patriot.)

More should be said on the relations between the enterprise and the society, especially if we take into account the ways to keep the organization healthy over a period of a hundred years. It then becomes most obvious about the mutual ties between the enterprise and the society – for one thing the healthy organization will need a steady supply of fairly well-matured and well-educated personalities (it cannot use delinquents, criminals, cynical kids, spoiled and indulged kids, hostile people, warmongers, destroyers, vandals, etc., but exactly these people are the products of a poor society). This is very much like saying that a poor society cannot support healthy enterprises, in the long run at least. (Although it probably is true that some kinds of products can be well made in the authoritarian society or the authoritarian enterprise, or under conditions of fear and starvation. I really should find out what kinds of exports for instance, can come from Spain today, or how good are Negro workers in South Africa? What kind of production do they have?)

It is also true that the healthy enterprise cannot function at all well under conditions of riots and civil war, of epidemics, of sabotage and murder, of class warfare, or caste warfare. The culture itself has to be healthy for this reason as well. Also there cannot be conditions of corruption, political corruption, nor can there be religious corruption or religious domination. The enterprise must be free to develop itself in all ways which do not interfere with the goodness and the health of the society. This means also that there ought not to be too much political domination either.

In effect any company that restricts its goals purely to its own profits, its own production, and its own sales is getting a kind of a free ride from me and other taxpayers. I help pay for the schools and the police departments and the fire departments and the health departments and everything else in order to keep the society healthy, which in turn supplies high-level workers and managers to such companies at little expense to them. I feel that they should, in order to be fair, make more returns to the society than they are making—that is, in terms of producing good citizens, people who because of their good work situation can themselves be benevolent, charitable, kind, altruistic, etc., etc., in the community.

I am impressed again with the necessity, however difficult the job may be, of working out some kind of moral or ethical accounting scheme. Under such a scheme tax credits would be given to the company that helps to improve the whole society, that helps to improve the local population, and helps to improve the democracy by helping to create more democratic individuals. Some sort of tax penalty should be assessed against enterprises that undo the effects of a political democracy, of good schools, etc., etc., and that make their people more paranoid, more hostile, more nasty, more malevolent, more destructive, etc. This is like sabotage against the whole society. And they should be made to pay for it.

Partly it must be put up to the accountants to try to figure out some way of turning into balance sheet terms the intangible personnel values that come from improving the personality level of the workers, making them more cooperative, better workers, less destructive, etc. It does cost money to hire this kind of personnel; it costs money to train and teach them and to build them into a good team, and there are all sorts of other costs involved in making the enterprise attractive to this kind of worker and this kind of engineer, etc. All these real expenditures of money and effort ought somehow to be translated into accounting terms so that the greater value of the enterprise that contributes to the improvement of the whole society can somehow be put on the balance sheets. We all know that such a company for instance, is a better credit risk and lending banks will take this into account. So will investors. The only ones who don't take these things into account are the accountants.

BIBLIOGRAPHY

1. *Motivation and Personality* (New York: Harper & Row, Publishers, 1954).
2. The Need to Know and the Fear of Knowing. *Journ. General Psychol.* 1963, *68,* 11-25.

Frederick Herzberg

ONE MORE TIME: HOW DO YOU MOTIVATE EMPLOYEES?

How many articles, books, speeches, and workshops have pleaded plaintively, "How do I get an employee to do what I want him to do?"

The psychology of motivation is tremendously complex, and what has been unraveled with any degree of assurance is small indeed. But the dismal ratio of knowledge to speculation has not dampened the enthusiasm for new forms of

Herzberg, Frederick "one More Time: How Do You Motivate Employees?" *Harvard Business Review, 46,* (January-February, 1968): 53-62. © by the President and Fellows of Harvard College; all rights reserved. Reprinted by permission.

snake oil that are constantly coming on the market, many of them with academic testimonials. Doubtless this article will have no depressing impact on the market for snake oil, but since the ideas expressed in it have been tested in many corporations and other organizations, it will help—I hope—to redress the imbalance in the aforementioned ratio.

"MOTIVATING" WITH KITA

In lectures to industry on the problem, I have found that the audiences are anxious for quick and practical answers, so I will begin with a straightforward, practical formula for moving people.

What is the simplest, surest, and most direct way of getting someone to do something? Ask him? But if he responds that he does not want to do it, then that calls for a psychological consultation to determine the reason for his obstinacy. Tell him? His response shows that he does not understand you, and now an expert in communication methods has to be brought in to show you how to get through to him. Give him a monetary incentive? I do not need to remind the reader of the complexity and difficulty involved in setting up and administering an incentive system. Show him? This means a costly training program. We need a simple way.

Every audience contains the "direct action" manager who shouts, "Kick him!" And this type of manager is right. The surest and least circumlocuted way of getting someone to do something is to kick him in the pants—give him what might be called the KITA.

There are various forms of KITA, and here are some of them:

Negative physical KITA. This is a literal application of the term and was frequently used in the past. It has, however, three major drawbacks: (1) it is inelegant; (2) it contradicts the precious image of benevolence that most organizations cherish; and (3) since it is a physical attack, it directly stimulates the autonomic nervous system, and this often results in negative feedback—the employee may just kick you in return. These factors give rise to certain taboos against negative physical KITA.

The psychologist has come to the rescue of those who are no longer permitted to use negative physical KITA. He has uncovered infinite sources of psychological vulnerabilities and the appropriate methods to play tunes on them. "He took my rug away"; "I wonder what he meant by that"; "The boss is always going around me"—these symptomatic expressions of ego sores that have been rubbed raw are the result of application of:

Negative Psychological KITA. This has several advantages over negative physical KITA. First, the cruelty is not visible; the bleeding is internal and comes much later. Second, since it affects the higher cortical centers of the brain with its inhibitory powers, it reduces the possibility of physical backlash. Third, since the number of psychological pains that a person can feel is almost infinite, the direction and site possibilities of the KITA are increased many times. Fourth, the person administering the kick can manage to be above it all and let the system accomplish the dirty work. Fifth, those who practice it receive some ego satisfaction (one-upmanship), whereas they would find drawing blood abhorrent. Finally, if the employee does complain, he can always be accused of being paranoid, since there is no tangible evidence of an actual attack.

Now, what does negative KITA accomplish? If I kick you in the rear (physically or psychologically), who is motivated? I am motivated; you move! Negative KITA does not lead to motivation, but to movement. So:

Positive KITA. Let us consider motivation. If I say to you, "Do this for me or the company, and in return I will give you a reward, an incentive, more status, a promotion, all the quid pro quos that exist in the industrial organization," am I motivating you? The overwhelming opinion I receive from management people is, "Yes, this is motivation."

I have a year-old Schnauzer. When it was a small puppy and I wanted it to move, I kicked it in the rear and it moved. Now that I have finished its obedience training, I hold up a dog biscuit when I want the Schnauzer to move. In this instance, who is motivated—I or the dog? The dog wants the biscuit, but it is I who want it to move. Again, I am the one who is motivated, and the dog is the one who moves. In this instance all I did was apply KITA frontally; I exerted a pull instead of a push. When industry wishes to use such positive KITAs, it has available an incredible number and variety of dog biscuits (jelly beans for humans) to wave in front of the employee to get him to jump.

Why is it that managerial audiences are quick to see that negative KITA is *not* motivation, while they are almost unanimous in their judgment that positive KITA *is* motivation? It is because negative KITA is rape, and positive KITA is seduction. But it is infinitely worse to be seduced than to be raped; the latter is an unfortunate occurrence, while the former signifies that you were a party to your own downfall. This is why positive KITA is so popular: it is a tradition; it is in the American way. The organization does not have to kick you; you kick yourself.

Myths about motivation

Why is KITA not motivation? If I kick my dog (from the front or the back), he will move. And when I want him to move again, what must I do? I must kick him again. Similarly, I can charge a man's battery, and then recharge it, and recharge it again. But it is only when he has his own generator that we can talk about motivation. He then needs no outside stimulation. He *wants* to do it.

With this in mind, we can review some positive KITA personnel practices that were developed as attempts to instill "motivation":

1. Reducing time spent at work. This represents a marvelous way of motivating people to work—getting them off the job! We have reduced (formally and informally) the time spent on a job over the last 50 or 60 years until we are finally on the way to the "6½-day weekend." An interesting variant of this approach is the development of off-hour recreation programs. The philosophy here seems to be that those who play together, work together. The fact is that motivated people seek more hours of work, not fewer.

2. Spiraling wages. Have these motivated people? Yes, to seek the next wage increase. Some medievalists still can be heard to say that a good depression will get employees moving. They feel that if rising wages don't or won't do the job, perhaps reducing them will.

3. Fringe benefits. Industry has outdone the most welfare-minded of welfare states in dispensing cradle-to-the-grave succor. One company I know of had an informal "fringe benefit of the month club" going for a while. The cost of fringe benefits in this country has reached approximately 25 percent of the wage dollar, and we still cry for motivation.

People spend less time working for more money and more security than ever before, and the trend cannot be reversed. These benefits are no longer rewards; they are rights. A six-day week is inhuman, a ten-hour day is exploitation, extended medical coverage is a basic decency, and stock options are the salvation of American initiative. Unless the ante is continuously raised, the psychological reaction of employees is that the company is turning back the clock.

When industry began to realize that both the economic nerve and the lazy nerve of their employees had insatiable appetites, it started to listen to the behavioral scientists who, more out of a humanist tradition than from scientific study, criticized management for not knowing how to deal with people. The next KITA easily followed.

4. Human relations training. Over 30 years of teaching and, in many instances, of practicing psychological approaches to handling people have resulted in costly human relations programs and, in the end, the same question: How do you motivate workers? Here, too, escalations have taken place. Thirty years ago it was necessary to request, "Please don't spit on the floor." Today the same admonition requires three "please"s before the employee feels that his superior has demonstrated the psychologically proper attitudes toward him.

The failure of human relations training to produce motivation led to the conclusion that the supervisor or manager himself was not psychologically true to himself in his practice of interpersonal decency. So an advanced form of human relations KITA, sensitivity training, was unfolded.

5. Sensitivity training. Do you really, really understand yourself? Do you really, really, really trust the other man? Do you really, really, really, really cooperate? The failure of sensitivity training is now being explained, by those who have become opportunistic exploiters of the technique, as a failure to really (five times) conduct proper sensitivity training courses.

With the realization that there are only temporary gains from comfort and economic and interpersonal KITA, personnel managers concluded that the fault lay not in what they were doing, but in the employee's failure to appreciate what they were doing. This opened up the field of communications, a whole new area of "scientifically" sanctioned KITA.

6. Communications. The professor of communications was invited to join the faculty of management training programs and help in making employees understand what management was doing for them. House organs, briefing sessions, supervisory instruction on the importance of communication, and all sorts of propaganda have proliferated until today there is even an International Council of Industrial Editors. But no motivation resulted, and the obvious thought occured that perhaps management was not hearing what the employees were saying. That led to the next KITA.

7. Two-way communication. Management ordered morale surveys, suggestion plans, and group participation programs. Then both employees and management were communicating and listening to each other more than ever, but without much improvement in motivation.

The behavioral scientists began to take another look at their conceptions and their data, and they took human relations one step further. A glimmer of truth was beginning to show through in the writings of the so-called higher-order-need psychologists. People, so they said, want to actualize themselves. Unfortunately, the "actualizing" psychologists got mixed up with the human relations psychologists, and a new KITA emerged.

8. Job participation. Though it may not have been the theoretical intention, job participation often became a "give them the big picture" approach. For example, if a man is tightening 10,000 nuts a day on an assembly line with a torque wrench, tell him he is building a Chevrolet. Another approach had the goal of giving the employee a *feeling* that he is determining, in some measure, what he does on his job. The goal was to provide a *sense* of achievement rather than a substantive achievement in his task. Real achievement, of course, requires a task that makes it possible.

But still there was no motivation. This led to the inevitable conclusion that the employees must be sick, and therefore to the next KITA.

9. Employee counseling. The initial use of this form of KITA in a systematic fashion can be credited to the Hawthorne experiment of the Western Electric Company during the early 1930s. At that time, it was found that the employees harbored irrational feelings that were interfering with the rational operation of the factory. Counseling in this instance was a means of letting the employees unburden themselves by talking to someone about their problems. Although the counseling techniques were primitive, the program was large indeed.

The counseling approach suffered as a result of experiences during World War II, when the programs themselves were found to be interfering with the operation of the organizations; the counselors had forgotten their role of benevolent listeners and were attempting to do something about the problems that they heard about. Psychological counseling, however, has managed to survive the negative impact of World War II experiences and today is beginning to flourish with renewed sophistication. But, alas, many of these programs, like all the others, do not seem to have lessened the pressure of demands to find out how to motivate workers.

Since KITA results only in short-term movement, it is safe to predict that the cost of these programs will increase steadily and new varieties will be developed as old positive KITAs reach their satiation points.

HYGIENE VS. MOTIVATORS

Let me rephrase the perennial question this way: How do you install a generator in an employee? A brief review of my motivation-hygiene theory of job attitudes is required before theoretical and practical suggestions can be offered. The theory was first drawn from an examination of events in the lives of engineers and accountants. At least 16 other investigations, using a wide variety of populations (including some in the Communist countries), have since been completed, making the original research one of the most replicated studies in the field of job attitudes.

The findings of these studies, along with corroboration from many other investigations using different procedures, suggest that the factors involved in producing job satisfaction (and motivation) are separate and distinct from the factors that lead to job dissatisfaction. Since separate factors need to be considered, depending on whether job satisfaction or job dissatisfaction is being examined, it follows that these two feelings are not opposites of each other. The opposite of job satisfaction is not job dissatisfaction but, rather, *no* job satisfaction; and, similarly, the opposite of job dissatisfaction is not job satisfaction, but *no* job dissatisfaction.

Stating the concept presents a problem in semantics, for we normally think of satisfaction and dissatisfaction as opposites—i.e., what is not satisfying must be dissatisfying, and vice versa. But when it comes to understanding the behavior of people in their jobs, more than a play on words is involved.

Two different needs of man are involved here. One set of needs can be thought of as stemming from his animal nature—the built-in drive to avoid pain from the environment, plus all the learned drives which become conditioned to the basic biological needs. For example, hunger, a basic biological drive, makes it necessary to earn money, and then money becomes a specific drive. The other set of needs relates to that unique human characteristic, the ability to achieve and, through achievement, to experience psychological growth. The stimuli for the growth needs are tasks that induce growth; in the industrial setting, they are the *job content*. Contrariwise, the stimuli inducing pain-avoidance behavior are found in the *job environment*.

The growth or *motivator* factors that are intrinsic to the job are: achievement, recognition for achievement, the work itself, responsibility, and growth or advancement. The dissatisfaction-avoidance or *hygiene* (KITA) factors that are extrinsic to the job include: company policy and administration, supervision, interpersonal relationships, working conditions, salary, status, and security.

A composite of the factors that are involved in causing job satisfaction and job dissatisfaction, drawn from samples of 1,685 employees, is shown in Exhibit I. The results indicate that motivators were the primary cause of satisfaction, and hygiene factors the primary cause of unhappiness on the job. The employees, studied in 12 different investigations, included lower-level supervisors, professional women, agricultural administrators, men about to retire from management positions, hospital maintenance personnel, manufacturing

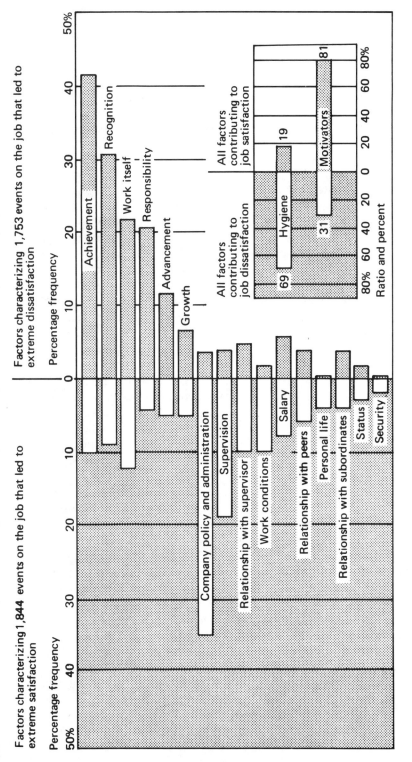

Factors characterizing 1,844 events on the job that led to extreme satisfaction | Factors characterizing 1,753 events on the job that led to extreme dissatisfaction

Percentage frequency

- Achievement
- Recognition
- Work itself
- Responsibility
- Advancement
- Growth
- Company policy and administration
- Supervision
- Relationship with supervisor
- Work conditions
- Salary
- Relationship with peers
- Personal life
- Relationship with subordinates
- Status
- Security

All factors contributing to job dissatisfaction | All factors contributing to job satisfaction

Hygiene 69   31   19   Motivators 81

Ratio and percent

EXHIBIT 1. Factors affecting job attitudes, as reported in 12 investigations.

supervisors, nurses, food handlers, military officers, engineers, scientists, housekeepers, teachers, technicians, female assemblers, accountants, Finnish foremen, and Hungarian engineers.

They were asked what job events had occurred in their work that had led to extreme satisfaction or extreme dissatisfaction on their part. Their responses are broken down in the exhibit into percentages of total "positive" job events and of total "negative" job events. (The figures total more than 100 percent on both the "hygiene" and "motivators" sides because often at least two factors can be attributed to a single event; advancement, for instance, often accompanies assumption of responsibility.)

To illustrate, a typical response involving achievement that had a negative effect for the employee was, "I was unhappy because I didn't do the job successfully." A typical response in the small number of positive job events in the Company Policy and Administration grouping was, "I was happy because the company reorganized the section so that I didn't report any longer to the guy I didn't get along with."

As the lower right-hand part of the exhibit shows, of all the factors contributing to job satisfaction, 81 percent were motivators. And of all the factors contributing to the employees' dissatisfaction over their work, 69 percent involved hygiene elements.

Eternal triangle

There are three general philosophies of personnel management. The first is based on organizational theory, the second on industrial engineering, and the third on behavioral science.

The organizational theorist believes that human needs are either so irrational or so varied and adjustable to specific situations that the major function of personnel management is to be as pragmatic as the occasion demands. If jobs are organized in a proper manner, he reasons, the result will be the most efficient job structure, and the most favorable job attitudes will follow as a matter of course.

The industrial engineer holds that man is mechanistically oriented and economically motivated and his needs are best met by attuning the individual to the most efficient work process. The goal of personnel management therefore should be to concoct the most appropriate incentive system and to design the specific working conditions in a way that facilitates the most efficient use of the human machine. By structuring jobs in a manner that leads to the most efficient operation, the engineer believes that he can obtain the optimal organization of work and the proper work attitudes.

The behavioral scientist focuses on group sentiments, attitudes of individual employees, and the organization's social and psychological climate. According to his persuasion, he emphasizes one or more of the various hygiene and motivator needs. His approach to personnel management generally emphasizes some form of human relations education, in the hope of instilling healthy employee attitudes and an organizational climate which he considers to be felicitous to human values. He believes that proper attitudes will lead to efficient job and organizational structure.

There is always a lively debate as to the overall effectiveness of the approaches of the organizational theorist and the industrial engineer. Manifestly they have achieved much. But the nagging question for the behavioral scientist has been: What is the cost in human problems that eventually cause more expense to the organization—for instance, turnover, absenteeism, errors, violation of safety rules, strikes, restriction of output, higher wages, and greater fringe benefits? On the other hand, the behavioral scientist is hard put to document much manifest improvement in personnel management, using his approach.

The three philosophies can be depicted as a triangle, as is done in Exhibit II, with each persuasion claiming the apex angle. The motivation-hygiene theory claims the same angle as industrial engineering, but for opposite goals. Rather than rationalizing the work to increase efficiency, the theory suggests that work be *enriched* to bring about effective utilization of personnel. Such a systematic attempt to motivate employees by manipulating the motivator factors is just beginning.

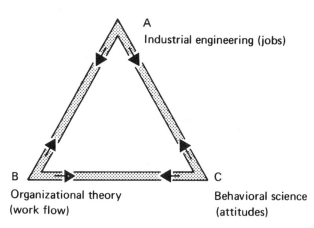

A
Industrial engineering (jobs)

B
Organizational theory
(work flow)

C
Behavioral science
(attitudes)

EXHIBIT II. 'Triangle' of philosophies of personnel management

The term *job enrichment* describes this embryonic movement. An older term, job enlargement, should be avoided because it is associated with past failures stemming from a misunderstanding of the problem. Job enrichment provides the opportunity for the employee's psychological growth, while job enlargement merely makes a job structurally bigger. Since scientific job enrichment is very new, this article only suggests the principles and practical steps that have recently emerged from several successful experiments in industry.

Job loading

In attempting to enrich an employee's job, management often succeeds in reducing the man's personal contribution, rather than giving him an opportunity for growth in his accustomed job. Such an endeavor, which I shall call horizontal job loading (as opposed to vertical loading, or providing motivator factors), has been the problem of earlier job enlargement programs. This activity merely enlarges the meaninglessness of the job. Some examples of this approach, and their effect, are:

Challenging the employee by increasing the amount of production expected of him. If he tightens 10,000 bolts a day, see if he can tighten 20,000 bolts a day. The arithmetic involved shows that multiplying zero by zero still equals zero.

Adding another meaningless task to the existing one, usually some routine clerical activity. The arithmetic here is adding zero to zero.

Rotating the assignments of a number of jobs that need to be enriched. This means washing dishes for a while, then washing silverware. The arithmetic is substituting one zero for another zero.

Removing the most difficult parts of the assignment in order to free the worker to accomplish more of the less challenging assignments. This traditional industrial engineering approach amounts to subtraction in the hope of accomplishing addition.

These are common forms of horizontal loading that frequently come up in preliminary brainstorming sessions on job enrichment. The principles of vertical loading have not all been worked out as yet, and they remain rather general, but I have furnished seven useful starting points for consideration in Exhibit III.

A successful application

An example from a highly successful job enrichment experiment can illustrate the distinction between horizontal and vertical loading of a job. The subjects of this study were the stockholder correspondents employed by a very large corporation. Seemingly, the task required of these carefully selected and highly trained correspondents was quite complex and challenging. But almost all indexes of performance and job attitudes were low, and exit interviewing confirmed that the challenge of the job existed merely as words.

A job enrichment project was initiated in the form of an experiment with one group, designated as an achieving unit, having its job enriched by the principles described in Exhibit III. A control group continued to do its job in the traditional way. (There were also two "uncommitted" groups of correspondents formed to measure the so-called Hawthorne Effect—that is, to gauge whether productivity and attitudes toward the job changed artificially merely because employees sensed that the company was paying more attention to them in doing something different or novel. The results for these groups were substantially the same as for the control group, and for the sake of simplicity I do not deal with them in this summary.) No changes in hygiene were introduced for either group other than those that would have been made anyway, such as normal pay increases.

The changes for the achieving unit were introduced in the first two months, averaging one per week of the seven motivators listed in Exhibit III. At the end of six months the members of the achieving unit were found to be

EXHIBIT III. Principles of vertical job loading

Principle	*Motivators involved*
A. Removing some controls while retaining accountability	Responsibility and personal achievement
B. Increasing the accountability of individuals for own work	Responsibility and recognition
C. Giving a person a complete natural unit of work (module, division, area, and so on)	Responsibility, achievement, and recognition
D. Granting additional authority to an employee in his activity; job freedom	Responsibility, achievement, and recognition
E. Making periodic reports directly available to the worker himself rather than to the supervisor	Internal recognition
F. Introducing new and more difficult tasks not previously handled	Growth and learning
G. Assigning individuals specific or specialized tasks, enabling them to become experts	Responsibility, growth, and advancement

outperforming their counterparts in the control group, and in addition indicated a marked increase in their liking for their jobs. Other results showed that the achieving group had lower absenteeism and, subsequently, a much higher rate of promotion.

Exhibit IV illustrates the changes in performance, measured in February and March, before the study period began, and at the end of each month of the study period. The shareholder service index represents quality of letters, including accuracy of information, and speed of response to stockholders' letters of inquiry. The index of a current month was averaged into the average of the two prior months, which means that improvement was harder to obtain if the indexes of the previous months were low. The "achievers" were performing less well before the six-month period started, and their performance service index continued to decline after the introduction of the motivators, evidently because of uncertainty over their newly granted responsibilities. In the third month, however, performance improved, and soon the members of this group had reached a high level of accomplishment.

Exhibit V shows the two groups' attitudes toward their job, measured at the end of March, just before the first motivator was introduced, and again at the end of September. The correspondents were asked 16 questions, all involving motivation. A typical one was, "As you see it, how many opportunities do you feel that you have in your job for making worthwhile contributions?" The answers were scaled from one to five with 80 as the maximum possible score. The achievers became much more positive about their job, while the attitude of the control unit remained about the same (the drop is not statistically significant).

How was the job of these correspondents restructured? Exhibit VI lists the suggestions made that were deemed to be horizontal loading, and the actual

Performance Index

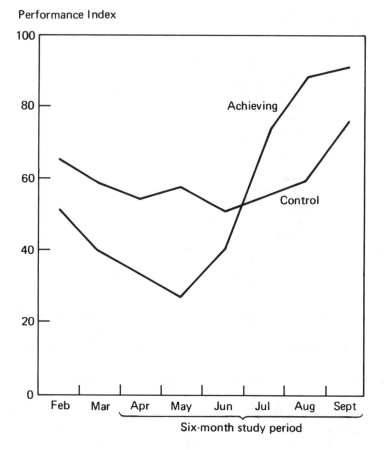

EXHIBIT IV. Shareholder service index in company experiment—
[Three-month cumulative average]

vertical loading changes that were incorporated in the job of the achieving unit.
The capital letters under "Principle" after "Vertical loading" refer to the
corresponding letters in Exhibit III. The reader will note that the rejected forms
of horizontal loading correspond closely to the list of common manifestations of
the phenomenon on page 75.

STEPS TO JOB ENRICHMENT

Now that the motivator idea has been described in practice, here are the steps
that managers should take in instituting the principle with their employees:
(1) Select those jobs in which

a. the investment in industrial engineering does not make changes too costly,
b. attitudes are poor,
c. hygiene is becoming very costly, and
d. motivation will make a difference in performance.

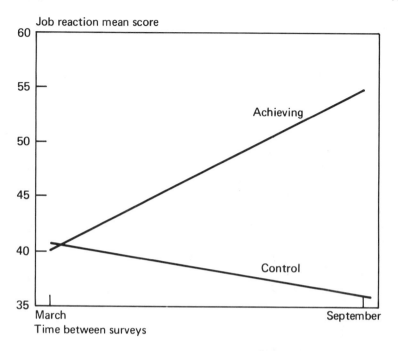

Job reaction mean score

March   September
Time between surveys

EXHIBIT V. Changes in attitudes toward tasks in company experiment [Changes in mean scores over six-month period]

(2) Approach these jobs with the conviction that they can be changed. Years of tradition have led managers to believe that the content of the jobs is sacrosanct and the only scope of action that they have is in ways of stimulating people.

(3) Brainstorm a list of changes that may enrich the jobs, without concern for their practicality.

(4) Screen the list to eliminate suggestions that involve hygiene, rather than actual motivation.

(5) Screen the list for generalities, such as "give them more responsibility," that are rarely followed in practice. This might seem obvious, but the motivator words have never left industry; the substance has just been rationalized and organized out. Words like "responsibility," "growth," "achievement," and "challenge," for example, have been elevated to the lyrics of the patriotic anthem for all organizations. It is the old problem typified by the pledge of allegiance to the flag being more important than contributions to the country—of following the form, rather than the substance.

(6) Screen the list to eliminate any *horizontal* loading suggestions.

(7) Avoid direct participation by the employees whose jobs are to be enriched. Ideas they have expressed previously certainly constitute a valuable source for recommended changes, but their direct involvement contaminates the process with human relations *hygiene* and, more specifically, gives them only a

Horizontal loading suggestions (rejected)	Vertical loading suggestions (adopted)	Principle
Firm quotas could be set for letters to be answered each day, using a rate which would be hard to reach.	Subject matter experts were appointed within each unit for other members of the unit to consult with before seeking supervisory help. (The supervisor had been answering all specialized and difficult questions.)	G
The women could type the letters themselves, as well as compose them, or take on any other clerical functions.	Correspondents signed their own names on letters. (The supervisor had been signing all letters.)	B
All difficult or complex inquiries could be channeled to a few women so that the remainder could achieve high rates of output. These jobs could be exchanged from time to time.	The work of the more experienced correspondents was proofread less frequently by supervisors and was done at the correspondents' desks, dropping verification from 100% to 10%. (Previously, all correspondents' letters had been checked by the supervisor.)	A
The women could be rotated through units handling different customers, and then sent back to their own units.	Production was discussed, but only in terms such as "a full day's work is expected." As time went on, this was no longer mentioned. (Before, the group had been constantly reminded of the number of letters that needed to be answered.)	D
	Outgoing mail went directly to the mailroom without going over supervisors' desks. (The letters had always been routed through the supervisors.)	A
	Correspondents were encouraged to answer letters in a more personalized way. (Reliance on the form-letter approach had been standard practice.)	C
	Each correspondent was held personally responsible for the quality and accuracy of letters. (This responsibility had been the province of the supervisor and the verifier.)	B,E

EXHIBIT VI. Enlargement vs. enrichment of correspondents' tasks in company experiment

sense of making a contribution. The job is to be changed, and it is the content that will produce the motivation, not attitudes about being involved or the challenge inherent in setting up a job. That process will be over shortly, and it is what the employees will be doing from then on that will determine their motivation. A sense of participation will result only in short-term movement.

(8) In the initial attempts at job enrichment, set up a controlled experiment. At least two equivalent groups should be chosen, one an experimental unit in which the motivators are systematically introduced over a period of time, and the other one a control group in which no changes are made. For both groups, hygiene should be allowed to follow its natural course for the duration of the experiment. Pre- and post-installation tests of performance and job attitudes are necessary to evaluate the effectiveness of the job enrichment program. The attitude test must be limited to motivator items in order to divorce the employee's view of the job he is given from all the surrounding hygiene feelings that he might have.

(9) Be prepared for a drop in performance in the experimental group the first few weeks. The changeover to a new job may lead to a temporary reduction in efficiency.

(10) Expect your first-line supervisors to experience some anxiety and hostility over the changes you are making. The anxiety comes from their fear that the changes will result in poorer performance for their unit. Hostility will arise when the employees start assuming what the supervisors regard as their own responsibility for performance. The supervisor without checking duties to perform may then be left with little to do.

After a successful experiment, however, the supervisor usually discovers the supervisory and managerial functions he has neglected, or which were never his because all his time was given over to checking the work of his subordinates. For example, in the R&D division of one large chemical company I know of, the supervisors of the laboratory assistants were theoretically responsible for their training and evaluation. These functions, however, had come to be performed in a routine, unsubstantial fashion. After the job enrichment program, during which the supervisors were not merely passive observers of the assistants' performance, the supervisors actually were devoting their time to reviewing performance and administering thorough training.

What has been called an employee-centered style of supervision will come about not through education of supervisors, but by changing the jobs that they do.

CONCLUDING NOTE

Job enrichment will not be a one-time proposition, but a continuous management function. The initial changes, however, should last for a very long period of time. There are a number of reasons for this:

The changes should bring the job up to the level of challenge commensurate with the skill that was hired.

Those who have still more ability eventually will be able to demonstrate it better and win promotion to higher-level jobs.

The very nature of motivators, as opposed to hygiene factors, is that they have a much longer-term effect on employees' attitudes. Perhaps the job will have to be enriched again, but this will not occur as frequently as the need for hygiene.

Not all jobs can be enriched, nor do all jobs need to be enriched. If only a small percentage of the time and money that is now devoted to hygiene, however, were given to job enrichment efforts, the return in human satisfaction and economic gain would be one of the largest dividends that industry and society have ever reaped through their efforts at better personnel management.

The argument for job enrichment can be summed up quite simply: If you have someone on a job, use him. If you can't use him on the job, get rid of him, either via automation or by selecting someone with lesser ability. If you can't use him and you can't get rid of him, you will have a motivation problem.

Charles L. Hulin
and Milton R. Blood

JOB ENLARGEMENT, INDIVIDUAL DIFFERENCES, AND WORKER RESPONSES

One of the most pervasive and dominant themes which exists in the attempts of industrial psychologists to provide guidelines and frameworks for the motivation of industrial workers is the notion of job enlargement. Job enlargement is a concerted attempt to stem and even reverse the current trends among industrial engineering programs toward job simplification and specialization. The attack on job specialization and job simplification has a long and impressive history going back nearly 200 years to the writings of Adam Smith. In 1776, Smith (reported in Lewis, 1963) stated that

It [division of labor] corrupts even the activity of his body, and renders him incapable of exerting his strength with vigour and perseverance, in any other employment than that to which he has been bred. His dexterity at his own particular trade seems, in this manner, to be acquired at the expense of his intellectual, social, and martial virtues [p.237].

Reprinted from the *Psychological Bulletin 69*, (1968): 41-55, by permission of the American Psychological Association.

Further early support for this position has been found in the writings of Durkheim (1933). However, the support from Durkheim is more in the eye of the reader than in the writings since Durkheim did not attack the division of labor per se, only the anomic division of labor. He stated that normally the division of labor produces social solidarity and that there is nothing noble about a man doing a large job in a mediocre fashion nor nothing debasing about a man doing a small job well. Unfortunately, most of the references to Durkheim are to his discussion of the anomic division of labor, which he considered a pathological state of society. The problem in the discussion presented by Durkheim is to define that point at which the division of labor ceases to be beneficial and becomes pathological and produces anomie. We raise the question of whether such a point exists and is indeed definable. If it does exist, can it be considered a constant or does it vary from worker to worker with some workers regarding extremely specialized, short-time-cycle, simple jobs as good jobs?

Most modern writers (Argyris, 1957; Kornhauser, 1965; Likert, 1961; MacGregor, 1957; Whyte, 1955) regard nearly all division of labor, with the resulting job simplification and specialization, as leading almost inevitably to monotony, boredom, job dissatisfaction, and inappropriate (from the point of view of management) behavior patterns. The evidence on this point will be reviewed in this paper, along with an analysis of the effects of the individual differences of workers on their responses to job enlargement and job simplification. An attempt will also be made to specify a model based on the cultural differences of workers which can be used to resolve the contradictions in the literature and to predict responses to larger (or enlarged) jobs.

DEFINITION

For the purposes of this review, job enlargement has been considered as the process of allowing individual workers to determine their own working pace (within limits), to serve as their own inspectors by giving them responsibility for quality control, to repair their own mistakes, to be responsible for their own machine setup and repair, and to attain choice of method. In this sense, job enlargement is qualitatively different from *job extension,* which consists of merely adding similar elements to the job without altering job content (e.g., soldering the red wires as well as the black wires). However, changing from a line-paced job to a self-paced job would be regarded as job enlargement. It can also be seen that the process of job enlargement produces jobs at a higher level of skill, with varied work content and relative autonomy for the worker. On the other hand, the process of job simplification results in jobs requiring less skill which are more repetitive and have less autonomy. The process of job simplification has progressed much further with some jobs than with others. Thus, jobs at different points in the process of simplification exist contemporaneously. While we do not normally think of differences between jobs in such terms, it seems to be a veridical way of organizing thinking about job levels. Also, such categorizations of jobs enable us to consider both experimental and correlational methods of analyzing differences or changes in worker responses. That is, changes in workers' responses which correlate with the degree of job simplification should also be observed if changes in job specialization are made experimentally.

TRADITIONAL MODEL

According to the theorists, as jobs become increasingly specialized the monotony (perception of the *sameness* of the job from minute-to-minute, perception of the unchanging characteristic of the job) increases. That is, short-time-cycle, simplified jobs lead to monotony. Monotony is supposedly associated with feelings of boredom and job dissatisfaction. Boredom and job dissatisfaction lead to undesirable (from management's point of view) behavior. This reasoning could be diagrammed as follows:

Stimulus condition	Perception	Affective response	Behavioral response
Simplified, low skill level, short-cycle jobs	Monotony	Boredom, job dissatis-faction	Absenteeism, turnover, restriction of output

Several assumptions in this line of reasoning deserve discussion. Consider the assumption that repetitiveness leads to monotony and, conversely, that uniqueness and change lead to a lack of monotony. Smith (1955) has demonstrated that there are important individual differences in susceptibility to monotony among workers on the same job. Apparently, some workers do not report monotony even in the face of a job with an extremely short work cycle. Baldamus (1961) has pointed out that repetitive work can often have positively motivating characteristics (traction) which tend to "pull the worker along" and are pleasant. This notion has been experimentally verified by Smith and Lem (1955) using a sample of industrial workers. Thus the assumption of repetitiveness leading to monotony could be questioned on two grounds—effects of individual differences and positive motivational characteristics of repetition.

The second assumption is that monotony leads to boredom and job dissatisfaction. Even granting that the physical reality of short time cycles or repetition leads to monotony, can we assume that workers respond with negative affect to this perception? This assumption can be questioned on much the same grounds as the first. At the very least, we should allow the possibility that some workers prefer the safety of not being required to make decisions. Vroom (1960) has demonstrated that not all workers are satisfied when they are allowed to take part in the decision-making process about their jobs, and there are significant individual differences (F scale scores) between workers who respond positively to the opportunity to make decisions and those who do not. While not exactly to the point, these data at least indicate that some workers prefer routine, repetition, and specified work methods to change, variety, and decision making.

The final assumption is that boredom and job dissatisfaction are associated with undesirable behavior patterns. This assumption is probably the least crucial to the argument since trite as it may seem, a high level of job satisfaction among industrial workers may be an appropriate goal in itself. If job enlargement had no other result than decreased boredom and increased job satisfaction, it would be appropriate. Also, there is evidence (Hulin, 1966; Weitz & Nuckols, 1953) that in certain circumstances, job satisfaction is significantly related to individual decisions to quit. The relationship between satisfaction and productivity and other on-the-job behaviors is somewhat more elusive. The fact that this relationship has been so difficult to obtain indicates the weakness of the final assumption of the traditional model.

EVIDENCE

Empirical studies linking job satisfaction to job size have a long history but have generally been poorly controlled, and most of the authors have attempted to generalize from severely limited data. In early study, Wyatt, Fraser, and Stock (1929a) reported that workers on a soap-wrapping job gave higher outputs when working conditions were uniform than when conditions were varied. Outputs were not different in the two conditions when the jobs were folding handkerchiefs and making bicycle chains. From this they concluded that varied conditions were better and they began studying optimum spacing of task changes! There are obvious problems with this study. The Ns were small and results did not reach statistical significance, most of the results do not support their conclusions, and they did not control for variations in output which may have been caused by the change per se as opposed to the particular variations of their hypotheses. Their writings also fail to distinguish among the effects of fatigue, inhibition, boredom, and monotony. In later studies, Wyatt, Fraser, and Stock (1929b) and Wyatt, Langdon, and Stock (1937) investigated the effects of jobs having short time cycles. Smith (1953) has pointed out "certain deviations from normally acceptable methods of scientific investigation . . . [p.69]." Part of their measure of boredom consisted of questions about slowing of output during the middle of the day. Those who reported such slowing were regarded as bored. Also, those who reported such slowing did indeed slow down at these times. Therefore, Wyatt et al. were able to obtain good matches between their measure of boredom and "typical" boredom output curves. The circularity is evident. The results relating boredom, IQ, and production cause concern. High-IQ workers were more bored and boredom reduced the rate of working, but high-IQ workers were more productive. Boredom was less likely to occur on fully automated work, and the experience of boredom was largely dependent on individual characteristics. The workers in all these studies were female, which serves as an additional restriction on generalization. All in all, both the measures and the conclusions of these studies are extremely suspect. Roethlisberger and Dickson (1941) and Smith (1953) were unable to replicate the original results of Wyatt et al. Generalizations from these data must, indeed, be cautious.

Walker (1950) presented a report of the benefits of a job-enlargement program which was undertaken at IBM. Though some might consider this article a heuristic success, it presented little in the way of data. There was no control for a Hawthorne effect, and no data were presented which concerned satisfaction, turnover, costs, etc.

Walker and Marriott (1951) provided data indicating that more than a third of the employees of mass production factories complained of boredom, but in rolling mills the proportion was only 8 percent. Boredom was more widespread among conveyor workers, and workers were less satisfied on such jobs if they had previously held a skilled job. Data came from interviews with 976 men from three large factories. This seems to be evidence supporting the traditional model which relates uniformity and repetition in work to dissatisfaction. While we have no disagreement with the results as presented, there are some problems associated with the generality of the conclusions. Individual differences in worker responses were considerable, and, in fact, "Many liked their work because it was simple, straightforward, and carried no responsibility." Differences between factories were attributed to differences in production techniques rather than to differences between the persons making up the work forces of the factories. A subsequent interview study (Walker & Guest, 1952) related increased dissatisfaction, increased absences, and increased turnover to assembly line work. The basic conclusion was that very little could be said in favor of assembly line work.

While Walker and Guest were careful not to generalize beyond their sample, their conclusions and recommendations were stated in very general terms, and sound as if they are cures for ills everywhere. In light of the sample described by Walker and Guest and the findings of Blood and Hulin (1967) and Turner and Lawrence (1965), there is little doubt that Walker and Guest's results would be anticipated by the model to be presented in this paper. Typical descriptive statements given by Walker and Guest (1952) are: "The area from which [the workers] were recruited has few mass production factories [p. 4]." "Only two in our sample had ever worked in an automobile plant before [p. 19]," and "
. . . 34.5 percent of all those [in the sample] with manual work experience were skilled persons. Considering the relatively unskilled nature of automobile assembly work, this high proportion of skilled workmen . . . is of interest [p. 31]." While our model would predict negative responses to simplified, line-paced jobs from workers such as those described by Walker and Guest, we would not expect such negative responses to be a general characteristic of the United States work force. In subsequent papers (Guest, 1955, 1957; Walker, 1954), these investigators have extolled the virtues of job flexibility, job rotation, and job enlargement without contributing any additional data. Their claims are unjustifiable because of the peculiarities of their sample and their lack of acceptable experimental controls.

The Detroit Edison Electric Utility Company carried out a program of job enlargement among first-line supervisors and clerical workers (Elliott, 1953). Though there were no controls and no statistical information was provided, Elliott claimed that job enlargement reduced costs and increased production. He then assumed a positive relationship between productivity and morale. On the basis of this assumed relationship, he argued that satisfaction had increased! Cost reduction and production increase are more easily explained in this case as a result of the elimination of duplications in the work process. The report did include the recognition that some workers prefer repetitive jobs.

Marks (1954) reported a study of 29 female employees in the manufacturing department of a company on the West Coast. A similar department was monitored as a control. Production was poorer with enlarged jobs, but quality improved.[1] After experience with the enlarged job, some workers disliked the lack of personal responsibility of an assembly line design. The conclusion, however, which is normally drawn from this study is that enlarged jobs are better.

When assembly operations were enlarged in the Maytag Company plant in Newton, Iowa, there were quantity and quality improvements in production (Biganne & Stewart, 1963). These workers would be expected by the model to be presented in this paper to be more satisfied with enlarged jobs. No statistical evidence was presented, but it was reported that most of the workers came to like their new jobs and they seemed to become involved.

In a study of the attitudes of skilled and semiskilled workers to job enlargement, Davis and Werling (1960) surveyed a West Coast plant employing 400 operating and 250 clerical and administrative personnel. The interests of skilled workers, similar to those of management, included company success, improvement of self, and improvement of operations. Semiskilled workers, on the other hand, lacked concern for company goals and they attached little importance to job content. From this, Davis and Werling concluded that semiskilled jobs are insufficiently enlarged. Such a conclusion requires evidence that the size of the job determines attitude. Of course there is no evidence of this sort, and, indeed, attitudes toward company goals and job content may be as influenced by many subcultural and personal background factors as by one aspect of the task. Further, the inference that the workers *should* think job content important is an evaluative asumption not necessary for empirical analysis of the data.

Argyris (1959) provided information from content analysis of interview with 34 employees from a department with high skill demands and 90 unskilled and semiskilled employees from another department. As compared with the skilled employees, those of lower skill expressed

a. less aspiration for high-quality work,
b. less need to learn more about their work,
c. more emphasis on money,

[1] Quality improvement would be expected in nearly all programs of job enlargement since the worker serves as his own inspector. If he makes a mistake and discovers it he can repair it on the spot. Such repairs on assembly line work are, of course, impossible since the worker cannot stop to make the repairs. This improvement in quality, however, should be regarded as a direct result of the technical changes in the jobs and not of changes in worker motivation or satisfaction. Kilbridge (1960b) has also pointed out that many of the positive results obtained in studies of job enlargement could be attributed to reductions in balance-delay time and nonproduction time and not to changes in worker motivations or satisfaction.

d. lower estimates of personal abilities,

e. less desire for variety and independence,

f. high work spoilage (subjectively judged since the tasks were different),

g. fewer lasting friendships formed on the job, and

h. less creative use of leisure time.

Also, the lower skilled employees expressed needs "to be left alone," "to be passive," and "to experience routine or sameness." According to the theories of Argyris, these differences are caused by the organization's stifling the maturity of individuals on the job. However, just as in the Davis and Werling study, there is no reason to believe that these differences were caused by the job rather than brought to the work situation.

In a study auspiciously titled "Job Enlargement: Antidote to Apathy," Reif and Schoderbek (1966) reported the results of a survey of companies regarding their use of job enlargement. Questionnaires were mailed to 276 companies. Replies were received from 210, and of these, 41 said they had used job enlargement. The most popular reasons for undertaking job enlargement were cost reduction and profit increase. Twenty-three respondents checked "increase in job satisfaction" as an advantage of job enlargement. It is significant that only 23 of the 41 companies which used job enlargement noted an increase in job satisfaction in spite of

a. the popularity of the traditional notion that workers want larger jobs, and

b. the opportunity for bias in this sample.

Reif and Schoderbek seemed unaware that their data may have been atypical even though the sample represented less than 15 percent of their initial population. Returns perhaps should not be expected from companies who have tried job enlargement unsuccessfully, and if an executive from such a company did reply he would probably be hesitant to admit that an executive policy of his firm had failed. Reif and Schoderbek's conclusions in favor of job enlargement and the proposal of job enlargement as an "antidote for apathy" are unjustified.

In a study of the effects of repetitive work on the mental health of industrial workers, Kornhauser (1965) found that many production workers from an urban area gave interview responses which he considered indicative of poor mental health. He showed that, in general, such indications of poor mental health increased as job level decreased (from skilled workers to semiskilled workers with repetitive tasks). He has gleaned a large amount of information from interviews with 655 men, and his data and his conclusions merit discussion. He convincingly showed that there are systematic differences in the interview responses of workers at different job levels. From the nature of the response differences he concluded that the persons in the lower skilled jobs were in poorer mental health and, furthermore, that their occupational situation caused this condition. He argued that job simplification is a cause of poor mental health. Before accepting these conclusions, some of the methods of his study must be examined.

First, all data were obtained from interview responses. Therefore, they are open to such biasing factors as social acceptability, interviewer bias, and bias of the coder who arranged the interview transcripts into quantitative material.

Social acceptability bias would enter the situation and distort responses in the obtained direction if the interviewee shaped his answers to his expectations of the responses desired by his middle-class-oriented interviewer. That is, persons in repetitive jobs may feel hesitant to admit that they are not dissatisfied with their work if they feel that such admission will lead to an unfavorable judgment from the interviewer. If the interviewer or coder was familiar with the hypothesis of the study (either explicitly or implicitly), there is the additional possibility that responses were systematically interpreted in the manner most favorable to the hypothesis. Since no information was presented which would either confirm or disconfirm the existence of these biases, we must approach the results with proper caution and the realization that such distortions *might* have taken place.

Second, Kornhauser attempted to generalize from an urban blue-collar sample to all production workers. Recent studies by Turner and Lawrence (1965) and Blood and Hulin (1967) have demonstrated that we cannot generalize from urban blue-collar workers to all blue-collar workers.

Further, Kornhauser chose to ignore differences in workers' personal backgrounds. Perhaps this is justified since he explained that these differences were not the point of his discussion. However, we should not overlook his data which show the relationship between personal background variables and the Mental Health Index score to be at least as strong as that between job level and the Mental Health Index score. He pointed to the relative independence of these influences, but his analytic techniques were such that they would not have been sensitive to interaction effects so this conclusion must be attributed to his personal judgment.

Finally, it is inevitable that the Mental Health Index depends on value judgments as to what constitutes good or poor health. In this case, good mental health seems to depend more on striving for personal betterment than on a realistic evaluation of the situation. For example, the interview response "There's such a thing as beating your brains against the wall. Some things you just can't change; might as well accept them and adjust yourself to them" was said by Kornhauser to "call attention to the very limited self-expectations, the degree of passivity, fatalism, and resignation that characterize many of the workers [p. 241]." Thus Kornhauser shows that he himself subscribes to what he considers to be a middle-class concept—that every person is responsible for his own situation rather than being influenced by forces beyond his control. He saw as evidence of poor mental health that members of a lower-class subculture do not hold middle-class ideals. What these data show most convincingly is that there are differences by job level among urban workers in the extent to which workers adhere to a middle-class value system. Another problem with the Mental Health Index results is that we are not able to compare them with any kind of base line. Some comparison data were provided from a small sample of low-ranking white collar workers and a small sample of production workers from outside Detroit. Because of the sample sizes, these comparison data are less trustworthy than the experimental data. Statistical probabilities of the differences between these comparison samples and the larger, Detroit blue-collar sample were not provided and in many cases the results look similar.

In several ways Kornhauser's study demonstrates the dangers of trying to index a culture-bound concept such as mental health when using a research sample which may contain subcultural differences and may be culturally different from the investigators and persons who are judging the validity of the research instrument. Nonetheless, the study confirms that there are response differences between different job levels. This is not a new concept, but whereas blue-collar and white-collar differences have been discussed in the past, Kornhauser showed that within the gross blue-collar category finer discriminations will provide additional information. Porter (1961) has shown that such differentiation is profitable in the white-collar realm. Certainly job level is an influential dimension in the determination of workers' responses and the extent to which class ideals prevail. If we can find other useful dimensions, we will increase our ability to understand, and hence predict, workers' reactions to job enlargement and other aspects of their work situation.

Scott (1966) has generalized the activation theory of vigilance behavior to the area of task and job design. The activation theory of vigilance behavior is a physiological explanation of behavior in situations characterized by low levels of stimulation and has been found to summarize much of the literature on vigilance decrement (Frankmann & Adams, 1962). Briefly, this theory holds that stimuli impinging on the human receptor serve two purposes. One is a cue or information function which is accomplished when the stimulation travels directly to the appropriate cortical projection area. The other is an arousal or activation function and is accomplished when the neural stimulation also travels through the ascending reticular formation and is diffused over a wide area of the cortex. This pathway serves no cue or information function but does serve to maintain the organism at a high state of arousal or activation. Generalizing from the activation theory and the results of vigilance studies, Scott argued that amount and variety of stimulation serve to motivate the worker and enable him to maintain a high level of performance. In short, nonroutine, nonrepetitive jobs are likely to serve as positive motivators of behavior. Basing a theory of industrial motivation in physiology would, of course, tend to give it the appearance of being more basic, general, and valid.

While we have no disagreement with the efficacy of the activation theory when applied to vigilance data, we do feel there are a number of problems involved with generalizing the theory to the area of industrial task design. First, the similarity between the experimental settings where vigilance decrements are reliably obtained and even the most routine and repetitive of industrial jobs is slight. The presence of other people, random intermittant noise, illumination changes, multiple tasks, the opportunity to move about, stretch, talk to other workers, etc., all summate to produce a situation far removed from the usual vigilance situations. Considering the fact that vigilance decrements can be eliminated by the introduction of multiple tasks, other people in the room, etc., industrial tasks are so different from vigilance tasks that any generalizations are exceedingly dangerous. Second, whenever tasks are enlarged, several derived social motivation variables are changed along with the desired changes in amount and variety of the physical stimulation. When more elements are added to a task, a greater variety of skills is required and, at the extreme, greater involvement in the job is required. Whether all or even most workers are willing to make this investment in their jobs is a matter for investigation, not assumption. Finally, while not an inherent problem of the activation theory, there is the matter of individual differences in the optimal levels of stimulation. While parameters for individual differences could be built into the theory, there are at present no such parameters nor are there any indications in the activation theory as to the source of information for predicting such individual differences parameters. Considering the variance controlled by these ubiquitous individual differences in the behavior and motivation of industrial workers, such an omission amounts to a very serious gap in the theory.

In addition to the references cited above, Worthy (1950), Argyris (1957, 1964), Davis (1957a, 1957b), and Davis and Canter (1955) presented the traditional viewpoint that larger jobs are "better" jobs. Though the human relations approach has gained widespread popular support, the data are unconvincing. These supportive data present us with severe restrictions either because of methodological problems or because of the nature of the samples. Warren (1958) reviewed the traditional literature and the research data and called for the research-team approach to the evaluation of job enlargement. He concurred in some of the human relations concepts, but he made clear the difference between monotony and boredom. An approach to the problem of disatisfaction with repetitive work which is notable for its novelty was presented by Behling (1964). He began with the human relations assumption that repetitive work leads to dissatisfaction. He then invoked the Maslow hierarchy of needs to explain this dissatisfaction, saying it results from the fact that our present civilization is able to satisfy our lower level needs thus making our higher level needs more potent. Of course while the lower level needs of workers are unsatisfied, these higher level needs are not motivators of behavior. He concluded that many of the needs of workers would be more properly fulfilled outside of the work organization. MacKinney, Wernimont, and Galitz (1962) reviewed the studies relating job specialization and job satisfaction, and they concluded that the issue was not settled by the data at that time. We obviously feel that the issue is still not structured, and also agree with MacKinney et al.'s (1962) statement:

> The most compelling argument against specialization as a major cause of job dissatisfaction lies in the fact of individual differences. This is the central fact of life in the behavioral sciences, and yet the would-be reformers apparently believe that all people must react in exactly the same way to the same job. The observer says to himself, "That job would drive me nuts in half an hour." From this he somehow concludes that it must drive everyone else nuts as well. This simply is not so! (For that matter, it's highly probable that many of the workers interviewed by sympathetic social scientists privately regard their questioners' activities as a pretty terrible way to earn a living, too) [p. 17].

More recent data presented by Whyte (1955), Kennedy and O'Neill (1958), Kilbridge (1960a), Katzell, Barrett, and Parker (1961), Kendall (1963), Conant and Kilbridge (1965), Kornhauser (1965), and Blood and Hulin (1967) indicate that the general conclusion regarding the effects of job enlargement on job satisfaction and/or motivation is overstated and may be applicable to only certain segments of the working population. Further, it seems that each of the assumptions in the job-enlargement model can be seriously questioned by numerous other studies.

Perhaps the most dramatic of these studies was done by Turner and Lawrence (1965). Turner and Lawrence attempted a comprehensive study of the attitudinal and behavioral responses of workers to different aspects of their jobs. The original hypotheses were that workers respond favorably (high satisfaction and low absence rates) to jobs which are more complex, have more responsibility, more authority, more variety, etc. In short, "good" responses would accompany high-level jobs. The hypothesis concerning attendance was confirmed for a sample of 470 workers from 11 industries working on 47 different jobs. The hypothesized positive relationship between job level and satisfaction was *not* supported. This finding plus the presence of a number of curvilinear relationships led Turner and Lawrence to the conclusion that the workers in the sample had been drawn from two separate and distinct populations whose members responded in different ways to similar job characteristics. The investigators, by splitting their group of workers on a succession of variables and analyzing the relationship between task attributes and job satisfaction, were able to determine that workers from factories located in small towns responded dramatically differently from workers who came from more urban settings. The workers from small-town settings tended to respond to task attributes in the manner predicted by Turner and Lawrence. Workers from cities indicated no relationship between task attributes and attendance and responded with *low* job satisfaction to suposedly desirable job attributes and with high satisfaction to such "undesirable" attributes as repetitiveness. Turner and Lawrence posited an explanation based on a notion of alienation qua anomie. They argued that workers in large cities with their extremely heterogeneous social cultures would be more likely to be normless (anomic). They would fail to develop strong group or subcultural norms and values due to the extreme size and heterogeneity of the city population and would fail to respond positively to the white-collar-oriented values attached to larger, more autonomous, more skilled jobs. Rather than ignoring the effects of individual differences or attributing them to chance, Turner and Lawrence were able to determine that the unexpected results could not be attributed to chance or poor mental health but could be attributed to differences in cultural backgrounds.

Blood and Hulin (1967) argued that workers from large cities could not be considered as being anomic on the basis of the evidence but could be considered to be alienated from the "work" norms of the middle calss (positive affect for occupational achievement, a belief in the intrinsic value of hard work, a striving for the attainment of responsible positions, and a belief in the work-related aspects of Calvinism and the Protestant ethic) and integrated with the norms of their own particular subculture. Simply because blue-collar workers do not share the work norms and values of the middle classes does not mean they have no norms. In the case of the industrial workers sampled by Turner and Lawrence, there is no compelling reason to suspect that workers in large industrialized cities would adhere to the dominant work value systems of the white middle-class groups. In fact, it would be somewhat surprising if these workers whose grandfathers and fathers had (likely) worked as unskilled or semiskilled laborers and had failed to rise above their initial job or, even worse, had been replaced by a machine or a younger worker at age 50 would behave in the way demanded by the Protestant ethic. (Work hard and you will get ahead. You are responsible for your own destiny. Acceptance into the Kingdom of Heaven is dependent on hard work on this mortal earth.) Starting from this position, Blood and Hulin reanalyzed some data gathered by Patricia C. Smith. These data had been gathered from some 1,300 blue-collar workers employed in 21 plants located throughout the eastern half of the United States. Using results of Kendall's (1963) principal component analysis based on variables available in the census tracts, Blood and Hulin ordered the 21 plants along a number of dimensions which they felt would reflect the degree to which the blue-collar workers in the communities would feel alienated from middle-class work norms. Kendall (1963) labeled the principal components which were chosen for this analysis as extent of slums, urbanization, population density, standard of living, etc. (see Kendall, 1963, or Blood and Hulin, 1967, for a description of how these variates were constructed). These community variates were then used to predict a number of variables obtained from each of the 21 plants. These dependent variables included extent of preparation for retirement, correlation between pay satisfaction and overall job satisfaction, etc. The predictions made were that blue-collar workers in communities where one could expect integration with and acceptance of middle-class work norms (small community, low standard of living, few slums, etc.) would respond as the human relations theory or the striving type of motivation theory (Maslow, 1943) would expect. However, workers in communities where we would expect alienation from middle-class work norms (large, industrialized communities with large slum areas, etc.) would not respond as expected and, in some cases, would respond in an opposite manner from the counterparts in the "integrated" communities. These predictions were confirmed beyond the chance level. Of particular interest to the present review are their finding regarding job level and work satisfaction. In the most "alienated" community the correlation between job level and work satisfaction was approximately $-.50$, while among the workers drawn from the plant located in the most "integrated" community the correlation between these two variables was approximately .40. These results raise questions for the generality of the job-enlargement model.

Similar evidence regarding the importance of plant location has been presented by Kendall (1963). While his analysis was not designed to answer the questions crucial to this review, he did present canonical regression variates indicating the role played by community characteristics in predicting different combinations of specific job satisfaction and general job satisfaction.

Katzell et al. (1961) determined that among a sample of warehouse workers drawn from a number of locations there existed strong relationships between both satisfaction and productivity on the response side and community characteristics on the input side. They demonstrated that the location of the plant and hence the backgrounds of the workers, since these would seem to be correlated variables, play important roles in shaping the attitudes of the workers and influencing their behavior.

Whyte's (1955) descriptions of rate busters and quota restricters also indicate the importance of the workers' cultural backgrounds. In his analysis, based on a group of workers working under a piece-rate bonus system, he found that workers who were likely to be "rate busters" (produce above the group standards) were those workers with rural or small-town backgrounds, whose fathers had been entrepreneurs or farmers, who were Protestants, who were Republicans, and who had tended to look "upward" toward their parents for authority sanctions rather than toward their peer group. Quota restricters were more likely to have been reared in large cities, have come from working-class families who were Catholic, have belonged to a boy's gang as a youth, and to be Democrats. It could be argued that the rate busters *rejected* the norms of their peer group and *accepted* the norms of management (middle-class norms). If this is true, then we can predict on the basis of background those workers who will be alienated from middle-class work norms and those who will be integrated with these norms.

Kilbridge (1960a) attacked the question of the preference of workers for larger versus smaller jobs and the issue of mechanical pacing versus self-pacing. Of a sample of 202 (141 females, 61 males) assembly line workers employed by a radio and television set factory in Chicago, 51 percent stated they would prefer a smaller job, 37 percent were indifferent, and only 12 percent preferred a larger job. Further, 84 percent stated they preferred mechanical pacing, 6 percent were indifferent, and only 10 percent preferred a self-paced job. Considering the location of this factory and the results of Turner and Lawrence (1965), Blood and Hulin (1967), and Whyte (1955), these results are not surprising.

TABLE 1 Plant-Location Index of Expected Worker
Alienation from Middle-Class Work Norms

Type of worker	Urban location	Rural location
Blue-collar	Alienated	Nonalienated
White-collar	Nonalienated	Nonalienated

Kennedy and O'Neill (1958) surveyed workers in four automotive production departments. They determined that assembly operators performing highly routine and repetitive tasks held opinions toward their supervisors or work situations no more negative than those held by utility men who were performing a much more varied set of tasks.

Finally, Turner and Miclette (1962) interviewed 115 female assembly workers from an electronics plant. Even though the work was extremely repetitive and routine, most of the workers expressed satisfaction with the work itself. The main sources of dissatisfaction came from the sense of being caught in a quantity-quality squeeze and the interruptions from staff and supervisory personnel. Object, batch, line, and process traction were discussed as sources of satisfaction (cf. Baldamus, 1961; Smith & Lem, 1955). Thus, repetition (job size) alone is a poor indicator of worker response and the various sources of positive motivations of repetitive work must be considered.

DISCUSSION

The studies reviewed appear to be of two types. Those which have used acceptable methodology, control groups, appropriate analysis, and multivariate designs have generally not yielded evidence which could be considered as supporting the job-enlargement thesis. Those studies which do appear to support such a thesis frequently contain a number of deviations from normally acceptable research practice. Unfortunately, the former studies are in the minority and the latter studies have generated the greatest fervor and have been accepted as gospel by a large number of psychologists and human relations theorists.

The case for job enlargement has been drastically overstated and overgeneralized. Further, the evidence of the simultaneous effects of plant location and job size (or job level) provides a means of summarizing the literature and resolving the contradictions. Specifically, the argument for larger jobs as a means of motivating workers, decreasing boredom and dissatisfaction, and increasing attendance and productivity is valid only when applied to certain segments of the work force—white-collar and supervisory workers and nonalienated blue-collar workers. That is, if we choose the urban-rural dimension of the location of the plant as a crude but useful index of the expected alienation of the blue-collar workers in the community we could construct Table 1.

We would expect the job-enlargement hypothesis to predict the behavior of the white-collar workers and the rural or small-town blue-collar workers. Such a hypothesis would not predict responses and behavior of the urban blue-collar workers. This interaction between job size, job satisfaction, and plant location could be further amplified by the following representation of a three-dimensional plot.

Figure 1 is based on data taken from Blood and Hulin (1967). The communities in which the 21 plants in their sample were located were ordered on one of the alienation indexes (or, more properly, dimensions of communities which may be used to index the extent of predicted alienation among the blue-collar workers), and the extremes of the alienation index were used to obtain the slopes of the front and back edge of the surface. In this instance, the back edge of the surface, which represents a community which should foster integration with middle-class work norms, has been drawn to indicate a correlation of .39 between job level and work satisfaction. The front edge of the surface, which represents a community which should develop feelings of alienation from middle-class norms among the blue-collar workers, has been drawn to indicate a correlation of -.52 between job level and work satisfaction.[2]

This response surface indicates that as we move from nonalienated to alienated communities, we should expect the relationship of job level to work satisfaction to change linearly from positive through zero to negative. It further

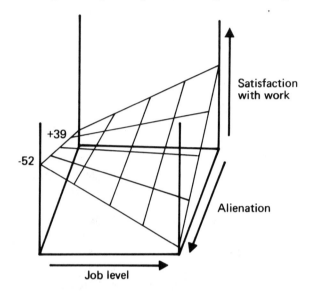

FIGURE 1. Response surface depicting the interrelationship between job level, satisfaction with work, and alienation of blue-collar workers from middle-class work norms. (Based on data from Blood and Hulin, 1967.)

indicates that if we hold job level constant at high-skill-level jobs, we would expect greater job satisfaction among nonalienated workers. However, if we look only at low levels of blue-collar jobs, we would expect greater work satisfaction among the alienated workers.

This response surface summarizes a great deal of the literature on job enlargement, job level, and job satisfaction. It seems evident, for example, that the rural workers sampled by Turner and Lawrence would have been drawn from the nonalienated end of the continuum while the urban workers would have come from plants located at the alienated end of the continuum. Likewise, those workers Katzell et al. found to be the most satisfied and the most productive should have been drawn from the nonalienated end of the continuum since they were located in small towns with nonunionized work forces. The workers interviewed by Walker and Guest (1952) seem to have been drawn from a plant located in a community which would be described as having workers who were

[2] A very convenient property of a response surface of this type is that any slice taken parallel to either of the stimulus planes results in a linear function relating the other stimulus variable to job satisfaction. This of course means we need not be concerned with any other than first degree functions with this particular model.

nonalienated since "The area from which [the workers] were recruited has few mass production factories [p. 4]," "Only two in our sample had ever worked in an automobile plant before [p. 8]," etc. Thus, the workers' negative responses to assembly line work would be predicted by the model. The workers in the Maytag study (Biganne & Stewart, 1963), being drawn from a small community, should have also responded positively to job enlargement. On the other hand, the workers studied by Kilbridge should have responded negatively to job enlargement since they were drawn from the Chicago metropolitan area (only 10 percent preferred a self-paced job and only 12 percent preferred a "larger" job). Whyte's (1955) descriptions of rate busters and quota restricters could also be explained by such a response surface. His rate busters appear to have been reared in an environment which would cause them to internalize the norms and value systems of the middle class. This was not true for the quota restricters. Also, this model would be expected to summarize the results of Blood and Hulin (1967) since these were the data used to verify the tenability of the response surface.

Finally, support for the part played by individual differences can be found even in those studies which make the strongest arguments for job enlargement. For example, Walker and Marriott reported that "many liked their [assembly line] work because it was simple, straightforward, and carried no responsibility." Argyris (1959) found lower skilled employees tending to express a desire "to experience routine or sameness." While these last two studies provide no direct support for such a model, they do indicate that the search for individual differences will be fruitful.

It would also seem that this response surface is reasonable from a theoretical point of view since it is consistent with most of the literature on anomie and alienation. Blue-collar workers living in small towns or rural areas would not be members of a work group large enough to develop and sustain its own work norms and values and would be more likely to be in closer contact with the dominant middle class. On the other hand, blue-collar workers living and working in large metropolitan areas would likely be members of a working-class population large enough to develop a set of norms particular to that culture. There is no compelling reason to believe that the norms developed by an urban working-class subculture would be the same or similar to those of the middle class.

If these arguments are correct, then we could expect that workers living in small towns would be more likely to be integrated with middle-class norms and workers in large cities would be more likely to feel alienated from the middle class and its norms and values. Turner and Lawrence (1965), provided discussion of the effects of heterogeneity and homogeneity of population on values and norms. However, it is not necessary to apply an argument based directly on number of blue-collar workers and social heterogeneity. One could argue that the dominant norms and values that all children learn in school and at home are those brought by the Anglo-Saxon Protestants from Europe in the seventeenth and eighteenth centuries. These norms and values have become the standard in American middle-class society. Children are taught these values in school by their middle-class teachers and attempt to reach goals defined in terms of these values by means of behavior consistent with these values. However, children raised in slums, where the cost of living is high, or where there is a great deal of migration are more likely to be frustrated in these attempts. Also, the lower-class American city dweller is less likely to be Anglo-Saxon Protestant (Turner & Lawrence, 1965) and less sympathetic to American middle-class values. Therefore, the acquisition by the lower-class city dweller of goals consistent with the Anglo-Saxon Protestant value system is likely to be met with criticism from his peer group (Whyte, 1955). Such frustration or negative reinforcement should extinguish behavior and beliefs consistent with American middle-class ideals.[3]

While we have cast our explanation of these results into a static model which implies fixed values of alienation from middle-class work norms, this is not a necessary aspect of the response surface. It would be possible to postulate a second moderating variable related to length of time since the job was enlarged or changed. This second moderator effect would be expected to indicate initial strong rejection of the enlarged job and initial dissatisfaction. As time on the enlarged job increases, however, we would expect less rejection and less dissatisfaction. The extent of the moderating effect of this latter variable is open to empirical study, but it does indicate the possibility of this model fitting into the current emphasis on dynamic as opposed to static models of work behavior (Vroom, 1966).

Even though such a model appears to summarize a great deal of the published evidence on job size and job satisfaction and is consistent with much of the theorizing regarding alienation and anomie, there are a number of unanswered problems. Nearly all of the data which have been published regarding the joint effects of job size and cultural variables on job satisfaction have used the environmental characteristics of the plant as one of the stimulus conditions. The assumption is that the environmental setting of the plant serves to index certain psychological variables of the individual workers. We have no disagreement with the use of index variables per se. However, the environmental setting of the plant or office is thoroughly confounded with the cultural backgrounds of the workers. Plants located in rural areas are more likely to have a work force with rural backgrounds who are Protestants, third or fourth generation Americans, etc. On the basis of the data, we have no way of disentangling the effects of plant location from the effects of the backgrounds of the workers. To attribute the changes in the relationship between job size and satisfaction to differences in the norms and value systems of the workers, as we have done, may not be warranted. On the other hand, the description of rate busters and quota restricters provided by Whyte does indicate that cultural and background differences are important. It would be incredible if the location of the plant had such an effect without operating through an intervening psychological variable. There is also evidence (Bronfenbrenner, 1958) that with socioeconomic status held constant, rural mothers adhere to more rigid patterns of socialization in their child-rearing practices. The probable effect of such practices (as opposed to

[3] The authors would like to thank Harry C. Triandis for pointing out this line of argument. We are, of course, fully responsible for its exposition.

permissiveness) is to result in children who are more likely to adopt the values of those who are in positions of authority (the middle-class oriented foremen and plant managers).

Finally, the writings of Durkheim, Weber, and Marx on the values and behavior of the industrial proletariat all point in the direction we have taken in the explanation of these findings.

There are also a number of problems raised by the studies relating job level to job satisfaction. For example, Ash (1954), Hoppock (1935), Hulin and Smith (1965), Inlow (1951), Katz (1949), Mann (1953), Miller (1940), and Morse (1953) have all presented data which indicate that higher satisfaction levels are associated with higher job levels. However, most of these studies contained problems mitigating against their being regarded as evidence negative to the model presented in Fig. 1. Many of these studies used white-collar as well as blue-collar workers as subjects. Others did not specify the location of the plant from which the workers were drawn. Thus, there is no way of knowing whether the findings are consistent with the model. Further, Blood and Hulin (1967) reanalyzed the data originally presented by Hulin and Smith (1965) and concluded that Hulin and Smith's conclusions had to be modified to take plant location into account. Finally, many of these studies did not separate the effects of job size from the effects of salary or wages.

In addition to the problems already mentioned, we are making the assumption that well-designed correlational studies can provide evidence on effects of basically manipulative programs. That is, the job-enlargement thesis states that if jobs are reengineered to make them larger, then certain desirable consequences will take place—notably decreases in monotony, increases in satisfaction, and decreases in turnover and restriction in output. We have made several inferences regarding this thesis and have based these inferences to a great extent on information contained in studies which have *correlated* job level or job size with satisfaction. Being *placed* on a high-skill-level job may be qualitatively different than having a present job *enlarged*. However, predictions based on a model (Fig. 1) which has been generated by such correlations appear to be valid for several of the job-enlargement studies. Second, we would expect differences between skilled and unskilled blue-collar workers to operate against the hypotheses. Highly skilled workers who have gone through an extensive training period should be more likely to adopt the norms and values of the middle class. Yet, we find that the highly skilled blue-collar workers do not necessarily report the higher satisfaction levels expected of them.

In summary, studies bearing on the job-enlargement thesis have been received and analyzed. These studies do not support the hypothesis that job size or job level is positively correlated *in general* with job satisfaction. Such hypotheses must be modified to take into account the location of the plant and the cultural backgrounds of the workers.

BIBLIOGRAPHY

Argyris, C. *Personality and organization*. New York: Harper, 1957.

Argyris, C. The individual and organization: An empirical test. *Administrative Science Quarterly* 1959, 4(2). 145—67.

Argyris, C. *Integrating the individual and the organization.* New York: John Wiley & Sons, 1964.

Ash, P. The SRA employee inventory—A statistical analysis. *Personnel Psychology,* 1954, 7, 337—60.

Baldamus, W. *Efficiency and effort.* London: Tavistock, 1961.

Behling, O. C. The meaning of dissatisfaction with factory work. *Management of Personnel Quarterly* 1964, 3(2). 11—16.

Biganne, J. F., and Stewart, P. A. Job enlargement: A case study. Research Series No. 25, 1963, State University of Iowa, Bureau of Labor and Management.

Blood, M. R., and Hulin, C. L. Alienation, environmental characteristics, and worker responses. *Journal of Applied Psychology,* 1967, 51, 284—90.

Bronfenbrenner, U. Socialization and social class through space and time. In E. E. Maccoby, T. M. Newcomb, and E. L. Hartley (Eds.), *Readings in social psychology.* New York: Holt, Rinehart and Winston, 1958. pp. 400—25.

Conant, E. H., and Kilbridge, M. D. An interdisciplinary analysis of job enlargement: Technology, costs, and behavioral implications. *Industrial and Labor Relations Review,* 1965, 18(3), 377-95.

Davis, L. E. Job design and productivity: A new approach. *Personnel,* 1957, 33, 418-30. (a)

Davis, L. E. Toward a theory of job design. *Journal of Industrial Engineering,* 1957, 8, 305-9. (b)

Davis, L. E., and Canter, R. R. Job design. *Journal of Industrial Engineering,* 1955, 6(1), 3-6, 20.

Davis, L., and Werling, R. Job design factors. *Occupational Psychology,* 1960, 34, 109-32.

Durkheim, E. *The division of labor.* Glencoe, Ill.: Free Press, 1933.

Elliott, J. D. Increasing office productivity through job enlargement. In, *The human side of the office manager's job.* (No. 134, Office Management Series) New York: American Management Association, 1953. Pp.3-15.

Frankmann, J. P., and Adams, J. A. Theories of vigilance. *Psychological Bulletin,* 1962, 59, 257-72.

Guest, R. H. Men and Machines: An assembly-line worker looks at his job. *Personnel,* 1955, 31, 496-503.

Guest, R. H. Job enlargement—A revolution in job design. *Personnel Administration,* 1957, 20(2), 9-16.

Hoppock, R. *Job satisfaction.* New York: Harper & Row, Publishers, 1935.

Hulin, C. L. Job satisfaction and turnover in a female clerical population. *Journal of Applied Psychology,* 1966, 50, 280-85.

Hulin, C. L., and Smith, P. C. A linear model of job satisfaction. *Journal of Applied Psychology,* 1965, 49, 209-16.

Inlow, G. M. Job satisfaction of liberal arts graduates. *Journal of Applied Psychology,* 1951, 35, 175-81.

Katz, D. Morale and motivation in industry. In W. Dennis (Ed), *Current trends in industrial psychology.* Pittsburgh: University of Pittsburgh Press, 1949. Pp.145-171.

Katzell, R. A., Barrett, R. S., and Parker, T. C. Job satisfaction, job performance, and situational characteristics. *Journal of Applied Psychology*, 1961, 45, 65-72.

Kendall, L. M. Canonical analysis of job satisfaction and behavioral, personal background, and situational data. Unpublished doctoral dissertation, Cornell University, 1963.

Kennedy, J. E., and O'Neill, H. E. Job content and worker's opinions. *Journal of Applied Psychology*, 1958, 42, 372-75.

Kilbridge, M. D. Do workers prefer larger jobs? *Personnel,* 1960, 37; 45-48. (a)

Kilbridge, M. D. Reduced costs through job enlargement. *Journal of Business* 1960, 33 (10); 357-62. (b)

Kornhauser, A. W. *Mental health of the industrial worker:* A Detroit study. New York: John Wiley & Sons, 1965.

Likert, R. *New patterns of management.* New York: McGraw-Hill Book Company, 1961.

MacGregor, D. M. Adventure in thought and action. In, *Proceedings of the fifth anniversary convocation of the school of industrial management.* Cambridge, Mass.: MIT Press, 1957.

MacKinney, A. C., Wernimont, P. F., and Galitz, W. O. Has specialization reduced job satisfaction? *Personnel,* 1962, 39(1), 8-17.

Mann, F. C. A study of work satisfaction as a function of the discrepancy between inferred aspirations and achievement. Unpublished doctoral disertation, University of Michigan, 1953.

Marks, A. R. N. An investigation of modifications of job design in an industrial situation and their effects on some measures of economic productivity. Unpublished doctoral dissertation, University of California, 1954. (Summarized in L. E. Davis & R. R. Canter, Job design research. *Journal of Industrial Engineering,* 1956, 7(6), 275-82.

Maslow, A. H. A theory of human motivation. *Psychological Review,* 1943, 50, 370-96.

Miller, D. C. Morale of college-trained adults. *American Sociological Review,* 1940, 5, 880-89.

Morse, N. C. *Satisfactions in the white-collar job.* Ann Arbor: University of Michigan, Institute for Social Research, Survey Research Center, 1953.

Porter, L. A study of perceived need satisfactions in bottom and middle management jobs. *Journal of Applied Psychology,* 1961, 45, 232-36.

Reif, W. E., and Schoderbek, P. P. Job enlargement: Antidote to apathy. *Management of Personnel Quarterly,* 1965, 5(1), 16-23.

Roethlisberger, F. J., and Dickson, W. J. *Management and the worker.* Cambridge: Harvard University Press, 1941.

Scott, W. E., Jr. Activation theory and task design. *Organizational Behavior and Human Performance,* 1966, 1, 3-30.

Smith, A. The education of the worker. (Orig. publ. 1776) Reported in A. O. Lewis (Ed.), *Of men and machines,* New York: Dutton, 1963. p.236-39.

Smith, P. C. The curve of output as a criterion of boredom. *Journal of Applied Psychology,* 1953, 37; 69-74.

Smith, P. C. Individual differences in susceptibility to industrial monotony. *Journal of Applied Psychology,* 1955, 39, 322-29.

Smith, P. C., and Lem, C. Positive aspects of motivation in repetitive work: Effects of lot size upon spacing of voluntary rest periods. *Journal of Applied Psychology,* 1955, 39, 330-33.

Turner, A. N., and Lawrence, P. R. *Industrial jobs and the worker: An investigation of response to task attributes.* Boston: Harvard University, Graduate School of Business Administration, 1965.

Turner, A. N., and Miclette, A. L. Sources of satisfaction in repetitive work. *Occupational Psychology,* 1962, 36, 215-31.

Vroom, V. H. *Some personality determinants of the effects of participation.* Englewood Cliffs, N. J.: Prentice-Hall Inc., 1960.

Vroom, V. H. A comparison of static and dynamic correlational methods in the study of organization. *Organizational Behavior and Human Performance,* 1966, 1, 55-70.

Walker, C. R. The problem of the repetitive job. *Harvard Business Review,* 1950, 28 (3), 54-58.

Walker, C. R. Work methods, working conditions, and morale. In A. Kornhauser, R. Dubin, & A. M. Ross (Eds.), *Industrial conflict.* New York: McGraw-Hill Book Company, 1954, p. 345-58.

Walker, C. R., and Guest, R. H. *The man on the assembly line.* Cambridge: Harvard University Press, 1952.

Karl W. Jackson
Dennis J. Shea

MOTIVATION TRAINING IN PERSPECTIVE

The naive psychology of everyday life is rich with an apparent understanding of human motivation (Heider, 1958; Schutz, 1963). Time after time we describe ourselves and others as being "motivated" or "unmotivated," and we frequently make sense out of motivated experiences and behavior by using motive-concepts. When we say things like "he's power-hungry," or "she has a strong need to be independent," we are attributing motives, thereby typifying the person by means of a causal shorthand that allows us to explain and predict his or her behavior. Yet with all of our personal knowledge of motivation, and with all of our skill in attributing motives, few psychological concepts have generated as much controversy as "motivation" and "motive." Some psychologists with a strong Behavioristic orientation (e.g., Skinner, 1964) argue that the concept of "motive" should be excluded from scientific psychology, while others (e.g., Koch, 1964) strongly urge that the concept is vital to an understanding of human behavior. Even among psychologists who espouse its value, there are vast differences in how they define the concept. For example, Hull's learning theory model (1943) defines a "motive" as a stimulating drive, while Tolman's (1959)

This article was prepared especially for this volume.

more cognitive approach to behavior defines motivation in terms of purposeful behavior. More recently, behavioral scientists have taken different approaches in attempts to increase human motivation. McClelland and Winter (1970) stress programs that emphasize individual change, while Herzberg's job enrichment approach (1968) suggests that a change in the environment leads to increased motivation.[1]

These controversies (and many more) are reflected in the theories, practices, and the effects of organizational psychologists. Nord (1969) and McGregor (1960), for example, disagree about whether the concept "motive" is needed at all. Nord's operant conditioning approach doesn't bother with the concept "motive," while McGregor's "theory" management depends on it. These approaches lead in turn to markedly different strategies for enhancing work productivity, and there is reason to believe that these different strategies will have different effects. For example, a sales manager who decided to apply operant conditioning principles to "motivate" his salesmen might employ a system of prizes or other extrinsic incentives as "motivators." If he decided to apply management based on "theory Y" assumptions, on the other hand, he would deemphasize the manipulation of extrinsic incentives and try to free his salesmen to set their own objectives and satisfy their own needs.

A study by Harlow (1950) suggests that these different strategies may lead to different motivational effects. He found that curiosity-motivated monkeys will manipulate puzzles ad infinitum without extrinsic reinforcers, but that when raisins were provided as reinforcers and were subsequently withdrawn the manipulative behavior stopped. This finding suggests that if a salesman is intrinsically motivated, he might suffer a decrement in sales after an incentive system is instituted and stopped, despite the fact that his sales performance may temporarily increase during the contest period. His performance may even decrease when the incentives are added.[2]

It is clear that different ways of resolving conceptual and theoretical controversies lead to different programs of action with potentially different effects. At the very time when organizations are turning more and more to social science for help, organizational psychology is fragmenting into a series of diverse schools, characterized by a proliferation of models and intervention strategies.

---

[1] These controversies in turn reflect more fundamental disagreements about the nature of man. Differing modes of resolving key philosophical problems have lead to different concepts and theories of motivation. See de Charms (1968) for a discussion of the philosophical issues revolving around (a) the mind-body problem, (b) the problem of causation, (c) the problem of hedonism, and (d) the problem posed by the subjective-objective dualities—and for a discussion of how these issues lead to different concepts and theories of motivation. Value differences also seem to play an important part in determining the way in which social scientists define and think about motivation. See Köhler (1928) and Polanyi (1958) for a discussion of values in the world of scientific theorizing.

[2] *We know of another example of a situation where the introduction of an "extrinsic" reinforcer interfered with the behavior it was designed to enhance. A "motivated" graduate* student was in the process of writing up an experiment he had been doing with one of his mentors. When the professor offered to pay him for writing up the article for publication, the "bribe" resulted in a great deal of negative feelings and the project was never completed.

These models and strategies in turn flow from different assumptions about motivation. Usually those assumptions are implicit, rather than explicit, so it is difficult for the student of organizational psychology (and for psychologists) to relate the approaches to each other in a systematic way and to evaluate and compare them in the light of the empirical support for their basic assumptions.

Our first major objective in this paper will be to share some key questions arising out of the study of motivation, show how answers to some of those questions have been translated into action with motivation training programs, and describe the effects of those kinds of training. Our second objective is to place the motivation training described here in perspective. We shall do so by presenting some of the problems associated with it and compare it to other programs and the problems associated with them. Finally, we shall suggest a broader approach to motivation training programs that would attempt to deal with the problems presented. We shall attempt to make our basic assumptions explicit so that they can be compared with those of other approaches.

KEY MOTIVATION CONCEPTS

What is it like to "be motivated?" When do we say of another that he is "motivated?" When do we attribute motives to another? How are motives related to experience? Answers to these questions will pave the way for a look at the basic motivation research which has led to motivation training.

What is it like to "be motivated?"

The words that we use in describing the state of "being motivated" are packed with energy—words like "drive," "desire," "concerned," and "engrossed." When we are motivated we are "turned on"—so actively concentrating on what we're doing that all else fades into the background. We are deeply committed to the task at hand, free of conflicting thoughts or preoccupations, polarized and unified toward a specific objective. Present thoughts are translated immediately and smoothly into action.

The contrasting condition of "being unmotivated" is a state of passivity or conflict. When we're unmotivated we're "turned off"—rather than being engrossed in anything or polarized toward a specific objective and free of conflicting thoughts, we tend to be inactive, or even if we're doing something, we have a difficult time concentrating on the task at hand. We are dull, uncreative, unspontaneous, or filled with anxiety. We hesitate about translating our thoughts into action.

"Being motivated" is a state characterized by three basic features not evident in "unmotivated" states. First, "being motivated" implies goal direction—a deep commitment toward some objective. In Heider's (1958) terms, a high level of *intention* is present. Second, when we're motivated we are energized, we are exerting ourselves. In other words (Heider), we're *trying*. Finally, we're conflict-free. We're not distracted by competing concerns.

When do we say of another, "He is really a motivated person?"

Let's take a look at John, a hypothetical worker who is employed at plant X as a lathe operator. We get out first view of him at midmorning. He is standing over his lathe concentrating intensely on the chair leg he is making. His body is alert, yet he seems relaxed. His eyes are glued to the leg he is carving as he deftly finishes the design. He moves quickly to the next block of wood and he begins to carve it without pause. The whistle for coffee break sounds but he doesn't seem to hear it. He is trying to finish the leg for the next shipment at noon and he continues to work quickly and effectively. He smiles as he works. He is achieving.

Our second view of John is at lunch. He is sitting at a corner table in the cafeteria talking with Laura, the sales manager's secretary. They are engrossed in a serious conversation. John is animated, alive, and obviously deeply pleased to be talking with Laura. He listens carefully to her and shares his reactions with her. Suddenly the whistle to end lunch blows but he continues to talk, oblivious to the sound. When his co-worker comes over to interrupt, John is momentarily startled and angry, but thanks his friend and continues his conversation. Finally, he and Laura get up together, he squeezes her hand, and they smile as they depart. He's been affiliating.

Later that evening we see John at a union meeting. He's caucusing with a group of workers who support him for the local presidency. His voice is loud as he tells the men what he will do for them if they support him. A man comes over and tells him that Laura is on the phone. He tells the men to wait for him. Once he reaches the telephone, he says, "Laura, I think I have them in the palm of my hand. They're doing everything that I want them to. I think you'll really be proud of me when I'm president. . .oh. . .sorry. . .I have to go. . .I see a guy and I need his vote." John wants power.

Based on our earlier description of individual motivation, it should be clear that in each of these three instances, John is highly motivated—he's intensely concerned, goal directed, committed to a specific task, and energetically pursuing it with little thought of anything else. In the first case his concern was with his work; in the second it was with his relationship with another person; in the third it was in reaching a position of high status, influence and power. In our terms his concern was with achievement, affiliation, and power, respectively.

We get knowledge of another person's level of motivation by observing the intensity of his behavior. The more actively he is pursuing an activity, the more we describe him as being motivated.[3] We attribute motivation (or concern,

[3] *When does a manager attribute motivation to a worker?* Organizations are polarized toward the attainment of specific objectives. "Motivated behavior," or "motivation" tend to be defined in terms of those objectives. Managers tend to attribute motivation to their workers when they are doing what they "ought" to be doing, i.e., when they are energetically pursuing the objectives of the organization. A manager looking at John in our three cases is likely to perceive him as "being motivated" in the first case, where his concern was with his work, but is much less likely to see him as being motivated in the other two (he

needs, desires, obsession. etc.) to him because we've known from personal experience that the intensity of *our* behavior is generally a function of the level of our motivation.

The specific motive that we attribute to another at any given time is a function of the direction in which we see him moving. If we see that a person is trying to make or repair a friendship we attribute to him a desire for that friendship. If we see him trying to dominate or impress another person we attribute to him a desire to have power over that person. We are able to make these attributions because of our own personal knowledge that our own motives lead us to particular kinds of activities.

When do we attribute motives to another?

It is one thing to say that a person is "motivated" at any given time and quite another to say that he's a highly motivated person. In one observation we can see that a person is "motivated," but it takes many observations for us to be sure that we can safely say, "He's really a motivated guy." Everyone is highly motivated from time to time, but only a few people will be highly motivated most of the time. We say that another is a motivated person when our experience with him indicates that he typically displays "motivated" behavior.

We use the same general procedure in attributing particular motives to people. Given that we have observed a person's motivated behavior several times, and that we have seen that he typically pursues objectives of a particular kind, we are able to categorize him with a particular motive concept. In the same way that everyone is "motivated" from time to time, but not everyone is a "motivated person"; everyone is concerned about a friendship from time to time, but not everyone is very frequently concerned about friendships. When we have the opportunity to observe another person several times, however, and when we have seen that he is frequently moved to establish and maintain friendships, then we summarize his behavior with a motive concept by saying, "He's really concerned with making friends," or "He's really an affiliative guy." We attribute particular motives to people, in short, when we see that they are *typically* motivated to reach a particular type of objective.

How are motives related to experience?

Human experience is a rich and varied stream of sights, sounds, smells, etc. Much of it is a representation of what is available to our direct perception at the moment. Night dreams, day dreams, and images of what was, will be, or could be available to perception, but is not, are all forms of fantasy. Our fantasy lives seem to reflect our obsessions and preoccupations. When we assign the "boy crazy" motive concept to a teenage girl we are implying not only that she typically engages in motivated behavior with respect to boys, but also that she is obsessed or preoccupied with thoughts of boys. Her fantasy life is filled with

---

may, in fact, accuse him of just "goofing off"). Managers (and teachers,) in short, tend to define motivation and motivated behavior by answering the question, "Is the behavior consistent with the demands of the job?"

boys, and observations of that aspect of her experience would indicate a typical fantasy pattern of boy-concern which corresponds with her behavior. Typical fantasy patterns, in short, seem to correspond with typical behavior patterns; and a person's typical fantasy patterns correspond with his motives.

We all have vast fantasy lives. The intensity of a person's obsessions or motives should be reflected by how frequently he thinks about the particular class of incentives defining the motive, and by how vivid the fantasies are. If we could somehow sample a person's thoughts or fantasies, we could learn a great deal about his motives; and if we could somehow change a person's typical fantasy patterns we could affect his motivated behavior.

REASEARCH OF INDIVIDUAL MOTIVATION—
THE WORK OF McCLELLAND, et al.

Can we measure individual motivation?

One of the major problems in the study of psychological variables is that of measurement. If we assume that "motivated behavior" is a function of thoughts or fantasies, the first problem becomes that of measuring a individual's thoughts. The second becomes that of relating those to measures of behavior. To go about that first task, Atkinson and McClelland (1948) provided some Navy men with a goal (to get something to eat) by creating a state of hunger. Some of the men had not eaten for an hour, some for four hours, and some had gone without food for 16 hours. The men were then asked to write some imaginative stories to picture cues that were flashed on a screen. To help them in the writing of their stories, they were given the following questions as guides:

1. What is happening? Who are the persons?
2. What has led up to this situation? What has happened in the past?
3. What is being thought? What is wanted? By whom?
4. What will happen? What will be done? By whom? (Atkinson, 1958, p. 48).

This technique of measurement, borrowed from Murray's (1943) thematic apperception test (TAT), is now called the method of thought sampling (de Charms, 1968).[4] The assumption behind the technique is that the writer "projects" his thoughts into the characters in his story. When the writer composes the story, he is giving us a sample of the way he thinks, i.e., a sample of his fantasy pattern. If he is concerned or obsessed about something, he should express that concern in his stories.

Once the story had been written, we may analyze the stories to see if their content fits our categories. Atkinson and McClelland analyzed the sailors' stories and they found the predicted relationship between the concern for food and the content of the stories. The more hungry the men, the more they wrote stories about characters being hungry, expressing a need for food, and taking part in

---

[4] See de Charms (1968) for an analysis and critique of this technique of measurement.

activity that was successful in overcoming their hunger (Atkinson, 1958, p. 62). Not only had they demonstrated that the "motivated" men wrote stories about "motivated" people, Atkinson and McClelland had performed the first step in the development of a general measure of motivation.

How do we define (differentiate) specific motives?

Hunger is a physiological need and it and other primary drives have been studied quite extensively by experimental psychologists. When we look at learned or secondary needs we find that the number of defined needs or motives (e.g., the need to be independent or dependent; to be aggressive or submissive, etc.) increases, while the research on each is quite minimal.

Following their hunger study, McClelland, Atkinson, and others set out to define and measure other motives in a similar manner. They confined their major efforts to the study of three motives, the needs for achievement, affiliation and power. In defining each, they had to answer two questions: (1) How do we define and measure the goal associated with each motive? and (2) How do we define and measure the intensity of the obsession associated with each motive?

After a great deal of research with the measurement instrument[5], the following definitions were derived for the three motives:

1. *Power motivation* (abbreviated "*n* Pow") was defined in terms of influence and control. A power goal is manifested in a story when a character shows concern about controlling, advising, or influencing another person (Winter, 1968).
2. *Affiliation motivation* (*n* Aff) is defined in terms of friendship. An affiliation goal is manifested in a story when one of the characters display concern about creating a friendly relationship with another or when he is concerned with losing a friend (Shipley & Veroff, 1958).
3. *Achievement motivation* (*n* Ach) is defined in terms of concern about success in competiton with some standard of excellence (McClelland, et al., 1953).

Comprehensive scoring manuals have been developed (Atkinson, 1958; Winter, 1968) for determining when a story contains a power, affiliation, or achievement goal. Because the majority of the research on individual motivation by the McClelland group has concentrated on the achievement motive, we shall elaborate on the recognition and measurement of that particular need.

A story is recognized as containing achievement imagery and receives a point in the scoring system if one or more characters in the story exhibits:

1. Concern with competing with some outside standard of excellence (e.g., doing better than another; surpassing a record)
2. Concern with competing with a self standard (e.g., improving one's performance)
3. Concern with engaging in a long-term effort
4. Concern with doing something unique

[5] See McClelland, et al., 1953 and Atkinson, 1958 for a detailed analysis of the development of the measure.

If an individual's story contains one or more of these concerns, we say that the story has an achievement goal, an indication of the writer's need for achievement. Once this has been indicated, we may look further at the story for an indication of the level of intensity of that concern. The more intense the concern, the more obsessed the writer is with achievement, the more he will write about the kinds of things that move him toward an achievement goal. A story is scored for the intensity of the obsession with achievement when a character:

1. Expresses a desire for excellence as a *need* (N)
2. Expresses some instrumental *activity* (ACT) that will move him toward his goal
3. Expresses hope that he will succeed in reaching his goal—*hope of success* (HOS)
4. Expresses a fear that he might fail, for he sets goals that require effort—*fear of failure* (FOF)
5. Expresses a feeling of success when he achieves his goal—*success feelings* (SF)
6. Expresses knowledge about things in the world that might keep him from reaching his goal—*world obstacles* (WO)
7. Express a feeling of failure when he fails to reach his goal—*failure feelings* (FF)
8. Expresses knowledge about personal inadequacies that might prevent him from reaching his goal—*personal obstacles* (PO)
9. Expresses the fact that he can get *help* (H) in reaching his goal
10. Expresses only a concern for achievement in his story (and not, e.g., affiliation, power, etc.)—*thema* (TH)

These scoring categories, then, define operationally an individual's level or intensity of achievement motivation. Using other categories we can also measure an individual's level of affiliation or power motivation. The more the individual is concerned (obsessed) with the thoughts reflected in those categories, the more we say that he has a particular level of motivation.

> *What do people with high achievement motivation do*
> *(i.e., what kind of motivated behavior do they emit) that*
> *distinguishes them from others?*

In defining very specifically what we mean by an individual's "achievement motivation," as we have here, we have simply said that people who have high achievement motivation are those who are concerned about competing with some standard of excellence and that they write stories that manifest that concern. The test of the concept and the measure comes when we validate it by relating it to "behavior."[6] The data indicate that both in the laboratory and in the real world, people with high achievement motivation perform differently than those with low achievement motivation.

[6] See McClelland, et al., 1953; Atkinson, 1958; and de Charms, 1968 for an extended discussion and evaluation of the measure's reliability and other features.

First of all, in the laboratory, it has been demonstrated that in relation to those who score low on the measure, those who have high n Achievement do better at a number of activities—they complete more paper and pencil tasks, they solve more mathematical problems, and they solve more verbal problems (unscrambling words) in a given amount of time (de Charms, 1968).

While these results are interesting and provide support for the validity of the measure, other data from the field are more impressive, especially to those in the business community. For example, early in the development of the measure at Wesleyan University, McClelland collected stories from a group of males. He reports (1965b) that upon checking the alumni directory he found that 83 percent of the men who could be classified as entrepreneurs had high n Achievement scores as Sophomores in college. In contrast, only 21 percent of those classified as non-entrepreneurs had high n Achievement. These data indicate that men who have a high need to achieve actually go on to be successful in their careers, especially in the business world.

How do they do it? What are the characteristics of an "achiever?" In answering these questions, McClelland has developed the concept of the "achievement syndrome" (1961), a cluster of behavioral indices that distinguishes the individual with high n Achievement.

1. *To begin with, he likes situations in which he takes personal responsibility for finding solutions to problems* (McClelland, 1962, p. 104). The achiever, in setting his goals, likes to be in charge of his fate.

2. *Another characteristic of a man with a strong achievement concern is his tendency to set moderate achievement goals and to take calculated risks* (McClelland, 1962), p. 104). Probably the most replicated finding in the achievement motivation literature is that the high achiever avoids "sure things" by setting goals that require some effort (i.e., they are challenging) on his part, while he avoids "pie-in-the-sky" goals over which he has little control.[7]

3. *The man who has a strong concern for achievement also wants concrete feedback as to how well he is doing* (McClelland, 1962, p. 105). The high achiever plans his life very carefully. He sets goals that he can reach and he makes them quite specific. In doing so, he is constantly aware of his progress.

How is an individual's achievement motivation developed?

We view achievement motivation as a learned, rather than as an innate motive. The question that follows from this assumption is: How does one learn the motive? The answer to this question is important, for historically it opened the door to an enormous expansion in research interests. Roger Brown (1965) says that "probably the single research result that was most crucial in effecting the expansion of scope was Marian Winterbottom's study of the childhood origins of achievement motivation" (p. 446). What Winterbottom (1958) did was to find a relationship between childhood training and achievement motivation. Mothers of

---

[7] See Atkinson and Feather (1966) for an extensive review of the risk-taking literature.

boys with high *n* Achievement expected that their children should do more things independently at an earlier age than mothers of boys with low need achievement. In another similar study, Rosen and D'Andrade (1959) found that parents of high scorers tended to give their children more responsibility in a block stacking task. Both of these studies are important in that they stress the relationship between childhood experiences and the achievement motive.

Once McClelland and his co-workers had discovered the relationship between childhood independence training and achievement motivation, they looked at other sources that might influence the development of individuals with high achievement motivation. Since the reading that a child does may influence his fantasies, McClelland investigated that relationship.

In what Brown (1965) calls " . . . one of the more audacious investigations in the history of social science" (p. 450), McClelland (1961) assembled fourth and fifth grade readers for children from about 30 countries all over the world. Those stories (after they were translated into English) were then scored for *n* Achievement and those scores were related to indices of economic development. The results showed that those countries with high *n* Achievement present in their children's readers were more developed (in terms of per capita income and the amount of electricity produced) than those countries with low *n* Achievement. Later (1962), de Charms and Moeller found a similar relationship between *n* Achievement in children's readers in the United States and economic activity. The higher the *n* Achievement content in the children's readers, the more those children went on to increase the economic productivity in the country.

In summary, these data show that achievement motivation is developed by learning how to work independently (which assumes taking personal responsibility, planning, and learning from experience—the elements of the achievement syndrome) in a cultural milieu that stresses thoughts about achievement. When achievement motivation is developed in individuals, they perform relatively successfully, especially in entrepreneurial roles.

Can achievement motivation be increased?

What we have done here is to present evidence that indicates that individuals do differ along the dimension of motivation, and in particular achievement motivation, that we can measure the variable scientifically, and that we have some knowledge about how it is learned. In addition, we know from a great deal of research that people who have high achievement motivation are more "successful" in their endeavors (especially business endeavors) than those who have low *n* Achievement.

Over the last ten years, McClelland and his students have devoted a great deal of their efforts to attempts to increase achievement motivation by means of training courses, based on the assumption that *n* Ach is a learned motive. Burris (1958) presented the first data that indicated that *n* Achievement counseling of college underachievers improved their grades. Kolb (1965), in the summer of 1961, conducted the first full-scale achievement motivation training program. In the program, 57 underachieving high school boys (I. Q. 120, average grade D+)

attended a summer school instruction course. From these, Kolb randomly selected 20 boys from lower and middle classes, put them on the floor of a dormitory, acted as their counselor, and conducted a training course with them. At the end of the semester, the trained students had significantly improved their grades. The effect was especially true for those boys who initially had low n Achievement.

Aronoff and Litwin (1966) conducted an achievement motivation training course with 16 middle-level executives in business. They had a control group of 11 untrained men who took part in a management development course. The authors devised an advancement score for the two-year period prior to the training and the two-year period after the course. The men who were trained in achievement motivation showed significantly greater advancement than the men who took part in the corporation course.

McClelland (1969) presented data showing the effects of achievement motivation training with a group of 49 Black businessmen from the Washington, D. C. area. His results showed that on every index of performance (from new business starts to promotion to new capital invested) that the trained men were at least twice as successful as a comparable group of 63 untrained men after six months.

Finally, the training has been shown to be effective in other countries besides the United States. In 1963, 34 Indian businessmen from the Bombay area attended a training course. Data on 30 of the trained men and 11 untrained men were collected from two years prior to and two years after the training. They found the trained group had significantly increased their activity over their previous behavior and that they were significantly more active than the group which had not had the training.

In 1969, McClelland and Winter presented the results of still another motivation change study in their book, *Motivating Economic Achievement.* In the study presented there, over 70 businessmen in two cities in India were trained. After an extended and very complex analysis of the effects of the training, the results may be summarized as follows: The course participants

1. were more active after the course, while the untrained individuals stayed about the same,
2. became more vigorous in their activity (in terms of working longer and harder),
3. made more attempts to start new businesses and were more successful in starting new businesses,
4. invested more capital, and
5. showed a greater increase in gross income.

   How is achievement motivation and "motivated behavior" increased in the training courses?

   Some of the basic principles upon which the training courses are built are presented by McClelland in his paper: *Toward a theory of motive acquisition* (1965a). A careful description of the training itself may be found in Shea and

Jackson (in preparation). Basically, the training course employs four training principles:

1. Participants are trained to examine themselves carefully—their behavior, their needs, and their feelings.
2. Participants are trained to be aware of the thoughts and actions of "motivated" individuals and are helped to learn how to think and behave like those individuals.
3. Participants are trained to set realistic goals that they can responsibly achieve.
4. Participants, in a group setting, are supported in their attempt at personal change.

We have found that any attempt to describe the training without going into a great deal of detail is doomed to failure. The training course is composed of well over 20 "psychological inputs" (Shea and Jackson) that are designed to facilitate motivation change based on the four principles outlined above. The course as now developed is composed of a three-to ten-day experiential workshop in a retreat setting. The training involves an intensive self-examination and change process in which the participants and trainers work for about 12 hours per day.

OTHER RESEARCH ON INDIVIDUAL MOTIVATION—
THE WORK OF DE CHARMS. ET AL.

One of McClelland's former students, Richard de Charms, has recently developed a fresh approach to the study of individual motivation (1968), and an expanded form of motivation training (in preparation). De Charms' key concept is "person causation" which he defines as " . . .*the initiation by an individual of behavior intended to produce a change in his environment"* (1968, p. 6). He asserts that one of the first concepts that an individual learns is that he can be effective in producing (causing) changes in his life and that man's striving to be a causal agent is his primary motivational propensity.

De Charms uses two terms to represent the polar extremes of personal causation representing idealized personality types. A person who typically sees himself as powerless, at the mercy of external events and people, is called a *Pawn*. A person who usually sees himself as a potent master of his own destiny is called an *Origin*. A *Pawn* is constrained, his behavior is determined by external forces beyond his control. An *Origin* feels that the locus of control of his behavior lies within himself—he makes the choices, and the effects of his behavior are determined by him.

In studies based on his theory, de Charms found that we attribute "Origin" and "Pawn" behavior to others and that feeling like an Origin rather than a Pawn has marked effects on one's behavior. Individuals seen as Pawns are not seen as responsible for their behavior; those seen as Origins are seen to "own" their behavior and are responsible for its consequences. People feeling like Origins enjoy their behavior more than when they act as Pawns. When they choose to act, rather than being forced to, they are more creative and more productive (de Charms, 1968).[8]

Plimpton (1970) has developed a scoring system for measuring the Origin-Pawn variable. Like the measure of *n* Achievement, the system is applied to the content analysis of TAT stories. It has the following six categories:

1. Internal control
2. Goal setting
3. Instrumental activity
4. Reality perception
5. Personal responsibility
6. Self confidence[9]

Can personal causation be increased?

De Charms does not define personal causation as a "motive"; however, he notes that the feeling that one can control his fate is primary to any experience of motivation and any motivated behavior that might accompany that experience. One must feel that his energy is "worth it"—that it will result in the desired consequences—before he will expend that energy. Over the past several years de Charms and his co-workers have been engaged in a long-term research program designed to investigate the question: Can we train individuals to act more like Origins?

Origin training attempts to allow the trainee to develop the ability and desire to be independent by gradually training him to take increasing responsibility for his behavior by setting his own goals and planning and structuring his own life. It does so by providing the trainee with the skills and personal characteristics required for such independence, i.e., a realistic, accepted, and accurate self-concept, a disposition to think like an Origin, and ability and desire to set realistic objectives, etc. In its objectives, the training is similar to achievement motivation and self-esteem training.[10]

De Charms (in preparation) describes the effects of the first extensive Origin-training program that was conducted with several hundred low-income, Black elementary school children. The program was designed as a two-step process in which teachers were given Origin training (in conjunction with achievement motivation training) in a small group setting and then designed with the investigators a training program that they used in the schools. They were trained to act as trainers in their classrooms.

The program resulted in significant positive effects on both the teachers and their students. More trained than untrained teachers either went on to graduate

---

[8] Readers familiar with Rotter's (1966) internal-external control of reinforcements variable will see striking similarities between it and personal causation (Origin-Pawn). See de Charms (1968) for a discussion of the differences between the concepts.

[9] See Plimpton (1970) for a description of the development, reliability, and validity of the measure.

[10] The Origin concept is very similar to prevailing conceptions of high self-esteem (Coopersmith, 1967) or a positive self-esteem (Wylie, 1961). Coopersmith is now developing self-esteem training programs which are quite similar to Origin-training.

work or advanced to more responsible positions. In addition, the program resulted in substantial and significant increases in achievement motivation, Origin fantasies, realistic and successful goal setting, and academic performance for those children who participated in the training program.[11]

PROBLEMS IN MOTIVATION TRAINING

Psychologists, educators, parents, and many others have struggled for years with the question, "How can we motivate people?" While the programs described here have been quite successful, they have not been without problems. By discussing some of those problems, we hope to shed additional light on this complex question.

The major problems that occur center around the issue of the relationship between the individual and his environment. Simply instituting individual motivation training does not necessarily mean that the individual will benefit completely in terms of maximizing his potential; nor does it mean that the organization will benefit from the training.

Addressing ourselves to the second of those issues, we know of instances where individual motivation training has actually interfered with the objectives of the organization. McCowan (personal communication) found that unskilled workers in achievement motivation training programs were quite likely to quit the job that they held in favor of another job that provided the opportunity for more advancement. As we noted earlier, de Charms and his co-workers have found that when motivation training courses have been conducted with teachers (with the assumed goal of increasing the ability of the teachers to "motivate" their students to learn), a good number of the teachers either leave the teaching profession or move to "more advanced" positions in the profession where they have little contact with children (de Charms, in preparation). Finally, Jackson found that when he conducted a motivation training workshop in his education psychology course, his students became so "motivated" that they have moved in the direction of changing the educational system (Jackson, in press). In each of these cases, while the training has appeared to have been "successful," the sponsoring organization has, in some way, suffered from its success.

At least two other examples indicated that when the newly acquired "motivation" is not supported by the environment, the program has not led to optimal results. Kolb (1965), in his study of motivation training with middle- and lower-class students, found that the performance of the lower-class children fell back to its earlier level when the trained students remained in their old environment. De Charms' data indicate that when trained children return to classes with untrained teachers, their accelerated learning drops off, although not to its earlier level. Trained children in a supportive environment continue to exhibit the accelerated effects of earlier training.

These problems are at least partially explained if we note that "motivated"

[11] See de Charms, Collins, Jackson and Shea (1968), Shea (1969), Plimpton (1970), and Coor (1970) for detailed analyses of the results of the program. De Charms (in preparation) will present a comprehensive analysis of the entire project.

people seem to perform most effectively in relatively free situations in which available acitvities allow them to satisfy their achievement or personal causation needs. When the worker (or the student) is given that freedom he can satisfy his needs by selecting his own objectives, designing his own procedures, and evaluating his own work. If organizational objectives provide the opportunity for that "motivated" behavior, the organization benefits from the training; if not, the effects of the training may be debilitating.

Most organizations are organized around objectives and procedural recipes that limit the freedom of individual members. However, organizations, and specific positions within them, vary in terms of how much these objectives limit individual member freedom (Likert, 1967). The specific objective-classes available to any given member also vary with respect to how much they are consistent with his motive-hierarchy. Some positions prescribe achievement-related objectives, while others (e.g., manager, supervisor, teacher, etc.) prescribe power or affiliation objectives.

Highly motivated people tend to gravitate toward positions in which they feel free and in which they may pursue objectives consistent with their most intense motive-related concerns.[12] If a worker in an achievement motivation training course comes back to a position which does not allow him to satisfy his need to achieve because it doesn't allow him the freedom of choice necessary for the fulfillment of that need, he will be likely to seek a position where there is a better fit or match between his needs and the structure of his environment. If the alternative of locomotion to another environment does not exist for the individual, it seems that he is left with one of two courses of action. He can attempt to change the organization by attempting to move it in the direction of opening up to the needs of its members. If the environment cannot be changed, then it is quite likely that the newly trained individual will exhibit little "motivated behavior" and the program will appear useless, both for the organization and the individual.

MOTIVATION TRAINING: DEMOCRATIC MANAGEMENT

The notion that behavior is a function of both the individual and his environment is far from being new. Kurt Lewin, one of the first social scientists to propose that psychologists could and even should study change or intervention tactics in organizations, described the relationship in his famous equation: $B = f(P,E)$ (1966, p. 12). As a function of the theory presented in that equation, Lewin predicted that individuals will be more productive and experience higher morale when they operate in an environment which allows them the freedom to participate in decisions that affect their behavior. The now

---

[12] This is probably why people with intense concerns with achievement tend to become entrepreneurs. As an entrepreneur one is in a position to establish one's own objectives and procedures, and to satisfy one's competetive needs, without being constrained by organizational objectives—unless, of course, the objectives of one's organization are a direct reflection of one's own needs

classic studies by Lippitt and White (1943) and Coch and French (1948) lended great support to his theory. Marrow (1970) in his excellent biography of Lewin, cites those as he traces the development of the theory and research that led to contemporary programs which stress democratic (or participatory) management, worker-centered" climate, etc., as techniques to facilitate the motivation of the individual.

We briefly mention this approach to training because it appears to us that it places emphasis on the environmental (e.g., situational climate) effects on individual motivation, while McClelland's approach emphasizes individual change. Where *n* Achievement training neglects the environment, the "job enrichment" (see Herzberg, 1968) type of training seems to neglect the individual.

The latter approach, like the former, results in problems for the individual and the organization. Some individuals ("theory-X" types?) appear to need structure and completely fall apart in a "democratic" environment. Anecodotal evidence from the de Charms project indicated that when teachers began their school year committed to treating their students like "Origins" and gave them complete freedom, the students reacted with a great deal of anxiety to the new responsibility. The teachers had to modify their leadership behavior in terms of returning to a more structured environment until the students were trained (motivated?) to respond to a more free climate. When the classroom was gradually transformed into an "Origin" atmosphere as the teachers "loosened the reins" (de Charms, in press), the "motivated behavior" in terms of increased academic performance was enhanced. We would think that the same general phenomenon would occur in a work situation. An "unmotivated" individual who is accustomed to tight direction is likely to suffer greatly in a "democratic" climate.

MOTIVATION TRAINING IN PERSPECTIVE

Motivation trainers who espouse the "individual" approach in motivation training have implicitly assumed what we could call a"one-factor" theory of motivation. They have either considered the other factor (the environment or the situation) to be unimportant or they have assumed that it is a constant. This approach is captured in the equation: Motivated Behavior = f (Individual Motivation, K), where K is a constant describing the environment in which the individual resides. Motivation training derived out of this assumption (e.g., achievement motivation training) would predict that the higher the individual motivation, the greater the evidence of motivated behavior. Based on the problems we have outlined earlier, it seems clear that this kind of equation does not suffice to predict behavior.

It seems quite interesting to us that most "motivation training programs" that have been developed in the "democratic management" tradition are also "one-factor" theories. Such training seems to assume that the individual factor is either unimportant or is constant (e.g. McGregor (1966) assumes that all people are "highly motivated"). The motivation assumptions behind such programs seem to be captured in the equation: Motivated behavior $= f$ (Environment, K), where K is again a constant, this time applying to individual characteristics.

This type of training, which predicts that a "more democratic" (more free?) climate leads to more responsibility, more motivation, and more productivity, appears, like the achievement motivation training, to be quite successful (Herzberg, 1968; Likert, 1967). As we mentioned before, however, not everyone responds to increased responsibility in a positive manner, and the programs are not without problems.

This evidence indicates to us that if we are to predict motivated behavior we must pay attention to both the motivation of the individual *and* to the properties of the environment. But it seems important to note from the evidence presented that an increase in either of these two "factors" will not necessarily result in an increase in "motivated behavior." Man's "life space" cannot be viewed as a cookbook where an addition of x bits of individual motivation and y bits of a free environment will result in an increase in motivated behavior. The best results in motivation training seem to occur when there is a good fit (match) between individual motives and environmental opportunity. "Motivated" individuals perform quite well in an open environment; "unmotivated" individuals do not. The converse relationship seems to hold for closed or restricted environments. As we continue our efforts in the area of motivation training, we must focus our attention on the match or mismatch between individual needs and environmental opportunity.

In summary, we would note that individuals responsible for organizational development might take their cues from the behavior of de Charms' teachers. There are different perspectives in human motivation and motivation training. How he diagnoses the needs of his individuals and the structure of the job environment will determine the program he implements. The success or failure of his program will depend on his ability to match individual needs and environmental opportunity.

BIBLIOGRAPHY

Aronoff, J. and Litwin, G. H. *Achievement motivation training and executive advancement.* Unpublished paper, Harvard University, 1966.

Atkinson, J. W. *Motives in fantasy, action, and society.* Princeton: Van Nostrand, 1958.

Atkinson, J. W., and Feather, N. T. (eds.) *A theory of achievement motivation.* New York: John Wiley & Sons, 1966.

Atkinson, J. W. and McClelland, D. C. The projective expression of needs: II. The effect of differential intensities of the hunger drive on thematic apperception. *Journal of Experimental Psychology, 38,* 1948, 643-58.

Brown, R. *Social psychology.* New York: Free Press, 1965.

Burris, R. W. *The effect of counseling on achievement motivation.* Unpublished doctoral dissertation. University of Indiana, 1958.

Coch, L. and French, J. R. P. Overcoming resistance to change. *Human relations,* 11, 1948, 512-32.

Coopersmith, S. *The antecedents of self esteem.* San Francisco: W. H. Freeman, 1967.

Coor, Ina F. *The effects of grade level and motivation training on ego development.* Unpublished doctoral dissertation, Washington University, 1970.

de Charms, R. *Personal causation.* Reading, Mass: Addison-Wesley, 1968.

de Charms, R. From Pawns to Origins: Toward self motivation. In Lesser, G. S. (ed.) *Psychology and educational practice.* Glenview, Illinois: Scott, Foresman and Co. 1971.

de Charms, R. *Motivation in the schools.* (In preparation).

de Charms, R. and Moeller, G. H. Values expressed in American children's readers: 1890-1950. *Journal of Abnormal and Social Psychology.* 64, 1962, 136-42.

de Charms, R., Collins, Janet, Jackson, K. W., and Shea, D. J. *Can the motives of low income Black children be changed?* Paper presented in a symposium at the American Educational Research Association meetings, February, 1969, Los Angeles.

Harlow, H. F., Harlow, M. K., and Meyer, D. R. Learning motivated by a manipulative drive. *Journal of Experimental Psychology, 40,* 1950, 228-34.

Heider, F. *The psychology of interpersonal relations.* New York: John Wiley & Sons, 1958.

Herzberg, F. One more time: How do you motivate employees? *Harvard Business Review,* Jan.-Feb., 1968, 53-62.

Hull, C. L. *Principles of behavior.* New York: Appleton-Century-Crofts, 1943.

Jackson, K. A coparticipative, experiential learning design for educational psychology. In Rosenberg, M. *Educational therapy,* Vol III, (in press).

Koch, S. Psychology and emerging conceptions of knowledge as unitary. In T. W. Wann (ed.), *Behaviorism and phenomenology.* Chicago: University of Chicago Press, 1964.

Köhler, W. *The place of value in the world of facts.* New York: Liveright, 1928.

Kolb, D. A. Achievement motivation training for underachieving high school boys. *Journal of Personality and Social Psychology, 2,* 1965, 783-92.

Lewin, K. *Principles of topological psychology.* New York: McGraw-Hill Book Company, 1966.

Likkert, R. *The human organization: Its management and value.* New York: McGraw-Hill Book Company, 1967.

Lippitt, R., and White, R. K. The "social climate" of children's groups. In Barker, R. G., Kennin, J. S., and Wright, H. F. (eds.), *Child behavior and development.* New York: McGraw-Hill Book Company, 1943, 485-508.

Marrow, A. J. *The practical theorist: The life and work of Kurt Lewin.* New York: Basic Books, 1970.

McClelland, D. C. *The achieving society.* Princeton, N. J.: Van Nostrand, 1961.

McClelland, D. C. Business drive and national achievement. *Harvard Business Review,* July-August, 1962, 99-112.

McClelland, D. C. Toward a theory of motive acquisition. *American Psychologist.* 20, 1965a, 321-33.

McClelland, D. C. *N* Achievement and entrepreneurship: A Longitudinal study. *Journal of Personality and Social Psychology,* 1, 1965b, 389-92.

McClelland, D. C. Black capitalism: Making it work. In *Think* (an IBM publication). July-August, 1969, 6-11.

McClelland, D. C. Atkinson, J. W., Clark, R. A. and Lowell, E. L. *The achievement motive.* New York: Appleton-Century-Crofts, 1953.

McClelland, D. C. and Winter, D. G. *Motivating economic achievement.* New York: Free Press, 1969.

McGregor, D. The human side of enterprise. In *Leadership and motivation.* MIT Press, 1966, 3-20.

Murray, H. *Thematic apperception test manual.* Cambridge, Mass: Harvard University Press, 1943.

Nord, W. Beyond the teaching machine: The neglected area of operant condition in the theory and practice of management. *Organizational Behavior and Human Performance,* Vol. 4, 4, Nov., 1969.

Plimpton, Franziska H. *O-P manual: A content analysis coding system designed to assess the Origin Syndrome.* Unpublished paper: Washington University, 1970.

Polanyi, M. *Personal knowledge.* Chicago: University of Chicago Press, 1958.

Rosen, B. C., and D'Andrade, R. G. The psychosocial origin of achievement motivation. *Sociometry, 22,* 1959, 185-218.

Rotter, J. B. Generalized expectancies for internal versus external control of reinforcement. *Psychological Monographs 80* (1, Whole No. 609). 1966.

Schutz, A. *Collected papers, Vol. 1.* The Hague: Nijhoff, 1963.

Shea, D. J. *The effects of achievement motivation training on motivational and behavioral variables.* Unpublished doctoral dissertation, Washington University, 1969.

Shea, D. J. and Jackson, K. W. Motivation training with teachers—a description. To appear in de Charms, R. *Motivation in the schools* (in preparation).

Shipley, T. E., and Veroff, J. A projective measure of need for affiliation. In Atkinson, R. W. (ed.), *Motives in fantasy, action, and society.* Princeton, N. J.: Van Nostrand, 1958.

Skinner, B. F. Behaviorism at fifty. In Wann, T. W. (ed.) *Behaviorism and phenomenology.* Chicago: The University of Chicago Press, 1964.

Tolman, E. C. Principles of purposive behavior. In Koch, S. (ed.) *Psychology: A study of a science.* Vol. 2. New York: McGraw-Hill Book Company, 1959, 92-157.

Winter, D. G. *Scoring manual for n power.* Unpublished paper, 1968.

Winterbottom, Marian R. The relation of need for achievement to learning experiences in independence and mastery. In Atkinson, J. W. (ed.) *Motives in fantasy, action, and society,* Princeton, N. J.: Van Nostrand, 1958.

Wylie, Ruth C. *The self concept: a critical survey of pertinent research literature. Lincoln: University of Nebraska Press, 1961.*

chapter 4

Learning and Personality Development

When an individual enters an organization, he brings with him his own, unique ways of interpreting and responding to his environment. The process through which these characteristics evolve may be termed personality development. Why should we be concerned with this process? Why don't we just hire a psychologist to develop a personality test and select people for the organization who have the type of personality we want? The fact that so many people think that the implications of personality for organizations end with selection is itself a strong argument for exploring the concept at some depth.

Even if selection were the only issue, the concept of personality would still be important. First of all, we need to know what characteristics will be most helpful for the jobs we wish to fill now and in the future. We also need to know how to test for these characteristics. Therefore, we require a basic understanding of the characteristics themselves and of personality in general. Unfortunately, a truly adequate, overall concept of personality has not yet been formulated.

So far, we have been considering personality as it exists at one point in time. However, does personality remain fixed? Most students of personality would argue that one's personality changes constantly. Individuals are influenced by situational factors; they learn new ways and vary their behavior in many of their more accustomed roles. Thus, the individual who enters an organization, even though he does bring with him a well-established pattern of responses to his environment, will be significantly influenced by the demands of that environment. His personality will change as a result. In essence, personality development may occur as a result of everyday experience within an organization. Different demands bring different responses, which may be either strengthened or weakened as a result of their consequences. Different consequences bring changes in self-perception and self-esteem. Thus the concept of personality and the process of personality development have continuing significance for management.

All explanations of personality are based on observations of the behavior of humans and other animals; proponents of the different theories disagree mainly on how the empirical data fit into a unified schema. One need not choose any one theory or set of theories but may use all of them as a basis for insights into himself and others. With this as a general background, let us explore the concept of personality itself.

In the reading that follows, Lazarus summarizes and compares several important personality theories. For present purposes, little need be added to his discussion except for some attention to the definition of personality itself. Perhaps the most widely used definition comes from Gordon Allport (1937), who defined personality as ". . . the dynamic organization within the individual of those psycho-physical systems that determine his unique adjustments to his environment (p. 48)." Lazarus (1963) viewed personality in a similar way, ". . . as an organization of stable structures within a person that dispose him to act in certain ways (p. 49)." These definitions imply some underlying structure which an individual carries with him but also stress the role of the environment in determining or influencing the behavior which will occur. Thus, both the prior experiences in the individual and his current situation become co-determinants of his behavior. It is within this framework that Lazarus, in the following selection, examines the issues of personality theory. The Lazarus reading is followed by a short paper prepared by the editor which explores some implications of personality for organizations and introduces the selections on learning by Bigge and Nord.

REFERENCES

Allport, G. W. *Personality: A Psychological Interpretation.* New York: Holt, Rinehart and Winston, 1937.

Lazarus, R. S. *Personality and Adjustment.* Englewood Cliffs, N.J.: Prentice-Hall, Inc. 1963.

McGregor, D. *The Human Side of Enterprise.* New York: McGraw-Hill Book Company, 1960.

Richard S. Lazarus

PERSONALITY THEORY

THEORETICAL FRAMES OF REFERENCE

We must first consider the nature of a psychological event in order to identify some of the frames of reference in which it may be regarded. There are three components of any psychological event. The first is the *stimulus* to which a person responds. The last is his *response*. The other component is made up of the states and activities in the *organism* in between the first and last. We cannot directly observe these states and activities, which are sometimes called mediating structures and processes, but we assume that they intervene between stimulus and response. We have already seen examples of them in the form of motivation and control.

The exact definition of stimulus is a source of controversy. Some hold that we can identify a stimulus only by physical measurements, such as wave lengths of light or decibels of sound. Others hold that we must define a stimulus by the reactions it induces, such as the interpretations a person gives some physical object. The meaning of response is broad: It can include not only obvious actions like reaching for something, but also, what is more difficult to identify, the styles of action. We may include as a response even the internal physiological accompaniments of a psychological event, such as the changes in heart activity or respiration that are associated with emotional states such as fear or anger. Still, in spite of the ambiguity of these terms, psychologists in analyzing psychological events have found it useful to think in terms of stimulus, the intervening structures and processes of the organism, and response.

The S-O-R analysis also turns out to be an excellent way of distinguishing among different frames of reference in personality theory. A frame of reference in itself is not precisely a theory, rather it is the philosophic basis of a theory because it delineates assumptions and emphases. Some theorists, for instance, tend to focus on responses, others on the intervening processes (such as subjective interpretations of stimuli), and still others on the physical qualities of stimuli. Although these variations in assumption and emphasis are not, as we shall see, the only sources of disagreement among persons with differing theoretical orientations, they are fundamental and important. Sometimes, however, several specific theories can be grouped together because they agree in their basic S-O-R frame of reference.

Richard S. Lazarus, *Personality and Adjustment,* © 1963. Reprinted by permission of Prentice-Hall, Inc., Englewood Cliffs, New Jersey.

Now we shall examine three frames of reference that diverge with respect to stimulus, organism, and response. The first, trait-and-type, falls on the response side of the S-O-R analysis; the second, the stimulus-response-associative-learning frame of reference, centers around physical stimuli and how habits of response are acquired; finally, the phenomenological approach, which defines the stimulus subjectively—that is, how a person apprehends it—focuses mainly on the intervening structures and processes. All current personality theories may in fact, be subsumed under these three basic frames of reference. Although a given theory may incorporate more than one frame of reference, any theory or part of a theory can be analyzed along these lines.

The Trait-and-Type Frame of Reference

The simplest and most traditional way of describing a person's personality is to identify his consistent patterns of behavior and label them with trait names. Every language contains large numbers of words that define traits of personality. We describe people as shy, aggressive, submissive, lazy, melancholy, easy-going, ambitious, and so on. But what do we mean when we use such terms? And how can this common sense approach to the description of personality become a systematic scientific enterprise?

The Trait Approach. If we observe a person in a variety of situations and note that he always allows someone else to take the initiative in deciding what to do, we have reason to think that this tendency is a consistent part of his personality. We have only to interpret it and to find a term that describes it—say, "submissiveness." If such a descriptive term applies to a person in a wide variety of situations, then we can fairly claim it as a trait. The more consistent the behavior and the more frequent its occurrence in dissimilar situations, the more clearly and importantly characteristic the trait. In the trait approach to personality, then, we identify the most important characteristics in human personality and analyze their organization.

We said earlier that the trait approach is largely oriented to response characteristics. Let us consider how this is so. We know that we identify traits by observing a person behave consistently in response to a variety of stimuli. Thus, to identify a trait we must observe characteristic responses occurring independently of the stimulus context (pattern of stimuli to which the person is exposed). For it is just those responses that are not governed by the stimulus context and therefore recur in a variety of circumstances that define a trait. The trait approach to personality requires, then, that stimuli be held constant or ruled out and that a person's responses be clearly attributes or dispositions that belong to him rather than the situation. To the degree that a trait theorist is interested in forces within personality that determine consistent patterns of behavior, he introduces intervening structures and processes into his system.

* * *

The Type Approach. Personality typologies are built on a response-oriented frame of reference that is very similar to that involved in traits. The difference is that whereas in the latter approach we assign a variety of traits to a person, as in a psychogram, in the type approach we adopt a much broader, unifying scheme of classification, or pigeonholing. The type approach, then, is an extension of the trait approach. By the pattern of his traits we can classify a person. If he shares a trait pattern with a large group of other individuals, we can simplify the description: Instead of listing each trait according to the extent he has it, we use a few categories for characteristic patterns. Thus, we observe that shyness tends to go with other qualities, such as an inclination to be introspective, easily hurt, and so on, and we can identify this grouping of traits by a single inclusive category called introversion. And we can identify a complementary type called extroversion. Having isolated these two categories, we can say that because such-and-such a person has such-and-such traits he is a member of one or the other type.

Just as the vocabulary of traits has existed for thousands of years, so have typologies. The best known typology in ancient Greece was that of Hippocrates, in the fifth century B.C. Conceiving that the body contained four fluids, or humors—yellow bile, black bile, phlegm, and blood—Hippocrates speculated that personality depended on which of these humors predominated in a person's constitution. Thus, yellow bile went with a choleric or irascible temperament, black bile with melancholy, phlegm with the sluggish, apathetic, or phlegmatic person, and blood with the cheerful, active, sanguine personality.

Among the best-known modern typologies of personality is that of Carl Jung, an early associate of Freud. Jung's typology includes two broad categories—the *extrovert,* who is oriented primarily toward others and the external world, and the *introvert,* who is more preoccupied with himself and his subjective world. Extroversion and introversion are expressed in a variety of functions, including thinking, feeling, sensing, and intuiting, so that, in actuality, Jung's typology is more complex than people usually realize. For example, one could be a thinking extrovert, but an introvert in the intuitive function. Another familiar personality typology is that of Freud himself, who conceived of types according to his theory of psychosexual development. In this theory Freud proposed that everyone passes through three infantile psychosexual stages distinguished according to the primary means of sexual gratification. In the oral stage erotic activity centers around the lips and mouth, in the anal stage on bowel activity and the stimulation of the mucous membranes of the anus, and in the phallic stage on the genital organs.

In the course of development some individuals, because of traumatic experiences at one or another stage, fail to progress normally to the next stage. When they are adults, the primitive psychosexual tendencies characteristic of the respective immature stages continue to remain active, governing their personalities and producing characteristic psychological traits. Thus, Freud identified three types: oral, anal, and phallic. The *oral type* is characterized by dependent attitudes toward others. He continues to seek sustenance, or feeding, from others, and, depending on when during the oral stage fixation occurred, is either optimistic, immature, and trusting, or pessimistic, suspicious, and sarcastic, about the prospects of continuing support. The *anal type* is also characterized by two substages, the first identified by outbursts of aggression, sloppiness, and petulance, the second associated with obstinacy, orderliness, and parsimoniousness. The *phallic type* is characterized by an adolescent immaturity in which the predominant conflicts are heterosexual, stemming from the Oedipus complex and the anxieties associated with it. The phallic period is stormy, with sharp emotional swings and preoccupation with love object choices. Adults with severe disturbances in childhood development can be classified into oral, anal, and phallic types according to when the psychosexual disturbance occurred and what types of behavior pattern they display as a result.

There are many other personality typologies. Usually, as with those of Jung and Freud, rather than being merely simple, independent classification schemes of behavior, they are also based on theoretical propositions about the structure, dynamics, and development of personality. The reader should consult the other sources listed at the end of the volume for elaboration of these systems.

From a practical standpoint, the trait-and-type approach is most useful when the pertinent behavior patterns are absolutely consistent—that is, characteristic of a person regardless of circumstances. What limits the usefulness of any trait or type system is the problem of degree of trait generality. The statement that a person has the trait of submissiveness is useful for prediction only insofar as he is submissive in all or most situations. If he is submissive only in certain circumstances, then we can predict his behavior accurately only if we know what those circumstances are.

This puts the finger on the most serious deficiency of the trait-and-type approach to personality, namely, that it largely ignores the dynamic interchange between a person and his environment. For the stimulus context normally limits the manifestations of trait characteristics.

The problem of prediction also suggests the weakness of typologies: They are likely to be so excessively broad that a classification will apply to a person only to a limited degree except in extreme instances. Identifying someone as anal, for example, is useful so long as it permits us to expect such characteristic behavior as obstinacy or orderliness. But few people are so inordinately typical that they are obstinate or orderly in every situation that may arise.

Thus, the trait-and-type approach is limited by focusing exclusively on responses and assuming that personality structures are static properties that can be inferred from consistencies of response, rather than adaptive transactions with the environment. Because of this critical limitation, psychologists have constructed other frames of reference that pay more attention to the stimulus context. Let us now turn to one of these, the stimulus-response-associative-learning approach, and examine how it handles this difficulty in the trait-and-type frame of reference.

Stimulus-Response-Associative-Learning Theory (SRAL)

The central concern of SRAL theorists is the problem of how organisms acquire habits of response. They have traditionally attempted to discover the details of the learning process, to find out how connections are established between stimuli and responses in juxtaposition (association) so that when a given stimulus, or one similar to it, recurs, it will induce the same, or similar, response. In their theories of learning they try to specify *how* these connections are made, strengthened, or broken.

Besides elevating the question of how habits or traits are acquired, the SRAL frame of reference stands on the physical stimulus side of the S-O-R sequence. Instead of being built around correlations among responses as the trait-and-type frame of reference is, associative-learning approaches rest on correlations between physical stimuli and responses.

Although SRAL theorists were originally concerned entirely with principles of learning, some came to recognize that their propositions might have general application to other fields, such as personality. Personality psychologists have, in fact, tended simply to accept the learning process as given, without much concern about its details, even though they usually assume that personality structure develops, in part, through learning. To fill the gap, therefore, learning theoreticians with broad concerns such as Edwin Guthrie in past years and John Dollard and Neal Miller in recent years have attempted to carry associative-learning theory into the realm of personality. But exactly how does personality become established through the learning process?

Dollard and Miller identify four concepts of prime importance in the learning process—drive, response, cue, and reinforcement. *Drive* is what initiates responses. It originates as tissue needs, which, when unsatisfied, produce internal discomforts that lead a person to activities that may or may not satisfy it. *Reinforcement* of a drive is the product of responses that do satisfy the need. Thus, if the need for food produces drive, the response of eating reinforces the hunger drive by fulfilling it and so terminates that behavior sequence. Learning, then, is the establishment of *responses* that reinforce under conditions of drive—that is, responses which reduce or eliminate the drive. Learning also requires the establishment of connections between such responses and certain *cues*, or stimuli, in the environment. Thus, if the reinforcing response is eating, a person must identify those stimuli to which the response is appropriate. These situations may involve the presence of food or environmental circumstances under which food may be found—for instance, a refrigerator can be an appropriate cue for obtaining food. In sum, under conditions of drive, and in the presence of cues, or stimuli, a person makes responses that reinforce the drive, and those responses that do are learned in association with those cues.

In addition to these fundamental factors, Dollard and Miller identify certain other characteristics of learning. The strengthening of connections between certain cues and drive-reinforcing responses implies the converse weakening of other connections and the elimination of inappropriate responses that may have been tried before. This elimination of previously learned responses is called *extinction.* This process is essential to learning, for learning could not take place unless, along with the establishment and strengthening of desired responses, unwanted acts were extinguished.

According to still another principle of SRAL theory, *stimulus generalization,* responses that have been learned in association with one specific cue may be transferred to other similar situations. If we have learned to be afraid of speaking up in one particular social situation, the response of fear is likely to be induced by other social situations as well. The greater the similarity between stimuli, the more the likelihood that a response that has been learned to one stimulus will generalize to the other; and conversely, the less the similarity, the less the likelihood. Since no two situations are ever precisely the same, consistency of behavior would never occur without stimulus generalization. The perception of stimulus similarity, it is generally thought, is based on the physical features of the stimuli. But actually specifying which physical quality is critical remains one of the most perplexing unsolved problems in learning theory, since we can respond similarly to stimuli on the basis of many physical dimensions. The cues of similarity to which a person responds or fails to respond are difficult, if not impossible, to predict without a knowledge of intervening structures and processes.

If responses learned to one stimulus tended to generalize indiscriminately to others, learning could not occur, since the same response could then be made to all. For adaptive behavior to develop, a person must learn to distinguish among stimuli so that he makes reinforcing responses to the correct one. To give a concrete example, he must learn to differentiate a refrigerator that contains food from a cabinet that contains material incapable of reducing his hunger drive. The process by which we differentiate appropriate from inappropriate cues is called *discrimination.* Just as stimulus generalization is required in order for a person to spread a given response to all members of a class of appropriate cues, so discrimination is required to permit him to select the proper class of cues that will produce drive reduction.

Finally, through *anticipation,* another process postulated by associative-learning theory, we identify the probable consequences of a stimulus or response; thereby we can learn to perform actions that will reduce a drive in the future and to avoid those that will have painful or dangerous consequences. Anticipation, which involves making a response earlier than it would normally occur, helps the individual react appropriately to an impending situation about which he has been alerted.

According to SRAL theory, complex social motives, such as the desire to achieve or to be liked, are learned in the same way as any other simpler type of response, such as tying a shoe or hitting a typewriter key. Rewards can also be learned. Thus, we learn to accept expressions of approval as rewards because the approval has become associated in childhood with the reinforcement, by parents or other adults, or primary drives like hunger and thirst. In other words, we have learned that approval is connected with desirable consequences even though social approval itself originally had no intrinsic value.

According to the principles of learning briefly sketched above, it is plain that we can learn complex patterns of response, including neurotic symptoms, such as phobias and hysterical paralyses characteristic of certain types of neurotic disorder as well as the defense mechanisms connected with these disorders. Defense mechanisms as responses—although they are maladjustments in the sense that, in using them, we distort reality in our perceptions and judgments—do reduce the drives of anxiety and fear. Clearly, then, any characteristic of personality—motives, control processes, defense mechanisms, and so on—is learned according to the same set of laws specified by learning theorists.

For *our* analysis of frames of reference, the important feature of SRAL theory is its emphasis on the physical stimulus. The point is that from this position the stimulus to a behavioral act can be defined in terms of physical dimensions (such as wave lengths, shape, weight, size, and distance) and completely independently of the person behaving—that is, responding. And since it is these objective characteristics to which the person presumably responds, we can construct behavioral laws by separately identifying the physical characteristics of environmental stimuli and the characteristics of responses made in association with these stimuli. The basic unit of description is the stimulus-response connection.

It is a direct attack on this emphasis on the physical stimulus that identifies the phenomenological point of view, the third major frame of reference in personality theory.

Personality from a Phenomenological Point of View

For a theorist in the phenomenological camp, defining a stimulus physically immediately poses a problem, namely, that our perception of objects is not necessarily identical with the objects themselves. Our senses do not directly transmit physical objects. Rather, we respond to representations of objects—that is, objects as mediated by our perceptual apparatuses and by our individual interpretations. In an effort to articulate the distinction, psychologists interested in perception have termed the physical object itself the "distal stimulus," and the the object as mediated by intervening mechanisms the "proximal stimulus." The phenomenologist argues that what determine responses are not physical objects themselves but the intervening structures and processes within a person that mediate the physical stimuli. He reconstructs the causes of action through inferences about these psychological representations of external stimuli. Thus, in phenomenological approaches to personality the stimulus in the S-O-R analysis is still significant, but as a psychological representation within a person, not as an external physical condition. Here the emphasis is on the O, and the psychological representation of a physical stimulus may deviate sharply from physical reality.

The essence of the phenomenological frame of reference to personality is this: The cause of action is the world as a person apprehends it privately. This privately apprehended world is the core construct of the theoretical systems of such phenomenologists as Kurt Lewin and Carl Rogers. In Lewin's system the term employed for the construct is *life space,* in Rogers' it is *phenomenal field.*

For Lewin the psychological representation of the world (the life space) consists of the person's needs and the potentialities of action available, as he apprehends them. Every aspect of a person's physical environment that is not part of the life space and to which he does not directly respond is the "foreign hull" of the life space. To understand his behavior at any point in time we must reconstruct and describe the life space, which means that we must understand the psychological forces in operation at that moment.

These forces are described by a Lewinian graphically in diagrams that include: goal regions (shown as enclosed places); positive and negative valences (designated by plus or minus signs), which identify desirable or undesirable aspects of the life space; vectors (arrows), which point out the directions to which a person is pulled; and barriers (lines separating the person from positive goals), which block or slow down a person's approach to any goal region. Many forces may affect the person, and his behavior at any time is a resultant of them. Not only can the total psychological field (called the life space) be thus represented diagrammatically, but the structure of the individual personality can also be diagrammed. . . .

The important elements in the Lewinian system are these: Psychological events are considered in terms of the construct of life space, which comprises subjective definitions of the environment, and some of the psychodynamic laws that pertain to it are identified diagrammatically. The system makes use of both motivational and cognitive structures in continual interplay. Inferences about a person's life space are always derived from systematic observation of his behavior in his environment. Yet the terms of the analysis of behavior and setting are not static traits and stationary objects but the person's own subjective apprehension of his environment and his relationship to it.

In contrast with Lewin's brand of phenomenology is the self theory of Rogers, whose concepts are also couched in the language of subjective experience (for example, what we want and how we think and feel). The Rogerian concept that is analogous to life space is phenomenal field, and the core (or most important aspect) of that field is the *self-concept* of the individual, that is, his notion of who he is in relation to his environment. It is this self-concept that determines his behavior. This phenomenal self is, for a person himself, reality. He does not respond to the objective environment but to what he perceives it to be, regardless of how distorted or personalized his perception may be. These subjective realities are tentative hypotheses that a person entertains about environmental situations.

Thus, one person will conceive of himself as a reformer with the mission of correcting certain worldly ills and helping others to "see the light." Another will view himself as a "realist," able to accept gracefully, and even benefit from the weaknesses of human nature and man's social institutions. Self-concepts are complex and variable and they determine how persons will react to and deal with a wide variety of situations. These conceptions of who and what one is not only comprise central values and belief systems, but also include images of oneself as physically strong or weak, attractive or unattractive, popular or unpopular, and so on, based partly on the reflected appraisals of other people with whom one has had contact. According to self theorists, this differentiated portion of the phenomenal field, the self-concept, determines all behavior. And most behavior, indeed, is organized around efforts to preserve and enhance this phenomenal self.

While Lewin goes about the task of reconstructing a person's life space, with its multiplicity of psychological forces, from observing how he acts in different situations, Rogers identifies the self-concept largely from introspection. That is, a Rogerian learns about someone's self-system by listening to his introspective report about himself and his perceptions of the world. Lewin systematically observed behavior in various naturalistic and experimental situations, but Rogers developed his theoretical constructions primarily from psychotherapy. He argued that to the degree that he could provide an environment of permissiveness and support, a patient's reports would validly reflect his whole phenomenal field and his narrower self-concept.

Regardless of the exact form of the phenomenological system, however, it is clear that it shifts theoretical attention from the physical stimulus itself to the way a person apprehends it and, therefore, to the properties of the person that mediate between the physical stimulus and behavior. Thus, to recapitulate, although trait-and-type theory is response-centered and associative-learning theory is stimulus-response-centered, phenomenological theory revolves around the properties of the person that intervene between the stimulus and the behavioral response.

All theories of personality are variations of one sort or another of the three main frames of reference derived from the stimulus, organism, and response sequence. Some theories, as we have seen, are in the main anchored to one or another of these three points of view. Other systems, such as that of Freud, are mixtures, in that they draw on features of all three frames of reference. For example, psychoanalysis contains features of the trait-and-type approach, yet its essential character does not fall in that category. The point to remember is that the frames of reference described do not specify individual theoretical systems, but rather orientations or emphases that vary among them.

* * *

Walter R. Nord

PERSONALITY AND ORGANIZATIONS[1]

Of the many concepts employed in the study of personality, three are especially important for understanding behavior of people in organizations. First, *psychological defense* is a term which helps a manager understand responses, of both himself and others, to psychological threat. The notion of self-concept is valuable as an aid to understanding how people see themselves and the consequences of attacks on this perception. Finally, in considering

---

[1] The personality vs. organization issue is treated in Part II.

personality change, a manager will obtain ideas which will be useful in understanding the relationship of the organizational context to personality and personnel development.

PSYCHOLOGICAL DEFENSE

Freud noted that the perception of threats produces anxiety. Typically, people attempt to defend themselves from anxiety by distorting, falsifying, or even denying reality. To the organizational observer, such behavior appears to be irrational. While these defenses do not directly help the individual to deal with external reality, they are adaptive, since they maintain the internal tension at a manageable level.

Most textbooks in introductory psychology include an extensive list of defense mechanisms. One commonly listed ego defense is *repression,* by which threatening information is forced out of consciousness without awareness. Another common defense, known as *projection,* is the attribution of one's own problems or motives to someone else. The third defense, called *denial,* is the failure to acknowledge that certain threats or feelings exist. There are many more defense mechanisms; most people employ a variety, though they tend to favor one defense or another as characteristic of themselves. In addition, the more intense the anxiety or threat experienced by the individual, the more likely it becomes that these defenses will play an important part in much of his behavior.[2] These defenses create problems for human interaction because they often seem irrational. Commonly, would-be helpers attempt to give aid on the rational level or respond with defenses of their own. Success is seldom achieved, and greater tensions often result.

Perhaps no psychological concept has more importance for administrators than psychological defense. Ideas and actions that appear to be rational and quite functional from the manager's point of view are often perceived as threats by other members of the organization. These participants attempt to reduce their anxiety through some type of ego defense. The manager often responds in turn by accusing the participants of being irrational. As a result, without realizing what he has done, the manager often increases the amount of anxiety and the operation of defense mechanisms. Of course, not all opposition to management actions takes the form of a psychological defense; however, much opposition may well do so. Awareness of such behavior may lead to the development of management behavior and organizational designs that prevent and deal effectively with defenses. An understanding of personality theory may contribute to better management by providing means of anticipating, recognizing, and preventing the operation of costly defenses.

SELF-CONCEPT

A second major contribution of personality theory is the idea of *self-concept,* the individual's view of himself. The self-concept often takes the form of the "good me," the "bad me," and the "not me." The "good me" includes things

[2] This direct relation is probable at least within some range, until perhaps bodily harm or survival is involved.

about me for which I have been rewarded, the "bad me" includes things for which I have been punished, and the "not me" includes those things which are not part of me.

More recently, the self-concept has been applied to personality in some creative ways. For example, Rotter (1966) suggested that some people see themselves as able to control their environment (internal control), while others see themselves as controlled by the environment (external control). De Charms (1968) has developed a similar notion in distinguishing between "orgins," those who can be expected to initiate change in the world, and "pawns," who are more apt to accept things as they are. These concepts, suggesting important differences in how people react to their surroundings, have important implications for selection and training in organizations.

Goffman (1967) has argued that the self-concept has important sociological as well as psychological importance. He noted that society sanctions elaborate rituals of behavior patterns which enable people to save face. For example, individuals employ jokes, politeness, and other ceremonies to prevent social offenses. Furthermore, people avoid discussing certain topics and avoid noticing or calling attention to certain embarrassing behaviors in order to allow others to maintain their role or the self which they expect to maintain. Thus, social mechanisms exist to protect the self-concept of individuals. These mechanisms may serve important social functions. Nevertheless, attempts to maintain self-esteem can also have negative consequences for organizations.

Bennis, Schein, Steele, and Berlew (1968) suggested that attempts to maintain self-esteem lead to three sets of outcomes which may be dysfunctional for organizations. First, people respond to threats to self-esteem by trying to hide those parts of themselves which they feel are less than totally acceptable. Secondly, attempts to maintain self-esteem lead individuals to pretend to be something that they are not. Finally, efforts to maintain self-esteem often result in cautious and ritualized behavior. Organizations which expect creative, innovative behavior may find that they encourage caution instead by inadvertently threatening individuals.

An example of these consequences was demonstrated by the case of an organizational merger. The details of the problems in the merger of a company manufacturing high-status, expensive furniture with a company producing relatively inexpensive furniture were reported by Nord (1968). The workers from the former plant viewed themselves as craftsmen. They had been accustomed to working on prestigious furniture and making each piece individually in the manner of a traditional craft. One of the consequences of the merger was to put these men on an assembly-line operation. Many workers expressed the feeling that they had lost a great deal of status. One worker commented that management had cheapened the furniture, and another mentioned that he had felt like a craftsman before but now was working on a job which required very little skill. Even the lower-skilled workers empathized with the threat to self-esteem felt by the more skilled group. Although this loss of status and esteem was not the sole cause of problems in the merger, it appeared to be an important contributing factor.

In general, people respond to threats to their self-concept in much the same way that they might respond to other psychological threats. An important variable for managers to consider is the way people think of themselves. Changes which threaten a person's perception of himself or of a group to which he belongs can produce defensive reactions. The manager's own self-perception, of course, is also of great import. His defenses may produce behavior which appears irrational to his subordinates and other co-workers; the result may be costly for the functioning of the organization.

THE SOCIAL NATURE OF PERSONALITY AND CHANGE

A third contribution of personality theory to management is derived from the social nature of personality and personality change. Kurt Lewin's description of the process of personal change as "unfreezing," "changing," and "refreezing," is especially important in recent thinking. Lewin hypothesized that, for change to occur, some forces had to be introduced that would encourage the individual to *want* a change. Then other forces were needed to produce the change. Finally, after the charge had occurred, support was required for maintenance of the new behavior. This "refreezing" process is often neglected, because the social factors in change are not considered. Lewin's work, however, stressed the social environment which surrounds the change.

Often, personality and personality change are, to an important degree, interpersonal or social processes. Other people are important sources of an individual's identity and self-concept. It is widely recognized that other people's approval can have substantial effects on individual behavior. Many studies have demonstrated the pressures for conformity which a group can exert. Other studies have shown that an individual will seek out others for support of his own views or for definition of his own position by comparison with others. In addition, the particular features a person exhibits depend on others. Robert Tannenbaum has conceptualized this process through a "hooking" metaphor. He suggests that people have various facets of personality which are "hooked" or drawn out by certain facets of the personality of others.[3] Thus, a person is in part a product of the characteristics of those around him. Other people become a potential source of individual growth rather than conformity or inhibition. In any case, personality is in part a function of interpersonal relationships rather than a set of character traits.

Two important implications for organizational management stem from this perspective on personality: First, because the development and maintenance of individual behavior depends on other people, personality is not fixed. Second, attempts to change individuals require attention to the existing social environment, not just to individual behavior patterns in isolation. Selection procedures, training programs, and management policies that consider only the individual are doomed to very limited success.

[3] This model was presented by Robert Tannenbaum in an informal talk at an organizational development training group at UCLA in July, 1970.

LEARNING

Personal change can be better understood through the concept of learning. Although there is no one universally accepted definition of learning, most theorists would agree that learning involves actual and/or potential changes in behavior which result from the interaction of an individual with his environment. Generally, changes that result from fatigue and maturation are excluded.

Major differences within the field of learning are concerned with the basic question of how people learn to come to terms with their environment. Many psychologists rely heavily on conditioning processes, using the notion of reinforcement or reward and punishment as the basis for behavior change. In this view, people learn by being rewarded or punished for their behavior. Another group of psychologists relies heavily on the mental apparatus of man to explain learning. These cognitive theorists employ inferred mental processes to explain changes in individual thought and behavior.

These are certainly not the only approaches to learning, but they do provide contrasting ways of understanding the issues on which major theories of learning diverge. The following selection by Bigge highlights these contrasts.

BIBLIOGRAPHY

Bennis, W. G., Schein, E. H., Steele, F. I., and Berlew, D. E. *Interpersonal Dynamics.* Homewood, Ill.: Dorsey Press, 1968.

DeCharms, R. *Personal Causation.* New York: Academic Press, 1968.

Goffman, E. *Interaction Ritual.* New York: Doubleday & Company, 1967.

Lazarus, R. S. *Personality and Adjustment.* Englewood Cliffs, N.J.: Prentice-Hall, Inc., 1963.

Nord, W. "Individual and Organizational Conflict in an Industrial Merger." In *Proceedings of the 11th Midwest Management Conference.* Madison, Wisc.: Academy of Management, 1968. pp. 50-66.

Rotter, J. B. "Generalized Expectancies for Internal versus External Control of Reinforcement." *Psychological Monographs* 80 (1, whole no. 609), 1966.

Morris L. Bigge

DESCRIBING
THE LEARNING PROCESS

WHAT ARE THE TWO MAJOR CONTEMPORARY
VERSIONS OF THE NATURE OF LEARNING?

Whereas contemporary S-R associationists—the neobehaviorists—conceive of learning as *conditioning* or *reinforcement,* Gestalt-field psychologists think of it as *development of insight.*

Is Learning Conditioning-Reinforcement?

In the eyes of neobehaviorists, learning is more or less permanent change of behavior which occurs as a result of practice. Thus, the learning process consists of impressions of new reaction patterns on pliable, passive organisms. Since learning arises, in some way, from an interplay of organisms and their environments, the key concepts of neobehaviorists are *stimulus* (that excitement which is provided by an environment) and *response* (that reaction which is made by an organism). Consequently, the problem of the nature of the learning process is centered in a study of the relationships of processions of stimuli and responses and what occurs between them. Since the focus always is upon behavior, in practical application, a neobehavioristically oriented teacher strives to change behaviors of his students in the desired direction by providing the right stimuli at the proper time.

Neobehaviorists use "conditioning" or "reinforcement" to describe the learning process as they understand and interpret it. "Conditioning" is so called because it results in formation of conditioned responses. A conditioned response is a response which is associated with, or evoked by, a new—conditioned—stimulus. Conditioning implies a principle of adhesion; one stimulus or response is attached to another stimulus or response so that revival of the first evokes the second.

Reinforcement is a special kind or aspect of conditioning within which the tendency for a stimulus to evoke a response on subsequent occasions is increased by reduction of a *need* of a *drive stimulus.* A "need," as used here, is an objective, biological requirement of an organism which must be met if the

Abridged from pp. 94-110 in LEARNING THEORIES FOR TEACHERS by Morris L. Bigge. Copyright © 1964 by Morris L. Bigge. Reprinted by permission of Harper & Row, Publishers.

organism is to survive and grow. Examples of needs are an organism's requirement for food, sex, or escape from pain. A "drive stimulus" is an aroused state of an organism. It is closely related to the need which sets the organism into action, and may be defined as a strong, persistent stimulus which demands an adjustive response. When an organism is deprived of satisfaction of a need, drive stimuli occur.

What Are the Possible Kinds of Conditioning?

There are two kinds of positive conditioning—*classical* and *instrumental*—and a negative conditioning process—*extinction.* Through classical and instrumental conditioning, an organism *gains* responses or habits; through extinction it *loses* them.

Classical Conditioning. Classical conditioning usually is associated with such incidents as Pavlov's teaching a dog to salivate at the ringing of a bell; it is *stimulus substitution.* In Pavlov's conditioning experiment, the sound of a bell occurred prior to, or simultaneously with, the dog's salivation, which was caused by the presence of food. Then in the future the dog salivated at the ringing of the bell, even when the food was not present.

In classical conditioning a new stimulus is presented along with an already adequate, unconditioned stimulus—such as the smell of food—and just prior to the response, which is evoked by the unconditioned stimulus. The new stimulus becomes the conditioned stimulus, and the response which follows both stimuli becomes the conditioned response. Thus, in classical conditioning, an organism learns to respond to a new stimulus in the same, or similar, way it responds to the old, unconditioned stimulus. In Pavlov's experiment, the sound of the bell became the new, conditioned stimulus which evoked the old, unconditioned response—salivation. Then, salivation was a conditioned response.

Classically conditioned learning is revealed in the behavior of an organism by the increasing capacity of a previously neutral stimulus, with successive training trials to evoke a response which originally was evoked by some other (unconditioned) stimulus. A "neutral stimulus" is one whose first occurrence does nothing toward evoking or reinforcing the response which is under study.

Instrumental Conditioning. Just as classical conditioning theory derives from the early work of Pavlov, instrumental condition theory has emerged from the foundation built by Thorndike. Instrumental conditioning usually is equated with reinforcement; it is response modification or change. An animal first makes a response, then receives a "reward;" the response is instrumental in bringing about its reinforcement. There is a *feedback* from the "rewarding" stimulus which follows the response that the organism is learning; a dog is fed after he "speaks" and, thereby, the likelihood of his "speaking" in the future is increased.

Extinction. Extinction is the process whereby an organism gradually loses a response or habit through repeating the response a number of times while no reinforcing stimulus accompanies it. Any habits gained through either classical or instrumental conditioning may be lost through extinction.

How Does Reinforcement Occur?

Neobehaviorists, who emphasize the importance of reinforcement in learning, assume that some psychological conclusions are fairly well established: (1) patterns of action and expectation develop through an organism's responses to repeated stimuli accompanied by "fumble and success" type of trial and error learning under conditions of positive or negative reinforcement; (2) reinforcement occurs through satisfaction of either basic biological needs like hunger or sex, or secondary needs such as a need for security, recognition, or aesthetic gratification; and (3) educational encouragement must take the form of positive and negative reinforcers. A positive reinforcer is a stimulus which strengthens a behavior; a negative one is a stimulus whose withdrawal strengthens a behavior. Note that negative reinforcement, psychologically, is different from punishment.

Primary Reinforcement. Reinforcement may be either *primary* or *secondary*. Primary reinforcement strengthens a certain behavior through the satisfaction of a basic biological need or drive. Secondary reinforcement sometimes is called high-order reinforcement. The reinforcers of secondary or high-order reinforcement have acquired their power of reinforcement indirectly through learning; poker chips for which a chimpanzee will work and money for which man will do almost anything are secondary reinforcers.

The drive reduction sequence of primary reinforcement proceeds as follows: (1) deprivation of satisfaction of a basic requirement, such as that for food, produces a state of need in an organism, (2) the need expresses itself as a tension state or drive stimulus which energizes the organism into action (a food-deprived animal shows the restless activity whose manifestation is called the hunger drive), (3) the activity achieves satisfaction of the need and relieves the tension state, and (4) the form of the activity which immediately preceded the satisfaction of the need or reduction of the drive is reinforced.

Within a drive reduction sequence, a response is closely associated with a drive stimulus and the stimulus-response conjunction is associated with a rapid decrease in the drive produced stimuli—hunger pangs. Thus the response is reinforced; the tendency for hunger to evoke it is increased. This, supposedly, is how we learn to like our various kinds of food.

Secondary Reinforcement. Secondary reinforcement is reinforcement which is brought about by occurrence of an originally neutral stimulus. When a neutral stimulus such as a sound or light is repeatedly paired with food in the presence of a food-deprived (hungry) animal, the formerly neutral stimulus becomes a secondary, conditioned reinforcer. Thus, secondary reinforcement results when originally neutral stimuli become closely associated with primary reinforcing stimuli and thereby become effective in reducing needs. In this way, neutral stimuli acquire the power of acting as reinforcing agents; a chimpanzee learns to accept poker chips as a "reward" just as readily as he accepts food. Consequently, actions of the chimpanzee are reinforced by his receiving poker chips when he performs them; this is secondary reinforcement.

How May We Group S-R Associationists?

On the basis of their position in regard to the associationistic nature of learning, we may divide neobehaviorists into three groups. One group makes conditioning the heart of the learning process but holds that reinforcement is not necessary for conditioning to occur. A second group is committed to reinforcement or law of effect theories. The third group consists of two-factor theorists who contend that there are two basically different learning processes—conditioning independent of reinforcement and conditioning governed by principles of reinforcement.

Edwin R. Guthrie's *contiguous conditioning* is most representative of the first—conditioning, nonreinforcement—group. The names of Clark L. Hull (1884-1952) and B. F. Skinner are most often associated with the *reinforcement* group. However, Hull and Skinner have differed sharply in regard to the nature of the reinforcement process. Three prominent *two-factor psychologies* are those of Kenneth W. Spence (1907-), Edward C. Tolman (1886-1959), and O. H. Mowrer (1907-). Hence, four representative neobehaviorisms are Guthrie's *contiguous conditioning*, Hull's *deductive behaviorism or reinforcement theory*, Skinner's *operant conditioning*, and Spence's *quantitative S-R theory*. All four are alike in their emphasis upon a mechanical treatment of stimuli and responses. They agree that at no time is purposiveness to be assumed. Problems of "purposes" must be explained by natural laws or principles whereby organisms mechanically develop "purposes." However, they differ in their interpretations of stimulus-response relationships in learning procedures. Guthrie is convinced that learning occurs when a stimulus and a response happen simultaneously; Hull centered the essence of learning in what occurs between the stimulus and the response; and Skinner places his emphasis upon the stimulus which follows a response. When we express these serial relationships symbolically, using S for stimulus, R for response, and O for organism, Guthrie holds to an S-R, Hull to an S-O-R, and Skinner to an R-S learning theory. Since Spence incorporates both contiguity and reinforcement into his theory, it cannot be categorized in this way.

Although there are clear-cut psychological theories of learning, neo-behaviorists in education tend not to adhere rigidly to any one of the S-R patterns but to intermix them in applying psychology to teaching procedures. In this way they attempt to achieve an integration of the earlier works of Pavlov, Watson, and Thorndike with that of contemporary associationists. . . .Let us now examine very briefly three representative, systematic neobehavioristic theories of learning and see how each would color teaching procedures in a school learning situation.

Guthrie's Contiguous Conditioning. Guthrie's learning theory is classical conditioning, not reinforcement. Furthermore, it is a special kind of conditioning which we may identify as *simultaneous contiguous condition*. *Contiguity* means that stimuli acting *at the time* of a response, on their recurrence, tend to evoke that response. Furthermore, if a stimulus occurs contiguously with a response, the response to that stimulus will continue to occur with it until some other response becomes conditioned to that stimulus.

Strengthening of individual connections of stimuli and response—the actual conditioning—supposedly takes place with a single simultaneous occurrence of a stimulus and response. This does not mean that repetition has no place in learning, but that within repetition an increasing number of stimuli are made into conditioners; there is no strengthening of individual connections, but there is enlistment of more.

Guthrie thinks that, since association can occur with one connection and last for life, there is no need for anything like reward, pleasure, or need reduction to explain learning. Thus, there is no place for reinforcement in his contiguity theory. To Guthrie, scientific laws deal with observable phenomena only. In psychology these are physical stimuli, and responses in the form of contractions of muscles and secretions of glands, but there is no place for hypothetical intervening variables between stimuli and responses. We only need to know that "... a combination of stimuli which has accompanied a movement will on its recurrence tend to be followed by that movement."[1]

A proponent of contiguous conditioning in teaching people first gets them to perform in a certain way, then while they are doing so gives them the stimuli which he wants associated with that behavior. To teach that man is *Homo sapiens,* a Guthriean would induce his student to say *Homo sapiens* and while he was saying it stimulate him with *man* either spelled out, pictured, or both. The more "man" stimuli he could give the student while he was saying *Homo sapiens* the better it would be. In this teaching-learning process *man* is the conditioned stimulus and *Homo sapiens* is the conditioned response.

Hull's Reinforcement Theory. Hull's learning theory also is stimulus-response conditioning, but of a special kind, called *reinforcement.* In presenting his theory of learning Hull stated,

> Whenever a reaction (R) takes place in temporal contiguity with an afferent receptor impulse (s) resulting from the impact upon a receptor of a stimulus energy (S) and this conjunction is followed closely by the diminution in a need (and the associated diminution in the drive, D, and in the drive receptor discharge, s_D), there will result an increment Δ $(s- \rightarrow R)$, in the tendency for that stimulus on subsequent occasions to evoke that reaction.[2]

Within Hullian reinforcement, the stimulus and the response are not simultaneous; the stimulus precedes the response. Furthermore, learning does not take place with a single trial; it is stamped in through a process of repeated need or drive stimulus reductions.

Hull thought that learning occurs through biological adaptation of an organism to its environment in a way to promote survival. A state of need means

---

[1] Edwin R. Guthrie, *The Psychology of Learning,* rev. ed. (New York: Harper & Row, Publishers, 1952), p. 23.

[2] Clark L. Hull, *Principles of Behavior* (New York: Appleton-Century-Crofts, 1943), p. 71.

that survival of the organism is not being adequately served. Drive is a general condition of organic privation arising from lack of food, water, or air, from unhealthful temperatures, from tissue injury, from sex-linked conditions, or from other deficiencies. When needs or drive stimuli develop, the organism acts and the action brings reduction in needs or drive stimuli. Actions—responses— which lead to reduction of needs or drive stimuli are reinforced; thus reinforcement is centered in adaptation for survival. However, in life situations there are many reinforcers which do not contribute directly to biological adaptation of an organism. Through higher-order conditioning many things and actions come to have value and can serve as reinforcers. Higher-order conditioning is conditioning based upon previous conditioning; it more often is called secondary conditioning . . . .

A child is conditioned to think—say to himself "man" when he sees a man or a picture of a man. This conditioning could have been based upon reduction of drive stimuli. Perhaps he wanted a piece of candy and his parents withheld it from him until he said "man." Now, in ninth grade, "stimulus man" evokes *Homo sapiens,* perhaps through the satisfaction of curiosity, and curiosity is a product of higher-order conditioning; the youth previously had been conditioned to be curious.

Skinner's Operant, Instrumental Conditioning. The unique feature of operant conditioning is that the reinforcing stimulus occurs not simultaneously with or preceding the response but following the response. In operant conditioning, an organism must first make the desired response and then a "reward" is provided. The reward reinforces the response—makes it more likely to recur. The response is instrumental in bringing about its reinforcement. The essence of learning is not stimulus substitution but response modification. In learning, there is a feedback from the reinforcing stimulus to the previous response. To illustrate, in the training of pets a desired response is reinforced after it occurs—a dog is fed after it "speaks," and this increased the likelihood of its "speaking" in the future.

Note that in operant conditioning the stimulus which produced the response in the first place is not in any way involved in the learning process. The original response is a result of a stimulus, but the nature of this stimulation is irrelevant to operant conditioning. It is only necessary that some—any—stimulus elicit the response for operant conditioning to function. Emphasis is on reinforcing agents, not on original causative factors.

An operant-reinforcement approach to teaching a ninth-grader that man is *Homo sapiens* would be to show the student *man* along with several other more complicated words, one of which is *Homo sapiens.* If the student chooses *"non sequitur,"* or any expression other than *Homo sapiens,* nothing happens. If he chooses *"homo sapiens,"* the teacher says "wonderful." This is reinforcement, and they proceed to a new "problem."

Within neobehaviorism, learning is nonpurposive habit formation. Habits are formed through conditioning, which attaches desired responses to specific stimuli. A stimulus triggers an action or response, which can take only one form because of the nature of the stimulus, the condition of the organism, and the "laws of learning" involved. Teachers who adopt this mechanistic approach to learning decide specifically what behaviors they want their students, when finished products, to manifest, and they proceed to stimulate them in such a way as to evoke and fix those behaviors.

Is Learning Development of Insight?

The key word of Gestalt-field psychologists in describing learning is *insight.* They regard learning as a process of developing new insights or modifying old ones. Insights occur when an individual, in pursuing his purposes, sees new ways of utilizing elements of his environment, including his own bodily structure. The noun *learning* connotes the new insights—or meanings—which are acquired.

Gestalt-field theorists attack two weaknesses in the theory that learning is conditioning: (1) the attempt of S-R associationists to explain complex interrelated organizations in terms of simpler elements, that is, to insist that learning consists of an accumulation of individual conditioned responses, each relatively simple in itself, but eventuating in a complicated pattern of habits; and (2) the tendency of S-R associationists to attribute learning to reduction of basic organic drives.

Gestalt-field psychologists view learning as a purposive, explorative, imaginative, and creative enterprise. This conception breaks completely with the idea that learning consists of linking one thing to another according to certain principles of association. Instead, the learning process is identified with thought or conceptualization; it is a nonmechanical development or change of insight.

S-R associationists also sometimes use the term *insight,* but when they do they mean something quite different from what a Gestalt-field theorist means. When used by associationists, the term describes a special and rare kind of learning. To use Woodworth's definition, insight is ". . . some penetration into the [absolutely] true nature of things."[3] But to Woodworth and other associationists, the ordinary form which learning takes is conditioning. The most systematic of the associationists would deny that there can be two entirely different kinds of learning; therefore they prefer to describe *all* learning as conditioning. Since insight obviously implies something very different from conditioning, many associationists do not use the term at all. To them it connotes something intuitive and mystical, something which cannot be described operationally. In contrast, Gestalt-field psychologists do not like to use the term *conditioning;* they regard *development of insight* as the most descriptive phrase available to describe the manner in which learning actually takes place.

The Gestalt-field definition of insight is a sense of, or feeling for, pattern or relationships. To state it differently, insight is the "sensed way through" or "solution" of a problematic situation. Insights often first appear as vague "hunches." We might say that an insight is a kind of "feel" we get about a situation which permits us to continue actively serving our purposes, or trying

---

[3] R. S. Woodworth, *Psychology* (New York: Holt, Rinehart & Winston, Inc., 1940), pp. 299-300.

to. When are insights verbalized? Perhaps at once; perhaps never. We probably know many things which we never manage to put into words. This is a problem on which animal experimentation sheds some light. Animals below man cannot talk; they can communicate, but not by putting sounds together in coherent subject-predicate sentences. Yet the evidence indicates beyond much doubt that they learn insightfully when confronted with what to them are problems.

If we define *hypothesis* broadly, we may refer to insights as hypotheses. However, a hypothesis usually is defined as a special kind of verbalized insight. It is a statement which takes the form of a declarative sentence, or in many cases an "if-then" sentence. For example, one might say, "Most redheaded girls have violent tempers" (a declarative statement), or one might say, "If most redheaded girls reach a certain frustration level, they then display a violent temper" (an if-then statement). Hypotheses, defined as verbal statements, are the only kind of insight which we can test in a strictly scientific fashion.

This brings us to a crucial question: Are insights necessarily true? Gestalt-field psychologists do not use the term "insights" in a way to imply that they are necessarily true. Granted, the term sometimes is used this way by others—Woodworth, for one. . . . But the relativistic orientation of Gestalt-field theorists necessarily leads them to think of insights as trial answers which may or may not help a person toward his goal; they may or may not be true. Truth, relativistically defined, "is that quality of an insight which enables its possessor to design behavior which is successful in that it achieves what it is designed to achieve."[4] Insights derive from a person's best interpretations of what comes to him; they may be deeply discerning or they may not. They may serve as dependable guides for action or they may prove ruinous. Sultan, one of Köhler's chimpanzees, held a box in the air beneath a hanging banana. He then suddenly released his hold on the box and attempted to jump on it to reach the food. Sultan had an insight, but not a true one.

Insights are to be considered, not as literal descriptions of objective physical-social situations, but as interpretations of one's perceived environment on the basis of which subsequent action can be designed. Although insights are not physicalistic descriptions of objects or processes in the environment, they necessarily take account of the physical environment. Their usability depends in part on how well this is done. Insights may misinterpret a physical environment so badly that they are useless as rules of action, in which case they are to be regarded as false.

It is important to understand that insights are always a learner's own. It is true, of course, that they may become his own through adoption. An insight is usable to a learner only if he can "fit it in." He must understand its significance—for him. A teacher cannot give an insight to a student as we serve a person meat on a platter. He may acquaint students with his insights, but they do not become insights for students until students see their meaning for themselves and adopt them as their own.

[4] Ernest E. Bayles, *Democratic Educational Theory* (New York: Harper & Row, Publishers, 1960), p. 80.

One objection frequently raised to the Gestalt-field tendency to construe all learning as insightful is that some learning tasks are performed successfully without apparent development of insight—as, for example, when a child memorizes the multiplication tables. A field psychologist concedes that some learning appears highly mechanical, but he goes on to say that it is not necessarily as mechanical as it appears. He argues that even though a child may repeat the multiplication tables until he appears to have memorized them by rote, what the child actually has done is to get the feel of some pattern which is present in the tables. The pattern may lie in the relationship of numbers or perhaps merely in the order in which the student placed the numbers to "memorize" them.

Insight does not imply that for a person to learn something he must understand all aspects of its use. Any degree of "feel for a pattern" is sufficient to constitute insightful learning. For example, in learning to extract the square root of a number, one might develop insight as to *why* the method works. Or the insight gained might be much more superficial; it might be merely a "feel" for the method—the pattern of steps—with no real understanding of the basic algebraic formula

$$(x + y)^2 = x^2 + 2xy + y^2$$

Some Examples of Insightful Learning

Before he can become a sharpshooter, a rifleman must get a "feel" for his rifle. Often a Tennessee squirrel hunter was slow in learning to be an army rifleman. He had an excellent feel for his squirrel gun, but a squirrel gun was not an army rifle. In his army training he had to change old insights as well as develop new ones. On his squirrel gun his sights were fixed immovably to the barrel. To hit a squirrel he had to take wind and distance into consideration and move the rifle away from a line on the target (windward and upward) to give "Tennessee windage" and "Kentucky elevation." He had developed insights to the point that he could behave intelligently without thinking; he could aim his gun and pull the trigger while giving very little attention to what he was doing.

Since his army rifle had movable sights which, prior to aiming, were to be adjusted to allow for windage and elevation, he was supposed to set his sights and then line them directly on his target. But under pressure of target practice he used his new insights to adjust his sights correctly, then when he began to fire he gave his rifle Tennessee windage and Kentucky elevation. In army terminology he got a "Maggie"—he missed the target completely. He had used two sets of incompatible insights. He could learn to shoot his army rifle accurately only by getting complete feel for his army rifle and leaving most of his squirrel-gun-aiming insights out of the picture.

What is the answer to $\sqrt{(\text{dog})^2}$=? How did you know it was "dog"? Had you ever before worked with square root and dog at the same time? If you knew the answer was "dog," you had an insight into the problem. Perhaps you had never put the insight into words, but you knew that $\sqrt{x^2}$=x and $\sqrt{4^2}$=4. Your insight, when verbalized, would run something like, "The square root of anything squared is that thing." Conversely, you may have "learned"—memorized—"The square root of a quantity squared is that quantity" and still not know the answer to $\sqrt{(\text{dog})^2}=?$

How would students study spelling so as to develop insight? Teaching for insight has definite implication for methods in spelling. Groups or families of words might be studied in such a way that students develop feeling for a certain spelling pattern. Once a pattern is discovered other words will be sought which conform to it. *Cat, fat,* and *bat* are "at" words. Now what about *hat, mat, pat, rat,* and *sat?* As students, working cooperatively with their teacher, find other word families, they soon will encounter words which apparently should, but do not, fit a certain family—they find some limitations to an insight. They then seek other words with the same divergence from the "rule" and make a family of them. Or in case there is only one divergent word, they think of it as an exception. As the insights into patterns of spelling are put into words, a class can formulate rules. But now rules will be verbalizations of students' insight as contrasted with meaningless statements memorized at the beginning of study.

Insight and Generalization

Often when an insight is first "caught" it applies to a single case. Even so, a person is likely to assume that the insight may work in similar situations. Suppose, for example, that, after studying a particular situation, we hypothesize, "Mary became a shoplifter because she felt unwanted by her parents." The natural next step is to think, "Boys and girls who feel unwanted at home tend to become thieves." Of course, this generalization is only *suggested.* It is not *warranted* by evidence from a single case. Before generalizations become reliable it is usually necessary that they rest on a number of specific insights, all suggesting the same conclusion. In short, dependable generalizations are usually products of considerable experience. Further, they are prone to change in the course of experience, evolving continuously in the direction of greater usefulness as tools of thought.

A tested generalization is assumed to be valid in any future situation similar to the situations in which it was tested. Tested generalizations have the character of *rules, principles,* or *laws.* Syntactically, generalizations are frequently if-then statements: if we take a given action, then the probability is high that a given consequence will follow. We emphasize that tested generalizations should be regarded as *probabilities.* Although, to behave with foresight, we must assume that our generalizations have predictive value, the predictions are to some degree always based on probability.

As suggested earlier, if-then statements usually also may be expressed in present-tense declarative sentences. For example, when a person says, "An increase in the quantity of money is likely to produce a rise in prices," he may mean exactly the same as if he said, "If the quantity of money in circulation is increased, then prices are likely to rise." In using generalizations as hypotheses in scientific procedure, the if-then form often is preferable. It is more likely than is a simple declarative sentence to suggest operations to be performed, and therefore throw emphasis upon experimental tests.

WHAT IS THE RELATIONSHIP
OF BEHAVIOR TO LEARNING?

Behavioristically defined, *"Behavior* is the publicly observable activity of muscles or glands of external secretion as manifested in movements of parts of the body or in the appearance of tears, sweat, saliva and so forth."[5] Gestalt-field psychology gives "behavior" a quite different meaning. It is any change in a person, his perceived environment, or the relation between the two which is subject to *psychological* principles or laws. Psychological behavior involves purpose and intelligence; hence it is not correlated with physical movement. From a Gestalt-field point of view, psychological behavior is not directly observable; it must be inferred.[6]

Learning and change in observable behavior usually occur side by side and obviously are interrelated in some way. Accordingly, S-R associationists contend that any change of behavior is learning, and conversely, that learning is a change of behavior. Thus, the current practice among many educators of defining learning as "change in behavior" usually reflects an associationist psychology.

Gestalt-field theorists counter that S-R associationists err in making synonymous the observable results of learning and the learning itself. They argue that a change in physiological behavior does not necessarily mean that learning has occurred. A person who is struck from behind and knocked down may gain from this experience a healthy respect for dark alleys, but the change in behavior—falling down—is not equivalent to a change in insight. Furthermore, a person may use insights he has had for some time as a basis for change in his present behavior. An author may know that too much coffee is not good for him but persist in drinking coffee until he completes a manuscript and then reduce the amount of coffee he drinks. Probably many changes in the behavior of school children do not reflect change of insight, or at least not the kind of change which the teacher assumes. Johnny may start saying "please" and "thank you" without an insightful grasp of the implications. He may labor hours every night over homework without having his work produce any change of mind about matters embraced in the homework itself. (Of course, the assignments may cause changes in his attitudes toward teachers and school.)

Gestalt-field psychologists maintain that not only may change in behavior occur without learning, but also learning may occur without observable changes in behavior. This is true in any of innumerable situations. There may be no opportunity or occasion for a change in behavior, as when a person decides it would be nice to give more to charity but doesn't have the money to do so. New insights may fail to change a person's behavior if they are competing with old insights which have a stronger hold. Thus, one may decide that racial discrimination is bad but continue to practice it. In summary, when a person

---

[5] D. O. Hebb, *A Textbook of Psychology,* (Philadelphia: W. B. Saunders Company, 1958), p. 2.

[6] See Morton Deutsch, "Field Theory in Social Psychology," in Gardner Lindzey (ed.), *Handbook of Social Psychology* (Reading, Mass.: Addison-Wesley, 1954), p. 191.

learns, his behavior usually changes; but it does not follow that for learning to take place a change in observable behavior must take place at the same time, or that from a change in overt behavior we can always accurately infer the full nature of the insight behind it.

Many people with a behavioristic orientation think that doing something a number of times will necessarily affect future behavior. Thus, if one smokes a pack of cigarettes a day for a few weeks he is likely to become a habitual smoker. Gestalt-field theorists deny that this is the case. Doing a thing once or many times will affect subsequent behavior only in the degree to which doing it gives the doer a feeling for the act or insight into the consequences of its performance. It is the thought process, not the action, which is crucial. For this reason, Gestalt-field psychologists emphasize experience rather than behavior, with experience defined as an interactive event in which a person comes to see and feel the consequences of a given course of action, through acting and seeing what happens.

The emphasis of S-R associationists upon overt behavior has led to school practices designed to produce a desired kind of behavior and to methods of evaluation which measure overt behavior—and nothing else. Teachers, or other school authorities, decide which specific behaviors they want students to display. They then stimulate the students in such a way as to evoke the desired behaviors. The success of the process is judged by how dependably the behavior can be invoked in the future (usually on tests). Field psychologists protest this approach to education; they argue that a student may learn little more from it than the insights he gains about teachers and schools and about how to play the memory-work game successfully.

Walter R. Nord

BEYOND THE TEACHING MACHINE

The work of B. F. Skinner and the operant conditioners has been neglected in management and organizational literature. The present paper is an attempt to eliminate this lacuna. When most students of management and personnel think of Skinner's work, they begin and end with programmed instruction. Skinner's

From Walter R. Nord, "Beyond the Teaching Machine: The Neglected Area of Operant Conditioning in the Theory and Practice of Management," *Organizational Behavior and Human Performance*, Vol. 4, (1969), pp. 375-401. Reprinted by permission.

ideas, however, have far greater implications for the design and operation of social systems and organizations than just the teaching machine. These additional ideas could be of great practical value.

While neglecting conditioning, writers in the administrative, management, and personnel literature have given extensive attention to the work of other behavioral scientists. McGregor and Maslow are perhaps the behavioral scientists best known to practitioners and students in the area of business and management. Since the major concern of managers of human resources is the prediction and control of the behavior of organizational participants, it is curious to find that people with such a need are extremely conversant with McGregor and Maslow and totally ignorant of Skinner. This condition is not surprising since leading scholars in the field, of what might be termed the applied behavioral sciences, have turned out book after book, article after article, and anthology after anthology with scarcely a mention of Skinner's contributions to the design of social systems. While many writers who deal with the social psychology of organizations are guilty of the omission, this paper will focus primarily on the popular positions of Douglas McGregor, Abraham Maslow, and Frederick Herzberg to aid in exposition.

Almost every book in the field devotes considerable attention to Maslow and McGregor. These men have certainly contributed ideas which are easily understood and "make sense" to practitioners. Also, many practitioners have implemented some of these ideas successfully. However, the belief in the Maslow-McGregor creed is not based on a great deal of evidence. This conclusion is not mine alone, but in fact closely parallels Maslow's (1965) own thoughts. He wrote:

> After all, if we take the whole thing from McGregor's point of view of a contrast between a Theory X view of human nature, a good deal of the evidence upon which he bases his conclusions comes from my researches and my papers on motivations, self-actualization, et cetera. But I of all people should know just how shaky this foundation is as a final foundation. My work on motivations came from the clinic, from a study of neurotic people. The carry-over of this theory to the industrial situation has some support from industrial studies, but certainly I would like to see a lot more studies of this kind before feeling finally convinced that this carry-over from the study of neurosis to the study of labor in factories is legitimate. The same thing is true of my studies of self-actualizing people—there is only this one study of mine available. There were many things wrong with the sampling, so many in fact that it must be considered to be, in the classical sense anyway, a bad or poor or inadequate experiment. I am quite willing to concede this—as a matter of fact, I am eager to concede it—because I'm a little worried about this stuff which I consider to be tentative being swallowed whole by all sorts of enthusiastic people, who really should be a little more tentative in the way that I am (p. 55-56).

By contrast, the work of Skinner (1953) and his followers has been supported by millions of observations made on animals at all levels of the phylogenetic scale, including man. Over a wide variety of situations, behavior has been reliably predicted and controlled by operant and classical conditioning techniques.

Why then have the applied behavioral sciences followed the McGregor–Maslow approach and ignored Skinner? Several reasons can be suggested. First is the metaphysical issue. Modern Americans, especially of the managerial class, prefer to think of themselves and others as being self-actualizing creatures operating near the top of Maslow's need-hierarchy, rather than as animals being controlled and even "manipulated" by their environment. McGregor (1960) developed his argument in terms of Maslow's hierarchy. Skinner's position is unattractive in the same way the Corpernican theory was unattractive. Second, Skinner's work and stimulus-response psychology in general appear too limited to allow application to complex social situations. Certainly, this point has much merit. The application of S-R theory poses a terribly complex engineering problem, perhaps an insoluble one in some areas. Nevertheless, the designs of some experimental social systems, which will be discussed later in this paper, demonstrate the feasibility of the practical application of Skinnerian psychology to systems design. A third possible reason for the acceptance of the McGregor and Maslow school and rejection of Skinner may stem from the fact that the two approaches have considerable, although generally unrecognized overlap. As will be shown below, McGregor gave primary importance to the environment as the determinant of individual behavior. Similarly, although not as directly, so does Maslow's hierarchy of needs. The major issue between Skinner and McGregor-Maslow has to do with their models of man. Skinner focuses on man being totally shaped by his environment. Maslow-McGregor see man as having an essence or intrinsic nature which is only congruent with certain environments. The evidence for any one set of metaphysical assumptions is no better than for almost any other set. Empirically, little has been found which helps in choosing between Skinner's and McGregor's assumptions. Further, since most managers are concerned mainly with behavior, the sets of assumptions are of limited importance. It should be noted, however, that if McGregor's writings were stripped of Maslow's model of man, his conclusions on the descriptive and proscriptive levels would remain unchanged. Such a revision would also make McGregor's ideas almost identical with Skinner's. With more attention to contingencies of reinforcement and a broader view of the possibilities of administering reinforcement, the two sets of ideas as they apply to prediction and control of action would be virtually indistinguishable.

The remainder of this paper will be devoted to three areas. First, the similarities and differences between McGregor and Skinner will be discussed. Then, a summary of the Skinnerian position will be presented. Finally, the potential of the Skinnerian approach for modern organizations will be presented with supporting evidence from social systems in which it has already been applied.

McGREGOR AND SKINNER COMPARED

The importance of environmental factors in determining behavior is the crucial and dominant similarity between Skinner and McGregor. As will be shown below, environmental determination of behavior is central to both men.

McGregor (1960) gave central importance to environmental factors in determining how a person behaves. For example, he saw employee behavior as a consequence of organizational factors which are influenced by managerial strategy. In a sense, Theory X management leads to people behaving in a way which confirms Theory X assumptions, almost as a self-fulfilling prophecy. In addition, McGregor's statement of Theory Y assumptions places stress on "proper conditions," rewards and punishments, and other environmental factors. Further, he recognized the importance of immediate feedback in changing behavior. Also, he noted that failure to achieve results is often due to inappropriate methods of control. These are the very terms a behaviorist such as Skinner uses in discussing human actions. Finally, McGregor (1966) noted stimulus-response psychology as a possible model for considering organizational behavior. However, he discarded the reinforcement approach because it did not permit intrinsic rewards to be dealt with. Such a view not only led him to discard a model which describes, by his own admission, important behaviors, but is based on an incomplete view of reinforcement.

McGregor's basic arguments could have been based on Skinner rather than Maslow. The major difference would be the assumption of fewer givens about human nature. In view of this similarity one need not choose either Skinner or McGregor. Rather, there is considerable overlap in that both focus on changing the environmental conditions to produce changes in behavior. Further, both writers place substantial emphasis on the goals of prediction and control. Both are quite explicit in suggesting that we often get undesired results because we use inappropriate methods of control. In fact, the emphasis that McGregor's (1960) first chapter gives to the role of environment in controlling behavior seems to place him clearly in the behavioral camp.

Certainly there are important differences between Skinner and McGregor as well as the marked similarities noted above. For example, McGregor's (1960) use of Maslow's hierarchy of needs implies a series of inborn needs as a focus of the causal factors of behavior whereas Skinner (1953) views environmental factors as the causes of behavior. This difference does not, however, suggest an unresolvable conflict on the applied level. Skinner too allows for satiation on certain reinforcers which will be subject to species' and individual differences. Proceeding from this premise, Skinner focuses on the environmental control of behavior in a more rigorous and specific fashion than did McGregor. For example, McGregor (1960) advocated an agricultural approach to development which emphasizes the provision of the conditions for behavioral change as a management responsibility. He noted in a general way that features of the organization, such as a boss, will influence behavioral change. He added that the change would not be permanent unless the organizational environment reinforced the desired behavior pattern. Such a general approach is an assumed basis for Skinner, who proceeds to focus on the types of reinforcement, the details of the administration of reinforcement, and the outcomes which can be expected from the administration of various types of reinforcement. Thus, changes in behavior which are predicted and achieved by Skinnerian methods can be viewed as empirical support for the work of McGregor.

There are other commonalities in the thinking of the two men. Both assume that there are a wide number of desirable responses available to a person which he does not make, because the responses are not rewarded in the environment. Both suggest that many undesired responses are repeated because they are rewarded. Both are clearly advocating a search for alternatives to controlling behavior which will be more effective in developing desired responses.

At this same level of analysis, there seems to be one major difference which revolves around the issue of self-control. However, this difference may be more apparent than real. Skinner (1953) wrote "It appears, therefore, that society is responsible for the larger part of the behavior of self-control. If this is correct, little ultimate control remains with the individual (p. 240)." Continuing on self-control, Skinner adds: "But it is also behavior; and we account for it in terms of other variables in the environment and history of the individual. It is these variables which provide the ultimate control (p. 240)."

In apparent contrast, McGregor (1960) stated: "Theory *Y* assumes that people will exercise self-direction and self-control in the achievement of organizational objectives *to the degree that they are committed to those objectives* (p. 56)." Seemingly this statement contradicts Skinner in placing the locus of control inside the individual. However, this conflict is reduced a few sentences later when McGregor (1960) added "Managerial policies and practices materially affect this degree of commitment (p. 56)." Thus, both writers, Skinner far more unequivocally than McGregor, see the external environment as the primary factor in self-control. While McGregor polemicized against control by authority, he was not arguing that man is "free." Perhaps the more humanistic tone of McGregor's writing or his specific attention to managerial problems faced in business is responsible for his high esteem among students of management relative to that accorded Skinner. While metaphorically there is great difference, substantively there is little. It would seem, however, that metaphors have led practitioners and students of applied behavioral science to overlook some valuable data and some creative management possibilities.

One major substantive difference between the two approaches exists: it involves intrinsic rewards. McGregor (1960) saw a dicotomy in the effects of intrinsic and extrinsic rewards, noting research which has shown intrinsic ones to be more effective. He concludes the "mechanical" view (reinforcement theory) is inadequate, because it does not explain the superior outcomes of the use of "intrinsic" over "extrinsic" rewards. Here, as will be discussed in more detail later in connection with Herzberg, the problem is McGregor's failure to consider scheduling of reinforcement. "Intrinsic" rewards in existing organizations may be more effective because they occur on a more appropriate schedule for sustaining behavior than do "extrinsic" rewards. Intrinsic rewards are given by the environment for task completion or a similar achievement, and often occur on a ratio schedule. The implications of this crucial fact will be discussed shortly in considering Skinner's emphasis on the scheduling of rewards. For the present, it is suggested that McGregor gave little attention to reinforcement schedules and made a qualitative distinction between external and internal rewards. He seems to agree with Skinner that achievement, task completion, and control of the environment are reinforcers in themselves. Skinner's work suggests, however, that these rewards have the same consequences as "extrinsic" rewards, if they are given on the same schedule.

By way of summary to this point, it appears that more humanistic social scientists have been preferred by managers to behaviorists such as Skinner in their efforts to improve the management of human resources. Perhaps the oversight has been due to the congruence between their values and the metaphysics of people such as McGregor and Maslow. The differences between McGregor and Skinner do not appear to involve open conflict.

To the extent the two approaches agree, the major criterion in employing them would seem to be the degree to which they aid in predicting and controlling behavior toward organizational goals. The work of Skinner and his followers has much to offer in terms of the above criterion. In particular, McGregor's followers might find Skinner's work an asset in implementing Theory Y. The remainder of this paper will develop some of the major points of the Skinnerian approach and seek to explore their potential for industrial use.

CONDITIONING–A SYNTHESIS
FOR ORGANIZATIONAL BEHAVIOR

The behavioral psychology of Skinner assumes, like Theory Y that rate of behavior is dependent on the external conditions in which the behavior takes place. Like Theory X, it stresses the importance of the administration of rewards and punishments. Unlike Theory X, Skinnerian psychology places emphasis on rewards. Like Theory Y it emphasizes the role of interdependence between people in a social relationship and thus views the administration of rewards and punishments as an exchange. For those who are unfamiliar with the work of Skinner and his followers, a brief summary follows. Like any summary of an extensive body of work, this review omits a lot of important material. A more detailed, yet simple, introduction to conditioning can be found in Bijou and Baer (1961) and Skinner (1953). Extensions of this work by social exchange theorists such as Homans (1961) suggest that the conditioning model can be extended to a systems approach, contrary to McGregor's (1966) belief.

Generally, conditioned responses can be divided into two classes. Each class is acquired in a different fashion. The first class, generally known as respondent or classically conditioned behavior, describes the responses which are controlled by prior stimulation. These responses, generally thought of as being involuntary or reflexive, are usually made by the "smooth muscles." Common ones are salivation and emotional responses. Initially, the presentation of an unconditioned stimulus will elicit a specific response. For example, food placed on one's tongue will generally cause salivation. If a bell is sounded and then food is placed on the tongue, and this process is repeated several times, the sound of the bell by itself will elicit salivation. By this process, stimuli which previously did not control behavior such as the bell, can become a source of behavior control. Many of our likes and dislikes, our anxieties, our feelings of patriotism, and other emotions can be thought of as such involuntary responses. The implications of emotional responses are of major importance to the management of human resources and more will be said about them later. However, the second class of responses, the operants, are of even greater importance.

The rate of operant responses is influenced by events which follow them. These events are considered to be the consequences of behavior. The responses, generally thought to be voluntary, are usually made by striped muscles. All that is necessary for the development of an operant response is that the desired response has a probability of occurring which is greater than zero for the individual involved. Most rapid conditioning results when the desired response is "reinforced" immediately (preferably about one-half second after the response). In other words, the desired response is followed directly by some consequence. In simple terms, if the outcome is pleasing to the individual, the probability of his repeating the response is apt to be increased. If the consequence is displeasing to the individual, the probability of his repeating the response is apt to be decreased. The process of inducing such change (usually an increase) in the response rate, is called operant conditioning. In general, the frequency of a behavior is said to be a function of its consequences.

The above description of operant conditioning is greatly simplified. The additional considerations which follow will only partially rectify this state. One crucial factor has to do with the frequency with which a given consequence follows a response. There are several possible patterns. Most obviously, the consequence can be continuous (for example, it follows the response every time the response is made). Alternatively a consequence might follow only some of the responses. There are two basic ways in which such partial reinforcement can be administered. First, the consequence can be made contingent on a certain number of responses. Two sub-patterns are possible. Every nth response may be reinforced or an average of $1/n$ of the responses may be reinforced in a random pattern. These two related patterns are called ratio schedules. The former is known as a fixed ratio and the latter is known as a variable ratio. Ratio schedules tend to generate a high rate of response, with the variable ratio schedule leading to a more durable response than both the fixed-ratio and continuous patterns. A second technique of partial reinforcement can be designed where the consequence follows the response only after a certain amount of time has elapsed. The first response made after a specified interval is then reinforced, but all other responses produce neutral stimulus outcomes. This pattern can also be either fixed or variable. Generally, interval schedules develop responses which are quite long lasting when reinforcement is no longer given, but do not yield as rapid a response rate as ratio schedules do. Obviously, mixed patterns of ratio and interval schedules can also be designed.

A second consideration about operant conditioning which deserves brief mention is the concept of a response hierarchy. All the responses which an individual could make under a given set of conditions can be placed in order according to probability that they will be made. In this view, there are two basic strategies for getting an individual to make the desired response. First, one could attempt to reduce the probability of all the more probable responses. Second, one could attempt to increase the probability of the desired response. Of course, some combination of these two approaches may often be used.

Strategies for changing the probability of a response can be implemented by punishment, extinction, and positive reinforcement. Generally punishment and extinction are used to decrease the occurrence of a response whereas positive reinforcement is used to increase its probability. An understanding of these three operations in behavior control is important, not only for knowing how to use them, but chiefly because of their unanticipated consequences or their side-effects.

Punishment is the most widely used technique in our society for behavior control. Perhaps, as Reese (1966) said, the widespread use of punishment is due to the immediate effects it has in stopping or preventing the undesired response. In this sense, the punisher is reinforced for punishing. Also, many of us seem to be influenced by some notion of what Homans (1961) called distributive justice. In order to reestablish what we believe to be equity, we may often be led to punish another person. This ancient assumption of ". . . an eye for an eye . . ." has been widely practiced in man's quest for equity and behavior control.

Whatever the reason for punishing, it can be done in two ways, both of which have unfortunate side-effects. First, punishment can be administered in the form of some aversive stimulus such as physical pain or social disapproval. Secondly, it can be administered by withdrawing a desired stimulus. The immediate effect is often the rapid drop in frequency of the punished response. The full effects, unfortunately, are often not clearly recognized. Many of these consequences are crucial for managers of organizations.

Punishment may be an inefficient technique for controlling behavior for a number of reasons. First, the probability of the response may be reduced only when the threat of punishment is perceived to exist. Thus, when the punishing agent is away, the undesired response may occur at its initial rate. Secondly, punishment only serves to reduce the probability of the one response. This outcome does not necessarily produce the desired response, unless that response is the next most probable one in the response hierarchy. Really, what punishment does is to get the individual to do something other than what he has been punished for. A third effect is that the punishment may interfere with the response being made under desired circumstances. For example, if an organizational member attempts an innovation which is met with punishment by his superiors because they did not feel he had the authority to take the step, it is quite possible that his creative behavior will be reduced even in those areas where his superiors expect him to innovate.

In addition to these effects there are some other important by-products of punishment. Punishment may result in a person making responses which are incompatible with the punished response. Psychological tension, often manifested in emotional behavior such as fear or anxiety, is often the result. Secondly, punishment may lead to avoidance and dislike of the punishing agent. This effect can be especially important to managers who are attempting to build open, helping relationships with subordinates. The roles of punishing agent and helper are often incompatible. Many line-staff conflicts in organizations undoubtedly can be explained in these terms. Finally, punishment may generate counter-aggression. Either through a modeling effect or a justice effect, the punished person may respond with aggressive responses towards the punishing agent or towards some other stimulus.

The second technique for behavior change, commonly called extinction, also focuses primarily on reducing the probability of a response. Extinction arises from repeated trials where the response is followed by a neutral stimulus. This technique generates fewer by-products than punishment. However, like punishment, it does not lead to the desired response being developed. Furthermore, to the extent that one has built up an expectation of a reward for a certain response, a neutral consequence may be perceived as punishing. Thus, extinction may have some advantages over punishment, but has many of the same limitations.

Positive reinforcement is the final technique for changing behavior. Under conditions of positive reinforcement, the response produces a consequence that results in an increase in the frequency of the response. It is commonly stated that such a consequence is rewarding, pleasing, or drive-reducing for the individual. The operant conditioners, however, avoid such inferences and define positive reinforcers as stimuli which increase the probability of a preceding response. Positive reinforcement is efficient for several reasons. First, it increases the probable occurrence of the desired response. The process involves rewarding approximation of desired response itself immediately after it is made. The desired behavior is being directly developed as opposed to successive suppression of undesired acts. Secondly, the adverse emotional responses associated with punishment and extinction are apt to be reduced and in fact favorable emotions may be developed. Since people tend to develop positive affect to others who reward them, the "trainer" is apt to become positively valenced in the eyes of the "learner."

By way of summary, Skinner's (1953) approach suggested that the control of behavior change involves a reduction in the probability of the most prepotent response and/or an increase in the probability of some desired response. Punishment and extinction may be used. These means can only reduce the probability of the unwanted response being made. Also, they may have undesired side-effects. The third technique, positive reinforcement, has the important advantage of developing the desired response rather than merely reducing the chances of an undesired one. Also, positive reinforcement is apt to produce favorable rather than unfavorable "side-effects" on organizational relationships.

This approach seems to suggest that both or neither Theory X and Theory Y assumptions are useful. This section suggested that conditioning may be both Theory X and Theory Y. Perhaps since the operant view does not make either set of assumptions, it is neither Theory X nor Theory Y. Operant conditioning is consistent with Theory Y in suggesting that the limits on human beings are a function of the organizational setting, but like Theory X, implies something about human nature; namely that deprivation or threat of some sort of deprivation is a precondition for behavior to be controlled. From the managerial perspective, however, the nomonological question is of little significance. The important thing to managers is behavior and the major point of this approach is that behavior is a function of its consequences. Good management is that which leads to the desired behavior by organizational members. Management must see to it that the consequences of behavior are such as to increase the frequency of desired behavior and decrease the frequency of undesired behaviors. The question becomes, how can managers develop a social system which provides the appropriate consequences? In many ways the answer to this question is similar to what Theory Y advocates have suggested. However, there are some new possibilities.

APPLICATIONS OF CONDITIONING IN ORGANIZATIONS

The potential uses of the Skinnerian framework for social systems are increasing rapidly. The approach has far more applicability to complex social systems than has often been recognized. McGregor's rejection of the stimulus-response or the reward-punishment approach as inadequate for management because it does not allow for a systems approach is quite inconsistent with this general trend and his own environmentally based approach. Recent work in the field of behavioral control has begun to refute McGregor's position. The Skinnerian view can be and has been used to redesign social systems.

The most complete redesign was envisioned by Skinner (1948) in his novel, *Walden Two*. In this book, Skinner developed a society based on the use of positive reinforcement and experimental ethics geared to the goal of competition of a coordinated social unit with its environment. In other words, the system is designed to reward behaviors which are functional for the whole society. Social change is introduced on the basis of empirical data. As a result of the success of this system, man is enabled to pursue those activities which are rewarding in themselves. Although the book is a novel, it can be a valuable stimulus for thought about the design of social organization.

In addition, Skinner (1954) has taken a fresh look at teaching and learning in conventional educational systems. He noted that the school system depends heavily on aversive control or punishment. The use of low marks and ridicule have merely been substituted for the "stick." The teacher, in Skinner's view, is an out of date reinforcing mechanism. He suggested the need to examine the reinforcers which are available in the system and to apply them in a manner which is consistent with what is known about learning. For example, control over the environment itself may be rewarding. Perhaps grades reinforce the wrong behavior and are administered on a rather poor schedule. It would seem that a search for new reinforcers and better reinforcement schedules is appropriate for all modern organizations.

These speculations suggest the potential for great advances. *Walden Two* is in many ways an ideal society but has been a source of horror to many readers. The thoughts about changes in teaching methods are also a subject of controversy. However, the environment can be designed to aid in the attainment of desired ends. People resist the idea that they can be controlled by their environment. This resistance does not change the fact that they are under such control. Recently, evidence has begun to accumulate that the Skinnerian approach can be employed to design social systems.

Much of this evidence was collected in settings far removed from modern work organizations. The reader's initial response is apt to be, "What relevance do these studies have to my organization?" Obviously, the relationship is not direct. However, if, as the operant approach maintains, the conditioning process describes the acquisition and maintenance of behavior, the same principles can be applied to any social organization. The problem of application becomes merely that of engineering. The gains may ˉwell be limited only by an administrator's ingenuity and resources.

Much of the evidence comes from studies of hospitalized mental patients and autistic children, although some has been based on normal lower class children. A few examples from these studies will serve to document the great potential of the conditioning methods for social systems. Allyon and Azrin (1965) observed mental patients' behavior to determine what activities they engaged in when they had a chance. They then made token contingent on certain responses such as work on hospital tasks. These tokens could be exchanged for the activities the patients preferred to engage in. The results of this approach were amazing. In one experiment five schizophrenics and three mental defectives served as Ss. They did jobs regularly and adequately when tokens were given for the job. Such performance was reported to be in sharp contrast to the erratic and inconsistent behavior characteristic of such patients. When the tokens were no longer contingent on the work, the performance dropped almost to zero. In a second experiment, a whole ward of 44 patients served as Ss. A similar procedure was followed and 11 classes of tasks observed. When tokens were contingent upon the desired responses, the group spent an average of 45 hours on the tasks daily. When tokens were not contingent on responses, almost no time was spent on the tasks. The implications seem rather clear. When desired behavior is rewarded, it will be emitted, when it is not rewarded, it will not be emitted.

A great deal of related work has been reported. Allyon (1966) and Wolf, Risley, and Mees (1966) have shown how a reinforcement procedure can be effective in controlling the behavior of a psychotic patient and of an autistic child respectively. These are but a few of the many studies in a growing body of evidence.

More important for present purposes are the application of this approach in more complex social situations. The work of Hamblin et al. (1967) shows some of the interesting possibilities of the conditioning approach for school classes and aggressive children. A token system was used to shape desired behavior. Through the application of the conditioning approach to the school system, gains may be made in educating children from deprived backgrounds. Two examples will illustrate these possibilities.

The first example comes from a recent newspaper story. A record shop owner in a Negro area of Chicago reported seeing the report card of a Negro boy. The owner thought the boy was bright, but the report card showed mostly unsatisfactory performance. He told the boy he would give him $5 worth of free records if he got all "excellents" on the next report card. Ten weeks later the boy returned with such a card to collect his reward. The owner reported that similar offers to other children had a remarkable effect in getting them to study and do their homework. The anecdote demonstrates what everyone knows anyway: people will not work if rewards do not exist. The problems of education in the ghetto and motivation to work in general, may be overcome by appropriate reinforcement. Further support for this statement comes from the work of Montrose Wolf.

Wolf (1966) ran a school for children, most of whom were sixth graders, in a lower class Negro area of Kansas City. The children attended this school for several hours after school each day and on Saturday. Rewards were given in the form of tickets which could be saved and turned in for different kinds of things like toys, food, movies, shopping trips, and other activities. Tickets were made contingent on academic performance within the remedial school itself, and on performance in the regular school system. The results were remarkable. The average regular school grade of the students was raised to C from D. The results on standard achievement tests showed the remedial group progressed over twice as much in one year as they had done the previous year. They showed twice as much progress as a control group. Other gains were also noted. Wolf reported that a severe punishment was not to let the children attend school. They expressed strong discontent when school was not held because of a holiday. He further noted that when reading was no longer rewarded with tickets, the students still continued to read more than before the training. Arithmetic and English did not maintain these increments. Thus, to some extent, reading appeared to be intrinsically rewarding.

A final point concerns the transferability of skills learned in such a school to society at large. Will the tasks that are not rewarding in themselves be continued? The answer is probably not, unless other rewards are provided. The task then becomes to develop skills and behavior which society itself will reward. If this method is applied to develop behavior which is rewarded by society, the behavior is apt to be maintained. The same argument holds for organizational behavior. It will be fruitless to develop behavior which is not rewarded in the organization.

In summary, evidence has been presented to show the relevance of the Skinnerian approach to complex social systems. Certainly the evidence is only suggestive of future possibilities. The rest of this paper attempts to suggest some of these implications for organizational management.

MANAGEMENT THROUGH POSITIVE REINFORCEMENT

The implications of the systematic use of positive reinforcement for management range over many traditional areas. Some of the more important areas include training and personnel development, compensation and alternative rewards, supervision and leadership, job design, organizational design, and organizational change.

Training and Personnel Development

The area of training has been the first to benefit from the application of conditioning principles with the use of programmed learning and the teaching machine. An example of future potential comes from the Northern Systems Company Training Method for assembly line work. In this system, the program objectives are broken down into sub-objectives. The training employs a lattice which provides objective relationships between functions and objectives, indicates critical evaluation points, and presents a visual display of go-no-go functions. Progress through various steps is reinforced by rewards. To quote from a statement of the training method ". . . the trainee gains satisfaction only by demonstrated performance at the tool stations. Second, he quickly perceives that correct behaviors obtain for him the satisfaction of his needs, and that incorrect behaviors do not (p. 20)." Correct performance includes not only job skills, but also the performance of social interaction which is necessary in a factory setting. The skills taught are designed to allow for high mobility in the industrial world. The Northern System's method develops behavior which the economic and social system will normally reinforce and has been successful in training people in a wide variety of skills. Its potential in training such groups as the "hard-core" unemployed seems to be limited only by the resources and creativity of program designers.

The Skinnerian approach seems to have potential for all areas of personnel development, not only for highly programmed tasks. Reinforcement theory may be useful in the development of such behaviors as creativity. The work of Maltzman, Simon, Raskin, and Licht (1960) demonstrated this possibility. After a series of experiments employing a standard experimental training procedure with free association materials, these investigators concluded that a highly reliable increase in uncommon responses could be produced through the use of reinforcement. The similarity of their results to those of operant experiments with respect to the persistance of the responses and the effect of repetitions, led them to conclude that originality is a form of operant behavior. Positive reinforcement increased the rate at which original responses were emitted.

Support is also available for the efficacy of operant conditioning to more conventional personnel and leadership development. Three such contributions are discussed below. The first concerns the organizational environment as a shaper of behavior of which Fleishman's (1967) study is a case in point. He found that human relations training programs were only effective in producing on-the-job changes if the organizational climate was supportive of the content of the program. More generally it would appear that industrial behavior is a function of its consequences. Those responses which are rewarded will persist: those responses which are not rewarded or are punished will decrease in frequency. If the organizational environment does not reward responses developed in a training program, the program will be, at best, a total waste of time and money. As Sykes (1962) has shown, at worst, such a program may be highly disruptive. A second implication of operant conditioning concerns the content of personnel development programs in the area of human relations. If, as

Homans (1961) and others have suggested, social interaction is also influenced by the same operant principles, then people in interaction are constantly "shaping" or conditioning each other. The behavior of a subordinate is to some degree developed by his boss and vice-versa. What more sensible, practical point could be taught to organizational members than that they are teaching their fellow participants to behave in a certain manner? What more practical, sensible set of principles could be taught than that, due to latent dysfunctions generated, punishment and extinction procedures are less efficient ways to influence behavior than positive reinforcement? Clearly, the behavioral scientists who have contributed so greatly to organizational practice and personnel development have not put enough emphasis on these simple principles. The third implication for personnel development is added recognition that annual merit interviews and salary increments are very inefficient development techniques. The rewards or punishments are so delayed that they can be expected to have little feedback value for the employees involved. More frequent appraisals and distribution of rewards are apt to be far more effective, especially to the degree that they are related to specific tasks or units of work.

Job Design

Recently, behavioral scientists have emphasized the social psychological factors which need to be attended to in job design. McGregor and others have suggested job enlargement. Herzberg (1968) has argued that job enlargement just allows an individual to do a greater variety of boring jobs and suggests that "job enrichment" is needed. For present purposes, job enlargement and job enrichment will be lumped together. Both of these approaches are consistent with the conditioning view if two differences can be resolved. First, the definitions of motivation must be translated into common terms. Second, reinforcers operating in the newly designed jobs must be delineated and tested to see if the reinforcers postulated in the newly designed jobs are really responsible for behavioral changes or if there are other reinforcers operating.

With respect to the definitions of motivation, the two approaches are really similar in viewing the rate of behavior as the crucial factor. The major differences exist on the conceptual level. Both job enlargement and job enrichment are attempts to increase motivation. Conceptually, McGregor and Herzberg tend to view motivation as some internal state. The conditioning approach does not postulate internal states but rather deals with the manipulation of environmental factors which influence the rate of behavior. Actually, some combination of the two approaches may be most useful theoretically as Vinacke (1962) has suggested. However, if both approaches are viewed only at the operational level, it is quite probable that rates of behavior could be agreed on as an acceptable criterion. Certainly from the practitioners viewpoint, behavior is the crucial variable. When a manager talks about a motivated worker, he often means one who frequently makes desired responses at a high rate without external prompting from the boss. The traditional view of motivation as an inner-drive is of limited practical and theoretical value.

If both approaches could agree on the behavioral criterion, at least on an operational level, the operant approach could be employed to help resolve some practical and theoretical problems suggested by the work of McGregor and Herzberg. Since, generally speaking, the external conditions are most easily manipulated in an organization, attention can be focused on designing an environment which increases the frequency of the wanted responses. As a result, practitioners and students of organization could deal with motivation without searching for man's essence. We can avoid the metaphysical assumptions of Maslow and McGregor until they are better documented. The issue of a two-factor theory of motivation proposed by Herzberg which recently has been severely challenged by Lindsay, Marks, and Gorlow (1967) and Hulin and Smith (1967) among others can also be avoided. Attention can be confined to developing systems which produce high rates of desired behavior. Thus the conceptual differences about motivation do not cause unresolvable conflict at the present time.

The second area of difference between McGregor-Herzberg and the operant explanation of the effects of job enrichment stems from the failure of Herzberg and McGregor to recognize the great variety of possible rewards available in job design. The Skinnerian approach leads to the development of a more comprehensive discussion of the rewards from enriched or enlarged jobs. In terms of the operant approach, both job enrichment and job enlargement are apt to lead to what would generally be called greater motivation or what we will call higher rates of desired behavior. McGregor and Herzberg suggest feelings of achievement and responsibility explain these results. The reinforcement approach leads to a search for specific rewards in these newly designed jobs.

Job enlargement can be viewed simply as increasing the variety of tasks a person does. Recent research on self-stimulation and sensory deprivation has suggested that stimulation itself is reinforcing, especially when one has been deprived of it. The increased variety of tasks due to job enlargement may thus be intrinsically rewarding due to a host of reinforcers in the work itself rather than to any greater feeling of responsibility or achievement. These feelings may be a cause of greater productivity or merely correlates of the receipt of these intrinsic rewards from stimulation. The evidence is not clear, but the effects of job enlargement can at least be partially explained in operant terms.

Some additional support from this idea comes from Schultz's (1964) work on spontaneous alternation of behavior. Schultz suggested that spontaneous alternation of human behavior is facilitated (1) when responses are not reinforced and/or are not subjected to knowledge of correctness, (2) by the amount of prior exercise of one response alternative, and (3) by a short intertrial interval. Low feedback and reinforcement, short intervals between responses, and the frequent repetition of one response are all characteristic of many jobs which need enlargement. Merely making different responses may be rewarding to a worker, thereby explaining some of the benefits noted from job enlargement. It has also been noted that people create variation for themselves in performing monotonous tasks. For example, ritualized social interaction in the form of social "games" is a form of such alternation workers developed noted by Roy (1964).

By way of summary, much of the current work on job enlargement and enrichment has attributed the effects to feelings of achievement or responsibility, without taking into account numerous other possible reinforcers which may be more basic. Further research to determine the efficacy of these various possibilities is needed before definite conclusions can be drawn. Do the feelings of achievement or responsibility operate as reinforcers in an operant manner? Do these feelings come from other more basic rewards as task variety? Present data do not permit answers to these questions.

With respect to the benefits noted from job enrichment, an operant model may provide further insights. Herzberg (1968) maintained that some jobs can not be "enriched" or made more motivating in themselves. It is the contention of this paper that it is not the tasks which are the problem, but it is the reinforcement schedules. For example, what could be more boring, have less potential for achievement and realization of Herzberg's satisfiers, than the game of bingo. Yet people will sit for hours at bingo, often under punishing conditions (since the house takes in more than it pays out) and place tokens on numbers. Similar behavior is exhibited at slot-machines and other gambling devices. Most operational definitions of motivation would agree that these players are highly motivated. The reason is clear from the operant viewpoint. The reinforcement schedule employed in games of chance, the variable ratio schedule, is a very powerful device for maintaining a rapid rate of response. With respect to job design, the important requirement is that rewards follow performance on an effective schedule.

The type of rewards Herzberg (1968) called satisfiers may be important motivators because they are distributed on a variable ratio schedule. Herzberg's data do not rule out this explanation. Take achievement, for example. If a person is doing a job from which it is possible to get a feeling of achievement, there must be a reasonably large probability that a person will not succeed on the task. Often times, this condition means that some noncontinuous schedule or reinforcement is operating. An individual will succeed only on some variable ratio schedule. In addition, successful completion of the task is often the most important reward. The reward is, of course, immediate. A similar statement could be made about tasks which are said to yield intrinsic satisfaction, such as crossword puzzles or enriched jobs. Thus the factors Herzberg called motivators may derive their potency from the manner in which the rewards are administered. The task is immediately and positively reinforced by the environment on a variable ratio schedule. Often the schedule is one which rewards a very small fraction of a large number of responses. Since behavior is a function of its consequences, if jobs can be designed to reinforce desired behavior in the appropriate manner, "motivated" workers are apt to result. Some of Herzberg's results may be explained without resort to a two-factor theory more parsimoniously in terms of schedules of reinforcement. Herzberg's (1966) finding that recognition is only a motivator if it is contingent on performance further documents the operant argument.

Another suggestion for job design from the operant tradition was suggested by Homans. He explored the relationship of the frequency of an activity and satisfaction to the amount of a reward. He concluded that satisfaction is generally positively related to the amount of reward whereas frequency of an activity is negatively related to the amount of reward the individual has received in the recent past. In order to have both high satisfaction and high activity, Homans (1961) suggested that tasks need to be designed in a manner such that repeated activities lead up to the accomplishment of some final result and get rewarded at a very low frequency until just before the final result is achieved. Then the reinforcement comes often. For example, consider the job of producing bottled soda. An optimal design would have the reward immediate on the completion of putting the caps on the bottles, but the task would be designed such that all the operations prior to capping were completed before any capping was done. Near the end of a work day, all the capping could be done. High output and satisfaction might then exist simultaneously. In general then, the operant approach suggests some interesting possibilities for designing jobs in ways which would maximize the power of reinforcers in the job itself.

A similar argument can be applied to some problems faced in administration and management. For example, it is commonly recognized that programmed tasks tend to be attended to before unprogrammed ones. It is quite obvious that programmed functions produce a product which is often tangible. The product itself is a reinforcer. An unprogrammed task often requires behavior which has not been reinforced in the past and will not produce a reward in the near future. It may be beneficial to provide rewards relatively early for behavior on unprogrammed tasks. This suggestion will be difficult to put into practice because of the very nature of unprogrammed tasks. Perhaps the best that can be done is to reward the working on such tasks.

Compensation and Alternative Rewards

Although whether money is a true "generalized reinforcer" as Skinner suggests, has not been demonstrated conclusively, for years operant principles have been applied in the form of monetary incentive systems. Opsahl and Dunnette (1966) concluded that such programs generally do increase output. However, the restriction of output and other unanticipated consequences are associated with these programs. Many writers have attributed these consequences to social forces, such as the desire for approval from one's peers. Gewitz and Baer (1958), for example, have shown that social approval has the same effects as other reinforcers in an operant situation. Dalton's (1948) famous study on rate-busters may be interpreted to show that people who are more "group-oriented" may place a higher value on social approval and hence are more apt to abide by group production norms than are less "group-oriented" people. Thus, it is not that money in piece-rate systems is not a potential reinforcer, but rather other reinforcers are more effective, at least after a certain level of monetary reward.

The successful use of the Scanlon Plan demonstrates the value of combining both economic and social rewards. This plan rewards improved work with several types of reinforcers, and often more immediately and directly than many incentive systems. The Scanlon Plan combines economic rewards, often given monthly, with social rewards. The latter are given soon after an employee's idea has been submitted or used.

Related arguments can be made for other group incentive programs. Often jobs are interdependent. The appropriate reinforcement for such tasks should be contingent upon interdependent responses, not individual ones. Even if the jobs are independent, the workers are social-psychologically interdependent. Social rewards are often obtainable by restricting output. It is hardly surprising that individual incentive programs have produced the unanticipated consequences so often noted. Further, since rewards and punishments from the informal group are apt to be administered immediately and frequently they are apt to be very powerful in controlling behavior.

In general then, money and other rewards must be made contingent on the desired responses. Further, the importance of alternative rewards to money must be recognized and incorporated into the design of the work environment. The widely known path-goal to productivity model expresses a similar point.

Another problem of compensation in organizations is also apparent in an operant context. Often, means of compensation, especially fringe benefits, have the unanticipated consequence of reinforcing the wrong responses. Current programs of sick pay, recreation programs, employee lounges, work breaks, and numerous other personnel programs all have one point in common. They all reward the employee for not working or for staying away from the job. These programs are not "bad," since often they may act to reduce problems such as turnover. However, an employer who relies on them should realize what behavior he is developing by establishing these costly programs. Alternative expenditures must be considered. If some of the money that was allocated for these programs was used to redesign jobs so as to be more reinforcing in themselves, more productive effort could be obtained. This idea is certainly not new. A host of behavioral scientists have suggested that resources devoted to making performance of the job itself more attractive will pay social and/or economic dividends.

Another interesting application of conditioning principles has to do with the schedule on which pay is distributed. The conventional pay schedule is a fixed interval one. Further, pay often is not really contingent on one's performance. The response needed to be rewarded is often attending work on pay day. Not only is pay often not contingent upon performance, but the fixed interval schedule is not given to generating a high response rate. In a creative article, Aldis (1966) suggested an interesting compensation program employing a variable ratio schedule. Instead of an annual Christmas bonus or other types of such expected salary supplements, he suggested a lottery system. If an employee produced above an agreed-upon standard, his name would be placed in a hat. A drawing would be held. The name(s) drawn would receive an amount of money proportionate to the number of units produced during that period of time. This system would approximate the desired variable ratio schedule.

In addition to the prosperity of the owners of gambling establishments, there is some direct evidence that variable ratio schedules will be of use to those charged with predicting and controlling human behavior. A leading St. Louis hardware company,[1] although apparently unaware of the work of the operant conditioners, has applied an approximate variable ratio schedule of reinforcement to reduce absenteeism and tardiness. Although the complete data is not available, the personnel department has reported surprising success. A brief description of the system will be presented below and a more detailed study will be written in the near future.

Under the lottery system, if a person is on time (that is, not so much as a half minute late) for work at the start of his day and after his breaks, he is eligible for a drawing at the end of the month. Prizes worth approximately $20 to $25 are awarded to the winners. One prize is available for each 25 eligible employees. At the end of six months, people who have had perfect attendance for the entire period are eligible for a drawing for a color television set. The names of all the winners and of those eligible are also printed in the company paper, such that social reinforcement may also be a factor. The plan was introduced because tardiness and absenteeism had become a very serious problem. In the words of the personnel manager, absenteeism and tardiness ". . . were lousy before." Since the program was begun 16 months ago, conditions have improved greatly. Sick leave costs have been reduced about 62 percent. After the first month, 151 of approximately 530 employees were eligible for the drawing. This number has grown larger, although not at a steady rate to 219 for the most recent month. Although the comparable figures for the period before the program were unfortunately not available, management has noted great improvements. It would appear that desired behavior by organization participants in terms of tardiness and absenteeism can be readily and inexpensively developed by a variable ratio schedule of positive reinforcement. The possibilities for other areas are limited largely by the creativity of management.

The operant approach also has some additional implications for the use of money as a reward. First, many recent studies have shown money is not as important as other job factors in worker satisfaction. Herzberg, (1968) among others, has said explicitly that money will not promote worker satisfaction. Undoubtedly, in many situations, Herzberg is correct. However, crucial factors of reward contingencies and schedules have not been controlled in these studies. Again, it appears that the important distinction that can be made between Herzberg's motivators and hygiene factors is that the former set of rewards are contingent on an individual's responses and the latter are not. If a work situation were designed so that money was directly contingent on performance, the results might be different. A second point has to do with the perception of money as a reward. Opsahl and Dunnette (1966) have recently questioned pay secrecy policies. They maintained that pay secrecy leads to misperception of the amount of money that a promotion might mean. The value of the reinforcers are underestimated by the participants suggesting that they are less effective than they might otherwise be. Certainly, alternative rewards are likely to be "over chosen." By following policies of pay secrecy, organizations seem to be failing to utilize fully their available monetary rewards.

[1] The author wishes to thank Mr. C. for making this information available and one of his students, Richard Weis, for informing him about this program.

In addition to under utilization of money rewards, organizations seem to be almost totally unaware of alternative reinforcers, and in fact see punishment as the only viable method of control when existing reinforcers fail. What are some alternatives to a punishment centered bureaucracy? Some, such as job design, improved scheduling of reinforcement, and a search for new reinforcers have already been suggested. There are other possible reinforcers, a few of which are discussed below.

The important thing about reinforcers is that they be made immediately contingent on desired performance to the greatest degree possible. The potential reinforcers discussed here also require such a contingent relationship, although developing such relationships may be a severe test of an administrator's creativity. One of the more promising reinforcers is leisure. It would seem possible in many jobs to establish an agreed upon standard output for a day's work. This level could be higher than the current average. Once this amount is reached, the group or individual could be allowed the alternative of going home. The result of experiments in this direction would be interesting to all concerned. Quite possibly, this method might lead to a fuller utilization of our labor force. The individual may be able to hold two four-hour jobs, doubling his current contribution. Such a tremendous increase in output is quite possible as Stagner and Rosen (1966) have noted, when the situation possesses appropriate contingencies. Certainly, the problems of industrial discipline, absenteeism, and grievances which result in lower productivity might be ameliorated. Another possible reinforcer is information. Guetzkow (1965) noted that people have a strong desire to receive communication. Rewarding desired performance with communication or feedback may be a relatively inexpensive reinforcer. Graphs, charts, or even tokens which show immediate and cumulative results may serve this function. Some of the widely accepted benefits from participative management may be due to the reinforcing effect of communication. Certainly the "Hawthorne effect" can be described in these terms. In addition, social approval and status may be powerful reinforcers. Blau's classic study described by Homans (1961) on the exchange of approval and status for help is but one example. People will work for approval and status. If these are made contingent on a desired set of responses, the response rate can be increased. At present, often social approval is given by one's peers, but is contingent on behavior which is in conflict with organizational goals.

In addition to these reinforcers, there are certain social exchange concepts such as justice, equity, reciprocity, and indebtedness which deserve attention. Recent research has demonstrated that an unbalanced social exchange, such as one which is inequitable or leaves one person indebted to someone else, may be tension producing in such a way that individuals work to avoid them. In other words, unbalanced exchanges are a source of punishment. Relationships, such as those involving dependency, which result in such social imbalance can be expected to have the same latent consequences as punishment. Techniques which employ social imbalance to predict and control behavior can be expected to be less efficient in most respects than ones based on positive reinforcement.

The crucial variable in distributing any reward is contingency. Managers have been quick to point out that the problem with a "welfare-state" is that rewards do not depend on desired behavior. This point is well taken. It is surprising that the same point has not been recognized in current management practices.

Organizational Climate and Design

Important aspects of human behavior can be attributed to the immediate environment in which people function. The potential then exists to structure and restructure formal organizations in a manner to promote the desired behavior. Once this point is recognized and accepted by managers, progress can begin. The reaction of managers to this approach is often, "You mean my organization should reward people for what they ought to do anyway?" The answer is that people's behavior is largely determined by its outcomes. It is an empirical fact rather than a moral question. If you want a certain response and it does not occur, you had better change the reinforcement contingencies to increase its probable occurrence.

The first step in the direction of designing organizations on this basis involves defining explicitly the desired behaviors and the available reinforcers. The next step is to then make these rewards dependent on the emission of the desired responses. What are some of the implications of such reasoning for organizational design?

Already the importance of organizational climate has been discussed in connection with human development. Some additional implications merit brief consideration. A major one concerns conformity. Often today the degree to which people conform to a wide variety of norms is lamentably acknowledged and the question is asked, "Why do people do it?" The reasons in the operant view are quite clear: conformity is rewarded, deviance is punished. People conform in organizations because conformity is profitable in terms of the outcomes the individual achieves. In fact, Nord (in press) and Walker and Heyns (1962) presented considerable evidence that conformity has the same properties as other operant responses. If managers are really worried about the costs of conformity in terms of creativity and innovation, they must look for ways to reward deviance, to avoid punishing nonconformity, and to avoid rewarding conformity. Furthermore, the way in which rewards are administered is important. Generally, if rewards are given by a person or group of people, a dependency relationship is created, with hostility, fear, anxiety, and other emotional outcomes being probable. Dependence itself may be a discomforting condition. It is therefore desirable to make the rewards come from the environment. Rewards which have previously been established for reaching certain agreed-upon goals are one such means. Meaningful jobs, in which achievement in itself is rewarding are another way. In general, to the degree that competition is with the environment or forces outside the organization, and rewards come from achievement itself, the more effective the reinforcers are apt to be in achieving desired responses.

A final point concerns the actual operation of organizations. Increasingly it is recognized that a formal organization, which aims at the coordination of the efforts of its participants, is dependent on informal relationships for its operation. As Gross (1968) noted,

> In administration, also, "the play's the thing" and not the script. Many aspects of even the simplest operation can never be expressed in writing. They must be sensed and felt . . . Daily action is the key channel of operational definition. In supplying cues and suggestions, in voicing praise and blame, in issuing verbal instructions, administrators define or clarify operational goals in real life (p.406).

More generally, what makes an organization "tick" is the exchange of reinforcers within it and between it and its environment. The nature of these exchanges involves both economic and social reinforcers. Many of these are given and received without explicit recognition or even awareness on the part of the participants. The operant approach, focuses attention on these exchange processes. As a result, it may prove to be an invaluable asset to both administrators and students of administration and organization.

A final advantage of the operant approach for current organizational theory and analysis may be the attention it focuses on planned and rational administration. Gouldner (1966) noted "Modern organizational analysis by sociologists is overpreoccupied with the spontaneous and unplanned responses which organizations make to stress, and too little concerned with patterns of planned and rational administration (p. 397)." The Skinnerian approach leads to rational planning in order to control outcomes previously viewed as spontaneous consequences. This approach could expand the area of planning and rational action in administration.

BIBLIOGRAPHY

Aldis, O. Of pigeons and men. In R. Ulrich, T. Stachnik and J. Mabry (Eds), *Control of Human Behavior,* Glenview, Ill.: Scott, Foresman, 1966. Pp. 218-221.

Ayllon, T. Intensive treatment of psychotic behavior by stimulus satiation and food reinforcement. In R. Ulrich, T. Stachnik and T. Mabry (Eds), *Control of Human Behavior,* Glenview, Ill.: Scott, Foresman, 1966, 170-176.

Ayllon, T., and Azrin, N. H. The measurement and reinforcement of behavior of psychotics. *Journal of Experimental Analysis of Behavior,* 1965, 8, 357-83.

Bijou S. W., and Baer, D. M. *Child Development.* Vol. 1. New York: Appleton-Century-Crofts, 1961.

Dalton M. The Industrial "rate-buster": a characterization. *Applied Anthropology* 1948, 7, 5-18.

Fleishman, E. A. Leadership climate, human relations training, and supervisory behavior. In *Studies in Personnel and Industrial Psychology.* Homewood, Ill.: Dorsey, 1967, 250-63.

Free records given for E's, pupils report cards improve. *St. Louis Post Dispatch,* December 3, 1967.

Gewirtz. J. L., and Baer, D. M. Deprivation and satiation of social reinforcers as drive conditions. *Journal of Abnormal and Social Psychology,* 1958, 57, 165-172.

Gouldner, A. W. Organizational analysis. In Bennis, W. G., Benne, K. D., and Chin, R. (Eds.), *The Planning of Change,* New York: Holt, Rinehart and Winston, 1966. 393-99.

Gross, B. M. *Organizations and their Managing.* New York: Free Press, 1968.

Guetzkow, H. Communications in Organizations. In March, J. G. (Ed.), *Handbook of Organizations,* Chicago: Rand McNally, 1965. 534-73.

Hamblin, R. L., Bushell, O. B., Buckholdt, D., Ellis D., Ferritor, D., Merritt, G., Pfeiffer, C., Shea, D., and Stoddard, D. Learning, problem children and a social exchange system. Annual Report of the Social Exchange Laboratories, Washington University, and Student Behavior Laboratory, Webster College, St. Louis, Mo. August, 1967.

Herzberg, F. One more time: How do you motivate employees. *Harvard Business Review,* January-February 1968, Pp.53-62.

———*Work and the Nature of Man.* Cleveland: World, 1966.

Homans, G. C. *Social Behavior: Its Elementary Forms.* New York: Harcourt Brace Jovanovich, Inc., 1961.

Hulin, C. L., and Smith, P. A. An empirical investigation of two implications of the two-factor theory of job satisfaction. *Journal of Applied Psychology,* 1967, 51, 396-402.

Lindsay, C. A., Marks, E., and Gorlow, L. The Herzberg theory: a critique and reformulation. *Journal of Applied Psychology,* 1967, 51, 330-39.

Maltzman, I., Simon, S., Roskin, D., and Licht, L. Experimental studies in the training of originality. Psychological Monographs: General and Applied, 1960, 74 (6, Whole No. 493).

Maslow, A. *Eupsychian Management.* Homewood, Ill.: Dorsey, 1965.

McGregor, D. *The Human Side of Enterprise.* New York: McGraw-Hill Book Company, 1960.

McGregor, D. *Leadership and Motivation.* Cambridge, Mass.: M. I. T. Press, 1966.

Nord, W. R. Social exchange theory: an integrative approach to social conformity. *Psychological Bulletin,* (in press).

Northern Systems Company, A proposal to the department of labor for development of a prototype project for the new industries program. Part one.

Opsahl, R. L., and Dunnette, M. D. The role of financial compensation in industrial motivation. *Psychological Bulletin,* 1966, 66, 94-118.

Reese, E. P. *The Analysis of Human Operant Behavior.* Dubuque, Ia.: William C. Brown, 1966.

Roy, D. F. "Banana time"—job satisfaction and informal interaction. In Bennis, W. G., Schein, E. H., Berlew, D. E., and Steele, F. I. (Eds.), *Interpersonal Dynamics.* Homewood, Ill.: Dorsey, 1964, Pp.583-600.

Schultz, D. P. Spontaneous alteration behavior in humans, implications for psychological research. *Psychological Bulletin,* 1964, 62, 394-400.

Skinner, B. F. *Science and Human Behavior,* New York: The MacMillan Company, 1953.

Skinner, B. F. The science of learning and the art of teaching. *Harvard Educational Review,* 1954, 24, 86-97.

Skinner, B. F. *Walden Two.* New York: The MacMillian Company, 1948.

Stagner, R., and Rosen, H. *Psychology of Union-Management Relations.* Belmont, Cal.: Wadsworth, 1966.

Sykes, A. J. M. The effect of a supervisory training course in changing supervisors' perceptions and expectations of the role of management. *Human Relations* 1962, 15, 227-43.

Vinacke, E.W. Motivation as a complex problem. *Nebraska Symposium on Motivation,* 1962, 10, 1-45.

Walker, E. L., and Heyns, R. W. *An Anatomy of Conformity.* Englewood Cliffs, N. J.: Prentice-Hall Inc., 1962.

Wolf, M. M., Risley, T., and Mees, H. Application of operant conditioning procedures to the behavior problems of an autistic child. In R. Ulrich, T. Stachnik and T. Mabry, (Eds.), *Control of Human Behavior.* Glenview, Ill.: Scott, Foresman, 1966, p. 187-93.

chapter 5

Personality, Culture, and Management

Personality development is influenced by interaction among members of a society. This section explores the process by which values and behavioral tendencies are transmitted within a culture. Linton, in the following selection, describes the relationship between personality and culture. One of the major functions of culture, in Linton's view, is the preparation or training of people for social positions, such as work and organizational roles that they will occupy in the future. In this view, culture has broad implications for the management of people in organizations. Nord, in the following selection, explores some of the implications of culture for organizational behavior.

THE CONCEPT OF CULTURE

Linton's (1945) definition of culture as "... the configuration of learned behavior and results of behavior whose component elements are shared and transmitted by the members of a particular society (p.32)," is widely accepted. Importantly, this definition refers only to learned behaviors organized into a patterned whole. In other words, the behaviors in question are acquired and are part of a series of acts related to each other in a recurring way. Further, Linton used "behavior and results of behavior" broadly to include overt behavior (i.e., physical and muscular movements) and covert or psychological behavior (i.e., attitudes, values, and knowledge). Finally, this definition includes only transmitted behaviors which are "shared," (held in common by two or more members of society).

Transmission of behavior

For Linton, imitation was an important source of socialization. Support for this view has come from recent studies which have shown that people learn responses by watching other people interacting with the environment. It is quite likely that much role behavior, such as appropriate work behavior, is learned from observation of the actions of people who play those roles. Thus, much cultural learning may occur vicariously and informally as a result of imitation.[1]

---

1. An excellent discussion of modeling and initative learning can be found in Bandura (1969).

This mode of transmission is central in the view of Linton and other sociologically oriented approaches to personality development.

REFERENCES

Bandura, A. *Principles of Behavior Modification.* New York: Holt, Rinehart and Winston, 1969.

Linton, R. *The Cultural Background of Personality.* New York: Appleton-Century-Crofts, 1945.

Ralph Linton
CULTURE
AND PERSONALITY FORMATION

*   *   *

Our discussion of the possible role of hereditary factors in determining the personality norms for various societies should have made it clear that these factors are quite inadequate to account for many of the observable differences. The only alternative is to assume that such differences are referable to the particular environments within which the members of various societies are reared. As has been pointed out elsewhere, the environmental factors which appear to be most important in connection with personality formation are people and things. The behavior of the members of any society and the forms of most of the objects which they use are largely stereotyped and can be described in terms of culture patterns. When we say that the developing individual's personality is shaped by culture, what we actually mean is that it is shaped by the experience which he derives from his contact with such stereotypes. That it actually is shaped by such contacts to a very large extent will hardly be doubted by anyone familiar with the evidence; however, the literature on the subject seems to have largely ignored one important aspect of the shaping process.

The influences which culture exerts on the developing personality are of two quite different sorts. On the one hand we have those influences which derive from the culturally patterned behavior of other individuals *toward* the child. These begin to operate from the moment of birth and are of paramount importance during infancy. On the other hand we have those influences which derive from the individual's observation of, or instruction in, the patterns of behavior characteristic of his society. Many of these patterns do not affect him directly, but they provide him with models for the development of his own habitual responses to various situations. These influences are unimportant in early infancy but continue to affect him throughout life. The failure to distinguish between these two types of cultural influence has led to a good deal of confusion.

It must be admitted at once that the two types of influence overlap at certain points. Culturally patterned behavior directed toward the child may serve as a model for the development of some of his own behavior patterns. This factor

From THE CULTURAL BACKGROUND OF PERSONALITY by Ralph Linton. Copyright© 1945. Abridged by permission of Appleton-Century-Crofts, Educational Division, Meredith Corporation.

becomes operative as soon as the child is old enough to observe and remember what other people are doing. When, as an adult, he finds himself confronted by the innumerable problems involved in rearing his own children, he turns to these childhood memories for guidance. Thus in almost any American community we find parents sending their children to Sunday School because they themselves were sent to Sunday School. The fact that, as adults, they greatly prefer golf to church attendance does little to weaken the pattern. However, this aspect of any society's patterns for child-rearing is rather incidental to the influence which such patterns exert upon personality formation. At most it insures that children born into a particular society will be reared in much the same way generation after generation. The real importance of the patterns for early care and child training lies in their effects upon the deeper levels of the personalities of individuals reared according to them.

It is generally accepted that the first few years of the individual's life are crucial for the establishment of the highly generalized value-attitude systems which form the deeper levels of personality content. The first realization of this fact came from the study of atypical individuals in our own society and the discovery that certain of their peculiarities seemed to be rather consistently linked with certain sorts of atypical childhood experiences. The extension of personality studies to other societies in which both the normal patterns of child-rearing and the normal personality configurations for adults were different from our own only served to emphasize the importance of very early conditioning. Many of the "normal" aspects of European personalities which were accepted at first as due to instinctive factors are now recognized as results of our own particular patterns of child care. Although study of the relations between various societies' techniques for child-rearing and the basic personality types for adults in these societies has barely begun, we have already reached a point where certain correlations seem to be recognizable. Although a listing of all these correlations is impossible in a discussion as brief as the present one, a few examples may serve for illustration.

In societies in which the culture pattern prescribes absolute obedience from the child to the parent as a prerequisite for rewards of any sort, the normal adult will tend to be a submissive individual, dependent and lacking in initiative. Even though he has largely forgotten the childhood experiences which led to the establishment of these attitudes, his first reaction to any new situation will be to look to someone in authority for support and direction. It is worth noting in this connection that there are many societies in which the patterns of child-rearing are so effective in producing adult personalities of this type that special techniques have been developed for training a few selected individuals for leadership. Thus, among the Tanala of Madagascar, eldest sons are given differential treatment from birth, this treatment being designed to develop initiative and willingness to assume responsibility, while other children are systematically disciplined and repressed. Again, individuals who are reared in very small family groups of our own type have a tendency to focus their emotions and their anticipations of reward or punishment on a few other individuals. In this they are harking back unconsciously to a childhood in which all satisfactions and frustrations derived from their own fathers and mothers. In societies where the child is reared in an extended family environment, with numerous adults about, any one of whom may either reward or punish, the normal personality will tend in the opposite direction. In such societies the average individual is incapable of strong or lasting attachments or hatreds toward particular persons. All personal interactions embody an unconscious attitude of: "Oh well, another will be along presently." It is difficult to conceive of such a society embodying in its culture such patterns as our concepts of romantic love, or of the necessity for finding the one and only partner without whom life will be meaningless.

Such examples could be multiplied indefinitely, but the above will serve to show the sort of correlations which are now emerging from studies of personality and culture. These correlations reflect linkages of a simple and obvious sort, and it is already plain that such one-to-one relationships between cause and effect are in the minority. In most cases we have to deal with complex configurations of child-training patterns which, as a whole, produce complex personality configurations in the adult. Nevertheless, no one who is familiar with the results which have already been obtained can doubt that here lies the key to most of the differences in basic personality type which have hitherto been ascribed to hereditary factors. The "normal" members of different societies owe their varying personality configurations much less to their genes than to their nurseries.

While the culture of any society determines the deeper levels of its members' personalities through the particular techniques of child-rearing to which it subjects them, its influence does not end with this. It goes on to shape the rest of their personalities by providing models for their specific responses as well. This latter process continues throughout life. As the individual matures and then ages, he constantly has to unlearn patterns of response which have ceased to be effective and to learn new ones more appropriate to his current place in the society. At every step in this process, culture serves as a guide. It not only provides him with models for his changing roles but also insures that these roles shall be, on the whole, compatible with his deep seated value-attitude systems. All the patterns within a single culture tend to show a sort of psychological coherence quite aside from their functional interrelations. With rare exceptions, the "normal" individual who adheres to them will not be required to do anything which is incompatible with the deeper levels of his personality structure. Even when one society borrows patterns of behavior from another, these patterns will usually be modified and reworked until they become congruous with the basic personality type of the borrowers. Culture may compel the atypical individual to adhere to forms of behavior which are repugnant to him, but when such behavior is repugnant to the bulk of a society's members, it is culture which has to give way.

Turning to the other side of the picture, the acquisition of new behavior patterns which are congruous with the individual's generalized value-attitude systems tends to reinforce these systems and to establish them more firmly as time passes. The individual who spends his life in any society with a fairly stable culture finds his personality becoming more firmly integrated as he grows older. His adolescent doubts and questionings with respect to the attitudes implicit in his culture disappear as he reaffirms them in his adherence to the overt behavior which his culture prescribes. In time he emerges as a pillar of society, unable to understand how anyone can entertain such doubts. While this process may not make for progress, it certainly makes for individual contentment. The state of such a person is infinitely happier than that of one who finds himself compelled to adhere to patterns of overt behavior which are not congruous with the value-attitude systems established by his earliest experiences. The result of such incongruities can be seen in many individuals who have had to adapt to rapidly changing culture conditions such as those which obtain in our own society. It is even more evident in the case of those who, having begun life in one culture, are attempting to adjust to another. These are the "marginal men" whose plight is recognized by all who have worked with the phenomenon of acculturation. Lacking the reinforcement derived from constant expression in overt behavior, the early-established value-attitude systems of such individuals are weakened and overlaid. At the same time, it seems that they are rarely if ever eliminated, still less replaced by new systems congruous with the cultural milieu in which the individual has to operate. The acculturated individual can learn to act and even to think in terms of his new society's culture, but he cannot learn to feel in these terms. At each point where decision is required he finds himself adrift with no fixed points of reference.

In summary, the fact that personality norms differ for different societies can be explained on the basis of the different experience which the members of such societies acquire from contact with their cultures. In the case of a few small societies whose members have a homogeneous heredity, the influence of physiological factors in determining the psychological potentialities of the majority of these members cannot be ruled out, but the number of such cases is certainly small. Even when common hereditary factors may be present, they can affect only potentialities for response. They are never enough in themselves to account for the differing content and organization which we find in the basic personality types for different societies.

Early in this chapter I cited three conclusions which anthropologists had arrived at as a result of their studies of personality in a wide range of societies and cultures. That personality norms differ for different societies is only the first of these. It is still necessary to explain why the members of any society always show considerable individual variation in personality and also why much the same range of variation and much the same personality types seem to be present in all societies. The first of these problems presents few difficulties. No two individuals, even identical twins, are exactly alike. The members of any society, no matter how closely inbred it may be, differ in their genetically determined potentialities for growth and development. Moreover the working out of these potentialities is affected by all sorts of environmental factors. From the moment of birth on, individuals will differ in size and vigor, while a little later differences in intelligence and learning ability will become apparent. It has already been said that the process of personality formation seems to be mainly one of the integration of experience. This experience, in turn, derives from the interaction of the individual with his environment. It follows that even identical environments, if such things are conceivable, will provide different individuals with different experiences and result in their developing different personalities.

Actually, the situation is much more complicated than this. Even the best-integrated society and culture provides the individuals who are reared in it with environments which are far from uniform. Culture expresses itself to the individual in terms of the behavior of other people and of his contacts with the objects which members of his society habitually make and use. The latter aspect of the cultural environment may be fairly uniform in some of the simpler societies where a combination of general poverty and patterns of sharing prevents the development of marked differences in living standards, but such societies certainly are in the minority. In most communities the various households vary in their equipment and thus provide the children reared in them with somewhat different physical environments. We do not know in how far differences of this sort are significant in personality formation, but everything indicates that they are of rather secondary importance. People have an infinitely greater effect on the developing individual than do things. In particular, the close and continuous contact which the child has with members of his own family, whether parents or siblings, seems to be crucial in establishing his generalized value-attitude systems. Needless to say, the experience which he may derive from such contacts is as varied as the individuals themselves. Even the most rigid culture patterns allow a certain amount of latitude in individual behavior, while the patterns for family relationships can never be too rigid in practice. Someone has said, "Nothing is as continuous as marriage," and the same would apply to parent-child relations. Repeated personal interactions lead to the development of individual patterns of behavior whose range of variation is limited only by fear of what the neighbors may say. Even while acting within the limits imposed by culture, it is possible for parents in any society to be affectionate or indifferent, strict or permissive, sources of aid and security in the child's dealings with outsiders or additional dangers in a generally hostile world. Individual differences and environmental differences can enter into an almost infinite series of permutations and combinations, and the experience which different individuals may derive from these is equally varied. This fact is quite sufficient to account for the differences in personality content which are to be found among the members of any society.

Why much the same range of variation and much the same personality types seem to be present in all societies presents a more difficult problem. Anthropologists themselves are in much less complete agreement on these points than on the preceding ones. Most anthropologists who have had intimate contacts with a number of different societies believe that such is the case, but any real proof or disproof must await the development of much better techniques for personality diagnosis. It must also be understood that when anthropologists say that much the same personality types seem to be present in all societies, in spite of marked differences in their frequencies, the term *personality* is used in a special sense. Most of the specific responses of individuals always fall within the limits set by culture, and it would be too much to expect to find them duplicated in members of different societies. What the anthropologist means is that when one becomes sufficiently familiar with an alien culture and with the individuals who share it, one finds that these individuals are fundamentally the same as various people whom he has known in his own society. While the specific, culturally patterned responses of the two will differ, their abilities and their basic value-attitude systems will be very much the same. This sort of matching does not require any elaborate typing of personalities in technical terms. What it does require is an intimate and sympathetic knowledge of the individuals and cultures involved. One must become exceedingly familiar with the culture of another group before the differences between individual norms of behavior and cultural norms become sufficiently obvious to serve as a guide in judging the deeper levels of individual personalities.

Similarities in the ability levels of members of different societies are not difficult to explain. All human beings are, after all, members of a single species, and the potential range of variations in this respect must be much the same for all societies. Similarities in the generalized value-attitude systems of individuals reared in different cultural environments are more difficult to account for, but there can be no question that they do occur. In the light of our present knowledge the most probable explanation seems to be that they are primarily a result of similar family situations operating upon individuals with similar levels of ability. It has already been noted that culture patterns for the interactions of family members always permit a considerable range of individual variation. In all societies the personalities involved in family situations tend to arrange themselves in much the same orders of dominance and to develop much the same patterns of private, informal interaction. Thus even in the most strongly patriarchal societies one encounters a surprising number of families in which the wife and mother is the dominant member. She may accord her husband exaggerated respect in public, but neither he nor the children will have any doubt as to where real power lies. Again, there are a whole series of biologically conditioned situations which repeat themselves irrespective of the cultural setting. In every society there will be eldest children and youngest children, only children and those reared as members of a large sibling group, feeble, sickly children and strong, vigorous ones. The same thing holds for various sorts of parent-child relationships. There are favorite children, wanted or unwanted children, good sons and black sheep who are constantly subject to suspicion and discipline. Even while operating within the culturally established limits of parental authority, various parents may be affectionate and permissive or take a sadistic delight in exercising their disciplinary functions to the full. Each of these situations will result in a particular sort of early experience for the individual. When essentially similar individuals in different societies are exposed to similar family situations, the result will be a marked similarity in the deeper levels of their personality configurations.

Although the family situations just discussed operate at what might be termed a subcultural level, the frequency with which a particular situation arises in a particular society will be influenced by cultural factors. Thus it is much more difficult for a wife to establish control in a strongly patriarchal society than in a matriarchal one. In the former case she has to work counter to the accepted rules for the marital relationship and to brave all sorts of social pressures. Only a woman of very strong character, or one with a very weak husband, will be able to establish dominance. In the latter case any woman with ordinary strength of character can dominate her household with the aid of social pressures. In every society the bulk of the families will approximate the culturally established norms in their members' interpersonal relationships. It follows that most of the children reared in a particular society will be exposed to similar family situations and will emerge with many elements of even the deeper levels of their personalities in common. This conclusion seems to be borne out by the study of a wide range of societies. In every case numerous correlations can be established between the culture patterns for family organization and child-rearing and the basic personality type for adult members of the society.

In summary, culture must be considered the dominant factor in establishing the basic personality types for various societies and also in establishing the series of status personalities which are characteristic for each society. It must be remembered that basic personality types and status personalities, like culture construct patterns, represent the modes within certain ranges of variation. It is doubtful whether the actual personality of any individual will ever agree at all points with either of these abstractions. With respect to the formation of individual personalities, culture operates as one of a series of factors which also includes the physiologically determined potentialities of the individual and his relations with other individuals. There can be little doubt that in certain cases factors other than the cultural ones are primarily responsible for producing a particular personality configuration. However, it seems that in a majority of cases the cultural factors are dominant. We find that in all societies the personalities of the "average," "normal" individuals who keep the society operating in its accustomed ways can be accounted for in cultural terms. At the same time we find that all societies include atypical individuals whose personalities fall outside the normal range of variation for the society. The causes of such aberrant personalities are still imperfectly understood. They unquestionably derive in part from accidents of early environment and experience. In how far still other, genetically determined factors may be involved we are still unable to say.

In bringing this discussion to a close I am keenly conscious of the number of problems which I have indicated without being able to provide solutions. I am also conscious of the extent to which I have had to depend on techniques which will appear unscientific to those who regard science as something inseparably linked with the laboratory and slide rule. Those who are investigating culture, society and the individual and the complex interrelations of these phenomena are pioneers and, like all pioneers, they have to live by rough and ready methods. They are laboring in the lonely outposts which science has set up on the fringes of a new continent. Even their longest expeditions into the unknown have been mere traverses leaving great unexplored areas between. Those who come after them will be able to draw maps in the terms required by exact science and to exploit riches. The pioneers can only press on, sustained by the belief that somewhere in this vast territory there lies hidden the knowledge which will arm man for his greatest victory, the conquest of himself.

Walter R. Nord

CULTURE
AND
ORGANIZATIONAL BEHAVIOR [1]

Linton (1945) described the influence of culture on personality formation. He emphasized that the shaping of personality promotes the stability of a social system by developing human beings who are compatible with the demands made on them by the role requirements of the social system. Since work roles are an important part of most social systems, one major aspect of the socialization process is the means by which individuals are prepared for functioning in work organizations. To some degree this process determines the types of organizational structure and management which can be effective in any given society.

Often, managers attribute organizational problems to individuals who do not behave in an expected manner. While organizational difficulties do arise from individual personality differences, many difficulties are more a function of differences between classes or large groups of people. The behavior of a member of a particular social class may appear deviant to a manager who is accustomed to dealing with members of a different group. Managers may benefit from concepts which direct their thinking toward behavior common to large groups of people in addition to behavior unique to one or a few individuals. The concepts of culture and subculture may serve this function by helping the manager to recognize sources of problems resulting from variations in social learning among societies or among subgroups within a society. Much training in organizational behavior and management focuses mainly on individuals and small groups. This paper attempts to increase the amount of attention given to larger groups in contemporary training in organizational behavior.

The relevance of culture to organizational behavior is treated in two parts. The first part of the paper reviews some of the effects of culture on the

This paper was prepared especially for this volume.

[1] The helpful comments of Ken Runyon, a doctoral student at Washington University, are gratefully acknowledged.

development and abilities of people. Attention is directed to the implications of culture for international management. The second portion of the paper seeks to show the relevance of the concept for domestic management in our contemporary, complex society. Since the same processes which explain cross-cultural differences operate within our society, it is believed that many of our current problems can best be understood and dealt with in cultural terms.

I–CULTURAL FACTORS AND CROSS–CULTURAL MANAGEMENT

Most people with experience in international management can tell of many incidents documenting the cultural relativity of management practices. These managers find that the role behaviors which are shared and transmitted in our society to prepare people for complex organizations do not take the same form in other cultures. Often, however, problems resulting from cultural factors are not recognized as cultural.

Cultural problems are difficult to diagnose because so many crucial elements are hidden from the participants of the system itself. Often cultural patterns exist as unrecognized assumptions. It is generally only by looking at other cultures that people become aware of having taken their own cultural patterns for granted.

Cultural patterns have many powerful, although often subtle, consequences for organizations. Although broad demographic and geographic factors have important effects, attention here will be primarily limited to the consequences of social learning. Existing research has explored such topics as the effects of culture on perception, use of space in personal interaction, time perspective, attitudes toward authority, organizational structure and process and motivation.

Culture and Perception. Cultural patterns influence the perception of reality. Segall, Campbell, and Herskovits (1966) found that people in different societies are differentially susceptible to certain geometric illusions. For example, people from Western societies are more accustomed than non-Westerners to three-dimensional structures which have straight lines and precise right angles. As a result it could be predicted that Westerners would be more apt to see obtuse angles on a two-dimensional drawing as being extended in space and therefore would mis-estimate the length of lines embedded in such figures. Support for this prediction and similar findings concerning other geometric illusions suggest that different environmental factors may produce experiences and expectations which generate certain distortions in perception.

Other work has shown that language is also an important factor in perception. For example, Carroll and Casagrande (1958) found that language differences between Navajo-dominant and English-dominant Navajo children were associated with perceptual differences. They found that the children who responded in the Navajo language tended to classify objects on the basis of form, whereas the English-speaking Navajo children tended to classify by size and color. The researchers attributed this contrast to the central role played by form and material in the grammatical structure of the Navajo language. Similarly, Whorf

(1947) noted the linguistic determination of conceptual processes. For example, Eskimo languages, which have a relatively large number of words for snow, facilitate the discrimination among types of snow. Similarly, Brown and Lenneberg (1958) concluded that "... languages of the world, like the professional vocabularies within one language, are so many different windows on reality (p.18)." It seems clear that intercultural differences in perception are in part due to differences in how people see the world and which parts of the world they are exposed to.

Culture, Space, and Interaction. Culture also influences the way people use and feel about space. Hall (1959) argued convincingly that in the socialization process people learn many small cues which have significant meaning in a particular context.[2] These cues play the same role as any conditioned stimulus in a classical conditioning situation. They are culture bound, since the associations and feelings they elicit in one culture are not elicited in others.

The use of space affects interaction patterns. One of Hall's examples compared the arrangement of offices in France and the United States. Americans tend to divide space equally among people and to distribute their desks and positions around the wall, leaving the center open for group activities. In contrast, the French are apt to place the key figure in the center and to divide the remaining space unequally. As a result, a newcomer from another culture may perceive his new French peers as hostile, since they may give him a desk crowded in a corner and may not move to give him "equal space." This is but one example of how people coming from another culture may experience feelings of discomfort without awareness of the cultural cause.

Similar discomforts may result from cultural differences in interpersonal distances. For example, Hall noted that the common interaction distance is much smaller in Latin America than it is in the United States. People in Latin America stand closer to each other for a particular type of conversation. Someone from the U.S. may be very uncomfortable talking to Latin Americans, because he may feel that Latin Americans stand "too close" when talking.

Time and Culture. The complex organizations of modern America depend on adherence to precise time schedules. In fact, some observers have suggested that the clock is the most important machine for the existence of complex organizations and industrial societies.

Americans are socialized, usually by their families and school systems, to be very sensitive to time. Such norms about time are not shared by other cultures. Again Hall reported that members of many cultures do not plan or schedule events very far in advance and are much less precise in meeting time deadlines. For example, many people of the Middle East tend to lump all time beyond a week into one undifferentiated category, the future. As a result, they are apt not to keep appointments set too far ahead, much to the dismay of Americans who attempt to plan with them. Similarly, Americans tend to arrive very promptly (i.e., within a few minutes of the hour agreed upon) for an appointment. In

---

[2] Schulman's discussion of channels of communication in Part III of this book treats these cues in more depth.

other cultures it may not be considered impolite to keep someone waiting for hours.

Authority and Culture. Differences in perception and attitudes about authority are other important sources of intercultural variation. The magnitude of these differences can be demonstrated by two examples. First, in Japanese organizations it is looked upon as quite legitimate, and in fact it is expected that members of management will play an active role in the personal life of employees. Obviously, Americans have a narrower definition of appropriate behavior for their organizational superiors.

A second example comes from Miller (1955), who noted that in European cultural traditions power and formal authority tend to be associated with height or elevation. Such associations are related to European religious conceptions, which place supernatural beings above people. Early European visitors to America were struck by what appeared to them to be the lack of authority among Indians known as the Central Algonkians. The deities of these Indians were thought to be on the same level as humans, at the corners of the universe. This religious symbolism was paralleled by an authority structure which differed radically from the European model. In fact, there appeared to be almost no authority structure in the traditional European sense. Miller noted that power in Algonkian society did not descend from a hierarchy but was perceived as being everywhere and equally accessible to all. Furthermore, the possession of power was temporary, being gained and lost through performance. In Algonkian society effort was coordinated without a hierarchy as we know it. Miller observed that coordination was achieved by people doing what was needed without being told, recalling what they had done the year before.

Organizational Structure, Process, and Culture. Differences in attitudes toward authority are often paralleled by contrasts in organizational structure and processes of decision making and communication. Japan provides a useful example. Although Prasad (1968) argued that the Japanese system of industrial organization is becoming somewhat more like our own, the fact remains that Japan developed and maintains a complex industrial system based on management practices which most American managers would brand as inefficient. For example, an employee of a Japanese firm can expect lifetime tenure, wages based on seniority, a great deal of emphasis on loyalty to his employer, and vaguely defined lines of authority and job responsibility. Nevertheless, the success of Japan in building a mighty industrial system in a very short period of time is undisputed. In its cultural context the Japanese style or organization has been an instrument of progress rather than inefficiency.

Emphasis again must be placed on cultural context. As Brown (1969) has pointed out, a variety of factors make the Japanese system functional. For example, the potential costs of incompetence as a result of the permanent employment system are dealt with by a very careful selection system and a relatively early retirement age—55. Furthermore, Brown argued that the communication system, which appears chaotic by our standards, in essence places the decision making in the hands of a qualified few. The real decision making is carried on by an informal process which distributes responsibility almost automatically to employees in proportion to their relevant expertise.[3] The people in the system are acutely sensitive to the behavior and feelings of others, and a very smooth-running, yet informal, system is maintained. To quote Brown,

> To the westerner, the lack of work rules, job analysis, lack of definition of responsibility, etc., are evidence of the Oriental's lack of a sense of individualism. The Japanese approach to the work situation is not only an illustration of a certain degree of individualism but a means of preserving it and developing it. The executives of companies are instinctively aware of this trait. On paper all authority appears to be in their hands, but . . . the trust and approbation of subordinates' collective good sense of initiative is the most accurate delegation of authority possible (p.441).

The process through which decisions are communicated in Japanese organizations has also been baffling to many Western managers. For instance, one American manager in Japan found that many of his Japanese colleagues were so polite in saying "no" that he often thought they were saying "Yes."[4] In this case, the absence of formal procedures and misunderstood personal communication resulted in significant organizational problems. Probably better than any other society, Japan provides a radical demonstration of the relativity of management practices. The European examples which follow, however, show the importance of the relativity concept in more homogeneous cultures.

Widely varied practices of administration and management can thrive in different cultural contexts. From the cross-cultural study of organizations, we may be able to discern some of the essentials of coordination of effort which are hidden from us in our own culture. The writing of Levinson (1968) is extremely informative in this context.

Arguing from a psychonalytical perspective, Levinson discussed the relationship of organizational and cultural practices. He noted that participants' expectations about organizations parallel their early experiences with such power figures as their parents. For example, he observed that there are national commonalities between patterns of parental behavior and attitudes and managerial practices of organizations. Levinson demonstrated this point by comparing the child-rearing practices and typical managerial behavior in Germany, England, and the United States. In Germany, the father is the primary source of socialization. He is generally viewed as being authoritative and directive. Paralleling this parental behavior are authoritarian and directive management practices. In contrast to Germany, in England, where the mother plays a more important role in socialization, management practices are more "feminine." For example, protective arrangements which prevent open

---

[3] It is interesting to note that current management theory stresses allocation of responsibility according to function. In some ways, perhaps we have much to learn from the Japanese system.

[4] The author is indebted to Ken Runyon for this example.

competition are more characteristic of industry in Britain than in other countries.

Levinson extended his analysis to the United States. Socialization practices in the United States are highly child-centered. American children have considerable freedom, and the parental role is often at least partially that of "servant" to the child. American views of government and attitudes toward organizational authority, are consistent with such parental relationships. Levinson noted that the American government is symbolized by a "benign Uncle Sam," who has the role of helping people help themselves. Similarly, other organizations are primarily seen as serving individual interests. This view of organizations, which stresses the value of the individual, helps to explain the emphasis on decentralization and the rapid growth of the human-relations movement in American organizations. Since the parent has the major objective of helping the child grow toward independence, the executive is similarly expected to help the individual grow.

Although Levinson warns that these analogies are only suggestive, they do imply that parental relationships develop attitudes and expectations about a person's future interaction with organizations and sources of power. Observation of family structure may provide valuable insights into the expectations people have of organizations and hence may be a useful guide to people in international management. In fact, a worthwhile training vehicle for managers assigned to posts abroad might be experience with families of the culture to which they will be moving.

Motivation and Culture. One of the most important effects of culture is its influence on individual motivation. Earlier in this book Jackson and Shea discussed achievement motivation and its relationship to behavior in organizations. McClelland (1962) argued that differences in socialization practice between cultures produce national differences in achievement orientation which have consequences for economic growth. He found that increasing themes of achievement motivation in a nation's popular literature are often followed by increases in economic growth.

McClelland's thesis suggests that socialization practices of the family and other institutions differ in the emphases given to independence training. The resulting differences in achievement motivation are in turn reflected in industrial growth rates. People who have a high need for achievement tend to exhibit an affinity for taking personal responsibility for solutions to problems, a desire for concrete feedback, and a tendency to set moderate goals and take calculated risks. These are entrepreneurial characteristics, important ingredients for successful industrialization. Other writers have postulated similar relationships between economic growth and cultural motivation patterns. Best known is Weber's (1930) explanation for the rise of capitalism. He maintained that the value orientation of Protestantism was instrumental in producing behavior conducive to the accumulation of capital necessary for industrial development.

Whyte and Braun (1966) approached the relationship of the socialization process and industrial growth empirically. On the basis of case observations, Whyte and Braun concluded that the school system in nonindustrialized nations produced behavioral characteristics and attitudes incompatible with industrial growth. First of all, the heroes in the texts were military men, who did not model sustained efforts to achieve long-range goals. Second, successful industrial leaders and entrepreneurs were not considered worthy of respect, much less heroic. Third, Whyte and Braun reported that the schools were characterized by autocratic teachers and submissive children. The children were only infrequently rewarded for taking risks. Furthermore, the teachers were reluctant to have the students confront novel situations. In McClelland's terms, independence training was low. The teachers felt that it was unfair to ask students to attempt problems that had not first been explained in depth by the teacher.[5] Finally, the authors found that the teachers used group members to maintain discipline by rewarding the "squealer." One consequence was the students' failure to develop trust of other people, making it very difficult for coordinated effort to exist. In general, Whyte and Braun's data suggested that the models and processes used in education influence the potential for economic growth.

To here, our discussion of cultural effects on motivation has revealed that subtle socialization practices have important consequences for industrial development and organization. Many of these consequences are unintended side effects, some consistent with industrialization as we know it and others making economic development very difficult. In addition, there is some evidence concerning the influence of culture on the motivation patterns of organizational participants.

One of the most widely known studies of the effects of culture on motivation was reported by Haire, Ghiselli, and Porter (1963). Questionnaires were distributed in eleven countries[6] to 2800 managers to survey their views on leadership, management roles and practices, and their own job satisfaction. When asked what they wanted from their jobs, the respondents exhibited marked uniformity across cultural lines. In every case self-actualization needs were deemed the most important. Furthermore, in almost all countries the need for autonomy was second in importance, the need for security was generally third, social needs were generally fourth, and the need for esteem was generally fifth.

These managers from different cultures varied widely, however, in what they thought they were getting from their jobs. Whereas Maslow's hierarchy of needs fits the data quite well for satisfaction in England and the United States, it did not describe the results for other countries. The authors concluded:

> This suggests, perhaps, that the theoretical formulation is especially relevant to the cultural conditions existing in these two English-speaking countries. It also may suggest that industrial and business firms in these two countries have succeeded in satisfying basic needs first and are currently in a position where employees, at least managerial employees,

[5] Whyte and Braun seem to be on the side of many critics of contemporary American education, who contend that, while content is important, it is the way people are taught, the process, the way they "learn how to learn" that influences their ability to deal with problems in the future.

[6] The nations included were Belgium, Denmark, England, France, Germany, Italy, Japan, Norway, Spain, Sweden, and the United States.

are directing their efforts increasingly to each higher step on the scale of need prepotency. In other countries but these two, past conditions in business organizations may not have led to such a systematic, step-by-step fulfillment of needs from most basic to the least basic. In essence, then, this part of the findings for need satisfaction indicates either that the theory of prepotency of needs is particularly well adapted to organizational behavior in the U.S. and England, or that industrial firms in these countries have created conditions to fit the theory (p. 116).

The authors further noted that the similarity in estimates of importance and the wide differences in the degree of need satisfaction suggest that human nature gives rise to universal needs, the satisfaction of which is influenced by the situation. They stated:

There is little evidence here to suggest that the basic motivational equipment with which the manager approaches his job varies from country to country. What does vary is what he finds there (p. 117).[7]

The Haire et al. study reiterates the point that a psychology of individual behavior is not, by itself, an adequate guide for management practice. Each manager must be concerned with situational and cultural variables, which will influence such factors as the degree to which individual needs are satisfied. It is useful, then, to consider management—domestic as well as international—in a cultural context.

IMPLICATIONS OF STUDY OF SUBCULTURES FOR DOMESTIC MANAGEMENT

The study of subcultures may be helpful for domestic management by directing attention to behavior which is shared and transmitted by large groups of people within a complex culture. The term "culture" was advanced by early anthropologists, who dealt primarily with social systems far less complex than contemporary industrialized societies. In the United States it would be very difficult to discover many patterns shared throughout the society. "Modal" personality would be hard to define. Rather, there are many attitudes, values, and behavioral characteristics which are shared within sub-groups of our society. The term "sub-culture" (a culture within a larger culture) provides the advantages of the concept of culture but allows the unit of social analysis to be smaller than the general society. In our society many important sub-cultural distinctions can be made which have direct implications for organizational behavior. A few of these distinctions are treated below, including those based on regional, ethnic, religious, sexual, and occupational differences.[8]

[7] While this statement may appear somewhat inconsistent with McClelland's data, it should be remembered that the study of Haire et. al. deals with managers in highly industrialized nations, where as McClelland seems to be most concerned with distinguishing industrial from nonindustrial nations.

[8] This list is not intended to be comprehensive. Missing are some obvious distinctions which exist on economic, occupational, and other related dimensions commonly considered in studies of social stratification.

Age and Correlates of Age. One of the major divisions in our society today appears to be along age lines. There seems to be little doubt that many younger people share values and behaviors more closely with each other than they do with older people, even their parents. These sub-cultural differences between age groups are a major source of social tension.

Although the reasons for the "generation gap" are much more complex than those mentioned here, the scope of this paper permits only brief comments. Some writers have attributed the gap to such technological changes as the advent of television, which communicates very quickly, making the individual aware of his interdependence with almost all areas of the world. Others, such as Berrelson and Steiner (1967), suggest that differences between generations may result from an interaction of physiological and institutional factors. They quote Washburn as noting,

> Modern medicine and diet have accelerated puberty by about three years over what it was at the beginning of the nineteenth century. On the other hand, social developments have tended to postpone the age at which people take responsible positions. For example, if puberty is at fifteen and a girl is married at seventeen, there is a minimum delay between biology and society. However, if puberty is at twelve and marriage at twenty, the situation is radically different. In terms of college entrance, people tend to enter older but to have grown up younger than formerly and nothing in our system takes account of these facts . . . (p.130).

Generational differences are providing strong challenges to organizations. College administrators and professors are being asked (even coerced) to redefine the substance and process of education. Businessmen are prompted to ask, "Why are young people's feelings about business so different from mine:" [9]

Some of the implications of these differences in attitudes toward business were noted by Webber (1969). Webber's data revealed that contemporary college students admired a person most for his commitment to a cause. In contrast, contemporary executives were most apt to admire a person for his decisiveness. Furthermore, the students wanted business to be more involved in the community, more personal, and interested in societal improvement rather than just personal advancement. Incidentally, these views are not representative of a "radical fringe"; Webber reported that they are shared by master's degree candidates at the Wharton School of Finance and Commerce.

Many observers have noted that today's young people are typically more concerned with personal experience, authentic interpersonal relationships, and the development and enjoyment of their feelings than were youths 10 or 20 years ago. These are important differences. Such values are more apt to produce conflict with than commitment to traditional bureaucratic organizations.

Employees' lack of commitment to organizational goals seems to be a growing problem for management. Part of this problem is attributable to the generational differences under consideration. Managers may find it useful to

[9] Of course, for many the question is phrased in more evaluative terms: "What's wrong with today's youth?"

view the problem in cultural terms. To some degree today's human input comes from a sharply different culture than that of even a few years ago.

Rural v Urban Backgrounds. Subcultures resulting from regional differences, such as rural *v* urban backgrounds, have also been shown to have important consequences for organizations. For example, Dalton (1948) noted certain characteristics of the industrial "rate-buster." Often people who violated group norms against high productivity were from rural backgrounds. By contrast, the non-rate-busters were more apt to have come from urban backgrounds. This cultural interpretation was supported by Turner and Lawrence's (1965) finding that sharply different reactions to job characteristics occurred as a function of the rural-urban variable. Satisfaction for rural workers was associated with more complex or "enriched" jobs, whereas satisfaction for urban workers was more positively related to such job characteristics as repetitiveness. These findings suggest that different types of technology and management strategies might be called for, depending on whether the work force has a predominantly "town" or "city" orientation.

Employing the Culturally Different. Another implication of culture for modern organizations involves the so-called "hard-core unemployed" or "the culturally different." The latter term is preferable for several reasons. First, it is more general. Second, it is more value free. Third, and most significantly, it implies that we must examine the behaviors and values expected of people in modern organizations and compare them with behavior and value patterns of the groups which we are trying to integrate into the work force. Rather than leading into value judgments, such as an approach leads to a focus on both what is desired and what is—and, beyond that, to more fruitful diagnosis and therapy, since it implies accomodation rather than a molding of people.

There are two polar types of therapy: One type emphasizes changing organizational structures; the other stresses changing the people who participate. Often the second approach has been blindly taken, under the assumption that the organization is fixed and that the only therapy is therefore to change the people. A more viable approach is to develop systems which achieve coordination of effort through means which are compatible with the cultural system.

Recently a great deal of attention has been focused on speeding the entry of the culturally different into the work force. Many of these people are known to suffer from disease and deficient nutrition and to have a long history of failure in organizational situations. Further, their socialization experiences have not included contacts with models of "good" work habits and attitudes. In fact, many have a long history of reward for nonwork activities and punishment for attempts to better themselves by conventional means.

Heims (1964), talking particularly of Negroes, suggested some cultural "deprivations" [10] which account for many work-related problems. For example, he noted that Negroes were often said to be uncouth, to be improperly dressed,

---

[10] The quotation marks indicate that these deprivations were not absolute, but rather are relative to what members of the mainstream of the culture would consider normal.

to have limited knowledge, or to be unsophisticated, and so forth. In other words, they differed significantly in their normal behavior from the generally accepted standard of the mainstream of society. In addition they were handicapped by a lack of such basic skills as reading. Heims also suggested some other culturally determined, work-related deprivations. He noted that the social contacts of many Negroes exclude them from the work ethos. As a result they do not learn the work values which the typical American is assumed to acquire in the socialization process. Many black youths may be alienated from certain distinctive ways that factories and offices operate because they do not have the childhood experiences which give them the general atmosphere of daily work and occupational routines. In general, they lack the socialization assumed for most employees.

Staats and Staats (1963) presented a similar argument about reinforcement. They suggested that certain common achievement stimuli are far less reinforcing for lower-class boys than for middle-class boys. Rewards that ordinarily can be counted on to reinforce such achievement behavior as acquiring formal education may not be effective for lower-class boys. Staats and Staats used an operant perspective to provide an additional way of dealing with problems of the culturally different. The factors which constitute effective reward systems differ among cultures. The combination of a cultural perspective and the operant view leads directly to a search for variables in the social system which function as reinforcers.

The cultural view also focuses attention on criteria for entry into organizations. The problems of selection and promotion of culturally different people go far beyond deliberate discrimination. Although intentional discrimination is still an important problem, a great deal of discrimination is very subtle and often may be unrecognized by the organizations involved. The selection process may often screen out valuable human assets on the basis of irrelevant cultural factors.

Selection procedures must be reconsidered in the light of subcultural differences. It is commonly recognized that psychological tests and other selection devices are valid only for populations on which they have been validated. Tests developed for measuring individual mental and psychological differences are apt to be culture bound. Since there are cultural differences within our society, we risk widespread underutilization of human resources unless we follow selection procedures validated on the relevant populations. [11] The potential loss from such discrimination against many minority groups, the sum of unused human resources, is great. However, the potential loss from discrimination against a majority group —women—may be even greater.

Cultural Definition of the Role of Women. In most cultures roles are allocated at least partially on the basis of sex. In our society, despite our rhetoric of equal opportunity and laws against job discrimination on the basis of sex,[12] few

[11] An excellent discussion of job testing and the disadvantage was prepared by the APA Task Force on Employment Testing of Minority Groups (1969).

[12] The first federal government suit aimed at giving women job rights equal to those of men, in compliance with the 1964 Civil Rights Act, was not filed until July, 1970.

managers would maintain that women in fact have equal opportunity for advancement at all levels. It is common in many organizations for someone to say, "Sally sure is an intelligent, capable woman. If she were only a man, she'd be vice president by now." Further, hidden cultural assumptions about what roles and role behaviors are appropriate for females influence the actions of nearly everyone and the consequences of those actions for females. The women's liberation movement is seeking to change the operation of these social forces.[13]

Women comprise an increasing proportion of the work force and a majority of the population. One of the criteria for effectiveness of any social organization is the degree to which it can utilize its resources (human included) to carry on profitable exchanges with its environment. To the degree that socio-cultural factors cause underutilization of the potential of over half of society's human assets, the social system is operating at less than full effectiveness. Furthermore, such a system can be questioned on moral grounds and is certainly prone to latent social tension and mental health problems.

The changing role of women may well turn out to be the most vital social issue of our lifetime. Truly equal job opportunities for women could mean changes in our cultural patterns of childrearing, family structure, power distribution, and organizational management. The concept of culture may be valuable, both to society as a whole and to managers of organizations in particular, for dealing with this cultural change. If nothing else, viewing the role of women in cultural terms may help us to develop an awareness of the assumptions which have heretofore been unrecognized but have had dysfunctional consequences.

CONCLUSIONS

A cultural perspective is a valuable asset to management of human resources. The concept of culture may help a manager to diagnose and deal with classes of human differences both among and within social systems. People differ in important ways as a result of their culture.

The more that managers are aware of the widely shared cultural backgrounds, values, sets of assumptions, and ways of viewing reality which distinguish members of their organizations, the better they are apt to manage.

BIBLIOGRAPHY

Allport, G. W. *Personality: A Psychological Interpretation.* New York: Holt, Rinehart & Winston, 1937.

[13] Many groups in society which are forces for change in other areas have been slow to accept equality for women. For example, some observers have noted that many women in the women's liberation movement were initially active in seeking civil rights for blacks. However, male civil-rights activists refused to accept the women as equals. The resulting feelings of discrimination experienced by the women contributed to their becoming active in women's liberation. Furthermore, the behavior of both black and white male "liberals" who champion the cause of an open society for blacks but either explicitly or implicitly assume that women should play certain roles and not others seems paradoxical.

APA Task Force on Employment Testing of Minority Groups, "Job Testing and the Disadvantages." *American Psychologist* 24 (1969):637-50.

Berrelson, B., and Steiner, G. A. *Human Behavior: Shorter Edition.* New York: Harcourt Brace Jovanovich, Inc., 1967.

Brown, W. Japanese Management: The Cultural Background. *Monumenta Nipponica—Studies in Japanese Culture,* 21:47-60. R. A. Webber, ed., *Culture and Management.* Homewood, Ill,: Richard D. Irwin, Inc., 1969. pp. 428-42.

Brown, R. W., and Lenneberg, E. H. "The Function of Language Classifications in Behavior." In E. E. Maccoby, T. M. Newcomb, and E. L. Hartley, eds., *Readings in Social Psychology.* 3rd ed. New York: Holt, Rinehart & Winston, 1958. pp. 9-18.

Carroll, J. B., and Casagrande, J. B. "The Function of Language Classifications in Behavior." In E. E. Maccoby, T. M. Newcomb, and E. L. Harteley, eds., *Readings in Social Psychology.* 3rd ed. New York: Holt, Rinehart & Winston, 1958. pp.62-112.

Dalton, M. "The Industrial 'Rate-Buster': A Characterization." *Applied Anthropology* 7 (1948):5-18.

DeCharms, R. *Personal Causation.* New York: Academic Press, 1968.

Goffman, E. *Interaction Ritual.* New York: Doubleday & Company, Inc., 1967.

Haire, M., Ghiselli, E., and Porter, L. "Cultural Patterns in the Role of the Manager." *Industrial Relations* 2 (1963): 95-117.

Himes, J.S. "Some Work-Related Cultural Deprivations of Lower-Class Negro Youths." in L. A. Ferman, J. L. Kornbluh, and J. A. Miller, eds., *Negroes and Jobs.* Ann Arbor: University of Michigan Press, 1968. pp. 187-93.

Lazarus, R. S. *Personality and Adjustment.* Englewood Cliffs, N.J.: Prentice-Hall, Inc., 1963.

Levinson, H. *The Exceptional Executive: a Psychological Conception.* Cambridge, Mass.: Harvard University Press, 1968.

Linton, R. *The Cultural Background of Personality.* New York: Appleton-Century-Crofts, 1945.

McClelland, D. "Business Drive and National Achievement." *Harvard Business Review* 40 (July-August, 1962):99-112.

McGregor, D. *The Human Side of Enterprise.* New York: McGraw-Hill Book Company, 1960.

Miller, W. B. "Two Concepts of Authority." *The American Anthropologist.* April, 1955. In N. J. Leavitt, L. R. Pondy, eds., *Readings in Managerial Psychology.* Homewood, Ill,: Richard D. Irwin, Inc., 1964. pp.557-76.

Nord, W. "Industrial and Organizational Conflict in an Industrial Merger." *Midwest Management Conference.* Madison, Wisc.: Academy of Management, 1968. pp.50-66.

Prasad, S. B. "A New System of Authority in Japanese Management." *Journal of Asian and African Studies* 3 (1968):216-25.

Rotter, J. B. "Generalized Expectancies for Internal versus External Control of Reinforcement." *Psychological Monographs* 80 (1966) no. 1.

Segall, M. H., Campbell, D. T., and Herskovits, M. J. *The Influence of Culture on Visual Perception.* Indianapolis: Bobbs-Merrill, 1966.

Staats, A. W., and Staats, C. K. *Complex Human Behavior.* New York: Holt, Rinehart & Winston, 1963.

Turner, A. N., and Lawrence, P. R. *Industrial Jobs and the Worker.* Boston: Harvard University Press, 1965.

Webber, R. A., ed., *Culture and Management,* Homewood, Ill.: Richard D. Irwin, 1969.

Weber, M. *The Protestant Ethic and the Spirit of Capitalism.* London: George Allen & Unwin Ltd., 1930.

Whorf, B. L. "Science and Linguistics." *Technology Review* 44 (1940):229-31, 247, 248.

Whyte, W. F., and Braun, R. R. "Heroes, Homework, and Industrial Growth." *Columbia Journal of World Business* 1 (Spring, 1966):51-57. In R. A. Webber, ed., *Culture and Management.* Homewood, Ill.: Richard D. Irwin, 1969. pp. 286-94.

chapter 6

Psychology, Power, and People: Value Dilemmas in Applied Behavioral Science

While the use of the scientific method to test theories and propositions is central in organizational behavior, knowledge in this field, as in any other, is influenced by value judgments. Every author has certain metaphysics that influence what he will write and perhaps even whether he will write. The earlier papers on perception support the idea that "facts" and data do not describe reality absolutely. Rather, what the viewer brings to the situation contributes a great deal of variance to what he "actually sees." Students of organizational behavior are no exception.

Earlier it was argued that operant conditioning differs from the more humanistic approaches to organizational behavior primarily in its underlying values. One of the most frequently voiced objections to the operant approach is, "It denies individual freedom." This statement reveals some of the metaphysical assumptions of the speaker. He holds a value position, shared by many in our culture, which stresses the dignity and freedom of the individual. This section focuses on the issue of human dignity *v* applied science. It concludes with a debate between two of the foremost contemporary psychologists, B. F. Skinner and Carl Rogers, concerning the issue of control.

Skinner and Rogers focus on some of the basic philosophical issues in the control of human behavior in general. While the importance of their arguments goes far beyond the primary focus of this book, the same issues have been raised repeatedly in the history of the application of scientific knowledge to organizations and people. The issue, simply stated, is, "When does influence and coordination of effort toward common goals become manipulation that violates human dignity?" Closely related is the question, "What is the role of behavioral science in the control of behavior?" Similarly, physical scientists are asked, "What is the responsibility of the scientist for the use of his data?" All of these questions raise important metaphysical issues.

The influence of metaphysics on social science was convincingly argued by Gouldner (1965). He suggested that metaphysics involves a person's ". . . most primitive beliefs and feelings and most general hypotheses about the world (p. 349)." These assumptions influence our theories, without our realizing it. Furthermore, since these assumptions about the total universe were not derived from a systematic sampling of the universe itself, they often introduce unrecognized error. In this sense, metaphysics, like other cultural elements, makes it difficult for a scientist to see and report objectively. To quote Gouldner, these metaphysics "... are all-purpose cognitive tools with which a scholar selects from and creates the particular tools of his specialized craft (p. 350)." Since values and science are inseparably interwoven, the nature of this relationship must be studied. Even though many scientists maintain their work is "value free," this notion of "value free" science is now commonly recognized as a myth.

The atomic bomb brought into sharp focus the notion of the social responsibility of the physical scientist. Many have taken the position that science is objective and that the scientist's role is to study reality and not be any more responsible than any other citizen for how his data are used. Other scientists, such as Bridgman (1948), have argued strongly that scientists are responsible for the uses of scientific discoveries. He stated, "... I believe ... that each and every scientist has a moral obligation to see to it that the uses society makes of scientific discoveries are beneficent (p. 69)." As the social sciences develop, the issue of values and science is apt to be vital, since the subject matter is man himself.

Those who apply social science to organizational behavior have run into the value question head-on. For example, the Hawthorne studies, which will be dealt with in depth in part II, are an important landmark in the development of current thought. As Landsberger (1958) pointed out, these studies have been widely criticized because of value judgments made by the researchers in their *other* writings! Critics have charged that the researchers were anti-union, guilty of introducing manipulation of people into industry, biased in accepting primarily a management view of the worker, and callous in treating the individual more as an object than as a human.

A more comprehensive indictment of the whole field of industrial social science was provided by Baritz (1960). He contended that industrial social scientists, particularly psychologists, have accepted the norms of American managers. Baritz charged that as a consequence social scientists in industry have almost universally avoided dealing with the political and ethical implications of their work. Furthermore, psychologists have at least implicitly, by refusing to take a value stance concerning the uses of their work, accepted management's ends. Baritz charged that most firms have employed social scientists explicitly to increase management's control over people. To him, the types of controls offered by psychologists were extremely dangerous, since they resulted in the manipulation of people without the people being aware of it. Baritz's fear was heightened because, in his view, social scientists were devising increasingly effective means of controlling conduct. Certainly, Baritz is not alone in his fear of such power placed in the hands of managers.

These charges are inconsistent with the explicit aims of many behavioral scientists who see their work as promoting individual growth. Most of the authors cited in this book share a commitment to the democratic values and the respect for individuals which characterize our cultural values. Herzberg, Maslow, McGregor, Maier, Likert, and others are centrally concerned with the individual as a human being, not as a tool for manipulation. Most of them have argued strongly that their techniques and ideas are quite the opposite of manipulation and in fact depend for their success on commitment to a positive view of human nature. Nevertheless, the issue of human dignity and control remains.

The question of behavior control and the role of the social scientist in organizations is apt to become more important in the future. As more managers acquire sophisticated knowledge of behavioral techniques and as more powerful behavioral techniques are developed, the issues will become even more serious. What should be the role of the behavioral scientist in society and in organizations? What is the relationship of applied behavioral science to individual freedom? What is freedom? These are some of the issues that Skinner and Rogers wrestle with in the selection which follows.

REFERENCES

Baritz, L. *The Servants of Power.* Middletown, Conn.: Wesleyan University, 1960.

Bridgman, P. W. "Scientists and Social Responsibility." *Bulletin of the Atomic Scientists,* 4 (March 1948): 69-72.

Gouldner, A. W. *Enter Plato.* New York: Basic Books, 1965.

Landsberger, H. A. *Hawthorne Revisited.* Ithaca, N. Y.: Cornell University, 1958.

Carl R. Rogers
and B.F. Skinner

SOME ISSUES CONCERNING THE CONTROL OF HUMAN BEHAVIOR: A SYMPOSIUM

I [SKINNER]

Science is steadily increasing our power to influence, change, mold—in a word, control-human behavior. It has extended our "understanding" (whatever that may be) so that we deal more successfully with people in nonscientific ways, but it has also identified conditions or variables which can be used to predict and control behavior in a new, and increasingly rigorous, technology. The broad disciplines of government and economics offer examples of this, but there is special cogency in those contributions of anthropology, sociology, and psychology which deal with individual behavior. Carl Rogers has listed some of the achievements to date in a recent paper. (1). Those of his examples which show or imply the control of the single organism are primarily due, as we should expect, to psychology. It is the experimental study of behavior which carries us beyond awkward or inaccessible "principles," "factors," and so on, to variables which can be directly manipulated.

It is also, and for more or less the same reasons, the conception of human behavior emerging from an experimental analysis which most directly challenges traditional views. Psychologists themselves often do not seem to be aware of how far they have moved in this direction. But the change is not passing unnoticed by others. Until only recently it was customary to deny the possibility of a rigorous science of human behavior by arguing, either that a lawful science was impossible because man was a free agent, or that merely statistical predictions would always leave room for personal freedom. But those who used to take this line have become most vociferous in expressing their alarm at the way these obstacles are being surmounted.

Now, the control of human behavior has always been unpopular. Any undisguised effort to control usually arouses emotional reactions. We hesitate to admit, even to ourselves, that we are engaged in control, and we may refuse to control, even when this would be helpful, for fear of criticism. Those who have explicitly avowed an interest in control have been roughly treated by history. Machiavelli is the great prototype. As Macaulay said of him, "Out of his surname

"Some Issues Concerning the Control of Human Behavior: A Symposium, . Rogers, C. R. and Skinner, B. F. *Science* 124: 1057-66, 30 November 1956.

they coined an epithet for a knave and out of his Christian name a synonym for the devil." There were obvious reasons. The control that Machiavelli analyzed and recommended, like most political control, used techniques that were aversive to the controllee. The threats and punishments of the bully, like those of the government operating on the same plan, are not designed—whatever their success—to endear themselves to those who are controlled. Even when the techniques themselves are not aversive, control is usually exercised for the selfish purposes of the controller and, hence, has indirectly punishing effects upon others.

Man's natural inclination to revolt against selfish control has been exploited to good purpose in what we call the philosophy and literature of democracy. The doctrine of the rights of man has been effective in arousing individuals to concerted action against governmental and religious tyranny. The literature which has had this effect has greatly extended the number of terms in our language which express reactions to the control of men. But the ubiquity and ease of expression of this attitude spells trouble for any science which may give birth to a powerful technology of behavior. Intelligent men and women, dominated by the humanistic philosophy of the past two centuries, cannot view with equanimity what Andrew Hacker was called "the specter of predictable man" (2). Even the statistical or actuarial prediction of human events, such as the number of fatalities to be expected on a holiday weekend, strikes many people as uncanny and evil, while the prediction and control of individual behavior is regarded as little less than the work of the devil. I am not so much concerned here with the political or economic consequences for psychology, although research following certain channels may well suffer harmful effects. We ourselves, as intelligent men and women, and as exponents of Western thought, share these attitudes. They have already interfered with the free exercise of a scientific analysis, and their influence threatens to assume more serious proportions

Three broad areas of human behavior supply good examples. The first of these—*personal control*—may be taken to include person-to-person relationships in the family, among friends, in social and work groups, and in counseling and psychotherapy. Other fields are *education* and *government*. A few examples from each will show how nonscientific preconceptions are affecting our current thinking about human behavior.

Personal Control

People living together in groups come to control one another with a technique which is not inappropriately called "ethical." When an individual behaves in a fashion acceptable to the group, he receives admiration, approval, affection, and many other reinforcements which increase the likelihood that he will continue to behave in that fashion. When his behavior is not acceptable, he is criticized, censured, blamed, or otherwise punished. In the first case the group calls him "good"; in the second, "bad." This practice is so thoroughly ingrained in our culture that we often fail to see that it is a technique of control. Yet we are almost always engaged in such control, even though the reinforcements and punishments are often subtle.

The practice of admiration is an important part of a culture, because behavior which is otherwise inclined to be weak can be set up and maintained with its help. The individual is especially likely to be praised, admired, or loved when he acts for the group in the face of great danger, for example, or sacrifices himself or his possessions, or submits to prolonged hardship, or suffers martyrdom. These actions are not admirable in any absolute sense, but they require admiration if they are to be strong. Similarly, we admire people who behave in original or exceptional ways, not because such behavior is itself admirable, but because we do not know how to encourage original or exceptional behavior in any other way. The group acclaims independent, unaided behavior in part because it is easier to reinforce than to help.

As long as this technique of control is misunderstood, we cannot judge correctly an environment in which there is less need for heroism, hardship, or independent action. We are likely to argue that such an environment is itself less admirable or produces less admirable people. In the old days, for example, young scholars often lived in undesirable quarters, ate unappetizing or inadequate food, performed unprofitable tasks for a living or to pay for necessary books and materials or publication. Older scholars and other members of the group offered compensating reinforcement in the form of approval and admiration for these sacrifices. When the modern graduate student receives a generous scholarship, enjoys good living conditions, and has his research and publication subsidized, the grounds for evaluation seem to be pulled from under us. Such a student no longer *needs* admiration to carry him over a series of obstacles (no matter how much he may need it for other reasons), and, in missing certain familiar objects of admiration, we are likely to conclude that such *conditions* are less admirable. Obstacles to scholarly work may serve as a useful measure of motivation—and we may go wrong unless some substitute is found—but we can scarcely defend a deliberate harassment of the student for this purpose. The productivity of any set of conditions can be evaluated only when we have freed ourselves of the attitudes which have been generated in us as members of an ethical group.

A similar difficulty arises from our use of punishment in the form of censure or blame. The concept of responsibility and the related concepts of foreknowledge and choice are used to justify techniques of control using punishment. Was So-and-So aware of the probable consequences of his action, and was the action deliberate? If so, we are justified in punishing him. But what does this mean? It appears to be a question concerning the efficacy of the contingent relations between behavior and punishing consequences. We punish behavior because it is objectionable to us or the group, but in a minor refinement of rather recent origin we have come to withhold punishment when it cannot be expected to have any effect. If the objectionable consequences of an act were accidental and not likely to occur again, there is no point in punishing. We say that the individual was not "aware of the consequences of his action" or that the consequences were not "intentional." If the action could not have been avoided—if the individual "had no choice"—punishment is also withheld if the individual is incapable of being changed by punishment because he is of "unsound mind." In all of these cases—different as they are—the individual is held "not responsible" and goes unpunished.

Just as we say that it is "not fair" to punish a man for something he could not help doing, so we call it "unfair" when one is rewarded beyond his due or for something he could not help doing. In other words, we also object to wasting *reinforcers* where they are not needed or will do no good. We make the same point with the words *just* and *right*. Thus we have no right to punish the irresponsible, and a man has no right to reinforcers he does not earn or deserve. But concepts of choice, responsibility, justice, and so on, provide a most inadequate analysis of efficient reinforcing and punishing contingencies because they carry a heavy semantic cargo of quite different sort, which obscures any attempt to clarify controlling practices or to improve techniques. In particular, they fail to prepare us for techniques based on other than aversive techniques of control. Most people would object to forcing prisoners to serve as subjects of dangerous medical experiments, but few object when they are induced to serve by the offer of return privileges—even when the reinforcing effect of these privileges has been created by forcible deprivation. In the traditional scheme the right to refuse guarantees the individual against coercion or an unfair bargain. But to what extent *can* a prisoner refuse under such circumstances?

We need not go so far afield to make the point. We can observe our own attitude toward personal freedom in the way we resent any interference with what we want to do. Suppose we want to buy a car of a particular sort. Then we may object, for example, if our wife urges us to buy a less expensive model and to put the difference into a new refrigerator. Or we may resent it if our neighbor questions our need for such a car or our ability to pay for it. We would certainly resent it if it were illegal to buy such a car (remember Prohibition); and if we find we cannot actually afford it, we may resent governmental control of the price through tariffs and taxes. We resent it if we discover that we cannot get the car because the manufacturer is holding the model in deliberately short supply in order to push a model we do not want. In all this we assert our democratic right to buy the car of our choice. We are well prepared to do so and to resent any restriction on our freedom.

But why do we not ask *why* it is the car of our choice and resent the forces which made it so? Perhaps our favorite toy as a child was a car, of a very different model, but nevertheless bearing the name of the car we now want. Perhaps our favorite TV program is sponsored by the manufacturer of that car. Perhaps we have seen pictures of many beautiful or prestigeful persons driving it—in pleasant or glamorous places. Perhaps the car has been designed with respect to our motivational patterns: the device on the hood is a phallic symbol; or the horsepower has been stepped up to please our competitive spirit in enabling us to pass other cars swiftly (or, as the advertisements say, "safely"). The concept of freedom that has emerged as part of the cultural practice of our group makes little or no provision for recognizing or dealing with these kinds of control. Concepts like "responsibility" and "rights" are scarcely applicable. We are prepared to deal with coercive measures, but we have no traditional recourse with respect to other measures which in the long run (and especially with the help of science) may be much more powerful and dangerous.

Education

The techniques of education were once frankly aversive. The teacher was usually older and stronger than his pupils and was able to "make them learn." This meant that they were not actually taught but were surrounded by a threatening world from which they could escape only by learning. Usually they were left to their own resources in discovering how to do so. Claude Coleman has published a grimly amusing reminder of these older practices (3). He tells of a schoolteacher who published a careful account of his services during 51 years of teaching, during which he administered: ". . .911,527 blows with a cane; 124,010 with a rod; 20,989 with a ruler; 136,715 with the hand; 10,295 over the mouth; 7,905 boxes on the ear; [and] 1,115,800 slaps on the head. . ."

Progressive education was a humanitarian effort to substitute positive reinforcement for such aversive measures, but in the search for useful human values in the classroom it has never fully replaced the variables it abandoned. Viewed as a branch of behavioral technology, education remains relatively inefficient. We supplement it, and rationalize it, by admiring the pupil who learns for himself; and we often attribute the learning process, or knowledge itself, to something inside the individual. We admire behavior which seems to have inner sources. Thus we admire one who *recites* a poem more than one who simply *reads* it. We admire one who *knows* the answer more than one who *knows where to look it up*. We admire the *writer* rather than the *reader*. We admire the arithmetician who can do a problem in his head rather than with a slide rule or calculating machine, or in "original" ways rather than by a strict application of rules. In general we feel that any aid or "crutch"—except those aids to which we are now thoroughly accustomed—reduces the credit due. In Plato's *Phaedus*, Thamus, the king, attacks the invention of the alphabet on similar grounds! He is afraid "it will produce forgetfulness in the minds of those who learn to use it, because they will not practice their memories. . ." In other words, he holds it more admirable to remember than to use a memorandum. He also objects that pupils "will read many things without instruction. . .[and] will therefore seem to know many things when they are for the most part ignorant." In the same vein we are today sometimes contemptuous of book learning, but, as educators, we can scarcely afford to adopt this view without reservation.

By admiring the student for knowledge and blaming him for ignorance, we escape some of the responsibility of teaching him. We resist any analysis of the educational process which threatens the notion of inner wisdom or questions the contention that the fault of ignorance lies with the student. More powerful techniques which bring about the same changes in behavior by manipulating *external* variables are decried as brainwashing or thought control. We are quite unprepared to judge *effective* educational measures. As long as only a few pupils learn much of what is taught, we do not worry about uniformity or regimentation. We do not fear the feeble technique; but we should view with dismay a system under which every student learned everything listed in a syllabus—although such a condition is far from unthinkable. Similarly, we do not fear a system which is so defective that the student must *work* for an education; but we are loath to give credit for anything learned without effort—although this could well be taken as an ideal result—and we flatly refuse to give credit if the student already knows what a school teaches.

A world in which people are wise and good without trying, without "having to be," without "choosing to be," could conceivably be a far better world for everyone. In such a world we should not have to "give anyone credit"—we should not need to admire anyone—for being wise and good. From our present point of view we cannot believe that such a world would be admirable. We do not even permit ourselves to imagine what it would be like.

Government

Government has always been the special field of aversive control. The state is frequently defined in terms of the power to punish and jurisprudence leans heavily upon the associated notion of personal responsibility. Yet it is becoming increasingly difficult to reconcile current practice and theory with these earlier views. In criminology, for example, there is a strong tendency to drop the notion of responsibility in favor of some such alternative as capacity or controllability. But no matter how strongly the facts, or even practical expedience, support such a change, it is difficult to make the change in a legal system designed on a different plan. When governments resort to other techniques (for example, positive reinforcement), the concept of responsibility is no longer relevant and the theory of government is no longer applicable.

The conflict is illustrated by two decisions of the Supreme Court in the 1930's which dealt with, and disagreed on, the definition of control or coercion (4, p. 233). The Agricultural Adjustment Act proposed that the Secretary of Agriculture make "rental or benefit payments" to those farmers who agreed to reduce production. The government agreed that the Act would be unconstitutional if the farmer had been *compelled* to reduce production but was not, since he was merely *invited* to do so. Justice Roberts (4) expressed the contrary majority view of the court that "The power to confer or withhold unlimited benefits is the power to coerce or destroy." This recognition of positive reinforcement was withdrawn a few years later in another case in which Justice Cardozo (4, p.244) wrote "To hold that motive or temptation is equivalent to coercion is to plunge the law in endless difficulties." We may agree with him, without implying that the proposition is therefore wrong. Sooner or later the law must be prepared to deal with all possible techniques of governmental control.

The uneasiness with which we view government (in the broadest possible sense) when it does not use punishment is shown by the reception of my utopian novel, *Walden Two* (4a). This was essentially a proposal to apply a behavioral technology to the construction of a workable, effective, and productive pattern of government. It was greeted with wrathful violence. Life magazine called it "a travesty on the good life," and "a menace . . . a triumph of mortmain or the dead hand not envisaged since the days of Sparta . . . a slur upon a name, a corruption of an impulse." Joseph Wood Krutch devoted a substantial part of his book, *The Measure of Man* (5), to attacking my views and those of the protagonist, Frazier, in the same vein, and Morris Viteles has recently criticized the book in a similar manner in *Science* (6). Perhaps the reaction is best expressed in a quotation from *The Quest for Utopia* by Negley and Patrick (7):

> Halfway through this contemporary utopia, the reader may feel sure, as we did, that this is a beautifully ironic satire on what has been called 'behavioral engineering.' The longer one stays in this better world of the psychologist, however, the plainer it becomes that the inspiration is not satiric, but messianic. This is indeed the behaviorally engineered society, and while it was to be expected that sooner or later the principle of psychological conditioning would be made the basis of a serious construction of utopia—Brown anticipated it in *Limanora*— yet not even the effective satire of Huxley is adequate preparation for the shocking horror of the idea when positively presented. Of all the dictatorships espoused by utopists, this is the most profound, and incipient dictators might well find in this utopia a guidebook of political practice.

One would scarcely guess that the authors are talking about a world in which there is food, clothing, and shelter for all, where everyone chooses his own work and works on the average only four hours a day, where music and the arts flourish, where personal relationships develop under the most favorable circumstances, where education prepares every child for the social and intellectual life which lies before him, where—in short—people are truly happy, secure, productive, creative, and forward-looking. What is wrong with it? Only one thing: someone "planned it that way." If these critics had come upon a society in some remote corner of the world which boasted similar advantages, they would undoubtedly have hailed it as providing a pattern we all might well follow—provided that it was clearly the result of a natural process of cultural evolution. Any evidence that intelligence had been used in arriving at this version of the good life would, in their eyes, be a serious flaw. No matter if the planner of *Walden Two* diverts none of the proceeds of the community to his own use, no matter if he has no current control or is, indeed, unknown to most of the other members of the community (he planned that, too), somewhere back of it all he occupies the position of prime mover. And this, to the child of the democratic tradition, spoils it all.

The dangers inherent in the control of human behavior are very real. The possibility of the misuse of scientific knowledge must always be faced. We cannot escape by denying the power of a science of behavior or arresting its development. It is no help to cling to familiar philosophies of human behavior simply because they are more reassuring. As I have pointed out elsewhere (8), the new techniques emerging from a science of behavior must be subject to the explicit countercontrol which has already been applied to earlier and cruder forms. Brute force and deception, for example, are now fairly generally suppressed by ethical practices and by explicit governmental and religious agencies. A similar countercontrol of scientific knowledge in the interests of the group is a feasible and promising possibility. Although we cannot say how devious the course of its evolution may be, a cultural pattern of control and countercontrol will presumably emerge which will be most widely supported because it is most widely reinforcing.

If we cannot forsee all the details of this (as we obviously cannot), it is important to remember that this is true of the critics of science as well. The dire consequences of new techniques of control, the hidden menace in original cultural designs—these need some proof. It is only another example of my present point that the need for proof is so often overlooked. Man has got himself into some pretty fixes, and it is easy to believe that he will do so again. But there is a more optimistic possibility. The slow growth of the methods of science, now for the first time being applied to human affairs, *may* mean a new and exciting phase of human life to which historical analogies will not apply and in which earlier political slogans will not be appropriate. If we are to use the knowledge that a science of behavior is now making available with any hope of success, we must look at human nature as it is brought into focus through the methods of science rather than as it has been presented to us in a series of historical accidents.

If the advent of a powerful science of behavior causes trouble, it will not be because science itself is inimical to human welfare but because older conceptions have not yielded easily or gracefully. We expect resistance to new techniques of control from those who have heavy investments in the old, but we have no reason to help them preserve a series of principles that are not ends in themselves but rather outmoded means to an end. What is needed is a new conception of human behavior which is compatible with the implications of a scientific analysis. All men control and are controlled. The question of government in the broadest possible sense is not how freedom is to be preserved but what kinds of control are to be used and to what ends. Control must be analyzed and considered in its proper proportions. No one, I am sure, wishes to develop new master-slave relationships or bend the will of the people to despotic rulers in new ways. These are patterns of control appropriate to a world without science. They may well be the first to go when the experimental analysis of behavior comes into its own in the design of cultural practices.

II[ROGERS]

There are, I believe, a number of matters in connection with this important topic on which the authors of this article, and probably a large majority of psychologists, are in agreement. These matters then are not issues as far as we are concerned, and I should like to mention them briefly in order to put them to one side.

Points of Agreement

I am sure we agree that men—as individuals and as societies—have always endeavored to understand, predict, influence, and control human behavior—their own behavior and that of others.

I believe we agree that the behavioral sciences are making and will continue to make increasingly rapid progress in the understanding of behavior, and that as a consequence the capacity to predict and to control behavior is developing with equal rapidity.

I believe we agree that to deny these advances, or to claim that man's behavior cannot be a field of science, is unrealistic. Even though this is not an issue for us, we should recognize that many intelligent men still hold strongly to the view that the actions of men are free in some sense such that scientific knowledge of man's behavior is impossible. Thus Reinhold Niebuhr, the noted theologian, heaps scorn on the concept of psychology as a science of man's behavior and even says, "In any event, no scientific investigation of past behavior can become the basis of predictions of future behavior" (9). So, while this is not an issue for psychologists, we should at least notice in passing that it is an issue for many people.

I believe we are in agreement that the tremendous potential power of a science which permits the prediction and control of behavior may be misused, and that the possibility of such misuse constitutes a serious threat.

Consequently Skinner and I are in agreement that the whole question of the scientific control of human behavior is a matter with which psychologists and the general public should concern themselves. As Robert Oppenheimer told the American Psychological Association last year (10) the problems that psychologists will pose for society by their growing ability to control behavior will be much more grave than the problems posed by the ability of physicists to control the reactions of matter. I am not sure whether psychologists generally recognize this. My impression is that by and large they hold a laissez-faire attitude. Obviously Skinner and I do not hold this laissez-faire view, or we would not have written this article.

Points at Issue

With these several points of basic and important agreement, are there then any issues that remain on which there are differences? I believe there are. They can be stated very briefly: Who will be controlled? Who will exercise control? What type of control will be exercised? Most important of all, toward what end or what purpose, or in the pursuit of what value, will control be exercised?

It is on questions of this sort that there exist ambiguities, misunderstandings, and probably deep differences. These differences exist among psychologists, among members of the general public in this country, and among various world cultures. Without any hope of achieving a final resolution of these questions, we can, I believe, put these issues in clearer form.

Some Meanings

To avoid ambiguity and faulty communication, I would like to clarify the meanings of some of the terms we are using.

Behavioral science is a term that might be defined from several angles but in the context of this discussion it refers primarily to knowledge that the existence of certain describable conditions in the layman being and/or in his environment is followed by certain describable consequences in his actions.

Prediction means the prior identification of behaviors which then occur. Because it is important in some things I wish to say later, I would point out that one may predict a highly specific behavior, such as an eye blink, or one may predict a class of behaviors. One might correctly predict "avoidant behavior," for example, without being able to specify whether the individual will run away or simply close his eyes.

The word *control* is a very slippery one which can be used with any one of several meanings. I would like to specify three that seem most important for our present purposes. *Control* may mean: (i) The setting of conditions by B for A, A having no voice in the matter, such that certain predictable behaviors then occur in A. I refer to this as external control. (ii) The setting of conditions by B for A, A giving some degree of consent to these conditions, such that certain predictable behaviors then occur in A. I refer to this as the influence of B on A. (iii) The setting of conditions by A such that certain predictable behaviors then occur in himself. I refer to this as internal control. It will be noted that Skinner lumps together the first two meanings, external control and influence, under the concept of control. I find this confusing.

Usual Concept of Control
of Human Behavior

With the underbrush thus cleared away (I hope), let us review very briefly the various elements that are involved in the usual concept of the control of human behavior as mediated by the behavioral sciences. I am drawing here on the previous writings of Skinner, on his present statements, on the writings of others who have considered in either friendly or antagonistic fashion the meanings that would be involved in such control. I have not excluded the science fiction writers, as reported recently by Vandenburg (11), since they often show an awareness of the issues involved, even though the methods described are as yet fictional. These then are the elements that seem common to these different concepts of the application of science to human behavior.

(1) There must first be some sort of decision about goals. Usually desirable goals are assumed, but sometimes, as in George Orwell's book *1984,* the goal that is selected is an aggrandizement of individual power with which most of us would disagree. In a recent paper Skinner suggests that one possible set of goals to be assigned to the behavioral technology is this: "Let men be happy, informed, skillful, well-behaved and productive" (12). In the first draft of his part of this article, which he was kind enough to show me, he did not mention such definite goals as these, but desired "improved" educational practices, "wider" use of knowledge in government, and the like. In the final version of his article he avoids even these value-laden terms, and his implicit goal is the very general one that scientific control of behavior is desirable, because it would perhaps bring "a far better world for everyone."

Thus the first step in thinking about the control of human behavior is the choice of goals, whether specific or general. It is necessary to come to terms in some way with the issue, "For what purpose?"

(2) A second element is that, whether the end selected is highly specific or is a very general one such as wanting "a better world," we proceed by the methods of science to discover the means to these ends. We continue through further experimentation and investigation to discover more effective means. The method of science is self-correcting in thus arriving at increasingly effective ways of achieving the purpose we have in mind.

(3) The third aspect of such control is that as the conditions or methods are discovered by which to reach the goal, some person or some group establishes these conditions and uses these methods, having in one way or another obtained the power to do so.

(4) The fourth element is the exposure of individuals to the prescribed conditions, and this leads, with a high degree of probability, to behavior which is in line with the goals desired. Individuals are now happy, if that has been the goal, or well-behaved, or submissive, or whatever it has been decided to make them.

(5) The fifth element is that if the process I have described is put in motion then there is a continuing social organization which will continue to produce the types of behavior that have been valued.

Some Flaws

Are there any flaws in this way of viewing the control of human behavior? I believe there are. In fact the only element in this description with which I find myself in agreement is the second. It seems to me quite incontrovertibly true that the scientific method is an excellent way to discover the means by which to achieve our goals. Beyond that, I feel many sharp differences, which I will try to spell out.

I believe that in Skinner's presentation here and in his previous writings, there is a serious underestimation of the problem of power. To hope that the power which is being made available by the behavioral sciences will be exercised by the scientists, or by a benevolent group, seems to me a hope little supported by either recent or distant history. It seems far more likely that behavioral scientists, holding their present attitudes, will be in the position of the German rocket scientists specializing in guided missiles. First they worked devotedly for Hitler to destroy the U.S.S.R. and the United States. Now, depending on who captured them, they work devotedly for the U.S.S.R. in the interest of destroying the United States, or devotedly for the United States in the interest of destroying the U.S.S.R. If behavioral scientists are concerned solely with advancing their science, it seems most probable that they will serve the purposes of whatever individual or group has the power.

But the major flaw I see in this review of what is involved in the scientific control of human behavior is the denial, misunderstanding, or gross underestimation of the place of ends, goals or values in their relationship to science. This error (as it seems to me) has so many implications that I would like to devote some space to it.

Ends and Values in Relation to Science

In sharp contradiction to some views that have been advanced, I would like to propose a two-pronged thesis: (i) In any scientific endeavor—whether "pure" or applied science—there is a prior subjective choice of the purpose or value which that scientific work is perceived as serving. (ii) This subjective value choice which brings the scientific endeavor into being must always lie outside of that endeavor and can never become a part of the science involved in that endeavor.

Let me illustrate the first point from Skinner himself. It is clear that in his earlier writing (12) it is recognized that a prior value choice is necessary, and it is specified as the goal that men are to become happy, well-behaved, productive, and so on. I am pleased that Skinner has retreated from the goals he then chose, because to me they seem to be stultifying values. I can only feel that he was choosing these goals for others, not for himself. I would hate to see Skinner become "well-behaved," as that term would be defined for him by behavioral scientists. His recent article in the *American Psychologist* (13) shows that he certainly does not want to be "productive" as that value is defined by most psychologists. And the most awful fate I can imagine for him would be to have him constantly "happy." It is the fact that he is very unhappy about many things which makes me prize him.

In the first draft of his part of this article, he also included such prior value choices, saying for example, "We must decide how we are to use the knowledge which a science of human behavior is now making available." Now he has dropped all mention of such choices, and if I understand him correctly, he believes that science can proceed without them. He has suggested this view in another recent paper, stating that "We must continue to experiment in cultural design ... testing the consequences as we go. Eventually the practices which make for the greatest biological and psychological strength of the group will presumably survive" (8, p. 549).

I would point out, however, that to choose to experiment is a value choice. Even to move in the direction of perfectly random experimentation is a value choice. To test the consequences of an experiment is possible only if we have first made a subjective choice of a criterion value. And implicit in his statement is a valuing of biological and psychological strength. So even when trying to avoid such choice, it seems inescapable that a prior subjective value choice is necessary for any scientific endeavor, or for any application of scientific knowledge.

I wish to make it clear that I am not saying that values cannot be included as a subject of science. It is not true that science deals only with certain classes of "facts" and that these classes do not include values. It is a bit more complex than that, as a simple illustration or two may make clear.

If I value knowledge of the "three R's" as a goal of education, the methods of science can give me increasingly accurate information on how this goal may be achieved. If I value problem-solving ability as a goal of education, the scientific method can give me the same kind of help.

Now, if I wish to determine whether problem-solving ability is "better" than knowledge of the three R's, then scientific method can also study those two values but *only*—and this is very important—in terms of some other value which I have subjectively chosen. I may value college success. Then I can determine whether problem-solving ability or knowledge of the three R's is most closely associated with that value. I may value personal integration or vocational success or responsible citizenship. I can determine whether problems-solving ability or knowledge of the three R's is "better" for achieving any one of these values. But the value or purpose that gives meaning to a particular scientific endeavor must always lie outside of that endeavor.

Although our concern in this symposium is largely with applied science, what I have been saying seems equally true of so-called "pure" science. In pure science the usual prior subjective value choice is the discovery of truth. But this is a subjective choice, and science can never say whether it is the best choice, save in the light of some other value. Geneticists in the U.S.S.R., for example, had to make a subjective choice of whether it was better to pursue truth or to discover facts which upheld a governmental dogma. Which choice is "better"? We could make a scientific investigation of those alternatives but only in the light of some other subjectively chosen value. If, for example, we value the survival of a culture, then we could begin to investigate with the methods of science the question of whether pursuit of truth or support of governmental dogma is most closely associated with cultural survival.

My point then is that any endeavor in science, pure or applied, is carried on in the pursuit of a purpose or value that is subjectively chosen by persons. It is important that this choice be made explicit, since the particular value which is being sought can never be tested or evaluated, confirmed or denied, by the scientific endeavor to which it gives birth. The initial purpose or value always and necessarily lies outside the scope of the scientific effort which it sets in motion.

Among other things this means that if we choose some particular goal or series of goals for human beings and then set out on a large scale to control human behavior to the end of achieving those goals, we are locked in the rigidity of our initial choice, because such a scientific endeavor can never transcend itself to select new goals. Only subjective human persons can do that. Thus if we chose as our goal the state of happiness for human beings (a goal deservedly ridiculed by Aldous Huxley in *Brave New World*), and if we involved all of society in a successful scientific program by which people became happy, we would be locked in a colossal rigidity in which no one would be free to question this goal, because our scientific operations could not transcend themselves to question their guiding purposes. And without laboring this point, I would remark that colossal rigidity, whether in dinosaurs or dictatorships, has a very poor record of evolutionary survival.

If, however, a part of our scheme is to set free some "planners" who do not have to be happy, who are not controlled, and who are therefore free to choose other values, this has several meanings. It means that the purpose we have chosen as our goal is not a sufficient and a satisfying one for human beings but must be supplemented. It also means that if it is necessary to set up an elite group which is free, then this shows all too clearly that the great majority are only the slaves—no matter by what high-sounding name we call them—of those who select the goals.

Perhaps, however, the thought is that a continuing scientific endeavor will evolve its own goals; that the initial findings will alter the directions, and subsequent findings will alter them still further, and that science somehow develops its own purpose. Although he does not clearly say so, this appears to be the pattern Skinner has in mind. It is surely a reasonable description, but it overlooks one element in this continuing development, which is that subjective personal choice enters in at every point at which the direction changes. The findings of a science, the results of an experiment, do not and never can tell us what next scientific purpose to pursue. Even in the purest of science, the scientist must decide what the findings mean and must subjectively choose what next step will be most profitable in the pursuit of his purpose. And if we are speaking of the application of scientific knowledge, then it is distressingly clear that the increasing scientific knowledge of the structure of the atom carries with it no necessary choice as to the purpose to which this knowledge will be put. This is a subjective personal choice which must be made by many individuals.

Thus I return to the proposition with which I began this section of my remarks—and which I now repeat in different words. Science has its meaning as the objective pursuit of a purpose which has been subjectively chosen by a person or persons. This purpose or value can never be investigated by the particular scientific experiment or investigation to which it has given birth and meaning. Consequently, any discussion of the control of human beings by the behavioral sciences must first and most deeply concern itself with the subjectively chosen purposes which such an application of science is intended to implement.

Is the Situation Hopeless?

The thoughtful reader may recognize that, although my remarks up to this point have introduced some modifications in the conception of the processes by which human behavior will be controlled, these remarks may have made such control seem, if anything, even more inevitable. We might sum it up this way: Behavioral science is clearly moving forward; the increasing power for control which it gives will be held by someone or some group; such an individual or group will surely choose the values or goals to be achieved; and most of us will then be increasingly controlled by means so subtle that we will not even be aware of them as controls. Thus, whether a council of wise psychologists (if this is not a contradiction in terms), or a Stalin or a Big Brother has the power, and whether the goal is happiness, or productivity, or resolution of the Oedipus complex, or submission, or love of Big Brother, we will inevitably find ourselves moving toward the chosen goal and probably thinking that we ourselves desire it.

Thus, if this line of reasoning is correct, it appears that some form of *Walden Two* or of *1984* (and at a deep philosophic level they seem indistinguishable) is coming. The fact that it would surely arrive piecemeal, rather than all at once does not greatly change the fundamental issues. In any event, as Skinner has indicated in his writings, we would then look back upon the concepts of human freedom, the capacity for choice, the responsibility for choice, and the worth of the human individual as historical curiosities which once existed by cultural accident as values in a prescientific civilization.

I believe that any person observant of trends must regard something like the foregoing sequence as a real possibility. It is not simply a fantasy. Something of that sort may even be the most likely future. But is it an inevitable future? I want to devote the remainder of my remarks to an alternative possibility.

Alternative Set of Values

Suppose we start with a set of ends, values, purposes, quite different from the type of goals we have been considering. Suppose we do this quite openly, setting them forth as a possible value choice to be accepted or rejected. Suppose we select a set of values that focuses on fluid elements of process rather than static attributes. We might then value: man as a process of becoming, as a process of achieving worth and dignity through the development of his potentialities; the individual human being as a self-actualizing process, moving on to more challenging and enriching experiences; the process by which the individual creatively adapts to an ever-new and changing world; the process by which knowledge transcends itself, as, for example, the theory of relativity transcended Newtonian physics, itself to be transcended in some future day by a new perception.

If we select values such as these we turn to our science and technology of behavior with a very different set of questions. We will want to know such things as these: Can science aid in the discovery of new modes of richly rewarding living? more meaningful and satisfying modes of interpersonal relationships? Can science inform us on how the human race can become a more intelligent participant in its own evolution—its physical, psychological and social evolution? Can science inform us on ways of releasing the creative capacity of individuals, which seem so necessary if we are to survive in this fantastically expanding atomic age? Oppenheimer has pointed out (14) that knowledge, which used to double in millenia or centuries, now doubles in a generation or a decade. It appears that we must discover the utmost in release of creativity if we are to be able to adapt effectively. In short, can science discover the methods by which man can most readily become a continually developing and self-transcending process, in his behavior, his thinking, his knowledge? Can science predict and release an essentially "unpredictable" freedom?

It is one of the virtues of science as a method that it is as able to advance and implement goals and purposes of this sort as it is to serve static values, such as states of being well-informed, happy, obedient. Indeed we have some evidence of this.

Small Example

I will perhaps be forgiven if I document some of the possibilities along this line by turning to psychotherapy, the field I know best.

Psychotherapy, as Meerloo (15) and others have pointed out, can be one of the most subtle tools for the control of A by B. The therapist can subtly mold individuals in imitation of himself. He can cause an individual to become a submissive and conforming being. When certain therapeutic principles are used in extreme fashion, we call it brainwashing, an instance of the disintegration of the personality and a reformulation of the person along lines desired by the controlling individual. So the principles of therapy can be used as an effective means of external control of human personality and behavior. Can psychotherapy be anything else?

Here I find the developments going on in client-centered psychotherapy (16) an exciting hint of what a behavioral science can do in achieving the kinds of values I have stated. Quite aside from being a somewhat new orientation in psychotherapy, this development has important implications regarding the relation of a behavioral science to the control of human behavior. Let me describe our experience as it relates to the issues of this discussion.

In client-centered therapy, we are deeply engaged in the prediction and influencing of behavior, or even the control of behavior. As therapists, we institute certain attitudinal conditions, and the client has relatively little voice in the establishment of these conditions. We predict that if these conditions are instituted, certain behavioral consequences will ensue in the client. Up to this point this is largely external control, no different from what Skinner has described, and no different from what I have discussed in the preceding sections of this article. But here any similarity ceases.

The conditions we have chosen to establish predict such behavioral consequences as these: that the client will become self-directing, less rigid, more open to the evidence of his senses, better organized and integrated, more similar to the ideal which he has chosen for himself. In other words, we have established by external control conditions which we predict will be followed by internal control by the individual, in pursuit of internally chosen goals. We have set the conditions which predict various classes of behaviors—self-directing behaviors, sensitivity to realities within and without, flexible adaptiveness—which are by their very nature unpredictable in their specifics. Our recent research (17) indicates that our predictions are to a significant degree corroborated, and our commitment to the scientific method causes us to believe that more effective means of achieving these goals may be realized.

Research exists in other fields—industry, education, group dynamics—which seems to support our own findings. I believe it may be conservatively stated that scientific progress has been made in identifying those conditions in an interpersonal relationship which, if they exist in B, are followed in A by greater maturity in behavior, less dependence on others, an increase in expressiveness as a person, an increase in variability, flexibility and effectiveness of adaptation, an increase in self-responsibility and self-direction. And, quite in contrast to the concern expressed by some, we do not find that the creatively adaptive behavior which results from such self-directed variability of expression is a "happy accident" which occurs in "chaos." Rather, the individual who is open to his experience, and self-directing, is harmonious not chaotic, ingenious rather than random, as he orders his responses imaginatively toward the achievement of his own purposes. His creative actions are no more a "happy accident" than was Einstein's development of the theory of relativity.

Thus we find ourselves in fundamental agreement with John Dewey's statement: "Science has made its way by releasing, not by suppressing, the elements of variation, of invention and innovation, of novel creation in individuals" (18). Progress in personal life and in group living is, we believe, made in the same way.

Possible Concept of the
Control of Human Behavior

It is quite clear that the point of view I am expressing is in sharp contrast to the usual conception of the relationship of the behavioral sciences to the control of human behavior. In order to make this contrast even more blunt, I will state this possibility in paragraphs parallel to those used before.

(1) It is possible for us to choose to value man as a self-actualizing process of becoming—to value creativity, and the process by which knowledge becomes self-transcending.

(2) We can proceed, by the methods of science, to discover the conditions which necessarily precede these processes and, through continuing experimentation, to discover better means of achieving these purposes.

(3) It is possible for individuals or groups to set these conditions, with a minimum of power or control. According to present knowledge, the only authority necessary is the authority to establish certain qualities of interpersonal relationship.

(4) Exposed to these conditions, present knowledge suggests that individuals become more self-responsible, make progress in self-actualization, become more flexible, and become more creatively adaptive.

(5) Thus such an initial choice would inaugurate the beginnings of a social system or subsystem in which values, knowledge, adaptive skills, and even the concept of science would be continually changing and self-transcending. The emphasis would be upon man as a process of becoming.

I believe it is clear that such a view as I have been describing does not lead to any definable utopia. It would be impossible to predict its final outcome. It involves a step-by-step development, based on a continuing subjective choice of purposes, which are implemented by the behavioral sciences. It is in the direction of the "open society," as that term has been defined by Popper (19), where individuals carry responsibility for personal decisions. It is at the opposite pole from his concept of the closed society, of which *Walden Two* would be an example.

I trust it is also evident that the whole emphasis is on process, not on end-states of being. I am suggesting that it is by choosing to value certain qualitative elements of the process of becoming that we can find a pathway toward the open society.

The Choice

It is my hope that we have helped to clarify the range of choice which will lie before us and our children in regard to the behavioral sciences. We can choose to use our growing knowledge to enslave people in ways never dreamed of before, depersonalizing them, controlling them by means so carefully selected that they will perhaps never be aware of their loss of personhood. We can choose to utilize our scientific knowledge to make men happy, well-behaved, and productive, as Skinner earlier suggested. Or we can insure that each person learns all the syllabus which we select and set before him, as Skinner now suggests. Or at the other end of the spectrum of choice we can choose to use the behavioral sciences in ways which will free, not control; which will bring about constructive variability, not conformity; which will develop creativity, not contentment; which will facilitate each person in his self-directed process of becoming; which will aid individuals, groups, and even the concept of science to become self-transcending in freshly adaptive ways of meeting life and its problems. The choice is up to us, and, the human race being what it is, we are likely to stumble about, making at times some nearly disastrous value choices and at other times highly constructive ones.

I am aware that to some, this setting forth of a choice is unrealistic, because a choice of values is regarded as not possible. Skinner has stated:

> Man's vaunted creative powers . . . his capacity to choose and our right to hold him responsible for his choice—none of these is conspicuous in this new self-portrait (provided by science). Man, we once believed, was free to express himself in art, music, and literature, to inquire into nature, to seek salvation in his own way. He could initiate action and make spontaneous and capricious changes of course. . . . But science insists that action is initiated by forces impinging upon the individual, and that caprice is only another name for behavior for which we have not yet found a cause (12, pp. 52-53).

I can understand this point of view, but I believe that it avoids looking at the great paradox of behavioral science. Behavior, when it is examined scientifically, is surely best understood as determined by prior causation. This is one great fact of science. But responsible personal choice, which is the most essential element in being a person, which is the core experience in psychotherapy, which exists prior to any scientific endeavor, is an equally prominent fact in our lives. To deny the experience of responsible choice is, to me, as restricted a view as to deny the possibility of a behavioral science. That these two important elements of our experience appear to be in contradiction has perhaps the same significance as the contradiction between the wave theory and the corpuscular theory of light, both of which can be shown to be true, even though incompatible. We cannot profitably deny our subjective life, any more than we can deny the objective description of that life.

In conclusion then, it is my contention that science cannot come into being without a personal choice of the values we wish to achieve. And these values we choose to implement will forever lie outside of the science which implements them; the goals we select, the purposes we wish to follow, must always be outside of the science which achieves them. To me this has the encouraging meaning that the human person, with his capacity of subjective choice, can and will always exist, separate from and prior to any of his scientific undertakings. Unless as individuals and groups we choose to relinquish our capacity of subjective choice, we will always remain persons, not simply pawns of a self-created science.

III [SKINNER]

I cannot quite agree that the practice of science *requires* a prior decision about goals or a prior choice of values. The metallurgist can study the properties of steel and the engineer can design a bridge without raising the question of whether a bridge is to be built. But such questions are certainly frequently raised and tentatively answered. Rogers wants to call the answers "subjective choices of values." To me, such an expression suggests that we have had to abandon more rigorous scientific practices in order to talk about our own behavior. In the experimental analysis of other organisms I would use other terms, and I shall try to do so here. Any list of values is a list of reinforcers—conditioned or otherwise. We are so constituted that under certain circumstances food, water, sexual contact, and so on, will make any behavior which produces them more likely to occur again. Other things may acquire this power. We do not need to say that an organism chooses to eat rather than to starve. If you answer that it is a very different thing when a man chooses to starve, I am only too happy to agree. If it were not so, we should have cleared up the question of choice long ago. An organism can be reinforced by—can be made to "choose"—almost any given state of affairs.

Rogers is concerned with choices that involve multiple and usually conflicting consequences. I have dealt with some of these elsewhere (20) in an analysis of self-control. Shall I eat these delicious strawberries today if I will then suffer an annoying rash tomorrow? The decision I am to make used to be assigned to the province of ethics. But we are now studying similar combinations of positive and negative consequences, as well as collateral conditions which affect the result in the laboratory. Even a pigeon can be taught some measure of self-control! And this work helps us to understand the operation of certain formulas—among them value judgments—which folk-wisdom, religion, and psychotherapy have advanced in the interests of self-discipline. The observable effect of any statement of value is to alter the relative effectiveness of reinforcers. We may no longer enjoy the strawberries for thinking about the rash. If rashes are made sufficiently shameful, illegal, sinful, maladjusted, or unwise, we may glow with satisfaction as we push the strawberries aside in a grandiose avoidance response which would bring a smile to the lips of Murray Sidman.

People behave in ways which, as we say, conform to ethical, governmental, or religious patterns because they are reinforced for doing so. The resulting behavior may have far-reaching consequences for the survival of the pattern to which it conforms. And whether we like it or not, survival is the ultimate criterion. This is where, it seems to me, science can help—not in choosing a goal, but in enabling us to predict the survival of mankind. Do not ask me why I want mankind to survive. I can tell you why only in the sense in which the physiologist can tell you why I want to breathe. Once the relation between a given step and the survival of my group has been pointed out, I will take that step. And it is the business of science to point out just such relations.

The values I have occasionally recommended (and Rogers has not led me to recant) are transitional. Other things being equal, I am betting on the group whose practices make for healthy, happy, secure, productive, and creative people. And I insist that the values recommended by Rogers are transitional, too, for I can ask him the same kind of question. Man as a process of becoming—*what?* Self-actualization—for what? Inner control is no more a goal than external.

What Rogers seems to me to be proposing, both here and elsewhere (1), is this: Let us use our increasing power of control to create individuals who will not need and perhaps will no longer respond to control. Let us solve the problem of our power by renouncing it. At first blush this seems as implausible as a benevolent despot. Yet power has occasionally been foresworn. A nation has burned its Reichstag, rich men have given away their wealth, beautiful women have become ugly hermits in the desert, and psychotherapists have become nondirective. When this happens, I look to other possible reinforcements for a plausible explanation. A people relinquish democratic power when a tyrant promises them the earth. Rich men give away wealth to escape the accusing finger of their fellowmen. A woman destroys her beauty in the hope of salvation. And a psychotherapist relinquishes control because he can thus help his client more effectively.

The solution that Rogers is suggesting is thus understandable. But is he correctly interpreting the result? What evidence is there that a client ever becomes truly *self*-directing? What evidence is there that he ever makes a truly *inner* choice of ideal or goal? Even though the therapist does not do the choosing, even though he encourages "self-actualization"—he is not out of control as long as he holds himself ready to step in when occasion demands—when, for example, the client chooses the goal of becoming a more accomplished liar or murdering his boss. But supposing the therapist does withdraw completely or is no longer necessary—what about all the other forces acting upon the client? Is the self-chosen goal independent of his early ethical and religious training? of the folk-wisdom of his group? of the opinions and attitudes of others who are important to him? Surely not. The therapeutic situation is only a small part of the world of the client. From the therapist's point of view it may appear to be possible to relinquish control. But the control passes, not to a "self," but to forces in other parts of the client's world. The solution of the therapist's problem of power cannot be *our* solution, for we must consider *all* the forces acting upon the individual.

The child who must be prodded and nagged is something less than a fully developed human being. We want to see him hurrying to his appointment, not because each step is taken in response to verbal reminders from his mother, but because certain temporal contigencies, in which dawdling has been punished and hurrying reinforced, have worked a change in his behavior. Call this a state of better organization, a greater sensitivity to reality, or what you will. The plain fact is that the child passes from a temporary verbal control exercised by his parents to control by certain inexorable features of the environment. I should suppose that something of the same sort happens in successful psychotherapy. Rogers seems to me to be saying this: Let us put an end, as quickly as possible, to any pattern of master-and-slave, to any direct obedience to command, to the submissive following of suggestions. Let the individual be free to adjust himself to more rewarding features of the world about him. In the end, let his teachers and counselors "wither away," like the Marxist state. I not only agree with this as a useful ideal, I have constructed a fanciful world to demonstrate its advantages. It saddens me to hear Rogers say that "at a deep philosophic level" *Walden Two* and George Orwell's *1984* "seem indistinguishable." They could scarcely be more unlike—at any level. The book *1984* is a picture of immediate aversive control for vicious selfish purposes. The founder of *Walden Two*, on the other hand, has built a community in which neither he nor any other person exerts any *current* control. His achievement lay in his original *plan*, and when he boasts of this ("It is enough to satisfy the thirstiest tyrant") we do not fear him but only pity him for his weakness.

Another critic of *Walden Two*, Andrew Hacker (21), has discussed this point in considering the bearing of mass conditioning upon the liberal notion of autonomous man. In drawing certain parallels between the Grand Inquisition passage in Dostoevsky's *Brothers Karamazov*, Huxley's *Brave New World*, and *Walden Two*, he attempts to set up a distinction to be drawn in any society between conditioners and conditioned. He assumes that "the conditioner can be said to be autonomous in the traditional liberal sense." But then he notes: "Of course the conditioner has been conditioned. But he has not been conditioned by the conscious manipulation of another *person.*" But how does this affect the resulting behavior? Can we not soon forget the origins of the "artificial" diamond which is identical with the real thing? Whether it is an "accidental" cultural pattern, such as is said to have produced the founder of *Walden Two*, or the engineered environment which is about to produce his successors, we are dealing with sets of conditions generating human behavior which will ultimately be measured by their contribution to the future, not the past, for the test of "goodness" or acceptability.

If we are worthy of our democratic heritage we shall, of course, be ready to resist any tyrannical use of science for immediate or selfish purposes. But if we value the achievements and goals of democracy we must not refuse to apply science to the design and construction of cultural patterns, even though we may then find ourselves in some sense in the position of controllers. Fear of control, generalized beyond any warrant, has led to a misinterpretation of valid practices and the blind rejection of intelligent planning for a better way of life. In terms which I trust Rogers will approve, in conquering this fear we shall become more mature and better organized and shall, thus, more fully actualize ourselves as human beings.

BIBLIOGRAPHY

1. C.R. Rogers, *Teachers College Record 57*, 316. (1956).
2. A. Hacker, *Antioch Rev.* 14, 195 (1954).
3. C. Coleman, *Bull. Am. Assoc. Univ. Professors* 39, 457, (1953).
4. P. A. Freund et al., *Constitutional Law: Cases and Other Problems*, vol. 1 (Little, Brown, Boston, 1954).
4a. B. F. Skinner, *Walden Two*, (Macmillan, New York, 1948).
5. J. W. Krutch, *The Measure of Man* (Bobbs-Merrill, Indianapolis, 1953).
6. M. Viteles, *Science* 122 1167 (1955).
7. G. Negley and J. M. Patrick, *The Quest for Utopia* (Schuman, New York: 1952):
8. B.F. Skinner, *Trans. N. Y. Acad. Sci.* 17, 547 (1955).
9. R. Niebuhr, *The Self and the Dramas of History* (Scribner, New York: 1955), p. 47.
10. R. Oppenheimer, *Am. Psychol. 11, 127 (1956)*.
11. S.G. Vandenberg, *ibid* 11, 339 (1956).
12. B.F. Skinner, *Am. Scholar* 25, 47 (1955-56).
13. —— *Am. Psychol.* 11, 221 (1956).
14. R. Oppenheimer, *Roosevelt University Occasional Papers* 2 (1956)
15. J.A.M. Meerloo, *J. Nervous Mental Disease 122, 353 (1955)*.
16. C.R. Rogers, *Client-Centered Therapy* (Houghton-Mifflin, Boston: 1951).
17. —— and R. Dymond, Eds. *Psychotherapy and Personality Change* (Univ. of Chicago Press, Chicago, 1954).
18. J. Ratner, Ed., *Intelligence in the Modern World: John Dewey's Philosophy* (Modern Library, New York, 1939), p. 359.
19. K. R. Popper, *The Open Society and Its Enemies* (Rutledge and Kegan Paul, London: 1945).
20. B. F. Skinner, *Science and Human Behavior* (Macmillan, New York; 1953).
21. A Hacker, *J. Politics* 17 590 (1955).

part 2

FORMAL ORGANIZATIONS IN THEORY AND PRACTICE

C. Wright Mills in *The Power Elite* quotes a statement by Mr. John L. McCaffrey, the chief executive of International Harvester, "The biggest trouble with industry is that it is full of human beings . . . (p. 135)". Part 1 of this book centered around what is known about how and why individuals behave. Most of the selections agreed that a significant portion of the variance in individual behavior is attributable to environmental factors.

Formal organizations create a multitude of environmental conditions which have important consequences for individual participants. As Mr. McCaffrey's statement implies, the behavior of participants is often detrimental to the realization of organizational goals. His diagnosis is basically psychological; directing attention to changes in individuals that might improve organizational effectiveness. However, a second view must be noted. An alternative, sociological diagnosis directs attention to properties of a social system that evoke various behavior patterns. It states, "The trouble with individuals is that they must function in formal organizations." Perrow (1970) introduces his exposition of the sociological view by noting certain "prejudices" in the field of organizational behavior.

The most important prejudice . . . is that organizational problems are people problems, and that good leadership is the answer. The second, minor prejudice is that current work in psychology, social psychology, and sociology has demolished classical management theory and replaced it with new and true principles. I try to show that many people problems and leadership problems are really due to organizational structure and that while classical management theory is quite deficient, it does deal with important problems that the other approaches neglect (p. viii-ix).

The psychological and sociological diagnoses are complementary rather than mutually exclusive. Individuals, in attempting to satisfy their needs, often follow paths other than those expected by the organization's planners and directors. The readings in part 1 suggest that the choice of paths is "psychologically lawful" and, to some degree, can be predicted and controlled by environmental forces. Part 2 focuses on formal organization as a means for coordination of individual behavior.

An organization's performance is affected by the complex interaction of many forces originating inside and outside its boundaries. Economic, cultural, psychological, sociological, technological, and historical factors form only a partial list of the variables. The only way for both managers and students of organizations to deal adequately with this complexity is to view organizations as social systems.

THE STUDY OF FORMAL ORGANIZATIONS PAST AND PRESENT

Formal organizations hold a position of central importance in the life of almost every American. The United States has long been characterized as a society which stresses formal organizations, and Americans have pioneered in the theory and practice of management. Most members of our society are familiar with many concepts and principles of organization management. Line-staff, organization charts, authority, job descriptions, and span of control are almost everyday phrases to many organizational participants.

The foregoing terms are characteristic of classical management or organization theory which emphasizes "action-oriented" principles appropriate for structuring and administering an organization. As numerous writers have pointed out, a major shortcoming of classical theory was its tendency to deal with the human factor only through implicit assumptions. Recent work has attempted to compensate for this lacuna in classical thought by stressing social and psychological variables. However, the newer approach may have made an equally serious omission. The so-called "human relations school," in stressing the human factor, makes implicit, simplified assumptions about technological and structural considerations. More recently, integrative approaches have evolved which seek to encompass the dynamic interaction of people, culture, structure, technology, and tasks.

Unfortunately, popular knowledge about organization theory seems to be based heavily on classical theory and only to a limited extent on the more recent trends. The thinking of beginning students in organizational behavior often reflects these popular notions. Therefore, as Gross (1968) has suggested, the training of administrators often needs to begin with unlearning.

The modern view is well summarized by Leavitt (1964), who suggested that organizations can be understood in terms of the interaction of the task, structure, technology, and people. Levels and changes in levels of any of these four variables have potential consequences for the other three. Although Leavitt's model does not explicitly show the important interaction between an organization and the larger social system, it does describe how people, technology, a task or problem, and structure are dynamically related within an organization. However, a more complete view is provided by an "open systems" model, which would focus attention on the dynamic interaction of the organizational elements with the environment.[1] Leavitt's model and the readings in this section should help the student see both the limits of classical theory and its relationship to modern theory.[2]

The role of goals deserves more specific attention than is suggested by the simple summary of Leavitt's model. Perrow (1970) demonstrated how goals can be an important independent variable. For example, envision two companies in the textile business. Company A places heavy emphasis on maximizing profit, whereas Company B places considerable importance on being a leader in introducing new fabrics. This difference in goals is apt to be associated—and maybe causative of—important differences between the two organizations. If the original goals are subsequently modified, vestiges of the differences can still be observed long afterward.

We have said that formal organizations are characterized by a deliberately planned structure and specifically stated goals. These two factors may make formal organizations more difficult to understand than other social systems. However, formal organizations do foster more homogeneous and predictable behavior on the part of their participants, making them easier to study than most other forms of social organization. Researchers have taken advantage of these fortunate circumstances, and a substantial amount of empirical data has been published about the behavior of people in formal organizations. This research is practically and theoretically important. The study of organizations is both a part of general social and psychological theory and a distinct field in and of itself.

The readings which follow introduce the student to the rapidly growing literature of formal organizations. Emphasis is given to the sociological view; the major focus is on properties of social systems as independent variables. However, as will be seen in the readings themselves, the nature of the topic precludes exclusive emphasis on any one discipline.

Part 2 is divided into two chapters. The first chapter reviews the history of organizational study. The second chapter stresses the unanticipated consequences which an organization generates and documents these outcomes with examples of conflicts and tensions from the study of formal organizations.

REFERENCES

Gross, B. M. *Organizations and Their Managing.* Ney York: Free Press, 1968.

Leavitt, H. J. *Managerial Psychology.* Rev. ed. Chicago: University of Chicago Press, 1964.

1. The work of Lawrence and Lorsch (1967) on the organization-environment interface is exceptionally helpful.
2. Missing from this discussion is the important work of Woodward (1965), which is fully treated by Dubin in the section on leadership in Part 3.

Lawrence, P., and J. Lorsch, *Organization and Enviroment: Managing Differentiation and Integration.* Boston: Division of Research, Harvard Business School, 1967.

Mills, C. W. *The Power Elite.* New York: Oxford University Press, 1959.

Perrow, C. *Organizational Analysis: A Sociological View.* Belmont, Calif.: Wadsworth, 1970.

Woodward, J. *Industrial Organization.* London: Oxford University Press, 1965.

chapter 7

Formal Introduction
And Theory

This chapter introduces some of the primary trends in the study of organizations. Some of the conflicts among approaches have their roots in what was taken as problematic and what was assumed by various scholars. The first selection explores a variety of contrasting approaches. Scott takes the reader on a well-planned, concise, and clearly narrated tour through the literature of modern organization theory, ending with a description of the state of existing knowledge and unresolved questions for the future.

The next two articles deal with the Hawthorne studies, which have proven to be the most important research in the history of organizational behavior. As Homans points out, these studies grew out of research designed to test the influence of light intensity on output. Thus, in a sense, the Hawthorne studies developed from an attempt to test ideas suggested by the "scientific management" approach of Frederick W. Taylor and his followers. It is commonly believed that the Hawthorne research "discovered" the informal work group which Taylor supposedly neglected. However, Taylor was very aware of informal groups and their restriction of output; much of his work was intended to overcome this phenomenon, which he called "soldiering." While the Hawthorne studies demonstrated many things about the behavior of people in formal organizations, they did not "discover" informal groups. They did emphasize problems which had received little systematic attention in the literature and practice of management. They were a major stimulus to the widespread introduction of human relations, counseling, and social-psychological awareness in management. To many, the Hawthorne studies demonstrate the efficacy of considerate, democratic, or humanistic management.

Carey's paper challenges the conclusions of the Hawthorne researchers by re-examining their data. Carey was not the first to question the Hawthorne studies, but most of the other attacks have been more concerned with the values and assumptions of the researchers than with the data. Carey's paper can not take away from the historical importance of the Hawthorne research; it does, however, demonstrate that one of the foundation studies of the whole field of organizational behavior is open to dispute.

William G. Scott

ORGANIZATION THEORY: AN OVERVIEW AND AN APPRAISAL

Man is intent on drawing himself into a web of collectivized patterns. "Modern man has learned to accommodate himself to a world increasingly organized. The trend toward ever more explicit and consciously drawn relationships is profound and sweeping; it is marked by depth no less than by extension."[1] This comment by Seidenberg nicely summarizes the pervasive influence of organization in many forms of human activity.

Some of the reasons for intense organizational activity are found in the fundamental transitions which revolutionized our society, changing it from a rural culture, to a culture based on technology, industry, and the city. From these changes, a way of life emerged characterized by the *proximity* and *dependency* of people on each other. Proximity and dependency, as conditions of social life, harbor the threats of human conflict, capricious antisocial behavior, instability of human relationships, and uncertainty about the nature of the social structure with its concomitant roles.

Of course, these threats to social integrity are present to some degree in all societies, ranging from the primitive to the modern. But, these threats become dangerous when the harmonious functioning of a society rests on the maintenance of a highly intricate, delicately balanced form of human collaboration. The civilization we have created depends on the preservation of a precarious balance. Hence, disrupting forces impinging on this shaky form of collaboration must be eliminated or minimized.

Traditionally, organization is viewed as a vehicle for accomplishing goals and objectives. While this approach is useful, it tends to obscure the inner workings and internal purposes of organization itself. Another fruitful way of treating organization is as a mechanism having the ultimate purpose of offsetting those forces which undermine human collaboration. In this sense, organization tends to minimize conflict, and to lessen the significance of individual behavior which deviates from values that the organization has established as worthwhile. Further, organization increases stability in human relationships by reducing

From William G. Scott, "Organization Theory: An Overview and an Appraisal," *Academy of Management Journal* 4 (April, 1961): 7-26. Reprinted by permission.

[1] Roderick Seidenburg, *Post Historic Man* (Boston: Beacon Press, 1951), p. 1.

uncertainty regarding the nature of the system's structure and the human roles which are inherent to it. Corollary to this point, organization enhances the predictability of human action, because it limits the number of behavioral alternatives alailable to an individual. As Presthus points out:

> Organization is defined as a system of structural interpersonal relations . . . individuals are differentiated in terms of authority, status, and role with the result that personal interaction is prescribed . . . Anticipated reactions tend to occur, while ambiguity and spontaneity are decreased.[2]

In addition to all of this, organization has built-in safeguards. Besides prescribing acceptable forms of behavior for those who elect to submit to it, organization is also able to counterbalance the influence of human action which transcends its established patterns.[3]

Few segments of society have engaged in organizing more intensively than business.[4] The reason is clear. Business depends on what organization offers. Business needs a system of relationships among functions; it needs stability, continuity, and predictability in its internal activities and external contacts. Business also appears to need harmonious relationships among the people and processes which make it up. Put another way, a business organization has to be free, relatively, from destructive tendencies which may be caused by divergent interests.

As a foundation for meeting these needs rests administrative science. A major element of this science is organization theory, which provides the grounds for management activities in a number of significant areas of business endeavor. Organization theory, however, is not a homogeneous science based on generally accepted principles. Various theories of organization have been, and are being evolved. For example, something called "modern organization theory" has recently emerged, raising the wrath of some traditionalists, but also capturing the imagination of a rather elite avant-garde.

The thesis of this paper is that modern organization theory, when stripped of its irrelevancies, redundancies, and "speech defects," is a logical and vital evolution in management thought. In order for this thesis to be supported, the reader must endure a review and appraisal of more traditional forms of organization theory which may seem elementary to him.

In any event, three theories of organization are having considerable influence on management thought and practice. They are arbitrarily labeled in this paper

---

[2] Robert V. Presthus, "Toward a Theory of Organizational Behavior," *Administrative Science Quarterly,* June, 1958, p. 50.

[3] Regulation and predictability of human behavior are matters of degree varying with different organizations on something of a continuum. At one extreme are bureaucratic-type organizations with tight bonds of regulation. At the other extreme are voluntary associations, and informal organizations with relatively loose bonds of regulation.

This point has an interesting sidelight. A bureaucracy with tight controls and a high degree of predictability of human action appears to be unable to distinguish between destructive and creative deviations from established values. Thus the only thing which is safeguarded is the *status quo.*

[4] The monolithic institutions of the military and government are other cases of organizational preoccupation.

as the classical, the neoclassical, and the modern. Each of these is fairly distinct; but they are not unrelated. Also, these theories are on-going, being actively supported by several schools of management thought.

THE CLASSICAL DOCTRINE

For lack of better method of identification, it will be said that the classical doctrine deals almost exclusively with the *anatomy of formal organization.* This doctrine can be traced back to Frederick W. Taylor's interest in functional foremanship and planning staffs. But most students of management thought would agree that in the United States, the first systematic approach to organization, and the first comprehensive attempt to find organizational universals, is dated 1931 when Mooney and Reiley published *Onward Industry.*[5] Subsequently, numerous books, following the classical vein, have appeared. Two of the more recent are Brech's *Organization*[6] and Allen's *Management and Organization.*[7]

Classical organization theory is built around four key pillars. They are the division of labor, the scalar and functional processes, structure, and span of control. Given these major elements just about all of classical organization theory can be derived.

(1). The *division of labor* is without doubt the cornerstone among the four elements.[8] From it the other elements flow as corollaries. For example, *scalar* and *functional* growth requires specialization and departmentalization of functions. Organization *structure* is naturally dependent upon the direction which specialization of activities travels in company development. Finally, *span of control* problems result from the number of specialized functions under the jurisdiction of a manager.

(2). The *scalar and functional processes* deal with the vertical and horizontal growth of the organization, respectively.[9] The scalar process refers to the growth of the chain of command, the delegation of authority and responsibility, unity of command, and the obligation to report.

The division of the organization into specialized parts and the regrouping of the parts into compatible units are matters pertaining to the functional process. This process focuses on the horizontal evolution of the line and staff in a formal organization.

---

[5] James D. Mooney and Alan C. Reiley, *Onward Industry* (New York: Harper & Row, Publishers, 1931). Later published by James D. Mooney under the title *Principles of Organization.*

[6] E.F.L. Brech, *Organization* (London: Longmans, Green and Company, 1957).

[7] Louis A. Allen, *Management and Organization* (New York: McGraw-Hill Book Company, 1958).

[8] Usually the division of labor is treated under a topical heading of departmentation, see for example: Harold Koontz and Cyril O'Donnell, *Principles of Management* (New York: McGraw-Hill Book Company, 1959), Chapter 7.

[9] These processes are discussed at length in Ralph Currier Davis, *The Fundamentals of Top Management* (New York: Harper & Row, Publishers, 1951), Chapter 7.

(3). *Structure* is the logical relationship of functions in an organization, arranged to accomplish the objectives of the company efficiently. Structure implies system and pattern. Classical organization theory usually works with two basic structures, the line and the staff. However, such activities as committee and liaison functions fall quite readily into the purview of structural considerations. Again, structure is the vehicle for introducing logical and consistent relationships among the diverse functions which comprise the organization.[10]

(4). The *span of control* concept relates to the number of subordinates a manager can effectively supervise. Graicunas has been credited with first elaborating the point that there are numerical limitations to the subordinates one man can control.[11] In a recent statement on the subject, Brech points out, "span" refers to " . . . the number of persons, themselves carrying managerial and supervisory responsibilities, for whom the senior manager retains his over-embracing responsibility of direction and planning, coordination, motivation, and control."[12] Regardless of interpretation, span of control has significance, in part, for the shape of the organization which evolves through growth. Wide span yields a flat structure; short span results in a tall structure. Further, the span concept directs attention to the complexity of human and functional interrelationships in an organization.

It would not be fair to say that the classical school is unaware of the day-to-day administrative problems of the organization. Paramount among these problems are those stemming from human interactions. But the interplay of individual personality, formal groups, intraorganizational conflict, and the decision-making processes in the formal structure appears largely to be neglected by classical organization theory. Additionally, the classical theory overlooks the contributions of the behavioral sciences by failing to incorporate them in its doctrine in any systematic way. In summary, classical organization theory has relevant insights into the nature of organization, but the value of this theory is limited by its narrow concentration on the formal anatomy of organization.

NEOCLASSICAL THEORY OF ORGANIZATION

The neoclassical theory of organization embarked on the task of compensating for some of the deficiencies in classical doctrine. The neoclassical school is commonly identified with the human relations movement. Generally, the neoclassical approach takes the postulates of the classical school, regarding the pillars of organization as givens. But these postulates are regarded as modified by people, acting independently or within the context of the informal organization.

One of the main contributions of the neoclassical school is the introduction of behavioral sciences in an integrated fashion into the theory of organization.

[10] For a discussion of structure see: William H. Newman, *Administrative Action* (Englewood Cliffs: Prentice-Hall, Inc., 1951), Chapter 16.
[11] V.A. Graicunas, "Relationships in Organization," *Papers on the Science of Administration* (New York: Columbia University Press, 1937).
[12] Brech, op. cit. p. 78.

Through the use of these sciences, the human relationists demonstrate how the pillars of the classical doctrine are affected by the impact of human actions. Further, the neoclassical approach includes a systematic treatment of the informal organization, showing its influence on the formal structure.

Thus, the neoclassical approach to organization theory gives evidence of accepting classical doctrine, but superimposing on it modifications resulting from individual behavior, and the influence of the informal group. The inspiration of the neoclassical school were the Hawthorne studies.[13] Current examples of the neoclassical approach are found in human relations books like Gardner and Moore, *Human Relations in Industry,*[14] and Davis, *Human Relations in Business.*[15] To a more limited extent, work in industrial sociology also reflects a neoclassical point of view.[16]

It would be useful to look briefly at some of the contributions made to organization theory by the neoclassicists. First to be considered are modifications of the pillars of classical doctrine; second is the informal organization.

Examples of the Neoclassical Approach to the Pillars of Formal Organization Theory

(1). The *division of labor* has been a long standing subject of comment in the field of human relations. Very early in the history of industrial psychology study was made of industrial fatigue and monotony caused by the specialization of the work.[17] Later, attention shifted to the isolation of the worker, and his feeling of anonymity resulting from insignificant jobs which contributed negligibly to the final product.[18]

Also, specialization influences the work of management. As an organization expands, the need concomitantly arises for managerical motivation and coordination of the activities of others. Both motivation and coordination in turn relate to executive leadership. Thus, in part, stemming from the growth of industrial specialization, the neoclassical school has developed a large body of theory relating to motivation, coordination, and leadership. Much of this theory is derived from the social sciences.

(2). Two aspects of the *scalar and functional* processes which have been treated with some degree of intensity by the neoclassical school are the delegation of authority and responsibility, and gaps in or overlapping of

[13] See F. J. Roethlisberger and William J. Dickson, *Management and the Worker* (Cambridge: Harvard University Press, 1939).

[14] Burleigh B. Gardner and David G. Moore, *Human Relations in Industry* (Homewood, Ill.: Richard D. Irwin, Inc., 1955).

[15] Keith Davis, *Human Relations in Business* (New York: McGraw-Hill Book Company, 1957).

[16] For example see Delbert C. Miller and William H. Form, *Industrial Sociology* (New York: Harper & Row, Publishers, 1951).

[17] See Hugo Munsterberg, *Psychology and Industrial Efficiency* (Boston: Houghton Mifflin Company, 1913).

[18] Probably the classic work is Elton Mayo, *The Human Problems of an Industrial Civilization* (Cambridge: Harvard University Press, 1946, first printed 1933).

functional jurisdictions. The classical theory assumes something of perfection in the delegation and functionalization processes. The neoclassical school points out that human problems are caused by imperfections in the way these processes are handled.

For example, too much or insufficient delegation may render an executive incapable of action. The failure to delegate authority and responsibility equally may result in frustration for the delegatee. Overlapping of authorities often causes clashes in personality. Gaps in authority cause failures in getting jobs done, with one party blaming the other for shortcomings in performance.[19]

The neoclassical school says that the scalar and functional processes are theoretically valid, but tend to deteriorate in practice. The ways in which they break down are described, and some of the human causes are pointed out. In addition the neoclassicists make recommendations, suggesting various "human tools" which will facilitate the operation of these processes.

(3). *Structure* provides endless avenues of analysis for the neoclassical theory of organization. The theme is that human behavior disrupts the best laid organizational plans, and thwarts the cleanness of the logical relationships founded in the structure. The neoclassical critique of structure centers on frictions which appear internally among people performing different functions.

Line and staff relations is a problem area, much discussed, in this respect. Many companies seem to have difficulty keeping the line and staff working together harmoniously. Both Dalton[20] and Juran[21] have engaged in research to discover the causes of friction, and to suggest remedies.

Of course, line-staff relations represent only one of the many problems of structural frictions described by the neoclassicists. As often as not, the neoclassicists will offer prescriptions for the elimination of conflict in structure. Among the more important harmony-rendering formulae are participation, junior boards, bottom-up management, joint committees, recognition of human dignity, and "better" communication.

(4). An executive's *span of control* is a function of human determinants, and the reduction of span to a precise, universally applicable ratio is silly, according to the neoclassicists. Some of the determinants of span are individual differences in managerial abilities, the type of people and functions supervised, and the extent of communication effectiveness.

Coupled with the span of control question are the human implications of the type of structure which emerges. That is, is a tall structure with a short span or a flat structure with a wide span more conducive to good human relations and high morale? The answer is situational. Short span results in tight supervision; wide span requires a good deal of delegation with looser controls. Because of individual and organizational differences, sometimes one is better than the other.

---

[19] For further discussion of the human relations implications of the scalar and functional processes see Keith Davis, op. cit., pp. 60-66.

[20] Melville Dalton, "Conflicts between Staff and Line Managerial Officers," *American Sociological Review,* June, 1950, pp. 342-51.

[21] J. M. Juran, "Improving the Relationship between Staff and Line," *Personnel,* May, 1956, pp. 515-24.

There is a tendency to favor the looser form of organization, however, for the reason that tall structures breed autocratic leadership, which is often pointed out as a cause of low morale.[22]

The Neoclassical View of the Informal Organization

Nothing more than the barest mention of the informal organization is given even in the most recent classical treatises on organization theory.[23] Systematic discussion of this form of organization has been left to the neoclassicists. The informal organization refers to people in group associations at work, but these associations are not specified in the "blueprint" of the formal organization. The informal organization means natural groupings of people in the work situation.

In a general way, the informal organization appears in response to the social need—the need of people to associate with others. However, for analytical purposes, this explanation is not particularly satisfying. Research has produced the following, more specific determinants underlying the appearance of informal organizations.

(1). The *location* determinant simply states that in order to form into groups of any lasting nature, people have to have frequent face-to-face contact. Thus, the geography of physical location in a plant or office is an important factor in predicting who will be in what group.[24]

(2). *Occupation* is a key factor determining the rise and composition of informal groups. There is a tendency for people performing similar jobs to group together.[25]

(3). *Interests* are another determinant for informal group formation. Even though people might be in the same location, performing similar jobs, differences of interest among them explain why several small, instead of one large, informal organizations emerge.

(4). *Special issues* often result in the formation of informal groups, but this determinant is set apart from the three previously mentioned. In this case, people who do not necessarily have similar interests, occupations, or locations may join together for a common cause. Once the issue is resolved, then the tendency is to revert to the more "natural" group forms.[26] Thus, special issues give rise to a rather impermanent informal association; groups based on the other three determinants tend to be more lasting.

When informal organizations come into being they assume certain characteristics. Since understanding these characteristics is important for management practice, they are noted below:

[22] Gardner and Moore, op. cit., pp. 237-43.

[23] For example, Brech, op. cit., pp. 27-29; and Allen, op. cit., pp. 61-62.

[24] See: Leon Festinger, Stanley Schachter, and Kurt Back, *Social Pressures in Informal Groups* (New York: Harper & Row, Publishers 1950), pp. 153-63.

[25] For example see W. Fred Cottrell, *The Railroader* (Palo Alto: The Stanford University Press, 1940), Chapter 3.

[26] Except in cases where the existence of an organization is necessary for the continued maintenance of employee interest. Under these conditions the previously informal association may emerge as a formal group, such as a union.

(1). Informal organizations act as agencies of *social control.* They generate a culture based on certain norms of conduct which, in turn, demands conformity from group members. These standards may be at odds with the values set by the formal organization. So an individual may very well find himself in a situation of conflicting demands.

(2). The form of human interrelationships in the informal organization requires *techniques of analysis* different from those used to plot the realtionships of people in a formal organization. The method used for determining the structure of the informal group is called sociometric analysis. Sociometry reveals the complex structure of interpersonal relations which is based on premises fundamentally unlike the logic of the formal organization.

(3). Informal organizations have *status and communication* systems peculiar to themselves, not necessarily derived from the formal systems. For example, the grapevine is the subject of much neoclassical study.

(4). Survival of the informal organization requires stable continuing relationships among the people in them. Thus, it has been observed that the informal organization *resists change.*[27] Considerable attention is given by the neoclassicists to overcoming informal resistance to change.

(5). The last aspect of analysis which appears to be central to the neoclassical view of the informal organization is the study of the *informal leader.* Discussion revolves around who the informal leader is, how he assumes this role, what characteristics are peculiar to him, and how he can help the manager accomplish his objectives in the formal organization.[28]

This brief sketch of some of the major facets of informal organization theory has neglected, so far, one important topic treated by the neoclassical school. It is the way in which the formal and informal organizations interact.

A conventional way of looking at the interaction of the two is the "live and let live" point of view. Management should recognize that the informal organization exists, nothing can destroy it, and so the executive might just as well work with it. Working with the informal organization involves not threatening its existence unnecessarily, listening to opinions expressed for the group by the leader, allowing group participation in decision-making situations, and controlling the grapevine by prompt release of accurate information.[29]

While this approach is management centered, it is not unreasonable to expect that informal group standards and norms could make themselves felt on formal organizational policy. An honestly conceived effort by managers to establish a working relationship with the informal organization could result in an association where both formal and informal views would be reciprocally modified. The danger which at all costs should be avoided is that "working with

[27] Probably the classic study of resistance to change is Lester Coch and John R. P. French, Jr., "Overcoming Resistance to Change," in Schuyler Dean Hoslett (ed.), *Human Factors in Management* (New York: Harper & Row Publishers, Inc., 1951) pp. 242-68.

[28] For example see Robert Saltonstall, *Human Relations in Administration* (New York: McGraw-Hill Book Company, 1959), pp. 330-31; and Keith Davis, op. cit., pp. 99-101.

[29] For an example of this approach see: John T. Doutt, "Management Must Manage the Informal Group, Too," *Advanced Management,* May, 1959, pp. 26-28.

the informal organization" does not degenerate into a shallow disguise for human manipulation.

Some neoclassical writing in organization theory, especially that coming from the management-oriented segment of this school, gives the impression that the formal and informal organizations are distinct, and at times, quite irreconcilable factors in a company. The interaction which takes place between the two is something akin to the interaction between the company and a labor union, or a government agency, or another company.

The concept of the social system is another approach to the interactional climate. While this concept can be properly classified as neoclassical, it borders on the modern theories of organization. The phrase "social system" means that an organization is a complex of mutually interdependent, but variable, factors.

These factors include individuals and their attitudes and motives, jobs, the physical work setting, the formal organization, and the informal organizations. These factors, and many others, are woven into an overall pattern of interdependency.

From this point of view, the formal and informal organizations lose their distinctiveness, but find real meaning, in terms of human behavior, in the operation of the system as a whole. Thus, the study of organization turns away from descriptions of its component parts, and is refocused on the system of interrelationships among the parts.

One of the major contributions of the Hawthorne studies was the integration of Pareto's idea of the social system into a meaningful method of analysis for the study of behavior in human organizations.[30] This concept is still vitally important. But unfortunately some work in the field of human relations undertaken by the neoclassicists has overlooked, or perhaps discounted, the significance of this consideration.[31]

The fundamental insight regarding the social system, developed and applied to the industrial scene by the Hawthorne researchers, did not find much extension in subsequent work in the neoclassical vein. Indeed, the neoclassical school after the Hawthorne studies generally seemed content to engage in descriptive generalizations, or particularized empirical research studies which did not have much meaning outside their own context.

The neoclassical school of organization theory has been called bankrupt. Criticisms range from, "human relations is a tool for cynical puppeteering of people," to "human relations is nothing more than a trifling body of empirical and descriptive information." There is a good deal of truth in both criticisms, but another appraisal of the neoclassical school of organization theory is offered here. The neoclassical approach has provided valuable contributions to lore of organization. But, like the classical theory, the neoclassical doctrine suffers from incompleteness, a shortsighted perspective, and lack of integration among the

[30] See Roethlisberger and Dickson, op. cit., Chapter 24.

[31] A check of management human relations texts, the organization and human relations chapters of principles of management texts, and texts on conventional organization theory for management courses reveals little or no treatment of the concept of the social system.

many facets of human behavior studied by it. Modern organization theory has made a move to cover the shortcomings of the current body of theoretical knowledge.

MODERN ORGANIZATION THEORY

The distinctive qualities of modern organization theory are its conceptual analytical base, its reliance on empirical research data and, above all, its integrating nature. These qualities are framed in a philosophy which accepts the premise that the only meaningful way to study organization is to study it as a system. As Henderson put it, the study of a system must rely on a method of analysis. " . . . involving the simultaneous variations of mutually dependent variables."[32] Human systems, of course, contain a huge number of dependent variables which defy the most complex simultaneous equations to solve.

Nevertheless, system analysis has its own peculiar point of view which aims to study organization in the way Henderson suggests. It treats organization as a system of mutually dependent variables. As a result, modern organization theory, which accepts system analysis, shifts the conceptual level of organization study above the classical and neoclassical theories. Modern organization theory asks a range of interrelated questions which are not seriously considered by the two other theories.

Key among these questions are:

(1). What are the strategic parts of the system?
(2). What is the nature of their mutual dependency?
(3). What are the main processes in the system which link the parts together, and facilitate their adjustment to each other?
(4). What are the goals sought by systems?[33]

Modern organization theory is in no way a unified body of thought. Each writer and researcher has his special emphasis when he considers the system. Perhaps the most evident unifying thread in the study of systems is the effort to look at the organization in its totality. Representative books in this field are March and Simon, *Organizations,*[34] and Haire's anthology, *Modern Organization Theory.*[35]

Instead of attempting a review of different writers' contributions to modern organization theory, it will be more useful to discuss the various ingredients involved in system analysis. They are the parts, the interactions, the processes, and the goals of systems.

[32] Lawrence J. Henderson, *Pareto's General Sociology* (Cambridge: Harvard University Press, 1935), p. 13.
[33] There is another question which cannot be treated in the scope of this paper. It asks, what research tools should be used for the study of the system?
[34] James G. March and Herbert A. Simon, *Organizations* (New York: John Wiley & Sons, 1958).
[35] Mason Haire, (ed.) *Modern Organization Theory* (New York: John Wiley & Sons, Inc. 1959).

The Parts of the System and Their Interdependency

The first basic part of the system is the *individual,* and the personality structure he brings to the organization. Elementary to an individual's personality are motives and attitudes which condition the range of expectancies he hopes to satisfy by participating in the system.

The second part of the system is the formal arrangement of functions, usually called the *formal organization.* The formal organization is the interrelated pattern of jobs which make up the structure of a system. Certain writers, like Argyris, see a fundamental conflict resulting from the demands made by the system, and the structure of the mature, normal personality. In any event, the individual has expectancies regarding the job he is to perform; and, conversely, the job makes demands on, or has expectancies relating to, the performance of the individual. Considerable attention has been given by writers in modern organization theory to incongruencies resulting from the interaction of organizational and individual demands.[36]

The third part in the organization system is the *informal organization.* Enough has been said already about the nature of this organization. But it must be noted that an interactional pattern exists between the individual and the informal group. This interactional arrangement can be conveniently discussed as the mutual modification of expectancies. The informal organization has demands which it makes on members in terms of anticipated forms of behavior, and the individual has expectancies of satisfaction he hopes to derive from association with people on the job. Both these sets of expectancies interact, resulting in the individual modifying his behavior to accord with the demands of the group, and the group, perhaps, modifying what it expects from an individual because of the impact of his personality on group norms.[37]

Much of what has been said about the various expectancy systems in an organization can also be treated using status and role concepts. Part of modern organization theory rests on research findings in social-psychology relative to reciprocal patterns of behavior stemming from role demands generated by both the formal and informal organizations, and role perceptions peculiar to the individual. Bakke's *fusion process* is largely concerned with the modification of role expectancies. The fusion process is a force, according to Bakke, which acts to weld divergent elements together for the preservation of organizational integrity.[38]

The fifth part of system analysis is the *physical setting* in which the job is performed. Although this element of the system may be implicit in what has been said already about the formal organization and its functions, it is well to separate it. In the physical surroundings of work, interactions are present in

[36] See Chris Argyris, *Personality and Organization* (New York: Harper & Row, Publishers 1957), esp. Chapters 2, 3, 7.

[37] For a larger treatment of this subject see George C. Homans, *The Human Group* (New York: Harcourt Brace Jovanovich, Inc., 1950), Chapter 5.

[38] E. Wight Bakke, "Concept of the Social Organization," in *Modern Organization Theory,* Mason Haire, (ed.) (New York: John Wiley & Sons, 1959) pp. 60-61.

complex man machine systems. The human "engineer" cannot approach the problems posed by such interrelationships in a purely technical, engineering fashion. As Haire says, these problems lie in the domain of the social theorist.[39] Attention must be centered on responses demanded from a logically ordered production function, often with the view of minimizing the error in the system. From this standpoint, work cannot be effectively organized unless the psychological, social, and physiological characteristics of people participating in the work environment are considered. Machines and processes should be designed to fit certain generally observed psychological and physiological properties of men, rather than hiring men to fit machines.

In summary, the parts of the system which appear to be of strategic importance are the individual, the formal structure, the informal organization, status and role patterns, and the physical environment of work. Again, these parts are woven into a configuration called the organizational system. The processes which link the parts are taken up next.

The Linking Processes

One can say, with a good deal of glibness, that all the parts mentioned above are interrelated. Although this observation is quite correct, it does not mean too much in terms of system theory unless some attempt is made to analyze the processes by which the interaction is achieved. Role theory is devoted to certain types of interactional processes. In addition, modern organization theorists point to three other linking activities which appear to be universal to human systems of organized behavior. These processes are communication, balance, and decision making.

(1). Communication is mentioned often in neoclassical theory, but the emphasis is on description of forms of communication activity, i.e., formal-informal, vertical-horizontal, line-staff. Communication, as a mechanism which links the segments of the system together, is overlooked by way of much considered analysis.

One aspect of modern organization theory is the study of the communication network in the system. Communication is viewed as the method by which action is evoked from the parts of the system. Communication acts not only as stimuli resulting in action, but also as a control and coordination mechanism linking the decision centers in the system into a synchronized pattern. Deutsch points out that organizations are composed of parts which communicate with each other, receive messages from the outside world, and store information. Taken together, these communication functions of the parts comprise a configuration representing the total system.[40] More is to be said about communication later in the discussion of the cybernetic model.

(2). The concept of *balance* as a linking process involves a series of some rather complex ideas. Balance refers to an equilibrating mechanism whereby the

---

[39] Mason Haire, "Psychology and the Study of Business: Joint Behavioral Sciences," in *Social Science Research on Business: Product and Potential* (New York: Columbia University Press, 1959), pp. 53-59.

[40] Karl W. Deutsch, "On Communication Models in the Social Sciences," *Public Opinion*

various parts of the system are maintained in a harmoniously structured relationship to each other.

The necessity for the balance concept logically flows from the nature of systems themselves. It is impossible to conceive of an ordered relationship among the parts of a system without also introducing the idea of a stabilizing or an adapting mechanism.

Balance appears in two varieties—quasi-automatic and innovative. Both forms of balance act to insure system integrity in face of changing conditions, either internal or external to the system. The first form of balance, quasi-automatic, refers to what some think are "homeostatic" properties of systems. That is, systems seem to exhibit built-in propensities to maintain steady states.

If human organizations are open, self-maintaining systems, then control and regulatory processes are necessary. The issue hinges on the degree to which stabilizing processes in systems, when adapting to change, are automatic. March and Simon have an interesting answer to this problem, which in part is based on the type of change and the adjustment necessary to adapt to the change. Systems have programs of action which are put into effect when a change is perceived. If the change is relatively minor, and if the change comes within the purview of established programs of action, then it might be fairly confidently predicted that the adaptation made by the system will be quasi-automatic.[41]

The role of innovative, creative balancing efforts now needs to be examined. The need for innovation arises when adaptation to a change is outside the scope of existing programs designed for the purpose of keeping the system in balance. New programs have to be evolved in order for the system to maintain internal harmony.

New programs are created by trial and error search for feasible action alternatives to cope with a given change. But innovation is subject to the limitations and possibilities inherent in the quantity and variety of information present in a system at a particular time. New combinations of alternatives for innovative purposes depend on:

a. the possible range of output of the system, or the capacity of the system to supply information.
b. the range of available information in the memory of the system.
c. the operating rules (program) governing the analysis and flow of information within the system.
d. the ability of the system to "forget" previously learned solutions to change problems.[42] A system with too good a memory might narrow its behavioral choices to such an extent as to stifle innovation. In simpler language, old learned programs might be used to adapt to change, when newly innovated programs are necessary.[43]

Much of what has been said about communication and balance brings to mind

Quarterly 16 (1952): 356-80.

[41] March and Simon, op. cit., pp. 139-40.

[42] Mervyn, L. Cadwallader, "The Cybernetic Analysis of Change in Complex Social Organization," *The American Journal of Sociology*, September, 1959, p. 156.

[43] It is conceivable for innovative behavior to be programmed into the system.

a cybernetic model in which both these processes have vital roles. Cybernetics has to do with feedback and control in all kinds of systems. Its purpose is to maintain system stability in the face of change. Cybernetics cannot be studied without considering communication networks, information flow, and some kind of balancing process aimed at preserving the integrity of the system.

Cybernetics directs attention to key questions regarding the system. These questions are: How are communication centers connected, and how are they maintained? Corollary to this question: what is the structure of the feedback system? Next, what information is stored in the organization, and at what points? And as a corollary: how accessible is this information to decision-making centers? Third, how conscious is the organization of the operation of its own parts? That is, to what extent do the policy centers receive control information with sufficient frequency and relevancy to create a real awareness of the operation of the segments of the system? Finally, what are the learning (innovating) capabilities of the system?[44]

Answers to the question posed by cybernetics are crucial to understanding both the balancing and communication processes in systems.[45] Although cybernetics has been applied largely to technical-engineering problems of automation, the model of feedback, control, and regulation in all systems has a good deal of generality. Cybernetics is a fruitful area which can be used to synthesize the processes of communication and balance.

(3). A wide spectrum of topics dealing with types of decisions in human systems makes up the core of analysis of another important process in organizations. Decision analysis is one of the major contributions of March and Simon in their book *Organizations.* The two major classes of decisions they discuss are decisions to produce and decisions to participate in the system.[46]

Decisions to produce are largely a result of an interaction between individual attitudes and the demands of organization. Motivation analysis becomes central to studying the nature and results of the interaction. Individual decisions to participate in the organization reflect on such issues as the relationship between organizational rewards versus the demands made by the organization. Participation decisions also focus attention on the reasons why individuals remain in or leave organizations.

March and Simon treat decisions as internal variables in an organization which depend on jobs, individual expectations and motivations, and organizational structure. Marschak[47] looks on the decision process as an independent variable upon which the survival of the organization is based. In this case, the organization is viewed as having, inherent to its structure, the ability to maximize survival requisites through its established decision processes.

---

[44] These are questions adapted from Deutsch, op. cit., 368-70.
[45] Answers to these questions would require a comprehensive volume. One of the best approaches currently available is Stafford Beer, *Cybernetics and Management* (New York: John Wiley & Sons, 1959).
[46] March and Simon, op. cit., Chapters 3 and 4.
[47] Jacob Marschak, "Efficient and Viable Organizational Forms" in Mason Haire (ed.), *Modern Organization Theory,* (New York: John Wiley & Sons, Inc. 1959), pp. 307-20.

The Goals of Organization

Organization has three goals which may be either intermeshed or independent ends in themselves. They are growth, stability, and interaction. The last goal refers to organizations which exist primarily to provide a medium for association of its members with others. Interestingly enough these goals seem to apply to different forms of organization at varying levels of complexity, ranging from simple clockwork mechanisms to social systems.

These similarities in organizational purposes have been observed by a number of people, and a field of thought and research called general system theory has developed, dedicated to the task of discovering organizational universals. The dream of general system theory is to create a science of organizational universals, or if you will, a universal science using common organizational elements found in all systems as a starting point.

Modern organization theory is on the periphery of general system theory. Both general system theory and modern organization theory study:

1. The parts (individuals) in aggregates, and the movement of individuals into and out of the system.
2. The interaction of individuals with the environment found in the system.
3. The interactions among individuals in the system.
4. General growth and stability problems of systems.[48]

Modern organization theory and general system theory are similar in that they look at organization as an integrated whole. They differ, however, in terms of their generality. General system theory is concerned with every level of system, whereas modern organizational theory focuses primarily on human organization.

The question might be asked, what can the science of administration gain by the study of system levels other than human? Before attempting an answer, note should be made of what these other levels are. Boulding presents a convenient method of classification:

1. The static structure—a level of framework, the anatomy of a system; for example, the structure of the universe.
2. The simple dynamic system—the level of clockworks, predetermined necessary motions.
3. The cybernetic system—the level of the thermostat, the system moves to maintain a given equilibrium through a process of self-regulation.
4. The open system—level of self-maintaining systems, moves toward and includes living organisms.
5. The genetic-societal system—level of cell society, characterized by a division of labor among cells.
6. Animal systems—level of mobility, evidence of goal-directed behavior.
7. Human systems—level of symbol interpretation and idea communication.
8. Social system—level of human organization.
9. Transcendental systems—level of ultimates and absolutes which exhibit systematic structure but are unknowable in essence.[49]

---

[48] Kenneth E. Boulding, "General System Theory—The Skeleton of a Science," *Management Science,* April, 1956, pp. 200-02.

[49] Ibid., pp. 202-5.

This approach to the study of systems by finding universals common at all levels of organization offers intriguing possibilities for administrative organization theory. A good deal of light could be thrown on social systems if structurally analogous elements could be found in the simpler types of systems. For example, cybernetic systems have characteristics which seem to be similar to feedback, regulation, and control phenomena in human organizations. Thus, certain facets of cybernetic models could be generalized to human organization. Considerable danger, however, lies in poorly founded analogies. Superficial similarities between simpler system forms and social systems are apparent everywhere. Instinctually based ant societies, for example, do not yield particularly instructive lessons for understanding rationally conceived human organizations. Thus, care should be taken that analogies used to bridge system levels are not mere devices for literary enrichment. For analogies to have usefulness and validity, they must exhibit inherent structural similarities or implicity identical operational principles.[50]

Modern organization theory leads, as it has been shown, almost inevitably into a discussion of general system theory. A science of organization universals has some strong advocates, particularly among biologists.[51] Organization theorists in administrative science cannot afford to overlook the contributions of general system theory. Indeed, modern organization concepts could offer a great deal to those working with general system theory. But the ideas dealt with in the general theory are exceedingly elusive.

Speaking of the concept of equilibrium as a unifying element in all systems, Easton says, "It (equilibrium) leaves the impression that we have a useful general theory when in fact, lacking measurability, it is a mere pretence for knowledge."[52] The inability to quantify and measure universal organization elements undermines the success of pragmatic tests to which general system theory might be put.

Organization Theory: Quo Vadis?

Most sciences have a vision of the universe to which they are applied, and administrative science is not an exception. This universe is composed of parts. One purpose of science is to synthesize the parts into an organized conception of its field of study. As a science matures, its theorems about the configuration of its universe change. The direction of change in three sciences,

---

[50] Seidenberg, op. cit., p. 136. The fruitful use of the type of analogies spoken of by Seidenberg is evident in the application of thermodynamic principles, particularly the entropy concept, to communication theory. See Claude E. Shannon and Warren Weaver, *The Mathematical Theory of Communication,* (Urbana: The University of Illinois Press, 1949). Further, the existence of a complete analogy between the operational behavior of thermodynamic systems, electrical communication systems, and biological systems has been noted by Y. S. Touloukian, *The Concept of Entropy in Communication, Living Organisms, and Thermodynamics,* Research Bulletin 130, Purdue Engineering Experiment Station.

[51] For example see Ludwig von Bertalanffy, *Problem of Life* (London: Watts and Company, 1952).

[52] David Easton, "Limits of the Equilibrium Model in Social Research," in *Profits and Problems of Homeostatic Models in the Behavioral Sciences,* Publication 1, Chicago Behavioral Sciences, 1953, p. 39.

physics, economics, and sociology, are noted briefly for comparison with the development of an administrative view of human organization.

The first comprehensive and empirically verifiable outlook of the physical universe was presented by Newton in his *Principia.* Classical physics, founded on Newton's work, constitutes a grand scheme in which a wide range of physical phenomena could be organized and predicted. Newtonian physics may rightfully be regarded as "macro" in nature, because its system of organization was concerned largely with gross events of which the movement of celestial bodies, waves, energy forms, and strain are examples. For years classical physics was supreme, being applied continuously to smaller and smaller classes of phenomena in the physical universe. Physicists at one time adopted the view that everything in their realm could be discovered by simply subdividing problems. Physics thus moved into the "micro" order.

But in the nineteenth century a revolution took place motivated largely because events were being noted which could not be explained adequately by the conceptual framework supplied by the classical school. The consequences of this revolution are brilliantly described by Eddington:

> From the point of view of philosophy of science the conception associated with entropy must I think be ranked as the great contribution of the nineteenth century to scientific thought. It marked a reaction from the view that everything to which science need pay attention is discovered by microscopic dissection of objects. It provided an alternative standpoint in which the centre of interest is shifted from the entities reached by the customary analysis (atoms, electric potentials, etc.) to qualities possessed by the system as a whole, which cannot be split up and located—a little bit here, and a little bit there. . . . We often think that when we have completed our study of *one* we know all about *two,* because "two" is "one and one." We forget that we have still to make a study of "and." Secondary physics is the study of "and"—that is to say, of organization.[53]

Although modern physics often deals in minute quantities and oscillations, the conception of the physicist is on the "macro" scale. He is concerned with the "and," or the organization of the world in which the events occur. These developments did not invalidate classical physics as to its usefulness for explaining a certain range of phenomena. But classical physics is no longer the undisputed law of the universe. It is a special case.

Early economic theory, and Adam Smith's *Wealth of Nations* comes to mind, examined economic problems in the macro order. The *Wealth of Nations* is mainly concerned with matters of national income and welfare. Later, the economics of the firm, micro-economics, dominated the theoretical scene in this science. And, finally, with Keynes' *The General Theory of Employment Interest and Money,* a systematic approach to the economic universe was reintroduced on the macro level.

The first era of the developing science of sociology was occupied by the great social "system builders." Comte, the so-called father of sociology, had a macro

---

[53] Sir Arthur Eddington, *The Nature of the Physical World* (Ann Arbor: The University of Michigan Press, 1958), pp. 103-4.

view of society in that his chief works are devoted to social reorganization. Comte was concerned with the interrelationships among social, political, religious, and educational institutions. As sociology progressed, the science of society compressed. Emphasis shifted from the macro approach of the pioneers to detailed, empirical study of small social units. The compression of sociological analysis was accompanied by study of social pathology or disorganization.

In general, physics, economics, and sociology appear to have two things in common. First, they offered a macro point of view as their initial systematic comprehension of their area of study. Second, as the science developed, attention fragmented into analysis of the parts of the organization, rather than attending to the system as a whole. This is the micro phase.

In physics and economics, discontent was evidenced by some scientists at the continual atomization of the universe. The reaction to the micro approach was a new theory or theories dealing with the total system, on the macro level again. This third phase of scientific development seems to be more evident in physics and economics than in sociology.

The reason for the "macro-micro-macro" order of scientific progress lies, perhaps, in the hypothesis that usually the things which strike man first are of great magnitude. The scientist attempts to discover order in the vastness. But after macro laws or models of systems are postulated, variations appear which demand analysis, not so much in terms of the entire system, but more in terms of the specific parts which make it up. Then, intense study of microcosm may result in new general laws, replacing the old models of organization. Or, the old and the new models may stand together, each explaining a different class of phenomenon. Or, the old and the new concepts of organization may be welded to produce a single creative synthesis.

Now, what does all this have to do with the problem of organization in administrative science? Organization concepts seem to have gone through the same order of development in this field as in the three just mentioned. It is evident that the classical theory of organization, particularly as in the work of Mooney and Reiley, is concerned with principles common to all organizations. It is a macro-organizational view. The classical approach to organization, however, dealt with the gross anatomical parts and processes of the formal organization. Like classical physics, the classical theory of organization is a special case. Neither are especially well equipped to account for variation from their established framework.

Many variations in the classical administrative model result from human behavior. The only way these variations could be understood was by a microscopic examination of particularized, situational aspects of human behavior. The mission of the neoclassical school thus is "microanalysis."

It was observed earlier, that somewhere along the line the concept of the social system, which is the key to understanding the Hawthorne studies, faded into the background. Maybe the idea is so obvious that it was lost to the view of researchers and writers in human relations. In any event, the press of research in the microcosmic universes of the informal organization, morale and productivity, leadership, participation, and the like forced the notion of the social system into limbo. Now, with the advent of modern organization theory, the social system has been resurrected.

Modern organization theory appears to be concerned with Eddington's "and." This school claims that its operational hypothesis is based on a macro point of view; that is, the study of organization as a whole. This nobility of purpose should not obscure, however, certain difficulties faced by this field as it is presently constituted. Modern organization theory raises two questions which should be explored further. First, would it not be more accurate to speak of modern organization theor*ies*? Second, just how much of modern organization theory is modern?

The first question can be answered with a quick affirmative. Aside from the notion of the system, there are few, if any, other ideas of a unifying nature. Except for several important exceptions,[54] modern organization theorists tend to pursue their pet points of view,[55] suggesting they are part of system theory, but not troubling to show by what mystical means they arrive at this conclusion.

The irony of it all is that a field dealing with systems has, indeed, little system. Modern organization theory needs a framework, and it needs an integration of issues into a common conception of organization. Admittedly, this is a large order. But it is curious not to find serious analytical treatment of subjects like cybernetics or general system theory in Haire's *Modern Organizational Theory*, which claims to be a representative example of work in this field. Beer has ample evidence in his book *Cybernetics and Management* that cybernetics, if imaginatively approached, provides a valuable conceptual base for the study of systems.

The second question suggests an ambiguous answer. Modern organization theory is in part a product of the past; system analysis is not a new idea. Further, modern organization theory relies for supporting data on microcosmic research studies, generally drawn from the journals of the last ten years. The newness of modern organization theory, perhaps, is its effort to synthesize recent research contributions of many fields into a system theory characterized by a reoriented conception of organization.

One might ask, but what is the modern theorist reorienting? A clue is found in the almost snobbish disdain assumed by some authors of the neoclassical human relations school, and particularly, the classical school. Reevaluation of the classical school of organization is overdue. However, this does not mean that its contributions to organization theory are irrelevant and should be overlooked in the rush to get on the "behavioral science bandwagon."

Haire announces that the papers appearing in *Modern Organization Theory* constitute, "the ragged leading edge of a wave of theoretical development."[56] Ragged, yes; but leading no! The papers appearing in this book do not represent a theoretical breakthrough in the concept of organization. Haire's collection is

---

[54] For example E. Wight Bakke, op. cit., pp. 18-75.

[55] There is a large selection including decision theory, individual-organization interaction, motivation, vitality, stability, growth, and graph theory, to mention a few.

[56] Mason Haire, "General Issues," in Mason Haire (ed.), *Modern Organization Theory (New York: John Wiley & Sons, Inc., 1959), p. 2.*

an interesting potpourri with several contributions of considerable significance. But readers should beware that they will not find vastly new insights into organizational behavior in this book, if they have kept up with the literature of the social sciences, and have dabbled to some extent in the esoteria of biological theories of growth, information theory, and mathematical model building. For those who have not maintained the pace, *Modern Organization Theory* serves the admirable purpose of bringing them up to date on a rather diversified number of subjects.

Some work in modern organization theory is pioneering, making its appraisal difficult and future uncertain. While the direction of this endeavor is unclear, one thing is patently true. Human behavior in organizations, and indeed, organization itself, cannot be adequately understood within the ground rules of classical and neoclassical doctrines. Appreciation of human organization requires a *creative* synthesis of massive amounts of empirical data, a high order of deductive reasoning, imaginative research studies, and a taste for individual and social values. Accomplishment of all these objectives, and the inclusion of them into a framework of the concept of the system, appears to be the goal of modern organization theory. The vitality of administrative science rests on the advances modern theorists make along this line.

Modern organization theory, 1960 style, is an amorphous aggregation of synthesizers and restaters, with a few extending leadership on the frontier. For the sake of these few, it is well to admonish that pouring old wine into new bottles may make the spirits cloudy. Unfortunately, modern organization theory has almost succeeded in achieving the status of a fad. Popularization and exploitation contributed to the disrepute into which human relations has fallen. It would be a great waste if modern organization theory yields to the same fate, particularly since both modern organization theory and human relations draw from the same promising source of inspiration—system analysis.

Modern organization theory needs tools of analysis and a conceptual framework uniquely its own, but it must also allow for the incorporation of relevant contributions of many fields. It may be that the framework will come from general system theory. New areas of research such as decision theory, information theory, and cybernetics also offer reasonable expectations of analytical and conceptual tools. Modern organization theory represents a frontier of research which has great significance for management. The potential is great, because it offers the opportunity for uniting what is valuable in classical theory with the social and natural sciences into a systematic and integrated conception of human organization.

George C. Homans

THE WESTERN ELECTRIC RESEARCHES

A word about the Western Electric Company is a necessary introduction to what follows. This company is engaged in manufacturing equipment for the telephone industry. Besides doing this part of its work, it has always shown concern for the welfare of its employees. In the matter of wages and hours, it has maintained a high standard. It has provided good physical conditions for its employees; and it has tried to make use of every established method of vocational guidance in the effort to suit the worker to his work. The efforts of the company have been rewarded in good industrial relations: there has been no strike or other severe symptom of discontent for over 20 years. In short, there is no reason to doubt that while these researches were being carried out the morale of the company was high and that the employees, as a body, had confidence in the abilities and motives of the company management. These facts had an important bearing on the results achieved.

The program of research which will be described grew out of a study conducted at Hawthorne by the Western Electric Company in collaboration with the National Research Council, the aim of which was to determine the relation between intensity of illumination and efficiency of workers, measured in output. One of the experiments made was the following: Two groups of employees doing similar work under similar conditions were chosen, and records of output were kept for each group. The intensity of the light under which one group worked was varied, while that under which the other group worked was held constant. By this method the investigators hoped to isolate from the effect of other variables the effect of changes in the intensity of illumination on the rate of output.

In this hope they were disappointed. The experiment failed to show any simple relation between experimental changes in the intensity of illumination and observed changes in the rate of output. The investigators concluded that this result was obtained, not because such a relation did not exist, but because it was in fact impossible to isolate it from the other variables entering into any determination of productive efficiency. This kind of difficulty, of course, has been encountered in experimental work in many fields. Furthermore, the investigators were in agreement as to the character of some of these other variables. They were convinced that one of the major factors which prevented their securing a satisfactory result was psychological. The employees being tested were reacting to changes in light intensity in the way in which they assumed that they were expected to react. That is, when light intensity was increased they were expected to produce more; when it was decreased they were expected to produce less. A further experiment was devised to demonstrate this point. The light bulbs were changed, as they had been changed before, and the workers were allowed to assume that as a result there would be more light. They commented favorably on the increased illumination. As a matter of fact, the bulbs had been replaced with others of just the same power. Other experiments of the sort were made, and in each case the results could be explained as a "psychological" reaction rather than as a "physiological" one.

This discovery seemed to be important. It suggested that the relations between other physical conditions and the efficiency of workers might be obscured by similar psychological reactions. Nevertheless the investigators were determined to continue in their course. They recognized the existence of the psychological factors, but they thought of them only as disturbing influences. They were not yet ready to turn their attention to the psychological factors themselves. Instead, they were concerned with devising a better way of eliminating them from the experiments, and the experiments they wanted to try by no means ended with illumination. For instance, there was the question of what was called "fatigue." Little information existed about the effect on efficiency of changes in the hours of work and the introduction of rest pauses. The investigators finally came to the conclusion that if a small group of workers was isolated in a separate room and asked to cooperate, the psychological reaction would in time disappear, and they would work exactly as they felt. That is, changes in their rate of output would be the direct result of changes in their physical conditions of work and nothing else.

* * *

In April, 1927, six girls were selected from a large shop department of the Hawthorne works. They were chosen as average workers, neither inexperienced nor expert, and their work consisted of the assembling of telephone relays. A coil, armature, contact springs, and insulators were put together on a fixture and secured in position by means of four machine screws. The operation at that time was being completed at the rate of about five relays in six minutes. This particular operation was chosen for the experiment because the relays were being assembled often enough so that even slight changes in output rate would show themselves at once on the output record. Five of the girls were to do the actual assembly work; the duty of the sixth was to keep the others supplied with parts.

The test room itself was an area divided from the main department by a wooden partition eight feet high. The girls sat in a row on one side of a long workbench. The bench and assembly equipment were identical with those used in the regular department, except in one respect. At the right of each girl's place was a hole in the bench, and into this hole she dropped completed relays. It was the entrance to a chute, in which there was a flapper gate opened by the relay in its passage downward. The opening of the gate closed an electrical circuit which controlled a perforating device, and this in turn recorded the completion of the relay by punching a hole in a tape. The tape moved at the rate of one-quarter of an inch a minute and had space for a separate row of holes for each operator. When punched, it thus constituted a complete output record for each girl for each instant of the day. Such records were kept for five years.

In this experiment, then, as in the earlier illumination experiments, great emphasis was laid on the rate of output. A word of caution is needed here. The Western Electric Company was not immediately interested in increasing output. The experiments were not designed for that purpose. On the other hand, output is easily measured, i.e., it yields precise quantitative data, and experience suggested that it was sensitive to at least some of the conditions under which the employees worked. Output was treated as an index. In short, the nature of the experimental conditions made the emphasis on output inevitable.

From their experience in the illumination experiments, the investigators were well aware that factors other than those experimentally varied might affect the output rate. Therefore arrangements were made that a number of other records should be kept. Unsuitable parts supplied by the firm were noted down, as were assemblies rejected for any reason upon inspection. In this way the type of defect could be known and related to the time of day at which it occurred. Records were kept of weather conditions in general and of temperature and humidity in the test room. Every six weeks each operator was given a medical examination by the company doctor. Every day she was asked to tell how many hours she had spent in bed the night before and, during a part of the experiment, what food she had eaten. Besides all these records, which concerned the physical condition of the operators, a log was kept in which were recorded the principal events in the test room hour by hour, including among the entries snatches of conversation between the workers. At first these entries related largely to the physical condition of the operators: how they felt as they worked. Later the ground they covered somewhat widened, and the log ultimately became one of the most important of the test room records. Finally, when the so-called Interviewing Program was instituted at Hawthorne, each of the operators was interviewed several times by an experienced interviewer.

The girls had no supervisor in the ordinary sense, such as they would have had in a regular shop department, but a "test room observer" was placed in the room, whose duty it was to maintain the records, arrange the work, and secure a cooperative spirit on the part of the girls. Later, when the complexity of his work increased, several assistants were assigned to help him.

When the arrangements had been made for the test room, the operators who had been chosen to take part were called in for an interview in the office of the superintendent of the Inspection Branch, who was in general charge of the experiment and of the researches which grew out of it. The superintendent described this interview as follows:

The nature of the test was carefully explained to these girls and they readily consented to take part in it, although they were very shy at the first conference. An invitation to six shop girls to come up to a superintendent's office was naturally rather startling. They were assured that the object of the test was to determine the effect of certain changes in working conditions, such as rest periods, midmorning lunches, and shorter working hours. They were expressly cautioned to work at a comfortable pace, and under no circumstances to try and make a race out of the test.

This conference was only the first of many. Whenever any experimental change was planned, the girls were called in, the purpose of the change was explained to them, and their comments were requested. Certain suggested changes which did not meet with their approval were abandoned. They were repeatedly asked, as they were asked in the first interview, not to strain but to work "as they felt."

The experiment was now ready to begin. Put in its simplest terms, the idea of those directing the experiment was that if an output curve was studied for a long enough time under various changes in working conditions, it would be possible to determine which conditions were the most satisfactory. Accordingly, a number of so-called "experimental periods" were arranged. For two weeks before the operators were placed in the test room, a record was kept of the production of each one without her knowledge. In this way the investigators secured a measure of her productive ability while working in the regular department under the usual conditions. This constituted the first experimental period. And for five weeks after the girls entered the test room no change was made in working conditions. Hours remained what they had been before. The investigators felt that this period would be long enough to reveal any changes in output incidental merely to the transfer. This constituted the second experimental period.

The third period involved a change in the method of payment. In the regular department, the girls had been paid according to a scheme of group piecework, the group consisting of 100 or more employees. Under these circumstances, variations in an individual's total output would not be immediately reflected in her pay, since such variations tended to cancel one another in such a large group. In the test room, the six operators were made a group by themselves. In this way each girl received an amount more nearly in proportion to her individual effort, and her interests became more closely centered on the experiment. Eight weeks later, the directly experimental changes began. An outline will reveal their general character: Period IV: two rest pauses, each five minutes in length, were established, one occurring in midmorning and the other in the early afternoon. Period V: these rest pauses were lengthened to ten minutes each. Period VI: six five-minute rests were established. Period VII: the company provided each member of the group with a light lunch in the midmorning and another in the midafternoon, accompanied by rest pauses. This arrangement became standard for subsequent Periods VIII through XI. Period VIII: work stopped a half-hour earlier every day—at 4:30 P.M. Period IX: work stopped at 4 P.M. Period X: conditions returned to what they were in Period VII. Period XI: a five-day work week was established. Each of these experimental periods lasted several weeks.

Period XI ran through the summer of 1928, a year after the beginning of the experiment. Already the results were not what had been expected. The output curve, which had risen on the whole slowly and steadily throughout the year, was obviously reflecting something other than the responses of the group to the imposed experimental conditions. Even when the total weekly output had fallen off, as it could hardly fail to do in such a period as Period XI, when the group was working only five days a week, daily output continued to rise. Therefore, in accordance with a sound experimental procedure, as a control on what had been done, it was agreed with the consent of the operators that in experimental Period XII a return should be made to the original conditions of work, with no rest pauses, no special lunches, and a full-length working week. This period lasted for twelve weeks. Both daily and weekly output rose to a higher point than ever before: the working day and the working week were both longer. The hourly output rate declined somewhat but it did not approach the level of Period III, when similar conditions were in effect.

The conclusions reached after Period XII may be expressed in terms of another observation. Identical conditions of work were repeated in three different experimental periods: Periods VII, X, and XIII. If the assumptions on which the study was based had been correct, that is to say, if the output rate were directly related to the physical conditions of work, the expectation would be that in these three experimental periods there would be some similarity in output. Such was not the case. The only apparent uniformity was that in each experimental period output was higher than in the preceding one. In the Relay Assembly Test Room, as in the previous illumination experiments, something was happening which could not be explained by the experimentally controlled conditions of work.

There is no need here to go into the later history of the test room experiment, which came to an end in 1933. It is enough to say that the output of the group continued to rise until it established itself on a high plateau from which there was no descent until the time of discouragement and deepening economic depression which preceded the end of the test. The rough conclusions reached at the end of experimental Period XII were confirmed and sharpened by later research. T. N. Whitehead, Associate Professor of Business in the Graduate School of Business Administration, Harvard University, has made a careful statistical analysis of the output records. He shows that the changes which took place in the output of the group have no simple correlation with the experimental changes in working conditions. Nor can they be correlated with changes in other physical conditions of which records were kept, such as temperature, humidity, hours of rest, and changes of relay type. Even when the girls themselves complained of mugginess or heat, these conditions were not apparently affecting their output. This statement, of course, does not mean that there is never any relation between output rate and these physical conditions. There is such a thing as heat prostration. It means only that, within the limits in which these conditions were varying in the test room, they apparently did not affect the rate of work.

The question remains: With what facts, if any, can the changes in the output rate of the operators in the test room be correlated? Here the statements of the girls themselves are of the first importance. Each girl knew that she was producing more in the test room than she ever had in the regular department, and each said that the increase had come about without any conscious effort on her part. It seemed easier to produce at the faster rate in the test room than at the slower rate in the regular department. When questioned further, each girl stated her reasons in slightly different words, but there was uniformity in the answers in two respects. First, the girls liked to work in the test room; "it was fun." Secondly, the new supervisory relation or, as they put it, the absence of the old supervisory control, made it possible for them to work freely without anxiety.

For instance, there was the matter of conversation. In the regular department, conversation was in principle not allowed. In practice it was tolerated if it was carried on in a low tone and did not interfere with work. In the test room an effort was made in the beginning to discourage conversation, though it was soon abandoned. The observer in charge of the experiment was afraid of losing the cooperation of the girls if he insisted too strongly on this point. Talk became common and was often loud and general. Indeed, the conversation of the operators came to occupy an important place in the log. T. N. Whitehead has pointed out that the girls in the test room were far more thoroughly supervised than they ever had been in the regular department. They were watched by an observer of their own, an interested management, and outside experts. The point is that the character and purpose of the supervision were different and were felt to be so.

The operators knew that they were taking part in what was considered an important and interesting experiment. They knew that their work was expected to produce results—they were not sure what results—which would lead to the improvement of the working conditions of their fellow employees. They knew that the eyes of the company were upon them. Whitehead has further pointed out that although the experimental changes might turn out to have no physical significance, their social significance was always favorable. They showed that the management of the company was still interested, that the girls were still part of a valuable piece of research. In the regular department, the girls, like the other employees, were in the position of responding to changes the source and purpose of which were beyond their knowledge. In the test room, they had frequent interviews with the superintendent, a high officer of the company. The reasons for the contemplated experimental changes were explained to them. Their views were consulted and in some instances they were allowed to veto what had been proposed. Professor Mayo has argued that it is idle to speak of an experimental period like Period XII as being in any sense what it purported to me—a return to the original conditions of work. In the meantime, the entire industrial situation of the girls had been reconstructed.

Another factor in what occurred can only be spoken of as the social development of the group itself. When the girls went for the first time to be given a physical examination by the company doctor, someone suggested as a joke that ice cream and cake ought to be served. The company provided them at the next examination, and the custom was kept up for the duration of the experiment. When one of the girls had a birthday, each of the others would bring her a present, and she would respond by offering the group a box of chocolates. Often one of the girls would have some good reason for feeling tired. Then the others would "carry" her. That is, they would agree to work especially fast to make up for the low output expected from her. It is doubtful whether this "carrying" did have any effect, but the important point is the existence of the practice, not its effectiveness. The girls made friends in the test room and went together socially after hours. One of the interesting facts which has appeared from Whitehead's analysis of the output records is that there were times when variations in the output rates of two friends were correlated to a high degree. Their rates varied simultaneously and in the same direction—something, of course, which the girls were not aware of and could not have planned. Also, these correlations were destroyed by such apparently trivial events as a change in the order in which the girls sat at the workbench.

Finally, the group developed leadership and a common purpose. The leader, self-appointed, was an ambitious young Italian girl who entered the test room as a replacement after two of the original members had left. She saw in the experiment a chance for personal distinction and advancement. The common purpose was an increase in the output rate. The girls had been told in the beginning and repeatedly thereafter that they were to work without straining, without trying to make a race of the test, and all the evidence shows that they kept this rule. In fact, they felt that they were working under less pressure than in the regular department. Nevertheless, they knew that the output record was considered the most important of the records of the experiment and was always closely scrutinized. Before long they had committed themselves to a continuous increase in production. In the long run, of course, this ideal was an impossible one, and when the girls found out that it was, the realization was an important element of the change of tone which was noticeable in the second half of the experiment. But for a time they felt that they could achieve the impossible. In brief, the increase in the output rate of the girls in the Relay Assembly Test Room could not be related to any changes in their physical conditions of work, whether experimentally induced or not. It could, however, be related to what can only be spoken of as the development of an organized social group in a peculiar and effective relation with its supervisors.

Many of these conclusions were not worked out in detail until long after the investigators at Hawthorne had lost interest in the Relay Assembly Test Room, but the general meaning of the experiment was clear at least as early as Period XII. A continuous increase in productivity had taken place irrespective of changing physical conditions of work. In the words of a company report made in January, 1931, on all the research which had been done up to that date:

Upon analysis, only one thing seemed to show a continuous relationship with this improved output. This was the mental attitude of the operators. From their conversations with each other and their comments to the test observers, it was not only clear that their attitudes were improving but it was evident that this area of employee reactions and feelings was a fruitful field for industrial research.

At this point the attention of the investigators turned sharply from the test room to the regular shop department from which the girls had come. Why was the mental attitude of the girls different in the test room from what it had been in the department? In their conversations with one another and in their comments to the observers, the girls were full of comparisons between the test room and the department, very much to the disadvantage of the latter. They felt relief from some form of constraint, particularly the constraint of supervision. They were exceedingly disparaging about the supervisors in the department, although management felt that the department had particularly good supervisory personnel. These facts suggested that the management of the company really knew very little about the attitudes which employees took toward conditions in the plant and very little also about what constituted good supervisory methods. Such was the atmosphere in which the so-called Interviewing Program, the third phase of the work at Hawthorne, was planned. So far the interests of the investigators had been centered on the question of what were good physical conditions of work. Now they shifted definitely in the direction of a study of human relations.

Briefly, the new plan called for interviewing a much larger group of employees than any hitherto studied, with the object of learning more about their feelings and attitudes. A beginning was to be made in the Inspection Branch, representing about 1,600 skilled and unskilled employees in both shop and office work. In the report of January, 1931, the investigators stated that their purposes had been the following:

> First, we wanted to know how employees felt about their work and the way they were treated; second, we desired to learn the manner in which the company policies were being applied and employees' reactions to them; third, we were hopeful that something would come out of these employee expressions which could be used to develop and improve the training of supervisors.

The supervisors in the Inspection organization were called together, and the project was described to them. Their criticism was invited, and various points in the plan were discussed at this meeting. Five interviewers were chosen from among the supervisors to conduct the interviews. Women were selected to interview women, and men to interview men. The interviewers were not to interview employees whom they knew, since their acquaintanceship might influence what was said. In particular, it was obvious that no one should interview any worker over whom he had administrative authority. Records of the interviews were to be kept, and comments on the working situation were to be set down as nearly verbatim as possible, but all records were to be confidential. The names of the persons interviewed were not to be associated with the records, and any identifying statements were to be omitted. This rule was kept so well that it limited the usefulness of the records. It meant that the details of particular interviews could not be put together to give a picture of an entire working group or department.

In accordance with these plans, the interviewing of employees in the Inspection organization was begun in September, 1928, a year and a half after the beginning of the Relay Assembly Test Room experiment. It was completed early in 1929. So favorable were the results that the decision was made to extend the program to the Operating Branch. For this purpose, the Division of Industrial Research was organized on February 1, 1929, with functions which were stated as follows:

1. To interview annually all employees to find out their likes and dislikes relative to their working status.
2. To study the favorable and unfavorable comments of employees.
   a. To initiate correction or adjustment of causes of unfavorable comments.
   b. To determine upon benefits to be derived from favorable comments and to instigate ways and means of acquiring these benefits.
3. To conduct supervisory training conferences for all supervisors using employee interviews as a basis.
4. To conduct test studies relative to employee relations, fatigue and efficiency.

*   *   *

The results of the Interviewing Program were interesting from the first. The program was received with enthusiasm by both supervisors and operators. "This is the best thing the Company ever did" and "The Company ought to have done this long ago" were the sort of comments commonly encountered. The employees seemed to enjoy the opportunity of expressing their thoughts. They felt some kind of release, as if feelings which had long been pent up within them had at last found an outlet. Requests for interviews were received, some from the supervisors themselves. Accordingly, the interviewing was extended beyond its original bounds to group and section chiefs, that is, those supervisors immediately in charge of the rank and file.[1] In the course of their interviews, these supervisors were asked what they thought of the program and its effect. They were in its favor. They felt that it had not embarrassed them, that the employees liked it, and that it ought to be kept up and extended.

Evidence soon accumulated that the interviews not only gave expression to attitudes hitherto pent up but also, in giving them expression, changed them. The report of 1931 explained this rather unexpected result by an analogy:

It has long been known that one who writes a memorandum greatly clears his thought upon the material to be presented. Exaggerations, distortions,

---

[1] The name "supervisor" is often given at Hawthorne to all ranks of supervision above the worker. The first-line supervisor, in direct contact with the operators, is the group chief. The three ranks above him are section chief, assistant foreman, and foreman. A foreman is in charge of a department.

emotional reactions, defenses, etc., are largely dissolved when thus viewed objectively. In a similar way employees who express their thought and feeling to a critical listener discharge emotional and irrational elements from their minds. Many personal and individual problems and attitudes have been improved by the verbal expression which the interview affords. Taking account of the employee expressions recorded in 20,000 interviews, we feel that this value in interviewing cannot be lightly overlooked.

The observation has been made, perhaps too cynically, that in building up good industrial relations it makes little difference what measures are taken to improve working conditions as long as the rank and file realize what the purpose of the measures is. The important factor is the conviction of the workers that the management is concerned about their welfare. Something of this sort Whitehead had in mind when he said of the Relay Assembly Test Room that, though the experimental changes might turn out to have no physical significance, their social significance was always favorable. In the same way in the Interviewing Program, the discovery that management was taking an interest in what they thought and felt was new and stimulating for many of the employees. It may be well to repeat here that the Western Electric Company has had a long record of intelligent treatment of its workers, which is reflected in the confidence the workers have in the Company. Without this confidence many of the results of the investigations at Hawthorne could not have been achieved. At the same time the investigations strengthened this confidence.

The effect of the Interviewing Program on the supervisors was not less interesting. The opinion of the management was that supervision improved almost simultaneously with the beginning of interviewing. This improvement was not the result of fear on the part of supervisors that their methods would be disclosed and shown to be faulty. There was apparently no such fear. It was the result rather of an increased knowledge of and interest in the method of supervision which came from the knowledge that it was being made a subject for research. The records of the interviews were used as illustrative material for the training of supervisors and for conferences on supervision. An effort was made to see that as many supervisors as possible should have temporary experience as interviewers. Those who took part felt that they acquired a new understanding of the human problems of industry and, not less important, a new understanding of themselves. In fact the two must go together in any study of human behavior. A man can carry his analysis of other men no further than he has carried his analysis of himself. Finally, the men who were most closely associated with the Interviewing Program felt great enthusiasm for the work. They felt that they were acquiring new understanding, that they were free to move wherever the facts led them, and that in the end they would come out with something useful. The Chairman of the Committee pointed out that there seemed to be the same disinterested curiosity among the investigators as there is in any scientific research laboratory when the work is going well.

The investigators came away from the Relay Assembly Test Room with the feeling that management really knew very little about what constituted good supervision or what the employees thought about their conditions of work. The

Interviewing Program was designed to provide such knowledge. It is significant that, in the original plan for the interviews, orders were given that comments on the working situation were to be recorded as nearly verbatim as possible. This material was the sort which was supposed to be important. The interviewers went to their early interviews with something like a series of questions in their heads which they expected the employees to answer. The questions concerned such matters as working conditions, job, supervision, and so forth. The interview was to consist in effect of a series of answers to these questions. It is true that the interviewers were cautioned against putting these questions directly to the person being interviewed. Instead they were to enter into conversation with the employee and lead him around to the appropriate subjects only as opportunity served. Nevertheless the questions existed. Unfortunately for this plan, the discovery was soon made that a series of questions did not form a satisfactory basis for an interview. Questions did produce opinions, but the opinions were of unequal value. For one thing, comments on persons were less likely to produce information on which action could be based than were comments on material conditions of work. Whenever a number of employees working in the same neighborhood complained of cold, smoke and fumes, insufficient locker space, or some other physical source of irritation, an investigation could be made. In many instances the complaints were found to be justified and the conditions were corrected. But complaints about persons and about supervision in general usually had to be disregarded. Investigation showed that they had more reference to the attitudes people took toward situations than to the situations themselves.

* * *

These conclusions were very general and seemed to be rather questions for further investigation than statements of observed fact. Nevertheless the experience of the interviewers did have one immediate result: a change in the method of interviewing. In order that the flow of the narrative may not be interrupted, the final form of the method as it was developed at Hawthorne will be described in a separate part of this report, but a word or two about it will not be out of place here. The report of 1931 described it as follows:

> The interviewer is introduced to the employee, and the interviewer "catches on" in a conversational way at any starting point mentioned by the employee. As long as an employee talks the interviewer follows his comments, displaying a real interest in what the employee has to say and taking sufficient notes to recall the employee's various comments. While the employee continues, no attempt is made on the part of the interviewer to change the subject, because it is a basic assumption of the method that, where the employee chooses his own topics, he chooses them largely in their order of importance for him. If the interviewer were to ask questions or to redirect the employee's comment to other topics or subjects he would in a sense ask the employee to talk about a subject important perhaps to the interviewer, but not necessarily at all important to the employee. The interviewer takes part in the conversation only in so far as it is necessary to keep the employee talking and to stimulate confidence.

This is a description of the interviewing method as used by an interviewer assigned temporarily at the Industrial Research Division from a line organization. The permanent staff interviewers would carry the technique one step further.

> They would listen very carefully for indications of stress and strain in the expressed thought of the individual. They would identify this unusual or exaggerated feeling on the part of the employee by such symptoms as expressions made with unusual emotion, exaggeration, or reiteration. These more skilled interviewers would then, carefully perhaps, press these topics further by questions and suggestions after the employee seemed to be otherwise "talked out." By this subsequent probing of these "spots" in the attitude and feeling of employees, new levels of meaning and interpretation are discovered both for the interviewer and the employee.

Clearly the set of questions with which the early investigators had gone to their interviews had wholly disappeared, and instead of regarding the personal preoccupations of the employees as in a sense irrelevant, the investigators were carefully following them up as a source of important understanding of the person interviewed and the human situation in the plant.

It is obvious that the Western Electric researches were all interrelated. One led to another. In planning each experiment, the investigators had in their minds hypotheses which they wished to test; but more important than any hypotheses was the simple desire to find out more about the employees. The factors which led to the next development of the research program were complicated and certainly were not fully realized at the time by the investigating group. The program had begun with a simple attempt to discover by experimentation the effect of changes in physical conditions on efficiency of work. The technique used was a standard one: other factors were to be held constant in order to isolate the effect on the output rate of changes in working conditions. The Relay Assembly Test Room showed that this method would not yield the expected results. In the very process of setting up the experiment, one of the important factors affecting output was being varied rather than held constant. But full realization of this fact did not come until later. The point which emerged at once from the Relay Assembly Test Room was that management really knew very little about the employees' reaction to physical conditions of work and methods of supervision. The Interviewing Program was undertaken with the object of finding out more about these matters, but once more the expectations of the investigators were not realized. The comments elicited from the employees in the interviews were of only limited use in improving working conditions and methods of supervision, and attempts to analyze the material statistically in terms of likes and dislikes came to no significant conclusions.

On the other hand, the comments did acquire meaning if they were taken in their context, as symptoms of sentiments, beliefs, unconscious assumptions held by the persons interviewed; and for a time the investigators were much interested in studying the employees as individuals, each with a personal history which, properly understood, explained much of his behavior. Members of the Department of Industrial Research in the Graduate School of Business Administration, Harvard University, had advised the company in the researches and had followed them closely. The next suggestion came from W. L. Warner, at that time Assistant Professor of Anthropology in Harvard University. It was that the comments secured in the interviews could not be treated as products of individual human beings. They were the precipitate of interaction between people in organized social groups: families, neighborhoods, working groups, and so forth. The investigators were naturally most interested in the social organization of the employees at the Hawthorne Works; and as a result of this new understanding, they gradually lost interest in individual interviews, just as they had lost interest in the Relay Assembly Test Room. They took another step away from their original point of departure and turned to what they were fond of calling the "actual working situation." They were beginning to study the social relations between people actually at work on the job.

Furthermore, the investigators were turned in this direction by certain practical problems which had arisen in the course of the Interviewing Program. The interviewers were receiving a more thorough training. The plan of interviewing all employess once a year had been adopted, but the interviews had grown longer and therefore more expensive. And there were employees who needed interviewing more often than once a year. A good picture of their situation could not be applied as a regular program all over the plant. There seemed to be a need both to limit and to concentrate the effort of interviewing.

Finally, the investigators discovered, in the course of the regular interviews, evidence here and there in the plant of a type of behavior which strongly suggested that the workers were banding together informally in order to protect themselves against practices which they interpreted as a menace to their welfare. This type of behavior manifested itself in (a) "straight-line" output, that is, the operators had adopted a standard of what they felt to be a proper day's work and none of them exceeded it by very much; (b) a resentment of the wage incentive system under which they worked—in most cases, some form of group piecework; (c) expressions which implied that group piecework as a wage incentive plan was not working satisfactorily; (d) informal practices by which persons who exceeded the accepted standard, that is, "rate killers," could be punished and "brought into line"; (e) informal leadership on the part of individuals who undertook to keep the working group together and enforce its rules; (f) preoccupations of futility with regard to promotion; and (g) extreme likes and dislikes toward immediate superiors, according to their attitude toward the behavior of the operators. The investigators felt that this complex of behavior deserved further study.

In view of these considerations, the decision was taken in May, 1931, to assign selected interviewers to particular groups of employees and allow them to interview the employees as often as they felt was necessary. The story of one of these groups is characteristic of the findings reached by this new form of interviewing. The work of the employees was the adjustment of small parts which went into the construction of telephone equipment. The management thought that the adjustment was a complicated piece of work. The interviewer found that it was really quite simple. He felt that anyone could learn it, but that the operators had conspired to put a fence around the job. They took pride in telling how apparatus which no one could make work properly was sent in from the field for adjustment. Then telephone engineers would come in to find out from the operators how the repairs were made. The latter would fool around, doing all sorts of wrong things and taking about two hours to adjust the apparatus, and in this way prevented people on the outside from finding out what they really did. They delighted in telling the interviewer how they were pulling the wool over everybody's eyes. It followed that they were keeping the management in ignorance as to the amount of work they could do. The output of the group, when plotted, was practically a straight line.

Obviously this result could not have been gained without some informal organization, and such organization in fact there was. The group had developed leadership. Whenever an outsider—engineer, inspector, or supervisor—came into the room, one man always dealt with him. Whenever any technical question was raised about the work, this employee answered it. For other purposes, the group had developed a second leader. Whenever a new man came into the group, or a member of the group boosted output beyond what was considered the proper level, this second leader took charge of the situation. The group had, so to speak, one leader for dealing with foreign and one for dealing with domestic affairs. The different supervisors were largely aware of the situation which had developed, but they did not try to do anything about it because in fact they were powerless. Whenever necessary, they themselves dealt with the recognized leaders of the group.

Finally, the investigator found that the group was by no means happy about what it was doing. Its members felt a vague dissatisfaction or unrest, which showed itself in a demand for advancements and transfers or in complaints about their hard luck in being kept on the job. This experience of personal futility could be explained as the result of divided loyalties—divided between the group and the company.

In order to study this kind of problem further, to make a more detailed investigation of social relations in a working group, and to supplement interview material with direct observation of the behavior of employees, the Division of Industrial Research decided to set up a new test room. But the investigators remembered what happened in the former test room and tried to devise an experiment which would not be radically altered by the process of experimentation itself. They chose a group of men—nine wiremen, three soldermen, and tow inspectors—engaged in the assembly of terminal banks for use in telephone exchanges, took them out of their regular department and placed them in a special room. Otherwise no change was made in their conditions of work, except that an investigator was installed in the room, whose duty was simply to observe the behavior of the men. In the Relay Assembly Test Room a log had been kept of the principal events of the test. At the beginning it consisted largely of comments made by the workers in answer to questions about their physical condition. Later it came to include a much wider range of entries, which were found to be extremely useful in interpreting the changes in the output rate of the different workers. The work of the observer in the new test room was in effect an expansion of the work of keeping the log in the old one. Finally, an interviewer was assigned to the test room; he was not, however, one of the population of the room but remained outside and interviewed the employees from time to time in the usual manner. No effort was made to get output records other than the ones ordinarily kept in the department from which the group came, since the investigators felt that such a procedure would introduce too large a change from a regular shop situation. In this way the experiment was set up which is referred to as the Bank Wiring Observation Room. It was in existence seven months, from November, 1931, to May, 1932.

The method of payment is the first aspect of this group which must be described. It was a complicated form of group piecework. The department of which the workers in the observation room were a part was credited with a fixed sum for every unit of equipment it assembled. The amount thus earned on paper by the department every week made up the sum out of which the wages of all the men in the department were paid. Each individual was then assigned an hourly rate of pay, and he was guaranteed this amount in case he did not make at least as much on a piecework basis. The rate was based on a number of factors, including the nature of the job a worker was doing, his efficiency, and his length of service with the company. Records of the output of every worker were kept, and every six months there was a rate revision, the purpose of which was to make the hourly rates of the different workers correspond to their relative efficiency.

The hourly rate of a given employee, multiplied by the number of hours worked by him during the week, was spoken of as the daywork value of the work done by the employee. The daywork values of the work done by all the employees in the department were then added together, and the total thus obtained was subtracted from the total earnings credited to the department for the number of units of equipment assembled. The surplus, divided by the total daywork value, was expressed as a percentage. Each individual's hourly rate was then increased by this percentage, and the resulting hourly earnings figure, multiplied by the number of hours worked, constituted that person's weekly earnings.

Another feature of the system should be mentioned here. Sometimes a stoppage which was beyond the control of the workers took place in the work. For such stoppages the workers were entitled to claim time out, being paid at their regular hourly rates for this time. This was called the "daywork allowance claim." The reason why the employees were paid their hourly rate for such time and not their average hourly wages was a simple one. The system was supposed to prevent stalling. The employees could earn more by working than they could by taking time out. As a matter of fact, there was no good definition of what constituted a stoppage which was beyond the control of the workers. All stoppages were more or less within their control. But this circumstance was supposed to make no difference in the working of the system, since the assumption was that in any case the workers, pursuing their economic interests, would be anxious to keep stoppages at a minimum.

This system of payment was a complicated one, but it is obvious that there was a good logical reason for every one of its features. An individual's earnings would be affected by changes in his rate or in his output and by changes in the output of the group as a whole. The only way in which the group as a whole could increase its earnings was by increasing its total output. It is obvious also that the experts who designed the system made certain implicit assumptions about the behavior of human beings, or at least the behavior of workers in a large American factory. They assumed that every employee would pursue his economic interest by trying to increase not only his own output but the output of every other person in the group. The group as a whole would act to prevent slacking by any of its members. One possibility, for instance, was that by a few weeks' hard work an employee could establish a high rate for himself. Then he could slack up and be paid out of all proportion with the amount he actually contributed to the wages of the group. Under these circumstances, the other employees were expected to bring pressure to bear to make him work harder.

Such was the way in which the wage incentive scheme ought to have worked. The next question is how it actually did work. At first the workers were naturally suspicious of the observer, but when they got used to him and found that nothing out of the ordinary happened as a result of his presence in the room, they came to take him for granted. The best evidence that the employees were not distrustful of the observer is that they were willing to talk freely to him about what they were doing, even when what they were doing was not strictly in accord with what the company expected. Conversation would die down when the group chief entered the room, and when the foreman or the assistant foreman entered everyone became serious. But no embarrassment was felt at the presence of the observer. To avoid misunderstanding, it is important to point out that the observer was in no sense a spy. The employees were deliberately and obviously separated from their regular department. The observer did not, and could not, pass himself off as one of them. And if only from the fact that a special interviewer was assigned to them, the members of the group knew they were under investigation.

The findings reached by the observer were more detailed but in general character the same as those which had emerged from the early interviews of other groups. Among the employees in the observation room there was a notion of a proper day's work. They felt that if they had wired two equipments a day they had done about the right amount. Most of the work was done in the morning. As soon as the employees felt sure of being able to finish what they considered enough for the day, they slacked off. This slacking off was naturally more marked among the faster than among the slower workmen.

As a result, the output graph from week to week tended to be a straight line. The employees resorted to two further practices in order to make sure that it should remain so. They reported more or less output than they performed and they claimed more daywork allowances than they were entitled to. At the end of the day, the observer would make an actual count of the number of connections wired—something which was not done by the supervisors—and he found that the men would report to the group chief sometimes more and sometimes less work than they actually had accomplished. At the end of the period of observation, two men had completed more than they ever had reported, but on the whole the error was in the opposite direction. The theory of the employees was that excess work produced on one day should be saved and applied to a deficiency on another day. The other way of keeping the output steady was to claim excessive daywork allowance. The employees saw that the more daywork they were allowed, the less output they would have to maintain in order to keep the average hourly output rate steady. The claims for daywork allowance were reported by the men to their group chief, and he, as will be seen, was in no position to make any check. These practices had two results. In the first place, the departmental efficiency records did not represent true efficiency, and therefore decisions as to grading were subject to errors of considerable importance. In the second place, the group chief was placed in a distinctly awkward position.

The findings of the observer were confirmed by tests which were made as a part of the investigation. Tests of intelligence, finger dexterity, and other skills were given to the workers in the room, and the results of the tests were studied in order to discover whether there was any correlation between output on the one hand and earnings, intelligence, or finger dexterity on the other. The studies showed that there was not. The output was apparently not reflecting the native intelligence or dexterity of the members of the group.

Obviously the wage incentive scheme was not working in the way it was expected to work. The next question is why it was not working. In this connection, the observer reported that the group had developed an informal social organization, such as had been revealed by earlier investigations. The foreman who selected the employees taking part in the Bank Wiring Observation Room was cooperative and had worked with the investigators before. They asked him to produce a normal group. The men he chose all came out of the same regular shop department, but they had not been closely associated in their work there. Nevertheless, as soon as they were thrown together in the observation room friendships sprang up and soon two well-defined cliques were formed. The division into cliques showed itself in a number of ways: in mutual exclusiveness, in differences in the games played during off-hours, and so forth.

What is important here is not what divided the men in the observation room but what they had in common. They shared a common body of sentiments. A person should not turn out too much work. If he did, he was a "rate-buster." The theory was that if an excessive amount of work was turned out, the management would lower the piecework rate so that the employees would be in the position of doing more work for approximately the same pay. On the other hand, a person should not turn out too little work. If he did, he was a "chiseler"; that is, he was getting paid for work he did not do. A person should say nothing which would injure a fellow member of the group. If he did, he was a "squealer." Finally, no member of the group should act officiously.

The working group had also developed methods of enforcing respect for its attitudes. The experts who devised the wage incentive scheme assumed that the group would bring pressure to bear upon the slower workers to make them work faster and so increase the earnings of the group. In point of fact, something like the opposite occurred. The employees brought pressure to bear not upon the slower workers but upon the faster ones, the very ones who contributed most to the earnings of the group. The pressure was brought to bear in various ways. One of them was "binging." If one of the employees did something which was not considered quite proper, one of his fellow workers had the right to "bing" him. Binging consisted of hitting him a stiff blow on the upper arm. The person who was struck usually took the blow without protest and did not strike back. Obviously the virtue of binging as punishment did not lie in the physical hurt given to the worker but in the mental hurt that came from knowing that the group disapproved of what he had done. Other practices which naturally served the same end were sarcasm and the use of invectives. If a person turned out too much work, he was called names, such as "Speed King" or "The Slave."

It is worth while pointing out that the output of the group was not considered low. If it had been, some action might have been taken, but in point of fact it was perfectly satisfactory to the management. It was simply not so high as it would have been if fatigue and skill had been the only limiting factors.

In the matter of wage incentives, the actual situation was quite different from the assumptions made by the experts. Other activities were out of line in the same way. The wiremen and the soldermen did not stick to their jobs; they frequently traded them. This was forbidden, on the theory that each employee ought to do his own work because he was more skilled in that work. There was also much informal helping of one man by others. In fact, the observation of this practice was one means of determining the cliques into which the group was divided. A great many things, in short, were going on in the observation room which ought not to have been going on. For this reason it was important that no one should "squeal" on the men.

A group chief was in immediate charge of the employees. He had to see that they were supplied with parts and that they conformed to the rules and standards of the work. He could reprimand them for misbehavior or poor performance. He transmitted orders to the men and brought their requests before the proper authorities. He was also responsible for reporting to the foreman all facts which ought to come to his attention. The behavior of the employees put him in an awkward position. He was perfectly well aware of the devices by which they maintained their production at a constant level. But he was able to do very little to bring about a change. For instance, there was the matter of claims for daywork allowance. Such claims were supposed to be based on stoppages beyond the control of the workers, but there was no good definition of what constituted such stoppages. The men had a number of possible excuses for claiming daywork allowance: defective materials, poor and slow work on the part of other employees, and so forth. If the group chief checked up on one type of claim, the workers could shift to another. In order to decide whether or not a particular claim was justified, he would have to stand over the group all day with a stop watch. He did not have time to do that, and in any case refusal to honor the employees' claims would imply doubt of their integrity and would arouse their hostility. The group chief was a representative of management and was supposed to look after its interests. He ought to have put a stop to these practices and reported them to the foreman. But if he did so, he would, to use the words of a short account of the observation room by Roethlisberger and Dickson, "lose sympathetic control of his men, and his duties as supervisor would become much more difficult."[2] He had to associate with the employees from day to day and from hour to hour. His task would become impossible if he had to fight a running fight with them. Placed in this situation, he chose to side with the men and report unchanged their claims for daywork. In fact there was very little else he could do, even if he wished. Moreover he was in a position to protect himself in case of trouble. The employees always had to give him a reason for any daywork claims they might make, and he entered the claims in a private record book. If anyone ever asked why so much daywork was being claimed, he could throw the blame wherever he wished. He could assert that materials had been defective or he could blame the inspectors, who were members of an outside organization. In still another respect, then, the Bank Wiring Observation Room group was not behaving as the logic of management assumed that it would behave.

Restriction of output is a common phenomenon of industrial plants. It is usually explained as a highly logical reaction of the workers. They have increased their output, whereupon their wage rates for piecework have been reduced. They are doing more work for the same pay. They restrict their output in order to avoid a repetition of this experience. Perhaps this explanation holds good in some cases, but the findings of the Bank Wiring Observation Room suggest that it is too simple. The workers in the room were obsessed with the idea that they ought to hold their production level "even" from week to week, but they were vague as to what would happen if they did not. They said that "someone" would "get them." If they turned out an unusually high output one week, that record would be taken thereafter as an example of what they could do if they tried, and they would be "bawled out" if they did not keep up to it. As a matter of fact, none of the men in the room had ever experienced a reduction of wage rates. What is more, as Roethlisberger and Dickson point out, "changes in piece rates occur most frequently where there is a change in manufacturing process, and changes in manufacturing process are made by engineers whose chief function is to reduce unit cost wherever the saving will justify the change. In some instances, changes occur irrespective of direct labor cost. Moreover, where labor is a substantial element, reduction of output tends to increase unit costs and instead of warding off a change in the piece rate may actually induce one."

What happened in the observation room could not be described as a logical reaction of the employees to the experience of rate reduction. They had in fact had no such experience. On the other hand, the investigators found that it could be described as a conflict between the technical organization of the plant and its social organization. By technical organization the investigators meant the plan, written or unwritten, according to which the Hawthorne plant was supposed to operate, and the agencies which gave effect to that plan. The plan included

---

[2] F. J. Roethlisberger and W. J. Dickson, "Management and the Worker," Harvard Business School: Division of Research, Business Research Studies, No. 9 (a monograph). (All quotations relating to the Western Electric researches are from this study as well as from the book of the same title by the same authors.)

explicit rules as to how the men were to be paid, how they were to do their work, what their relations with their supervisors ought to be. It included also implicit assumptions on which the rules were based, one of the assumptions being that men working in the plant would on the whole act so as to further their economic interests. It is worth while pointing out that this assumption was in fact implicit, that the experts who devised the technical organization acted upon the assumption without ever stating it in so many words.

There existed also an actual social situation within the plant: groups of men, who were associated with one another, held common sentiments and had certain relations with other groups and other men. To some extent this social organization was identical with the technical plan and to some extent it was not. For instance, the employees were paid according to group payment plans, but the groups concerned did not behave as the planners expected them to behave.

* * *

The Bank Wiring Observation Room seemed to show that action taken in accordance with the technical organization tended to break up, through continual change, the routines and human associations which gave work its value. The behavior of the employees could be described as an effort to protect themselves against such changes, to give management the least possible opportunity of interfering with them. When they said that if they increased their output, "something" was likely to happen, a process of this sort was going on in their minds. But the process was not a conscious one. It is important to point out that the protective function of informal organization was not a product of deliberate planning. It was more in the nature of an automatic response. The curious thing is that, as Professor Mayo pointed out to the Committee, these informal organizations much resembled formally organized labor unions, although the employees would not have recognized the fact.

Roethlisberger and Dickson summarize as follows the results of the intensive study of small groups of employees:

> According to our analysis the uniformity of behavior manifested by these groups was the outcome of a disparity in the rates of change possible in the technical organization, on the one hand, and in the social organization, on the other. The social sentiments and customs of work of the employees were unable to accommodate themselves to the rapid technical innovations introduced. The result was to incite a blind resistance to all innovations and to provoke the formation of a social organization at a lower level in opposition to the technical organization.

It is curious how, at all points, the Relay Assembly Test Room and the Bank Wiring Observation Room form a contrast. In the former, the girls said that they felt free from the pressure of supervision, although as a matter of fact they were far more thoroughly supervised than they ever had been in their regular department. In the latter, the men were afraid of supervision and acted so as to nullify it. The Bank Wiremen were in the position of having to respond to technical changes which they did not originate. The Relay Assemblers had periodic conferences with the superintendent. They were told what experimental changes were contemplated; their views were canvassed, and in some instances they were allowed to veto what had been proposed. They were part of an experiment which they felt was interesting and important. Both groups developed an informal social organization, but while the Bank Wiremen were organized in opposition to management, the Relay Assemblers were organized in cooperation with management in the pursuit of a common purpose. Finally, the responses of the two groups to their industrial situation were, on the one hand, restriction of output and, on the other, steady and welcome increase of output. These contrasts carry their own lesson.

*   *   *

Alex Carey

THE HAWTHORNE STUDIES: A RADICAL CRITICISM

There can be few scientific disciplines or fields of research in which a single set of studies or a single researcher and writer has exercised so great an influence as was exercised for a quarter of a century by Mayo and the Hawthorne studies. Although this influence has declined in the last ten years as a result of the widespread failure of later studies to reveal any reliable relation between the social satisfactions of industrial workers and their work performance, reputable textbooks still refer almost reverentially to the Hawthorne studies as a classic in the history of social science in industry.

One might have expected therefore that the Hawthorne studies would have been subjected to the most searching and skeptical scrutiny; that before the remarkable claims of these studies, especially about the relative unimportance of financial rewards compared with purely social rewards, became so widely influential, the quality of the evidence produced and the validity of the inferences from it would have been meticulously examined and assessed. There have been broad criticisms of Mayo's approach and assumptions, many of them cogent. They include charges of promanagement bias, clinical bias, and scientific naivete.[1] But no one has applied systematically and in detail the method of critical doubt to the claim that there is scientific worth in the original reports of the Hawthorne investigators.

Abridged from Alex Carey, "The Hawthorne Studies: A Radical Criticism," *American Sociological Review* 32 (1967): 403-16. Reprinted by permission.

[1] For a review of these charges and criticisms see Delbert Miller and William Form, *Industrial Sociology* (New York: Harper & Row, Publishers, 1951), pp. 74-83. For a defense

BACKGROUND

The Hawthorne studies comprise a long series of investigations into the importance for work behavior and attitudes of a variety of physical, economic, and social variables. The principal investigations were carried out between 1927 and 1932, whereafter economic depression caused their suspension. The component studies may be distinguished as five stages:

> Stage I: The Relay Assembly Test Room Study. (New incentive system and new supervision).
> Stage II: The Second Relay Assembly Group Study. (New incentive system only).
> Stage III: The Mica Splitting Test Room Study. (New supervision only).
> Stage IV: The Interviewing Program
> Stage V: The Bank-Wiring Observation Room Study.

Stages I to III constitute a series of partially controlled studies which were initially intended to explore the effects on work behavior of variations in physical conditions of work, especially variations in rest pauses and in hours of work, but also in payment system, temperature, humidity, etc.

However, after the studies had been in progress for at least 12 months the investigators came to the entirely unanticipated conclusion that social satisfactions arising out of human association in work were more important determinants of work behavior in general and output in particular than were any of the physical and economic aspects of the work situation to which their attention had originally been limited.[2] This conclusion came as "the great *éclaircissement* . . . an illumination quite different from what they had expected from the illumination studies."[3] It is the central and distinctive finding from which the fame and influence of the Hawthorne studies derive.

This "éclaircissement" about the predominant importance of social satisfactions at work occurred during Stage I of the studies. In consequence, all the later studies are in important ways subordinate to Stage I: "It was the origin from which all the subsequent phases sprang. It was also their main focal point. It gave to these other phases their significance in relation to the whole enquiry."[4]

---

see Henry A. Landsberger, *Hawthorne Revisited* (New York: Cornell, 1958). Landsberger's defense is restricted to the report of the Hawthorne studies by Fritz J. Roethlisberger and William Dickson, *Management and the Worker* (Cambridge, Harvard University Press, 1939). Even this report, in Landsberger's view, has "done the field of human relations in industry an amount of harm which, in retrospect, appears to be almost irreparable." Landsberger, op. cit., p. 64.

[2] George A. Pennock, "Industrial Research at Hawthorne," *Personnel Journal* 8 (February, 1930): 296-313; Mark L. Putman, "Improving Employee Relations," *Personnel Journal* 8 (February, 1930): 314-25.

[3] Fritz J. Roethlisberger, *Management and Morale* (Cambridge: Harvard University Press, 1941), p. 15.

[4] Lyndall Urwick and Edward Brech, *The Making of Scientific Management* III, (London: Management Publications Trust, 1948): 27. See also Roethlisberger and Dickson, op. cit., p. 29.

Stages II and III were "designed to check on" (and were taken to supplement and confirm) the Stage I conclusion "that the observed production increase was a result of a change in the *social situation* . . . (and) not primarily because of wage incentives, reduced fatigue or similar factors."[5] Stage IV was an interviewing program undertaken to explore worker attitudes. Stage V was a study of informal group organization in the work situation.

The two later studies (IV and V) resulted directly from conclusions based on Stages I-III about the superior influence of social needs. Observations made in both were interpreted in the light of such prior conclusions. Hence it is clear that, as maintained by Urwick, Stage I was the key study, with Stages II and III adding more or less substantial support to it. The present paper will therefore be limited to a consideration of the evidence produced in Stages I-III for the famous Hawthorne conclusions about the superior importance for work behavior of social needs and satisfactions.

THE PREFERRED INCENTIVE
SYSTEM AND OUTPUT

Stage I: Relay Assembly Test Room (new incentive and new supervision). In Stage I of the Hawthorne studies, five girls who were employed assembling telephone relays were transferred from the factory floor to a special test room. Here their output of relays was recorded for over two years during which a large number of alterations were made in their working conditions. These alterations included a much less variable assembly task,[6] shorter hours, rest pauses, freer and more friendly supervision, and a preferred incentive system.[7] These changes were introduced cumulatively and no control group was established. Nonetheless, it was originally expected that the study would yield information about the influence of one or another physical condition of work.[8]

At the end of two years, the girls' output had increased by about 30 percent.[9] By this time, the investigators were confident that the physical changes in work conditions had been of little importance, and that the observed increase was due primarily to a change in "mental attitude" of the employees resulting from changed methods of supervision.[10] This change in mental attitude was chiefly characterized by a more relaxed "relationship of confidence and friendliness . . . such . . . that practically no supervision is required."[11]

However, the standard report of the study recognizes that any of several changes introduced concurrently could, hypothetically, have caused both the observed change in mental outlook and the associated increase in output. The authors of the report list the following as providing possible "hypotheses to

[5] Morris S. Viteles, *Motivation and Morale in Industry* (London: Staples, 1954), p. 185.

[6] Roethlisberger and Dickson, op. cit., pp. 21, 26.

[7] Ibid., pp. 22, 30-73.

[8] Ibid., p. 129; Pennock, op. cit., p. 299.

[9] Roethlisberger and Dickson, op. cit., p. 160.

[10] Ibid., pp. 189-190; Pennock, op. cit., pp. 297-309.

[11] Pennock, op. cit., p. 309.

explain major changes" in work behavior.[12] (1) changes in the character and physical context of the work task; (2) reduction of fatigue and monotony consequent upon introduction of rest pauses and reduced hours of work;[13] (3) change in the payment system; and (4) changes in supervision with consequent social changes in group relations.

The remainder of this paper will critically examine the evidence and arguments from which the investigators reached conclusions favorable to the last of these alternative hypotheses.

First hypothesis: changes in work task and physical context. The investigators allow that "the fact that most of the girls in the test room had to assemble fewer types of relays could not be entirely ignored. Operator 5's performance offered a convincing example. Of all the girls in the room she had had more different types of relays to assemble and of all the girls her output rate had shown the least improvement."[14] Whitehead reports that "later (1930-31) her (Operator 5's) working conditions were in line with the rest of the group and her comparative standing in the group definitely improved."[15]

However, it was subsequently found that statistical analysis of the relevant data (i.e., the varying output of five girls who were subjected to numerous cumulatively introduced experimental changes) did not show "any *conclusive* evidence in favor of the first hypothesis." On this ground the investigators "concluded that the change from one type of relay to another familiar type did not sufficiently slow up output to explain the increased output of the relay test room assemblers as compared with the assemblers in the regular department."[16] This conclusion leads the investigators to dismiss from further consideration the possibility that changes in task and conditions played any part at all in the observed increase in output.[17]

Second hypothesis: reduced fatigue due to rest pauses and shorter hours. The investigators recognize that "the rest pauses and shorter hours (may have) provided a relief from cumulative fatigue" resulting in higher output. They acknowledge that the fact that the rate of output of all but the slowest worker declined once the girls were returned to standard hours is "rather convincing evidence in favor of this argument."[18] Yet the investigators eventually dismiss

---

[12] Roethlisberger and Dickson, op. cit., pp. 86-89.

[13] The investigators list fatigue and monotony as separate hypotheses. For brevity, these have been combined as one hypothesis. The same sort of critical objections are relevant to the arguments and evidence advanced by the investigators with respect to both.

[14] Ibid., p. 87

[15] T. North Whitehead; *The Industrial Worker*, (London: Oxford University Press, 1938) I: 65.

[16] Roethlisberger and Dickson, op. cit., p. 89. (Italics added.)

[17] The scientifically illiterate procedure of dismissing non-preferred explanations on the grounds that (1) the experimenters had found no *conclusive* evidence in favor of them and/or (2) there was no evidence that any *one* of these explanations, considered by itself, accounted for *all* the effect observed, recurs throughout Roethlisberger and Dickson's report of the Hawthorne studies. This procedure is never applied to preferred hypotheses, which are assumed to be well-founded provided only that the evidence *against* them is less than conclusive. See, e.g., Roethlisberger and Dickson, op. cit., p. 160 and pp. 96, 108, 127.

[18] Ibid., p. 87

these factors on the grounds that under the new conditions of work neither work curves nor medical examinations provided evidence that fatigue effects were present. Viteles has commented bluntly in this connection: "It is interesting to note that (these grounds) are exactly the same used by other investigators in illustrating the effectiveness of rest pauses *by reason of reduced fatigue.*"[19]

By these arguments, the investigators eliminated the first two of the four hypotheses originally proposed as alternative explanations of the 30 percent increase in output observed in Stage I. This left two contending "explanations," the new incentive system, and the new kind of supervision and related social factors. The problem of choosing between these explanations led directly to the next major experiments.

Stage II: Second Relay Assembly Group (new incentive system only). The aim of (this experiment) was to reproduce the testroom situation (i.e., Stage I) only in respect to the one factor of method of payment, using another group of operators. Since method of payment was to be the only alteration from the usual situation, it was thought that any marked changes in output could be reasonably related to this factor."[20]

Five girls who were employed on the same sort of task as the girls in Stage I under normal conditions on the factory floor were given the preferred incentive system which had been used throughout Stage I. Under this sytem, the earnings of each girl were based on the average output of the five. Under the regular payment system, the earnings of each girl were based on the average output of the whole department (i.e., about 100 girls).

Almost at once the Stage II girls' output increased by 12.6 percent.[21] But the experiment caused so much discontent among the rest of the girls in the department, who wanted the same payment conditions,[22] that it was discontinued after only nine weeks. The output of the five girls promptly dropped by 16 percent.[23]

As Viteles comments, "the increase in output during the period when the wage incentive was in effect, followed by a production decrease with the elimination of the wage incentive, represents evidence ordinarily interpreted as indicative of the direct and favorable influence of financial incentives upon output."[24] However, the investigators reject this interpretation and, without producing supporting evidence of any substance, conclude firmly[25] that the increase was due to intergroup rivalry resulting from the setting up of this second small group.

[19] Morris S. Viteles, *Industrial Psychology* (New York: W. W. Norton & Company, Inc., 1932), p. 476. Italics in original.

[20] Roethlisberger and Dickson, op. cit., p. 129.

[21] Ibid., pp. 131-132, 577; Pennock, op. cit., p. 307.

[22] Ibid., p. 133.

[23] According to an earlier report (Pennock, op. cit., p. 307), the increase in output was 13.8 percent, the experiment was discontinued after five weeks, and output then fell by 19-24 percent.

[24] Viteles, Motivation . . ., op. cit., p. 187.

[25] Roethlisberger and Dickson, op. cit., pp. 133-34, 158, 577.

The change in payment system alone (Stage II) produced as much increase in output in nine weeks (possibly five weeks[26]) as was produced in about nine months by change in payment system together with a change to genial supervision (Stage I).[27] Yet this comparison appears not to have made any impression on the investigators' confidence about the superior importance of social factors.[28]

Stage III: Mica Splitting Test Room (new supervision but no change in payment system). In Stage I. numerous changes had been introduced, resulting in a 30 percent increase in output. In Stage II, only one of these changes (the preferred incentive system) was introduced and a rapid 12 percent increase in output resulted. In Stage III, "the test-room situation was to be duplicated in all respects except for the change in pay incentive. If . . . output showed a trend similar to that noted in (Stage I), it would suggest that the wage incentive was not the dominant factor in the situation."[29] Stage III, then, sought to test the combined effect on output of change to a separate room, change in hours, and the introduction of rest pauses and friendly supervision. Again a selected group of five girls was closely studied and an increase in output was recorded—15.6 percent in 14 months[30] or, if one follows Pennock, 20 percent in 12 months.[31]

A comparison between Stage III and Stage I has little prospect of scientific usefulness since in Stage III (1) the incentive system was different from both the disliked system used at the beginning of Stage I and the preferred system introduced shortly afterwards, (2) the type of work was quite different from Stage I, and (3) the experimental changes were quite different.[32] However, it is this comparison which has been taken by reporters of the studies[33] and by textbook authors[34] to provide the principal experimental evidence about the relative importance of financial and social motives as influences on output. Assuming with Roethlisberger and Dickson that Stage I and Stage III have some minimum comparability, it is important to examine precisely how the investigators dealt with the evidence from these stages for the purpose of the comparison.

Comparison Between Results in Stages I, II, and III. (1). Stage III produced a claimed 15 percent increase in rate of output over fourteen months. Thereafter

[26] Pennock, op. cit., p. 307.

[27] That is, by the end of Experimental Period 7 in Roethlisberger and Dickson's output chart, op. cit., p. 78.

[28] Roethlisberger and Dickson, op. cit., pp. 160, 577.

[29] Ibid., p. 129.

[30] Ibid., p. 148.

[31] Pennock, op. cit., p. 307.

[32] Roethlisberger and Dickson, op. cit., pp. 156, 159.

[33] Ibid., pp. 146-49, 159-60; Pennock, op. cit., p. 307.

[34] For example, "we cannot avoid being impressed by the fact that a wage incentive alone (Stage II) increased production 12 percent, a change in the social situation raised output 15 percent, (Stage III) and a combination of the two gave an increase of 30 percent. This looks surprisingly like an additive effect, with the social rewards being somewhat more potent in influencing behavior than the monetary reward." Ross Stagner, *Psychology of Industrial Conflict* (New York: John Wiley & Sons, Inc., 1956), pp. 131-32. See also Milton Blum, *Industrial Psychology and Its Social Foundations* (New York: Harper & Row, Publishers, 1949), p. 26.

the group's average rate of output declined for twelve months before the study was terminated due to the depression and lay-offs. The investigators attribute this decline *entirely* to anxieties induced by the depression,[35] ignoring the possibility that the preceding increase might also have been influenced by changing general economic and employment conditions. They do this despite evidence that output among a group of 5,500 Hawthorne workers rose by 7 percent in the two years preceding the experiment.[36]

(2). In Stage III, the output rate for each girl shows continuous and marked fluctuations over the whole two years of the study.[37] To obtain the percentage increase to be attributed to each girl the investigators chose, for each girl, a "peak" output period within the study period and measured her increase as the difference between this peak and her output rate at the outset of the study.[38] These peaks occur at different dates for different girls. To secure the 15 percent increase that is claimed, the study is, in effect, terminated at different conveniently selected dates for different girls. There is *no one period* over which the group achieved the 15 percent average increase claimed.[39]

(3). In Stage I, two measures of the workers' performance are used: total output per week,[40] and hourly rate of output by weeks.[41] It is not clear from Roethlisberger and Dickson's report of Stage I whether the increase is in *total output* or *rate of output*. It is described only as "increase in output," and "output rose . . . roughly 30 percent,"[42] which would ordinarily be taken to mean an increase in *total output*. But the investigators make it clear in passing[43] that throughout the studies they used rate of output per hour as "the most common arrangement of output data" by which to "portray the general trend in efficiency of each operator and of the group." Whitehead, who produced a two-volume statistical study of Stage I as companion volumes to Roethlisberger and Dickson's standard report, is very clear on this point: "All output will be expressed in the form of a *rate* . . . as so many relays per hour."[44]

However, Whitehead employs throughout his study the description *"weekly rate of output"* when he means *rate of output per hour by weeks.*[45] This practice, coupled with his habit of not labelling the ordinates of his charts dealing with changes in output, and added to by Roethlisberger and Dickson's use of phrases such as "increase in output" to mean both *increase in rate of*

<hr/>

[35] Viteles comments on this period of declining output: "Both 'the investigators and the operators were of the opinion that the rates on the new piece parts were not high enough in comparison with the old.' Nevertheless scant consideration is given to the possibility that . . . a reduced appeal to economic motives could readily account in large part for the very severe drop in output observed during this final phase of the *Mica Splitting Room experiment.*" Viteles, Motivation . . ., op. cit., p. 191.

[36] Whitehead, op. cit., vol. II, Chart J-53.

[37] Roethlisberger and Dickson, op. cit., p. 147.

[38] Ibid., p. 148.

[39] Ibid., pp. 146-48, 159-60.

[40] Ibid., p. 78.

[41] Ibid., p. 76.

[42] Ibid., p. 160.

[43] Ibid., pp. 55, 77.

[44] Whitehead, op. cit., vol. I, p. 34.

[45] Ibid., vol. II, Chart B4.

output per hour and *increase in total output*, has led to widespread misinterpretation of the Hawthorne results, and textbook accounts which are seriously in error.[46]

Several points are of present importance. For Stage I, it is not clear whether the 30 percent increase in output claimed refers to *rate of output* or *total output*. It does not matter which measure is used to calculate percent increase in output in Stage I since the total hours worked per week at the end of the study period is only 4.7 percent less than at the beginning.[47] Thus, an increase of the order of 30 percent would result from either method of calculation. In Stage III, however, it makes a great deal of difference which method is used, and hourly rate of output is the only measure used. Thus, the 15 percent "increase in output"[48] claimed for Stage III is an increase in *rate of output per hour worked*, not in *total output*. Indeed, it is only by this measure that any increase *at all* in output can be shown.

If *total output per week* is used to measure performance in Stage III, the 15 percent increase claimed for Stage III reduces to less than zero because although output per hour increased by 15 percent, the weekly hours decreased by 17 percent, from 55 1/2 to 46 1/6.[49]

From Evidence to Conclusions. By subtracting the 15 percent increase in Stage III (which is an increase in *rate* of output) from the 30 percent increase in output in Stage I (which is all, or nearly all, an increase in *total* output), the investigators conclude that 15 percent remains as "the maximum amount (of increase in output) to be attributed to the change in wage incentive" introduced in Stage I. The investigators acknowledge the wholly speculative nature of this calculation, yet go on to assert in a summary of events to date that the conclusion "seemed to be warranted from the test room studies so far . . . that it was impossible to consider (a wage incentive system) as a thing in itself having an independent effect on the individual."[50]

It is important to appreciate just how invalid are the inferences made. In Stage I, friendly supervision and a change to a preferred incentive system led to an increase in total output of about 30 percent. In Stage III, friendly supervision without a change in payment system led to no increase in total output, but to a less than compensating increase in output per hour over a period during which working hours were reduced from 55 1/2 to 46 1/6. This could be interpreted to mean that when working hours exceed about 48 per week such extra

[46] For example, Edwin Ghiselli and Clarence Brown, *Personnel and Industrial Psychology* (New York: McGraw-Hill Book Company, 1948) pp. 435-37; and James A. C. Brown, *Social Psychology of Industry* (Harmondsworth: Penguin, 1954), pp. 71-72. These authors incorrectly report an almost continuous increase in total weekly output over the first nine months of Stage I. In fact, there was no increase except in the period of eight weeks immediately following the introduction of the preferred incentive system. There was no improvement in weekly output in either the preceding period or the four experimental periods extending over six months which followed it.

[47] Roethlisberger and Dickson, op. cit., pp. 76-77.

[48] Ibid., pp. 159-60.

[49] Ibid., pp. 136-39.

[50] Ibid., p. 160. Viteles bluntly rejects this inference as invalid, but textbook treatments of the Hawthorne studies generally accept it without demur. Viteles, *Motivation* . . . op. cit., p. 193.

working-time may bring little or no increase in total output—a finding which had been well-established many years before.[51] This interpretation would have left the way clear to attribute the 30 percent increase in Stage I entirely to the preferred incentive system. Instead, by the rather special method of analysis and argument that has been outlined, the investigators reached the conclusion that the effect of a wage incentive system is so greatly influenced by social considerations that it is impossible to consider it capable of independent effect.

A similar situation holds with regard to Stage II. As Stage II was planned, the "method of payment was to be the only alteration from the usual situation" with the express intention that "any marked changes in output" could then be "related to this factor."[52] There *was* a marked change in output—an immediate 12 percent increase; There *was* an immediate change in behavior—the other girls in the department demanded the same conditions. This would seem to require a conclusion in favor of the importance of a preferred incentive system, but no such conclusion was reached.

As a first step in the interpretation of the Stage II results, Roethlisberger and Dickson noticed, *post hoc,* that somewhere in the "daily history record" of the Stage I group was a reference to a comment by one member of that group that a "lively interest" was being taken in their output by members of the new Stage II group.[53] At this point, the investigators simply note this and hint at significance to come. Twenty-four pages later we are told that "although output had risen an average of 12 percent in (Stage II) it was *quite apparent* that factors other than the change in wage incentive contributed to that increase . . . *There was some evidence* to indicate that the operators in (Stage II) had seized upon this test as an opportunity to prove to everyone that they could do as well as the (Stage I) operators. They were out to equal the latters' record. In view of this, even the most liberal estimate would put the increase in output due to the change in payment alone at somewhat less than 12 percent." (Italics added). Since no additional evidence had been produced, this judgment lacks any serious foundation.

Much later (p. 577) the matter is returned to and, with no additional evidence, we are given to understand that the increase in output in Stage II was due to certain "social consequences" of the "basic social situation." This situation is simply asserted to have been one in which "rivalry (with the Stage I group) was brought to a focus" by setting up the Stage II group whose "output rose rapidly" in consequence.

Stage II was "designed to test the effect of a (change in) wage incentive" on output.[54] The preferred incentive system was introduced and output immediately rose 12 percent. It was withdrawn and output immediately dropped

[51] Horace M. Vernon, *Industrial Fatigue and Efficiency* (London: Dutton, 1921). Ghiselli and Brown have summarized Vernon's findings as follows: "In a munitions plant, when the working week was reduced from 66 to 48.6 hours (a reduction of 26 percent) hourly output was increased by 68 percent and total output for the week by 15 percent. This instance could be multiplied many times." Ghiselli and Brown, op. cit., p. 242.
[52] Roethlisberger and Dickson, op. cit., p. 129.
[53] Ibid., p. 134.
[54] Ibid., p. 576.

17 percent. Not encouraging results for anyone who believed that wage incentives were relatively unimportant and incapable of "independent effects." Yet these awkward results were not only explained away but converted to positive support for just such conclusions, all on the basis of a single hearsay comment by one girl.

The investigators carry the day for the hypothesis that "social factors were the major circumstances limiting output." They conclude that "none of the results (in Stages I, II and III) gave the slightest substantiation to the theory that the worker is primarily motivated by economic interest. The evidence indicated that the efficacy of a wage incentive is so dependent on its relation to other factors that it is impossible to separate it out as a thing in itself having an independent effect."[55] This conclusion is a striking contrast to the objective results obtained in Stages I, II, and III as these bear on incentive systems: (1) when a preferred wage incentive system was introduced, total weekly output per worker rose (Stage I and Stage (II); (2) when the preferred incentive system was withdrawn, output promptly dropped (Stage II); (3) when changes in supervision, hours, etc., were introduced but with *no change in incentive system,* no increase in weekly output per worker resulted (Stage III).

Viteles, an unusually perceptive critic of the Hawthorne studies, has commented caustically on Stage III: "This increase in output, representing an average rise of 15 percent in the first 14 months of the experiment, would ordinarily be accepted as evidence that the introduction of rest pauses and the shortening of the work day can in themselves result in increased output, even in the absence of changes in the way of enhancing the wage incentive."[56] Yet Viteles misses the important point that there was no overall increase in total weekly output in Stage III—only a less than compensating increase in output per hour when shorter hours were worked. It is clear that he supposes the 15 percent increase to be an increase in total output.[57] Viteles' patience is great, and his criticism of the Hawthorne studies restrained. But they eventually draw from him a testy general protest about "the more 'subtle'—certainly more subjective—form of analysis and interpretation which has generally characterized interpretation of the Hawthorne data by the Harvard group."[58]

It remains to consider more closely the complementary Hawthorne claim that it was friendly supervision and social factors which were the principal influences leading to the large rise in output in Stage I.

A CLOSER LOOK AT FRIENDLY
SUPERVISION IN ACTION

The *whole* of the Hawthorne claim that friendly supervision and resulting workgroup social relations and satisfactions are overwhelmingly important for work behavior rests on whatever evidence can be extracted from Stage I, since

[55] Ibid., pp. 575-76.
[56] Viteles, op. cit., *Motivation* . . ., p. 190.
[57] Ibid., p. 5.
[58] Ibid., p. 256.

that is the only study in the series which exhibits even a surface association between the introduction of such factors and increased output.

Stage I began with five girls specially selected[59] for being both "thoroughly experienced" and "willing and cooperative,"[60] so there was reason to expect this group to be more than ordinarily cooperative and competent. Yet from very early in the study "the amount of talking indulged in by all the operators" had constituted a "problem," because it "involved a lack of attention to work and a preference for conversing together for considerable periods of time."[61] The first indication in the report that this might be a serious matter occurs on August 2nd, 1927, twelve weeks after the girls' installation in the test-room, when four of the five operators were brought before the foreman[62] and reprimanded for talking too much.[63] Until November, however, "no attempt had been made to do away with this privilege, although several attempts had been made by the foreman to diminish what seemed to him an excessive amount of talking." But Operators 1A and 2A in particular continued to fail to display "that 'wholehearted cooperation' desired by the investigators." "Any effort to reprimand them would bring the reply 'We thought you wanted us to work as we feel,' "[64] since that was what the supervisors had told them at the beginning of the study.[65]

By November 17th, 1927, the situation had not improved and disciplinary rules were resorted to. All of the operators were required to call out whenever they made mistakes in assembly, and they were prevented from talking. By December, "the lack of cooperation on the part of some of the operators was seriously alarming a few of the executives concerned." Supervisors were asked to give the girls a "hint" by telling them that they were not doing as well as expected of them and that if they didn't improve they would lose their free lunches.[66]

From now on the girls, but especially 1A and 2A, were "threatened with disciplinary action" and subjected to "continual reprimands." "Almost daily" 2A was "reproved" for her "low output and behavior" (sic).[67] The investigators decided 1A and 2A did not have "the 'right' mental attitude." 2A was called up before the test-room authorities "and told of her offenses of being moody and inattentive and not cooperative." She was called up again before the superintendent.[68] Throughout this period output for all five girls remained

[59] Note, however, that while the five girls were "all chosen from among those with a considerable experience in the assembly of this kind of relay" ... "the actual method of selection was quite informal and somewhat obscure; it appears to have been determined by the girls themselves in conjunction with their shop foreman." Whitehead, op. cit., vol. I, p. 14.

[60] Roethlisberger and Dickson, op. cit., p. 21.

[61] Ibid., p. 53.

[62] Foremen were on a par with departmental chiefs and four ranks above operatives. Ibid., p. 11.

[63] Ibid., p. 38.

[64] Ibid., p. 53.

[65] Ibid., p. 21; Whitehead, op. cit., vol. I, p. 26.

[66] Whitehead, op. cit., vol. I, p. 16.

[67] Ibid., pp. 116-18.

[68] Roethlisberger and Dickson, op. cit., p. 55. Superintendents controlled a branch of the works and were seven ranks above operators. Ibid., p. 11.

static or falling.[69] After eleven weeks of serious but ineffective disciplinary measures and eight months after the beginning of the study, 1A and 2A were dismissed from the test room for "gross insubordination" and declining or static output.[70] Or, as Whitehead puts it, they "were removed for a lack of cooperation, which would have otherwise necessitated greatly increased disciplinary measures."[71]

1A and 2A were replaced by two girls chosen by the foreman[72] "who were experienced relay assemblers and desirous of participating in the test." These two girls (designated Operators 1 and 2) were transferred to the test room on January 25th, 1928.[73] They *both* immediately produced an output much greater (in total and in rate per hour) than that achieved by *any* of the original five girls on their transfer to the test room and much above the performance *at any time* of the two girls they replaced.[74]

Operators 1 and 2 had been friends in the main shop. Operator 2 was the only Italian in the group; she was young (21) and her mother died shortly after she joined the test room;[75] after this "Operator 2 earned the larger part of the family income." "(F)rom now on the history of the test room revolves around the personality of Operator 2."[76] Operator 2 rapidly (i.e., without any delay during which she might have been affected by the new supervision) adopted and maintained a strong and effective disciplinary role with respect to the rest of the group,[77] and led the way in increased output in *every* period from her arrival till the end of the study. In this she was closely followed by the other new girl, Operator 1.[78]

At the time that Operators 1 and 2 were brought into the test room, daily hours of work were shortened by half an hour but it was decided to *pay the operators the day rate for the half hour of working time lost.* A little later, the working day was reduced by a further half hour, and again the girls were paid for

[69] Ibid., p. 78. See Experimental Period 7 in Figure 7.

[70] Ibid., pp. 53-57.

[71] Whitehead, op. cit., vol. I, p. 118. In Mayo's accounts it is first said that these two operators "dropped out" (Elton Mayo, *The Human Problems of an Industrial Civilization,* [Boston: Harvard Business School, 1946], p. 56) and later that they "retired." (Elton Mayo, *The Social Problems of an Industrial Civilization* [London: Routledge and Kegan Paul, 1949], p. 62.) It is also interesting to compare the above account of events in the test room and drawn from the standard reports with Mayo's picture of the test room. According to Mayo's account, success was achieved "largely because the experimental room was in charge of an interested and sympathetic chief observer. He understood clearly from the first that any hint of the 'supervisor' in his methods might be fatal to the interests of the inquiry ... He helped the group to feel that its duty was to set its own conditions of work, he helped the workers to find the 'freedom' of which they so frequently speak ... At no time in the (whole period of the study) did the girls feel that they were working under pressure." (Mayo, *The Human Problems . . . ,* op. cit., pp. 68-69).

[72] Roethlisberger and Dickson, op. cit., p. 60.

[73] Ibid., pp. 55, 56, 60.

[74] Ibid., Figure 6, p. 76 and Figure 7, p. 78. Compare output curves during the first seven Experimental Periods with output from the second week of Experimental Period 8.

[75] Ibid., pp. 61-62.

[76] Whitehead, op. cit., vol. I, p. 120.

[77] Ibid., pp. 120-29; Roethlisberger and Dickson, op. cit., pp. 63, 74, 86, 156, 167.

[78] Roethlisberger and Dickson, op. cit., p. 162.

the time (one hour per day) they didn't work.[79] Later still, the girls were given Saturday mornings off and again they were paid for the time not worked.[80]

Summing up the experience in the test room up to *exactly* the time when the two operators were dismissed,[81] the investigators claim that "it is clear" that over this period there was "a gradual change in social interrelations among the operators themselves, which displayed itself in the form of new group loyalties and solidarities . . . (and) . . . a change in the relations between the operators and their supervisors. The test room authorities had taken steps to obtain the girls' cooperation and loyalty and to relieve them of anxieties and apprehensions. From this . . . arose . . . a change in human relations which came to be of great significance in the next stage of the experiment, when it became necessary to seek a new hypothesis to explain certain unexpected results of the inquiry."[82] In view of the evidence reviewed here this would seem to be a somewhat sanguine assessment of developments in the test room up to this point. It is, therefore, necessary to examine more systematically the way in which the behavior of the supervisors on the one hand and of the operators on the other (including their changing output) varied during the period under consideration.

It is already clear that whatever part satisfying social relations at work—resulting from free and friendly supervision—may have played in producing the increase in output, there were other influences likely to have been important, e.g., a period of fairly stern discipline, the dismissal of two workers, and their replacement by people of rather special personality and motivation. In order to assess these various influences on output it is necessary to consider how work performance varied during the periods when these changes were introduced. This is difficult because none of the reports of the Hawthorne studies provides actual figures covering the way in which output changed throughout Stage I. Consequently, one must work with such estimates as can be derived from the various graphs and charts of output-change that are supplied, and supplemented by occasional statements in the texts which give additional quantitative information.

AN EXAMINATION OF THE EVIDENCE: VARIATIONS IN SUPERVISORY PRACTICE AND VARIATIONS IN OUTPUT

For present purposes, Stage I may be divided into three phases: Phase I: the first three and a half months in the test room during which supervision seems to

[79] Whitehead, op. cit., vol. I, pp. 121-22. Roethlisberger and Dickson (op. cit., pp. 60, 62) give no indication that the operators were paid for these hours not worked. Indeed, their account clearly implies that they were not so paid (ibid., pp. 63-64). But Whitehead is quite explicit on this point.

[80] Roethlisberger and Dickson do report (op. cit., p. 68) that the girls were paid for the half day on Saturdays which was not worked. They acknowledge that this "added a new factor to the situation which cannot be disregarded and which has to be taken into account in comparing this period with any other" (ibid., p. 69). They take no further account of it, however, just as they take no further account of the unworked hours paid for on the occasions when the work day was shortened.

[81] That is, up to the end of Experimental Period 7 in Roethlisberger and Dickson's terminology.

[82] Roethlisberger and Dickson, op. cit., pp. 58-59.

have been fairly consistently friendly, casual, and at low pressure; Phase II: a further interval of about seven months during which supervision became increasingly stern and close. This phase culminates in the dismissal of two of the five operators and their replacement by workers of rather special character and motivation. Phase III: a final long period during which output rose rapidly and there was a return to free and friendly supervision.

Supervision during Phase I. "Besides the girls who composed the group under study there was a person in the experimental room who was immediately in charge of the test." This was the test room observer whose twofold function was "to keep accurate records . . . and to create and maintain a friendly atmosphere in the test room." He "assume(d) responsibility for most of the day to day supervision" while in other matters such as accounting, rate revision, and promotion, responsibility rested with the foreman.[83]

It is quite clear from Roethlisberger and Dickson's account that during Phase I the supervisors did everything in their power to promote a free, cooperative, and noncoercive relationship.[84] At the outset of the study the girls "were asked to work along at a comfortable pace" and were assured "that no attempt would be made to force up production." They were led to expect changes in working conditions which might be "beneficial and desirable from the employees' point of view," and were told that there was no reason why "any (such) change resulting in greater satisfaction of employees" should not be maintained, and this "regardless of any change in production rate."[85] "The test room observer was chiefly concerned with creating a friendly relation with the operators which would ensure their cooperation. He was anxious to dispel any apprehensions they might have about the test and, in order to do this, he began to converse informally with them each day."[86] Some weeks after the study began, there was a friendly talk with the doctor about the physical examinations and ice cream was provided and a party planned. Also, the girls were "invited to the office of the superintendent who had talked to them, and in various other ways they had been made the object of considerable attention."[87] Although there had been from almost the beginning a good deal of talking among the girls, a fairly permissive attitude had been taken about this.[88]

Output during Phase I. There was "no appreciable change in output" on transfer to the test room,[89] but there was a "downward tendency" during the first five weeks thereafter,[90] despite facilities which "made the work slightly easier."[91]

At the end of five weeks, the new wage incentive system was introduced and

[83] Ibid., pp. 22, 37.
[84] Ibid., pp. 32-39.
[85] Ibid., p. 33.
[86] Ibid., p. 37.
[87] Ibid., pp. 34, 39.
[88] Ibid., p. 53.
[89] Pennock, op. cit., pp. 301, 304.
[90] Roethlisberger and Dickson, op. cit., p. 58.
[91] Ibid., pp. 33-34, 39.

output increased.[92] From the output chart[93] this increase may be estimated at 4 or 5 percent. However, this increase must be accepted with some caution, for the investigators report that the "change in method of payment necessitated a change in piece-rates."[94] It was apparently judged that under the new conditions of work, (which did not include all of the types of relay assembled on the shop floor, and where there was one layout operator to five assemblers instead of one to six or seven as on the shop floor) new rates were necessary. We are told that "the chief consideration in setting the new piece rates was to determine a rate for each relay type which would pay the operators the same amount of money they had received in the regular department for an equivalent amount of work."[95] But it is well-established that the unreliability of time-study ratings can be expected to yield errors of at least 5 percent between different ratings of similar tasks.[96] So no great reliance can be placed on the observed 4 or 5 percent increase in output following the introduction of the new incentive system and the associated new piece-rates. Indeed, there is perhaps some recognition of this in Roethlisberger and Dickson's introductory comment that early in the study "a change in wage payment was introduced, a necessary step before the *experiment proper* could begin."[97] Phase I ends after 15 weeks of friendly supervision with a somewhat doubtful increase of 5 percent which occurred with the introduction of a preferred incentive system.

Supervision during Phase II. "The second phase . . . covering an interval of approximately seven months was concerned with the effects of various kinds of rest pauses."[98] The investigators emphasize that by the *beginning* of this phase not only was supervision friendly, but the relation between workers and supervisors was "free and easy."[99] Their account of actual supervisory behavior during succeeding months supports these claims. (1) On each of the four occasions when rest pauses were varied, the girls were consulted in advance, and on all but one occasion their expressed preferences were accepted. (2) The investigators decided to pay the girls their bonuses monthly instead of weekly, but when the girls were told about this decision they objected and the plan was dropped. That the girls "felt free to express their attitudes" and that the investigators altered their plans out of regard for these attitudes is said to be "typical of the supervisory technique employed" which "proved to be a factor of utmost importance in interpreting the results of the study." (3) Later the girls were given free lunches and were consulted about what should be served.[100]

However, the problem of excessive talking among the girls worsened. No attempt had been made to prohibit talking, although four of the girls had been

[92] Ibid., p. 58.
[93] Ibid., p. 56.
[94] Ibid., p. 34.
[95] Ibid., p. 35.
[96] Viteles, *Motivation* . . ., op. cit., pp. 30-38.
[97] Roethlisberger and Dickson, op. cit., p. 29, italics added.
[98] Ibid., p. 40. This phase actually extends from Aug. 8, 1927 to January 21, 1928, a period of 24 weeks.
[99] Ibid., pp. 45-46.
[100] Ibid, pp. 48-9, 51.

"given a talk regarding their behavior."[101] Now this "lack of attention to work and preference for conversing together for considerable periods" was judged to be reaching such proportions that the "experiment was being jeopardized and something had to be done."[102] A variety of disciplinary procedures of increasing severity were applied, but with little effect. Finally, the leaders in talking (operators 1A and 2A) were dismissed from the test room "for lack of cooperation which would have otherwise necessitated greatly increased disciplinary measures."

Output during Phase II. There was no change in weekly output during this six-month period. "Total weekly output does not decline when rest pauses are introduced, but remains practically the same during all the rest period experiments."[103]

Supervision during Phase III. At the beginning of Phase III,[104] the two dismissed girls were replaced by two girls chosen by the foreman. Something has already been said about the way in which these girls at once took and maintained the lead in output and about how one of them, who had a special need for more money, took over the general leadership and discipline of the rest of the group. These points will bear underlining by direct quotation:

> When Operator 2 joined the group, her home was largely dependent upon her earnings, and within a few weeks her father lost his job and became temporarily unemployed. Thus, to her natural sense of responsibility was added the factor of poverty; and Operator 2 began to urge the remainder of the group to increase their output.[105]
> Operators 1 and 2 were very definitely the fastest workers of the group in 1928, and this was freely recognized by the others."[106]
> On the whole, from January to November 1928, the Relay Test Group showed no very marked developments apart from a growing tendency for the discipline to pass from the hands of the supervisor to those of the group itself, largely as represented in the person of Operator 2.[107]
> Operator 2 became recognized as the leader of the group, both by the operators themselves and by the supervisor. It is doubtful whether any operator could have secured this position unless she had been the fastest worker, but the other qualifications possessed by Operator 2 were a high sense of the importance of the work for the group and a forceful personality.[108]
> Op. 2 "Oh! what's the matter with those other girls. I'll kill them."[109] (This expostulation was provoked by the output curves showing operators 3, 4, and 5 on a downward trend.)

[101] Ibid., p. 38.
[102] Ibid., pp. 53-54.
[103] Ibid., p. 79.
[104] Actually on January 25, 1928, two days after the beginning of Phase III. Thus, the resulting sharp rise in output does not show fully on Roethlisberger and Dickson's weekly output charts (op. cit., pp. 76, 78) until the second week of their Experimental Period 8.
[105] Whitehead, op. cit., vol. I, pp. 122-23.
[106] Ibid., p. 126.
[107] Ibid., p. 124.
[108] Ibid., p. 129.
[109] Ibid., p. 127.

From then on supervision again became increasingly friendly and relaxed. This friendliness of supervision often had a very tangible character. From the arrival of the new workers in the test room, the observer "granted them (all) more and more privileges." The preferred incentive system, the rest pauses, the free lunches, and the "parties" following the regular physical examinations all continued.[110] In addition, within the next eight months the girls were first paid for half an hour per day not worked, and then for an hour a day not worked, and finally for Saturday mornings not worked. Approximately eight months after the arrival of the new girls, all these privileges except the preferred incentive system and the parties were withdrawn. The girls were warned in advance about this withdrawal of privileges and were assured that the new and heartily disliked conditions "would terminate after approximately three months." Despite this promise, the girls' work deteriorated immediately: they wasted time in various ways such as reading newspapers, eating candy, and going for drinks and the observer shortly "discovered that the girls were attempting to keep the output rate low . . . so as to make sure that rest pauses would be reinstated." The observer "again tried to stop the excessive talking" by "reprimand and threat." He told the girls that "unless excessive talking ceased it might become necessary to continue the experiment without rest pauses for a longer period."[111]

At this point, the girls had been in the test room 18 months and had achieved nearly all the eventual 30 percent increase in output. Yet it would seem that Operator 2, the incentive system, and the other privileges, as well as "reprimand and threat" played a significant part in determining the work behavior and output of the group. It is also clear from Roethlisberger and Dickson's account that for a great part of the time following the arrival of Operators 1 and 2, the girls worked very well and happily and that while they did so, supervision was relaxed and friendly and relations continued to be satisfactory. But there would seem to be good grounds for supposing that supervision became more friendly and relaxed because output increased rather than vice versa.

Output during Phase III. Output for the whole group rose markedly during the several months after the dismissal of 1A and 2A, owing chiefly to the contributions from the new operators.[112] Thereafter, the group's total output rose more slowly for a further year (with a temporary drop when the Saturday morning shift was discontinued for a time).

SUMMARY OF EVIDENCE ABOUT SUPERVISION AND OUTPUT

(1). Apart from a doubtful 4-5 percent increase following the introduction of a preferred incentive system, there was no increase in weekly output during the first nine months in the test room, despite a great deal of preoccupation on the

[110] Roethlisberger and Dickson, op. cit., pp. 71, 72, 77.
[111] Ibid., pp. 70-72.
[112] Ibid., Figure 7, p. 78.

part of the supervisors with friendliness towards the workers, with consultation, and the provision of a variety of privileges not enjoyed on the factory floor.

(2). From the beginning of what Roethlisberger and Dickson describe aş the "experiment proper," that is, after the period in which the new incentive system was introduced, there was no increase in weekly output during the next six months. When it became apparent that free and friendly supervision was not getting results, discipline was tightened, culminating in the dismissal of two of the five girls.

(3). The dismissed girls were replaced by two girls of a special motivation and character who *immediately* led the rest in a sustained acceleration of output. One of these girls who had a special need for extra money rapidly adopted and maintained a strong disciplinary role with respect to the rest of the group. The two new girls led the way in increased output from their arrival till the end of the study.

(4). Total output per week showed a significant and sustained increase only after the two girls who had the lowest output[113] were dismissed and replaced by selected output leaders who account for the major part of the groups' increase, both in output rate and in total output, over the next seventeen months of the study.

(5). After the arrival of the new girls and the associated increase in output, *official* supervision became friendly and relaxed once more. The investigators, however, provide no evidence that output increased because supervision became more friendly rather than vice versa. In any case, since friendly supervision took a very tangible turn by paying the girls for time not worked, the piece-rate was in effect increased.

DISCUSSION AND CONCLUSIONS

The critical examination attempted here by no means exhausts the gross error and the incompetence in the understanding and use of the scientific method which permeate the Hawthorne studies from beginning to end. Three further studies were conducted: the Bank Wiring Observation Room Study; the Interviewing Program; and the Counselling Program. These studies cannot be discussed here, but I believe them to be nearly as worthless scientifically as the studies which have been discussed.[114] This should not be surprising, for they arose out of "evidence" found and conclusions reached in the earlier studies and were guided by and interpreted in the light of the strongest preconceptions based on the conclusions of the earlier studies.

There are major deficiencies in Stages I, II and III which have hardly been touched on: (1) There was no attempt to establish sample groups representative of any larger population than the groups themselves. Therefore, no generalization is legitimate. (2) There was no attempt to employ control data

[113] Ibid., p. 162.
[114] For substantiation of this judgment with respect to the Bank Wiring Observation Room Study see A. J. Sykes, "Economic Interest and the Hawthorne Researches: A Comment," *Human Relations* 18 (August, 1965): 253-63.

from the output records of the girls who were *not* put under special experimental conditions. (3) Even if both of these points had been met, the experiments would still have been of only minor scientific value since a group of five subjects is too small to yield statistically reliable results. Waiving all these points, it is clear that the objective evidence obtained from Stages I, II, and III does not support any of the conclusions derived by the Hawthorne investigators. The results of these studies, far from supporting the various components of the "human relations approach," are surprisingly consistent with a rather old-world view about the value of monetary incentives, driving leadership, and discipline. It is only by massive and relentless reinterpretation that the evidence is made to yield contrary conclusions. To make these points is not to claim that the Hawthorne studies can provide serious support for any such old-world view. The limitations of the Hawthorne studies clearly render them incapable of yielding serious support for any sort of generalization whatever.

If the assessment of the Hawthorne studies offered here is cogent, it raises some questions of importance for university teachers, especially for teachers concerned with courses on industrial organization and management. How is it that nearly all authors of textbooks who have drawn material from the Hawthorne studies have failed to recognize the vast discrepancy between evidence and conclusions in those studies, have frequently misdescribed the actual observations and occurrences in a way that brings the evidence into line with the conclusions, and have done this even when such authors based their whole outlook and orientation on the conclusions reached by the Hawthorne investigators? Exploration of these questions would provide salutary insight into aspects of the sociology of social scientists.

chapter 8

Unanticipated Consequences and Dysfunctions in Formal Organizations

To be successful, organizations must somehow elicit from their participants a commitment to the realization of the organization's goals. Methods of evoking commitment range from extreme coercion to laissez-faire. Almost every strategy has worked well in some situations, adequately in many, and not at all in others. Generally the success (functional outcomes) is mixed with dysfunctional consequences, those which run counter to organizational objectives.

FUNCTIONAL ANALYSIS AND UNANTICIPATED CONSEQUENCES

Many sociologists have classified consequences in another way, following Merton's distinction between manifest and latent consequences (Loomis and Loomis, 1965). Manifest outcomes are intended and recognized by participants in the system, while latent consequences are unintended and unrecognized.[1] Many organizational problems can be described as latent consequences of actions taken to produce functional outcomes. The division of labor is a classic example. As jobs have been broken down into small operations, the nature of work has changed. Many people have argued that, while productivity has increased, the commitment, self-esteem, and mental health of workers have been damaged.[2]

Most organizations attempt to achieve their goals not only by the division of labor but also by establishing rules, procedures, hierarchies, and other formal mechanisms. These steps generally contribute to organizational success as measured by certain criteria. At the same time, there generally are unanticipated consequences which are dysfunctional from the organization's viewpoint.[3]

Many of the dysfunctional consequences seem to result from attempts by participants to protect themselves or to satisfy their individual needs. Mathewson (1931), in a book written before the publication of the Hawthorne

1. For our purposes, latent and unanticipated consequences are used synonymously.
2. The personality *v* the organization issue is discussed further by Argyris and Strauss in this section.
3. It is important to specify for what system a consequence is functional or dysfunctional. For example, many outcomes which are functional for an organization may be dysfunctional for some other unit, such as society.

studies, discussed how workers developed an informal social system to protect themselves and their group from other individuals and other groups in the organization. In addition, Mathewson showed that often supervisors were involved in informal behavior contrary to the formal goals of the organization. More recently, Orth (1963) found that graduate business students at Harvard engaged in similar restrictive behavior. The cross-cultural nature of this behavior was shown by Ryapolov's (1966) discussion of how informal relationships in the Soviet Union served to protect organizational participants from managers and planners.

These examples, in addition to the "soldiering" noted in Taylor, the groups in the Hawthorne plant, and numerous other reported experiences, have demonstrated one set of latent consequences which occur in formal organizations. Planners and managers set up a formal system to coordinate effort for the achievement of organizational goals. The system does not permit the satisfaction of many participant needs. In fact, often the organization generates new needs and tensions. Lower-level participants can often best satisfy these needs through behavior which conflicts directly with the formal goals of the organization.

It is important to recall that the examples cited above included workers, supervisors, managers from different cultures, and even future organizational leaders. Not just a particular class, but people in a variety of positions respond with protective and restrictive practices under conditions of distrust and fear. Defensive responses by individuals to complex organizations are pervasive.

Unions are associated with another latent dysfunction of formal organizations for managers. Often, members of one organization will join or form another organization for protection or enhancement of their position. In this manner, the rise of unions shares important features with the development of informal groups in organizations and serves similar functions for lower-level participants and even management. Managers tend to stress the dysfunctional consequences of unions and overlook some of the important functions unions serve for the firm. In fact, many scholars have argued that on balance unions have more functional consequences than dysfunctional ones for many business organizations. For example, unions may serve as valuable means for conflict resolution, communication, and industrial discipline. While this topic requires another book, the parallels between the formation of unions and other responses of participants to formal organizations should be recognized.[4]

In addition to restrictive practices, informal groups, and unions, the latent dysfunctions of formal organizations take other forms. Jasinski (1956) documented some of the latent dysfunctions of efficiency controls. He reported

---

4. It is important to realize that unions, like other formal organizations have their own unanticipated consequences. For example, many unions are formally structured to be democratic and to satisfy the interests of their members. However, often the union leaders develop sets of personal needs and organizational interests at variance with the needs of the union membership. As a result, the behavior of many unions runs counter to the needs of the members whom they are presumed to represent. In general, organizations seem to develop needs of their own and to allocate their resources in ways which are inconsistent with their formally stated goals.

that people in organizations strive to do well according to the criteria by which they are evaluated. For example, evaluation criteria may take the form of monthly productivity ratings. If productivity is down toward the end of the month, individuals in the system will often turn to some of the easier jobs before attending to the more difficult ones. However, it may well be that satisfaction of the organization's best client requires immediate attention to the unattended, more difficult job. Under the existing reward systems, the individuals are rewarded for attending to the easier job and, in effect, punished for attending to the most organizationally relevant task. Maintenance, quality control, planning, and many other crucial activities may be rewarded insufficiently or not at all because they are difficult to measure. The results of misdirecting the efforts of organizational participants may be increased costs, reduced quality, unmet production schedules, and overdue orders.

Ridgway (1956) presented supporting data on the latent consequences of performance measurements. He reported that many rating systems are based on a single criterion which does not fully represent the behavior that the organization really needs from the person. Under such conditions, an individual can maximize his own benefit by performing well the tasks on which he is evaluated, and failing to attend to the tasks which are not included in his evaluation. Thus an organization may fail as a result of each person performing his job "well." Further, Ridgway noted that stressing certain criteria, such as applying pressure to increase performance, may have costly side effects: tensions, conflicts, and lower morale. Short-run gains may be paid for by unanticipated outcomes apparent only later or not at all. Often, the costly outcomes are difficult to diagnose, because they are not evident.

Argyris (1964) and Ryapolov (1966) showed how certain types of evaluation procedures may result in hardly noticeable but wasteful managerial behavior. For example, Argyris noted that many managers maintained "JIC" files, collections of documents kept "Just In Case" their bosses should ask. The cost of such defensive behavior is great in many organizations. Similarly, Ryapolov noted that Soviet managers sent a multitude of formal directives as a tactic to protect themselves from the planners, who evaluated the actions of the managers more vigorously than the outcomes. These Soviet managers found it far more advantageous to document their actions than to display goal-oriented behavior. Again, attempts by organizations to coordinate the efforts of participants to reach goals often produce quite different results. The same outcomes also occur in non-profit-oriented organizations.

Rogers (1968) argued that the evaluation of students interferes with the realization of the educational goals of universities. Rather than encouraging students to generate creative and innovative ideas and research, the current allocation of rewards develops individuals who are prone to memorize, deviate little from the mainstream, and agree with the professor or other authority. By their evaluation procedures, even organizations relatively free from the short-run pressures of the market mechanism generate forces in opposition to their own goals.

No discussion of the latent dysfunctions of bureaucratic structure would be complete without mention of the work of Robert Merton (1957). He pointed out, for example, that, when organizations develop specialists for a certain job, are they implicitly training those people to ignore other ways of doing the job and to ignore changed conditions. This "trained incapacity" is one source of inflexibility in bureaucratic organizations. Another source of latent dysfunctions in organizations are the rules which bureaucracies develop to increase the reliability of responses from participants. Pressures for strict adherence to rules tends to make them become absolute and thereby interfere with the ability of people to adapt to new situations. The devotion to rules produces results similar to what Merton called "goal displacement," through which evaluation procedures or particular techniques of goal achievement become ends for the organizational participants. It is through goal displacement that the common problem of bureaucratic "red tape" enters. The organizational participants are rewarded and safe if they follow certain procedures, even though these procedures may actually conflict with organizational efficiency and success.

In a sense, a great deal of the organizational behavior literature attempts merely to recognize, prevent, and overcome the latent dysfunctions of formal organizational procedures. Recently, the latent consequences of organizational structure have been seen to affect the actual organizational goals themselves. In other words, the way organizational resources are actually allocated in business indicates that many goals are being pursued which are, at most, only partially consistent with the assumed goal of profit maximization.

PROFIT MAXIMIZATION AS A GOAL

While an organization may have one overriding stated goal, such as profit maximization, the behavior of the people in the system cannot be accurately described or understood in terms of this one goal. In other words, while the economists' assumption of profit maximization may be good enough for their purposes, it certainly is not sufficient here. Although it may be assumed that each individual and each department within an organization does attempt to maximize profit in some way, it is doubtful whether the sum of these efforts yields maximization for the total organization.

How do we define the profits being maximized? Certainly, economic profit is one aspect. But people in organizations pursue many other goals including status, esteem, security, power, knowledge, approval, and the means of satisfying other human wants. Maximization of economic profit is an inadequate description of these pursuits.

Allocation of an organization's resources is political as well as economic. In many ways, the size of a departmental budget is used as a measure of status or value.[5] For a variety of organizationally relevant and irrelevant reasons, an

5. An advertising executive once confided his disappointment that his budget had not been increased despite general agreement about the success of his division. He had overlooked the possibility that his superiors might have allocated scarce financial resources elsewhere precisely because they recognized how much he could accomplish on a limited budget.

individual may be able to "oversell" his function to the budgeting panel beyond the best economic interest of the organization.

It may be to a manager's advantage to maximize the number of people on his staff or the amount of funds available for his favorite projects, but it may not be consistent with profit maximization. For example, Galbraith (1967) has argued that the various elements within organizations achieve their own individual ends at the expense of the organization's economic objectives, seeking only enough profit to keep top management and stockholders content. If Galbraith's description is correct, organizations can hardly be described as maximizing their profits. While his argument has been rejected as polemical and unscholarly by many economists, the related arguments of two other social scientists are not so easily discarded.

Cyert and March (1963) questioned the contemporary economic view of organizational decision making by attacking the economic assumptions that firms seek to maximize profits and operate with perfect knowledge. They concurred with our earlier statement that individuals have a host of personal as well as purely economic ends. Furthermore they noted that business decision-makers seek satisfactory rather than maximum profits. The level which is viewed to be satisfactory is determined by the organization's past goals and performance and by the past performance of comparable organizations. In addition to seeking satisfactory profit, Cyert and March argued that decision makers also attempt to avoid uncertainty. Moreover, Cyert and March argued that, in gathering information for making decisions, organizational participants engage in only limited search behavior often determined by factors other than rational profit maximization. For example, search behavior is stimulated by a problem or a crisis rather than an overall strategy aimed at maximum utility. Second, the search tends to be concentrated in the vicinity of the symptom and current practice. When causes are sought, efforts focus on vulnerable parts of the organization rather than on the more powerful elements. In addition, the search reflects the special training of the searchers and their hopes and expectations. Further, unresolved conflict in the organization effects communication patterns, which influence the search process systematically. As a result, actual decisions made by organizations are not rational in the purely economic sense. While space does not permit a complete summary of the Cyert and March position, it is hoped that this treatment stimulates exploration and discussion of their important argument. Organization decisions are not "rational" in the traditional economic sense.

Since individuals appear to pursue psychological as well as economic profits, it may be that organizations cannot maximize profit in the economic sense. The issue of social responsibility of business may be an important case in point. Concern for community problems may or may not be in the best economic interests of the organization. However, increasingly the social and moral pressures felt by organizational participants may dictate that an organization devote some of its resources to certain social problems. These pressures generate psychological needs for organizational decision makers. The decision makers may attempt to satisfy these needs by influencing the organization to become involved with solutions to broader social issues. When individual psychological profit requires organizations to behave "uneconomically," these pressures may be rationalized as having long-run public relations value but in fact may be unavoidable even if they have no economic payoff.

THE READINGS

The readings in this section generally represent a challenge to the classical view of organizations by focusing on unanticipated consequences and conflict. For the most part, the authors are questioning whether our traditional models of hierarchical organization and bureaucracy produce viable forms of organization. Bennis describes and summarizes the traditional arguments for bureaucracy and questions the inability of such organizations in modern society. The selection by Gross suggests that organizations can best be understood and managed if we realize that their operations reflect a variety of purposes. The goals of the organization are a product of the interests of some participants but are in conflict with the interests of others. Gross implies that organizations are more like coalitions than teams and that a multidisciplinary approach is necessary for understanding them. Certainly if classical economics, classical organization theory, or the human-relations view is taken alone as a basis for describing organizations, the picture will be distorted. The delightful short story by Barrett, based on a real series of incidents, shows how lower-level participants can respond to organizational rules.

The final two papers by Argyris and Strauss deal with the consequences of formal organizations for the psychological state of man. The issues they discuss underlie many of the controversies in the entire field. Argyris has been a leading exponent of the view that formal organizations are in conflict with the potential of man. This view is challenged by Strauss, co-author of one of the leading personnel books in the field, which stresses the human relations approach. While the Argyris-Strauss controversy may be resolved only at the metaphysical level or by a definitive answer to the nature-nuture controversy, its implications are vast. The relationship of the current structure of organizations to mental health and the possible alienation of individuals from the general social system as a result of the organization of work is a vital concern. Significant social problems—including mental illness, alcoholism, drug addiction, social unrest, and others—may in fact be partially described as latent consequences of the modern organization of work.

REFERENCES

Argyris, C. *Integrating the Individual and the Organization.* New York: John Wiley & Sons, 1964.

Cyert, R. M., and J. G. March, *A Behavioral Theory of the Firm.* Englewood Cliffs, N.J.: Prentice-Hall, Inc., 1963.

Galbraith, J. K. *The New Industrial State.* Boston: Houghton-Mifflin, 1967.

Jasinski, F. J. "Use and Misuse of Efficiency Controls." *Harvard Business Review* 34, (July-Aug. 1956): 105-12.

Loomis, C. P., and Z. K. Loomis, *Modern Social Theories.* Princeton, N.J.: Van Nostrand, 1965.

Mathewson, S. B. *Restriction of Output among Unorganized Workers.* New York: Viking Press, 1931.

Merton, R. K. *Social Theory and Social Structure.* Rev. ed. New York: Free Press, 1957.

Orth, Charles D., III, *Social Structure and Learning Climate: The First Year at the Harvard Business School.* Boston: Harvard University, 1963.

Ridgway, V. F. "Dysfunctional Consequences of Performance Measurements." *Administrative Science Quarterly* 1 (1956): 240-47.

Rogers, C. "Graduate Education in Psychology: A Passionate Statement." In W. G. Bennis, E. H. Schein, F. I. Steele, and D. E. Berlew eds., *Interpersonal Dynamics,* Rev. ed. Homewood, Ill.: Dorsey, 1968, pp. 687-703.

Ryapolov, G. "I Was a Soviet Manager." *Harvard Business Review* 44 (June-Feb. 1966): 117-25.

Warren G. Bennis

THE COMING DEATH
OF BUREAUCRACY

Not far from the new Government Center in downtown Boston, a foreign visitor walked up to a sailor and asked why American ships were built to last only a short time. According to the tourist, "The sailor answered without hesitation that the art of navigation is making such rapid progress that the finest ship would become obsolete if it lasted beyond a few years. In these words which fell accidentally from an uneducated man, I began to recognize the general and systematic idea upon which your great people direct all their concerns."

The foreign visitor was that shrewd observer of American morals and manners, Alexis de Tocqueville, and the year was 1835. He would not recognize Scollay Square today. But he had caught the central theme of our country: its preoccupation, its *obsession* with change. One thing is, however, new since de Tocqueville's time: the *acceleration* of newness, the changing scale and scope of change itself. As Dr. Robert Oppenheimer said,". . . the world alters as we walk in it, so that the years of man's life measure not some small growth or rearrangement or moderation of what was learned in childhood, but a great upheaval."

How will these accelerating changes in our society influence human organizations?

A short while ago, I predicted that we would, in the next 25 to 50 years, participate in the end of bureaucracy as we know it and in the rise of new social systems better suited to the twentieth-century demands of industrialization. This forecast was based on the evolutionary principle that every age develops an organizational form appropriate to its genius, and that the prevailing form, known by sociologists as bureaucracy and by most businessmen as "damn bureaucracy," was out of joint with contemporary realities. I realize now that my distant prophecy is already a distinct reality so that prediction is already foreshadowed by practice.

I should like to make clear that by bureaucracy I mean a chain of command structured on the lines of a pyramid—the typical structure which coordinates the business of almost every human organization we know of: industrial, governmental, of universities and research and development laboratories,

From Warren G. Bennis, "The Coming Death of Bureaucracy," *Think*, (November-December, 1966), pp. 30-35. ©1966 by IBM.

military, religious, voluntary. I do not have in mind those fantasies so often dreamed up to describe complex organizations. These fantasies can be summarized in two grotesque stereotypes. The first I call "Organization as Inkblot"—an actor steals around an uncharted wasteland, growing more restive and paranoid by the hour, while he awaits orders that never come. The other specter is "Organization as Big Daddy"—the actors are square people plugged into square holes by some omniscient and omnipotent genius who can cradle in his arms the entire destiny of man by way of computer and TV. Whatever the first image owes to Kafka, the second owes to George Orwell's 1984.

Bureaucracy, as I refer to it here, is a useful social invention that was perfected during the industrial revolution to organize and direct the activities of a business firm. Most students of organizations would say that its anatomy consists of the following components:

1. A well-defined chain of command.
2. A system of procedures and rules for dealing with all contingencies relating to work activities.
3. A division of labor based on specialization.
4. Promotion and selection based on technical competence.
5. Impersonality in human relations.

It is the pyramid arrangement we see on most organizational charts.

The bureaucratic "machine model" was developed as a reaction against the personal subjugation, nepotism and cruelty, and the capricious and subjective judgements which passed for managerial practices during the early days of the industrial revolution. Bureaucracy emerged out of the organizations' need for order and precision and the workers' demands for impartial treatment. It was an organization ideally suited to the values and demands of the Victorian era. And just as bureaucracy emerged as a creative response to a radically new age, so today new organizational shapes are surfacing before our eyes.

First I shall try to show why the conditions of our modern industrialized world will bring about the death of bureaucracy. In the second part of this article I will suggest a rough model of the organization of the future.

FOUR THREATS

There are at least four relevant threats to bureaucracy:

1. Rapid and unexpected change.
2. Growth in size where the volume of an organization's traditional activities is not enough to sustain growth. (A number of factors are included here, among them: bureaucratic overhead; tighter controls and impersonality due to bureaucratic sprawls; outmoded rules and organizational structures.)
3. Complexity of modern technology where integration between activities and persons of very diverse, highly specialized competence is required.
4. A basically psychological threat springing from a change in managerial behavior.

It might be useful to examine the extent to which these conditions exist *right now:*

(1). Rapid and unexpected change. Bureaucracy's strength is its capacity to efficiently manage the routine and predictable in human affairs. It is almost enough to cite the knowledge and population explosion to raise doubts about its contemporary viability. More revealing, however, are the statistics which demonstrate these overworked phrases:

   a. Our productivity output per man hour may now be doubling almost every 20 years rather than every 40 years, as it did before World War II.
   b. The Federal Government alone spent $16 billion in research and development activities in 1965; it will spend $35 billion by 1980.
   c. The time lag between a technical discovery and recognition of its commercial uses was: 30 years before World War 1, 16 years between the Wars, and only 9 years since World War II.
   d. In 1946, only 42 cities in the world had populations of more than one million. Today there are 90. In 1930, there were 40 people for each square mile of the earth's land surface. Today there are 63. By 2000, it is expected, the figure will have soared to 142.

Bureaucracy, with its nicely defined chain of command, its rules and its rigidities, is ill-adapted to the rapid change the environment now demands.

(2). Growth in size. While, in theory, there may be no natural limit to the height of a bureaucratic pyramid, in practice the element of complexity is almost invariably introduced with great size. International operation, to cite one significant new element, is the rule rather than exception for most of our biggest corporations. Firms like Standard Oil Company (New Jersey) with over 100 foreign affiliates, Mobil Oil Corporation, The National Cash Register Company, Singer Company, Burroughs Corporation and Colgate-Palmolive Company derive more than half their income or earnings from foreign sales. Many others—such as Eastman Kodak Company, Chas. Pfizer & Company, Inc., Caterpillar Tractor Company, International Harvester Company, Corn Products Company and Minnesota Mining & Manufacturing Company—make from 30 to 50 percent of their sales abroad. General Motors Corporation sales are not only nine times those of Volkswagen, they are also bigger than the Gross National Product of the Netherlands and well over the GNP of a hundred other countries. If we have seen the sun set on the British Empire, we may never see it set on the empires of General Motors, ITT, Shell and Unilever.

LABOR BOOM

(3). Increasing diversity. *Today's activities require persons of very diverse, highly specialized competence.*

Numerous dramatic examples can be drawn from studies of labor markets and job mobility. At some point during the past decade, the U.S. became the first nation in the world ever to employ more people in service occupations than in the production of tangible goods. Examples of this trend:

   a. In the field of education, the *increase* in employment between 1950 and 1960 was greater than the total number employed in the steel, copper and aluminum industries.

b. In the field of health, the *increase* in employment between 1950 and 1960 was greater than the total number employed in automobile manufacturing in either year.

c. In financial firms, the *increase* in employment between 1950 and 1960 was greater than total employment in mining in 1960.

These changes, plus many more that are harder to demonstrate statistically, break down the old, industrial trend toward more and more people doing either simple or undifferentiated chores.

Hurried growth, rapid change and increase in specialization—pit these three factors against the five components of the pyramid structure described on page 30, and we should expect the pyramid of bureaucracy to begin crumbling.

(4). Change in managerial behavior. There is, I believe, a subtle but perceptible change in the philosophy underlying management behavior. Its magnitude, nature and antecedents, however, are shadowy because of the difficulty of assigning numbers. (Whatever else statistics do for us, they most certainly provide a welcome illusion of certainty.) Nevertheless, real change seems underway because of:

a. A new concept of *man*, based on increased knowledge of his complex and shifting needs, which replaces an over simplified, innocent, push-button idea of man.

b. A new concept of *power*, based on collaboration and reason, which replaces a model of power based on coercion and threat.

c. A new concept of *organizational values*, based on humanistic-democratic ideals, which replaces the depersonalized mechanistic value system of bureaucracy.

The primary cause of this shift in management philosophy stems not from the bookshelf but from the manager himself. Many of the behavioral scientists, like Douglas McGregor or Rensis Likert, have clarified and articulated—even legitimized—what managers have only half registered to themselves. I am convinced, for example, that the popularity of McGregor's book, *The Human Side of Enterprise,* was based on his rare empathy for a vast audience of managers who are wistful for an alternative to the mechanistic concept of authority, i.e., that he outlined a vivid utopia of more authentic human relationships than most organizational practices today allow. Furthermore, I suspect that the desire for relationships in business has little to do with a profit motive per se, though it is often rationalized as doing so. The real push for these changes stems from the need, not only to humanize the organization, but to use it as a crucible of personal growth and the development of self-realization.[1]

---

[1] Let me propose an hypothesis to explain this tendency. It rests on the assumption that man has a basic need for transcendental experiences, somewhat like the psychological rewards which William James claimed religion provided—"an assurance of safety and a temper of peace, and, in relation to others, a preponderance of living affections." Can it be that as religion has become secularized, less transcendental, men search for substitutes such as close interpersonal relationships, psychoanalysis—even the release provided by drugs such as LSD?

The core problems confronting any organization fall, I believe, into five major categories. First, let us consider the problems, then let us see how our twentieth-century conditions of constant change have made the bureaucratic approach to these problems obsolete.

(1). **Integration.** The problem is how to integrate individual needs and management goals. In other words, it is the inescapable conflict between individual needs (like "spending time with the family") and organizational demands (like meeting deadlines).

Under twentieth-century conditions of constant change there has been an emergence of human sciences and a deeper understanding of man's complexity. Today, integration encompasses the entire range of issues concerned with incentives, rewards and motivations of the individual, and how the organization succeeds or fails in adjusting to these issues. In our society, where personal attachments play an important role, the individual is appreciated, and there is genuine concern for his well-being, not just in a veterinary-hygiene sense, but as a moral, integrated personality.

PARADOXICAL TWINS

The problem of integration, like most human problems, has a venerable past. The modern version goes back at least 160 years and was precipitated by an historical paradox: the twin births of modern individualism and modern industrialism. The former brought about a deep concern for and a passionate interest in the individual and his personal rights. The latter brought about increased mechanization of organized activity. Competition between the two has intensified as each decade promises more freedom and hope for man and more stunning achievements for technology. I believe that our society *has* opted for more humanistic and democratic values, however unfulfilled they may be in practice. It will "buy" these values even at loss in efficiency because it feels it can now afford the loss.

(2). **Social influence.** This problem is essentially one of power and how power is distributed. It is a complex issue and alive with controversy, partly because of an ethical component and partly because studies of leadership and power distribution can be interpreted in many ways, and almost always in ways which coincide with one's biases (including a cultural leaning toward democracy).

The problem of power has to be seriously reconsidered because of dramatic situational changes which make the possibility of one-man rule not necessarily "bad" but impractical. I refer to changes in top management's role.

Peter Drucker, over 12 years ago, listed 41 major responsibilities of the chief executive and declared that "90 percent of the trouble we are having with the chief executive's job is rooted in our superstition of the one-man chief." Many factors make one-man control obsolete, among them: the broadening product base of industry; impact of new technology; the scope of international operation; the separation of management from ownership; the rise of trade unions and general education. The real power of the "chief" has been eroding in most organizations even though both he and the organization cling to the older concept.

(3). **Collaboration.** This is the problem of managing and resolving conflicts. Bureaucratically, it grows out of the very same process of conflict and stereotyping that has divided nations and communities. As organizations become more complex, they fragment and divide, building tribal patterns and symbolic codes which often work to exclude others (secrets and jargon, for example) and on occasion to exploit differences for inward (and always fragile) harmony.

Recent research is shedding new light on the problem of conflict. Psychologist Robert R. Blake in his stunning experiments has shown how simple it is to induce conflict, how difficult to arrest it. Take two groups of people who have never before been together, and give them a task which will be judged by an impartial jury. In less than an hour, each group devolves into a tightly-knit band with all the symptoms of an "in group." They regard their product as a "master-work" and the other group's as "commonplace" at best. "Other" becomes "enemy." "We are good, they are bad; we are right, they are wrong."

RABBIE'S REDS AND GREENS

Jaap Rabbie, conducting experiments on intergroup conflict at the University of Utrecht, has been amazed by the ease with which conflict and stereotype develop. He brings into an experimental room two groups and distributes green name tags and pens to one group, red pens and tags to the other. The two groups do not compete; they do not even interact. They are only in sight of each other while they silently complete a questionnaire. Only ten minutes are needed to activate defensiveness and fear, reflected in the hostile and irrational perceptions of both "reds" and "greens."

(4). **Adaptation.** This problem is caused by our turbulent environment. The pyramid structure of bureaucracy, where power is concentrated at the top, seems the perfect way to "run a railroad." And for the routine tasks of the nineteenth and early twentieth centuries, bureaucracy was (in some respects it still is) a suitable social arrangement. However, rather than a placid and predictable environment, what predominates today is a dynamic and uncertain one where there is a deepening interdependence among economic, scientific, educational, social and political factors in the society.

(5). **Revitalization.** This is the problem of growth and decay. As Alfred North Whitehead has said: "The art of free society consists first in the maintenance of the symbolic code, and secondly, in the fearlessness of revision. . . Those societies which cannot combine reverence to their symbols with freedom of revision must ultimately decay. . . "

Growth and decay emerge as the penultimate conditions of contemporary society. Organizations, as well as societies, must be concerned with those social structures that engender buoyancy, resilience and a "fearlessness of revision."

I introduce the term "revitalization" to embrace all the social mechanisms that stagnate and regenerate, as well as the process of this cycle. The elements of revitalization are:

1. An ability to learn from experience and to codify, store and retrieve the relevant knowledge.
2. An ability to "learn how to learn," that is, to develop methods for improving the learning process.
3. An ability to acquire and use feed-back mechanisms on performance, in short, to be self-analytical.
4. An ability to direct one's own destiny.

These qualities have a good deal in common with what John Gardner calls "self-renewal." For the organization, it means conscious attention to its own evolution. Without a planned methodology and explicit direction, the enterprise will not realize its potential.

Integration, distribution of power, collaboration, adaptation and *revitalization*—these are the major human problems of the next 25 years. How organizations cope with and manage these tasks will undoubtedly determine the viability of the enterprise.

Against this background I should like to set forth some of the conditions that will dictate organization life in the next two or three decades.

(1). The environment. Rapid technological change and diversification will lead to more and more partnerships between government and business. It will be a truly mixed economy. Because of the immensity and expense of the projects, there will be fewer identical units competing in the same markets and organizations will become more interdependent.

The four main features of this environment are:

a. Interdependence rather than competition.
b. Turbulence and uncertainty rather than readiness and certainty.
c. Large-scale rather than small-scale enterprises.
d. Complex and multinational rather than simple national enterprises.

"NICE"—AND NECESSARY

(2). Population characteristics. The most distinctive characteristic of our society is education. It will become even more so. Within 15 years, two-thirds of our population living in metropolitan areas will have attended college. Adult education is growing even faster, probably because of the rate of professional obsolescence. The Killian report showed that the average engineer required further education only ten years after getting his degree. It will be almost routine for the experienced physician, engineer and executive to go back to school for advanced training every two or three years. All of this education is not just "nice." It is necessary.

One other characteristic of the population which will aid our understanding of organizations of the future is increasing job mobility. The ease of transportation, coupled with the needs of a dynamic environment, change drastically the idea of "owning" a job—or "having roots." Already 20 percent of our population change their mailing address at least once a year.

(3). **Work values.** The increased level of education and mobility will change the values we place on work. People will be more intellectually committed to their jobs and will probably require more involvement, participation and autonomy.

Also, people will be more "other-oriented," taking cues for their norms and values from their immediate environment rather than tradition.

(4). **Tasks and goals.** The tasks of the organization will be more technical, complicated and unprogrammed. They will rely on intellect instead of muscle. And they will be too complicated for one person to comprehend, to say nothing of control. Essentially, they will call for the collaboration of specialists in a project or a team-form of organization.

There will be a complication of goals. Business will increasingly concern itself with its adaptive or innovative-creative capacity. In addition, supragoals will have to be articulated, goals which shape and provide the foundation for the goal structure. For example, one might be a system for detecting new and changing goals; another could be a system for deciding priorities among goals.

Finally, there will be more conflict and contradiction among diverse standards for organizational effectiveness. This is because professionals tend to identify more with the goals of their profession than with those of their immediate employer. University professors can be used as a case in point. Their inside work may be a conflict between teaching and research, while more of their income is derived from outside sources, such as foundations and consultant work. They tend not to be good "company men" because they divide their loyalty between their professional values and organizational goals.

KEY WORD: "TEMPORARY"

(5). **Organization.** The social structure of organizations of the future will have some unique characteristics. The key word will be "temporary." There will be adaptive, rapidly changing *temporary* systems. These will be task forces organized around problems to be solved by groups of relative strangers with diverse professional skills. The group will be arranged on an organic rather than mechanical model; they will evolve in response to a problem rather than to programmed role expectations. The executive thus becomes a coordinator or "linking pin" between various task forces. He must be a man who can speak the polyglot jargon of research, with skills to relay information and to mediate between groups. People will be evaluated not vertically according to rank and status, but flexibly and functionally according to skill and professional training. Organizational charts will consist of project groups rather than stratified functional groups. (This trend is already visible in the aerospace and construction industries, as well as many professional and consulting firms.)

Adaptive, problem-solving, temporary systems of diverse specialists, linked together by coordinating and task-evaluating executive specialists in an organic flux—this is the organization form that will gradually replace bureaucracy as we know it. As no catchy phrase comes to mind, I call this an organic-adaptive structure. Organizational arrangements of this sort may not only reduce the intergroup conflicts mentioned earlier; it may also induce honest-to-goodness creative collaboration.

(6). Motivation. The organic-adaptive structure should increase motivation and thereby effectiveness, because it enhances satisfactions intrinsic to the task. There is a harmony between the educated individual's need for tasks that are meaningful, satisfactory and creative and a flexible organizational structure.

There will also be, however, reduced commitment to work groups, for these groups will be, as I have already mentioned, transient structures. I would predict that in the organic-adaptive system, people will learn to develop quick and intense relationships on the job, and learn to bear the loss of more enduring work relationships. Because of the added ambiguity of roles, time will have to be spent on continual rediscovery of the appropriate organizational mix.

I think that the future I describe is not necessarily a "happy" one. Coping with rapid change, living in temporary work systems, developing meaningful relations and then breaking them—all augur social strains and psychological tensions. Teaching how to live with ambiguity, to indentify with the adaptive process, to make a virtue out of contingency, and to be self-directing—these will be the tasks of education, the goals of maturity, and the achievement of the successful individual.

NO DELIGHTFUL MARRIAGES

In these new organizations of the future, participants will be called upon to use their minds more than at any other time in history. Fantasy, imagination and creativity will be legitimate in ways that today seem strange. Social structures will no longer be instruments of psychic repression but will increasingly promote play and freedom on behalf of curiosity and thought.

One final word: While I forecast the structure and value coordinates for organizations of the future and contend that they are inevitable, this should not bar any of us from giving the inevitable a little push. The French moralist may be right in saying that there are no delightful marriages, just good ones; It is possible that if managers and scientists continue to get their heads together in organizational revitalization, they *might* develop delightful organizations—just possibly.

I started with a quote from de Tocqueville and I think it would be fitting to end with one: "I am tempted to believe that what we call necessary institutions are often no more than institutions to which we have grown accustomed. In matters of social constitution, the field of possibilities is much more extensive than men living in their various societies are ready to imagine."

Bertram M. Gross

WHAT ARE YOUR ORGANIZATION'S OBJECTIVES?

A General-Systems Approach
to Planning

There is nothing that managers and management theorists are more solidly agreed on than the vital role of objectives in the managing of organizations. The daily life of executives is full of such exhortations as:

"Let's plan where we want to go . . . ."
"You'd better clarify your goals . . . ."
"Get those fellows down (or up) there to understand what our (or their) purposes really are . . . ."

Formal definitions of management invariably give central emphasis to the formulation or attainment of objectives. Peter Drucker's (1954) idea of "managing by objectives" gave expression to a rising current in administrative theory. Any serious discussion of planning, whether by business enterprises or government agencies, deals with the objectives of an organization.

Yet there is nothing better calculated to embarrass the average executive than the direct query: "Just what are your organization's objectives?" The typical reply is incomplete or tortured, given with a feeling of obvious discomfort. The more skillful response is apt to be a glib evasion or a glittering generality.

To some extent, of course, objectives cannot be openly stated. Confidential objectives cannot be revealed to outsiders. Tacit objectives may not bear discussion among insiders. The art of bluff and deception with respect to goals is part of the art of administration.

But the biggest reason for embarrassment is the lack of a well-developed language of organizational purposefulness. Such a language may best be supplied by a general-systems model that provides the framework for "general-systems accounting", or "managerial accounting" in the sense of a truly generalist

From Bertram M. Gross, "What Are Your Organization's Objectives? A General Systems Approach to planning," *Human Relations* 18 (Aug. 1965): 195-215. Reprinted by permission.

approach to all major dimensions of an organization. It is now possible to set forth-even if only in suggestive form—a general-systems model that provides the basis for clearly formulating the performance and structural objectives of any organization.

Let us now deal with these points separately—and conclude with some realistic observations on the strategy of planning.

THE NEED FOR A
LANGUAGE OF PURPOSEFULNESS

Many managers are still too much the prisoners of outworn, single-purpose models erected by defunct economists, engineers, and public administration experts. Although they know better, they are apt to pay verbal obeisance to some single purpose: profitability in the case of the business executive, efficiency in the case of the public executive.

If profitability is not the sole objective of a business—and even the more tradition-ridden economists will usually accept other objectives in the form of constraints or instrumental purposes—just what are these other types? If efficiency is not the only objective of a government agency—and most political scientists will maintain that it cannot be—what are the other categories? No adequate answers to these questions are provided by the traditional approaches to economics, business administration, or public administration. Most treatises on planning—for which purpose formulation is indispensable—catalogue purposes by such abstract and nonsubstantive categories as short-range and long-range, instrumental and strategic (or ultimate), general and specific. One book on planning sets forth 13 dimensions whithout mentioning anything so mundane as profitability or efficiency (LeBreton & Henning, 1961). Indeed, in his initial writings on management by objectives, Drucker never came to grips with the great multiplicity of business objectives. In his more recent work Drucker (1964) deals with objectives in terms of three "result areas": product, distribution channels, and markets. But this hardly goes far enough to illuminate the complexities of purpose multiplicity.

Thus far, the most systematic approach to organizational purposes is provided by budget experts and accountants. A budget projection is a model that helps to specify the financial aspects of future performance. A balance sheet is a model that helps to specify objectives for future structure of assets and liabilities. Yet financial analysis—even when dignified by the misleading label 'managerial accounting'—deals only with a narrow slice of real-life activities. Although it provides a way of reflecting many objectives, it cannot by itself deal with the substantive activities underlying monetary data. Indeed, concentration upon budgets has led many organizations to neglect technological and other problems that cannot be expressed in budgetary terms. Overconcentration on the enlargement of balance-sheet assets has led many companies to a dangerous neglect of human and organizational assets.

The great value of financial analysis is to provide a doorway through which one can enter the whole complex domain of organizational objectives. To explore this domain, however, one needs a model capable of dealing more fully with the multiple dimensions of an organization's performance and structure. To facilitate the development of purposefulness in each of an organization's subordinate units, the model should also be applicable to internal units. To help executives to deal with the complexities of their environment, it should also be applicable to external competitors or controllers.

THE GENERAL-SYSTEMS APPROACH

As a result of the emerging work in systems analysis, it is now possible to meet these needs by developing a "general systems model" of an organization. A general systems model is one that brings together in an ordered fashion information on all dimensions of an organization. It integrates concepts from all relevant disciplines. It can help to expand financial planning to full-bodied planning in as many dimensions as may be relevant. With it, executives may move from financial accounting to "systems accounting." It can provide the basis for "managerial accounting" in the sense of the managerial use not only of financial data (which is the way the term has been recently used) but of all ideas and data needed to appraise the state of a system and guide it towards the attainment of desirable future system states.[1]

Before outlining a general-systems model, it is important to set aside the idea that a system is necessarily something that is fully predictable or tightly controlled. This impression is created whenever anyone tries to apply to a human organization the closed or nonhuman models used by physicists and engineers. A human organization is much more complicated.

Specifically, when viewed in general systems terms, a formal organization (whether a business enterprise or a government agency) is

1. a man-resource system in space and time,
2. open, with various transactions between it and its environment,
3. characterized by internal and external relations of conflict as well as cooperation,
4. a system for developing and using power, with varying degrees of authority and responsibility, both within the organization and in the external environment,
5. a "feedback" system, with information on results of past performance activities feeding back through multiple channels to influence future performance,
6. changing, with static concepts derived from dynamic concepts rather than serving as a preliminary to them,
7. complex, that is, containing many subsystems, being contained in larger systems, and being criss-crossed by overlapping systems,

---

[1] "General-systems theory" often refers to theories dealing broadly with similarities among all kinds of systems—from atoms and cells to personalities, formal organizations, and populations. In this context the term refers to a special application of general systems theory to formal organizations—an application that deals not merely with a few aspects but generally with all aspects of formal organizations.

8. loose, with many components that may be imperfectly coordinated, partially autonomous, and only partially controllable,
9. only partially knowable, with many areas of uncertainty, with "black regions" as well as "black boxes" and with many variables that cannot be clearly defined and must be described in qualitative terms, and
10. subject to considerable uncertainty with respect to current information, future environmental conditions, and the consequences of its own actions.

THE PERFORMANCE-STRUCTURE MODEL

The starting-point of modern systems analysis is the input-output concept. The flow of inputs and outputs portrays the system's performance. To apply the output concept to a formal organization, it is helpful to distinguish between two kinds of performance: producing outputs of services or goods and satisfying (or dissatisfying) various interests. To apply the input concept, a three-way breakdown is helpful: acquiring resources to be used as inputs, using inputs for investment in the system, and making efficient use of resources. In addition, we may note that organizational performance includes efforts to conform with certain behaviour codes and concepts of technical and administrative rationality.

These seven kinds of performance objective may be put together in the following proposition:

The performance of any organization or unit thereof consists of activities to (1) satisfy the varying interests of people and groups by (2) producing outputs of services or goods, (3) making efficient use of inputs relative to outputs, (4) investing in the system, (5) acquiring resources, and (6) doing all these things, in a manner that conforms with various codes of behaviour and (7) varying conceptions of technical and administrative rationality.

In simplified form, the relations between these categories of performance may be visualized as follows:

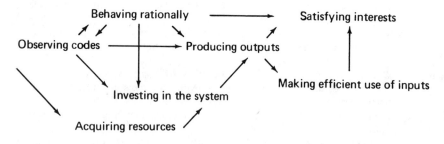

Let us now turn to system structure. The minimum elements in a machine system are certain physical components, including a "governor" (or "selector"), an "effector," a "detector," and lines of communication between them and the environment. For a formal organization these may be spelled out more specifically as subsystems in general, a central guidance subsystem, internal relations among the subsystems, and relations with the external environment. It is helpful at times to consider separately the people and the physical assets grouped together in the subsystems. It may also be helpful to give separate attention to the values held by individuals and the various subsystems.

These seven sets of structural objectives may be put together in the following proposition:

> The structure of any organization or unit thereof consists of (1) people and (2) nonhuman resources, (3) grouped together in differentiated subsystems that (4) interrelate among themselves and (5) with the external environment, (6) and are subject to various values and (7) to such central guidance as may help to provide the capacity for future performance.

In the language of matrix algebra, one can bring the two elements of system performance and system structure together into a 2 X 1 "nested" vector which may be called the "system state vector." Let P symbolize system performance and S system structure. Then the following sequence of vectors may symbolize changing system states over a period of time:

$$\begin{bmatrix} P \\ \underline{S} \end{bmatrix}^1 \qquad \begin{bmatrix} P \\ \underline{S} \end{bmatrix}^2 \qquad \begin{bmatrix} P \\ \underline{S} \end{bmatrix}^n$$

The vector is "nested" because both the performance element and the structure element consist of seven subelements and are themselves 7 X 1 vectors. Each subelement, in turn, is a multidimensional matrix.

The performance vector, it should be noted, includes among its many components the basic elements in income statements and revenue-expenditure budgets. The structure vector includes all the assets (and claims against them) measured in a balance sheet. Indeed, the former may be regarded as a greatly enlarged performance budget, the latter a balance sheet that includes human and institutional assets as well as financial assets. The relations between the two are even closer than those between an income statement and a balance sheet. Almost any aspect of system performance will have some effect on system structure. Any important plans for future performance inevitably require significant changes in system structure. Changes in system structure, in turn, are invariably dependent upon some types of system performance. In everyday affairs, of course, executives often make the mistake of

—planning for major improvements in performance without giving attention to the structural prerequisites, and
—planning for major changes in structure (sometimes because of outworn or unduly abstract doctrines of formal organization) without considering their presumed connection with performance.

The skillful use of a performance-structure model may help to avoid these errors.[2]

---

[2] This performance-structure model represents a major adaptation of what has long been known as "structural-functional" analysis. It is more dynamic than traditional structural-functional analysis, however, since it starts with action (performance) and works back to structure as the more regularized aspect of action. Also, instead of assuming a single function such as "system maintenance," it broadens the idea of function to cover the major dimensions of performance.

The first elements in both structure and performance, let it be noted, are human: people and the satisfaction of people's interests. All the other elements and their many decisions—both financial and technological—are ways of thinking about people and their behaviour. An organization's plans for the future are always plans made by people for people—for their future behaviour and for their future relations with resources and other people. Financial and technological planners may easily lose sight of these human elements. Another virtue of general systems analysis, therefore, is that it helps to bring together the "soft" information of human relations people with the "hard" data of accountants and engineers.

PERFORMANCE OBJECTIVES

Any one of the seven elements of system performance, as baldly stated above, may be used in a statement of "where we want to go" or as a criterion of "doing an effective job." But none of them is meaningful unless broken down into its subelements. When this is done, indeed, the basic subelements may be rearranged in many ways. There is no magic in any one ordering.

Within the present space limits I shall merely touch upon some of the major dimensions of each element and subelement. Additional details are available in *The Managing of Organizations* (Gross, 1964, Pt. V. Chs. 20-29).

Some random illustrations for both an organization (an aircraft company) and a unit thereof (its personnel office) are provided in Table 1. Tables 2 and 3 provide more detailed illustrations in two areas of special complexity: output objectives and input-output objectives. In these tables "goal" refers to a specific type of subelement and "norm" to a more specific formulation of a goal. To save space, reference to the tables will not be made in the text.

1. Satisfying Interests

Although the satisfaction of human interests is the highest purpose of any organization, interest-satisfaction objectives (often referred to as *benefits, welfare, utility, value,* or *payoff*) are the most difficult to formulate.

First of all, such objectives always involve a multiplicity of parties at interest—or "interesteds." These include the members of the organization, the organization's "clientele network," and other external groups and individuals. They vary considerably in visibility and in the extent to which their interests are affected by an organization's performance.

Second, their interests are usually multiple, often hard to identify, always divergent, and sometimes sharply conflicting. In psychological terms these interests may be described in terms of the human needs for security, belonging, status, prestige, power, and self-development. Many of these needs are expressed in terms of services and goods designed to meet them and the monetary income which, in a market economy, is necessary to provide such services and goods. They may also be expressed in terms of the needs for both employment and leisure. The terms "public interest" or "national interest" are ways of referring

TABLE 1. Performance Objectives: Some General Illustrations

Performance Objectives	Aircraft Company		Personnel Unit	
	Goals	Norms	Goals	Norms
1. Satisfying Interests				
(a) Members	Higher morale	Reducing labour turnover to 6%	Professional prestige	Leadership in professional organizations
(b) Clientele network	Meeting airlines' needs	5% rise in total sales	Meeting needs of line	Fewer complaints
(c) Others	Investors	Maintaining 3% yield on common stock	Serving all employees	Reducing labour turnover to 10%
2. Producing Output				
(a) Output mix	Adding short-range jets	End-product production schedule	New management training programme	End-product services
(b) Quantity	Increased market penetration	15% of industry sales	Greater coverage	150 "trainees" per year
(c) Quality	Safer planes	Wing improvements	Better designed courses	Better consultants
(d) Output flow	Work-flow	Detailed schedules	Work-flow	Detailed schedules
3. Making Efficient Use of Inputs				
(a) Profitability	Higher profits on net worth (or total assets)	20% on net worth	—	—
(b) Costs per unit	Lower engine costs	8% reduction	Total costs per trainee	$200 per week
(c) Partial input ratios	More output per man-hour	10% increase	Teacher costs	$150 per training-hour
(d) Portion of potential used	Reducing idle equipment-time	5% reduction	Full participation in training programme	No vacancies
4. Investing in the Organization				
(a) Hard goods	Re-equipment programme	Detailed specifications	New files	No vacancies
(b) People	Management training programme	50 trainees per year	"Retooling" of old-timers	Participation in "refresher" courses
(c) Internal units	Reorganization of personnel unit	Higher status for training section	Maintenance of existing organization	Maintaining present status for training section
(d) External relations	More support in Congress	Support by specific senators	More support from "line" executives	Support by specific executives
5. Acquiring Resources				
(a) Money	More equity	Selling securities	Larger budget	5% increase
(b) People	Better managers	Recruitment programme	More professional staff	Recruitment programme
(c) Goods	New machines	Procurement programme	New files	Procurement programme
6. Observing Codes				
(a) External codes	Obeying anti-trust laws	Competition within limits	Living within budgets	Controls on commitments
(b) Internal codes	Obeying company regs.	Control of deviations	Loyalty to unit	Social exclusiveness
7. Behaving Rationally				
(a) Technical rationality	Aeronautical research	Specific studies	Personnel research	Specific studies
(b) Administrative rationality	Formal reorganization	More decentralization	More "democracy"	Monthly staff meetings

TABLE 2. Output Performance Objectives: Some Detailed Illustrations

Output Production Objectives	Aircraft Company		Personnel Unit	
	Goals	Norms	Goals	Norms
A. Output Mix	Continued output of long-range jets New short-range jet Parts production Research for government Advisory services for users	Detailed production schedule	Maintaining personnel records Recruitment services Classification system Job analysis and evaluation Training programme	Operating programme
B. Output Quality				
1. Client satisfactions				
(a) Presumed results	Planes: Faster, safer flights	Specific speed and safety standards	Training programme: Better managers	Subsequent performance of trainees
(b) Choices made	Popularity among passengers	Prosperity of airline customers	Popularity of programme	Backlog of applications
(c) Payments given	Rising volume of airline sales	15% of industry sales	Budgets allocated	Specific budget figures
(d) Opinions expressed	Low complaint level	Decline in pilots' complaints	Trainees' opinions	Specific statements
2. Product characteristics	Conformance with specifications	Detailed specifications	Improved curriculum	Emphasis on decision-making skills
3. Production processes	Careful testing	Specific tests	Improved teaching methods	Use of field studies
4. Input quality	Outstanding productive personnel	Acquiring best designers	Outstanding teachers	Acquiring teachers of high repute
C. Output Quantity				
1. Monetary value				
(a) Total sales value	Planes: 15% of industry sales Lower proportion of value added with more sub-contracting	X million dollars	—	—
(b) Value added		$\dfrac{X}{3}$	—	—
(c) Value added adjusted for price changes	20% beyond 1960	$\dfrac{X^9}{3}$ (price deflator)	—	—
(d) Imputed value of nonmarketed output	Advisory services: Input value		Input value Training programme:	
2. Physical volume				
(a) Tangible units	Planes: Number to be produced	Specific cost figures		Specific cost figures
(b) Surrogates for intangible services	Advisory services:	Detailed production schedule		
(i) clients (ii) duration (iii) intermediate or subsequent products	More clients Longer periods Memoranda produced	Specific figures	More trainees Longer courses Field studies undertaken	Specific figures
(iv) input value	Total costs		Total costs	

304

TABLE 3. Input-Output Performance Objectives: Some Detailed Illustrations

Efficiency (Input-Output) Objectives	Aircraft Company		Personnel Unit	
	Goals	Norms	Goals	Norms
A. Profitability				
1. Unit profits	Short-range jet: higher profits with rising volume	Specific figures		—
2. Total profits				
Before taxes	Higher profits	10% increase		—
After taxes	Higher profits	12% increase		—
Total profits	Lower (with replacement of debt by equity)	10% decrease		—
3. Net worth	Higher	10% increase		—
4. Total assets				
5. Sales	Lower (with higher volume of sales)	10% decrease		—
B. Costs per unit	New short-range jets: Declining total costs with rising volume	10% decline per unit over first year	Training programme: Rising costs with longer duration and higher quality	20% more per trainee
C. Partial Input-Output Relations				
1. Labour-output ratios				
(a) Labour time	For a specific output unit: More output per direct man-hour	10% increase	More teacher-time per trainee	10% more per trainee
(b) Labour cost	No increase in direct costs	Same	Higher teacher fees	20% more per trainee
	Small increase in direct plus indirect labour costs	5% increase	Higher overhead costs	5% increase
(c) Output per $1 of labour cost	Lower total value	−6%	—	—
	Lower added value	−29%	—	—
2. Capital output ratio	For specific machines: fuller use of rated capacity	Specific figures	Low-cost residential facilities	Specific figures
D. Portion of Output Potential Used				
1. Waste	Less scrap material	Specific figures	Less waste	Elimination of unnecessary paperwork
2. Gap between actual and potential	Better utilization of scrap			
	Fuller use of capacity	Reaching 80% in 2 shifts	Fuller use of computers (on personnel records)	Reaching 35% of capacity
	Higher fulfilment of profit potential	8% on total assets	Higher fulfilment of service potential	Specific data on quality and quantity of end-products

305

to the great multiplicity of interests that many people and groups throughout a society have in common. There are always conflicting views concerning the nature of "public interests."

Third, it is immensely difficult to specify the extent of satisfactions desired or attained. Satisfactions themselves are locked in the hearts and minds of the people whose interests are presumed to be satisfied. They are inextricably associated with dissatisfactions and frustration. The most we can do is use certain indirect indicators expressed in terms of the observable behaviour of the behaviour of "interesteds." Two of the most immediate forms of behaviour are the choices they make (in participating in the organization or using its product) and the money they are willing to pay (in the form of consumer purchases, taxes, or dues). Other indicators are their expressed opinions (complaints or praise) and their subsequent behaviour as a presumed result of the satisfactions obtained. Such indicators with respect to clientele satisfactions provide the most important measures of output quality.

2. Producing Output

Output production objectives are much easier to formulate. They may best be expressed in terms of an "output mix" listing the types of services or goods supplied to the organization's (or unit's) clientele. For each type quality and quantity objectives may then be set.

Yet there are at least five major problems in this area. First of all, output quality has many dimensions. As already indicated, clientele satisfaction, the most important dimension of output quality, is exceedingly difficult to measure. Less direct indicators—such as product specifications, production processes, and the quality of input factors—may also be needed. The objective of higher quality often conflicts with the objective of higher quantity.

Second, although monetary aggregates are the only way of measuring total output, they must be used with considerable care. Important distinctions may be needed between the total value of output and value added, between marginal value and total or average value, between different ways of allocating value to time periods. For comparisons over time, adjustments for price changes may be needed; for international comparisons, adjustments in the value of international currencies.

Third, in the case of services and goods that are not sold (and this includes most of the intermediate output within business organizations) the only direct measure of output quantity is physical units. In most instances this means that there is no common denominator for the total quantity of different kinds of unit. All that can be done to aggregate quantity objectives is to use input costs or some administratively determined "price" (as in internal pricing systems) as an indirect quantity indicator.

Fourth, in the case of intangible services there are no physical units that can readily be identified. Here one can set objectives only in terms of such indirect indicators as the number of clients, the duration of services, certain intermediate products that are more tangible, and the volume or value of input factors.

Fifth, considerable confusion may develop between intermediate products and the end-products supplied to an organization's clientele. This readily happens with intangible end-product services that are provided on a nonsale basis to an intangible, unorganized, or reluctant clientele. More tangible intermediate products—particularly when supplied by hard-driving, ambitious units—may then receive disproportionate attention. One remedy is to formulate objectives in terms of work flow—that is, a series of intermediate outputs leading to the production of the organization's end products.

3. Making Efficient Use of Inputs

When resources available for use as inputs are perceived as scarce, an organization or unit usually becomes interested in making efficient use of inputs relative to outputs. Since there are many ways of calculating input and output and of relating the two, there are many varieties of input-output performance.

Profitability is the most useful input-output relation, since it provides a common measure of value for both input and output. Profitability measures may be used in many ways, however, depending upon whether one (1) relates profits to net worth, total assets, or sales, (2) focuses on unit profits or total profits, or (3) thinks in short- or long-range terms. Depending upon a variety of techniques for handling difficult accounting problems, they are subject to considerable statistical manipulation. They may also reflect an organization's monopoly power and its ability to obtain subsidies, as well as its efficiency. Nevertheless, in many circumstances—particularly over a long time period—profitability is the best single measure of efficiency, output quantity and quality, and interest satisfaction.

The most generally applicable efficiency objective is attaining the lowest possible total costs for a given unit of output. This cost-accounting measure is an essential instrument in attaining—even in formulating—profitability objectives. It is relevant to non-marketed products as well. In developing cost-accounting goals, however, it is essential not to neglect the quality dimensions of output. In the case of intangible services, as already indicated, the identification of the unit is extremely difficult. Where capital and material inputs are involved, it is necessary to make difficult—and sometimes arbitrary—decisions with respect to depreciation, the distinction between current and capital expenditures, and the value of withdrawals from inventories.

Partial input-output ratios are those relating some measure of input—usually either labour or capital—to some measure of total output. Such a ratio is particularly meaningful when the volume of other input factors may be presumed to remain unchanged. It will be very misleading, however, whenever there is any significant change in any other input factor—as when increased output per employee is counterbalanced, and in fact caused, by increased capital per unit of output.

Another efficiency measure is the proportion of potential actually used. This may be expressed in terms of a reduction in waste, a higher utilization of capacity (potential output), or profits in relation to potential profitability.

4. Investing in the System

In addition to producing current output, an organization must invest in its capacity for future production. Investment objectives involve the expansion, replacement, conservation, or development of assets. They are essential not only for survival, but to prevent decline or promote growth.

The most obvious investment objectives relate to hard goods and monetary reserves. The hard goods may include land, buildings, equipment and machinery, and stocks of materials. The monetary reserves may include cash, deposits, securities, receivables, and any other funds that can be drawn upon.

Less obvious, although equally important, is investment in people, subsystems, subsystem relations, external relations, and the development of values. Investment in the guidance subsystem itself—that is, in the management structure—is particularly important.

In other words, investment performance may deal directly with any element of system structure. Accordingly, the specifics of investment objectives may be presented in the subsequent discussion of system structure.

In general, however, it should be pointed out that investment objectives often mean a diversion of resources from use in current output. Thus there are often important conflicts not only among different forms of investment but between investment and output production.

5. Acquiring Resources

Neither output production nor investment is possible without resources that can be used as inputs. These must be obtained from the external environment or from within the organization. Under conditions of scarcity and competition this requires considerable effort. Thus resource-acquisition objectives usually receive high priority. Indeed, long-range planning is often oriented much more to acquiring resources than to utilizing them.

Organizations that sell their output may acquire external resources from the consumer market (through sales revenue), the capital market (through investment), and banks (through loans). Their sales, investment, and borrowing objectives are closely related to the extent of clientele satisfactions. Organizations and units that do not sell their output must depend mainly upon budgetary allocations.

In both cases monetary terms provide the most general expression of resource-mobilization objectives. But the monetary objectives are meaningful only when they reflect the specific resources to be acquired with money— people, information, facilities, goods, or organizations. In many circumstances it is also necessary to include (1) specifications for the resources desired, (2) specific terms and conditions, (3) selection methods, (4) the maintenance of supply lines, and (5) inspection of resources received.

The logical justification of an organization's "requirements" for additional resources is best provided by a set of objectives that moves back from (1) interest satisfactions and (2) output mix to (3) efficiency and (4) investment. In the budget-allocation process "acquisition logic" also requires efforts to appeal to the interests of those with most influence in the allocation decisions.

6. Observing Codes

Every organization aims at doing things in the "right" way. To some extent the "right" way is set forth in external codes—laws, regulations, moral and ethical prohibitions and prescriptions, and professional principles. It is also determined by the codes of the organization—its written and unwritten rules and rituals.

Some may prefer to think of code observance as a restraint upon efforts to attain other objectives. Nonetheless, a considerable amount of purposeful activity in organizations is involved in containing inevitable tendencies towards code deviation.

The greatest attention is usually given to internal codes. In the case of external codes that are not "internalized," the organization will often tolerate deviation. Indeed, the deception of external inspectors may itself become part of the internal code. Similarly, the deception of the organization's code-enforcement efforts may become part of the internal code of various units. These tendencies towards deviation are facilitated by the difficulty of understanding—or even keeping up with—complex regulations. They are promoted by recurring code conflicts.

These difficulties may be handled only in part by formal enforcement measures. Successful code observance also requires widespread internalization of codes and the continuing adjustment of conflicting and confusing codes.

7. Behaving Rationally

An organization or unit also aims at doing things "rationally." This means the selection of the most satisfactory means of attaining a given set of objectives—from interest satisfaction and output production down to rational behaviour itself. Thus rationality is an all-pervasive instrumental objective.

Perfect rationality is an impossible objective. The instruments of rational calculation—information, knowledge, and skill—are always imperfect. The dimensions of rational behaviour—desirability, feasibility, and consistency—are themselves frequently conflicting. The more desirable objective will frequently be less feasible, the more feasible objective less consistent with other goals, the more consistent objective less desirable.

Technical rationality involves the use of the best methods devised by science and technology. With rapid scientific and technological progress, it is constantly changing. On the one hand, the rational methods of a few years ago may be irrational today. On the other hand, new techniques are often adapted on the basis of "technological faddism" rather than truly rational choice. In either case, there are usually serious disputes among technicians, disputes that cannot be entirely settled within the confines of technical rationality.

Administrative rationality is a much broader type of rationality. It involves the use of the best methods of guiding or managing organizations. This involves the interrelated processes of planning, activating, and evaluating with respect to all significant dimensions of both performance and structure. It provides the framework for resolving technical disputes. Yet administrative rationality, although highly developed on an intuitive basis, still awaits systematic scientific formulation. Many so-called "principles" of administration neglect the major dimensions of performance, deal formalistically with structure, and ignore the relation between the two. Management theory has not yet gone far enough in encouraging managers to think and communicate explicitly in connection with such delicate subjects as the development and use of power and the management of internal and external conflict.

STRUCTURE OBJECTIVES

In thinking of system structure we should beware of images derived from the "nonhuman" structure of a building. The structure of an organization is based upon the expectations and behaviour of people and human groups. It has informal as well as formal aspects. It can never be understood (not even in its formal aspects) from an inspection of written decisions alone. It is never free from internal conflicts and inconsistencies. Unlike the frame of a building, it is always changing in many ways. Indeed, structure is merely the more stabilized aspect of activity. It consists of interrelations that provide the capacity for future performance and that can be understood only in terms of performance objectives. Some random illustrations of objectives for structural change are provided in Table 4.

1. People

The people in an organization are the first element in an organization's structure. Thus structural objectives may be formulated in terms of the types of personnel, their quality, and their quantity.

Personnel may be classified in terms of specific positions with such-and-such titles, salaries, and perquisites; abilities, knowledge, and interests; experience; educational background; health; and various personality characteristics. Other characteristics relate to age, sex, race, religion, geographical origins. Some combination of these dimensions is usually employed in objectives for recruitment, replacement, and promotion.

The formulation of quality objectives involves consideration of the place of various people within a specific subsystem. Without reference to any subsystem, however, it also involves attention to people's capacity for learning and self-development. It involves objectives for promoting the utilization of such capacity.

The number of people in an organization is one of the simplest measures of its size. Larger numbers are often sought as a prelude to obtaining other assets, as a substitute for them, or as a compensation for the lack of quality. Even with high-quality personnel and an adequate complement of non-human resources, larger numbers are often needed to supply essential reserves or the basis of major output expansion.

TABLE 4. Structural Objectives: Some General Illustrations

		Aircraft Company		Personnel Unit	
	Structural Objectives	Goals	Norms	Goals	Norms
1.	**People**				
	(a) Types	Fewer "blue-collars"	Specific manning tables	More professionals	Specific manning tables
	(b) Quantity	No overall increase	Specific manning tables	Larger staff	4 new positions
	(c) Quality	Better-educated staff	90% college graduates above supervisory level	Better educational background	All college graduates with a few PhDs
2.	**Non-human resources**				
	(a) Physical assets	More modern plant	Specific re-equipment programme	More adequate space	5 more rooms
	(b) Monetary assets	More liquid position	2 : 1 current ratio	Larger reserves	More transferable budget items
	(c) Claims against assets	Higher ratio of equity to long-term debt	$10 million equity increase	—	—
3.	**Subsystems**				
	(a) Units	Improved divisional structure	Stronger jet-plane divisions	Improved internal structure	Stronger training group
	(b) Committees	Improved committee structure	Inter-divisional task force on new jets	Better representation on committees	Participation in jet-plane task force
4.	**Subsystem relations**				
	(a) Cooperation-conflict	Settlement of inter-divisional disputes	Compromise on jet-plane design	Settlement of inter-unit disputes	Compromise on location of training division
	(b) Hierarchy	Stronger central control	Fewer levels	Stronger unit position	Direct line to top manager
	(c) Polyarchy	Dispersed responsibility	New clearance procedures	Dispersed responsibility	New clearance procedures
	(d) Communication	Better communication among divisions	Weekly paper	Better communication with line executives	Liaison units in line divisions
5.	**External relations**				
	(a) Clients and suppliers	Better distribution channels for parts	Relations with specific distributors	More support from line executives	Support by specific executives
	(b) Controllers and controllees	More support in Congress	Support by specific Senators	More support by budget unit	Support for 4 new positions
	(c) Associates and adversaries	Limits on completion	"Understandings" on division of markets	Rivalry with budget unit	Less budget opposition to training programme funds
6.	**Values**				
	(a) Internal-external orientation	Public service	Safer planes	Professionalism in personnel management	Advancement of unit's interests
	(b) Conformity and individualism	Initiative	Proposing of company policy by divisions	Loyalty to unit	Subordination of external interests
	(c) Activism-passivity	Progress	Faster planes	Progress	All-round improvement
7.	**System management**				
	(a) Higher level	More "professional" approach	Specific planning and control methods	More "human" approach	More emphasis on personnel management
	(b) Lower level	More effective supervision	Participatory activation methods	More effective supervision	Better check of supervisors

2. Nonhuman Resources

With advancing science and technology, nonhuman resources become increasingly essential as instruments of human activity.

Certain natural resources—if only a piece of land—are an essential foundation of human activity. Physical facilities provide the necessary housing for human activity. Equipment and machinery, particularly when driven by electrical energy, make it possible for people to move or process things with little expenditure of human energy. Data processing machinery replaces human labour in the processing of information. Thus investment objectives must deal with the structure of these physical assets.

As indicated in the discussion of investment performance, they may also include objectives with respect to monetary assets and—where balance-sheet accounting is used—to the structure of claims against them (liabilities).

3. Subsystems

Within any organization people and non-human resources are grouped together in various subsystems. Each subsystem, in turn, is often subdivided still further. The smallest subdivision is the individual person.

Each subsystem is identifiable mainly by its role or function. The major element in role definition is the output expected from the subsystem. In larger organizations, particularly those based upon advancing technology, role differentiation tends to become increasingly specific and detailed. It also tends to undergo change—but at uneven and varying rates in response to recurring new environmental conditions, new technology, and adjustments in the quantity and quality of the organization's output mix. This means an internal restructuring of the subsystems. With growth of the organization as a whole, the subsystems change in a disproportional manner. Some expand, some decline, and some must be liquidated.

Important distinctions must be made between individuals and roles. People may come and go, while a role remains. Moreover, one person may play a number of roles—that is, "wear many hats." Some roles are substantially developed by the people who play them. Most people are substantially affected by the roles they play.

There are many kinds of subsystems. Some are hierarchically organized units; others are committees. Some are organized to perform functions peculiar to a specific organization; others provide certain kinds of services (personnel, budgeting, accounting, procurement, methods analysis, public relations) that are widely used by many organizations. Some are called "line," others "staff." Some are informal only. The most important subsystem is the management or guidance subsystem (discussed separately under 7 below).

4. Internal Relations

By itself subsystem differentiation is divisive. The system as a whole exists only to the extent that the parts are brought together in a network of internal relations.

The first element in internal relations is cooperation among and within the subsystems. This cooperation must be based upon certain commonly accepted objectives for future performance. Otherwise work flows will not mesh. A large part of this cooperation may consist of routinized, habitual expectations and activity. At the same time cooperation is always associated with conflict relations within and among subsystems. If carried too far, conflict and tension may impair—even destroy—the internal structure. Within limits they may help to invigorate it.

Hierarchic relations are an indispensable element in the cooperation-conflict nexus. These consist of superior-subordinate relations, usually confined to certain spheres of behaviour. The lines of hierarchic authority provide formal channels of internal communication and ladders for career advancement. The upper positions in a hierarchy provide valuable points for conflict settlement and important symbols of organizational unity. At the same time, the growing role differentiation in modern organizations leads inevitably towards the subdivision of hierarchic authority and the growth of multiple hierarchy (see Gross, 1964, pp. 377-9).

Hierarchy is always accompanied by polyarchy—sometimes referred to as "lateral relations." One form of polyarchy is "joint authority." Thus committee members (often representing different units) may operate together as equals rather than as superiors and subordinates. Another is "dispersed authority." In budget procedures various units negotiate and bargain with each other—at least up to the point where hierarchic authority may be brought into play.

The communication network is an all-pervasive part of internal relations. A critical role in this network is always played by the various lines of hierarchic authority. But many other multi-directional channels and media—some of them informal—are also needed.

5. External Relations

The immediate environment of any organization includes not only individuals but also various groups that may be classified as enterprises, government agencies, and various types of association. The relations between an organization and this immediate environment may be expressed in terms of the roles played by such individuals and groups:

a. *Clients and suppliers*
   The clients are those who receive, or are supposed to benefit from, an organization's output. The suppliers those who supply the goods, services, information, or money acquired by the organization.

b. *Controllers and controllees*
   The controllers are the external regulators or "superiors." The controllees are the organization's regulatees or "subordinates."

c. *Associates and adversaries*
   The associates are partners or allies engaged in joint or cooperative undertakings. The adversaries include rivals for the same resources, competitors in producing similar outputs, and outright enemies interested in limiting or destroying the organization's performance or structure.

The same external organization often plays many—at times even all—of these roles. In so doing it will use many forms of external persuasion, pressure, or penetration.

Resistance to external influence usually involves an organization in preventive or counter measures of persuasion, pressure, or penetration. A more positive approach to external relations involves efforts to isolate, neutralize, or win over opponents and build up a farflung structure of external support through coalitions, alliances, and "deals." Such efforts may be facilitated by persuasive efforts aimed at unorganized publics.

6. Values

The individuals and subsystems in any organization are always guided by some pattern of values—that is, general attitudes towards what is desirable or undesirable and general ways of looking at the world. Some of the most important elements in this value structure may be defined in terms of the continua between.

   a. *Internal and external orientation*
   Internal orientation emphasizes the interests of members—in terms of their income, status, power, or self-development. External orientation emphasizes the interests of nonmembers; these may range from investors (owners) to clients to the society as a whole. Some organizations aim at integrating the two sets of values.

   b. *Conformity and individualism*
   In many organizations conformity is a high value—sometimes to the point of the complete subordination of individual initiative. Nevertheless, highly individualistic values may be hidden behind a facade of superficial conformism.

   c. *Passivity and activism*
   Among many members or organizations passivity is a highly cherished value. It leads to "playing it safe," "taking it easy," "following the book," and waiting for orders. Activist values, in contrast, lead to risk-taking, initiative, and innovation. Although apparently conflicting, the two are often intertwined.

Other values relate to freedom and control, authoritarianism and democracy, material and nonmaterial interests, equity and equality, impersonality and particularism, and ascription and achievement.

7. Guidance Subsystem

Some amount of coordinated action is always provided by the autonomous action—both routinized and spontaneous—of an organization's subsystems. But sufficient capacity for effective performance is not possible without the coordinating and promotional functions of a special subsystems with the responsibility for system guidance, or management. This guidance subsystem is composed of a network extending from a general directorate and top executives down through the middle and lower levels of managerial or supervisory personnel. At any level the members of this subsystem play various roles in decision making and communication with respect to the making of plans, the activating of people and groups, and the evaluating of plans made and action taken. The interrelation among these roles helps to determine the structure of the guidance subsystem.

An important aspect of management structure is the balance between centralization and decentralization. Both centralization and decentralization may be thought of in terms of the distribution of responsibility and authority by (a) vertical levels, (b) horizontal levels, and (c) geographical location. The extent of centralization or decentralization in any of these dimensions can best be specified with reference to specific roles or functions. The prerequisite for effective decentralization of some functions is the centralization of other functions. With increasing size and complexity, it usually becomes necessary to delegate greater responsibility and authority to lower levels and to field offices. This, in turn, requires the strengthening of certain planning, activating, and evaluating functions *of* the "centre," as well as various horizontal shifts in the centralization-decentralization balance *in* the centre.

Another vital aspect of management structure is its power base. This includes the resources at its disposal. It includes the support it obtains from the membership and major points of internal influence. It includes the support obtained externally—from associates, from clients and suppliers, and from controllers and controllees. Top business executives need support from their boards of directors and banks; government executives from President or Governor, legislators, and external interest groups.

Other important dimensions of management structure relate to managerial personnel and tenure. Admission to the upper ranks of management may be dependent upon a combination of such factors as sponsorship, ability, education, personality characteristics, and social origins. Some top managers seek a self-perpetuating oligarchy, with little or no provision made for inevitable replacement. Others set as major objectives the development of career and recruitment systems that make for high mobility within managerial ranks.

THE STRATEGY OF PLANNING

Planning is the process of developing commitments to some pattern of objectives.

The preceding section set forth the major categories of objectives.

Let us now turn to some of the strategic considerations involved in deriving a pattern from these categories.

1. The Selectivity Paradox

As specialists develop comprehensive ways of looking at systems, they often tend to overemphasize the role of comprehensive objectives in planning. Thus economists often give the false impression that national aggregates of income, product, investment, and consumption are the major goals in national policy-making. In the process of "selling their wares," budgeteers and accountants often give the impression that comprehensive projections of budgets, income statements, or balance cheets can define an organization's major goals. If this approach should be automatically transferred to general-systems accounting, we should then find ourselves recommending that an organization's planners should formulate comprehensive objectives for all the elements of system performance and system structure.

Yet this would be a misleading position. The essence of planning is the *selection of strategic objectives in the form of specific sequences of action to be taken by the organization.* These critical variables must be selected in terms of:

a. The major interest satisfactions that must be "promised" to obtain external and internal support.
b. Present, imminent, or foreseeable crises or emergencies. These may require "contingency plans."
c. Their decisive impact upon preceding, coordinate, or subsequent events.
d. The long-range implications of action in the present or the immediate future. These are the critical considerations with respect to the "sunk costs" of investment programmes and the immediate steps in extended production processes (such as the building of houses, ships, or aircraft).

With these strategic elements selected, many elements of performance and structure may be detailed in subsystem plans or handled on the basis of current improvisation. A passion for comprehensive detail by either the organization or its subsystems may undermine selectivity. It may easily result in a loss of perspective, in document-orientation instead of action-orientation, and in an information supply that overloads communication channels and processing capacity. It may thus lead to serious waste of resources.

But—and here is the paradox of selectivity—strategic objectives can be selected rationally *only if the planners are aware of the broad spectrum of possible objectives.* Otherwise, objectives may be set in a routinized, arbitrary, or superficial fashion. The very concept of selection implies the scanning of a broad range of possibilities.

The solution to this paradox may be found in the use of general systems accounting to provide *a comprehensive background for the selection of strategic objectives.*

2. The Clarity-Vagueness Balance

There is no need to labour the need for clarity in the formulation of an organization's objectives. Precise formulations are necessary for delicate operations. They provide the indispensable framework for coordinating complex activity. They often have great symbolic significance.

Yet in the wide enthusiasm for "crystal-clear goals," one may easily lose sight of the need for a fruitful balance between clarity and vagueness. The following quotation is an effort to contribute to this balance through a "crystal-clear" statement on the virtues of vagueness:

If all the points on a set of interrelated purpose chains were to be set forth with precise clarity, the result would be to destroy the subordination of one element to another which is essential to an operating purpose pattern. The proper focusing of attention on some goals for any particular moment or period in time means that other goals must be left vague. This is even more true for different periods of time. We must be very clear about many things we aim to do today and tomorrow. It might be dangerously misleading to seek similar clarity for our long-range goals.

Apart from its role in helping provide focus, vagueness in goal formation has many positive virtues. It leaves room for others to fill in the details and even modify the general pattern; over-precise goals stifle initiative. Vagueness may make it easier to adapt to changing conditions; ultraprecision can destroy flexibility. Vagueness may make it possible to work towards many goals that can only be attained by indirection. Some of the deepest personal satisfactions from work and cooperation come as by-products of other things. If pursued too directly, they may slip through one's fingers; the happiest people in the world are never those who set out to do the things that will make them happy. There is something inhuman and terrifying about ultrapurposeful action proceeding according to blueprint and schedule. Only vagueness can restore the precious element of humanity.

Above all, vagueness is an essential part of all agreements resulting from compromise. When a dispute is resolved, some degree of ambiguity enters into the terms of settlement. Hence the wide-open language often used in the final language of statutory law. Similar ambiguities are found in most constitutions, charters, declarations of purpose, policy manifestos, and collective bargaining agreements. Certain anticipated situations are always referred to in terms that mean different things to different people, and are valuable because of, not despite, this characteristic. (Gross, 1964, p. 497.)

3. Whose Objectives?

Whose objectives are an organization's objectives?

The crystal-clear answers to this question point to (1) the people who wrote the charter (law or articles of incorporation) under which the organization operates, (2) the holders of formal authority over the organization (legislators or stockholders), (3) the members of the organization as a whole, (4) the organization's specialized planning people, or (5) the organization's top managers.

Yet each of these answers is incomplete. The charter-writers and the holders of formal authority can deal with only a small portion of an organization's objectives. The members, the subsystems, and the specialized planners have or propose many objectives that the organization never accepts. The managers' objectives may be accepted only in part by the rest of the organization. All of these groups have many conflicting objectives.

A better, although vaguer, answer is one that defines an organization's objectives as those widely accepted by its members. These objectives may (to some extent, they *must*) reflect the objectives of charter-writers, the holders of formal authority, and other external groups. They must represent a common area of acceptance on the part of the organization's subsystems and members, albeit within a matrix of divergent and conflicting purposes. The technical planners play a major role in helping to formulate planning decisions. The top managers make (or legitimate) the decisions and play a major role in winning their acceptance throughout the organization. Whether recognized in formal planning procedures or not, the entire management structure is involved *de facto* in the daily operation of formulating and winning commitment to objectives for future performance and structure.

4. Conflict Resolving and Creating

As already indicated, the process of organizational planning involves dealing with many conflicting objectives and with divergent or conflicting parties at interest both inside and outside an organization.

Hence planning—rather than involving nothing but the sober application of technical rationality—is an exercise in conflict management. In this exercise systematic technical calculations are exceedingly valuable as a means both of narrowing areas of conflict and of revealing possibilities for conflict resolution. Yet technical calculations are never enough. Overreliance upon them can lead to administrative irrationality.

Rational planning, in contrast, requires realistic attention to the power for and against alternative plans. It requires the resolution of conflicts through the use of power in various combinations of persuasion and pressure. It also requires the building of a power base through various methods of conflict resolution.

The most widespread mode of conflict resolution is compromise, through which some interests are sacrificed. A more creative—but more difficult—method is integration. This involves a creative readjustment of interests so that all parties may gain and none lose. In some cases, total victory may be obtained for one point of view, with consequent defeat for its opposition. To prevent defeat on some objectives, it is often necessary to tolerate deadlock or avoid an issue entirely. Any real-life planning process may be characterized as *a stream of successive compromises punctuated by frequent occasions of deadlock or avoidance and occasional victories, defeats, and integrations.* All these outcomes lead to new conflicts to be handled by the planners and managers.

Successful planning is often possible only when the key members of an organization see themselves threatened by an imminent crisis. In noncrisis conditions the subsystems tend to move in their own directions. They will most readily accept common objectives when the alternative is perceived as an onslaught of acute dissatisfactions, that is, a crisis. With crisis as the alternative, conflicts may be more quickly and effectively resolved. This is particularly relevant to subsystem resistance against plans for significant structural change.

In developing an organization's purposes, therefore, managers are frequently involved in crisis management. They try to anticipate crises around the corner. They try to respond promptly to crises that emerge. They may even try to create crises by setting high aspirations and accentuating fears of failure. These are delicate activities. For managers without a broad perspective on an organization's performance, structure, and environmental relations, they are dangerous undertakings—with much to be lost on one front as the price of victory on another. Even with such a broad perspective, they involve considerations that may not always be publicly discussed with complete frankness.

Hence a better-developed language of organizational purposefulness will not provide an outsider with a satisfactory answer when he asks a manager, "Just what are your organization's purposes?" The most it can do is help the managers themselves in the difficult and unending process of asking the question and finding workable answers.

BIBLIOGRAPHY

Drucker, Peter F. *The practice of management.* New York: Harper & Row, Publishers, 1954.

Drucker, Peter F. *Managing for results.* New York: Harper & Row, Publishers, 1964.

Gross, Bertram M. *The managing of organizations.* 2 vols. New York: Free Press, 1964.

LeBreton, Preston P. and Henning, Dale A. *Planning theory.* Englewood Cliffs, N.J.: Prentice-Hall, Inc., 1961.

William E. Barrett

SEÑOR PAYROLL

Larry and I were Junior Engineers in the gas plant, which means that we were clerks. Anything that could be classified as paper work came to the flat double desk across which we faced each other. The Main Office downtown sent us a bewildering array of orders and rules that were to be put into effect.

Junior Engineers were beneath the notice of everyone except the Mexican laborers at the plant. To them we were the visible form of a distant, unknowable paymaster. We were Señor Payroll.

Those Mexicans were great workmen; the aristocrats among them were the stokers, big men who worked Herculean eight-hour shifts in the fierce heat of the retorts. They scooped coal with huge shovels and hurled it with uncanny aim at tiny doors. The coal streamed out from the shovels like black water from a high pressure nozzle, and never missed the narrow opening. The stokers worked stripped to the waist, and there was pride and dignity in them. Few men could do such work, and they were the few.

The Company paid its men only twice a month, on the fifth and on the

From William E. Barrett, Senor Payroll. *Southwest Review* 29 (Autumn, 1943): 25-29. Reprinted by permission of Southern Methodist University Press and of the author. Copyright© 1943 by Southern Methodist University Press.

twentieth. To a Mexican, this was absurd. What man with money will make it last 15 days? If he hoarded money beyond the spending of three days, he was a miser—and when, Señor, did the blood of Spain flow in the veins of misers? Hence it was the custom for our stokers to appear every third or fourth day to draw the money due to them.

There was a certain elasticity in the Company rules, and Larry and I sent the necessary forms to the Main Office and received an "advance" against a man's pay check. Then, one day, Downtown favored us with a memorandum:

"There have been too many abuses of the advance-against-wages privilege. Hereafter, no advance against wages will be made to any employee except in a case of genuine emergency."

We had no sooner posted the notice when in came stoker Juan Garcia. He asked for an advance. I pointed to the notice. He spelled it through slowly, then said, "What does this mean, this 'genuine emergency'?"

I explained to him patiently that the Company was kind and sympathetic, but that it was a great nuisance to have to pay wages every few days. If someone was ill or if money was urgently needed for some other good reason, then the Company would make an exception to the rule.

Juan Garcia turned his hat over and over slowly in his big hands. "I do not get my money?"

"Next payday, Juan. On the 20th."

He went out silently and I felt a little ashamed of myself. I looked across the desk at Larry. He avoided my eyes.

In the next hour two other stokers came in, looked at the notice, had it explained and walked solemnly out; then no more came. What we did not know was that Juan Garcia, Pete Mendoza and Francisco Gonzalez had spread the word and that every Mexican in the plant was explaining the order to every other Mexican. "To get the money now, the wife must be sick. There must be medicine for the baby."

The next morning Juan Garcia's wife was practically dying, Pete Mendoza's mother would hardly last the day, there was a veritable epidemic among children and, just for variety, there was one sick father. We always suspected that the old man was really sick; no Mexican would otherwise have thought of him. At any rate, nobody paid Larry and me to examine private lives; we made out our forms with an added line describing the "genuine emergency." Our people got paid.

That went on for a week. Then came a new order, curt and to the point: "Hereafter, employes will be paid ONLY on the fifth and the 20th of the month. No exceptions will be made except in the cases of employes leaving the service of the Company."

The notice went up on the board and we explained its significance gravely. "No, Juan Garcia, we cannot advance your wages. It is too bad about your wife and your cousins and your aunts, but there is a new rule."

Juan Garcia went out and thought it over. He thought out loud with Mendoza and Gonzalez and Ayala, then, in the morning, he was back. "I am quitting this company for different job. You pay me now?"

We argued that it was a good company and that it loved its employes like children, but in the end we paid off, because Juan Garcia quit. And so did Gonzalez, Mendoza, Obregon, Alaya and Ortez, the best stokers, men who could not be replaced.

Larry and I looked at each other; we knew what was coming in about three days. One of our duties was to sit on the hiring line early each morning, engaging transient workers for the handy gangs. Any man was accepted who could walk up and ask for a job without falling down. Never before had we been called upon to hire such skilled virtuosos as stokers for handy gang work, but we were called upon to hire them now.

The day foreman was wringing his hands and asking the Almighty if he was personally supposed to shovel this condemned coal, while there in a stolid, patient line were skilled men—Garcia, Mendoza and others—waiting to be hired. We hired them, of course. There was nothing else to do.

Every day we had a line of resigning stokers, and another line of stokers seeking work. Our paper work became very complicated. At the Main Office they were jumping up and down. The procession of forms showing Juan Garcia's resigning and being hired over and over again was too much for them. Sometimes Downtown had Garcia on the payroll twice at the same time when someone down there was slow in entering a resignation. Our phone rang early and often.

Tolerantly and patiently we explained: "There's nothing we can do if a man wants to quit, and if there are stokers available when the plant needs stokers, we hire them."

Out of chaos, Downtown issued another order. I read it and whistled. Larry looked at it and said, "It is going to be very quiet around here."

The order read: "Hereafter, no employee who resigns may be rehired within a period of 30 days."

Juan Garcia was due for another resignation, and when he came in we showed him the order and explained that standing in line the next day would do him no good if he resigned today. "Thirty days is a long time, Juan."

It was a grave matter and he took time to reflect on it. So did Gonzalez, Mendoza, Ayala and Ortez. Ultimately, however, they were all back—and all resigned.

We did our best to dissuade them and we were sad about the parting. This time it was for keeps and they shook hands with us solemnly. It was very nice knowing us. Larry and I looked at each other when they were gone and we both knew that neither of us had been pulling for Downtown to win this duel. It was a blue day.

In the morning, however, they were all back in line. With the utmost gravity, Juan Garcia informed me that he was a stoker looking for a job.

"No dice, Juan," I said. "Come back in 30 days. I warned you."

His eyes looked straight into mine without a flicker. "There is some mistake, Señor," he said. "I am Manuel Hernandez. I work as the stoker in Pueblo, in Santa Fe, in many places."

I stared back at him, remembering the sick wife and the babies without medicine, the mother-in-law in the hospital, the many resignations and the rehirings. I knew that there was a gas plant in Pueblo, and that there wasn't any in Santa Fe; but who was I to argue with a man about his own name? A stoker is a stoker.

So I hired him. I hired Gonzalez, too, who swore that his name was Carrera, and Ayala, who had shamelessly become Smith.

Three days later, the resigning started.

Within a week our payroll read like a history of Latin America. Everyone was on it: Lopez and Obregon, Villa, Diaz, Batista, Gomez, and even San Martin and Bolivar. Finally Larry and I, growing weary of staring at familiar faces and writing unfamiliar names, went to the Superintendent and told him the whole story. He tried not to grin, and said, "Damned nonsense!"

The next day the orders were taken down. We called our most prominent stokers into the office and pointed to the board. No rules any more.

"The next time we hire you *hombres,*" Larry said grimly, "come in under the names you like best, because, that's the way you are going to stay on the books."

They looked at us and they looked at the board; then for the first time in the long duel, their teeth flashed white. *"Si, Señores,"* they said.

And so it was.

Chris Argyris

HUMAN BEHAVIOR
IN ORGANIZATIONS

In this article, a discussion of some of the basic properties of personality will be followed by a similar discussion regarding formal organization, from which an attempt will be made to derive some of the basic characteristics of the relationship that will tend to arise when these two initial components are "married" to form the beginning of a social organization.[1]

The self, in this culture, tends to develop along specific developmental trends or dimensions which are operationally definable and empirically observable. The basic developmental trends may be described as follows. Human beings, in our culture:

Abridged from Chris Argyris, "Personal vs. Organizational Goals," *Yale Scientific,* (February, 1960), pp. 40-50. Reprinted by permission.

[1] This discussion is a short summary of the detailed analysis to be found in the report, *Personality and Organizations,* published by Harper & Bros., 1958.

(1). Tend to develop from a state of being passive as an infant to a state of increasing activity as an adult.

(2). Tend to develop from a state of dependence on others as an infant to a state of relative independence as an adult. Relative independence is the ability to "stand on one's own two feet" and simultaneously to acknowledge healthy dependencies.[2] It is characterized by the individual's freeing himself from his childhood determiners of behavior (e.g., family) and developing his own set of behavioral determiners. This individual does not tend to react to others (e.g., the boss) in terms of patterns learned during childhood. (1)

(3). Tend to develop from being capable of behaving in only a few ways as an infant to being capable of behaving in many different ways as an adult.[3]

(4). Tend to develop from having erratic, casual, shallow, quickly dropped interests as an infant to a deepening of interests as an adult. The mature state is characterized by an endless series of challenges in which the reward comes from doing something for its own sake. The tendency is to analyze and study phenomena in their full-blown wholeness, complexity and depth. (2)

(5). Tend to develop from having a short time perspective (i.e., the present largely determines behavior) as an infant to a much longer time perspective as an adult (i.e., behavior is more affected by the past and the future. (3,4)

(6). Tend to develop from being in a subordinate position in the family and society as an infant to aspiring to occupy a more equal and/or superordinate position relative to one's peers as an adult.

(7). Tend to develop from a lack of awareness of the self as an infant to an awareness of and control over one's self as an adult. The adult who tends to experience adequate and successful control over his own behavior tends to develop a sense of integrity (Erikson) and feelings of self-worth.

These dimensions are postulated as being descriptive of a basic multi-dimensional developmental process along which the growth of individuals in our culture may be measured. Presumably, every individual, at any given moment in time, could have his degree of development plotted along these dimensions. The exact location on each dimension will probably vary with each individual and even with the same individual at different times. Self-actualization may now be defined more precisely as the individual's plotted scores (or profile) along the above dimensions.[4]

A few words of explanation concerning these dimensions of personality development:

(1). The dimensions are continua in which the growth to be measured are assumed to be continuously changing in degree. An individual is presumed to

---

[2] This is similar to Erikson's sense of autonomy and Bronfenbrenner's state of creative interdependence.

[3] Lewin and Kounin believe that as the individual develops needs and abilities, the boundaries between them become more rigid. This explains why an adult is better able than a child to be frustrated in one activity and behave constructively in another.

[4] Another related but discrete set of developmental dimensions may be constructed to measure the protective (defense) mechanisms which individuals tend to create as they develop from infant to adulthood. Exactly how these would be related to the above model is not clear.

develop continuously in degree from the infant end to the adult end of each continuum.

(2). It is postulated that as long as one develops in a particular culture, one will never obtain maximum expression of these developmental trends. Clearly, all individuals cannot be maximally independent, active, and so forth, all the time and still maintain an organized society. It is the function of culture (e.g., norms, mores, etc.) to inhibit *maximum* expressions and to help an individual adjust and adapt by finding his *optimum* expression.

A second factor that prevents maximum expression and fosters optimum expression is the individual's own finite limits set by his personality. For example, some people fear the same amount of independence and activity that others desire. Also, it is commonplace to find some people who do not have the necessary abilities to perform specific tasks. No individual is known to have developed all known abilities to their full maturity.

Finally, defense mechanisms also are important factors operating to help an individual to deviate from the basic developmental trends.

(3). The dimensions described above are constructed in terms of latent or genotypical characteristics. If one states that an individual needs to be dependent, this need will probably be ascertained by clinical inference because it is one that individuals are not usually aware of. Thus, if one observes an employee acting as if he were independent, it is possible that if one goes below the behavioral surface, the individual may be quite dependent. The obvious example is the employee who seems to behave always in a manner contrary to that desired by management. Although this behavior may look as if he is independent, his contrariness may be due to his great need to be dependent on management, which he dislikes to admit to himself and to others.

One might say that an independent person is one whose behavior is not caused by the influence others have over him. Of course, no individual is completely independent. All of us have our healthy dependencies, i.e., those which help us to maintain our discreteness, to be creative, and to develop.

One operational criterion to ascertain whether an individual's desire to be, let us say, independent and active is a true manifestation is to ascertain the extent to which he permits others to express the same needs. Thus, an autocratic leader may say that he needs to be active and independent; he may also say that he wants subordinates who are the same; however, there is ample research to suggest that his leadership pattern only makes him and his subordinates more dependence ridden.

SOME BASIC PROPERTIES OF
FORMAL ORGANIZATION

The next step is to focus the analytic spotlight on the formal organization. What are its properties? What are its basic "givens"? What probable impact will they have on the human personality? How will the human personality tend to react to this impact? What sorts of "chain reactions" are probable when these two basic components are brought together?

Formal Organizations Are Rational Organizations. Probably the most basic property of formal organization is its logical foundation or, as it has been called by students of administration, its essential rationality. It is the "mirror image" of the planners' conception of how the intended consequences of the organization may be best achieved. The underlying assumption made by the creators of formal organization is that man within respectable tolerances will behave rationally, i.e., as the formal plan requires him to behave. Organizations are formed with particular objectives in mind, and their structure mirrors these objectives. Although man may not follow the prescribed paths, and consequently the objectives might never be achieved, Simon (6) suggests that, by and large, man does follow these prescribed paths. He points out:

> Organizations are formed with the intention and design of accomplishing goals, and the people who work in organizations believe, at least part of the time, that they are striving toward these same goals. We must not lose sight of the fact that, however far organization may depart from the traditional description . . . nevertheless most behavior in organizations is intendedly rational behavior. By "intended rationality" I mean the kind of adjustment of behavior to goals of which humans are capable—a very incomplete and imperfect adjustment, to be sure, but one which nevertheless does accomplish purposes and does carry out programs.

Most of these experts emphasize that although no organizational structure will exemplify the maximum expression of the principles, a satisfactory aspiration is for optimum expression, which means modifying the ideal structure to take into account the individual (and any environmental) conditions. Moreover, they urge that the people must be loyal to the formal structure if it is to work effectively. Thus Taylor emphasizes that scientific management would never succeed without a "mental revolution." Fayol has the same problem in mind when he emphasizes the importance of esprit de corps.

However, it is also true that these experts have provided little insight into *why* they believe that people should undergo a "mental revolution," or why an esprit de corps is necessary if the principles are to succeed. The only hints usually found are that resistance to scientific management occurs because human beings "are what they are," or "because it's human nature." But, *why* does "human nature" resist formal organizational principles? Perhaps there is something inherent in the principles which causes human resistance. Unfortunately, there exists too little research that specifically assesses the impact of the formal organizational principles on human beings.

The formal organizational experts believe that logical, rational design, in the long run, is more human than creating an organization haphazardly. They argue that it is illogical, cruel, wasteful, and inefficient not to have a logical design. It is illogical because design must come first. It does not make sense to pay a large salary to an individual without clearly defining his position and its relationship to the whole. It is cruel because, eventually, the participants suffer when no clear organizational structure exists. It is wasteful because, unless jobs are clearly predefined, it is impossible to plan logical training, promotion, resignation and retirement policies. It is inefficient because the organization becomes dependent on personalities. The "personal touch" leads to "playing politics," which Mary Follett has described as a "deplorable form of coercion" (7).

Unfortunately, the validity of these arguments tends to be obscured in the eyes of the behavioral scientist because it implies that the only choice left, if the formal, rational, predesigned structure is not accepted, is to have no organizational structure at all, with the organizational structure left to the whims, pushes and pulls of human beings. Some human-relations researchers, on the other hand, have unfortunately given the impression that formal structures are "bad" and that the needs of the individual participants should be paramount in creating and administering an organization. However, a recent analysis of the existing research points up quite clearly that the importance of the organization as an organism worthy of self-actualization is now being recognized by those who, in the past, have focused largely on the individual (8).

In the past, and for the most part in the present, the traditional organizational experts based their "human architectural creation" on certain basic principles (more accurately, assumptions) about the nature of organization.

Although these principles have been attacked by behavioral scientists, the assumption is made in this paper that to date no one has defined a more useful set of formal organization principles. Therefore, the principles are accepted as "givens." This frees us to inquire about their probable impact on people, *if they are used as defined.*

In introducing these principles, it is important to note that, as Gillespie suggests, the roots of these principles may be traced back to certain "principles of industrial economics," the most important of which is the basic economic assumption held by builders of the industrial revolution that, "the concentration of effort on a limited field of endeavor increases quality and quantity of output" (9). It follows from the above that the necessity for specialization should increase as the quantity of similar things to be done increases.

Task (Work) Specialization. If concentrating effort on a limited field of endeavor increases the quality and quantity of output, it follows that organizational and administrative efficiency is increased by the specialization of tasks assigned to the participants in the organization (10). Inherent in this assumption are three others. *First,* that the human personality will behave more efficiently as the task becomes specialized. *Second,* that there can be found a one best way to define the job so that it is performed at greater speed. (11). *Third,* that any individual differences in the human personality may be ignored by transferring more skill and thought to machines.

A number of difficulties arise with these assumptions when the properties of the human personality are recalled. *First,* the human personality, as we have seen, is always attempting to actualize its unique organization of parts resulting from a continuous, emotionally laden, ego-involving process of growth. It is difficult, if not impossible, to assume that this process can be choked off and the resultant unique differences of individuals ignored. This is tantamount to saying that self-actualization can be ignored. *Second,* task specialization requires the individual to use only a few of his abilities. Moreover, as specialization increases, it tends to require the use of the less complex doing or motor abilities which, research suggests, tend to be of lesser psychological importance to the individual. Thus the principle violates two basic "givens" of the healthy adult human personality. It inhibits self-actualization and provides expression for few, shallow, skin-surface abilities that do not provide the "endless challenge" desired by the healthy personality.

Chain of Command. The principle of task specialization creates an aggregate of parts, each performing a highly specialized task. However, an aggregate of parts busily performing their particular objective does not form an organization. A pattern of parts must be formed so that the interrelationships among the parts create the organization. Following the logic of specialization, the planners create a new function (leadership) whose primary responsibility is to control, direct and coordinate the interrelationships of the parts, and to make certain that each part performs its objective adequately. Thus the assumption is made that administrative and organizational efficiency is increased by arranging the parts in a determinate hierarchy of authority in which the part on top can direct and control the part on the bottom.

If the parts being considered are individuals, then they must be motivated to accept control, direction and coordination of their behavior. The leader, therefore, is assigned formal power to hire, discharge, reward and penalize the individuals in order that their behavior is molded toward the organization's objectives.

The impact of such a state of affairs is to make the individuals dependent on, passive and subordinate to the leader. As a result, the individuals have little control over their working environment. At the same time, their time perspective is shortened because they do not control the information necessary to predict their future. These requirements of formal organization act to inhibit four of the growth trends of personality because to be passive and subordinate and to have little control and short time perspective exemplify dimensions, in adults, of immaturity, not adulthood.

The planners of formal organization suggest three basic ways to minimize this admittedly difficult position. *First,* ample rewards should be given to those who perform well and who do not permit their dependence, subordination, passivity, etc., to influence them in a negative manner. The rewards should be material and psychological. Because of the specialized nature of the job, however, few psychological rewards are possible. It becomes important, therefore, that adequate material rewards are made available to the productive employee. This practice can lead to new difficulties, since the solution is, by its nature, not to do anything about the on-the-job situation (which is what is causing the difficulties) but to pay the individual for the dissatisfactions he experiences. The end result is that the employee is paid for his dissatisfaction while at work and his wages are given to him to gain satisfactions outside his immediate work environment.

Thus the management helps to create a psychological set which leads the employees to feel that basic causes of dissatisfaction are built into industrial life, that the rewards they receive are wages for dissatisfaction, and that if satisfaction is to be gained, the employee must seek it outside the organization.

To make matters more difficult, there are three assumptions inherent in the above solution that also violate the basic "givens" of human personality. *First,* the solution assumes that a whole human being can split his personality so that he will feel satisfied in knowing that the wages for his dissatisfaction will buy him satisfaction outside the plant. *Second,* it assumes that the employee is primarily interested in maximizing his economic gains. *Third,* it assumes that the employee is best rewarded as an individual producer. The work group in which he belongs is not viewed as a relevant factor. If he produces well, he should be rewarded. If he does not, he should be penalized even though he may be restricting production because of informal group sanctions.

The *second* solution suggested by the planners of formal organization is to have technically competent, objective, rational, loyal leaders. The assumption is made that if the leaders are technically competent, presumably they cannot have "the wool pulled over their eyes"; which should lead the employees to have a high respect for them. The leaders should be objective and rational and personify the rationality inherent in the formal structure. Being rational means that they must avoid becoming emotionally involved. As one executive states, "We must try to keep our personality out of the job." The leader must also be impartial. He does not permit his feelings to operate when he is evaluating others. Finally, the leader must be loyal to the organization so that he can inculcate the loyalty in the employees that Taylor, Fayol and others believe is so important.

Admirable as this solution may be, again it violates several of the basic properties of personality. If the employees are to respect an individual for what he does rather than for who he is, the sense of self-integrity, based on evaluation of the total self which is developed in people, is lost. Moreover, to ask the leader to keep his personality out of his job is to ask him to stop actualizing himself. This is not possible as long as he is alive. Of course, the executive may want to *feel* that he is not involved, but it is a basic "given" that the human personality is an organism always actualizing itself. The same problem arises with impartiality. No one can be completely impartial. As has been shown, the self concept always operates when we are making judgments. In fact, as May has pointed out, the best way to be impartial is to be as partial as one's needs predispose one to be but to be aware of this partiality in order to "correct" for it at the moment of decision (12). Finally, if a leader can be loyal to an organization under these conditions, there may be adequate grounds for questioning the health of his personality make-up.

The *third* solution suggested by many adherents to the formal organizational principles is to motivate the subordinates to have more initiative and to be more creative by placing them in competition with one another for the positions of power that lie above them in the organizational ladder. This solution is traditionally called "the rabble hypothesis." Acting under the assumption that employees will be motivated to advance upward, the formal organizational adherents add another assumption; that competition for the increasingly (as one goes up the ladder) scarcer positions will increase the effectiveness of the participants. Williams (13), conducting some controlled experiments, show that the latter assumption is not necessarily valid for people placed in competitive situations. Deutsch (14), as a result of extensive controlled experimental research, supports Williams' results and goes much further to suggest that competitive situations tend to lead to an increase in tension and conflict and to a decrease in human effectiveness. Levy and Freedman confirm Deutsch's observations and go further to relate competition to psychoneurosis (15).

Unity of Direction. If the tasks of everyone in a unit are specialized, then it follows that the objective or purpose of the unit must be specialized. The principle of unity of direction states that administrative and organizational efficiency increases if each unit has a single (or homogeneous set of) activity (activities) that is planned and directed by the leader[5]

This means that the work goal toward which the employees are working, the path toward the goal, and the strength of the barriers they must overcome to achieve the goal are defined and controlled by the leader. Assuming that the work goals do not ego-involve the employee (i.e., they are related to peripheral skin-surface needs), then ideal conditions for psychological failure have been created. The reader may recall that a basic "given" of a healthy personality is the aspiration for psychological success. Psychological success is achieved when each individual is able to define his own goals, in relation to his inner needs and the strength of the barriers to be overcome in order to reach these goals. Repetitive as it may sound, it is nevertheless true that the principle of unity of direction also violates a basic "given" of personality.

A BASIC INCONGRUENCY BETWEEN THE NEEDS OF A MATURE PERSONALITY AND THE REQUIREMENTS OF FORMAL ORGANIZATION

Bringing together the evidence regarding the impact of the formal organizational principles on the individual, it is concluded that there are some basic incongruencies between the growth trends of a healthy personality and the requirements of the formal organization. If the principles of formal organization are used as ideally defined, then the employees will tend to work in an environment where (1) they are provided control over their workaday world; (2) they are expected to be passive, dependent, subordinate; (3) they are expected to have a short-time perspective; (4) they are induced to perfect and value the frequent use of few skin-surface, shallow abilities; and (5) they are expected to produce under conditions leading to psychological failure.

All of these characteristics are incongruent to the ones healthy human beings

---

[5] The sacredness of these principles is questioned by a recent study. Herckscher concludes that the principles of unity of command and unity of direction are *formally* violated in Sweden. "A fundamental principle of public administration in Sweden is the duty of all public agencies to cooperate directly without necessarily passing through a common superior. This principle is even embodied in the constitution itself, and in actual fact it is being employed daily. It is traditionally one of the most important characteristics of Swedish administration that especially central agencies, but also central and local agencies of different levels, cooperate freely and that this is being regarded as a perfectly normal procedure."

are postulated to desire. They are much more congruent with the needs of infants in our culture. In effect, therefore, formal organizations are willing to pay high wages and provide adequate seniority if mature adults will for eight hours a day, behave in a less mature manner! *If the analysis is correct, this inevitable incongruency increases as (1) the employees are of increasing maturity; (2) as the formal structure, based on the above principles, is made more clear-cut and logically tight for maximum formal organizational effectiveness; (3) as one goes down the line of command; and (4) as jobs become more and more mechanized, i.e., take on assembly-line characteristics.*

The resultants of this lack of congruency are frustration, failure, short-time perspective and conflict. If the agents are predisposed to a healthy, more mature self-actualization:

(1). They will tend to experience frustration because their self-actualization will be blocked (16,17).

(2). They will tend to experience failure because they will not be permitted to define their own goals in relation to central needs, the paths of these goals, etc. (18,19).

(3). They will tend to experience short time perspective because they have no control over the clarity and stability of their future (20).

(4). They will tend to experience conflict because, as healthy agents, they will dislike frustration, failure and short-time perspective which are characteristic of the present job. However, if they leave, they may not find a new job easily; and/or even if a new job is found, it may not be much different (21).

It can be shown that under conflict, frustration, failure and short time perspective, the employees will tend to maintain self-integration by creating specific adaptive (informal) behavior such as:

1. Leaving the organization.
2. Climbing the organizational ladder.
3. Manifesting defense reactions such as daydreaming, aggression, ambivalence, regression, projection, etc.
4. Becoming apathetic and disinterested toward the organization, its make-up and goals. This leads to such phenomena as:
    a. Employees reduce the number and potency of the needs they expect to fulfill while at work.
    b. Employees "goldbrick," set rates, restrict quotas, make errors, cheat, slow down, etc.
5. Creating informal groups to sanction the defense reactions and apathy, distinterest and lack of self-involvement.
6. Formalizing the informal groups.
7. Evolving group norms that perpetuate the behavior outlined in items 3, 4, 5, and 6 above.
8. Evolving a psychological set that human or nonmaterial factors are becoming increasingly unimportant while material factors become increasingly important.
9. Acculturating the youth to accept the norms discussed in items 7 and 8.

The basic problem is to decrease the degree of dependency, subordination, submissiveness, etc. It can be shown that job enlargement, employee-centered (or democratic or participative) leadership are a few factors which, if used correctly, can go a long way toward ameliorating the situation. However, these are limited because their success depends on having employees who are ego-involved: highly interested in the organization. The adaptive behavior listed above predisposes the employee to disinterest, non-ego-involvement and apathy. The existence of such states of affairs, in turn, acts to require the more direct leadership pattern to "motivate" and control the disinterested employee. The directive leadership pattern, in turn, requires strong management controls if it is to succeed. But, as we have seen, directive leadership and management controls actually create the human problems that one is trying to solve.

This dilemma between the needs of the individuals and the demands of the organization is a basic, continual dilemma, posing an eternal challenge to the leader. How is it possible to create an organization in which it is possible for the individuals to obtain optimum expression and simultaneously, for the organization to obtain optimum satisfaction of its demands?

Although a few suggestions may be found in the literature, they are, by and large, untested and wanting in systematic rigor. Here lies a fertile field for future research in organizational behavior.

BIBLIOGRAPHY

1. White, R. W. *Lives in Progress,* p. 39 ff. New York, 1952.
2. White, R. W. *Op. cit.,* p. 347 ff.
3. Bakke, E. W. *Citizens Without Work* New Haven, Conn.: Yale University Press, 1940.
4. Lewin, K. Times Perspective and Morale. In Lewin, G. W. (ed.): *Resolving Social Conflicts,* p. 105. New York, 1948.
5. Rogers, C. R. *Client-Centered Therapy.* New York, 1951.
6. Simon, H. A. *Research Frontiers in Politics and Government,* ch. 2, p. 30. Washington, D. C., 1955.
7. Bendix, R. *Work and authority in Industry,* pp. 36-39.
8. Argyris, C. *The Present State of Research in Human Relations,* ch. 1. New Haven, Conn., 1954.
9. Gillespie, J. J. *Free Expression in Industry,* pp. 34-37. London, 1948.
10. Simon, H. A. *Administrative Behavior,* pp. 80-81. New York, 1947.
11. Friedman, G. *Industrial Society,* p. 54 ff. Glencoe, Ill., 1955.
12. May, R. *Historical and Philosophical Presuppositions for Understanding Therapy.* In Mowrer, O. H., *Psychotherapy Theory and Research,* pp. 38-39. New York, 1953.
13. Williams, L. C. S. Effects of Competition Between Groups in a Training Situation. *Occupational Psychology.* Vol. 30, no. 2 (April 1956), pp. 85-93.
14. Deutsch, M. The Effects of Cooperation and Competition Upon Group Process. *Human Relations* 2 (1949): 129-52.
15. Levy, S., and Freedman, L. Psychoneurosis and Economic Life. *Social Problems* Vol. 4, no. 1 (July 1956): 55-67.
16. Barker, R. B., Dembo, T., and Lewin, K. *Frustration and Regression.* Iowa City, Iowa: University of Iowa, 1941.

17. Dollard, J., et. al. *Frustration and Agression.* New Haven, Conn., 1939.
18. Lewin, K., et al. Level of Aspiration. In: Hunt, J. McV., ed. *Personality and the Behavior Disorders,* ch. 20, pp. 333-78.
19. Lippitt, R., and Bradford, L. Employee Success in Work Groups. *Personnel Administration,* Vol. 8 (Dec. 1945). ch. 4, pp. 6-10.
20. Lewin, K. Time Perspective and Morale. In: Lewin, G. W. ed.: *Resolving Social Conflicts,* pp. 103-24. New York, 1948.
21. Newcomb, T. M. *Social Psychology,* pp. 361-73. New York, 1950.

George Strauss

THE PERSONALITY–VERSUS ORGANIZATION HYPOTHESIS

Over the years, out of the contributions of individuals such as Argyris (1957), Hertzberg (1960), Maier (1955), Maslow (1954), and McGregor (1960) has come a consistent view of human motivation in industry.[1] With due credit to Chris Argyris, I would like to call it the "personality-versus-organization" hypothesis. I will state this hypothesis briefly first and then criticize it.

(1). Human behavior in regard to work is motivated by a hierarchy of needs, in ascending order: physical, safety, social, egoistic, and self-actualization. By "hierarchy" is meant that a higher, less basic need does not provide motivation unless all lower, more basic needs are satisfied, and that, once a basic need is satisfied, it no longer motivates.

Physical needs are the most fundamental, but once a reasonable (satisficing, as Simon would put it) level of physical-need satisfaction is obtained (largely through pay), individuals become relatively more concerned with other needs. First they seek to satisfy their security needs (through seniority, fringe benefits, and so forth). When these, too, are reasonably satisfied, social needs (friendship, group support, and so forth) take first priority. And so forth. Thus, for example, hungry men have little interest in whether or not they belong to strong social groups; relatively well-off individuals are more anxious for good human relations.

George Strauss, 'The Personality-Versus-Organization Hypothesis' from Harold J. Leavitt, Editor, THE SOCIAL SCIENCE OF ORGANIZATIONS: Four Perspectives © 1963. Reprinted by permission of Prentice-Hall, Inc., Englewood Cliffs, New Jersey.
[1] For an excellent summary of this hypothesis and its application, see Clark (1960-61). Somewhat the same position is taken by Merton (1957) and Selznick (1949); both suggest that organizational attempts to obtain conformity lead to unanticipated consequences, such as lack of innovation and even rebellion.

Only when most of the less pressing needs are satisfied will individuals turn to the ultimate form of satisfaction, self-actualization, which is described by Maslow (1943) as "the desire to become more and more what one is, to become everything that one is capable of becoming. . . . A musician must make music, an artist must paint, a poet must write, if he is to be ultimately happy. What a man *can* be, he *must* be." (p. 372.)

(2). Healthy individuals desire to mature, to satisfy increasingly higher levels of needs. This, in practice, means that they want more and more opportunity to form strong social groups, to be independent, creative, to exercise autonomy and discretion, and to develop and express their unique personality with freedom.

(3). The organization, on the other hand, seeks to program individual behavior and reduce discretion. It demands conformity, obedience, dependence, and immature behavior. The assembly-line worker, the engineer, and the executive are all subject to strong pressures to behave in a programmed, conformist fashion.[2] As a consequence, many individuals feel alienated from their work.

(4). Subordinates react to these pressures in a number of ways, most of which are dysfunctional to the organization. Individuals may fight back through union activity, sabotage, output restriction, and other forms of rational or irrational (aggressive) behavior. Or they may withdraw and engage in regression, sublimation, childish behavior, or failure to contribute creative ideas or to produce more than a minimum amount of work. In any case, employees struggle not to conform (at least at first). To keep these employees in line, management must impose still more restrictions and force still more immature behavior. Thus, a vicious cycle begins.

(5). Management pressures often lead to excessive competition and splintering of work groups and the consequent loss of cooperation and social satisfaction. Or work groups may become even stronger, but their norms may now be antimanagement, those of protecting individuals against pressures from above.

(6). A subtle management, which provides high wages, liberal employee benefits, "hygienic," "decent" supervision, and not too much pressure to work, may well induce employees to *think* they are happy and not *dissatisfied.*[3] But they are not (or should not be) truly *satisfied;* they are apathetic and have settled for a low level of aspiration. They do as little work as they can get away with and still hold their job. This is an unhealthy situation which is wasteful both to the individual and to the organization.

(7). There seem to be some differences in emphasis among authorities as to whether the behavior of the typical subordinate under these circumstances will be rational (reality-oriented) or irrational (frustration-oriented). In any case,

---

[2] These three groups are discussed in Walker and Guest (1952); Shepard (1960); and Whyte (1956).

[3] Hertzberg, Mausner, and Snyderman (1960) distinguish between dissatisfiers (basically, the absence of "hygienic" factors such as good "supervision, interpersonal relations, physical working conditions, salary, company policies, and administrative practices, benefits and job security") (p. 113) and motivators (basically challenge, autonomy, and interesting work). Similar conclusions are reached by Guerin, Vernoff, and Feld (1960). The Hertzberg, Mausner, and Snyderman analysis is critized by Vroom and Maier (1960).

organizational pressures, particularly being subjected to programmed work, may lead to serious personality disturbances and mental illness.[4] Thus, traditional organizational techniques not only prevent the organization from operating at maximum efficiency, but, in terms of their impact on individual adjustment, they are also very expensive to society as a whole.

(8). The only healthy solution is for management to adopt policies which promote intrinsic job satisfaction, individual development, and creativity, according to which people will willingly and voluntarily work toward organizational objectives because they enjoy their work and feel that it is important to do a good job.[5] More specifically, management should promote job enlargement, general supervision, strong cohesive work groups, and decentralization. In a nutshell, management should adopt "power-equalization techniques."

CRITICISM

The above is, in a sense, a hypothesis as to human behavior in organizations. But it is more than a coldly objective hypothesis: it is a prescription for management behavior, and implicit in it are strong value judgments.[6] With its strong emphasis on individual dignity, creative freedom, and self-development, this hypothesis bears all the earmarks of its academic origin.

Professors place high value on autonomy, inner direction, and the quest for maximum self-development. As much as any other group in society, their existence is work-oriented; for them, creative achievement is an end in itself and requires no further justification. Most professors are strongly convinced of the righteousness of their Protestant ethic of hard work and see little incongruity in feeling that everyone should feel as they do.

And yet there are many individuals (perhaps the bulk of the population) who do not share the professor's values and would not be happy in the professor's job. Further, the technical requirements of many lines of work are very different from those of academia. Academic work is best accomplished by those with academic values, but it is questionable whether these values are equally functional in other lines of work—where creativity is not required to get the job done, but only the ability to follow orders.

---

[4] Recent evidence suggests that unskilled workers are significantly more likely to suffer from personality disturbances anand psychosomatic illnesses than are skilled workers, and that these differences become manifest only after the individuals take up their work. (In other words, once individuals land in unskilled jobs, they tend to become more maladjusted.) (Kornhauser, 1962; French, Kahn, and Mann, 1962.)

[5] Perhaps the most general statement of this position is McGregor's Theory Y. See McGregor (1960).

[6] There seems to be a certain amount of confusion as to whether prescriptions for power-equalization are written from the point of view of organizational efficiency or that of mental health (and possibly the degree of confusion has increased since the primary source of research funds in this area has shifted from the military to the National Institute of Mental Health). There are those who claim that what is good for the individual will, in the long run, be good for the organization, and vice versa. Regardless, it is useful to keep one's criteria explicit.

In the pages which follow, I shall seek to revaluate personality-versus-organization hypothesis. I shall suggest, first, that it contains many debatable value judgments, and, second, that it ignores what Harold Leavitt has called "organizational economics." I shall conclude that a broad range of people do not seek self-actualization on the job—and that this may be a fortunate thing because it might be prohibitively expensive to redesign some jobs to permit self-actualization.

VALUE JUDGMENTS

It seems to me that the hypothesis, as often stated, overemphasizes (1) the uniqueness of the personality-organization conflict to large-scale industry, (2) the universality of the desire to achieve self-actualization, and (3) the importance of the job (as opposed to the community or the home) as a source of need satisfaction. Thus, too little attention is given to economic motivation.[7]

The uniqueness of the problem

At least some authors seem to overdramatize the personality-organization conflict as something unique to large-scale organization (particularly to mass-production industry). But this conflict is merely one aspect of what has been variously characterized as the conflict between individual and society, individual and environment, desire and reality, id and superego. "Thus the formal organization . . . is not truly the real villain; rather any kind of organized activity, from the most democratic to the most authoritarian contains within itself the necessary conditions for conflict."[8]

Similarly, the impact of the industrial revolution on work satisfaction can be overemphasized. Much is made of "alienation" (dictionary meaning: turning away) from work. Comparisons are constantly made between the old-time craftsman who did the entire job and the mass-production worker of today. But I doubt whether the medieval serf or the Egyptian slave enjoyed much sense of autonomy or creativity (although one might perhaps argue that he had more of a sense of identification and less of a feeling of anomie than does his better-fed modern counterpart). Perhaps there is less job satisfaction today than there was 100 years ago. Obviously, there are no objective ways of measuring this, but my surmise is that the "turning away" has been less dramatic than some have suggested. There have been boring, programmed jobs throughout history.

Others are as skeptical as I am regarding the theory of increased alienation. In his conclusion to a survey of job-satisfaction studies, Robert Blauner (1960) questions "the prevailing thesis that most workers in modern society are alienated and estranged. There is a remarkable consistency in the findings that the vast majority of workers, in virtually all occupations and industries, are

---

[7] I must confess that many of these criticisms apply to my own writing. See Strauss and Sayles (1960), especially Chapters 4-8 and 12, chapters for which I was responsible. See the review by Brayfield (1962).

[8] Bennis (1959, p. 281). Ironically, some of those most concerned with the tyranny of the organization would substitute for it the tyranny of the participative group.

moderately or highly satisfied, rather than dissatisfied with their jobs . . . The real character of the [pre-mass production] craftsman's work has been romanticized by the prevalent tendency to idealize the past . . . (pp.352-53). And J. A. C. Brown (1954) asserts "that in modern society there is far greater scope of skill and craftsmanship than in any previous society, and that far more people are in a position to use such skills" (p. 207).

The universality of the desire for self-actualization

The basic hypothesis implies a strong moral judgment that people should want freedom and self-actualization,[9] that it is somehow morally wrong for people to be lazy, unproductive, and uncreative. It seems to me that the hypothesis overemphasizes their desire for security. It can even be argued that some of the personality-versus-organization writing has a fairly antisocial, even nihilistic flavor; it seems to emphasize individual freedom and self-development as the all-important values. Yet "mature" behavior does not mean freedom from all restrictions; it means successful adjustment to them.

As Eric Fromm has suggested, most people do not want complete freedom. They want to know the limits within which they can act (and this is true both on and off the job). To put it another way: most people are willing to tolerate and may even be anxious for a few areas of their life which are unpredictable and exciting, but they insist that, in a majority of areas, events occur as expected. The research scientist, for example, may relish the novelty and uncertainty of laboratory work, but he insists that his secretary be always on call, that his technician give predictable responses, and that his car start with complete regularity.

True, some people seek much broader limits than do others, and some are not too upset if the limits are fuzzy. However, there are many who feel most comfortable if they work in a highly defined situation. For them, freedom is a burden; they want firm, secure leadership. And there are many more who, if not fully happy with programmed work, find it rather easy to accomodate themselves to it.

Argyris, for example, might reply that such individuals are immature personalities who have adjusted to organizational restrictions by becoming apathetic and dependent. Were the organizational environment healthy, these individuals would react differently. But in many cases, the restrictions which made these people this way occurred in childhood or are present in the culture. Such individuals may be "too far gone" to react well to power equalization, and their attitude is not likely to be changed short of intensive psychotherapy. Indeed, many people may have internalized and made part of their self-concept a low level of aspiration regarding their on-the-job responsibilities and their ability to handle these. What psychologists call the *theory of dissonance* suggests that

---

[9] Though the concept of self-actualization is insightful, I tend to agree with Bennis (1959) that it "is, at best, an ill-defined concept . . . [and that] self-actualized man seems to be more myth than reality" (p. 279).

sudden attempts to increase their sense of autonomy and self-determination might be quite disturbing.

Impressive evidence of the need for self-actualization is provided by the preliminary results of the mental health studies, which suggest that poor mental health is correlated with holding low-skilled jobs. And yet the evidence is still not complete. Apparently, not everyone suffers equally from unskilled work, and some adjust more easily than others. (Perhaps these studies will help us to improve the prediction process, so that we can do a better job of selecting and even training people for this kind of work.)

Further, it is far from clear whether this lower mental health is caused primarily by the intrinsic nature of unskilled work or by the fact that such work pays poorly and has low status both off and on the job.[10] In so far as mental disturbances are caused by economic and social pressures at home, higher wages may be a better solution than improved human relations on the job or a rearrangement of work assignments.

A hasty glance at the research in this field, as summarized in two reviews (Kasl and French, 1962; Vroom and Maier, 1960; see also Guerin, et. al., 1960), makes it abundantly clear that unskilled workers are not the only ones to suffer from poor mental health. Depending on which study one looks at or what mental health index is used, one can conclude that executives, clerical personnel, salespeople, and lower-level supervisors *all* suffer from below-average mental health. The evidence makes one sympathize with the old Quaker, "All the world is queer save me and thee; and sometimes I think thee is a little queer."

The job as the primary source of satisfaction

There is an additonal value judgment in the basic hypothesis that the *job* should be a primary form of need satisfaction for everyone (as it is for professors). But the central focus of many peoples' lives is not the job (which is merely a "way of getting a living"), but the home or the community. Many people find a full measure of challenge, creativity, and autonomy in raising a family, pursuing a hobby, or taking part in community affairs. As Robert Dubin (1959) puts it:

> Work, for probably a majority of workers, and even extending into the ranks of management, may represent an institutional setting that is not the central life interest of the participants. The consequence of this is that while participating in work a general attitude of apathy and indifference prevails . . . Thus, the industrial worker does not feel imposed upon by the tyranny of Organizations, company, or union (p. 161).[11]

[10] Both the Wayne State and the Michigan studies emphasize that no single factor explains the relationship. Kornhauser (1962) concludes: "Both on rational grounds and from empirical evidence, I see no reason to think that it is useful to single out one or a few of the job-related characteristics as distinctly important . . . If we are to understand why mental health is poorer in less-skilled, more routine factory jobs, we must look at the entire pattern of work and life conditions of people in these occupations—not just at single variables."

[11] Maslow (1954) himself suggests that self-actualization can be obtained off the job, as "an ideal mother[or] . . . athletically" (p. 373). Dubin's point may also be exaggerated. I

In my own interviewing experience in factories, I often ran across women who repeated variants of, "I like this job because it gets me away from all the kids and pressures at home." One girl even told me, "The job is good because it gives me a chance to think about God." Such individuals may feel little need for power equalization.

In any case, as Kerr, Dunlap, Harbison, and Myers (1960) predict, work, in the future, will doubtless be increasingly programmed and will provide fewer and fewer opportunities for creativity and discretion on the job. On the other hand, the hours will grow shorter and there will be a "new bohemianism" off the job. All this suggests the irreverent notion that *perhaps* the best use of our resources is to accelerate automation, shorten the work week just as fast as possible, forget about on-the-job satisfactions, and concentrate our energies on making leisure more meaningful.

Underemphasis on economic rewards

Since the hypothesis overemphasizes the job as a source of need satisfaction, it also underemphasizes the role of money as a means of motivation. The hypothesis says that, once employees obtain a satisficing level of economic reward, they go on to other needs and, presumably, are less concerned with money. However, the level of reward which is satisficing can rise rapidly over time. Further, money is a means of satisfying higher needs, too—ego, safety, and, for some, even self-actualization needs, for example, the individual who (perhaps misguidedly) seeks to live his life off the job engaging in "creative" consumption. True, employees expect much better physical, psychological, and social conditions on the job today than they did 50 years ago. But they also expect more money. There is little evidence that money has ceased to be a prime motivator.

"ORGANIZATIONAL ECONOMICS"

Perhaps the most fundamental criticisms of the personality-organization hypothesis is that it ignores (or at least misapplies) "organizational economics"; that it fails to balance carefully the costs and gains of power equalization. To be sure, most power-equalization advocates point out the hidden costs of autocracy: apathetic and resentful employees, turnover, absenteeism, sabotage, resistance to change, and all the rest. Traditional forms of supervision may be expensive in terms of the lost motivation and energy which might have been turned to organizational ends; they are even more expensive in terms of mental health. Yet some writers, in their moments of wilder enthusiasm, tend to overestimate the gain to be derived from eliminating autocracy and tend to underestimate the costs of power equalization.

---

would guess that for the most part those who participate actively (seek-self-actualization) off the job also seek to participate actively on the job, as "an ideal mother [or] ... athletically" (p. 373).

The gains from eliminating autocracy

Carried to excess, anxiety and aggression are undoubtedly harmful to both the organization and the individual. But many psychological studies suggest that dissatisfaction and anxiety (and even aggression, depending on how it is defined) spur individuals to work harder—particularly in simple, highly programmed tasks. Autocratic, work-oriented bosses very often get out high production: on occasion, their subordinates even develop high morale and cohesive work groups.[12]

Still, beyond certain limits, dissatisfaction, anxiety, and aggression are not in the organization's interest. There is much more doubt about apathy and conformity. It is often argued that an apathetic worker who is subject to "hygienic" supervision will only work enough so as not to get fired, that he will never exercise creativity or imagination or put out an outstanding performance.

On many jobs, however, management has no use for outstanding performance. What is outstanding performance on the part of an assembly-line worker? That he works faster than the line? That he shows creativity and imagination on the job? Management wants none of these. *Adequate* performance is all that can be used on the assembly line and probably on a growing number (I know no figures) of other jobs in our society. Here the conformist, dependent worker may well be the best.[13] As Leavitt and Whisler (12958) put it, "The issue of morale versus productivity that now worries us may pale as programming moves in. The morale of programmed personnel may be of less central concern because less (or at least a different sort of) productivity will be demanded of the." (p. 46)

Even at the management level, there may be an increasing need for conforming, unimaginative types of "organization men" if Leavitt and Whisler's prediction comes true that "jobs at today's middle-management levels will become highly structured. Much more of the work will be programmed, i.e., covered by sets of operating rules governing the day-to-day decisions that are made." (p. 41) Despite the *organization man* it might be argued that nonconformity will be useful to the organization only in increasingly limited doses.

The costs of power-equalization

On the other hand, power-equalization can be quite costly to the organization. To make general supervision or participative management work, many of the old-line autocratic supervisors must be retrained or replaced; this is an expensive process which may result in the demoralization or elimination of the organization's most technically competent individuals. Since it is extremely difficult to develop internalized motivation on many routine jobs, once the

[12] For a list of the conditions under which "authoritarian leadership might be as effective as its alternatives," see Wilensky (1957). Interestingly, the personality-organization hypothesis is strongly influenced by Freud. Yet Freud postulated that "productive work is partially a function of the expression hostility to the leader" (Bennis, 1959, p. 292).

[13] For an outstanding example, see Goode and Fowler (1949).

traditional, external sanctions (monetary rewards, fear of discharge, and so forth) are removed, *net motivation* may fall on balance. And it is fairly meaningless to talk of permitting exercise of discretion to assembly-line workers or girls on a punch-card operation; the very nature of the technology requires that all essential decisions be centrally programmed.

"But if the nature of the job makes power-equalization techniques impractical," some may argue, "change the nature of the job." Rensis Likert (1961) puts this well:

> To be highly motivated, each member of the organization must feel that the organization's objectives are of significance and that his own particular task contributes in an indispensable manner to the organization's achievement of its objectives. He should see his role as difficult, important, and meaningful. This is necessary if the individual is to achieve and maintain a sense of personal worth and importance. When jobs do not meet this specification they should be reorganized so that they do [p. 103, my emphasis.]

True, there are many opportunities to redesign jobs and work flows[14] so as to increase various forms of job satisfaction such as autonomy and achievement. But whether such changes should be made is a matter for organizational economics.

In many instances these changes, when accompanied by appropriate forms of supervision and proper selection of personnel, may result in substantial increases of productivity. (Purely technological losses in efficiency may be more than offset by increased motivation, less work-flow friction, and so forth.) Obviously, in such instances organizational economics would dictate that the changes should be introduced.

But there are other areas where technological changes can be made only at a substantial cost in terms of productivity—and the impact of automation and information technology seems to be increasing the number of jobs where this may be true. Should we scrap the advances of technology in these areas in order to foster good human relations? Or should we say, "Thank God for the number of people who have made an apparent adjustment to routine jobs. Would that there were more." Perhaps—as has been suggested earlier—it would be best to devote our resources to ever-shortening the work week and helping people to enjoy their leisure more fully.

There seems to be considerable evidence (Argyris, 1960, Chap. 5) that a relatively stable situation can exist in which workers perform relatively routine, programmed jobs under hygienic supervision. Although these workers may not be satisfied (in the Hertzberg sense) and may be immature, apathetic and dependent (in the Argyris sense), they are not actively dissatisfied, they do not feel a need for additional responsibility, and they seek meaning in life from their home and community rather than from their jobs. To be sure, these individuals are maximizing neither their productive efforts nor their possible job

---

[14] See, for example, Davis and Werling (1960); Friedmann (1955); Chapple and Sayles (1961); Strauss and Sayles (1960), Chapters 2 and 16.

satisfaction. But both management and employees find the situation satisficing (in the Simon sense). Barring sudden change, it is stable. It may well be the best we are likely to get in many situations without costly changes in technology, child upbringing, and so forth.

THE PERSONALITY–ORGANIZATION HYPOTHESIS SUMMARIZED

My concern in this section has been with the personality-versus-organization hypothesis. I have tried to demonstrate:

1. Although many individuals find relatively little satisfaction in their work, this may not be as much of a deprivation as the hypothesis would suggest, since many of these same individuals center their lives off the job and find most of their satisfactions in the community and the home. With these individuals, power-equalization may not liberate much energy.
2. Individuals are not motivated solely to obtain autonomy, self-actualization, and so forth. With various degrees of emphasis, individuals also want security and to know what is expected of them. Power-equalization may certainly stir up a good deal of anxiety among those who are not prepared for it, and at least some individuals may be reluctant to assume the responsibility that it throws upon them.
3. Power-equalization techniques are not too meaningful when management needs no more than an "adequate" level of production, as is often the case when work is highly programmed. Under such circumstances, the costs entailed by modification in job design and supervisory techniques may be greater than the gains obtained from increased motivation to work.

All of the above does not mean either that the personality-organization hypothesis is meaningless or that power-equalization techniques are not useful. Quite the contrary. What it does mean is that many individuals can accommodate themselves to the demands of the organization without too much psychological loss, and for them the personality-organization conflict is not particularly frustrating. Similarly, in many circumstances the gains to the organization from power equalization may be moderate and more than offset by its costs.

For other individuals (for example, scientists working in large companies), the personality-organization conflict may be felt quite acutely. For the most part, these are the very individuals whose work cannot be programmed and from whom management wants more than merely "adequate" production.

All this reemphasizes the often-made point that no single style of leadership can be universally appropriate. The techniques which work on the assembly line will almost certainly fail with research scientists. Indeed, it is fair to predict that, over time, the differences among supervisory styles may increase. Perhaps, in the future, we shall have at one extreme research scientists and others doing creative work who will be putting in a 40-hour or longer work week under conditions of relative power-equalization. At the other extreme may be those who submit to close supervision on highly programmed jobs, but for only 20 hours or so. Shades of Brave New World: the alphas and the gammas!

*   *   *

BIBLIOGRAPHY

Argyris, Chris. *Personality and Organization.* New York: Harper & Row, Publishers, 1957.

———*Understanding Organizational Behavior,* Homewood, Ill.: Irwin-Dorsey Press, 1960.

Bennis, Warren G. "Leadership Theory and Administrative Behavior." *Administrative Science Quarterly* 4 (December 1959).

Blauner, Robert "Work Satisfaction and Industrial Trends in Modern Society." In Walter Galenson and Seymour Martin Lipset, *Labor and Trade Unionism,* New York: John Wiley & Sons, 1960.

Brayfield, Arthur H. "Treating Faint Workers," *Contemporary Psychology* 2 (March 1962): 92-93

Brown, J. A. C. *The Social Psychology of Industry.* Baltimore: English Pelican edition, 1954.

Chapple, Elliot R., and Leonard Sayles. *The Measure of Management.* New York: The Macmillan Company, 1961.

Clark, James V., "Motivation and Work Groups: A Tentative View," *Human Organization,* 19 (Winter 1960-61): 199-208.

Davis, Louis E., and Richard Werling. "Job Design Factors," *Occupational Psychology* 34 (April 1960): 109-132.

Dubin, Robert "Industrial Research and the Discipline of Sociology." In *Proceedings of the 11th Annual Meeting,* Madison, Wisconsin: Industrial Relations Research Association, 1959.

French, John R. P., Jr., Robert L. Kahn, and Floyd C. Mann, eds., "Work Health and Satisfaction," *The Journal of Social Issues* 18 (July 1962).

Friedmann, George, *Industrial Society.* Glencoe, Ill.: The Free Press, 1955.

Goode, William J., and Irving Fowler, "Incentive Factors in a Low-Morale Plant." *American Sociological Review* 14 (October 1949): 619-24.

Guerin, Gerald, Vernoff, Joseph, and Feld, Sheila. *Americans View Their Mental Health.* New York: Basic Books, Inc., 1960.

Hertzberg, Fredrick, Mausner, Bernard, and Snydermann, Barbara. *The Motivation to Work.* New York: John Wiley & Sons, 1960.

Kasl, Stanislov V., and French, John R. P. Jr. "The Effects of Occupational Status on Physical and Mental Health" *Journal of Social Issues* 18 (July 1962): 67-89.

Kerr, Clark, Dunlap, John T., Harbison, Frederick H., and Myers, Charles A. *Industrialism and Industrial Man: The Problems of Labor and Management.* Cambridge: Harvard University Press, 1960.

Kornhauser, Arthur, "Mental Health of Factory Workers: A Detroit Study." *Human Organization* 21 (Spring 1962): 43-6.

Leavitt, Harold J. and Whisler, Thomas, "Management in the 1980's," *Harvard Business Review* (November 1958) 36.

Likert, R. *New Patterns of Management.* New York: McGraw-Hill Book Co., Inc., 1961.

McGregor, Douglas, *The Human Side of Enterprise.* New York: McGraw-Hill Book QCo., Inc., 1960.

Maier, Norman R. F., *Psychology in Industry,* 2nd ed. Boston: Houghton Mifflin Company, 1955.

Maslow, A. H. "A Theory of Human Motivation," *Psychological Review* 50 (July 1943): 372.

———,*Motivation and Personality.* New York: Harper & Row, Publishers, 1954.

Merton, Robert K. *Social Theory and Social Structure.* rev. enlarged ed. Glencoe: The Free Press, 1957.

Selznick, Philip, *TVA and the Grass Roots.* Berkeley: University of California Press, 1949.

Shepard, Herbert, "Nine Dilemmas in Industrial Research," *Administrative Science Quarterly* 1 (Fall 1960): 245-59.

Strauss, George, and Sayles, Leonard R., *Personnel: The Human Problems of Management.* Englewood Cliffs, N.J.: Prentice-Hall, Inc., 1960.

Vroom, Victor, and Maier, Norman R. F., "Industrial Social Psychology." *Annual Review of Psychology,* Paul Farnsworth, ed., Palo Alto: Annual Reviews, 1960, p. 12.

———, *Some Personality Determinants of the Effects of Participation,* Englewood Cliffs, N.J.: Prentice-Hall, Inc., 1960.

Walker, Charles R., and Guest, Robert H., *The Man on the Assembly Line.* Cambridge: Harvard University Press, 1952.

Whyte, William H., Jr., *The Organization Man.* New York: Simon and Schuster, Inc., 1956.

Wilensky, Harold W., "Human Relations in the Workplace." In *Research in Industrial Human Relations,* Arensberg and others, eds. New York: Harper and Row, Publishers, 1957, pp. 25-50.

part **3**

SOCIAL PSYCHOLOGY IN ORGANIZATIONAL BEHAVIOR

Parts I and II explored two complex sets of factors which are the basis for understanding the behavior of people in organizations. Part I treated individual behavior, and Part II viewed the properties of organizations themselves. Part III centers on the relationships among people in the context of organizations. Emphasis is given to the manner in which the behavior of one person influences the behavior of others either intentionally or unintentionally. Social power, communication, attitudes, groups and leadership are some of the topics studied by social psychologists which have proved most valuable to practicing managers.

The concept of influence is helpful in integrating these overlapping topics. One of the central problems of organizations—in fact, the reason for their existence—is the coordination of individual effort to achieve certain specified goals. In many ways the problem of coordination is a problem of influence. Simply stated, influence occurs when changes in the behavior of one person are produced by the behavior of one or more other persons. Organizations are social devices for influencing behavior[1] toward the achievement of specific goals. In this section we are concerned with the sources and consequences of influence in organizations.

The selections view influence under the headings of power, communication, attitudes, group behavior, and leadership. The reader may find it helpful to consider how each of these topics relates to influence within organizations rather than to highlight the differences among the topics.

1. Here, behavior is defined broadly to include both observable behavioral changes and internal changes, such as changes in perceptions, motives, attitudes, and expectations.

chapter 9

Power
and Influence

Most everyone who has participated in a formal organization has experienced the consequences of power. Power is perhaps the most important issue in most social units; its crucial role in human behavior has made it a focal point for theorists, researchers, and administrators. The disciplines of psychology, economics, political science, sociology, and anthropology have dealt extensively with the sources of power. Yet many students of organizational behavior have given little attention to the concept. Important management theorists such as Likert (1967) and Argyris (1964, 1970)[1] have written books on organizations and organizational change without referring to power in their indexes; other noted writers in the field have failed to give explicit attention to manifest and latent power in organizations. This lacuna is perhaps the "fatal flaw" in modern theories of organizational behavior.

It may be argued that since terms such as *influence* have been substituted for *power* that organizational behaviorists have in fact dealt extensively with the phenomenon of power. This may be the case, but the preference of theorists to avoid using "power" explicitly may provide valuable insights for a student in the sociology of knowledge. Is the failure to use "power" explicitly indicative of value positions which introduce systematic biases and omissions in the work of theorists? For example, it seems that organizational behaviorists who most clearly espouse the "power-equalization" or participative management position tend to hold Theory Y assumptions; they also appear to neglect the functional outcomes of power in organizations as well as the broad development of stratification structures and dominance hierarchies among animals, including man. It is suggested that the widespread inattention to power may be symptomatic of a value position which has led to incomplete theory and inadequate suggestions for the practice of management.

Again, it could be argued that these writers dealt with power by pointing to its dysfunctional consequences. At issue, however, is their relative failure to deal with the functional outcomes of power and reasons for pervasive and marked power differences among people. Many theorists have studied the undesired

---

1. These writers do, however, deal with the concept of power in their texts; in the above discussion it is the relative lack of specific attention to the concept that is being noted. For example, Argyris (1970) did view power explicitly in his treatment of entry points for intervention. While mentioning neither power nor influence in the index, such terms as *openness, trust* and *internal commitment* were cited no less than 53, 43, and 33 times respectively! Control systems were given 10 index citations, but their dysfunctional consequences were the major focus of discussion.

correlates of the use of power, but few currently fashionable models in organizational behavior incorporate the apparently successful use of power by such men as Vince Lombardi and by leaders in organizations such as the Marine Corps[2] and political "machines." How useful are Theory Y assumptions to a participant in the Democratic party in Chicago? The failure to deal with power seems to leave a void between currently accepted theory and currently existing organizations.

Gouldner (1970) has argued that in a utilitarian culture social theory may function to reduce the tension which is created by the realization" . . . that things of power may lack morality and that things of value may lack power (p. 85)." Social theories may be valued, especially by those with power, that reduce the conflict between what is considered good (ideal) and what is (real). Theorists who appear to view power as "bad" have developed theories which de-emphasize it and management strategies which advocate the reduction of power differentials. These systems, (e.g. management by objectives, Theory Y, System 4, participative management) all seem to indicate that power and goodness need not be in conflict. Such theories may be so widely accepted because they resolve the tension hypothesized by Gouldner. Theories that focus on power may increase this tension and hence be less acceptable. While this position is highly speculative, it is hoped that it will stimulate discussion of some neglected issues.

The following selection by French and Raven summarizes the types of social power. Their discussion explores the varied sources and effects of power and is a useful starting point in understanding the influence process in organizations. This selection is only intended as an introduction. For a more complete set of readings on power the book edited by Zald (1970) is suggested.

REFERENCES

Argyris, C. *Integrating the Individual and the Organization.* New York: John Wiley & Sons, 1964.

Argyris, C. *Intervention Theory and Method: A Behavioral Science View.* Reading, Mass. Addison-Wesley, 1970.

Gouldner, A. W. *The Coming Crisis of Western Sociology.* New York: Basic Books, 1970.

Likert, R. *The Human Organization: Its Management and Value.* New York: McGraw-Hill Book Company, 1967.

Zald, M. N., ed., *Power in Organization.* Nashville, Tenn.: Vanderbilt Univ. Press, 1970.

2. Recently, an ex-Marine Corps major told me of how he successfully trained a group which had been torn by strife due to racial and value differences. His primary device was to exercise his power in a manner to induce the men to hate him more than they did each other. Related strategies of training in the military are common knowledge and many people can be found who will attest to the success of Marine Corps training in terms of such common criteria as morale and productivity. The point here is not to advocate such approaches as either good nor generally applicable; it is rather to demonstrate how the values of behavioral scientists may have led them to omit important data from their thinking.

John R. P. French, Jr.
and Bertram Raven

THE BASES OF SOCIAL POWER

The process of power are pervasive, complex, and often disguised in our society. Accordingly one finds in political science, in sociology, and in social psychology a variety of distinctions among different types of social power or among qualitatively different processes of social influence (1, 6, 14, 20, 23, 29, 30, 38, 41). Our main purpose is to identify the major types of power and to define them systematically so that we may compare them according to the changes which they produce and the other effects which accompany the use of power. The phenomena of power and influence involve a dyadic relation between two agents which may be viewed from two points of view: (a) What determines the behavior of the agent who exerts power? (b) What determines the reactions of the recipient of this behavior? We take this second point of view and formulate our theory in terms of the life space of P, the person upon whom the power is exerted. In this way we hope to define basic concepts of power which will be adequate to explain many of the phenomena of social influence, including some which have been described in other less genotypic terms.

Recent empirical work, especially on small groups, has demonstrated the necessity of distinguishing different types of power in order to account for the different effects found in studies of social influence. Yet there is no doubt that more empirical knowledge will be needed to make final decisions concerning the necessary differentiations, but this knowledge will be obtained only by research based on some preliminary theoretical distinctions. We present such preliminary concepts and some of the hypotheses they suggest.

POWER, INFLUENCE, AND CHANGE

Psychological Change

Since we shall define power in terms of influence, and influence in terms of psychological change, we begin with a discussion of change. We want to define change at a level of generality which includes changes in behavior, opinions, attitudes, goals, needs, values and all other aspects of the person's psychological field. We shall use the word "system" to refer to any such part of

From John R. P. French and Bertram H. Raven, "The Bases of Social Power," In Darwin Cartwright, *Studies in Social Power,* pp. 150-67. Reprinted by permission of the Institute for Social Research. ©1959 The University of Michigan.

the life space.[1] Following Lewin (26, p. 305) the state of a system at time 1 will be denoted s_1 (a).

Psychological change is defined as any alteration of the state of some system *a* over time. The amount of change is measured by the size of the difference between the states of the system *a* at time 1 and at time 2: $ch(a) = s_2(a) - s_1(a)$.

Change in any psychological system may be conceptualized in terms of psychological forces. But it is important to note that the change must be coordinated to the resultant force of all the forces operating at the moment. Change in an opinion, for example, may be determined jointly by a driving force induced by another person, a restraining force corresponding to anchorage in a group opinion, and an own force stemming from the person's needs.

Social Influence

Our theory of social influence and power is limited to influence on the person, P, produced by a social agent, O, where O can be either another person, a role, a norm, a group or a part of a group. We do not consider social influence exerted on a group.

The influence of O on a system *a* in the life space of P is defined as the resultant force on system *a* which has its source in an act of O. This resultant force induced by O consists of two components: a force to change the system in the direction induced by O and an opposing resistance set up by the same act of O.

By this definition the influence of O does not include P's own forces nor the forces induced by other social agents. Accordingly the "influence" of O must be clearly distinguished from O's "control" of P. O may be able to induce strong forces on P to carry out an activity (i.e., O exerts strong influence on P); but if the opposing forces induced by another person or by P's own needs are stronger, then P will locomote in an opposite direction (i.e., O does not have control over P). Thus psychological change in P can be taken as an operational definition of the social influence of O on P only when the effects of other forces have been eliminated.

It is assumed that any system is interdependent with other parts of the life space so that a change in one may produce changes in others. However, this theory focuses on the primary changes in a system which are produced directly by social influence; it is less concerned with secondary changes which are indirectly effected in the other systems or with primary changes produced by nonsocial influences.

Commonly social influence takes place through an intentional act on the part of O. However, we do not want to limit our definition of "act" to such conscious behavior. Indeed, influence might result from the passive presence of O, with no evidence of speech or overt movement. A policeman's standing on a corner may be considered an act of an agent for the speeding motorist. Such acts of the inducing agent will vary in strength, for O may not always utilize all of his power. The policeman, for example, may merely stand and watch or act more strongly by blowing his whistle at the motorist.

---

[1] The word "system" is here used to refer to a whole or to a part of the whole

The influence exerted by an act need not be in the direction intended by O. The direction of the resultant force on P will depend on the relative magnitude of the induced force set up by the act of O and the resisting force in the opposite direction which is generated by that same act. In cases where O intends to influence P in a given direction, a resultant force in the same direction may be termed positive influence whereas a resultant force in the opposite direction may be termed negative influence.

If O produces the intended change, he has exerted positive control; but if he produces a change in the opposite direction, as for example in the negativism of young children or in the phenomena of negative reference groups, he has exerted negative control.

Social Power

The *strength of power* of O/P in some system a is defined as the maximum potential ability of O to influence P in a.

By this definition influence is kinetic power, just as power is potential influence. It is assumed that O is capable of various acts which, because of some more or less enduring relation to P, are able to exert influence on P.[2] O's power is measured by his maximum possible influence, though he may often choose to exert less than his full power.

An equivalent definition of power may be stated in terms of the resultant of two forces set up by the act of O: one in the direction of O's influence attempt and another resisting force in the opposite direction. Power is the maximum resultant of these two forces:

$$\text{Power of O/P(a)} = (f_{a,x} - f_{\overline{a,x}}) \max$$

where the source of both forces is an act of O.

Thus the power of) with respect to system a of P is equal to the maximum resultant force of two forces set up by any possible act of O: (a) the force which O can set up on the system a to change in the direction x, (b) the resisting force[3] in the opposite direction. Whenever the first component force is greater than the second, positive power exists; but if the second component force is greater than the first, then O has negative power over P.

It is necessary to define power with respect to a specified system because the power of O/P may vary greatly from one system to another. O may have great power to control the behavior of P but little power to control his opinions. Of

[2] The concept of power has the conceptual property of *potentiality;* but it seems useful to restrict this potential influence to more or less enduring power relations between O and P by excluding from the definition of power those cases where the potential influence is so momentary or so changing that it cannot be predicted from the existing relationship. Power is a useful concept for describing social structure only if it has a certain stability over time; it is useless if every momentary social stimulus is viewed as actualizing social power.

[3] We define resistance to an attempted induction as a force in the opposite direction which is set up by the same act of O. It must be distinguished from opposition which is defined as existing opposing forces which do not have their source in the same act of O. For example, a boy might resist his mother's order to eat spinach because of the manner of the induction attempt, and at the same time he might oppose it because he didn't like spinach.

course a high power of O/P does not imply a low power of P/O; the two variables are conceptually independent.

For certain purposes it is convenient to define the range of power as the set of all systems within which O has power of strength greater than zero. A husband may have a broad range of power over his wife, but a narrow range of power over his employer. We shall use the term "magnitude of power" to denote the summation of O's power over P in all systems of his range.

The dependence of s (a) on O.

Several investigators have been concerned with differences between superficial conformity and "deeper" changes produced by social influence (1, 5, 6, 11, 12, 20, 21, 22, 23, 26, 36, 37). The kinds of systems which are changed and the stability of these changes have been handled by distinctions such as "public vs. private attitudes," "overt vs. covert behavior," "compliance vs. internalization," and "own vs. induced forces." Though stated as dichotomies, all of these distinctions suggest an underlying dimension of the degree of dependence of the state of a system on O.

and the stability of these changes have been handled by distinctions such as "public vs. private attitudes," "overt vs. covert behavior," "compliance vs. internalization," and "own vs. induced forces." Though stated as dichotomies, all of these distinctions suggest an underlying dimension of the degree of dependence of the state of a system on O.

We assume that any change in the state of a system is produced by a change in some factor upon which it is functionally dependent. The state of an opinion, for example, may change because of a change either in some internal factor such as a need or in some external factor such as the arguments of O. Likewise the maintenance of the same state of a system is produced by the stability or lack of change in the internal and external factors. In general, then, psychological change and stability can be conceptualized in terms of dynamic dependence. Our interest is focused on the special case of dependence on an external agent, O (31).

In many cases the initial state of the system has the character of a quasi-stationary equilibrium with a central force field around s_1 (a) (26, p. 106). In such cases we may derive a tendency toward retrogression to the original state as soon as the force induced by O is removed.[4] Let us suppose that O exerts influence producing a new state of the system, s_2(a). Is s_2(a) now dependent on the continued presence of O? In principle we could answer this question by removing any traces of O from the life space of P and by observing the consequent state of the system at time 3. If s_3(a) retrogresses completely back to s_1(a), then we may conclude that maintenance of s_2(a) was completely dependent on O; but if s_3(a) equals s_2(a), this lack of change shows that s_2(a) has become completely independent of O. In general the degree of dependence

---

[4] Miller (33) assumes that all living systems have this character. However, it may be that some systems in the life space do not have this elasticity.

of $s_2(a)$ on O, following O's influence, may be defined as equal to the amount of retrogression following the removal of O from the life space of P:

$$\text{Degree of dependence of } s_2 \text{ (a) on O} = s_2 \text{ (a)} - s_3 \text{(a)}$$

A given degree of dependence at time 2 may later change, for example, through the gradual weakening of O's influence. At this later time, the degree of dependence of $s_4(a)$ on O, would still be equal to the amount of retrogression toward the initial state of equilibrium $s_1(a)$. Operational measures of the degree of dependence on O will, of course, have to be taken under conditions where all other factors are held constant.

Consider the example of three separated employees who have been working at the same steady level of production despite normal, small fluctuations in the work environment. The supervisor orders each to increase his production, and the level of each goes up from 100 to 115 pieces per day. After a week of producing at the new rate of 115 pieces per day, the supervisor is removed for a week. The production of employee A immediately returns to 100 but B and C return to only 110 pieces per day. Other things being equal, we can infer that A's new rate was completely dependent on his supervisor whereas the new rate of B and C was dependent on the supervisor only to the extent of 5 pieces. Let us further assume that when the supervisor returned, the production of B and C returned to 115 without further orders from the supervisor. Now another month goes by during which B and C maintain a steady 115 pieces per day. However, there is a difference between them: B's level of production still depends on O to the extent of 5 pieces whereas C has come to rely on his own sense of obligation to obey the order of his legitimate supervisor rather than on the supervisor's external pressure for the maintenance of his 115 pieces per day. Accordingly, the next time the supervisor departs, B's production again drops to 110 but C's remains at 115 pieces per day. In cases like employee B, the degree of dependence is contingent on the perceived probability that O will observe the state of the system and note P's conformity (5, 6, 11, 12, 23). The level of observability will in turn depend on both the nature of the system (e.g., the difference between a covert opinion and overt behavior) and on the environmental barriers to observation (e.g., O is too far away from P). In other cases, for example that of employee C, the new behavior pattern is highly dependent on his supervisor, but the degree of dependence of the new state will be related not to the level of observability but rather to factors inside P, in this case a sense of duty to perform an act legitimately prescribed by O. The internalization of social norms is a related process of decreasing degree of dependence of behavior on an external O and increasing dependence on an internal value; it is usually assumed that internalization is accompanied by a decrease in the effects of level of observability (37).

The concepts "dependence of a system on O" and "observability as a basis for dependence" will be useful in understanding the stability of conformity. In the next section we shall discuss various types of power and the types of conformity which they are likely to produce.

THE BASES OF POWER

By the basis of power we mean the relationship between O and P which is the source of that power. It is rare that we can say with certainty that a given empirical case of power is limited to one source. Normally, the relation between O and P will be characterized by several qualitatively different variables which are bases of power (30). Although there are undoubtedly many possible bases of power which may be distinguished, we shall here define five which seem especially common and important. These five bases of O's power are:

1. reward power, based on P's perception that O has the ability to mediate rewards for him;
2. coercive power, based on P's perception that O has the ability to mediate punishments for him;
3. legitimate power, based on the perception by P that O has a legitimate right to prescribe behavior for him;
4. referent power, based on P's identification with O;
5. expert power, based on the perception that O has some special knowledge or expertness.

Our first concern is to define the bases which give rise to a given type of power. Next, we describe each type of power according to its strength, range, and the degree of dependence of the new state of the system which is most likely to occur with each type of power. We shall also examine the other effects which the exercise of a given type of power may have upon P and his relationship to O. Finally, we shall point out the interrelationships between different types of power, and the effects of use of one type of power by O upon other bases of power which he might have over P. Thus we shall both define a set of concepts and propose a series of hypotheses. Most of these hypotheses have not been systematically tested, although there is a good deal of evidence in favor of several. No attempt will be made to summarize that evidence here.

Reward Power

Reward power is defined as power whose basis is the ability to reward. The strength of the reward power of O/P increases with the magnitude of the rewards which P perceives that O can mediate for him. Reward power depends on O's ability to administer positive valences and to remove or decrease negative valences. The strength of reward power also depends upon the probability that O can mediate the reward, as perceived by P. A common example of reward power is the addition of a piece-work rate in the factory as an incentive to increase production.

The new state of the system induced by a promise of reward (for example the factory worker's increased level of production) will be highly dependent on O. Since O mediates the reward, he controls the probability that P will receive it. Thus P's new rate of production will be dependent on his subjective probability that O will reward him for conformity minus his subjective probability that O will reward him even if he returns to his old level. Both probabilities will be greatly affected by the level of observability of P's behavior. Incidentally, a piece rate often seems to have more effect on production than a merit rating system because it yields a higher probability of reward for conformity and a much lower probability of reward for nonconformity.

The utilization of actual rewards (instead of promises) by O will tend over time to increase the attraction of P toward O and therefore the referent power of O over P. As we shall note later, such referent power will permit O to induce changes which are relatively independent. Neither rewards nor promises will arouse resistance in P, provided P considers it legitimate for O to offer rewards.

The range of reward power is specific to those regions within which O can reward P for conforming. The use of rewards to change systems within the range of reward power tends to increase reward power by increasing the probability attached to future promises. However, unsuccessful attempts to exert reward power outside the range of power would tend to decrease the power; for example if O offers to reward P for performing an impossible act, this will reduce for P the probability of receiving future rewards promised by O.

Coercive Power

Coercive power is similar to reward power in that it also involves O's ability to manipulate the attainment of valences. Coercive power of O/P stems from the expectation on the part of P that he will be punished by O if he fails to conform to the influence attempt. Thus negative valences will exist in given regions of P's life space, corresponding to the threatened punishment by O. The strength of coercive power depends on the magnitude of the negative valence of the threatened punishment multiplied by the perceived probability that P can avoid the punishment by conformity, i.e., the probability of punishment for nonconformity minus the probability of punishment for conformity (11). Just as an offer of a piece-rate bonus in a factory can serve as a basis for reward power, so the ability to fire a worker if he falls below a given level of production will result in coercive power.

Coercive power leads to dependent change also; and the degree of dependence varies with the level of observability of P's conformity. An excellent illustration of coercive power leading to dependent change is provided by a clothes presser in a factory observed by Coch and French (3). As her efficiency rating climbed above average for the group the other workers began to "scapegoat" her. That the resulting plateau in her production was not independent of the group was evident once she was removed from the presence of the other workers. Her production immediately climbed to new heights.[5]

At times, there is some difficulty in distinguishing between reward power and coercive power. Is the withholding of a reward really equivalent to a

---

[5] Though the primary influence of coercive power is dependent, it often produces secondary changes which are independent. Brainwashing for example, utilizes coercive power to produce many primary changes in the life space of the prisoner, but these dependent changes can lead to identification with the aggressor and hence to secondary changes in ideology which are independent.

punishment? Is the withdrawal of punishment equivalent to a reward? The answer must be a psychological one—it depends upon the situation as it exists for P. But ordinarily we would answer these questions in the affirmative; for P, receiving a reward is a positive valence as is the relief of suffering. There is some evidence that conformity to group norms in order to gain acceptance (reward power) should be distinguished from conformity as a means of forestalling rejection (coercive power) (5).

The distinction between these two types of power is important because the dynamics are different. The concept of "sanctions" sometimes lumps the two together despite their opposite effects. While reward power may eventually result in an independent system, the effects of coercive power will continue to be dependent. Reward power will tend to increase the attraction of P toward O; coercive power will decrease this attraction (11, 12). The valence of the region of behavior will become more negative, acquiring some negative valence from the threatened punishment. The negative valence of punishment would also spread to other regions of the life space. Lewin (25) has pointed out this distinction between the effects of rewards and punishment. In the case of threatened punishment, there will be a resultant force on P to leave the field entirely. Thus, to achieve conformity, O must not only place a strong negative valence in certain regions through threat of punishment, but O must also introduce restraining forces, or other strong valences, so as to prevent P from withdrawing completely from O's range of coercive power. Otherwise the probability of receiving the punishment, if P does not conform, will be too low to be effective.

Legitimate Power

Legitimate power is probably the most complex of those treated here, embodying notions from the structural sociologist, the group-norm and role oriented social psychologist, and the clinical psychologist.

There has been considerable investigation and speculation about socially prescribed behavior, particularly that which is specific to a given role or position. Linton (29) distinguishes group norms according to whether they are universals for everyone in the culture, alternatives (the individual having a choice as to whether or not to accept them), or specialties (specific to given positions). Whether we speak of internalized norms, role prescriptions and expectations (34), or internalized pressures (15), the fact remains that each individual sees certain regions toward which he should locomote, some regions toward which he should not locomote, and some regions toward which he may locomote if they are generally attractive for him. This applies to specific behaviors in which he may, should, or should not engage; it applies to certain attitudes or beliefs which he may, should, or should not hold. The feeling of "oughtness" may be an internalization from his parents, from his teachers, from his religion, or may have been logically developed from some idiosyncratic system of ethics. He will speak of such behaviors with expressions like "should," "ought to," or "has a right to." In many cases, the original source of the requirement is not recalled.

Though we have oversimplified such evaluations of behavior with a positive-neutral-negative trichotomy, the evaluation of behaviors by the person is really more one of degree. This dimension of evaluation, we shall call "legitimacy." Conceptually, we may think of legitimacy as a valence in a region which is induced by some internalized norm or value. This value has the same conceptual property as power, namely an ability to induce force fields (26, p. 40-41). It may or may not be correct that values (or the superego) are internalized parents, but at least they can set up force fields which have a phenomenal "oughtness" similar to a parent's prescription. Like a value, a need can also induce valences (i.e., force fields) in P's psychological environment, but these valences have more the phenomenal character of noxious or attractive properties of the object or activity. When a need induces a valence in P, for example, when a need makes an object attractive to P, this attraction applies to P but not to other persons. When a value induces a valence, on the other hand, it not only sets up forces on P to engage in the activity, but P may feel that all others ought to behave in the same way. Among other things, this evaluation applies to the legitimate right of some other individual or group to prescribe behavior or beliefs for a person even though the other cannot apply sanctions.

Legitimate power of O/P is here defined as that power which stems from internalized values in P which dictate that O has a legitimate right to influence P and that P has an obligation to accept this influence. We note that legitimate power is very similar to the notion of legitimacy of authority which has long been explored by sociologists, particularly by Weber (42), and more recently by Goldhammer and Shils (14). However, legitimate power is not always a role relation: P may accept an induction from O simply because he had previously promised to help O and he values his word too much to break the promise. In all cases, the notion of legitimacy involves some sort of code or standard, accepted by the individual, by virtue of which the external agent can assert his power. We shall attempt to describe a few of these values here.

Bases for legitimate power. Cultural values constitute one common basis for the legitimate power of one individual over another. O has characteristics which are specified by the culture as giving him the right to prescribe behavior for P, who may not have these characteristics. These bases, which Weber (42) has called the authority of the "eternal yesterday," include such things as age, intelligence, caste, and physical characteristics. In some cultures, the aged are granted the right to prescribe behavior for others in practically all behavior areas. In most cultures, there are certain areas of behavior in which a person of one sex is granted the right to prescribe behavior for the other sex.

Acceptance of the social structure is another basis for legitimate power. If P accepts as right the social structure of his group, organization, or society, especially the social structure involving a hierarchy of authority, P will accept the legitimate authority of O who occupies a superior office in the hierarchy. Thus legitimate power in a formal organization is largely a relationship between offices rather than between persons. And the acceptance of an office as *right* is a basis for legitimate power—a judge has a right to levy fines, a foreman should assign work, a priest is justified in prescribing religious beliefs, and it is the management's prerogative to make certain decisions (10). However, legitimate power also involves the perceived right of the person to hold the office.

Designation by a legitimizing agent is a third basis for legitimate power. An influencer O may be seen as legitimate in prescribing behavior for P because he has been granted such power by a legitimizing agent whom P accepts. Thus a department head may accept the authority of his vice-president in a certain area because that authority has been specifically delegated by the president. An election is perhaps the most common example of a group's serving to legitimize the authority of one individual or office for other individuals in the group. The success of such legitimizing depends upon the acceptance of the legitimizing agent and procedure. In this case it depends ultimately on certain democratic values concerning election procedures. The election process is one of legitimizing a person's right to an office which already has legitimate range of power associated with it.

Range of legitimate power of O/P. The areas in which legitimate power may be exercised are generally specified along with the designation of that power. A job description, for example, usually specifies supervisory activities and also designates the person to whom the job-holder is responsible for the duties described. Some bases for legitimate authority carry with them a very broad range. Culturally derived bases for legitimate power are often especially broad. It is not uncommon to find cultures in which a member of a given caste can legitimately prescribe behavior for all members of lower castes in practically all regions. More common, however, are instances of legitimate power where the range is specifically and narrowly prescribed. A sergeant in the army is given a specific set of regions within which he can legitimately prescribe behavior for his men.

The attempted use of legitimate power which is outside of the range of legitimate power will decrease the legitimate power of the authority figure. Such use of power which is not legitimate will also decrease the attractiveness of O (11, 12, 36).

Legitimate power and influence. The new state of the system which results from legitimate power usually has high dependence on O though it may become independent. Here, however, the degree of dependence is not related to the level of observability. Since legitimate power is based on P's values, the source of the forces induced by O include both these internal values and O. O's induction serves to activate the values and to relate them to the system which is influenced, but thereafter the new state of the system may become directly dependent on the values with no mediation by O. Accordingly this new state will be relatively stable and consistent across varying environmental situations since P's values are more stable than his psychological environment.

We have used the term legitimate not only as a basis for the power of an agent, but also to describe the general behaviors of a person. Thus, the individual P may also consider the legitimacy of the attempts to use other types of power by O. In certain cases, P will consider that O has a legitimate right to threaten punishment for nonconformity; in other cases, such use of coercion would not be seen as legitimate. P might change in response to coercive power of O, but it will make a considerable difference in his attitude and conformity if O is not seen as having a legitimate right to use such coercion. In such cases, the attraction of P for O will be particularly diminished, and the influence attempt will arouse more resistance (11). Similarly the utilization of reward power may vary in legitimacy; the word "bribe" for example, denotes an illegitimate reward.

Referent Power

The referent power of O/P has its basis in the identification of P with O. By identification, we mean a feeling of oneness of P with O, or a desire for such an identity. If O is a person toward whom P is highly attracted, P will have a desire to become closely associated with O. If O is an attractive group, P will have a feeling of membership or a desire to join. If P is already closely associated with O he will want to maintain this relationship (39, 41). P's identification with O can be established or maintained if P behaves, believes, and perceives as O does. Accordingly O has the ability to influence P, even though P may be unaware of this referent power. A verbalization of such power by P might be, "I am like O, and therefore I shall behave or believe as O does," or "I want to be like O, and I will be more like O if I behave or believe as O does." The stronger the identification of P with O the greater the referent power of O/P.

Similar types of power have already been investigated under a number of different formulations. Festinger (7) points out that in an ambiguous situation, the individual seeks some sort of "social reality" and may adopt the cognitive structure of the individual or group with which he identifies. In such a case, the lack of clear structure may be threatening to the individual and the agreement of his beliefs with those of a reference group will both satisfy his need for structure and give him added security through increased identification with his group (16, 19).

We must try to distinguish between referent power and other types of power which might be operative at the same time. If a member is attracted to a group and he conforms to its norms only because he fears ridicule or expulsion from the group for nonconformity, we would call this coercive power. On the other hand if he conforms in order to obtain praise for conformity, it is a case of reward power. The basic criterion for distinguishing referent power from both coercive and reward power is the mediation of the punishment and the reward by O: to the extent that O mediates the sanctions (i.e., has means control over P) we are dealing with coercive and reward power; but to the extent that P avoids discomfort or gains satisfaction by conformity based on identification, regardless of O's responses, we are dealing with referent power. Conformity with majority opinion is sometimes based on a respect for the collective wisdom of the group, in which case it is expert power. It is important to distinguish these phenomena, all grouped together elsewhere as "pressures toward uniformity," since the type of change which occurs will be different for different bases of power.

The concepts of "reference group" (40) and "prestige suggestion" may be treated as instances of referent power. In this case, O, the prestigeful person or group, is valued by P; because P desires to be associated or identified with O, he will assume attitudes or beliefs held by O. Similarly a negative reference group which O dislikes and evaluates negatively may exert negative influence on P as a result of negative referent power.

It has been demonstrated that the power which we designate as referent power is especially great when P is attracted to O (2, 7, 8, 9, 13, 23, 30). In our terms, this would mean that the greater the attraction, the greater the identification, and consequently the greater the referent power. In some cases, attraction or prestige may have a specific basis, and the range of referent power will be limited accordingly: a group of campers may have great referent power over a member regarding campcraft, but considerably less effect on other regions (30). However, we hypothesize that the greater the attraction of P toward O, the broader the range of referent power of O/P.

The new state of a system produced by referent power may be dependent on or independent of O; but the degree of dependence is not affected by the level of observability to O (6, 23). In fact, P is often not consciously aware of the referent power which O exerts over him. There is probably a tendency for some of these dependent changes to become independent of O quite rapidly.

Expert Power

The strength of the expert power of O/P varies with the extent of the knowledge or perception which P attributes to O within a given area. Probably P evaluates O's expertness in relation to his own knowledge as well as against an absolute standard. In any case expert power results in primary social influence on P's cognitive structure and probably not on other types of systems. Of course changes in the cognitive structure can change the direction of forces and hence of locomotion, but such a change of behavior is secondary social influence. Expert power has been demonstrated experimentally. (8, 33). Accepting an attorney's advice in legal matters is a common example of expert influence; but there are many instances based on much less knowledge, such as the acceptance by a stranger of directions given by a native villager.

Expert power, where O need not be a member of P's group, is called "informational power" by Deutsch and Gerard (4). This type of expert power must be distinguished from influence based on the content of communication as described by Hovland et al. (17, 18, 23, 24). The influence of the content of a communication upon an opinion is presumably a secondary influence produced after the *primary* influence (i.e., the acceptance of the information). Since power is here defined in terms of the primary changes, the influence of the content on a related opinion is not a case of expert power as we have defined it, but the initial acceptance of the validity of the content does seem to be based on expert power or referent power. In other cases, however, so-called facts may be accepted as self-evident because they fit into P's cognitive structure; if this impersonal acceptance of the truth of the fact is independent of the more or less enduring relationship between O and P, then P's acceptance of the fact is not an actualization of expert power. Thus we distinguish between expert power based on the credibility of O and informational influence which is based on characteristics of the stimulus such as the logic of the argument or the "self-evident facts."

Wherever expert influence occurs it seems to be necessary both for P to think that O knows and for P to trust that O is telling the truth (rather than trying to deceive him).

Expert power will produce a new cognitive structure which is initially relatively dependent on O, but informational influence will produce a more independent structure. The former is likely to become more independent with the passage of time. In both cases the degree of dependence on O is not affected by the level of observability.

The "sleeper effect" (18, 24) is an interesting case of a change in the degree of dependence of an opinion on O. An unreliable O (who probably had negative referent power but some positive expert power) presented "facts" which were accepted by the subjects and which would normally produce secondary influence on their opinions and beliefs. However, the negative referent power aroused resistance and resulted in negative social influence on their beliefs (i.e., set up a force in the direction opposite to the influence attempt), so that there was little change in the subjects' opinions. With the passage of time, however, the subjects tended to forget the identity of the negative communicator faster than they forgot the contents of his communication, so there was a weakening of the negative referent influence and a consequent delayed positive change in the subjects' beliefs in the direction of the influence attempt ("sleeper effect"). Later, when the identity of the negative communicator was experimentally reinstated, these resisting forces were reinstated, and there was another negative change in belief in a direction opposite to the influence attempt (24).

The range of expert power, we assume, is more delimited than that of referent power. Not only is it restricted to cognitive systems but the expert is seen as having superior knowledge or ability in very specific areas, and his power will be limited to these areas, though some "halo effect" might occur. Recently, some of our renowned physical scientists have found quite painfully that their expert power in physical sciences does not extend to regions involving international politics. Indeed, there is some evidence that the attempted exertion of expert power outside of the range of expert power will reduce that expert power. An undermining of confidence seems to take place.

SUMMARY

We have distinguished five types of power: referent power, expert power, reward power, coercive power, and legitimate power. These distinctions led to the following hypotheses.

1. For all five types, the stronger the basis of power the greater the power.
2. For any type of power the size of the range may vary greatly, but in general referent power will have the broadest range.

3. Any attempt to utilize power outside the range of power will tend to reduce the power.

4. A new state of a system produced by reward power or coercive power will be highly dependent on O, and the more observable P's conformity the more dependent the state. For the other three types of power, the new state is usually dependent, at least in the beginning, but in any case the level of observability has no effect on the degree of dependence.

5. Coercion results in decreased attraction of P toward O and high resistance; reward power results in increased attraction and low resistance.

6. The more legitimate the coercion the less it will produce resistance and decreased attraction.

BIBLIOGRAPHY

1. Asch, S. E. *Social psychology*, New York: Prentice-Hall, Inc., 1952.

2. Back, K. W. Influence through social communication. *J. abnorm. soc. Psychol.* 46 (1951): 9-23.

3. Coch,L., and French, J. R. P.,Jr. Overcoming resistance to change. *Hum. Relat.* 1 (1948: 512-32.

4. Deutsch,M., and Gerard, H. B. A study of normative and informational influences upon individual judgment. *J. abnorm. soc. Psychol.* 51 (1955) 629-36.

5. Dittes, J. E., and Kelley, H. H. Effects of different conditions of acceptance upon conformity to group norms. *J. abnorm. soc. Psychol.* 53 (1956): 100-107.

6. Festinger, L. An analysis of compliant behavior. In Sherif, M., and Wilson, M. O., (Eds.). *Group relations at the crossroads.* New York: Harper & Row, Publishers, 1953, 232-56.

7. Festinger, L. Informal social communication. *Psychol. Rev.* 57 (1950): 271-82.

8. Festinger,L.; Gerard, H. B.; Hymovitch, B.; Kelley, H. H.; and Raven, B. H. The influence process in the presence of extreme deviates. *Hum. Relat.* 5 (1952): 327-46.

9. Festinger, L.; Schachter, S.; and Back, K. The operation of group standards. In Cartwright, D., & Zander, A. *Group dynamics: research and theory.* Evanston: Row, Peterson, 1953, 204-23.

10. French, J. R. P., Jr.; Israel; Joachim: and As, Dagfinn "Arbeidernes medvirkning i industribedriften. En eksperimentell undersokelse." Institute for Social Research, Oslo, Norway, 1957.

11. French, J. R. P.; Jr.; Levinger, G.; and Morrison, H. W. The legitimacy of coercive power. In preparation.

12. French, J. R. P., Jr., and Raven, B. H. An experiment in legitimate and coercive power. In preparation.

13. Gerard, H. B. The anchorage of opinions in face-to-face groups. *Hum. Relat.* 7 (1954): 313-25.

14. Goldhammer, H., and Shils, E. A. Types of power and status. *Amer. J. Sociol.* 45 (1939) 171-78.

15. Herbst, P. G. Analysis and measurement of a situation. *Hum. Relat.* 2 (1953): 113-40.

16. Hochbaum, G. M. Self-confidence and reactions to group pressures. *Amer. soc. Rev.,* 19 (1954) 678-87.

17. Hovland, C. I., Lumsdaine, A. A., and Sheffield, F. D. *Experiments on mass communication.* Princeton: Princeton Univer. Press, 1949.

18. Hovland, C. I., and Weiss, W. The influence of source credibility on communication effectiveness. *Publ. Opin. Quart.* 15 (1951): 635-50.

19. Jackson, J. M., and Saltzstein, H. D. The effect of person-group relationships on conformity processes. *J. abnorm. soc. Psychol.* 57 (1958): 17-24.

20. Jahoda, M. Psychological issues in civil liberties. *Amer. Psychologist 11 (1956): 234-40.*

21. Katz, D., and Schank, R. L. *Social psychology.* New York: John Wiley & Sons, 1938.

22. Kelley, H. H., and Volkart, E. H. The resistance to change of group-anchored attitudes. *Amer. soc. Rev.,* 17 (1952): 453-65.

23. Kelman, H. Three processes of acceptance of social influence: compliance, identification and internalization. Paper read at the meetings of the American Psychological Association, August 1956.

24. Kelman, H., and Hovland, C. I. "Reinstatement" of the communicator in delayed measurement of opinion change. *J. abnorm. soc. Psychol. 48 (1953): 327-35.*

25. Lewin, K. *Dynamic theory of personality.* New York: McGraw-Hill Book Company, 1935, 114-70.

26. Lewin, K. *Field theory in social science.* New York: Harper & Row, Publishers, 1951.

27. Lewin, K., Lippitt, R., and White, R. K. Patterns of aggressive behavior in experimentally created social climates. *J. soc. Psychol.* 10 (1939): 271-301.

28. Lasswell, H. D., and Kaplan, A. *Power and society: A framework for political inquiry.* New Haven: Yale Univer. Press, 1950.

29. Linton, R. *The cultural background of personality.* New York: Appleton-Century-Crofts, 1945.

30. Lippitt, R.; Polansky, N.; Redl, F.; and Rosen, S. The dynamics of power. *Hum. Relat.* 5 (1952): 37-64.

31. March, J. G. An introduction to the theory and measurement of influence. *Amer. polit. Sci. Rev.* 49 (1955): 431-51.

32. Miller, J. G. Toward a general theory for the behavioral sciences. *Amer. Psychologist* 10 (1955): 513-31.

33. Moore, H. T. The comparative influence of majority and expert opinion. *Amer. J. Psychol.* 32 (1921): 16-20.

34. Newcomb, T. M. *Social psychology.* New York: Dryden, 1950.

35. Raven, B. H. The effect of group pressures on opinion, perception, and communication. Unpublished doctoral dissertation, University of Michigan, 1953.

36. Raven, B. H., and French, J. R. P., Jr. Group support, legitimate power, and social influence. *J. Person.,* 26, 1958, 400-09.

37. Rommetveit, R. *Social norms and roles.* Minneapolis: Univer. Minnesota Press, 1953.

38. Russell, B. *Power: A new social analysis.* New York: Norton, 1938.

39. Stotland, E., Zander, A., Burnstein, E., Wolfe, D., and Natsoulas, T. Studies on the effects of identification. University of Michigan, Institute for Social Reasearch. Forthcoming.

40. Swanson, G. E., Newcomb, T. M., and Hartley, E. L. *Readings in social psychology.* New York: Holt, Rinehart and Winston, 1952.

41. Torrance, E. P., and Mason, R. Instructor effort to influence: an experimental evaluation of six approaches. Paper presented at USAF-NRC Symposium on Personnel, Training, and Human Engineering. Washington, D.C., 1956.

42. Weber, M. *The theory of social and economic organization.* Oxford: Oxford Univer. Press, 1947.

chapter 10

Communication

It is fashionable to diagnose organizational maladies as communications problems. While on a general level this conclusion may be valid, it does not lead directly to an appropriate therapy. Instead, attention is often diverted to the development of writing or speaking skills, to courses in persuasion, or to the sending of more, better, or streamlined memoranda. Frequently these remedies are attempted without consideration of the basic dynamics of communication. The extent to which a message accomplishes its goal may be determined more by the social context than by the "quality" of the message. More generally, the point which so many people miss is that the social context, in addition to the characteristics of the transmitter, determines what techniques of communication will be effective. Furthermore, even the best transmitters will fail if the intended recipients are not able and/ or willing to receive and act on the messages.

HUMAN LIMITATIONS AND COMMUNICATION

Information theory is useful to an understanding of the technical process of communication. This approach, derived from engineering, attempts to quantify information and deal with the flow of messages through channels from the transmitter to the receiver. Communication is seen as the degree of overlap between the message sent and the message received. Sources of discrepancy are treated as "noise." Efficiency of transmission can be measured in terms of the energy input and the amount of information actually received.

Application of this model to human communication reveals a major problem: the human being is an inefficient processor of information. As Miller (1967) noted,

> ... The most glaring result has been to highlight man's inadequacy as a communication channel. As the amount of input information is increased, for example, by increasing the size of the set of alternative stimuli, the amount of information that the man transmits increases at first but then runs into a ceiling, an upper limit that corresponds roughly to his channel capacity. This ceiling is always very low. Indeed, it is an act of charity to call man a channel at all. Compared to telephone or television channels, man is better characterized as a bottleneck (p. 48).

Some communication errors as noted in Part 1. are perceptual in origin. The common party game in which people transmit a message in sequence derives its amusement value from such errors; after being passed by eight or ten people, the message usually bears little resemblance to its initial form. Other errors arise from more exclusively biological causes, such as the relatively limited human memory span. For example, most people can reliably repeat a string of only seven random digits. However, man's restricted channel capacity is only part of the story. Communication within organizations is complicated by social-psychological factors.

Organizations and social-psychological distortions. Communication is crucial to organizations. Only through information transmission can the efforts of people be coordinated so that the organization can respond effectively to its environment. However, organizations themselves introduce "noise" into human communication.

Guetzkow (1965), for example, reported the case of a production manager who recorded the themes of his mesages to his subordinates. Of 237 recorded incidents, the manager saw his messages as containing instructions or decisions in 165. However, in only 84 of these episodes did his subordinates perceive the messages in this way. The remainder of the time they viewed messages as merely giving information or advice. Such differences cannot always be resolved by a better choice of words, since the discrepancy may result from different perceptions of the whole social context. The subordinates may have given less weight to the manager's position of authority than he himself did. Alternatively, the supervisor may have been seen as uninformed or incompetent. Also, any message which had a high threat content for the receiver may have been distorted or ignored.

The hierarchical organizational structure can contribute directly to such distortions. While conducting a meeting of his subordinates, a vice president of one of our larger corporations made what he saw as a casual comment about a side issue which had arisen: "That's interesting; I'd like to hear more about that sometime." Much to his surprise, two weeks later one of his subordinates sent him a report on the topic which had obviously taken most of the subordinate's efforts since the meeting. This incident illustrates the extreme sensitivity of some people to cues from authority figures.[1] Downward information is often overweighted.

Another consequence of authority for intraorganizational communication is distortion of data sent upward. For example, it is very difficult for subordinates to convey unpleasant information to their superiors. When writing reports, which are condensations, the subordinates are more apt to omit undesirable elements than desirable ones. Carey (1951), after discussing his situation as a colonial administrator in Africa, concluded that his power created mistrust, which was manifested in the reluctance of his subordinates to give accurate information about unfavorable situations. Once he received several detailed

---

1. For example students are very sensitive to cues from the professor about what information is "really important."

reports about damage to a bridge. In checking on the reports, he found that the bridge was not just badly damaged but had been completely washed away.[2]

The foregoing examples demonstrate some of the sociological and psychological blocks to successful communication. The model discussed by Marshall Rosenberg, in a selection which follows, discusses ways to remove the social-psychological barriers. He is concerned with the feelings communicated by a message as a function of the way it is stated. If a method of communication can be devised which develops trust and communication of feelings, the blocks introduced by psychological threat can be reduced. Importantly, for Rosenberg, attention is devoted both to sending and receiving. Rosenberg's technique can be extremely valuable in dealing with sources that inhibit the transmission of information within organizations.

COMMUNICATION IN ORGANIZATIONS

Gross's (1968) informative discussion classified organizational barriers into five groups. One type is produced by certain motives of senders. Some senders are more interested in sounding good, influencing people, and building a record than in actually communicating. In fact, Gross suggested that many potential senders may not *want to* communicate, especially those who wish to avoid conflict.

A second group of barriers is in the messages themselves, which have a latent content of emotions, feelings, and attitudes more important than the overt message in influencing the response of the receiver.

Ambiguity—which frequently arises from the use of nonverbal or para-linguistic symbols which express the latent content—is the third source of error.[3] The nonverbal cues may be inconsistent with the verbal message. The responses to these inconsistencies often determine behavior, but the source of the behavior goes unrecognized by the participants. For example, an angry individual will often verbally deny his anger but communicate it in varied nonverbal ways. The receiver often responds with some sort of anxiety, anger, or other emotion, even though he is not aware of the reason. Interactions characterized by such tension reduce people's ability to work together.

A fourth source of error, according to Gross, stems from certain characteristics of receivers, such as the psychological variables discussed earlier. Information is distorted by perceptual processes and perceptual sets of the receiver. People tend to see what they want to and/or expect to see. Such behavior, while functional in some ways, has important dysfunctional consequences for communication.

A fifth set of barriers exists in the channels of communication themselves. For example, Gross cited evidence that the failure of the United States to be prepared for the Japanese attack on Pearl Harbor was the failure of

2. A student who wishes to learn for himself how these forces operate may compare his feelings about telling a fellow student the bad features of a professor's class and telling the professor himself. Also he may compare his feelings about confronting different professors. What characteristics of professors make it possible for them to get accurate feedback? What are the implications for managers?

3. The paper by Schulman in this section focuses on nonverbal communication.

communication channels. In this case, members of military intelligence failed to respond to a communication of the impending attack sent by lower-ranking officers in a unit which had low repute with the Intelligence Office. While the channels of communication existed in the formal sense, the value given to the information was affected by the channel through which it flowed. Messages must not only be sent and received, but they must be sent through the appropriate channels.

CHANNELS OF COMMUNICATION
IN ORGANIZATIONS

Classical theorists of management stressed lines of communication as a basic element in the design of the formal organization. For classical theorists, the lines on the organizational chart represented the communication channels. They advised that the channels of communication should be known, direct and short, and utilized consistently for all transmission of information. As noted above, however, communication which flows in the authority lines is often distorted by the responses of people to authority relationships. The influence of authority positions is not limited to subordinates; Gerard (1957) found the mere act of telling people that they are in a position of authority leads them to send more messages. Thus, the very structuring of hierarchical lines of communication introduces sources of "noise." Nevertheless, the authority channel is the most widely recognized line of communication in organizations.

Guetzkow pointed out another damaging effect of organizational hierarchy on communication by noting Read's (1962) finding that executives who aspired to higher positions were more inclined to withhold information that might be threatening to their status than were executives with lesser ambitions. Furthermore, this tendency was magnified by mistrust of superiors' motives and intentions concerning the executives' career and status.

Furthermore, the literature has shown that the structuring of communication

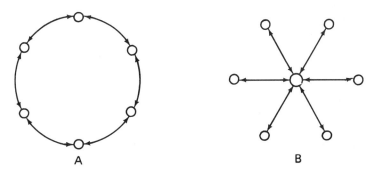

A   B

FIG. 1. Two types of communication network.

channels affects the accomplishment of group tasks and feelings of satisfaction of group members. Some of the most frequently cited work in the field reports the effect of communication networks on people's behavior and feelings. For example, the circle pattern, pictured in Fig. 1(a), provides members of the group with more chance to participate and be responsible for decisions than does the wheel configuration in Fig. 1(b). Groups organized in circle patterns generally experience higher satisfaction for all participants and are more adaptable but tend to be somewhat slower for routine tasks than those organized according to the configuration in Fig. 1(b). In 1(b), where all lines of communication are between the central person and one member, other members have no chance for intercommunication. Generally the central person is quite satisfied, but the rest of the group is less satisfied than members of a circle network. Network (b) groups have a great deal of difficulty adapting to newer tasks but are apt to be somewhat faster for routine tasks.

Leavitt (1964), who did much of the early research on these networks, suggested that there is not one best network of communication. The suitability of a network depends instead on the type of task and the characteristics of the people involved (such variables as the need to get started rapidly, the size of the group, the security and self-esteem of the leader, and the confidence, values, and expectations of all group members). One-way communication can satisfy important needs. For example, Leavitt noted one advantage of network (b) is that the leader can better hide his weaknesses from the group. Thus, while a great deal of the literature has argued for two-way, open communication, the issue is not clear cut. The "best" communication pattern is contingent on the situation, especially on the task. It should be noted, however, that the channels of communication are themselves independent variables with important consequences for organizational performance.

Although a great deal of attention has been given to formal channels, much communication does not follow the lines prescribed by organization charts. Guetzkow (1965) has classified other channels into the four categories of information exchanges, task expertise, friendship, and status.

Guetzkow's information and task expertise channels are closely related. Information exchange channels carry messages which involve knowledge about both the internal and external operations of the organization. Often, this channel runs parallel to the authority channel, but information moves in the opposite or upward direction. In the expertise channel, information moves mainly laterally and diagonally in organizations from those who have competence to those who need it. Jasinski (1959) pointed out how crucial the operation of lateral and diagonal communications is for organizational effectiveness. A factory may not provide formal channels between two foremen on the line or between the foremen of a line and the materials and maintenance departments. Yet, because it is necessary to correct mistakes immediately to avoid costly delays, the foremen develop channels to allow successful internal coordination.

Information and expertise channels are stressed in the current thinking on organization design. There is increasing recognition of the requirement that the interaction patterns of employees and the formal structure of the organization be consistent with the demands of the technology and the work flow. One of the important jobs of a manager is to aid in the establishment of communication networks that facilitate task performance by combining the channels of information exchange and expertise and transmitting both operational and technical knowledge.

Another of Guetzkow's categories is the "friendship channel" which overlaps all the other channels. This channel, often called the grapevine, is apt to carry messages which are more relevant to individual needs than to organizational goals. Since individual needs and organizational goals are often incongruent, this channel can be one of the greatest sources of frustration to a manager. "Noise" in this channel is often of a personal nature. That is to say, issues of relatively minor importance to the sender may become central for the receiver, or vice versa, and unexpected reactions may result. While there is evidence that the grapevine can be extremely rapid and accurate, its distribution of information is uneven and does not encourage or permit a check on accuracy by either the receiver or the original source of the message. In addition, because this channel often carries emotionally potent and unwritten messages, there is a high probability of mouth-to-mouth distortion.

The friendship channel poses a further problem for organizations. Since information is a scarce and valued commodity, it is a source of power and status. Status incongruity and other violations of expected norms occur when a lower-level participant has more of this valued resource than someone at a higher level. Consider, for example, the case of an individual who receives important new information, of direct concern to his job performance, from his secretary. The incongruity can produce tension, hostility and resentment. Such feelings, coupled with probable distortion, make it difficult for the individual to accept related information when he receives it through more formal channels. The tension must be dealt with before effective communication can be reestablished.

Recovery from tensions generated by a communications leak can take years. For example, Nord (1968) reported on the consequences of such a leak for the merger of two furniture companies. The problems of the merger were compounded by lower-level participants having the information well ahead of plant managers. So much anxiety was created by the leaked information that substantial mistrust and hostility toward management developed.

Nord's study revealed another complication introduced by the friendship channel. Once the merger had taken place, people still tended to exchange information with the same sources as before. In essence, it seems that the formal channels influence the development of the friendship channel. Once a friendship channel is developed, it may be resistant to organizational changes and create problems in the coordination of effort within a changed organization.

Finally, Guetzkow postulated the status channel, which transmits symbolic content. Although these cues are often fragmentary and ambiguous, they are important determinants of behavior in several ways. First, the transmission of nonsymbolic information is affected by and in turn affects status. As mentioned earlier, people who possess information are often esteemed by others. Symbolic information communicated through the status channel may also distort other information, as shown in the Pearl Harbor example. Information coming from low-status sources, even though accurate, often is not accepted or acted upon in the organization.

Status symbols may have some other direct, dysfunctional consequences, often for the very goals organizations seek. Universities, with their aim of educating students, offer a prime example. Students are frequently expected to address professors by a formal title and show "appropriate" respect. Does this practice reduce the open communication channels necessary for the free interchange of ideas? Clearly, the information carried in the status channel may inhibit the flow of information through other channels. Nevertheless, the information can also have functional outcomes by helping to define a stable social order.

Ethologists and other students of animal and human behavior have found that most social animals develop a status system, popularly known as a pecking order, which permits the dominant animals to assert their power symbolically, without physical conflict. Such status systems operate in human society. In small, face-to-face groups, one can observe a pecking order by noting who interrupts whom and who speaks to whom. In complex organizations the pecking order of the organizational hierarchy is supported by titles, size and location of office, dress, and a host of other status symbols. Patterns of expectation develop about how the people who possess these symbols should be treated. Adherence to these expectations can reduce anxiety, whereas violation of these expectations often produces tension. In many business organizations, the use of space and physical props operates to support the formal organizational hierarchy. In fact, a perceptive observer could walk into many organizations and accurately draw the organization chart just by observing the physical location and characteristics of the offices. Symbols thus communicate information which may help reduce tension by increasing each person's ability to predict what behavior will be shown toward him by others and what behavior of his own will be approved. Status symbols may have both functional and dysfunctional consequences.

People often appear to desire a high degree of predictability in their environment. Under conditions where intimate, face-to-face interaction is not possible, status symbols provide cues which help individuals to develop appropriate or at least tension-reducing expectations. Animals utilize similar cues. For example, bears are known to define their territory by scratching on trees, thus informing other bears that they can expect trouble if they violate the boundaries. Similarly, humans use "markers" to establish certain property rights. Engagement and wedding rings are common examples.

Goffman (1959) explored other functions of human symbols. People may employ props—such as a given model or brand of automobile—to convey a desired image to others. Thus, symbols may permit social definition of self in addition to tension reduction and social order.

The above discussion was written from a functional rather than from a moral perspective. Social critics who have pointed to the folly of status symbols have made important observations of the material waste and loss of human potential which the quest for status symbols often involves. Unfortunately, the social critics do not recognize the functional consequences of these symbols. More importantly, managers and others with power frequently are unaware of the dysfunctional consequences of these cues. Clearly, both functional and dysfunctional consequences are products of the large quantity of information which flows through the symbolic channel in organizations.

THE READINGS

The foregoing discussion has summarized many of the issues and problems of communication in organizations. Certainly, other readings in this book—especially those on perception, formal organization, and group behavior—are relevant to communication as well. Gibb's paper introduces some basic issues about communication within organizations by contrasting two conflicting approaches to communication. Gibb's position is shared by many of the leaders in the field. Rosenberg's paper presents a model for improving communication between people, which describes a method of implementing some of Gibb's ideas. Schulman summarizes the growing body of work on nonverbal communication. Some estimates suggest that over 80 percent of human communication is nonverbal. If, as many experts agree, the role of task groups and interpersonal relationships in organizations is of growing importance, the work on nonverbal communication has great practical relevance.

REFERENCES

Cary, S. "Africa Yesterday: One Ruler's Burden." *The Reporter* 10 (May, 1951): 21-24.

Gerard, H. B. "Some Effects of Status, Role Clarity, and Group Goal Clarity Upon the Individual's Relations to Group Process." *Journal of Personality* 25 (1957): 475-88.

Goffman, E. *The Presentation of Self in Everyday Life.* Garden City, N.Y.: Doubleday, 1959.

Gross, B. *Organizations and Their Managing.* New York: Free Press, 1968.

Guetzkow, H. "Communications in Organizations." In J. G. March (ed.), *Handbook of Organizations.* New York: Rand-McNally, 1965, pp. 534-73.

Jasinski, F. J. "Adapting Organization to New Technology." *Harvard Business Review* 37 (1959): 79-86.

Leavitt, H. J. *Managerial Psychology.* 2nd ed. Chicago: University of Chicago Press, 1964.

Miller, A. *The Psychology of Communication.* Baltimore: Penguin Books, 1967.

Nord, W. "Individual and Organizational Conflict in an Industrial Merger." In *Proceedings of the 11th Midwest Management Conference.* Madison, Wisc.: Academy of Management, 1968, pp. 50-66.

Read, W. H. "Upward Communication in Industrial Hierarchies." *Human Relations* 15 (1962): 3-16.

Jack R. Gibb

COMMUNICATION AND PRODUCTIVITY

Communication is a process of people relating to other people. As people relate to each other in doing work and in solving problems they communicate ideas, feelings and attitudes. If this communication is effective the work gets done better and the problems are solved more efficiently. Thus, in one sense, at this level of abstraction, there is an obvious relationship between communication and productivity.

Work and problem solving can each be viewed as the taking of appropriate roles at appropriate times as the task or problem evolves. Role taking *is* communication. This apparent and real relationship has caused management to take an increasing interest in all phases of communication. Books are written, training courses are devised, and communications specialists are created and demanded. The rapid growth of literature and programs has far out-distanced the relevant research and the clear knowledge that management can use in making decisions about communications programs. The literature is confusing, contradictory and voluminous.

Although in the most global sense it is fairly obvious that communication is related to productivity, it is very difficult to find satisfying evidence of clear relationships between specific communicative programs or acts, on the one hand, and measures of productivity, profit or corporate vitality on the other. Most studies of communication are short term in nature and relate aspects of communication to various personal and group variables that are perhaps assumed to be related to productivity in the long run, but whose relationships are tenuous at best.

It is the purpose of this paper to look at the overall problem from the standpoint of managerial decision making. What does top management or the individual manager do? The paper is organized around 9 fundamental communication issues that confront management in today's corporate world. These issues grow out of research, theory and management experience. While it is true that in both practice and theory there are many and varied legitimate positions on each issue, it is possible to distinguish two clusters of related managerial behaviors that are fairly consistently antithetical on each of the fundamental issues. In Table One are summarized the extreme positions of the

Reprinted by permission from PERSONNEL ADMINISTRATION, the January-February, 1964 issue. Copyright 1964, Society for Personnel Administration, 485-87 National Press Building, 14th & F Streets, Washington, D.C. 20004.

conflicting views—the views of the "persuasion manager" and of the "problem-solving manager"—on each of the nine issues. Each issue is stated in more detail at the beginning of each of the nine sections of the paper. The issues are practical, overlapping and in general are worded in the language of management rather than in the language of the specialist.

In general, the *persuasion approach* to communication tends to assume that it is the responsibility of management to regulate the flow of fact and feeling through the organization, to use such regulation as a convenient managerial tool, to build staff roles to work on communication problems, to spend a great deal of time and energy building "communications" programs, and to show a high concern about the information flow in the organization, particularly about verbal and written messages downward.

An alternative approach, designated for convenience as the *problem-solving approach,* is to assume that effective communication is an intrinsic component of effective work and efficient problem solving, that if communications problems exist they are symptoms of aberrant organization or poor line management, that communication is improved by more adequate line management action and problem solving rather than by staff action, and that by creating a managerial climate in which trust and openness is a norm, appropriate facts, attitudes and feelings tend to be spontaneously fed into the process of getting the job done.

In each of the following sections a focus or viewpoint consistent with each of the two above approaches is discussed.

1. SYMPTOM OR CAUSE

Is communication seen primarily as a symptom of more basic organizational processes or as itself a fundamental factor to be manipulated by management in the quest for greater productivity and organizational vitality? Is communication best viewed as a symptom or as a cause?

A manager with what might be termed a persuasion approach to management sees communication primarily as a management tool to be used in getting people to get the job dome. When he sees some defect in the work pattern that must be remedied he tends to attempt to manipulate the flow of communications as a remedial action. Communicative distortion is seen as a basic cause of poor work or problem solving and is worked on directly by altering managerial communications.

TABLE ONE. Two Alternative Views
of the Communication Processes

A Persuasian Approach— *The focus is on:*	*A Problem Solving Approach—* *The focus is on:*
1. Remedial programs	1. Diagnosis and etiology

2.	Staff responsibility	2.	Line responsibility
3.	Morale and hygiene	3.	Work product and job requirements
4.	Persuasion	4.	Problem solving
5.	Control of communi-cation flow	5.	Trust and openness
6.	Verbal communication	6.	Management action
7.	One-way messages	7.	Interaction and climate
8.	Knowledge and logic	8.	Attitudes and feelings
9.	Output and telling	9.	Input and listening

A manager with what might be termed a problem-solving approach to management tends to see communication primarily as a symptom or indicator of more basic organizational or managerial inadequacy. Information about communicative distortion is used as diagnostic data which will guide the manager in taking new managerial actions, reorganizing work patterns, or achieving new attitudes toward the organization or the people in it.

The evidence is fairly clear that when people are in an effective problem-solving or work relationship with each other they tend to communicate relevant feelings, ideas and perceptions with each other. When there is goal ambiguity, poor supervision or role inadequacy then communicative distortion occurs as a symptom of these more basic problems.

An analogy occurs in the concurrently flowering field of human relations. Human relations can be viewed as a symptom or as a cause. The growing awareness of human relations and communications problems is symptomatic of growing feelings of inadequacy on the part of management, and of a growing awareness of basic inadequacies in both management and organization theory and practice. When people have trouble getting along with each other and understanding each other, it is probably an indication that somehow they have been unable to create satisfactory jobs or a satisfying and effective work organization. The way to improve human relations and communications is to evolve new job prescriptions and more adequate work organizations—to change managerial actions. It may be a temporary solution to build human relations training programs and communications workshops—but this is at best a *temporary* or intermediate solution, a step that is getting at symptoms rather than more basic causes, and that is working on the shadow of the problem rather than on the problem itself.

2. STAFF OR LINE

Who is primarily responsible for effective communication—staff or line? The persuasion manager tends to emphasize the staff role in improvement of communications. The problem-solving manager tends to build responsibility for communications and human relations directly into the line functions.

A differentiating characteristic between the persuasion manager and the problem-solving manager is his emphasis upon one of two paths. The persuasion manager tends to build a communications staff with many responsibilities for studying communications, instituting programs, managing information and data flow within the organization, training people to communicate, and using various media to *persuade* people to change behavior or to communicate more adequately.

The problem-solving manager makes the assumption that communication is a direct line responsibility, that communication *must* occur in the process of doing work, solving problems, controlling distribution, or getting the job done. He works directly on the line causes of communicative errors. He works with others towards recomposing work groups, changing organizational patterns, re-organizing work space, or creating more adequate man-job relationships. He tends to change his behavior rather than his speech. He tends to control actions rather than to control talk.

It seems well at this point to call attention to the fact that we are describing two extreme typologies of management. In one sense the two types of managers being considered are hypothetical or "ideal" cases. The pure cases do not exist in the natural state. However, anyone with wide experience on the industrial scene can recognize the *genre*. The intent is to sharpen assumptions and to focus attention upon the implications of communications research for management practices. In practice, individual managers tend to show mixtures of the above patterns.

3. HYGIENE OR PRODUCTION

If there is a "communications program" is it primarily centered upon the requirements of the job and the product or is it primarily remedial in nature? Is it directed toward morale, hygiene and human relations or is it directed toward work and productivity?

The persuasion manager tends to direct the communication program toward improvement of morale and hygiene around the plant. He fights fires, drops verbal bombs where they are presumed to do the most good, centers upon remedial aspects of the situation, and directs plant and company campaigns toward curing ills such as absenteeism and waste.

The problem-solving manager tends to have no special communications program as such. When he does create such a program he tends to deal with analyses of job requirements, production schedules, goals of the enterprise, information storage and retrieval, efficiency of work flow, and other aspects of communication flow that are directly relevant to job performance and problem solving.

Hygiene-centered communication programs tend to send out information that is irrelevant, distorted to fit management goals, camouflaged to cover management errors, sent in too great a quantity, irrelevant to the concerns of the moment that *grow out of* task and problem demands or out of spontaneous group maintenance demands. Such programs are often met with suspicion and apathy, and may be seen as propaganda or as attempts to meet management needs rather than work needs or worker needs.

There is some evidence that communication is best when it is in response to natural interaction on the job between people who are learning appropriate trust, when it is in small groups or face-to-face situations, when it is asked for, and when it is between members who do not have too great psychological or hierarchical distance. The most effective communication thus tends to arise spontaneously out of situational demands.

Effective communication tends to be best in work units, where line managers and co-workers are learning a degree of trust appropriate to their relationship, and are learning to send and receive attitudes, feelings and information that are necessary for appropriate job performance. The interrelated assumptions here are that people like to do meaningful work, feel good when they have satisfactory job relationships, have good morale when they do challenging work that is related to their own choices, goals, and abilities, and that effective communication is a residual property of effective work and problem solving.

4. PERSUASION OR PROBLEM-SOLVING

Is the communication program focussed upon persuasion of people or upon individual and team problem solving?

The persuasion manager tends to see communication as primarily an influence process through which people can be changed, controlled, guided or influenced. Communication becomes education, propaganda, leadership, or guidance. Managers try to sell ideas, or to motivate others to work harder, feel better, have higher morale, and be more loyal.

> If one were to believe the public statements and writings of leading administrators, one could believe that most of them are genuinely anchored in the democratic style. Few will openly admit being autocratic or bureaucratic. After all, this is the age of the enlightened executive who assumes his social responsibility. However, upon close inspection they show a tendency to cling to the democratic theme out of feelings of inadequacy and uncertainty. They are democrats out of fear of public opinion rather than because they genuinely understand the needs and problems of people.
>
> —Eugene E. Jennings in
> The Executive—Autocrat,
> Bureaucrat, Democrat, 1962

The problem-solving manager sees communication primarily as a necessary adjunct of the process of doing work or solving problems. In order to solve the problem or get the job done certain information must be obtained, certain feelings must be expressed, and a certain amount of interpersonal perceptions must be exchanged in order for a team to be a healthy work or problem-solving unit. Job demands or team maintenance demands determine the amount and kind of communication that is necessary. Communication *is* problem solving.

The difference in the two approaches is one of *focus*. Communication is *both* influence and problem solving. The emphasis and the approach are the significant things. Persuasive communication tends to produce resistance, distrust, circumvention, or counter-persuasion. It is seen by the worker or subordinate as "news management," as propaganda, or as an effort to get him to do what he may not want to do. Research has shown persuasion-centered communications programs to be discouragingly ineffective in accomplishing management goals.

Problem-solving communication is subordinate to the demands of the job or the problem. The nature of the job or the problem calls forth certain bits of information, feelings or perceptions that are relevant to job accomplishment or problem solution. In general, the research shows that when conditions are created which produce relevant emergent communications out of the work situation, that communications problems are reduced. Thus, face-to-face communications in small groups tend to be superior to other forms of communication because there is a greater likelihood that communications will emerge from interactive job and problem demands.

5. REGULATION OR TRUST

Does one trust the manager and the worker or does one regulate the communication flow?

An increasingly clear body of evidence indicates that communication is related to the trust level in the relationship or in the organization. People who trust each other tend to be more open with each other. With high trust people are free to give information and feelings and to respond spontaneously to questions, are less apt to devise control strategies to manipulate others, are less apt to be closed and devious, are less apt to manufacture rumors or distortions, perhaps have less need to engage in extra communication, and thus they lay the groundwork for higher productivity. With low trust, people use more strategy, filter information, build interpersonal facades, camouflage attitudes, deliberately or unconsciously hold back relevant feelings and information in the process of interpersonal in-fighting, distort feedback upward in the direction of personal motivations, engage in extra communication, and thus indirectly sabotage productivity.

Managers tend to regulate the communication flow when distrust is high and tend to be more spontaneous and open with feelings and information when distrust is low. The persuasion manager tends to regulate communication flow—both in his personal actions and in his managerial policies. The problem-solving manager tends to create trust by allowing communications to follow the demands of the work situation. The openness-trusting stance is antithetical to the persuasion stance. Experimentation indicates that work and problem-solving efficiency is dependent upon the spontaneous flow of information and feelings through the system. Trust and openness are related to productivity.

6. TALK OR ACTION

Does a manager talk or act? Given a choice of where to focus effort, does management spend energies getting the problems solved and the jobs done or deciding what kinds of communications to send to the subordinate and the worker?

With articulate people words can become a fetish. What shall we say to the worker? What can I tell my subordinate? How shall I word the message? Part of this word-focus habit arises from a naive confidence that people will take the words at face value, part of it perhaps from an unconscious protest to one's intuitive understanding that talk will make little difference and that people won't listen at all. Interviews with managers indicate bimodal reactions of naive trust or equally naive cynicism about the effectiveness of words in communication.

Experimental and field studies can be interpreted to show that actions are more significant than words in communication. Gestures, bodily attitudes, empathic postures, and management actions communicate a great deal more than words do. A manager who says verbally that he trusts a subordinate and then proceeds to require detailed and frequent reports, or to make frequent checks on the subordinate's work, usually is *perceived* as distrusting the subordinate. Actions take priority over words in the communication channels.

The persuasion manager tends to ascribe an inordinately high value to words, symbols, pictures, and formal communications. Most people would perhaps agree that both words and actions communicate. The difference in management technologies lies in the relative emphasis in day-to-day management decision. The problem-solving manager tends to rely upon actions to communicate rather than upon words. He tends to use words more for information than for influence.

7. TRAFFIC OR CLIMATE

Is the "communication problem" basically a climate problem or a traffic problem? Do we focus attention upon refining the messages we send or upon creating a climate in which "messages" are decreasingly necessary? Is communication primarily directional or is it an interaction among people doing a job? Is the management problem one of creating a climate for interaction or one of regulating the message traffic?

The persuasion manager tends to be a traffic man, usually centering attention upon the one-way channels down the hierarchy or command channel. Great attention is paid to the mass media, refinement of the message, timing of the presentation, organizing the campaign, hitting at the psychological moment, and devising an appropriate propaganda strategy. Public relations, advertising and visual aids are in great demand. The problem is control of the traffic patterns of communication. Communication is often one-way.

The problem solving alternative to such action is to focus upon the interactive climate of work, to rely upon face-to-face interaction in line units who are working or solving problems together, to give all relevant information to line managers with maximum openness, to arrange the geography of work in such a way as to optimize relevant interaction, and to encourage questions, criticisms and all forms of informal interaction. Group discussions, small, flexible and overlapping work teams, and open channels are seen as communication tools. The problem is seen as one of creating a climate for work and problem solving. Communication is seen as flowing in a field of interaction, rather than as occurring on a one-way street—or even on a two-way street. Communication is a relationship.

8. KNOWLEDGE OR ATTITUDE

Which is more central in determining effective communication—information and logic or attitudes and feelings? If communication is seen as poor does the manager direct his energies toward refining the flow of information or toward changing the attitudes of persons engaged in communicating? Which is a more critical "leverage point" in adequate communication—knowledge and logic or attitudes and feelings?

The persuasion technologist tends to place an emphasis upon information and upon getting the "facts" to the right people. He tends to assume that information will change attitudes and behavior, and that information can be transmitted with acceptably high reliability through formal channels.

The evidence seems to point to the relative importance of attitudinal and motivational factors over informational factors in management and in behavior change. Campaigns to increase information usually accomplish considerably less than management would hope. Information does not necessarily change attitudes, value systems, or even perceptions. People tend to perceive information or reinterpret data in the direction of their motivations and wishes. People hear what they want to hear. They forget what they want to forget. There are various motivational reasons why people select from available information, ignore posters and pamphlets, overperceive or underperceive the "facts," and in general add their own distortions to the information that they receive.

The communication of intangibles like warmth, acceptance, respect, and trust are complex processes which are poorly correlated with the words people use and the information that is conveyed. The problem-solving manager tends to place emphasis upon feelings and perceptions of people, and to focus upon the work climate which will determine the way information is received and which may make special communication decreasingly necessary.

9. OUTPUT OR INPUT

If something goes wrong does the manager start telling or listening? If a manager wishes to take a diagnostic stance toward the communication problem in his company does he accomplish more by refining the outputs or the inputs? Supposing we knew no other information about the alternatives than the titles of the courses, which management development course would we keep going: "Management Public Speaking" or "Management Listening?"

The persuasion manager tends to think in terms of output. He tends to talk of getting the message across, telling subordinates about the goals of the company, motivating people to work, seeing that people understand what management is trying to do, and putting out the message efficiently and quickly with a minimum of effort.

The problem-solving manager tends to think more in terms of input. He may ask himself such questions as the following. What information is needed? How do others look at the problem? What other solutions are there to problems that face us? How can we get more data? How can we interpret what information is available? What cues are we failing to process?

In examining the above clusters of management behavior we find that tradition and precedent are on the side of the persuasion manager. Most of the scientific evidence where it is available is on the side of the problem-solving approach. The skills and habits of persuasion are readily available. The skills, habits, and attitudes appropriate to the problem-solving approach are less easily acquired. The paths to creative problem solving are unclear. The managerial rewards are presumably very great.

BIBLIOGRAPHY

1. Gibb, Jack R. "Defensive communication". *J. Commun.*, 11 (1961): 141-48.

2. Gibb, Jack R. "Climate for trust formation," in Bradford, Leland P., Gibb, Jack R., and Benne, Kenneth, eds., *T-group theory and laboratory method.* New York: John Wiley & Sons, 1963.

3. Jackson, Jay M. "The Organization and Its Communication Problems." *J. Commun.*, 9 (1959): 158-167, 189.

4. Johannsen, James R., and Edmunds, Carolyn Y. *Annotated bibliography on communication in organizations.* La Jolla, California: Western Behavioral Sciences Institute, 1962.

5. Mellinger, G. D. "Interpersonal Trust As a Factor In Communication." *J. Abnorm. Soc. Psychol.*, 52 (1956): 304-309.

6. Schutz, William C. Interpersonal Underworld. *Har. Bus. Rev.*, 36 (1958): 123-35.

Marshall B. Rosenberg

WORDS CAN BE WINDOWS OR WALLS

A friend of mine wrote a song entitled, "Words are Windows or They're Walls."[1] This phrase summarizes much that I have come to learn about the words people use in their relationships with one another. At times I see words

---

Prepared especially for this volume.

[1] Ruth Bebermeyer, *Words are Windows or They're Walls,* 1970.

serving as windows that allow me "to see into" the speaker's intentions and beliefs. At other times I see words serving as walls that obstruct the mutual understanding that will occur. In this article, I would like to outline a characteristic of language that serves to make words "walls," to describe how such language can interfere with working or living together, to outline characteristics that make words "windows" and to describe some of the procedures I use in helping people to learn to use words as windows rather than walls.

The main detriment to effective communication in working relationships involves the labeling of oneself or others. By labeling I refer to the use of words that describe static characteristics that exist "within" individuals. I would contrast words describing static characteristics that exist within persons with words describing processes or operations that go on between persons. For example, I would place the word "stupid" in the phrase, "John is stupid" in the category of words referring to static characteristics "within" John. In contrast, if I state "I am feeling frustrated because I do not know how to teach John," I am using words that describe processes or operations that exist in my *transactions* with John.

Associated with labels are expectations as to how a person should behave. For example, if I label John as stupid I might therefore expect that he would not be able to understand complicated messages. On the basis of this expectation I might then alter my behavior toward John by presenting information in a simplified way. My continuing to present information in this way could, of course, have consequences for John's behavior. His being exposed primarily to simplified information could prevent him from gaining experience in dealing with complicated messages. To the extent that intelligence is involved in learning to comprehend complicated messages, this sequence represents a self-fulfilling prophecy. I would like to diagram this process, since an understanding of it is crucial to an understanding of my concern about labels.

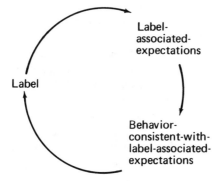

In the above example the label "stupid" led to label-associated expectations ("cannot comprehend complicated messages") which led to behavior consistent with label-associated expectations (presenting only simplified messages) which contributed to confirming the initial label ("stupid") by limiting the experience of the labeled person. The circle is complete and serves to perpetuate itself.

The nature of this "circular process has a number of implications about interpersonal relations that are important to me. For example, when I see this self-fulfilling process, which can be associated with labeling, I can appreciate why John Paul Sartre states that it violates the integrity of persons to label them. In addition, I am led to recall that in the field of education the dangers of self-fulfilling prophecies associated with labeling have been documented by Rosenthal and Jacobson[2] in their study, *Pygmalion in the Classroom.* They discovered that teachers often initiate a "self-fulfilling" prophecy when they label students; that is, teachers' expectations of a student's performance associated with labels such as "high achiever," in effect, determine that performance.

In the area of working relationships, I find certain labels showing up with great regularity regardless of the nature of the working relationship. Perhaps the most common labels are conservative-liberal (or variations thereof). The "conservative" member of the pair engages in the process by labeling the other as a "liberal" (of course choice adjectives may precede the label). He then tends to "expect" certain things from him such as failing to respect standardized procedures. On the basis of such expectation, the "conservative" acts to impress the "liberal" with the importance of procedures (for example, lecturing him about the value of roles and procedures, reminding him repeatedly of the procedures, etc.). Such behavior on the part of the "conservative" is likely to be annoying to the "liberal" and increases his resistance to "adhering to procedures." This of course confirms the prophecies of the "conservatives" about "liberals" not valuing procedures.

Or one can view this from the "liberal" point of view. Expecting that the "conservative" will resist innovation, the "liberal" does not openly communicate about the innovation, choosing to introduce it at the last moment, hopefully to minimize the opportunity for rebuttal. Such behavior on the part of the "liberal" is likely to provoke distrust on the part of the "conservative" and subsequent resistance to the innovation thereby confirming expectations of the "liberal" about "conservatives."

I would like to emphasize that labels can be equally self-defeating when applied to oneself as to others. Thus if an executive labels himself as an "organization man" he expects patterns of conformity from himself and rules out the possibility of his initiating or creating new patterns of behavior. The more he steeps himself in routine administrative activities, the more of an "organization man" he becomes.

I would also like to emphasize my belief that labels, whether "positive" or "negative," are limiting to one's development. Although labeling oneself as a "creative individual" in many organizations would be a "positive" label, I feel that it could be as limiting as labeling oneself as an "organization man." Labeling oneself as "creative" could lead one to ignore consideration and reverence of

[2] R. Rosenthal and L. Jacobson, *Pygmalion in the Classroom: Teacher Expectation and Pupils' Intellectual Ability* (New York: Holt, Rinehart & Winston, 1968).

traditional procedures. Although this may perpetuate a person's labeling of himself in a positive way, I doubt that it would lead to his functioning either in an effective way regarding the organization or in a way that was fulfilling to himself.

In order to make words used to describe oneself and others windows rather than walls, I recommend learning to translate the labels one used into a language of feelings and objectives. More specifically, this requires skill in four areas: ability to note time and situational contexts in which behavior occurs; ability to make observations of behavior without interpreting the behavior; ability to report on one's affective state; and the ability to report on one's desires. I would now like to describe each of these skills in greater detail.

Ability to note time and situation contexts in which behavior occurs. In many instances of interpersonal communication, I find it particularly helpful to clearly denote the time and situational context in which I am embedding my message. For example: Person A has been late with three out of five reports in the last month. Person B, his supervisor, states, "I'm concerned because you don't get your reports in on time." I find myself easily falling into the habit of making such absolutistic statements when I am in Person B's position, perhaps because I believe it emphasizes my concern more sharply. Unfortunately, it also tends to get me into picayune hassles because it often motivates the other person to defend himself against the absolute nature of the statement. For example, I would not be surprised if Person A were to respond, "What do you mean? I was on time with my report last week!" I believe Person B would be further ahead were he to be more specific in his time and situational referents; perhaps stating, "Last Tuesday, and Wednesday, and Thursday, I was concerned because I did not get your reports by the time I expected to receive them."

I offer the following two statements to exemplify what I mean by clarifying the situational contexts of messages.

Statement 1. I do not like the familiarity which you *often show in our relationship.*

Statement 2. I do not like how I feel in relationship to you during business meetings.

By being specific about the situational context in which the behavior occurs in Statement 2, I believe the listener's ease of understanding is facilitated.

Ability to make observations of behavior without labeling or interpreting the behavior. This skill involves the ability of the speaker to differentiate between observable behavior and inferences. By observable behavior I refer to behavior that can be perceived in contrast to statements making inferences and interpretations of the observable behavior. Following are examples of observations of behavior that avoid labeling and a contrasting statement in which labels and observable behavior are not differentiated.

John did not submit his reports on schedule the last two weeks.	John is irresponsible in his report writing.
John's department met its quota the last six months.	John is an asset to the company.

Ability to report on one's affective state.[3] I find the reporting of one's affective state to have several advantages in interpersonal communication. To begin with, I find trust increases in proportion to the degree to which people are able to openly acknowledge their present feelings. Second, I find it aids in keeping the communication in the present thereby avoiding the boredom and vagueness that I see quickly settling into communications in which feelings are absent. Third, I find that people feel more alive the more they are in touch with their feelings.

I differentiate three stages in teaching people to report on their affective state. To begin with, I help people to become aware that they have feelings. As strange as it may seem, I find many people who have been oriented to the world in such a way that they seem totally unaware that they have feelings. To help them become aware of their feelings, I conduct various exercises in which the person is given the opportunity to focus on his feelings at the moment. After awareness, I help people to develop a differentiated vocabulary for describing their feelings. This is a particularly difficult problem using the English language as the English vocabulary for describing affective states is relatively sparse. For example, I am told the Japanese language has approximately 75 different words to describe differential feelings of love whereas I routinely hear only about four or five describing this emotion in English. After awareness of feelings and developing a differentiated vocabulary to describe them is left the step of verbally reporting them to others. For many people this is a terrifying step as the reporting of feelings often leaves individuals feeling painfully vulnerable.

Ability to report one's desires. The final skill I would like to describe is the ability to report on one's desires as explicitly as possible. This involves being able to state in measurable terms what would lead to satisfaction of your desires. For example, if someone says to me, "I would like you to be more considerate," I would have more difficulty fulfilling his desires than if he were to say, "I would like you to give me at least a week's notice before setting up a meeting."

In daily conversation, all four of the skills previously described could be contained in a single, short message. To exemplify:

Yesterday, (specifying time context) during the business meeting (specifying situational context) when you brought up the matter of finances (observing behavior without labeling or interpreting) I was disappointed (reporting on one's affective state) because I wanted to finish the topic we started before going on to another (reporting on one's desires).

I frequently face the challenge of being asked to teach the communication skills described to teachers, parents, managers in industry and others as best I can in a relatively short time (usually two or three days). In learning these skills, the people I work with usually are changing from deeply ingrained habit patterns. I am far from solving the problems involved in making significant

---

[3] For those interested in a more thorough discussion of the advantages of reporting on one's affective state, I recommend John Powell, S.J., *Why Am I Afraid to Tell You Who I Am,* (Chicago: Argus Communication, 1969).

changes in longstanding communication patterns in a relatively short time,[4] but I would like to share some principles that have been helpful in bringing about the changes desired.

To begin with I try to be as explicit as possible about the objectives I have for the training sessions. I try to define in measurable terms what I would hope each participant would be able to accomplish by the end of the training program. The value of beginning an instructional program with measurable objectives has been described elsewhere and I won't go into it further at this point.[5] Second, I try to provide a learning environment that is as close to a real-life situation as possible. Thus through role playing and psychodrama I have people practice the communication skills in situations simulating real problems for them. Third, I try to maximize clear, concise feedback through the use of videotape and small group exercises. Fourth, I provide opportunity for as much actual practice of the new skills to be learned as possible. This practice involves immediately stopping a person if he departs from using the sought-for skills and enabling him to correct himself before going on. The concentration and attention that this requires usually leave participants exhausted physically and mentally.

At this point, I would like to mention two types of exercises that have not only been helpful in teaching the communication skills described, but which several participants also tell me have been very freeing to them psychologically.

The first type of exercise I call a *Label Detection Exercise*. I ask participants to detect and list the labels that they find themselves habitually applying to themselves and to others. Then I ask that the participant list the cost of this label; that is, I ask them to consider how labeling themselves as they do inhibits them from experiencing various possibilities in life, then I ask them to consider how labeling others as they do limits what they can experience with this other person. Thus one person labeled herself as "shy person" and she saw that by labeling herself as she did she expected "shy behavior" from herself and this kept her from approaching others at parties, limited the number of personal contacts she made in her work, and limited the initiative she exhibited even in intimate relationships. This same person frequently labeled others as "conceited." Labeling them in this way led her to expect that such persons would not be in need of any support or information from her. Thus, in these relationships she did not offer support or information even when she wanted to.

The other set of activities I call a *Label Transformation Exercise.* In this exercise I ask the participants to transform the labels in the Label Detection Exercise into the form of communication described in this paper; that is, I ask them to transform the label into a statement that (1) makes specific reference to time and situational contexts, (2) clearly differentiates between observations of behavior and labels, (3) reports on affective states, and (4) reports on desires.

Thus the label used by the person just referred to was transformed in the following way. The label of herself as "shy person" was transformed into the

---

[4] To complicate matters further, I often am asked to work with large numbers of people at a time.

[5] Robert F. Mager, *Preparing Instructional Objectives* (Palo Alto, Calif.: Fearon Publishers, Inc., 1962)

following statement, "Frequently when I am at parties (reference to time and situational context) I sit by myself and do not approach anyone (reference to observable behavior) and I'm afraid (reporting on affective state) because I want people to say that they like me and I don't want to chance this not happening" (report on desires). Once a label has been transformed in this way, I find people are freer to consider alternative possibilities of behavior than they were when labeling themselves.

The label this person used of others ("conceited") was transformed into the following statement, "Last week when we were working on the project (reference to time and situational context), Jack did not consult me (reference to observable behavior), and I was hurt (reporting on affective state) because I wanted to share what I had to offer in that project" (reporting on desires). Again I see this label transformation offering greater possibility of freedom of action than simply labeling the other person as "conceited."

In closing, when people read this article (reference to time and situation context) I'm afraid (reporting on affective state) that they might say "This is just a bunch of meaningless semantics" and not spend further time thinking about the article (reference to observable behavior) because I want them at least to spend time thinking to themselves, "I wonder how much of my life is being narrowed by how I label myself and others (reporting on desires).

Arthur D. Shulman

A MULTICHANNEL TRANSACTIONAL MODEL OF SOCIAL INFLUENCE

For the most part, past research concerned with social influence has assumed unjustly that the major sources of influence affecting an individual are carried on spoken and written communication channels. This overemphasis is evidenced by the almost exclusive use of verbal channels within social influence research. As Ray Birdwhistell (1971) points out, the erroneous abstraction of verbal and written communication:

> . . . is justified on the premise that the *significant* aspect of communication is contained within this data . . . since these verbal or syntactic forms are carried along the audio-aural channel, that channel is examined as *the* communication channel, and the speech and the auditory apparatus, by logical extention, the organs of communications. Other sensorily based

Prepared especially for this volume.

channels of interpersonal connection are either held constant as environmental variables of speech, . . . set aside as expressors of individual . . . states or dismissed as primitive contributors of interference . . . consistent with these premises and to this logic, communication is defended as a discontinuous single-channel process.

The purpose of this paper is to emphasize that nonverbal communications strongly influence and determine the course of social interaction. To facilitate this perspective a multichannel transactional model of social influence will be described. Though not independent, nor in any order of importance as will be stressed throughout this paper, the nonverbal channels of communication to be incorporated into a model of social influence processes are: the *proximic* mode concerned with spatial relations among interactants including eye contact and body orientation; *kinesic* modes or body motion; and *paralanguage* or the way in which things are vocalized, including pitch, range, intensity, hesitations, crying, etc. Other nonverbal modes as *dress, tactile, olfaction, temperature sensitivity,* and *extra sensory perception* which have not received as much attention as the above modes also will be considered potentially important nonverbal channels of social influence.

These categories are by no means exhaustive, nor mutually exclusive. For instance, either body orientation or eye contact could be considered separate channels of communication or each could be grouped under kinesic or under proximic modes. However, for the sake of simplifying this presentation, they will be considered aspects of the proximic channel of communication. Furthermore, the current state of knowledge of nonverbal communication factors in social influence is at a descriptive stage. This stage is not only characterized by arbitrary assignment of behaviors to generic categories, and arbitrary separation of channels, but most important, the units and methods of analysis are still being defined. Regardless of the methodological problems facing the social scientist, all of the nonverbal communications mentioned above are potential sources of influence and can best be put into perspective by briefly looking at the traditional ways social scientists have been formulating the social influence process.

In a recent social psychology text (1967), Edwin Hollander has elaborated on the idea that "all social influence appears to involve three essential elements which are not fixed but quite alterable in time." These elements are (1) an influence source, (2) a communication or message, and (3) the recipient of the communication. These basic elements are evident in a two-step flow of communication concept formulated by Katz and Lazarsfeld (1955). They emphasized the social characteristics of the recipient's reference group affiliations which act as filters for the message. Bauer (1964) expanded the two-step flow by giving greater weight to the interaction of motives and social identities of both communicator and recipient. He specified that a message is interpreted by the recipient within the context of his own motives and group affiliations as well as his perception of those of the communicator. This viewpoint explicitly sees social influence as a two-way interaction, a transaction.

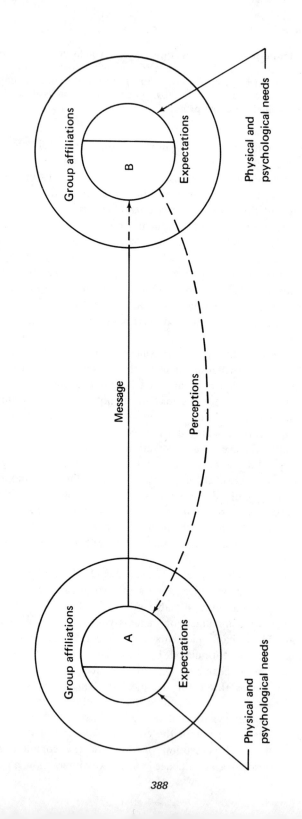

FIGURE 1. Transactional model of social influence. The message is interpreted by B within the context of his own group affiliations and needs and his expectation mediated perception of those of A. The message being sent by A is in part, determined by his perception of B.

Both parties adapt to and influence one another. Bauer's transactional model is presented graphically in Figure 1.

Implicit in Bauer's model is the idea that communication, whether written, verbal, or nonverbal, is given on a specific channel at a specific point in time. Only one message, which is being interpreted by the recipient in terms of past messages, is transmitted and reacted to at a particular time. It is these assumptions that the multichannel transactional model challenges. The multichannel transactional model assumes that in any social interaction, many messages are transmitted to the recipient at the same point of time. Each of these messages is capable, separately and in combination, of influencing and directing social interaction. As Birdwhistell (1965) has pointed out, communication is a continuous process made up of overlapping discontinuous segments. In multisensory arrangements, these segments maintain or modify the interaction, influencing the behavior of both parties. A graphic description of this perspective is presented in Figure 2. As can be seen, the major extensions of Bauer's model have been the amplification of the communication unit and the emphasis on the continuous interplay of the behavior of the individuals involved.

The implications of this multichannel expansion may not be evident from inspection of Figure 2. The position can be taken that each channel can be analyzed separately in terms of Bauer's transactional model. In fact, most of the research on nonverbal social influence processes has done just that. This procedure has unfortunately resulted in the study of units out of context. The crucial point, however, is that each channel's message is *not* necessarily independent or the same. They are interdependent, modifying, negating, or reinforcing each other. Furthermore, the multichannel perspective brings to light the need to study the patterning of messages along the various channels, for depending upon the situation, each channel can appear as the major vehicle of social influence.[1] Before explicating these points further, attention will be drawn to how one situational factor—role expectations—fits into the multichannel transactional model.[2]

The nonverbal messages that are perceived and have meaning for the interactants are to a substantial degree dependent upon the expectations an individual has for his behavior and for others' behavior. That is, within the multichannel transactional model, the expectations an individual has for his behavior within a given situation, his *role,* and the expectations he has for individuals occupying a *counter-role* position act as information filters. Furthermore, if we assume, as does Harry Stack Sullivan in his postulation of a need for consensual validation (1953) and Festinger (1951) in his presumption of a need for social reality, that expectation confirmation is a desired state, these

---

[1] That the situation can determine what channels carry what messages is readily seen in this writer's attempt to influence the reader within the confines of the written channel.

[2] Development of the multichannel model has been described elsewhere (Shulman, 1969a,b, 1970) and will not be presented here. Such factors as the amount of information a given individual can physically take in as well as such factors as physical and psychological need states are also recognized as important determinants of social influence, but will not be considered within the context of this paper.

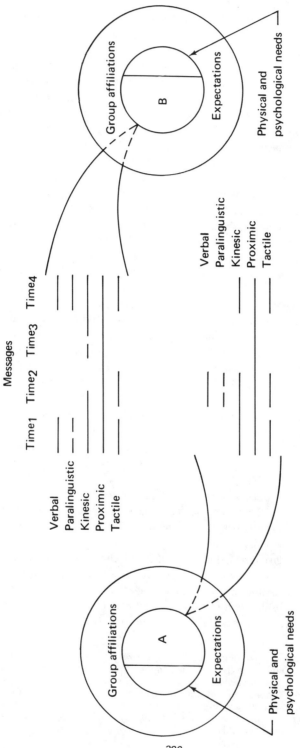

FIGURE 2. Multichannel transactional model of social influence. In any given time period (seconds, minutes, hours), A is sending many messages simultaneously over the various channels. These messages are interpreted by B within the context of his group affiliations, needs and his expectation mediated perception of those of A. Concurrently, B is sending multimessages over the channels which in part, determine what A is sending.

expectations take on a motivational quality, one that not only affects what is perceived and decoded, but also how individuals will act within a given situation.[3] This fact is exemplified by the work of Goffman.

Goffman (1959, 1961) has suggested that not only does the situation demand certain behaviors, but that nonverbal behaviors in part provide feedback for the adequacy of one's role enactment in the eyes of the other. Furthermore, Goffman suggests that these nonverbal channels are used to indicate the aceptance of the image of self that one projects as affecting the particular role position occupied. Goffman has labeled this phenomena role distance. Thus, the assembly-line worker appointed to an unwanted position of foreman may wear the required tie and jacket associated with his new position, but will wear the tie loosely, communicating his dissatisfaction with the new role assignment.[4]

Likewise, evidence that who the participants are, in terms of broad categories such as nationality, can determine how nonverbal behaviors are perceived and decoded is provided by the anthropologist, E. T. Hall.[5] Hall (1966) reports, for example, that Americans regard talking through a screen door while standing outside a house as not being inside the house or room in any sense of the word and act accordingly. On the other hand, Germans consider themselves as inside when talking through a screen door.[6] Similarly, within a culture, Jouraud (1968) cites evidence for what each of us have experienced. The meaning of messages along the tactile channel is in part determined by the sex of interactants and whether the participants are marital partners. Additional examples for each of the nonverbal channels can be found in the excellent reviews of Jaffe (1968), Matarozzo, Wien, Matarozzo and Saslow (1968), Duncan, (1969) and Mehrabian (1969). These examples provide further insight into the current state of knowledge of nonverbal social influence channels. As previously indicated, the state is one characterized by descriptions with little theory. In reviewing these descriptive advances, Duncan (1969) suggests that the research can be divided into three interlocking phases: (a) differentiating and specifying the behaviors in question through a transcription or notation system; (b) discovering the extent and nature of internal structure exhibited by the behaviors; and (c) seeking relationships between the behaviors and external variables, such as personality characteristics and the situation. However, as previously noted, the investigators of nonverbal communicants have tended to look at each channel separately and

---

[3] The motivational qualities of having one's expectations confirmed may not always be positive. Maddi (1961, 1968) and Clark and McClelland (1953) have evidence to suggest that only marked disconfirmation is viewed negatively with mild and moderate departure being viewed as positive.

[4] This example also demonstrates the need to include the nonverbal channel of dress within the multichannel transactional model. One of the few individuals who has started to explore this channel is Gregory Stone (1964).

[5] Hall is responsible for delineating the proximic channel and formulating a transcription system for these behaviors. Two other channels that have had much research also have their mentors, George Trager for paralanguage and Ray Birdwhistell for kinesics.

[6] Robert Sommer (1969) has experimentally verified Hall's observations of the potency of the proximic channel as a vehicle of social influence and has brought into focus the need for structural engineers and architects to take into consideration a behavioral basis for design.

in only a few instances, as in the more current work of Hall (1966) and of Scheflin (1965)[7], have investigators attempted to study the patterning of behavior via a multichannel perspective. The need for this perspective should be obvious to the reader who becomes conscious of the multimessages coming into him when interacting with another.

It is also becoming obvious to the social scientist who is finding that specific behaviors on each channel take on different connotations depending not only on the situation as previously mentioned, but also upon what else is being communicated. For instance, Mehrabian (1969) reports a number of instances where the external variables of attitude and status are curvilinearly related to proximic behaviors; his findings show the need to focus on the content, or patterning of behaviors across channels to understand the social influence process. For example, his summary of the research indicates that eye contact is slightly less than maximum for people who are either liked very much or slightly disliked. However, what attitude is being communicated can be described by looking at the distance between a communicator and his addressee. The more people like each other, the closer they will be.[8] These examples have been given to illustrate the level of sophistication of current description research. However, they give only minimal insight into the development of theory.

While there has been relatively little theory involved in the research on separate nonverbal channels and much less from a multichannel transactional perspective, what little there is can be related to the writings of G. H. Mead (1924). Mead concentrated on the importance of gestures as taking on symbolic meanings. More recently, Abrahamson (1966), Argyle (1967, 1969), Argyle and Kendon (1967), Rosenthal (1966) and others have implicitly called for a multichannel transactional perspective, but continue to work with the channels as if they were separate independent entities. Others as Hall, Bateson and Goffman have proposed models which can be incorporated into the multichannel perspective. Hall's (1963, 1966) programs are extensive and will not be reviewed here. Bateson's and Goffman's models are not only multichannel in nature, but also are to a minimal degree transactional in nature. Their own models, however, tend to classify the nonverbal behaviors in terms of an etiology of schizophrenia in Bateson's case, and in terms of impression formation and management in Goffman's case.

Bateson's model centers on the double-bind theory of schizophrenia.

---

[7] Scheflin, like other nonverbal communicator researchers, has concentrated on therapist-patient relationships. Within these relationships, Scheflin has found that nonverbal communications play at least one unique function, that of regulation. According to Scheflen, nonverbal communication via proximic and kinesic channels may be employed to indicate that a new point is about to be made, that the communicator is taking an attitude relative to several points being made by himself or by his addressee, and he is temporarily removing himself from the communication situation. Further work on he regulatory implications of nonverbal behaviors can be found in a study by Condon and Ogston (1966).

[8] Mehrabian reports that the sex of the individual involved will also interact with these communication channels in encoding the message.

For female communicators, body orientation toward the addressee, like their eye contact, is a parabolic function of attitude toward the addressee, such that the least direct orientation occurs for intensely disliked addressees, the highest degree occurs

According to this theory, conflicting messages from a significant source may create a "double-bind" situation which can lead to schizophrenia. An example of such behavior would be a child sensing hostility from his mother's physical withdrawal via the proximic channel despite her concurrent, overlapping verbalization of love.

The use of nonverbal sources of influence by Goffman have already been mentioned above in terms of role distance. Focusing on nonverbal sources which give information about the communicator, Goffman (1959) separates the behaviors into two classes which differ in the perceived intent of the communicator. Some of these behaviors are perceived as under the control of the communicator, others are perceived as actions for which the communicator has no control and is unaware of. According to Goffman, these latter behaviors are used by the recipient as a test of the credibility of the controlled impressions given off by the communicator. Recently, Eckman and Freisen (1969) have reported experimental confirmation of Goffman's intentional-unintentional behavior classifications. They found that psychotic patients could manage their facial expressions and hide anxiety during psychiatric interviews, but that the person who they were interacting with perceived the person was anxious via uncontrolled leg movements. These movements were in fact kinesic communications that the patient was unaware of and unable to control.

CONCLUSION

The purpose of this paper was to emphasize that nonverbal communications strongly influence and determine the course of social interaction. To facilitate this perspective a multichannel transactional model of social influence was described. The question remains, however, as to whether the model will be adapted or will social scientists continue to use the verbal, single channel perspective. This writer thinks the prospects of the adoption of the multichannel transactional model are good. Multichannel techniques that were unavailable before the widespread use of the computer are now readily available. Where ten years ago only a dozen investigators were concerned with nonverbal influence processes, there are over 100 who are researching the area today. Practicing psychologists as well as the general public have also started to reject the single-channel stimulus-response approach and adopt a multichannel transactional perspective. This can be seen in the growth of sensitivity training laboratories and their attempt to have us become aware of and use the many communication channels open to us.

---

for addressees who are liked very much. For male communicators, the only significant difference occurs with intensely liked addressees, who receive a less direct body orientation. The slight decrease in the directness of orientation of males or females toward intensely liked addressees may be understood in terms of the tendency of communicators to assume a side-by-side and very close position when they communicate to such addressees (p. 370).

REFERENCES

Abrahamson, M. *Interpersonal accommodation*. Princeton: D. Van Nostrand, 1966.

Argyle, M. *The psychology of interpersonal behavior*. Harmondsworth: Penguin Books, 1967.

Argyle, M. *Social interaction*. New York: Atherton Press, 1969.

Argyle, M., and Kendon, A. The experimental analysis of social performance, In L. Berkowitz, ed., *Advances in experimental social psychology*. New York: Academic Press, 1967.

Bauer, R. A. The obstinate audience: The influence process from the point of view of social communication. *American Psychologist* 19 (1964): 319-28.

Birdwhistell, R. L. Communication: A continuous multichannel process. In *Conceptual Bases and Applications of the Communicational Sciences* (New York: John Wiley & Sons, 1971).

Condon, W. S., and Ogston, W. D. Sound film analysis of normal and pathological behavior patterns. *Journal of Nervous and Mental Disease* 143 (1966): 338-47.

Duncan, S. D., Jr., Nonverbal communication, *Psychological Bulletin* 72 (1969): 118-37.

Ekman, P. and Friesen, W. V. Nonverbal leakage and clues to deception. *Psychiatry* 32 (1969): 88-106.

Festinger, L. Informal social communication. *Psychological Review* 57 (1950): 271-82.

Goffman, E. The presentation of self in everyday life. Garden City, N.J.: Doubleday Anchor, 1959.

Goffman, E. Encounters. Indiananapolis: Bobbs-Merrill, 1961.

Hall, E. T. A system for the notation of proximic behavior. *American Anthropologist* 65 (1963): 1003-26.

Hall, E. T. *The hidden dimension*. New York: Doubleday, 1966.

Hollander, E. P. *Principles and methods of social psychology,* New York: Oxford University Press, 1967.

Jaffe, J. Computer assessment of dyadic interaction rules from chronographic data. In J. Shlien, ed., *Research in psychotherapy, Vol. 3*. Washington, D.C.: American Psychological Association, 1968. Pp. 260-76.

Jourard, S. M. An exploratory study of body accessibility. *British Journal of Social and Clinical Psychology* 5 (1966): 221-31.

Katz, E. and Lazarsfeld, P. F. *Personal influence*. Glencoe, Ill.: Free Press, 1955.

Maddi, S. R. Unexpectedness, affective tone, and behavior. In D. W. Fiske and S. R. Maddi, eds., *Functions of varied experience*. Homewood, Illinois: Dorsey, 1961. Pp. 380-401.

Maddi, S. R. The pursuit of consistency and variety in R. P. Abelson, E. Aronson, W. J. McGuire, T. M. Newcomb, M. J. Rosenberg, and P. H. Tannenbaum, eds., *Theories of Cognitive Consistency*. Chicago, Rand McNally, 1968. Pp. 267-74.

Matarazzo, J. D.; Wiens, A. N.; Matarazzo, R. G.; and Saslow, G. Speech and silence behavior in clinical psychotherapy and its laboratory correlates. In J. Shlien, ed., *Research in psychotherapy, Vol. 3.* Washington, D.C.: American Psychological Association, 1968, pp. 347-94.

McClelland, D. and Clark, R. A. Antecedent conditions for affective arousal. In D. McClelland, J. W. Atkinson, R. A. Clark, and E. L. Lowell, *The achievement motive.* New York: Appleton-Century-Crofts, 1953. Sections 2 and 10.

Mead, G. H. *Mind, self, and society.* Chicago: University of Chicago Press, 1934.

Mehrabian, A. Significance of posture and position in the communication of attitude and status relationships. *Psychological Bulletin* 71 (1969): 359-72.

Rosenthal, R. *Experimenter effects in behavioral research.* New York: Appleton-Century-Crofts, 1966.

Scheflen, A. E. *Stream and structure of communicational behavior.* Philadelphia: Eastern Pennsylvania Psychiatric Institute, 1965.

Shulman, A. D. The effects of experimenters behavior on the subject: Role expectancy disconfirmation as a determinant of subject responses. Unpublished doctoral dissertation, State University of New York at Buffalo 1969.

Shulman, A. D. Effects of the experimenter's behavior on the subject—Affective valence of the experimenter's behavior and role expectancy confirmation-disconfirmation as determinants of the subject's affective state. Paper presented at Midwestern Psychological Association Meetings, May, 1969, Chicago, Ill.

Shulman, A. D. and Stone, M. Expectation confirmation-disconfirmation as a determinant of interpersonal behavior: A study of loudness of voice. Paper presented at Southwestern Psychological Association Meetings, April 1970, St. Louis, Mo.

Sommer, R. *Personal space.* Englewood Cliffs, New Jersey: Prentice-Hall, Inc., 1969.

Stone, G. P. Appearance and the self. In A. M. Rose, ed., *Human behavior and social processes.* Boston: Houghton Mifflin, 1962, pp. 128-47.

Sullivan, H. S. *The interpersonal theory of psychiatry,* New York: Norton, 1953.

chapter **11**

Attitudes

An enormous amount of research on attitude development and change has been published. This book offers only a brief introduction to the concepts, theories, and implications for organizations. The major portion of our treatment of attitudes is a selection by Secord and Backman, who review some of the major approaches to attitude development and change.[1]

Attitudes, like other concepts in the field of organizational behavior, may be defined in a variety of ways, depending on one's theoretical and/or practical orientation. Secord and Backman (1964) provided a widely used definition that alludes to the presence of affective, cognitive, and behavioral components in attitudes: "... certain regularities of an individual's feelings, thoughts, and predispositions to act toward some aspect of his environment" (p. 97).[2]

It is generally believed that the outward effect of attitudes is to induce or inhibit behavior. It is difficult, however, to isolate this influence from the influence of other phenomena. Furthermore, a full understanding of attitudes requires measurement of the two internal components, feelings and thoughts, which may not be communicated accurately. The problem is compounded in many studies by attempts to compare and/or add together the attitudes of different people. Thus, our knowledge of attitudes and their consequences is limited by their nature and may be clouded by efforts to "average" them.

Attitude research—a moral issue? Incomplete though our knowledge of attitudes may be, there is much interest in manipulating them to achieve desired behavioral results.

The Skinner-Rogers controversy in part I focused on the ethical implications of attempts to control behavior. Skinner and his followers are never sure (often giving the impression that they do not care) what the mental processes of their

1. In the chapter from which this reading was taken, Secord and Backman were mainly concerned with defining attitudes and explaining some theoretical approaches, reserving for later chapters their treatment of attitude change. The reader who wishes to pursue the subject of attitude change may find Chapters Four, Five and Six in their book very helpful. For a more up-to-date treatment of research on attitudes the reader may consult McGuire (1969); for more on the role of attitudes in organizational behavior, Vroom (1964) is suggested.

2. Recently, Zajonc (1968) emphasized that the cognitive organization of the component can have motivational properties as well.

subjects are. If attitudes do have important consequences for behavior, the potential ethical issues involved in attitude research are even greater than those involved in behavioral research. For example, when does attitude change become thought control? What constitutes legitimate inquiry and influence of an individual's attitudes? What are possible ways to protect individuals from manipulation of attitudes? It is thus surprising that so many people, psychologists in particular, have reacted so vigorously on ethical grounds against the operant conditioners but have viewed the research on attitudes with such apparent ethical neutrality.[3] Perhaps it is because the effects of operant conditioning have been demonstrated to be so powerful, whereas knowledge about attitudes has not permitted such a high degree of control—*yet*. At any rate, it is important that we understand this research and explore its possible ethical implications. Secord and Backman's selection provides a useful beginning.

REFERENCES

McGuire, W. J. "The Nature of Attitudes and Attitude Change." In G. Lindzey and E. Aronson, eds., *The Handbook of Social Psychology.* 2nd ed. Reading, Mass.: Addison-Wesley, 1969, *3*, pp. 136-314.

Secord, P. F., and C. W. Backman, *Social Psychology.* New York: McGraw-Hill Book Company, 1964.

Vroom, V. H. *Work and Motivation.* New York: John Wiley & Sons, 1964.

Zajonc, R. B. Cognitive Theories in Social Psychology." In G. Lindzey and E. Aronson (eds.), *The Handbook of Social Psychology.* 2nd ed. Reading, Mass.: Addison-Wesley, 1969, *1*, pp. 320-411.

---

3. Only when attitude change is called brainwashing does it excite people very much. When it is called therapy, education, rehabilitation, management development, etc., it is generally applauded rather than feared by the masses, governmental leaders, and the social science "establishment." In many ways, these change processes can reasonably be described as types of "brainwashing," which are legitimated by the social system.

Paul F. Secord
and Carl W. Backman

THEORIES OF ATTITUDE ORGANIZATION

In their enthusiasm for the new measurement techniques introduced by Thurstone in 1928 and Likert in 1932, investigators often studied attitudes almost apart from their relation to anything else. Today, psychologists and sociologists realize that the concept of attitude is most useful when studied in context: as a component of the personality of individuals, as serving functional or adjustive ends, or as a descriptive concept characterizing a prevailing mode of thought of the members of a category or subgroup. Context relating attitude to other variables is provided by theory. The years since World War II have seen the gradual development of theory appropriate to the study of attitude change. While none of the theories developed is as yet adequate, they nevertheless serve to integrate many investigations that formerly appeared to be unrelated. Moreover, much current research is generated by these theories.

Most of the theories are intrapersonal: they pertain to the relations of the three attitude components within an individual and specify various conditions that control these relations and produce changes in them. The remainder of this chapter will be devoted to a discussion of several representative theories in order to gain a perspective on the various empirical studies to be discussed in the chapters following.

CONSISTENCY AS AN ORGANIZING PRINCIPLE

One of the prevailing characteristics of human thought and behavior is its tendency to be consistent. If we like a person, we tend to attribute "good" traits to him, and we resist any suggestion that he might posess undesirable traits. We also have beliefs that are consistent with our behavior. Thus, after many news releases about the relation between lung cancer and smoking, a sample of respondents in Minneapolis were asked whether or not they believed the relation had been proved. Only 7 percent of the heavy smokers believed that it had, compared with 20 percent of the light smokers and 29 percent of the nonsmokers (Osgood, 1960). A good party Democrat is likely to give a friendly reception to speeches by any Democratic politician and unfriendly reception to speeches by any Republican politican.

* * *

In 1945 Lecky published a small book in which he attempted to explain much thought and behavior in terms of a single principle: the tendency of the individual to be self-consistent. He suggested that this single principle might substitute for the many principles of human behavior that had been developed for dealing with diverse areas of cognition and behavior. For example, he attempted to show how learning could be explained as well by a consistency principle as by conditioning. The process of forgetting was also explained by consistency: inconsistent elements drop out of memory. He even developed a theory of pleasure, based upon the idea that pleasure is experienced when the organism finds a way to make consistent some experience which is at first inconsistent.

Perhaps the father of modern consistency theory is Heider, who published an important paper on the topic in 1946 and in 1958 published a book-length monograph devoted to his "balance theory." In just the last decade, widespread interest in the principle of consistency has been evident. Many behavioral scientists are now assiduously devoting themselves to developing systematic theories based upon the principle, and many active research programs are in progress.

* * *

Only four of these theoretical approaches will be treated in any detail in this chapter: Rosenberg's theory of affective-cognitive consistency, Festinger's theory of cognitive dissonance, Katz and Stotland's motivational theory of attitude change, and Kelman's three-process theory of attitude change. Although Rosenberg's theory is not as broad as some . . . and has not produced as much extensive empirical study, it is chosen for discussion because it contributes to a better understanding of the nature of affective-cognitive components and the relation between them. Festinger's theory of cognitive dissonance has led to extensive research and has the special merit of demonstrating the relations between cognitive elements and behavior. The approaches of Katz and Stotland and of Kelman are discussed briefly in order to gain a broader perspective on approaches to attitude change other than consistency theory.

* * *

ROSENBERG'S THEORY OF
AFFECTIVE-COGNITIVE CONSISTENCY

Rosenberg (1960*a*, 1960*b*) has concerned himself primarily with conceptualizing what happens *within the individual* when attitudes change. He is particularly interested in the relation between affective and cognitive components of an attitude. In general, past treatments have recognized both of these components, but have been unconcerned with specifying in any precise way how they are organized with respect to each other. Rosenberg attempts to remedy this deficiency. In addition, he extends the cognitive component of an attitude to include not only cognitions about the attitude object, but also *beliefs about* *the relations between that object and other important values of the person.* The affective component is defined in the usual manner as the positive or negative feeling that the individual has toward the attitude object. Thus, a person might have a negative feeling toward Republican congressmen. He also has certain beliefs about them that relate to other positively or negatively valued conditions. He might believe that Republican congressmen obstruct progress, that they hamper the economy, that they have outmoded views on taxation, and that their views on social welfare are inappropriate in a democratic nation.

Rosenberg's principal hypothesis is that the nature and strength of the feeling toward an attitude object are correlated with the cognitions associated with the attitude object. He makes the following statement:

> Strong and stable positive affect toward a given object should be associated with beliefs that it leads to the attainment of a number of important values, while strong negative affect should be associated with beliefs that the object tends to block the attainment of important values. Similarly, moderate positive or negative affects should be associated with beliefs that relate the attitude object either to less important values or, if to important values, then with less confidence about the relationships between these values and the attitude object. (1960*b*, p. 18)

Rosenberg (1953, 1956) has developed a procedure for determining the cognitive components of attitudes. He uses a set of 35 value statements, such as "all human beings having equal rights," "people being well-educated," "making one's own decisions," and "attaining economic security." The subject first categorizes each item in terms of its *value importance,* that is, how satisfying it is to him. To do this, he considers each value statement separately and rates its value importance by placing it in a category ranging from "gives me maximum satisfaction" (+10) through "gives me neither satisfaction nor dissatisfaction" (0) to "gives me maximum dissatisfaction" (-10). For example, if he values education highly, he might give a rating of +8 to "people being well-educated."

Second, the subject rates these value statements with respect to how well a particular attitude contributes to their realization. Suppose, for example, that the attitude concerns Federal aid to education. Taking the first value statement, "people being well-educated," he would rate Federal aid to education on a scale from +5 to -5, positive ratings implying that Federal aid interferes with its attainment. Ratings of the value of statements obtained in this fashion are termed the *perceived instrumentality* of the attitude object.

From ratings of value importance and perceived instrumentality, a *cognitive index* for the attitude object "Federal aid to education" may be obtained. This index represents the subject's pattern of beliefs about the extent to which Federal aid to education results in the attainment of or interference with the individual's values, weighted according to their importance. It is a quantitative measure of the extent to which a person's attitude is consistent with his values.

A principal finding by Rosenberg (1956) is that the index of cognitive structure is consistent with the affect of an attitude, as measured by an attitude scale. That is, if a subject has strong positive affect toward an attitude object, he is likely to have a high cognitive index for that attitude, believing it to be instrumental in attaining his positive values and in blocking negative values. The association between the affective component of an attitude and the cognitive index has been found to be greatest for the person's most salient values. A person's attitudes, then, are anchored in his important values in a highly consistent manner.

Of particular importance are the implications of Rosenberg's theory and methodology for understanding attitude change. . . . A basic proposition in his theory is as follows (Rosenberg, 1960*b*):

> When the affective and cognitive components of an attitude are mutually consistent the attitude is in a stable state; when the affective and cognitive components are mutually inconsistent (to a degree that exceeds the individual's present tolerance for such inconsistency) the attitude is in an unstable state and will undergo spontaneous reorganizing activity until such activity eventuates in either (1) the attainment of affective-cognitive consistency or (2) the placing of an "irreconcilable" inconsistency beyond the range of active awareness. (P. 22).

From this proposition it follows that if certain external forces bring about a change in either the affective or cognitive components of a previously stable attitude, pressures will arise to change the remaining conponent. Most studies previous to Rosenberg have emphasized change in cognitive components as a cause of change in affective components, stressing *rational* processes in attitude change. A good illustration is provided by certain attempts to change racial prejudice. Some attempts to change prejudice toward the Negro use communications designed to convince the individual of the unfavorable consequences of prejudice and of the lack of evidence concerning racial differences on important attributes. But if the person changes his beliefs in response to direct attempts of this kind, his new beliefs would be inconsistent with his negative affect, hence, according to this theory, he resists such approaches. To be successful, such pressures toward change would have to be strong and persistent, creating strong inconsistency between affect and cognition.

While most attitude studies have stressed change in cognitive components as a cause of shifts in affective components, Rosenberg has concentrated on demonstrating that a change in *affect* will produce cognitive changes (Rosenberg and Gardner, 1958; Rosenberg, 1960 *c*). In one experiment, eight subjects who were in favor of the United States policy of giving economic aid to foreign nations were placed under deep hypnosis and their positive feeling reversed to a negative one. This was accomplished by giving each subject the following instructions while under deep hypnosis (Rosenberg, 1960*a*):

> After you awake, and continuing until our next meeting, you will feel very strongly opposed to the United States policy of giving economic aid to foreign nations. The mere idea of the United States giving economic aid to foreign nations will make you feel very displeased and disgusted. Until your next meeting with me you will continue to feel very strong and thorough opposition to the United States policy of economic aid to foreign nations. You will have no memory whatsoever of this suggestion's having been made . . . until the amnesia is removed by my giving you the signal at our next session. (P. 327)

Before and after hypnotic manipulation, subjects indicated the value importance and the perceived instrumentality on Rosenberg's 32 value statements with respect to their own attitude toward foreign aid and two other attitudes used as controls. As predicted, subjects made large-scale changes in both perceived instrumentality and value statements involving foreign aid. Since affect was not manipulated for the control attitudes, no appreciable changes occurred with respect to them. Typically, a subject changed from a position extremely supportive of foreign aid to one of extreme opposition. At the same time, many of his related beliefs changed. For example, if before the affect manipulation he believed that foreign aid would help to maintain such positive values as "the prevention of economic depression," he later believed that *abandonment* of foreign aid would prevent economic depression.

Sometimes, instead of changing the *instrumental* relation between attitude and value, a subject altered the strength or even the direction (positive or negative) of his values, to make them more consistent with the experimentally produced affect. For example, if a subject continued to believe that foreign aid would prevent economic depression, but shifted from extreme support of foreign aid to extreme opposition, he might change the value of economic depression from a negative one to a positive one, arguing that economic depression had certain beneficial effects upon the country. The effects observed in this experiment persisted in most instances for an entire week, at the end of which period the experimenter removed the affect change and explained the entire experiment to the subjects.

*   *   *

FESTINGER'S THEORY OF COGNITIVE DISSONANCE

The theory of cognitive dissonance, developed by Festinger (1957), has the great merit of linking attitude to overt behavior, a problem that has been troublesome throughout the history of attitude research. Critics often argued that the concept of attitude was useless, because no one could be sure that a person would behave in accordance with his verbally expressed attitudes. Dissonance theory recognizes this shortcoming and helps to remedy it by specifying the conditions under which attitudes and behavior do correspond.

Festinger introduces his theory by noting that the attitudes of an individual are normally consistent with each other, that he behaves in accordance with his attitudes, and that his various actions are consistent with each other. For example, if a person believes in democracy, he does not believe in fascism. If he believes a college education is a good thing, he tries to send his children to college. If he behaves conscientiously in doing his college assignments, he is likely to behave conscientiously on a job. Of particular interest is the question of what happens when inconsistencies occur.

By the term cognitive element is meant any knowledge, opinion, or belief about the environment, about oneself, or about one's behavior. The term *dissonance* is introduced to represent an inconsistency between two or more cognitive elements. Two cognitive elements are in a dissonant relation if, considering these two alone, *the obverse of one element would follow from the other.* For example, if a person knew that the most he could afford to pay for a new automobile was $2,500 and that he had just been persuaded to sign a contract to purchase one costing $3,000, there would be a dissonant relation between these two cognitive elements. On the other hand, two cognitive elements are consonant with one another if one follows from the other. Thus, the knowledge that you are getting wet is consonant with the knowledge that it is raining.

Relations between cognitive elements may be either relevant or irrelevant. Dissonance and consonance may only exist between relevant elements. Many cognitive elements have nothing to do with each other. A person may know that the cost of first-class mail is 5 cents an ounce and may also know that spark plugs ignite the gasoline in an engine. These elements are irrelevant to each other.

The magnitude of dissonance is a function of the proportion of all relevant cognitive elements that is dissonant. These elements are generally weighted according to their importance. Thus, the magnitude of dissonance may be expressed in terms of the following ratio:

$$\text{Dissonance} = \frac{\text{importance x no. of dissonant elements}}{\text{importance x no. of consonant elements}}$$

From this ratio,[1] it is clear that the more nearly equal the relative proportions of consonant and dissonant elements, the greater the dissonance is. If there are only a few dissonant elements and many consonant elements, dissonance is relatively low. The number of dissonant elements can never exceed the number of consonant elements, for this would lead to a change, removing the dissonance. Hence the maximum value that dissonance can reach is 1, which is approached when the proportions of dissonant and consonant elements are equal.

Actually, the magnitude of dissonance is represented in terms of a ratio in order to clarify the concept rather than to offer a measuring device. Dissonance cannot be directly measured, and in actual practice in experiments, conditions are compared only with respect to whether or not condition *A* represents a greater or a lesser amount of dissonance than condition *B*. At best, a series of conditions may be rank-ordered, but the exact quantities of dissonance present are not measured.

Reduction of dissonance

Several propositions in dissonance theory have been stated as follows (Festinger, 1957):

[1] Strictly speaking, not even the ratio presented is correct. If there are relatively equal proportions of trivial dissonant and consonant elements, dissonance should be smaller than in the case of relatively equal proportions of highly important dissonant and consonant elements. But the formula shown would yield equal amounts of dissonance in these two special cases. Thus the ratio should be further weighted by the mean importance of all of the relevant elements. But this is mainly an academic point, since the ratio is not used to actually measure dissonance.

The existence of dissonance, being psychologically uncomfortable, will motivate the person to try to reduce the dissonance and achieve consonance (p. 30).

When dissonance is present, in addition to trying to reduce it, the person will actively avoid situations and information which would likely increase the dissonance (p. 3).

The strength of the pressures to reduce the dissonance is a function of the magnitude of the dissonance (p. 18).

Three ways of reducing dissonance are:

1. Change of a behavioral cognitive element. When knowledge of one's own behavior is dissonant with a belief, it is often simplest to change one's behavior. Thus if a person smokes but thinks it is bad for his health, he may stop smoking. Or if he realizes that "goofing off" instead of studying is inconsistent with knowledge that he intends to apply for medical school, he may stop goofing off.

2. Change of an environmental cognitive element. Sometimes the behavior of a person is dissonant with some environmental factor that can be changed. For example, he may reduce the dissonance between his knowledge that smoking causes cancer and his use of cigarettes by changing to a filter-tip brand. Perhaps the easiest aspect of the environment to change is the social or interpersonal environment. Thus a smoker bothered by dissonance may seek support from other persons who also smoke and who can present arguments and reassurance against the view that lung cancer is caused by smoking. He may, for example, point to the fact that many doctors smoke.

3. Addition of new cognitive elements. Sometimes it is difficult to change any of the cognitive elements that are involved in dissonance. Under these circumstances it is often possible to add new elements to outweigh the dissonant ones. A person who has purchased an automobile he cannot afford may convince himself that he is likely to get a substantial raise in pay, that he can readily borrow the additional money, or that he has probably overestimated his expenses and underestimated his income. The smoker worried about lung cancer may tell himself that smoking is relaxing and thus beneficial to his health.

IMPLICATIONS OF DISSONANCE THEORY

Many studies have explored various facets of dissonance theory, and more are in progress. One of these will be described to illustrate the usefulness of the theory in predicting attitude change. The experiment (Festinger and Carlsmith, 1959) chosen is of particular interest because it bears out predictions from dissonance theory opposite to those of common sense. From dissonance theory, the following hypothesis may be derived.

1. If a person is induced to say or do something opposite to his private attitude, he will tend to modify his attitude so as to make it consonant with the cognition of what he has said or done.

This is clear and obvious, but a second hypothesis is as follows:

2. The greater the pressure used to elicit the behavior contrary to one's private attitude (beyond the minimum needed to elicit it), the *less* his attitude will change.

To illustrate, if a person having a strong preference for Democratic candidates in an election were paid $5,000 to go out and persuade other persons to vote for Republican candidates, he would be less likely to switch his personal political preference than if he were to perform the same behavior for a fee of only $100. If $100 were just sufficient to elicit his acceptance of the task, this degree of reward would be more likely to result in a change in his own political preference than any other amount of reward. A greater amount of reward would appreciably strengthen the elements involved in working for a Republican victory and thereby would result in less dissonance and less pressure to change. It is at the point where the pressure to comply and one's political leanings are in approximately equal opposition that dissonance is at a maximum.

The following procedure was used to test the two hypotheses stated above. After completing a dull, boring "experimental" task, subjects were informed that a student helper usually brought in the next experimental subject and told him how enjoyable the experiment was. It was implied that this helper had failed to show up, and the student who had just completed the task was asked to serve in this capacity. Two magnitudes of reward for serving in this role were used for different groups of students: $1 and $20.

Here, then, is an experimental situation where the subject forms a strong private opinion that the task he has just engaged in is dull and boring, but where for a price (and presumably other considerations, such as his desire to cooperate with the experimenter), he agrees to tell a new subject that it is an enjoyable task. After they had served as helpers, subjects were interviewed and asked to rate their opinions concerning the experiment on an 11-point scale from maximum negative opinion to maximum positive opinion. As predicted, those who had received a reward of only $1 rated the experiment higher in terms of its enjoyability than those who had received $20.

In other words, if monetary reward is used as the pressure to win such compliance from a person, the prediction is that the more money he receives for complying, the less his attitude will change. The key to understanding the second hypothesis is the point that *dissonance is at its maximum* when the opposing cognitive elements are equal in strength and importance. Since the amount of attitude change is a function of the amount of dissonance, it is at the point where these opposing elements are equal that the greatest attitude change will occur. If opposing elements are made unequal by appreciably strengthening one set of elements but not the other, dissonance will be somewhat less, and attitude change will be smaller.

* * *

A FUNCTIONAL THEORY OF ATTITUDES

Katz (1960), and Katz and Stotland (1959) in a somewhat more formal presentation, have offered a functional approach to the study of attitudes. From their point of view, the motivational basis of an attitude is the key to understanding change and resistance to change. They note that situational factors and the communication directed toward attitude change will have different effects depending on the motivational basis of the attitude. The motivational basis is conceptualized in terms of the function which an attitude performs for the person. Katz has described four major functions of attitudes as follows:

1. **The instrumental, adjustive, or utilitarian function.** By this is meant that the individual strives to maximize the rewards and minimize the penalties which he experiences. Thus, he develops favorable attitudes toward those objects which result in reward and unfavorable attitudes toward those which lead to punishment.

2. **The ego-defensive function.** Attitudes may function to protect the person from acknowledgment of unpleasant truths about himself or of the harsh realities in his environment. For example, a person with considerable insecurity about his own worth may develop strong prejudice against minority groups so that he can regard himself as superior.

3. **The value-expressive function.** A person may derive satisfaction from expressing himself in terms of attitudes that are appropriate to his personal values and to his self concept. Thus, an individual with strong democratic-liberal values may receive much gratification by engaging in actions that foster such values.

4. **The knowledge function.** The individual is presumed to have a basic drive to understand, to make sense out of, to "structure" his experience. Elements of experience that are at first inconsistent with what a person knows are rearranged or changed so as to achieve consistency.

The value-expressive function and the knowledge function tie in closely with Festinger's theory of cognitive dissonance, as well as other consistency theories. The value-expressive function concerns consistency between values (a form of cognitive element) and cognitive elements representing behavior. The knowledge function resembles Festinger's proposition that a person is motivated to reduce dissonance and achieve consonance. Katz and Stotland apply the consistency principle primarily to single attitude objects: They suggest that affective, cognitive, and behavioral components involving a single attitude object move toward consistency. In their system, different attitudes often may be inconsistent with each other without creating strain.

The instrumental, adjustive, or utilitarian function and the ego-defensive function represent some elements of attitude theory not yet discussed, and they deserve further elaboration here. Katz (1960) notes that to change an attitude that serves an adjustive function, one of the following two conditions must prevail:

(1) The attitude and the activities related to it no longer provide the satisfactions they once did, or (2) the individual's level of aspiration has been raised. The Chevrolet owner who had positive attitudes toward his old car may now want a more expensive car commensurate with his new status (P. 177)

Shifts in the satisfactions obtained from various behaviors, then, result in associated changes in attitudes. When new behaviors which are somewhat inconsistent with current attitudes are rewarded, existing attitudes are modified. Similarly, experiences which are punishing lead to unfavorable attitudes toward the communicators or objects which incite the punishment. . . . Communications that arouse considerable anxiety or fear are likely to create unfavorable attitudes toward the communicator and his communication, a result consistent with theory.

Ego-defensive attitudes are readily aroused by any situation that threatens the individual. Prejudice toward minority groups is an example of an attitude that is sometimes ego-defensive. This attitude would be aroused by excessive competition, derogatory remarks by others, or any other threat to a person's status. Other factors arousing such attitudes include the direct encouragement of their expression by other persons, especially those who hold authoritative positions, and the building up of inhibited drives or impulses in the person such as sexual or aggressive feelings.

Most important is the point that persuasive communications that are effective with attitudes having other motivational bases are often ineffective with ego-defensive attitudes. Thus, communications that provide a great deal of information in support of changing an attitude may not work because such a change deprives the person of an attitude that serves to bolster his ego-defenses. To take one example, an individual whose prejudice toward the Negro is rooted in his own sense of inferiority and his hostile feelings resulting from emotional conflict will be highly resistant to information supporting the view that there is no innate difference between white and Negro. Similarly, promise of rewards for change or the threat of punishment are unlikely to have much effect, unless they are more powerful than the ego-defense motives. Threat of punishment in particular, because it increases defensiveness, may boomerang, that is, effect a change opposite to that intended by the communicator.

Not content with the conclusion that ego-defensive attitudes are more resistant to change than other kinds of attitudes, Katz identifies the conditions and types of persuasive communications which should be effective with ego-defensive attitudes. Two necessary conditions are the reduction of threat and the ventilation of feelings. The communication must come not from a threatening or anxiety-arousing person, but from one who creates a relaxed atmosphere. Opportunities to "blow off steam" reduce the strength of impulses that otherwise provide strong support for ego-defensive attitudes. Communications that help the person to acquire insight in a nonthreatening way into his own mechanisms of defense have the best possibility of changing ego-defensive attitudes.

*   *   *

KELMAN'S THREE–PROCESS THEORY OF ATTITUDE CHANGE

The last theory to be discussed is one proposed by Kelman (1961). His conception of the various means by which attitudes may be changed is particularly useful because the theory itself suggests the conditions under which attitude change will be manifested and those under which it will not, and because it also identifies the conditions leading to temporary change and those producing permanent change. His ideas have some resemblance to those of French and Raven (1959) on power. . . . Kelman (1961) suggests that there are three distinct processes of social influence: compliance, identification, and internalization.

(1) *"Compliance* can be said to occur when an individual accepts influence from another person or from a group because he hopes to achieve a favorable reaction from the other" (p. 62). Here the expression of opinion, even though the person privately disagrees with what he is expressing, is instrumental to gaining some reward or avoiding punishment. Thus an employee aware that his boss is proud of the jokes he tells may laugh heartily at them even though he does not think they are funny. In this way he avoids incurring his boss's displeasure. As might be expected, opinions of this sort are expressed only when they may be observed by the influencing agent.

(2) *"Identification* can be said to occur when an individual adopts behavior derived from another person or a group because this behavior is associated with a satisfying self-defining relationship to this person or group" (p. 63). This is a means of establishing or maintaining a desirable relation to the other person or group and of supporting the self-definition that is part of the relation. One form which identification takes is shown in attempts to be like the other person or to actually be the other person. This is commonly observed in children who copy the behavior and attitudes of their parents or other models. In another form of identification, the individual does not attempt to be like another person, but forms a relation to him that demands behavior quite different from his. The individual behaves in terms of the expectations that the other person has with respect to his behavior. For example, a patient behaves in accordance with the expectations of his doctor and adopts his advice and suggestions. A final form of identification maintains the individual's relation to a group in which his self-definition is anchored. Thus, a physician adopts the attitudes and behavior expected of him by his fellow physicians.

Identification, like compliance, does not occur because the behavior or attitude itself is intrinsically satisfying to the individual. It occurs because of the satisfying relation to another person or group, and it requires the activation of the relation in order for it to occur. Thus, in particular settings, an individual performs his role as a doctor, but there are some situations to which this role is not relevant, as for example situations relating to his wife or children. Unlike the compliance situation, however, the individual actually believes in the attitudes and actions that he adopts as a result of identification.

(3) *"Internalization* can be said to occur when an individual accepts influence because the induced behavior is congruent with his value system" (p. 65). Here the content of the induced attitude or behavior is intrinsically rewarding. The attitude or behavior helps to solve a problem or is demanded by the values of the individual. Thus a person with a liberal political attitude is likely to support a government program for medical care of the aged because one of the values to which he subscribes is that government should promote the public welfare.

Which of these various processes are likely to occur depends in part upon the *source of power of the influencing agent.* If he has strong control over rewards and punishment that the individual might receive, compliance is likely. For example, a child may often comply with the strictures of a stern parent even though his private feelings are in other directions. If on the other hand, the relation to the influence agent is a satisfying one, identification is likely to occur. Thus a daughter enjoying an affectionate relation to her mother may adopt many of her attitudes and behaviors. Finally, internalization occurs when the communicator is highly credible or believable. The recommendations of an expert are accepted if they appear to be congruent with one's values.

In a similar fashion, the conditions leading to the reaction of the individual vary for the different influence processes. When the influencing agent is in a position to closely observe an action or a statement of opinion, compliance is likely to occur. The child behaves well when the stern parent is watching him. Identification requires that the relation to the influence agent be a salient one: the situation must be dominated by the relation. The daughter adopts her mother's attitudes, for example, when playing the mother role toward her younger sister. Finally, attitudes or actions that have been internalized are likely to be expressed only when the values that were relevant to the initial acquisition are activated. The values with regard to honesty become particularly salient when the individual is taking an examination, for example.

These processes have somewhat different implications for permanence of the attitude change. An attitude adopted through compliance is likely to be abandoned if the agent exerting the initial influence loses control over the individual. Such attitudes are also likely to remain isolated from other attitudes and values. Behavior or attitudes initiated as a result of identification are maintained only so long as the relation to the influencing agent remains a satisfying one—and so long as the agent himself retains the attitude. Internalized attitudes are likely to persist as long as the values relevant to their adoption are maintained. A final point of importance is that particular situations are not necessarily pure examples of just one of these processes. Often two or more processes occur simultaneously, or all three may operate together. Thus, if an agent has powerful control over a person, but the relation is also a satisfying one, both compliance *and* identification are likely to occur. In addition, if the attitudes or actions required by this situation are also congruent with other attitudes held, internalization may take place.

*   *   *

SUMMARY AND CONCLUSIONS

Rosenberg's approach provides an explicit means of relating affective and cognitive components and demonstrates that attitude cognitions are instrumentally related to values. Unlike Festinger, however, he explicitly limits himself to "internal consistency," excluding from consideration behavioral elements as well as the various external conditions that might facilitate or block attitude change. The strength of Festinger's dissonance theory is the linkage it provides between behavior and attitude. This is especially evident in the forced-compliance situation, where behavior discrepant with existing attitudes is experimentally elicited.

Although Katz accepts consistency as the basis of the value function and knowledge function, he believes that consistency has certain limits. Along with his collaborator Stotland, he suggests that the principle is especially applicable to single attitude objects: the affective, cognitive, and behavior components toward a *single* object move toward consistency. Much inconsistency, however, may exist among different attitudes, according to Katz and Stotland. In a sense, dissonance theory provides for this by declaring that many cognitive elements are irrelevant to each other. But perhaps a theoretical system is needed that handles irrelevant as well as relevant elements. Katz stresses the importance of motivational factors conceived in terms long familiar to psychologists. In a wider sense, his adjustive and ego-defensive functions stress a broader consistency principle, embracing motivation and action.

Kelman, like Festinger, Rosenberg, and Katz, recognizes the role of internal consistency in attitude change. Like Katz, he suggests two other processes by which attitudes may be changed. He differs from all the other theorists in making a sharper distinction between overt and covert behavior—between public expression and private opinion. His three-process theory treats these two aspects of behavior as relatively independent of each other.

In contrast, Festinger is very explicit about the relation between these two facets of behavior. Speaking of compliance brought about by reward or threat of punishment, he states that if the compliant behavior is at variance with private attitudes, "dissonance inevitably follows from such a situation." It is likely, but not inevitable, that such dissonance will move the individual in the direction of private conformity in order to reduce the dissonance.

Kelman's approach attempts to specify conditions under which situations produce public conformity with little "dissonance" and others that produce more "dissonance" and probably lead to changes in private attitudes. His approach seems best suited to understanding long-term shifts in attitude occurring as a result of ongoing associations with other persons.

These four theories are only a sample chosen from a larger number of theories that have many points of similarity but some important differences. As a group, they make major contributions to the problems of attitude organization and change. Perhaps the most important general contribution of attitude theory is that it helps to solve the problem of *validity*. Throughout the history of attitude research, some psychologists and sociologists have been skeptical because, they asserted, the concept of attitudes was of doubtful validity. By this was meant that, unless it could be demonstrated that a person holding a particular position on an attitude continuum behaved in accordance with that position, the measurement of attitude was invalid. It was more or less assumed that there should be a direct correspondence between a person's overt behavior and his feelings and thoughts as indicated by his responses to an attitude test.

The relation between attitude and behavior is no longer conceptualized in such simple terms. Today we understand that it is necessary to have a theoretical structure that defines the conditions and the manner in which cognitive, affective, and behavioral elements do correspond to each other. The various theories permit us to devise experiments to study the manifold relations between cognitive, affective, and behavioral elements and the conditions that affect these relations. Thus, these theories enable us to make sense out of a great many otherwise unrelated phenomena. Present-day attitude theory, however, is by no means complete. The very existence of so many competing theories suggests that many problems remain to be solved. For example, a recent review of the early research on dissonance theory offers alternative interpretations of findings and points up many inadequacies in experimental design and analysis (Chapanis and Chapanis, 1964).

In the following three chapters,[2] the various research findings on attitude change will be described, and the theories already discussed will often be referred to in the attempt to explain the results of the various experiments. It will also become apparent that consistency theories are not entirely representative of attitude theory. Some investigators have attempted to apply learning theory to attitude research. Such theory assumes a greater diversity of motivation underlying attitude change than simply the need to restore consistency. The learning-theory approach also emphasizes attitude change as a process covering a broader span of time than is generally dealt with by consistency theories. To some extent, the theories of Katz and Stotland and of Kelman take learning theory into account, but further applications of learning theory to attitude change will be introduced from time to time in the chapters which follow.

BIBLIOGRAPHY

Chapanis, Natalia P., and Chapanis, A. Cognitive dissonance: Five years later. *Psychol. Bull.* 61 (1964): 1-22.

Festinger, L. *A theory of cognitive dissonance.* New York: Harper and Row, Publishers, Incorporated, 1957.

[2] [These three chapters refer to the Secord and Backman book] —Ed.

Festinger, L., and Carlsmith, J. M. Cognitive consequences of forced compliance. *J. abnorm. soc. Psychol.* 58 (1959): 203-10.

French, J. R. P., Jr., and Raven, B. H. The bases of social power. In D. Cartwright, ed. *Studies in social power.* Ann Arbor, Mich.: University of Michigan Press, 1959. p. 118-49.

Katz, D. The functional approach to the study of attitude change. *Publ. Opin. Quart.* 24 (1960): 163-204.

Katz, D., and Stotland, E. A preliminary statement to a theory of attitude structure and change. In S. Koch, ed., *Psychology: A study of a science.* Vol. 3. *Formulations of the person and the social context.* New York: McGraw-Hill Book Company, 1959. p. 423-75.

Kelman, H. C Processes of opinion change. *Publ. Opin. Quart.* 25 (1961): 57-78.

Rosenberg, M. J. The experimental investigation of a value theory of attitude structure. Unpublished doctoral dissertation, University of Michigan, 1953.

Rosenberg, M. J. Cognitive structure and attitudinal affect. *J. abnorm. Soc. Psychol.* 53 (1956): 367-72.

Rosenberg, M. J. A structural theory of attitude dynamics. *Publ. Opin. Quart.* 24 (1960): 319-40. (a)

Rosenberg, M. J. An anlysis of affective-cognitive consistency. In C. I. Hovland & M. J. Rosenberg, eds., *Attitude organization and change.* New Haven, Conn.: Yale University Press, 1960. p. 15-64. (b)

Rosenberg, M. J. Cognitive reorganization in response to the hypnotic reversal of attitudinal affect. *J. Pers.* 28 (1960): 39-63. (c)

Rosenberg, M. J., and C. W. Gardner. Some dynamic aspects of post-hypnotic compliance. *J. abnorm. soc. Psychol.* 57 (1958): 351-66.

Walter R. Nord

ATTITUDES AND ORGANIZATIONAL EFFECTIVENESS

Despite an abundance of studies on attitudes, the practical contributions of this research have been far more limited than its potential. This situation prompted Weick (1969) to remark that we have paid too much attention to such factors as cognitions, plans, and beliefs and too little to actions. He suggested that attitudes may be determined by behavior rather than vice versa. Actions may merely summarize behavior of the past. Weick's admonition to study behavior in organizations is well founded. At the same time, the work on attitudes and related concepts has contributed and will continue to contribute some interesting data about people in organizations.

Attitudes have received wide attention in the literature of organizational behavior and management. Such terms as "sentiments," "degree of job satisfaction," and "morale" have been employed to describe phenomena closely akin to what we have termed attitudes. While managers may be interested in the attitudes of people outside the organization for purposes of marketing and public relations, our concern here is primarily with the attitudes of organizational participants.

Most people assume that good feelings toward the organization will lead to effective performance. However, researchers have given up the hope of finding an invarient, positive relationship between measures of attitudes and organizational effectiveness or performance. Vroom (1964) reviewed 20 studies on the relationship of attitudes or job satisfaction to various criteria of effectiveness. He reported correlations ranging from +.86 to −.31, with a median of +.14. Clearly, such variation argues that there is unlikely to be any simple relationship between attitudes and performance. Rather, most research suggests a need to look at more narrowly defined criteria and attitudes toward particular aspects of the work environment.

Vroom (1969) concluded that the factors which make organizational membership seem attractive and satisfying are not the same as those which induce dependable and effective performance within the system. Vroom reached conclusions similar to those of Brayfield and Crockett (1955) in their comprehensive review; although job satisfaction seemed to be negatively related to voluntary turnover, absenteeism, and accident rates, the relationships that were found between job satisfaction and performance were inconsistent from study to study, some negative and some positive. A search for the conditions under which particular relationships exist is required. Research on job attitudes must take into account situational variables and the individual's past experiences and present needs.

To the extent that the organization supports the satisfaction of needs by supporting productivity, a positive correlation between attitudes toward the organization and productivity might be expected. However, if the individual perceives the organization as reducing his need satisfaction by introducing barriers to his performance, he may have positive attitudes toward productivity and be a high producer but have negative attitudes toward the organization.

Other sources of need satisfaction must also be considered. As discussed earlier, an individual may experience need satisfaction from low productivity. When group norms restrict output, it is quite possible to have a high degree of participation (i.e., long tenure, low absenteeism) in the organization, favorable attitudes toward the organization, and at the same time low productivity. The crucial factor seems to be the individual's perception of what behaviors lead to need satisfaction. Only when organization goals or requirements and individual needs are viewed as being satisfied by the same behavior can favorable attitudes toward the organization and performance be expected to be positively related. This relationship could be predicted from balance models discussed by Secord and Backman.

The balance models suggest that behavioral tendencies are associated with only a particular element of the environment. Behavioral predispositions to produce are apt to be much more closely associated and consistent with feelings and thoughts about the job itself than with feelings and thoughts about the supervisor, the organization, fringe benefits, and other features of the work environment not directly related to the job. There is no reason to expect attitudes toward a company in general to have any necessary relationship to behavioral tendencies to produce. Prediction of behavioral predispositions from affective expressions is likely to be successful only in cases in which both components are dealing with the same aspect of the environment.

ATTITUDES AND MANAGEMENT

Given all the possible sources of variance in attitudes, organization, and tasks, it is unlikely that anyone could devise a system of attitude development which would increase the effectiveness of members of all organizations. With this reservation in mind, managers can still derive useful insights from management systems based on attitudes. Likert (1967) argued that attitudes of organizational participants contribute directly, at least in the long run, to organization effectiveness. He maintained that a determination of the actual worth of an organization must include measures of the human assets as well as normal accounting data, and he proposed that much of this supplemental information should come from attitude surveys of organizational participants.

Likert advocated a particular style of management for developing favorable attitudes and hence increasing the value of the human assets. Field studies, conducted mainly by University of Michigan researchers, have shown that democratic or participatory management styles are associated with more positive attitudes toward the organization on the part of organizational participants, more productive behavior, and a greater realization of organizational goals. Likert suggested that System 4 (his term for participatory management) will enhance organizational performance. System 4, in Likert's view, changes the causal variable — managerial behavior toward people. These changes affect the intervening variables of attitudes and motivation and thereby lead to changes in organizational performance. Thus, for Likert, attitudes are crucial intervening variables in organizational performance.

If reliable and valid measurement could be developed,[1] few behavioral scientists would be likely to disagree with Likert's argument for human-resource accounting. Organizational decisions often appear to overemphasize readily quantifiable variables. As a result, the effect of decisions on the human asset may often be underestimated. Human-asset accounting could modify this dysfunctional imbalance.

Further investigation is required, however, before the influence of attitudes on organizational performance can be clearly understood. It would therefore be unwise to depend exclusively on anything as specific as System 4. A more fruitful approach would be some type of situational thinking (Pigors and Myers, 1965) or, better yet, a true system view (Buckley, 1968; and Emery, 1968),

[1] Encouraging preliminary research in this direction was reported by Brummet, Flamholtz, and Pyle (1968).

which includes simultaneously the state of the individual's needs, his perceptions, the organizational structure and requirements, and many of the other variables treated in this book. All management systems influence the attitudes of participants. The type of attitudes each developes and the consequences of any particular set of attitudes depend on many factors.

Only if a particular style of management develops attitudes and behavior that are consistent with need satisfaction for the individual and the organization will that management style foster an increase in organization worth. Under many conditions an individual's needs and an organization's goals might be satisfied quite well by one of the other systems described by Likert, either the exploitive-authoritative or the benevolent-authoritative.

Unresolved issues. While the concept of attitudes has important practical possibilities, their realization is apt to be hindered by several factors. First, our measures are less than satisfactory for many practical purposes. Second, there are substantial value questions involved in any attempt to measure and change attitudes. Third, there is the haunting suggestion of Weick (1969) that attitudes may develop after actions rather than before and thereby contribute relatively little to performance. Finally, there are intra- and interorganizational differences which make questionable the attempt to generalize from specific findings.

REFERENCES

Brayfield, A. H. and W. H. Crockett, "Employee Attitudes and Employee Performance." *Psychological Bulletin* 52:(1955):396-424.

Buckley, W., ed. *Modern Systems Research for the Behavioral Scientist.* Chicago: Aldine, 1968.

Brummet, R. L.; E. G. Flamholtz, and W. C. Pyle, "Human Resource Measurement—A Challenge for Accountants." *The Accounting Review* 43 (1968); 217-24.

Emery, F. E. *Systems Thinking.* Middlesex, Eng.: Penguin, 1969.

Likert, R. *The Human Organization: Its Management and Value.* New York: McGraw-Hill Book Company, 1967.

Pigors, P., and C. A. Myers, *Personnel Administration: A Point of view and a Method.* 5th ed. New York: McGraw-Hill Book Company, 1965.

Vroom, V. H. "Inudstrial Social Psychology." In G. Lindzey and E. Aronson (eds.), *The Handbook of Social Psychology,* 2nd ed.vol. 5. Reading, Mass.: Addison-Wesley, 1969, pp. 196-268.

Vroom, V. H. *Work and Motivation.* New York: John Wiley & Sons, 1964.

Weick, K. E. *The Social Psychology of Organizing.* Reading, Mass.: Addison-Wesley, 1969.

chapter 12

Group Behavior and Organizations

Individualism is a central tenet of economic and social values in the United States. Many American politicians employ the rhetoric of personal initiative and freedom; few are elected on a platform advocating "from each according to his abilities, to each according to his needs." Our literature and history as taught in most public schools glorify rugged individualism. Politically and economically, individual dignity, freedom, power, and rewards are stressed at least in our explicit values.

In view of the widespread acceptance of these values and our parallel success with an economic system based on individual initiative, it is no surprise that some people react strongly to those who emphasize groups rather than individuals. For instance, one recent presidential cabinet member did not differentiate between sociology and socialism; William H. Whyte, in his *Organization Man,* lamented the decreasing role of the individual in organizations; many managers do not have the understanding or the willingness to deal with the social side of man's behavior in organizations.

Despite such reactions, the increasing role of groups at all levels of modern organizations is becoming an accepted fact.[1] Bennis's paper in Part II suggested that internal and external demands on modern organizations require much more interdependence and coordination of effort. Consider also Galbraith's (1967) description of the role of groups at middle and upper levels of management. He asserted that organizations are run by a technostructure, composed of everyone who participates in organizational decision making, and that the real accomplishments of large modern organizations depend on coordination of effort of many people rather than on genius. Further, " . . . the decision of modern

1. Groups themselves and awareness of groups are not new to organizations. As noted earlier, Frederick Taylor's "scientific management" was an outgrowth of his efforts to overcome "soldiering" (i.e., restrictive practices of informal groups). Mathewson (1931) described in great detail the role of groups in influencing individual behavior. Of course, the Hawthorne studies were most important in pointing to the influence of groups in organizations.

All of these efforts centered on blue-collar work groups. Although both Mathewson and the Hawthorne researchers reported that superiors as well as workers were involved in output restriction, generally output restriction has been considered a peer-group phenomenon.

business enterprises is the product not of individuals but of groups (p. 65)." According to Galbraith, such groups define the goals of the organization, and ultimately determine the allocation of resources. The resulting allocation may be more in line with the goals of the technostructure than with the stated goals of the organization. Often even the president and other very high-level officers lack control or knowledge of what is happening in the organization. Certainly, the stockholders and the board of directors are apt to have relatively little influence. Galbraith's view leaves little place for individualism, even at the managerial level. Other modern critics have made similar assertions. For example, C. W. Mills argued in his *Power Elite* (1959) that group decision making and group processes are extremely important in the shaping of national policy.

Both friends and critics of modern society have pointed to the important role of groups in management. While many have drawn conclusions from personal observation or data of uncertain reliability, a survey of subscribers to the *Harvard Business Review* provides more firm evidence.

The survey, reported by Tillman (1960), explored the amount of time the respondents spent in groups and how they felt about it. The results revealed that an average executive spent 3½ hours per week in formal committee meetings and about one working day (9½ hours) per week in informal conferences and consultations with other executives. Interestingly, group work was more important at higher levels. Generally, upper-level executives served on more committees than did either lower- or middle-managment people. Also, upper-level executives were more favorable toward committees than were lower-level executives. Overall, executives at all levels wholeheartedly agreed that committees are very useful for promoting coordination and sharing information. A variety of comments by the respondents reflected the theme that, in today's complex business world, committees are often the only way of coordinating the functions of the business and promoting communication among departments. In addition, committees were seen as means of inducing people to think about problems more clearly and deeply. Although there were many objections to committees, including feelings that they take too much time, prohibit the pinpointing of responsibility, and run the risk of undue compromises, the executives nevertheless perceived committees as contributing significantly to the realization of organizational goals. Tillman summarized their feelings by observing that

> The great majority of their suggestions led them to this conclusion: *the problem is not so much committees in management as it is the management of committees* (p. 68).

Committees and task groups serve an important function in the operation of modern organizations. As the degree of specialization and the correlated requirements for coordination become greater, the role of groups will become even more important. Management's attitudes toward groups are changing. Much of the earlier literature of administration was devoted to how management can fight, or at least neutralize, work groups. Increasingly, it is evident that work groups are essential for the success of the organization. The issue is now how to utilize groups effectively.

GROUPS: FUNCTIONAL VIEW

Simply stated, the functional view of groups is that groups arise and endure to serve the needs of their members. An individual finds a group attractive because other members provide him with rewards which he cannot obtain as easily from any other source. When several people find each other to be sources of positive reinforcement, they are apt to form common patterns of exchange. Groups tend to dissolve or to be characterized by stress when the exchange of benefits is no longer favorable to all or some members.

The types of needs which are satisfied vary from one individual or situation to another because of variations in group tasks, organization structure surrounding the group, available technology, personalities of the group's members, cultural environment, and the degree of crisis. These and other factors influence the group process through their effect on individual needs.

Functions of Groups for Individuals

Groups help to satisfy a number of individual needs. Our knowledge about the functions of groups comes from research into both human and animal behavior. Some functions of groups are merely physiological, while others involve complex coordination of effort. One important function seems to be stress reduction.

The presence of other animals of the same species may be functional for individual survival. Etkin (1967) noted that, in water which has small quantities of harmful chemicals, goldfish survive better when in groups than when alone. Mice in cold environments tend to be able to survive better in groups, presumably because of heat and shelter provided by the animals' own bodies. Other research found that animals in a threatening situation experience less anxiety when another animal of the same species is present than when alone. Bovard (1959) provided additional evidence to support the stress-reducing properties of the mere presence of other animals.

Human groups have also been found to serve important functions. Schachter (1959) reported that the presence of others was valued by people under conditions of stress. Stotland (1959) found that peer groups provided support for members, allowing individuals to express more direct and overt hostility toward threatening power figures. Thus work groups may be a source of strength for subordinates.

Groups may also provide a means of self-definition—either through shared beliefs or values, as in religious and ethnic groups, or through interpersonal comparison (Festinger, 1954). A reward or personal ability, such as a particular grade in school, often has little meaning until one finds out how it compares with the attainment of other people.

Thus we see that the presence or absence of groups of different types has important functional and dysfunctional consequences for individuals and hence for organizations. The issue is not "are groups good or bad?" but "how can groups be best used to meet individual and organizational goals?" The functional view, focusing on individual needs, may give some insights into this question.

Groups in Organizations

Formal organizations affect the development and characteristics of groups through the interplay of structural and technological factors on individual needs and group dynamics. The organization influences in two ways: individual needs by generating them (e.g., through introducing feelings of threat and competition) and by introducing bridges and/or barriers to their satisfaction. One source of need satisfaction is interaction within groups. The features of group structure (size, patterns of interaction, cohesion, etc.) are in part a function of such organizational variables as noise levels, the proximity of workers in the production process, and the degree of interdependence required by the work and by the formal structure itself. These same organizational factors influence the dynamics of the group through their continuing effects on the needs of individual members. Furthermore, the group structure itself has independent effects on individual needs and performance.

Tannenbaum (1966) summarized some of the important work on these effects. A central variable in this research is group cohesion—the degree of members' attraction to the group or the amount of "stick-togetherness' (Mikalachki, 1969) they exhibit. Considerable research has shown that membership in cohesive groups may serve to increase job satisfaction and to reduce absenteeism and turnover. Other studies have shown that groups whose members are strongly attracted to the group experience fewer work-related anxieties than do members of groups characterized by lower cohesiveness.

Recently Mikalachki (1969) reviewed the literature on group cohesion and productivity and added some relevent data. He argued that cohesion may be either task oriented or socially oriented. Only in the former case would we expect productivity to be enhanced by the cohesion.[2]

Attraction to a group is influenced by member qualities as well as organizational forces. For example, one is apt to be more attracted to people who share one's values than to others. Furthermore, personal relationships of individual members to the group affect its development. Aronson and Mills

---

2. Mikalachki also suggested some important implications of group cohesion on administrators. He noted that supervision of noncohesive groups requires a great deal of time, because group members must be treated more individually than collectively. Furthermore, lack of cohesion may lead to the additional disadvantages of high turnover and tension and may require a supervisor to develop and monitor channels of communication. By contrast, highly cohesive task groups can be dealt with collectively and have less tension and turnover and a more integrated structure, which facilitates communication. Mikalachki suggests that administrators and industrial engineers may be well-advised to introduce the conditions which are known to promote the development of highly cohesive task groups—". . . small groups whose members identify with its formal goals, perform interdependent task roles, and show a high degree of concern for one another (p. 79)."

(1959) demonstrated that a high "cost of entry" into a group may increase member commitment. In this sense, marine training, fraternity hazing, and the rough treatment given to pro football rookies may be functional for the group. Group processes are also affected by the tendency of people to define themselves in terms of a group. (Often, especially in religious and ethnic groups, personal identity of individual members, as shown earlier, is dependent on the group.) An attack on groups central to one's identity arouses vigorous defenses and counterattacks. The "irrational" behavior of unions, extremist political groups, and even management and other work groups can often be more readily understood in this light.

The Readings

The following selections discuss the consequences of groups for individuals and highlight some issues of central importance to organizations. Cartwright and Lippitt attempt to tie together central findings on the social psychology of groups. Their focus, on the relationship of individuals to groups, is helpful for a consideration of ways to utilize groups effectively. The following article looks at the same issue from a different point of view. Schutz helps us understand how personal needs are related to group functioning and how interpersonal relationships within work groups can be improved. The symposium by Campbell, Dunnette, and Argyris examines the value of T-groups, one of the most controversial topics in organizational behavior. Their discussion has major implications for general issues concerning the evaluation of training and managerial actions in general. A final selection by the editor examines some additional ideas about groups in organization.

REFERENCES

Aronson, E., and Mills, J. "The Effects of Severity of Initiation on Liking for a Group." *Journal of Abnormal and Social Psychology* 59 (1959): 177-81.

Bovard, E. W. "The Effects of Social Stimuli on the Response to Stress." *Psychological Review* 66 (1959): 267-77.

Etikin, W. *Social Behavior from Fish to Man.* Chicago: University of Chicago Press, 1967.

Festinger, L. "A Theory of Scoial Comparison Processes." *Human Relations* 7 (1954): 117-40.

Galbraith, J. K. *The New Industrial State.* Boston: Houghton Mifflin, 1967.

Mathewson, S. B. *Restriction of Output among Unorganized Workers.* New York: Viking, 1931.

Mikalachki, A. *Group Cohesion Reconsidered.* London, Ont.: University of Western Ontario, 1969.

Mills, C. W. *The Power Elite.* New York: Oxford University Press, 1959.

Schachter, S. *The Psychology of Affiliation: Experimental Studies of the Sources of Gregariousness.* Stanford, Ca.: Stanford University, 1959.

Stotland, E. "Peer Groups and Reactions to Power Figures." In D. Cartwright, ed., *Studies in Social Power*. Ann Arbor, Mich.: University of Michigan, 1959. pp. 53-68.

Tannenbaum, A. S. *Social Psychology of the Work Organization*. Belmont, Ca.: Wadsworth Publishing Co., Inc., 1966.

Tillman, R. "Problems in Review: Committees on Trial." *Harvard Business Review* 38 (1960): 6-12, 162-73.

Dorwin Cartwright and Ronald Lippitt

GROUP DYNAMICS
AND THE INDIVIDUAL

How should we think of the relation between individuals and groups? Few questions have stirred up so many issues of metaphysics, epistemology, and ethics. Do groups have the same reality as individuals? If so, what are the properties of groups? Can groups learn, have goals, be frustrated, develop, regress, begin and end? Or are these characteristics strictly attributable only to individuals? If groups exist, are they good or bad? How *should* an individual behave with respect to groups? How *should* groups treat their individual members? Such questions have puzzled man from the earliest days of recorded history.

In our present era of "behavioral science" we like to think that we can be "scientific" and proceed to study human behavior without having to take sides on these problems of speculative philosophy. Invariably, however, we are guided by certain assumptions, stated explicitly or not, about their observability, and about their good or bad value.

Usually these preconceptions are integral parts of one's personal and scientific philosophy, and it is often hard to tell how much they derive from emotionally toned personal experiences with other people and how much from coldly rational and "scientific" considerations. In view of the fervor with which they are usually defended, one might suspect that most have a small basis at least in personally significant experiences. These preconceptions, moreover, have a tendency to assume a homogeneous polarization—either positive or negative.

Consider first the completely negative view. It consists of two major assertions: first, groups don't really exist. They are a product of distorted thought processes (often called "abstractions"). In fact, social prejudice consists precisely in acting as if groups, rather than individuals, were real. Second, groups are bad. They demand blind loyalty, they make individuals regress, they reduce man to the lowest common denominator, and they produce what *Fortune* magazine has immortalized as "group-think."

In contrast to this completely negative conception of groups, there is the completely positive one. This syndrome, too, consists of two major assertions: first, groups really do exist. Their reality is demonstrated by the difference it

From Dorwin Cartwright and Ronald Lippitt, "Group Dynamics and the Individual," *International Journal of Group Psychotherapy* 7, (January, 1957): 86-102. Reprinted by permission of American Group Psychotherapy Association.

makes to an individual whether he is accepted or rejected by a group and whether he is part of a healthy or sick group. Second, groups are good. They satisfy deep-seated needs of individuals for affiliation, affection, recognition, and self-esteem; they stimulate individuals to moral heights of altruism, loyalty, and self-sacrifice; they provide a means, through cooperative interaction, by which man can accomplish things unattainable through individual enterprise.

This completely positive preconception is the one attributed most commonly, it seems, to the so-called "group dynamics movement." Group dynamicists, it is said, have not only *reified* the group but also *idealized* it. They believe that everything should be done by and in groups—individual responsibility is bad, man-to-man supervision is bad, individual problem-solving is bad, and even individual therapy is bad. The only good things are committee meetings, group decisions, group problem-solving, and group therapy. "If you don't hold the group in such high affection," we were once asked, "why do you call your research organization the Research Center FOR Group Dynamics? And, if you are for groups and group dynamics, mustn't you therefore be *against* individuality, individual responsibility, and self-determination?"

FIVE PROPOSITIONS ABOUT GROUPS

This assumption that individuals and groups must necessarily have incompatible interests is made so frequently in one guise or another that it requires closer examination. Toward this end we propose five related assertions about individuals, groups, and group dynamics, which are intended to challenge the belief that individuals and groups must necessarily have incompatible, or for that matter, compatible interests.

(1). Groups do exist; they must be dealt with by any man of practical affairs, or indeed by any child, and they must enter into any adequate account of human behavior. Most infants are born into a specific group. Little Johnny may be a welcome or unwelcome addition to the group. His presence may produce profound changes in the structure of the group and consequently in the feelings, attitudes, and behavior of various group members. He may create a triangle where none existed before or he may break up one which has existed. His development and adjustment for years to come may be deeply influenced by the nature of the group he enters and by his particular position in it—whether, for example, he is a first or second child (a personal property which has no meaning apart from its reference to a specific group).

There is a wealth of research whose findings can be satisfactorily interpreted only by assuming the reality of groups. Recall the experiment of Lewin, Lippitt, and White (15) in which the level of aggression of an individual was shown to depend upon the social atmosphere and structure of the group he is in and not merely upon such personal traits as aggressiveness. By now there can be little question about the kinds of results reported from the Western Electric study (18) which make it clear that groups develop norms for the behavior of their members with the result that "good" group members adopt these norms as their *personal* values. Nor can one ignore the dramatic evidence of Lewin, Bavelas, and others (14) which shows that group decisions may produce changes in individual behavior much larger than those customarily found to result from attempts to modify the behavior of individuals *as* isolated individuals.

(2). Groups are inevitable and ubiquitous. The biological nature of man, his capacity to use language, and the nature of his environment which has been built into its present form over thousands of years require that man exist in groups. This is not to say that groups must maintain the properties they now display, but we cannot conceive of a collection of human beings living in geographical proximity under conditions where it would be correct to assert that no groups exist and that there is no such thing as group membership.

(3). Groups mobilize powerful forces which produce effects of the utmost importance to individuals. Consider two examples from rather different research settings. Seashore (22) has recently published an analysis of data from 5,871 employees of a large manufacturing company. An index of group cohesiveness, developed for each 228 work groups, permitted a comparison of members working in high and in low cohesive groups. Here is one of his major findings: "Members of high cohesive groups exhibit less anxiety than members of low cohesive groups, using as measures of anxiety: (a) feeling 'jumpy' or 'nervous,' (b) feeling under pressure to achieve higher productivity (with actual productivity held constant), and (c) feeling a lack of support from the company" (p.98). Seashore suggests two reasons for the relation between group cohesiveness and individual anxiety: "1) that the cohesive group provides effective support for the individual in his encounters with anxiety-provoking aspects of his environment, thus allaying anxiety, and 2) that group membership offers direct satisfaction, and this satisfaction in membership has a generalized effect of anxiety-reduction" (p. 13).

Perhaps a more dramatic account of the powerful forces generated in groups can be derived from the publication by Stanton and Schwartz (24) of their studies of a mental hospital. They report, for example, how a patient may be thrown into an extreme state of excitement by disagreements between two staff members over the patient's care. Thus, two doctors may disagree about whether a female patient should be moved to another ward. As the disagreement progresses, the doctors may stop communicating relevant information to one another and start lining up allies in the medical and nursing staff. The patient, meanwhile, becomes increasingly restless until, at the height of the doctors' disagreement, she is in an acute state of excitement and must be secluded, put under sedation, and given special supervision. Presumably, successful efforts to improve the interpersonal relations and communications among members of the staff would improve the mental condition of such a patient.

In general, it is clear that events occurring in a group may have repercussions on members who are not directly involved in these events. A person's position in a group, moreover, may affect the way others behave toward him and such personal qualities as his levels of aspiration and self-esteem. Group membership itself may be a prized possession or an oppressive burden; tragedies of major proportions have resulted from the exclusion of individuals from groups, and equally profound consequences have stemmed from enforced membership in groups.

(4). Groups may produce both good and bad consequences. The view that groups are completely good and the view that they are completely bad are both based on convincing evidence. *The only fault with either is its one-sidedness.* Research motivated by one or the other is likely to focus on different phenomena. As an antidote to such one-sidedness it is a good practice to ask research questions in pairs, one stressing positive aspects and one negative: What are the factors producing conformity? and what are the factors producing nonconformity? What brings about a breakdown in communication? and what stimulates or maintains effective communication? An exclusive focus on pathologies or upon positive criteria leads to a seriously incomplete picture.

(5). A correct understanding of group dynamics permits the possibility that desirable consequences from groups can be deliberately enhanced. Through a knowledge of group dynamics, groups can be made to serve better ends, for knowledge gives power to modify human beings and human behavior. At the same time, recognition of this fact produces some of the deepest conflicts within the behavioral scientist, for it raises the whole problem of social manipulation. Society must not close its eyes to Orwell's horrible picture of life in 1984, but it cannot accept the alternative that in ignorance there is safety.

To recapitulate our argument: groups exist; they are inevitable and ubiquitous; they mobilize powerful forces having profound effects upon individuals; these effects may be good or bad; and through a knowledge of group dynamics there lies the possibility of maximizing their good value.

A DILEMMA

Many thoughtful people today are alarmed over one feature of groups: the pressure toward conformity experienced by group members. Indeed, this single "bad" aspect is often taken as evidence that groups are bad in general. Let us examine the specific problem of conformity, then, in order to attain a better understanding of the general issue. Although contemporary concern is great, it is not new. More than 100 years ago Alexis de Tocqueville wrote: "I know of no country in which there is so little independence of mind and real freedom of discussion as in America. . . In America the majority raises formidable barriers around the liberty of opinion. . . The master (majority) no longer says: 'You shall think as I do or you shall die'; but he says: 'You are free to think differently from me and to retain your life, your property, and all that you possess, but they will be useless to you, for you will never be chosen by your fellow citizens if you solicit their votes; and they will affect to scorn you if you ask for their esteem. You will remain among men, but you will be deprived of the rights of mankind. Your fellow creatures will shun you like an impure being; and even those who believe in your innocence will abandon you, lest they should be shunned in their turn'" (25, pp. 273-75).

Before too readily accepting such a view of groups as the whole story, let us invoke our dictum that research questions should be asked in pairs. Nearly everyone is convinced that individuals should not be blind conformers to group norms, that each group member should not be a carbon copy of every other member, but what is the other side of the coin? In considering why members of groups conform, perhaps we should also think of the consequences of the removal of individuals from group membership or the plight of the person who really does not belong to any group with clear-cut norms and values. The state of anomie, described by Durkheim, is also common today. It seems as if people who have no effective participation in groups with clear and strong value systems either crack up (as in alcoholsim or suicide) or they seek out groups which will demand conformity. In discussing this process, Talcott Parsons writes: "In such a situation it is not surprising that large numbers of people should ... be attracted to movements which can offer them membership in a group with a vigorous esprit de corps with submission to some strong authority and rigid system of belief, the individual thus finding a measure of escape from painful perplexities or from a situation of anomie" (17, pp. 128-29).

The British anthropologist, Adam Curle, has stressed the same problem when he suggested that in our society we need not four, but five freedoms, the fifth being freedom from that neurotic anxiety which springs from a man's isolation from his fellows, and which, in turn, isolates him still further from them.

We seem, then, to face a dilemma: the individual needs social support for his values and social beliefs; he needs to be accepted as a valued member of some group which *he* values; failure to maintain such group membership produces anxiety and personal disorganization. But, on the other hand, group membership and group participation tend to cost the individual his individuality. If he is to receive support from others and, in turn, give support to others, he and they must hold in common some values and beliefs. Deviation from these undermines any possibility of group support and acceptance.

Is there an avenue of escape from this dilemma? Certainly, the issue is not as simple as we have described it. The need for social support for some values does not require conformity with respect to all values, beliefs, and behavior. Any individual is a member of several groups, and he may be a successful deviate in one while conforming to another (think of the visitor in a foreign country or of the psychologist at a convention of psychiatrists). Nor should the time dimension be ignored; a person may sustain his deviancy through a conviction that his fate is only temporary. These refinements of the issue are important and should be examined in great detail, but before we turn our attention to them, we must assert that we do *not* believe that the basic dilemma can be escaped. To avoid complete personal disorganization man must conform to at least a minimal set of values required for participation in the groups to which he belongs.

PRESSURES TO UNIFORMITY

Some better light may be cast on this problem if we refer to the findings of research on conformity. What do we know about the way it operates?

Cognitive Processes. Modern psychological research on conformity reflects the many different currents of contemporary psychology, but the major direction has been largely determined by the classic experiment of Sherif (23) on the development of social norms in perceiving autokinetic movement and by the more recent study of Asch (1) of pressures to conformity in perceiving unambiguous visual stimuli.

What does this line of investigation tell us about conformity? What has it revealed, for instance, about the conditions that set up pressures to conformity? Answers to this question have taken several forms, but nearly all point out that social interaction would be impossible if some beliefs and perceptions were not commonly shared by the participants. Speaking of the origin of such cognitive pressures to uniformity among group members, Asch says: "The individual comes to experience a world that he shares with others. He perceives that the surroundings include him, as well as others, and that he is in the same relation to the surroundings as others. He notes that he, as well as others, is converging upon the same object and responding to its identical properties. Joint action and mutual understanding require this relation of intelligibility and structural simplicity. In these terms the 'pull' toward the group becomes understandable" (1, p. 484).

Consistent with this interpretation of the origin of pressures to uniformity in a perceptual or judgmental situation are the findings that the major variables influencing tendencies to uniformity are (a) the quality of the social evidence (particularly the degree of unanimity of announced perceptions and the subject's evaluation of the trustworthiness of the other's judgments), (b) the quality of the direct perceptual evidence (particularly the clarity or ambiguity of the stimuli), (c) the magnitude of the discrepancy between the social and the perceptual evidence, and (d) the individual's self-confidence in the situation (as indicated either by experimental manipulations designed to affect self-confidence or by personality measurements).

The research in this tradition has been productive, but it has emphasized the individual and his cognitive problems and has considered the individual apart from any concrete and meaningful group membership. Presumably any trustworthy people adequately equipped with eyes and ears could serve to generate pressures to conformity in the subject, regardless of his specific relations to them. The result of this emphasis has been to ignore certain essential aspects of the conformity problem. Let us document this assertion with two examples.

First, the origin of pressures to uniformity has been made to reside in the person whose conformity is being studied. Through eliminating experimentally any possibility that pressures might be exerted by others, it has been possible to study the conformity of people as if they existed in a world where they can see or hear others but not be reacted to by others. It is significant indeed, that conformity does arise in the absence of direct attempts to bring it about. But this approach does not raise certain questions about the conditions which lead to *social* pressures to conformity. What makes some people try to get others to conform? What conditions lead to what forms of pressure on others to get them to conform? The concentration of attention on the conformer has diverted attention away from the others in the situation who may insist on conformity and make vigorous efforts to bring it about or who may not exert any pressure at all on deviates.

A second consequence of this emphasis has been to ignore the broader social meaning of conformity. Is the individual's personal need for a social validation of his beliefs the only reason for conforming? What does deviation do to a person's acceptance by others? What does it do to his ability to influence others? Or, from the group's point of view, are there reasons to insist on certain common values, beliefs, and behavior? These questions are not asked nor asnwered by an approach which limits itself to the cognitive problems of the individual.

Group Processes. The group dynamics orientation toward conformity emphasizes a broader range of determinants. Not denying the importance of the cognitive situation, we want to look more closely at the nature of the individual's relation to particular groups with particular properties. In formulating hypotheses about the origin of pressures to uniformity, two basic sources have been stressed. These have been stated most clearly by Festinger and his co-workers (5), who propose that when differences of opinion arise within a group, pressures to uniformity will arise (a) if the validity or "reality" of the opinion depends upon agreement with the group (essentially the same point as Asch's), or (b) if locomotion toward a group goal will be facilitated by uniformity within the group.

This emphasis upon the group, rather than simply upon the individual, leads one to expect a broader set of consequences from pressures to uniformity. Pressures to uniformity are seen as establishing: (a) a tendency on the part of each group member to change his own opinion to conform to that of the other group members, (b) a tendency to try to change the opinions of others, and (c) a tendency to redefine the boundaries of the group so as to exclude those holding deviate opinions. The relative magnitudes of these tendencies will depend on other conditions which need to be specified.

This general conception of the nature of the processes that produce conformity emerged from two early field studies conducted at the Research Center for Group Dynamics. It was also influenced to a considerable extent by the previous work of Newcomb (16) in which he studied the formation and change of social attitudes in a college community. The first field study, reported by Festinger, Schachter, and Back (7), traced the formation of social groups in a new student housing project. As each group developed, it displayed its own standards for its members. The extent of conformity to the standards of a particular group was found to be related directly to the degree of cohesiveness of that group as measured by sociometric choices. Moreover, those individuals who deviated from their own group's norms received fewer sociometric choices than those who conformed. A process of rejection for nonconformity had apparently set in. The second field study, reported by Coch and French (3), observed similar processes. This study was conducted in a textile factory and was concerned with conformity to production standards set by groups of workers. Here an individual worker's reaction to new work methods was found to depend upon the standards of his group and, here too, rejection for deviation was observed.

The next phase of this research consisted of a series of experiments with groups created in the laboratory. It was hoped thereby to be able to disentangle the complexity of variables that might exist in any field setting in order to understand better the operation of each. These experiments have been reported in various publications by Festinger, Back, Gerard, Hymovitch, Kelley, Raven, Schachter, and Thibaut (2, 6, 8, 9, 11, 20). We shall not attempt to describe these studies in detail, but draw upon them and other research in an effort to summarize the major conclusions.

First, a great deal of evidence has been accumulated to support the hypothesis that pressures to uniformity will be greater the more members want to remain in the group. In more attractive or cohesive groups, members attempt more to influence others and are more willing to accept influence from others. Note that here pressures to conformity are high in the very conditions where satisfaction from group membership is also high.

Second, there is a close relation between attempts to change the deviate and tendencies to reject him. If persistent attempts to change the deviate fail to produce conformity, then communication appears to cease between the majority and the deviate, and rejection of the deviate sets in. These two processes, moreover, are more intense the more cohesive the group. One of the early studies which documented the process of rejection was conducted by Schachter (20) on college students. It has recently been replicated by Emerson(4) on high school students, who found essentially the same process at work, but he discovered that among his high school students efforts to influence others continued longer, there was a greater readiness on the part of the majority to change, and there was a lower level of rejection within a limited period of time. Yet another study, conducted in Holland, Sweden, France, Norway, Belgium, Germany, and England, found the same tendency to reject deviates in all of these countries. This study, reported by Schachter, et al. (21), is a landmark in cross-cultural research.

Third, there is the question of what determines whether or not pressures to uniformity will arise with respect to any particular opinion, attitude, and behavior. In most groups there are no pressures to uniformity concerning the color of necktie worn by the members. Differences of opinion about the age of the earth probably would not lead to rejection in a poker club, but they might do so in certain fundamentalist church groups. The concept of *relevance* seems to be required to account for such variations in pressures to uniformity. And, if we ask, "relevance for what?" we are forced again to look at the group and especially at the goals of the group.

Schachter (20) has demonstrated, for example, that deviation on a given issue will result much more readily in rejection when that issue is relevant to the group's goals than when it is irrelevant. And, the principle of relevance seems to be necessary to account for the findings of a field study reported by Ross (19). Here attitudes of fraternity men toward restrictive admission policies were studied. Despite the fact that there was a consistent policy of exclusion in these fraternities, there was, surprisingly, little evidence for the existence of pressures toward uniformity of attitudes. When, however, a field experiment was conducted in which the distribution of actual opinions for each fraternity house was reported to a meeting of house members together with a discussion of the relevance of these opinions for fraternity policy, attitudes then tended to change to conform to the particular modal position of each house. Presumably the experimental treatment made uniformity of attitude instrumental to group locomotion where it had not been so before.

SOURCES OF HETEROGENEITY

We have seen that pressures to uniformity are stronger the more cohesive the group. Shall we conclude from this that strong, need-satisfying, cohesive groups must always produce uniformity on matters that are important to the group? We believe not. We cannot, however, cite much convincing evidence since research has focused to date primarily upon the sources of pressures to uniformity and has ignored the conditions which produce heterogeneity. Without suggesting, then, that we can give final answers, let us indicate some of the possible sources of heterogeneity.

Group Standards about Uniformity. It is important, first, to make a distinction between conformity and uniformity. A group might have a value that everyone should be as different from everyone else as possible. Conformity to this value, then, would result not in uniformity of behavior but in nonuniformity. Such a situation often arises in therapy groups or training groups where it is possible to establish norms which place a high value upon "being different" and upon tolerating deviant behavior. Conformity to this value is presumably greater the more cohesive the group and the more it is seen as relevant to the group's objectives. Unfortunately, very little is known about the origin and operation of group standards about conformity itself. We doubt that the pressure to uniformity, which arises from the need for "social reality" and for group locomotion can simply be obliterated by invoking a group standard of tolerance, but a closer look at such processes as those of group decision making will be required before a deep understanding of this problem can be achieved.

Freedom to Deviate. A rather different source of heterogeneity has been suggested by Kelley and Shapiro (12). They reason that the more an individual feels accepted by the other members of the group, the more ready he should be to deviate from the beliefs of the majority under conditions where objectively correct deviation would be in the group's best interest. They designed an experiment to test this hypothesis. The results, while not entirely clear because acceptance led to greater cohesiveness, tend to support this line of reasoning.

It has been suggested by some that those in positions of leadership are freer to deviate from group standards than are those of lesser status. Just the opposite conclusion has been drawn by others. Clearly, further research into group properties which generate freedom to deviate from majority pressures is needed.

Subgroup Formation. Festinger and Thibaut (8) have shown that lower group-wide pressures to uniformity of opinion result when members of a group perceive that the group is composed of persons differing in interest and knowledge. Under these conditions subgroups may easily develop with a resulting heterogeneity within the group as a whole though with uniformity within each subgroup. This conclusion is consistent with Asch's (1) finding that the presence of a partner for a deviate greatly strengthens his tendency to be independent. One might suspect that such processes, though achieving temporarily a greater heterogeneity, would result in a schismatic subgroup conflict.

Positions and Roles. A more integrative achievement of heterogeneity seems to arise through the process of role differentiation. Established groups are usually differentiated according to "positions" with special functions attached to each. The occupant of the position has certain behaviors prescribed for him by the others in the group. These role prescriptions differ, moreover, from one position to another, with the result that conformity to them produces heterogeneity within the group. A group function, which might otherwise be suppressed by pressures to uniformity, may be preserved by the establishment of a position whose responsibility is to perform the function.

Hall (10) has recently shown that social roles can be profitably conceived in the context of conformity to group pressures. He reasoned that pressures to uniformity of prescriptions concerning the behavior of the occupant of a position and pressures on the occupant to conform to these prescriptions should be greater the more cohesive the group. A study of the role of aircraft commander in bomber crews lends strong support to this conception.

MORE THAN ONE GROUP

Thus far our analysis has proceeded as though the individual were a member of only one group. Actually we recognize that he is, and has been, a member of many groups. In one of our current research projects we are finding that older adolescents can name from 20 to 40 "important groups and persons that influence my opinions and behavior in decision situations." Indeed, some personality theorists hold that personality should be viewed as an "internal society" made up of representations of the diverse group relationships which the individual now has and has had. According to this view, each individual has a unique internal society and makes his own personal synthesis of the values and behavior preferences generated by these affiliations.

The various memberships of an individual may relate to one another in various ways and produce various consequences for the individual. A past group may exert internal pressures toward conformity which are in conflict with a present group. Two contemporaneous groups may have expectations for the person which are incompatible. Or an individual may hold a temporary membership (the situation of a foreign student, for example) and be faced with current conformity pressures which if accepted will make it difficult to readjust when returning to his more permanent memberships.

This constant source of influence from other memberships toward deviancy of every member of every group requires that each group take measures to preserve its integrity. It should be noted, however, that particular deviancy pressures associated with a given member may be creative or destructive when evaluated in terms of the integrity and productivity of the group, and conformity pressures from the group may be supportive or disruptive of the integrity of the individual.

Unfortunately there has been little systematic research on these aspects of multiple group membership. We can only indicate two sets of observations concerning (a) the intrapersonal processes resulting from multiple membership demands, and (b) the effects on group processes of the deviancy pressures which arise from the multiple membership status of individual members.

Marginal Membership. Lewin, (13), in his discussion of adolescence and of minority group membership, has analyzed some of the psychological effects on the person of being "between two groups" without a firm anchorage in either one. He says: "The transition from childhood to adulthood may be a rather sudden shift (for instance, in some of the primitive societies), or it may occur gradually in a setting where children and adults are not sharply separated groups. In the case of the so-called 'adolescent difficulties,' however, a third state of affairs is often prevalent: children and adults constitute two clearly defined groups; the adolescent does not wish any longer to belong to the children's group and, at the same time, knows that he is not really accepted in the adult group. He has a position similar to what is called in sociology the 'marginal man' . . . a person who stands on the boundary between two groups. He does not belong to either of them, or at least he is not sure of his belongingness in either of them" (p. 143). Lewin goes on to point out that there are characteristic maladjustive behavior patterns resulting from this unstable membership situation: high tension, shifts between extremes of behavior, high sensitivity, and rejection of low status members of both groups. This situation, rather than fostering strong individuality, makes belonging to closely knit, loyalty-demanding groups very attractive. Dependency and acceptance are a welcome relief. Probably most therapy groups have a number of members who are seeking relief from marginality.

Overlapping Membership. There is quite a different type of situation where the person does have a firm anchorage in two or more groups but where the group standards are not fully compatible. Usually the actual conflict arises when the person is physically present in one group but realizes that he also belongs to other groups to which he will return in the near or distant future. In this sense, the child moves between his family group and his school group every day. The member of a therapy group has some sort of time perspective of "going back" to a variety of other groups between each meeting of the therapy group.

In their study of the adjustment of foreign students both in this country and after returning home, Watson and Lippitt (26) observed four different ways in which individuals cope with this problem of overlapping membership.

(1). Some students solved the problem by "living in the present" at all times. When they were in the American culture all of their energy and attention was directed to being an acceptable member of this group. They avoided conflict within themselves by minimizing thought about and contact with the other group "back home." When they returned to the other group they used the same type of solution, quickly shifting behavior and ideas to fit back into the new present group. Their behavior appeared quite inconsistent, but it was a consistent approach to solving their problem of multiple membership.

(2). Other individuals chose to keep their other membership the dominant one while in this country. They were defensive and rejective every time the present group seemed to promote values and to expect behavior which they felt might not be acceptable to the other group "back home." The strain of maintaining this orientation was relieved by turning every situation into a "black and white" comparison and adopting a consistently rejective posture toward the present, inferior group. This way of adjusting required a considerable amount of distorting of present and past realities, but the return to the other group was relatively easy.

(3). Others reacted in a sharply contrasting way by identifying wholeheartedly with the present group and by rejecting the standards of the other group as incorrect or inferior at the points of conflict. They were, of course, accepted by the present group, but when they returned home they met rejection or felt alienated from the standards of the group (even when they felt accepted).

(4). Some few individuals seemed to achieve a more difficult but also more creative solution. They attempted to regard membership in both groups as desirable. In order to succeed in this effort, they had to be more realistic about perceiving the inconsistencies between the group expectations and to struggle to make balanced judgments about the strong and weak points of each group. Besides taking this more objective approach to evaluation, these persons worked on problems of how the strengths of one group might be interpreted and utilized by the other group. They were taking roles of creative deviancy in both groups, but attempting to make their contributions in such a way as to be accepted as loyal and productive members. They found ways of using each group membership as a resource for contributing to the welfare of the other group. Some members of each group were of course threatened by this readiness and ability to question the present modal ways of doing things in the group.

Thus it seems that the existence of multiple group memberships creates difficult problems both for the person and for the group. But there are also potentialities and supports for the development of creative individuality in this situation, and there are potentialities for group growth and achievement in the fact that the members of any group are also members of other groups with different standards.

SOME CONCLUSIONS

Let us return now to the question raised at the beginning of this paper. How should we think of the relation between individuals and groups? If we accept the assumption that individuals and groups are both important social realities, we can then ask a pair of important questions. What kind of effects do groups have on the emotional security and creative productivity of the individual? What kinds of effects do individuals have on the morale and creative productivity of the group? In answering these questions it is important to be alerted to both good and bad effects. Although the systematic evidence from research does not begin to provide full answers to these questions, we have found evidence which tends to support the following general statements.

Strong groups do exert strong influences on members toward conformity. These conformity pressures, however, may be directed toward uniformity of thinking and behavior, or they may foster heterogeneity.

Acceptance of these conformity pressures, toward uniformity or heterogeneity, may satisfy the emotional needs of some members and frustrate others. Similarly, it may support the potential creativity of some members and inhibit that of others.

From their experiences of multiple membership and their personal synthesis of these experiences, individuals do have opportunities to achieve significant bases of individuality.

Because each group is made up of members who are loyal members of other groups and who have unique individual interests, each group must continuously cope with deviancy tendencies of the members. These tendencies may represent a source of creative improvement in the life of the group or a source of destructive disruption.

The resolution of these conflicting interests does not seem to be the strengthening of individuals and the weakening of groups, or the strengthening of groups and the weakening of individuals, but rather a strengthening of both by qualitative improvements in the nature of interdependence between integrated individuals and cohesive groups.

BIBLIOGRAPHY

1. Asch, S. E. *Social Psychology*. New York: Prentice Hall Inc., 1952.
2. Back, K. W. Influence Through Social Communication. *J. Abn. & Soc. Psychol*. 46: 1951, 9-23.
3. Coch, L., and French, J. R. P. Overcoming Resistance to Change. *Hum. Relat*. 1: 1948, 512-32.
4. Emerson, R. M. Deviation and Rejection: An Experimental Replication. *Am. Sociol. Rev*. 19: 1954, 688-93.
5. Festinger, L. Informal Social Communication. *Psychol. Rev*. 57: 1950, 271-292.

6. Festinger, L.; Gerard, H. B.; Hymovitch, B.; Kelley, H. H.; and Raven, B. The Influence Process in the Presence of Extreme Deviates. *Hum. Relat.* 5: 1952, 327-46.

7. Festinger, L.; Schachter, S.; and Back, K. *Social Pressures in Informal Groups.* New York: Harper & Row, Publishers, 1950.

8. Festinger, L. and Thibaut, J. Interpersonal Communication in Small Groups. *J. Abn. & Soc. Psychol.,* 46: 1951, 92-99.

9. Gerard, H. B. The Effect of Different Dimensions of Disagreement on the Communication Process in Small Groups. *Hum. Relat.* 6: 1953, 249-71.

10. Hall, R. L. Social Influence on the Aircraft Commander's Role. *Am. Sociol. Rev.* 20: 1955, 292-99.

11. Kelley, H. H. Communication in Experimentally Created Hierarchies. *Hum. Relat.* 4: 1951, 39-56.

12. Kelley, H. H. and Shapiro, M. M. An Experiment on Conformity to Group Norms Where Conformity Is Detrimental to Group Achievement. *Am. Sociol. Rev.* 19: 1954, 667-77.

13. Lewin, K. *Field Theory in Social Science.* New York: Harper & Row, Publishers, 1951.

14. Lewin, K. Studies in Group Decision. In: *Group Dynamics: Research and Theory,* ed. D. Cartwright and A. Zander. Evanston: Row, Peterson, 1953.

15. Lewin, K.; Lippitt, R.; and White, R. Patterns of Aggressive Behavior in Experimentally Created "Social Climates." *J. Soc. Psychol.* 10: 1939, 271-99.

16. Newcomb, T. M. *Personality and Social Change.* New York: Dryden, 1943.

17. Parsons, T. *Essays in Sociological Theory.* rev. ed. Glencoe: Free Press, 1954.

18. Roethlisberger, F. J. and Dickson, W. J. *Management and the Worker.* Cambridge: Harvard University Press, 1939.

19. Ross, I. Group Standards Concerning the Admission of Jews. *Soc. Prob.* 2: 1955, 133-40.

20. Schachter, S. Deviation, Rejection, and Communication. *J. Abn. & Soc. Psychol.* 46: 1951, 190-207.

21. Schachter, S., et al. Cross-cultural Experiments on Threat and Rejection. *Hum. Relat.* 7: 1954, 403-39.

22. Seashore, S. E. *Group Cohesiveness in the Industrial Group.* Ann Arbor: Institute for Social Research, 1954.

23. Sherif, M. *The Psychology of Social Norms.* New York: Harper & Row, Publishers, 1936.

24. Stanton, A. H. and Schwartz, M. S.: *The Mental Hospital.* New York: Basic Books, 1954.

25. Tocqueville, A. *Democracy in America,* Vol. 1. New York: Alfred A. Knopf, 1945 (original publication, 1835).

26. Watson, J. and Lippitt, R. *Learning Across Cultures.* Ann Arbor: Institute for Social Research, 1955.

William C. Schutz

INTERPERSONAL UNDERWORLD

Although the businessman must spend a major part of his time dealing with other people, he has in the past had little help in overcoming the difficulties that inevitably arise when people get together. The terms which have been used to describe these problems—terms like "disciplinary problems," "human relations troubles," or the currently popular "communications difficulties"—have served only to hide the real difficulties, for they are descriptions of symptoms. The real causes must be sought at a deeper level; they lie in interpersonal relations.

In every meeting of two or more people two levels of interaction occur. One is the overt—the play that is apparently being played. The other is the covert—like a ballet going on in back of the performance on the interpersonal stage—a subtle struggle for attention and status, for control and influence, and for liking and warmth. This ballet influences the performance by pushing the overt players into unusual postures and making them say and do unusual things. Thus, the objective, hardheaded executive is overtly very resistant to a splendid idea suggested by the brash young fellow who may someday replace him. But this example is much too obvious. The ballet's effect on the actors is usually more subtle.

The importance of these covert factors can hardly be overestimated. The productivity of any particular group is profoundly influenced by them. One of the main functions of this article is to attempt to dispel the idea that strong interpersonal differences existing within a group setting can be effectively handled by ignoring them—as if by the magic of closing your eyes you could make problems go away. Rather, interpersonal problems must be understood and dealt with. If ignored, they are usually transformed so that they are not expressed directly as open hostility but find their expression through the task behavior of the group. Failure to allow these group processes to work in a direct fashion will decrease the group's productivity.

The types of behavior that result from interpersonal difficulties are various. In many cases it is difficult to recognize their connection with interpersonal relations in the work situation. To illustrate some of these more subtle

Abridged from William C. Schutz, "Interpersonal Underworld," *Harvard Business Review*, 36 (July-August, 1958): 123-35. © 1958 by the President and Fellows of Harvard College; all rights reserved. Reprinted by permission.

connections, I shall describe several behaviors resulting from, or symptomatic of, interpersonal difficulties, and then present a sampling of situations giving rise to these behaviors.

BEHAVIORAL SYMPTOMS

Generally, interpersonal problems lead individuals to resist each other and each other's influence in various overt, but more often covert, ways. Each individual may oppose, delay, fail to support, or sabotage another. The mechanisms to be discussed here are largely covert, or unconscious; the individual does these things without being aware of his intention to resist or obstruct.

Communications Problems

These days "communications problems" are greatly emphasized as a source of industrial difficulty. This emphasis, however, seems misplaced. For one thing, problems which are caused by communications are due not to *inadequate* communication but to *too adequate* communication, since what is transmitted most accurately between people is how they feel rather then what they say. Thus, if the boss really feels his research scientist is not very important, that feeling will be communicated to the scientist much more readily than any words that pass between them. For another thing, communications difficulties are primarily the *result* of interpersonal difficulties; they are seldom themselves a primary *cause* of problems. Resisting another person is often accomplished through the medium of communication. Thus:

A person may find it difficult to understand what is being said, or, sometimes, actually not hear what is said. Often a person feels confused; he just cannot follow all the things that are going on. Another sign of resistance is incoherent speech, mumbling, not bothering to make a point clear, or not making sure that the listener has heard. All of these occurrences impede the process of verbal communication.

Resistance may also take the form of forgetting to pick up a message that was to have been left on one's desk. Or one may forget to mail a memo or leave a message of importance to someone else; or the message may be garbled, ambiguous, or actually contain a factual error. Similarly, misreading and misinterpretation increase greatly in situations of interpersonal strife.

Individually, these behaviors all appear to be simple human failings and, indeed, in many cases may be only that. However, it is always a good bet, especially when the incidents recur, that they are unconsciously motivated by interpersonal differences. In short, interpersonal problems frequently find expression through the obstruction of valid communication. Excessive communications problems can usually be interpreted as a symptom of interpersonal trouble.

Loss of Motivation

Another expression of interpersonal problems is the loss of motivation to work on a task. In innumerable ways the individual's work becomes ineffective because he lacks the desire to produce. The accumulation of many minor inefficiencies amounts to the equivalent of losing the services of a group member or a part of one or more members' resources and abilities. For example:

If a group member is supposed to look up some information which is needed for other members of the group to complete their work, he may just miss getting to the company library before Friday night closing time. Therefore he will have to wait over the weekend and, in the meantime, hold up two other people who are waiting for his report. Or perhaps some morning he will oversleep when he should be at the committee meeting.

Another individual does only what is required of him and nothing extra. If he works from nine to five, he will leave promptly at five, for he considers his work a chore, a task to be accomplished and nothing more. If something goes wrong because of someone else's error, he will make no effort to compensate for it. If he is not very busy and someone else needs a hand, he will not lend it. All in all, he will do only the very minimum required to retain his job.

Another manifestation of a man's loss of motivation is a sudden realization that his outside interests and commitments are much stronger than he had thought when the group began. He finds that he has conflicting meetings and other things to do which force him to leave meetings early, to arrive late, or perhaps even to miss one. Or he may have reports to write that prevent him from coming or working for this committee.

Chronic absenteeism or lateness is still another manifestation of an interpersonal difficulty. Perhaps a group member has an actual illness or some commitment at home that prevents his coming; there may be any one of a large number of reasons for his absence or lateness, many of which are rational. But these situations may happen too often to make the whole pattern a rational one. If a man has a meeting and the snow is heavy, it may be that he cannot make the meeting because of the traffic situation; but if it were a meeting which he really wanted to attent, the snow would not be a great enough obstacle to prevent him from going.

Also, a loss of motivation very frequently expresses itself in an actual feeling of physical tiredness. Handling emotional and interpersonal difficulties is hard work, especially if it involves holding back certain strong feelings. This work actually makes the individual so tired that he has great difficulty in bringing himself to work and to persevere on a job once it is begun. It often happens that an individual who feels completely exhausted in one part of his work situation miraculously perks up when a new task comes along or when he goes home to a more enjoyable activity. Again, this is not a case of deliberate malingering. The person actually feels tired. When the conflict-inducing situation is removed, the tiredness lifts.

In general, what is happening is that a person suddenly finds that other groups in which his interpersonal relations are happier are more important than the present group, and hence his motivation to work in the situation is reduced.

A man will seek a situation in which, he is happiest and will attempt to avoid unpleasant situations as far as possible. In other words, he escapes the situation by withdrawing his involvement.

Indiscriminate Opposition

Another category of responses to interpersonal difficulties involves direct blockage of action. This mechanism is often quite overt and conscious, but it likewise has many covert and unconscious forms.

A symptom of a bad relationship is resistance to suggestions. It may happen that an individual in the group makes suggestions which are opposed by another member regardless of their merit. As soon as the first member begins to talk, the second man-because he feels hostile to the first—feels a surge of resistance or reluctance to accept anything he is going to hear. This is, of course, not beneficial from the standpoint of the group, because a very good suggestion may be rejected for irrelevant personal reasons.

The manner in which such opposition is manifested is often very subtle. If an antagonist makes a suggestion, rather than use direct attack an individual may say smilingly, "That sounds interesting, but perhaps if we tried this other method it would be even more effective." Another technique is to postpone a decision on an opponent's suggestion. The parliamentary procedure of "tabling" is one formal method, as are setting up investigating committees, considering other matters first, offering amendments, or being unavailable for a meeting to decide on the suggestion. Undoubtedly the experienced businessman can extend this list indefinitely. Again, it is important to note that, although the techniques are often deliberately used, they are perhaps used even more often without the user's awareness of his motivation.

Operational Problems

There are several ailments of total group functioning that are symptomatic of interpersonal difficulties. In most cases, difficulty in reaching decisions is a sure indication of interpersonal strife. This usually implies that the group is unable to tell anybody *no*, since to make such a decision involves saying *yes* to the proponents of another view. Compromises are then put through that satisfy neither side and that certainly do not accomplish the task as effectively as the group could under optimal conditions. The compromise is really one between the individuals who are in conflict, and not a compromise, essentially, of the issues of the case.

Another symptom of interpersonal problems in a group is inefficient division of labor. If the relationships among the men are poor, difficulties arise as soon as it comes time to assign different roles and divide the labor so that the group can operate more effectively. Strongly held interpersonal feelings prevent the group from saying *no* to somebody who wants to be in a particular position in the group but whom the other members consider unsuited to that position. This person may, therefore, be put into the role anyway, to the detriment of the functioning of the group. For example:

In one group of marketing personnel there was a man of clearly outstanding abilities regarding ideas for the solution of the group's problem. Because of his strength and dominance in the group he was accepted as the leader. One result of this was that he was not in a very good position to express his ideas, since as the leader he had to assume a conciliator role; thus, his virtue as a member who could contribute to the substance of the group's task was diminished.

A second result was that he could not act as a good administrator, that is, could not effectively coordinate the efforts of the other group members. So, by not being able to say *no* to this person, or by not being able to discuss more openly the best use to be made of his abilities, the group lost in two very important ways.

Another frequent instance of this difficulty is putting a man who is extremely capable in a subordinate role, with the result that his abilities cannot be utilized by the group. Thus:

In a different group the phenomenon opposite to the previous example occurred, resulting in equal injury to the group's performance. Because of personal hostility from several other members the most competent man was relegated to the role of secretary. There his time was consumed taking minutes, and his stellar abilities were wasted.

In general, then, ability to place men properly within a group is one indication of good basic interpersonal relations, while inability is a sign that there must be something wrong among the people that prevents them from using their resources optimally.

Task Distortions

Interpersonal difficulties are almost invariably reflected in a group's performance on its task, although at times these effects are more obvious than at others. Here are three examples of interpersonal problems being expressed directly in work behavior, taken from groups of eight graduate students working on actual industrial problems at the Harvard Business School:

One of these groups was working on the problem of bringing out a new product for a major manufacturer. The members developed a marketing strategy for this product in which the big stress was on the image that the product would present to consumers. In fact, they put so much stress on the image that they neglected certain other factors.

My observations of this group in operation indicated the reason for the inefficient emphasis. From the beginning certain men were assigned by the group, not to the actual task, but to the presentation to be made to the company at the completion of the work. Some of them became very concerned with the impression *they* would make—in fact more concerned with this than with the impression the product would make. Therefore, they unconsciously sought the aspect of their assigned task which would allow them to work on their interpersonal problem and anxiety and concentrated on it to the consequent neglect of other factors which were also important.

Another group evolved a marketing strategy for bringing out a family of products. On examination, it appeared that this product family was not particularly well integrated. In addition, there was reason to believe that a single product would be more effective.

From interviews with the individual members and from observations of their working as a group, it became clear that the family of products was a compromise solution. Certain members of the group had wanted one product; others had wanted a different one. Instead of trying to work out these differences of opinion in terms of marketing considerations, the group decided implicitly to bring out the whole family as a solution to their interpersonal problem.

Still another group devised a marketing solution with a heavy emphasis on a decentralized distribution system. But the company representatives immediately wondered about the wisdom of using such autonomous distributors, since company-hired distributors should lead to more profits. The group was at a loss to justify its own suggestion.

Again, observations of the group throughout the term indicated a possible reason. The group had had a serious interpersonal blowup at one point, and the members had decided to go their separate ways. The result of this decision was autonomous operation by the individual members of the group. Apparently the group members were unconsciously influenced by the fact that their group could operate more effectively as autonomous individuals.

Interpersonal problems are often worked out on some aspect of the task that closely approximates the relationship which is of concern to the group (company to dealer, company to consumer, and so forth). In this way the tensions generated by the interpersonal problems can be relieved by symbolically displacing them into the work situation. The drawback of this phenomenon is that, although it appears that the group is very task-oriented, its work may in fact be quite inappropriate and inefficient at many points.

COMMON ISSUES

We have looked at some of the behaviors which may be considered symptomatic of inadequate interpersonal relations. Certain problem situations that occur in group and interpersonal dealings with great frequency generate these symptoms. As an illustration of the nature of the problems and some of their vicissitudes, I shall now discuss three of them.

Consensus for Decision

In every group, sooner or later, a decision-making apparatus must be agreed on. Whether it be consensus, majority rule, unanimity, or any other method, there must be some *modus operandi* for the group to make decisions. By consensus I mean, here, that everyone in the group is agreed that a certain course of action is best for the group, regardless of whether or not he individually agrees with it. Ordinarily, if the group does not have consensus and a decision goes through, the group pays. For instance:

Let us suppose that a group, perhaps a committee, has gotten together with the task of deciding a particular issue. The issue has come to a vote, and the vote is fairly decisive, say six to two. The two people in the minority, however, do not really feel that they have had an opportunity to express their feelings about the issue. Although they are committed to go along with the decision, they have an inner reluctance to do so. This covert reluctance may manifest itself in any of the symptoms already mentioned. Perhaps the most common symptom is a loss of interest, although this situation could be expected to give rise to any of them.

The question of consensus is central in decision making. In a deeper sense, consensus means that everyone in a group feels that the group understands his position and his feelings about it; and he feels, then, that the group should take a particular course of action even though he does not personally agree. If the individual is not allowed to voice his own feelings and reasons for voting against the particular issue, he will, at least unconsciously, resist the efficient functioning of the group from that point on. If consensus is not required, decisions can often be made more quickly (for example, by majority rule or by fiat), but delay will probably result, due to the unacknowledged members having various ways of resisting once the decision has been made and the action is undertaken.

The ability to detect a lack of consensus is, of course, a very important attribute for a group leader. A few rules of thumb might be of help here. The clue is that it is very difficult to find out whether there is a consensus unless each person is allowed to speak; for lack of disagreement does not necessarily indicate that the group has consensus. Frequently people simply are reluctant to raise their objections. However, if each member is asked separately whether or not he assents to the issue, the group leader can usually pick up objections:

> He may be able to spot disagreement by noticing such things as changes in tone of voice. In one group the leader asked if everyone agreed on a suggested course of action. As he went around the room he got the following responses: *yes, yes, yes, yes, yes, okay.* This leader, being fairly astute, immediately began to question the man who had said *okay,*
> because this man apparently could not quite bring himself to be like the other members of the group with regard to this decision. This inability is usually a good indication of an objection. The individual is reluctant to object directly because of the weight of all the other members disagreeing with him.
> After this man had been quizzed for a while, it became clear that he did have a strong objection. Once he was allowed to talk it out, he went along with the group and was quite willing to say *yes* and, in fact, to pitch in and work with the decision that was finally made.
> Another good indicator of lack of consensus is any attempt by a member to postpone a decision by further discussion or by further action of some kind. Comments like, "What is it we are voting on?" or "Weren't we supposed to discuss something else first?" or "I have no objection to that, but . . . " all indicate that the individual is not yet ready to cast a positive vote for a given decision. He probably has an objection that ought to be brought out into the open and discussed.

Allowing the objector to raise his point for discussion is not just a hollow gesture. The objector will be more likely to go along with the final decision—or he may eventually carry the day because he reflects some objections that other people had but were not aware of. Whether the group actually changes its vote or not, it will be more likely to reach a correct decision. This opportunity for the group to discuss a previously covert factor is very important for its effectiveness.

Authority Problem

Another group phenomenon that leads to reduced effectiveness concerns the relationship of the group members to the leader of the group. (The term *leader* will be used loosely to mean the person who is, in the eyes of the group members, supposed to head the group—usually a formal leader, a designated person who has a higher title.) It is the nature of such relationships that members of the group have ambivalent feelings toward the authority figure—both positive and negative feelings. The negative feelings can be particularly disturbing since it usually is hard for people to express such feelings directly, because their jobs may be in jeopardy or because they feel that they should not attack an authority figure.

Since the hostility must be expressed, however, they often transfer it to another member of the group. Some other member, usually one with characteristics similar to those disliked in the leader, will be attacked more than he realistically should be for his behavior in the group. He will be attacked not only for what he does, but also because the attack that the group would like to level toward the leader is displaced onto him. The term *scapegoat* is often used for this person. For example, if the group members are dissatisfied because the leader is not giving sufficient direction to the group, the dissatisfaction may be vented toward a silent or nonparticipating member, the member in the group who comes closest to having the characteristic of the leader which the group members do not like. For example:

> In one marketing group the leader offered the group very little direction, far less than most members would have liked. Subsequently, everyone began to get very angry with one group member who did not say much and who occasionally missed meetings because of his other commitments. The group attacked him for his lack of interest and unwillingness to contribute to the group.
>
> A key to what was really happening is found in the fact that he was actually quite interested and was contributing a great deal, thus making the attack somewhat undeserved; but significantly, the characteristics which angered the group members were precisely those that covertly irritated them about the leader. Apparently they displaced their aggression from the leader, whom they felt they could not attack directly, onto a group member who had similar attributes.

This same mechanism operates when the boss is too *authoritarian*. Somebody in the group who has similar tendencies will be severely attacked, again as a displacement of the attack they would like to level at the boss.

With regard to dealing with this phenomenon, perhaps the most useful thing to be said is that there are times when a leader, in order to allow a group to operate more effectively, must himself become the scapegoat. If he can absorb some of the hostility that is really meant for him or perhaps in some cases even absorb some of the hostility meant for other group members, he can be most useful in helping a group to function more effectively. Of course, in order to do this the leader must be aware that the hostility is not necessarily directed at him personally; it is just an inevitable consequence of group activity that hostility does arise. If he can absorb the hostility directly, it does not have to be deflected into the group where it is most destructive to the group and to the group's ability to fulfill its purposes. An important part of a leader's role is to be a scapegoat occasionally in order that the group may proceed and operate more effectively. This situation brings to mind an old saying, "A good king is one whose subjects prosper."

The Problem Member

Another frequently occurring group difficulty is the presence of a problem member, one of the most difficult of all interpersonal problems for a group to deal with. Problem members are of two main types—the overactive member and the underactive member. Either can disrupt group functioning, and both are usually difficult to handle.

The overactive problem member dominates the group's attention far more than his abilities warrant. The difficulties arise partly because the apparent intensity of his feelings leads to a general reluctance of the group to hurt the individual while at the same time they cannot curtail his destructive activities. To illustrate what can happen in such a situation:

> In one five-man group of military personnel working on a series of tactical problems, Mac immediately took over control of the group. Because he was reasonably competent and highly forceful, he went unchallenged for several meetings. The other group members were not very compatible, so they had a difficult time handling Mac. Gradually some members began losing interest in the group until one discussion of a very trivial topic, the postal rates from Washington to Chicago, came up in one of their rest periods. The exchange that followed was amazing in that Mac was attacked severely and at length by the other group members for his dogmatically stated opinion about postal rates. The group used this topic to vent their stored-up feelings toward Mac. By this time, however, the group had no resources to cope with these strong feelings, and it quickly disintegrated after the conflict.

The optimal solution to the problem represented by this member is to handle him in such a way that he can be retained in the group and his resources made use of and still not be allowed to obstruct the group's functioning:

> Another group had this problem with Bob. But this group quickly deposed Bob and set up a leader of considerably less intellect but with superior coordinating abilities. For a short time after they had deposed Bob the group made sure he realized he was not going to run the group; then they gradually allowed him back into the group by paying more attention to his

ideas. Finally, after about ten meetings, his ideas were highly influential and sought by the group, although he was not allowed to dominate. In this way the group took care of the problem presented by an overactive member and was still able to utilize his abilities. This is an ideal solution and the sign of a strong, compatible group.

Someone who will not become integrated into the group also poses a problem for the group. The lack of commitment of this member, perhaps even a lack of willingness to work, constitutes a serious group problem. One solution is to eject the member from the group. This is a solution only insofar as it removes the source of a difficulty; it does not allow the group to utilize the man's abilities. The problem member often serves a useful function by enabling other members to direct their hostility toward him, so that they do not have to deal with the real differences among themselves. Thus, it is not unusual that if a chronically negative member is absent, the group finds that it still has disagreements.

FRAMEWORK FOR BEHAVIOR

Now that I have described examples of several interpersonal problem situations and various reactions to them, I shall present a brief outline of a theory of interpersonal behavior. In order to deal with interpersonal behavior it is necessary to have an understanding of the *general* principles of this behavior, since formulas for handling *specific* situations are of limited value at best. The following theory is by no means the only one extant in psychological literature, but it is offered as a possible framework for understanding phenomena of the type under discussion here.

Interpersonal Needs

The basis for evolving this theory of interpersonal behavior is the individual's *fundamental interpersonal relations orientation* or, to abbreviate, FIRO. The basic assumption of this approach is that people need people. Every human being, because he lives in a society, must establish an equilibrium between himself and his human environment — just as he must establish an equilibrium between himself and the physical world. This social nature of man gives rise to certain interpersonal needs, which he must satisfy to some degree while avoiding threat to himself. Although each individual has different intensities of need and different mechanisms for handling them, people have three basic interpersonal needs in common:

The Need for Inclusion. This is the need to maintain a satisfactory relation between the self and other people with respect to interaction or belongingness. Some people like to be with other people all the time; they want to belong to organizations, to interact, to mingle. Other people seek much less contact; they prefer to be alone, to interact minimally, to stay out of groups, to maintain privacy.

If a continuum were to be drawn between these two extremes, every person could be placed at a point (or region) at which he feels most comfortable. Thus, to a certain degree each individual is trying to belong to a group, but he is also trying to maintain a certain amount of privacy. From the other point of view he wishes to some degree to have people initiate interaction toward him through invitations and the like, and also wishes to some degree that people would leave him alone. For each dimension these two aspects may be distinguished: (1) the behavior he initiates toward others, his expressed behavior; and (2) the behavior he prefers others to express toward him, his wanted behavior. This distinction will prove valuable in the discussion of compatibility.

The Need for Control. This is the need to maintain a satisfactory relation between oneself and other people with regard to power and influence. In other words, every individual has a need to control his situation to some degree, so that his environment can be predictable for him. Ordinarily this amounts to controlling other people, because other people are the main agents which threaten him and create an unpredictable and uncontrollable situation. This need for control varies from those who want to control their entire environment, including all the people around them, to those who want to control no one in any situation, no matter how appropriate controlling them would be.

Here, again, everyone varies as to the degree to which he wants to control others. In addition, everyone varies with respect to the degree to which he wants to be controlled by other people, from those who want to be completely controlled and are dependent on others for making decisions for them to those who want to be controlled under no conditions.

The Need for Affection. This is the need to maintain a satisfactory relation between the self and other people with regard to love and affection. In the business setting this need is seldom made overt. It takes the form of friendship. In essence, affection is a relationship between two people only, a dyadic relationship. At one extreme individuals like very close, personal relationships with each individual they meet. At the other extreme are those who like their personal relationships to be quite impersonal and distant, perhaps friendly but not close and intimate.

Again between these two extremes everyone has a level of intimacy which is most comfortable for him. From the other side, each individual prefers that others make overtures to him in a way that indicates a certain degree of closeness.

To clarify the various orientations in these three areas, Exhibit 1 presents the extreme positions taken on each of the dimensions. Everyone fits somewhere between these two extremes, most of them in the middle.

EXHIBIT 1. **Extreme Types on the Three
Interpersonal Dimensions**

Expressed Behavior		*Dimension*	*Wanted Behavior*	
Extreme High Oversocial	Extreme Low Undersocial	Inclusion	Extreme High Social- Compliant	Extreme Low Countersocial
Autocrat Overpersonal	Abdicrat Underpersonal	Control Affection	Submissive Personal- Compliant	Rebellious Counterpersonal

GROUP COMPATIBILITY

This theory of interpersonal relations can be very useful to businessmen in determining the compatibility of the members of a group. If at the outset we can choose a group of people who can work together harmoniously, we shall go far toward avoiding situations where a group's efforts are wasted in interpersonal conflicts.

Our theoretical framework is designed to handle this problem. Suppose we consider in more detail the two aspects for each one of the three interpersonal dimensions. One aspect is what we *do* with relation to other people; let us call this "e" for *expressed* behavior. The second is what we *want* from other people, how we want them to act toward us; let us call this "w" for *wanted* behavior. Then we can use "e" and "w" to try to find out how people will relate to each other in the *inclusion* dimension ("I"), the *control* dimension ("C") and the *affection* dimension ("A"), as shown schematically in Exhibit 2.

EXHIBIT 2. **Schema of Interpersonal Behaviors**

Expressed Behavior	*Dimension*	*Wanted Behavior*
I initiate interaction with people	Inclusion	I want to be included
I control people	Control	I want people to control me
I act close and personal toward people	Affection	I want people to get close and personal to me

If we make a ten-point scale, from zero to nine, and say that in each of the two aspects of the three dimensions everyone has some propensity, some preferred behavior, we can characterize each person by six scores: e^I, w^I, e^C, w^C, e^A, w^A.

In the course of my research I have developed a questionnaire, called FIRO-B (the "B" refers to *behavior),* comprising a check list of 54 statements designed to measure an individual's propensities in each of these six categories. . . The resulting scores for each need area can be plotted on a diagram, as in Exhibit 3.

Two Kinds

Note that in Exhibit 3 there are two diagonals, which may be used to explain two different kinds of compatibility—"originator compatibility" (oK) and "interchange compatibility" (xK). Individuals can be located on these diagonals from their scores on FIRO-B.

In popular literature there are at least two well-known and apparently contradictory maxims relating to the bases of compatibility: "Opposites attract," and "Birds of a feather flock together." Considering the diagonals on Exhibit III might aid us in coming to a sensible resolution of these maxims, since there seems to be some truth in each of them:

Originator Diagonal. Let us take an example in the control dimension and consider the lower right to upper left line. The people who fall in the lower right quadrant are the ones who want to control others and do not want to be controlled themselves. These people can be called autocrat-rebels; they want to be the bosses and do not want anyone else to tell them what to do. In the upper left quadrant we have just the opposite. These are abdicrat-submissives; they want to be told what to do, and they do not want to control anyone else.

For smooth functioning it would appear that if we had one autocrat-rebel, we would not want another one, since they would both want to give orders and neither would want to take them. This is called *competitive* incompatibility. Also, if we had two abdicrat-submissives, a situation would be created wherein both people want someone to tell them what to do and neither wants to do the telling. This is called *apathetic* incompatibility. However, if we have one autocrat-rebel and one abdicrat-submissive, the relationship will probably be harmonious, since one person wants to give orders and the other wants to take them.

Interchange Diagonal. Now, consider the other diagonal on the diagram. Let us take affection for an example this time. In the upper right quadrant are the people who express a lot of close personal behavior, and want the same expressed to them. These are the people of "high interchange," and they can be called overpersonal-personal-compliants. They like an atmosphere in which there is a lot of affection; so, for instance, they would like a party better than a board of directors meeting. In the lower left quadrant are people of "low interchange," who like neither to give nor to receive affection. They can be called underpersonal-counterpersonals. They do not want anyone to get very close to them, nor do they want to get very close to anyone. They like their relations rather reserved, cool, and distant.

EXHIBIT 3. **Graphic Representation
of Interpersonal Dimensions**

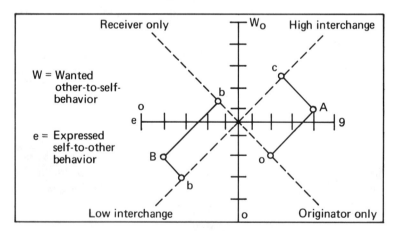

Here the complementary idea of the originator diagonal—that opposites attract—does not apply; for, if one person likes to be very close and personal and the other person does not, they are going to threaten each other. One who likes to keep his relations reserved is not going to like it when the other makes overtures; and, in the reverse direction, the one who wants very close relations is not going to be very happy if the other does not. So it seems reasonable that the situation would lead to harmony more readily if the people involved were close on this diagonal, unlike the situation on the originator diagonal.

In the inclusion dimension, again, it would be better if both interacting persons were very close to being either very high or very low on this diagonal so that one would not always want to be with people while the other wanted to stay home and read a book. Hence, on the interchange diagonal the "birds of a feather" maxim seems most appropirate; people should be similar in their values along this diagonal.

Predictable Relations

To exemplify the working of the technique let us consider Exhibit 3 for the control area.

From FIRO-B, we learn that A has a score of 8 on e^c, and 5 on w^c, while B has a score of 1 on e^c and 1 on w^c. These points are plotted on the diagram. Each score, for illustrative purposes, may be divided into two components, one on each diagonal. These components are represented by a_x and a^o and b_x and b^o on the diagram.

The measure of interchange compatibility (xK) of A and B is proportional to the distance between a^x and b^x. A smaller distance means a more similar orientation toward the amount of interchange of control that should exist in a relation. In the example, A believes that relations should involve a great deal of influence and control, while B's preference is for less structured, more laissez-faire relations. Their compatibility in this regard is reflected in he relatively large distance between a_x and b_x.

Originator compatibility (oK) is proportional to the sum of a^o and b^o. Optimal originator compatibility occurs when one score is to the left of the midpoint of the diagonal and the other score is exactly the same distance to the right of the midpoint. In our example this is almost exactly true; thus A and B have high originator compatibility. A wishes to control others but not to be controlled, while B wishes to be controlled but not to control or influence others very much. Hence they complement each other.

Our conclusion then about this pair is the following: they disagree as to the atmosphere they desire regarding mutual influence and control. A likes structured hierarchies while B prefers more permissive relations. However, when there is a situation of a certain structure, they are compatible with regard to the roles they will take in relation to each other. A will take the influential, responsible position, and B will take the subordinate role.

These psychological considerations can very easily be converted into formulas, and in research work and practical applications this is done. There have been several experiments performed which indicate the usefulness of this approach. These experiments demonstrate that groups of from two to eight can be composed—based on FIRO-B scores—in such a way that their productivity, and to some extent their interaction, is predictable. Much research is still to be done to improve the accuracy of these predictions, but the results are highly encouraging.[1]

[1] See William C. Schutz, op. cit. [FIRO, New York, 1958]

GROUP DEVELOPMENT

Another major point in the theory is that every group, no matter what its function or composition, given enough time, goes through the three interpersonal phases of inclusion, control, and affection in the same sequence. To illustrate:

Recently I was interviewing a member of a group, which had just completed 30 meetings, to get an idea of her feeling about the experience. In response to the question, "How would you describe what happened in this group?" she replied, "Well, first you're concerned about the problem of where you fit in the group; then you're wondering about what you'll accomplish. Finally, after a while, you learn that people mean something. Your primary concern becomes how people feel about you and about each other."

In or Out

First, *the inclusion phase centers around the question of "in or out."* It begins with the formation of the group. When people are confronted with each other, they must first find the place where they fit in. This involves being in or out of the group, establishing oneself as a specific individual, and seeing if one is going to be paid attention to and not be left behind or ignored. This anxiety area gives rise to individual-centered behavior such as overtalking, extreme withdrawal, exhibitionism, recitation of biographies and other previous experience.

At the same time the basic problem of commitment to the group is present. Each member is implicitly deciding to what degree he will become a member of the group, how much investment he will withdraw from his other commitments and invest in this new relationship. He is asking, "How much of myself will I devote to this group? How important will I be in this setting? Will they know who I am and what I can do, or will I be indistinguishable from many others?" This is, in short, the problem of identity. He is, in effect, deciding primarily on his preferred amount of inclusion initiation with the other members—just how much actual contact, interaction, and communication he wishes to have.

Hence, the main concerns of the formative process are "boundary problems," problems that have to do with entering into the boundaries of a group and belonging to that group. These are problems of inclusion.

Characteristic of groups in this phase is the occurrence of what have been called "goblet issues." The term is taken from an analogy to a cocktail party where people sometimes pick up their cocktail glass, or goblet, and figuratively peer through it to size up the other people at the party. Hence, they are issues that in themselves are of minor importance to the group members but serve as vehicles for getting to know people, especially in relation to oneself.

Often a goblet issue is made of the first decision confronting a group. In some groups discussions leading to a decision about such an issue continue for an unbelievably long time and then never reach a conclusion. But there has been a great deal of learning in that the members have gained a fairly clear picture of each other. Each member knows who responds favorably to him, who sees the things the way he does, how much he knows as compared to the others, how the leader responds to him, and what type of role he can expect to play in the group. Acquiring this knowledge is the unconscious purpose of the goblet issue.

The frustrating experience of having groups endlessly discuss topics of little real interest to anyone is very common. Every group finds its own goblet issues within the framework of its aim. "The weather" is fairly universal; "rules of procedure" is common in formal groups; "Do you know so-and-so?" often characterizes new acquaintances from the same location; relating incidents or telling stories has a goblet element for business gatherings; and "Where are you from?" often serves for military settings. Mark Twain apparently overlooked the fact that nobody really *wants* to "do anything about the weather"—they just want to use it as a topic for sizing up people. These discussions are inevitable, and, contrary to all outward appearances, they do serve an important function. Groups which are not permitted this type of testing out will search for some other method of obtaining the same personal information, perhaps using as a vehicle a decision of more importance to the work of the group.

Top or Bottom

After the problems of inclusion have been sufficiently resolved, control problems become prominent. *This phase centers around the problems of "top or bottom."* Once members are fairly well established as being together in a group, the issue of decision-making procedures arises. This involves problems of sharing responsibility and its necessary concomitant, distribution of power and control. Characteristic behavior at this stage includes leadership struggles; competition; and discussion of orientation to the task, structuring, rules of procedure, methods of decision marking, and sharing the responsibility for the group's work. The primary anxieties at this phase revolve around having too much or too little influence. Each member is trying to establish himself in the group so that he has the most comfortable amount of interchange and the most comfortable degree of initiation with the other members with regard to control, influence, and responsibility.

Near or Far

Finally, following a satisfactory resolution of these phases, problems of affection become focal. *This phase centers on the issue of "near or far."* The individuals have come together to form a group; they have differentiated themselves with respect to responsibility and power. Now they must become emotionally integrated. At this stage it is characteristic to see such behavior expressed through positive feelings, direct personal hostility, jealousies, pairing behavior, and, in general, heightened emotional feeling between pairs of people.

The primary anxieties at this stage have to do with not being liked or close enough to people or with being too intimate. Each member is striving to obtain his most favorable amount of affectional interchange and most comfortable position regarding initiating and receiving affection—deciding, like Schopenhauer's porcupines, how to get close enough to receive warmth, yet avoid the pain of sharp quills.

Tightening the Bolts

These are not distinct phases. The group development postulate asserts that these problem areas are *emphasized* at certain points in a group's growth, but all three problem areas are always present. Similarly, some people do not always go along with the central issue for the group. For certain individuals a particular problem area will be so personally potent that it will transcend the current group issue. The area of concern for any individual will result from his own problem areas and those of the group's current phase. Perhaps a close approximation to the developmental phenomena is given by the tire-changing model:

> When a person changes a tire and replaces the wheel, he first sets the wheel in place and secures it by tightening the bolts one after another just enough so the wheel is in place and the next step can be taken. Then the bolts are tightened further, usually in the same sequence, until the wheel is firmly in place. Finally each bolt is gone over separately to secure it.

In a similar way, the need areas are worked on until they are handled satisfactorily enough to continue with the work at hand. Later on they are returned to and worked over to a more satisfactory degree. If one need area has not been worked out well on the first sequence, it must receive more attention on the next cycle.

APPLICATIONS OF THEORY

The next question is: What can we do about these problems so as to utilize this information practically? This is more difficult. The above analysis is derived largely from experience with experimental research on small groups selected for this purpose. Solutions for the problems observed are largely, though not entirely, speculative and can only be offered as suggestions which should be explored carefully in each individual case before being adopted.

More specifically, the interpretations presented here can be looked upon as suggestions for *diagnosis*. The more men in business can become aware of the basic factors underlying their interpersonal difficulties, the better they will be able to meet these difficulties. As in the practice of medicine, if the disease is properly diagnosed, the doctor has a better chance of curing it than if it is improperly or superficially diagnosed, even though a correct diagnosis by no means guarantees a cure.

Clearing the Air

Serious interpersonal difficulties that are left covert only smolder and erupt at the expense of efficiency and productivity. The most effective way covert difficulties can be dealt with is by first making them overt. For example:

> In one marketing group, the leader finally told one member that he did not like the way he was acting in the group and that he felt he should contribute more. After a brief but difficult and bitter exchange the two began to tell each other their feelings about the situation. They managed to clear the air, and the situation improved markedly.

When successful, overt discussion is like a cold shower: it is approached with apprehension, the initial impact is very uncomfortable, but the final result justifies the tribulations.

To summarize, "interpersonal problems" include difficulties such as members who are withdrawn from a group; personal hostilities between members; problem members who are either inactive and unintegrated or overactive and destructive; power struggles between group members; members battling for attention; dissatisfaction with the leadership in the group; dissatisfaction with the amount of acknowledgment that an individual's contributions are getting, or dissatisfaction with the amount of affection and warmth exhibited in the group.

If it becomes quite clear to the group members that their difficulties are so severe that their activity is being impaired, then bringing the issues out in the open and talking about them will help. It is somewhat difficult, however, to tell exactly when a problem is so severe that it is holding the group up. Perhaps some of the earlier discussion of symptoms will be useful for assessing the effect of interpersonal factors on the group.

It might be helpful to view groups (including anywhere from two to twenty people) on a continuum—from those that are completely compatible, that is, able to work well together, to those that are completely incompatible, that is, incapable of working together. Any particular group can be placed somewhere along this continuum. To illustrate:

> The members of the group at the extreme compatible end of the continuum are able to work well together within a relatively short time with a minimum of difficulty and can operate effectively over a period of time on a wide variety of problems. They need no training or new awareness.
>
> The group at the incompatible end, however, cannot work effectively. The interpersonal problems that cause the task difficulties are so deepseated in the personalities of the individual members that no amount of outside assistance will be worthwhile. It would take so long before this group could operate effectively that, from a practical standpoint, any kind of training of the group members or any awareness of their problems would be unfruitful.
>
> Between these two extreme types are groups that profit more or less by the kind of awareness which has been discussed. If a group is relatively near the compatible end, with a minimum of awareness and a minimum of discussion of its difficult problems, it will become a smoothly functioning group. If interpersonal problems in a group are very minor, they can usually be ignored without impairing the group seriously; or, if the

problems exist between two members, they can often work out their difficulties by themselves outside the group.

With groups near the incompatible end much more intensive work has to be done to get through their problems so that they can function effectively. Such work should probably be guided by someone who is experienced with group process and can help group members to work out their difficulties.

Another advantage of this approach operates more through the individuals than the group. If the individual members can gain the kind of awareness of their own needs in situations as discussed in this article, then this in itself will help them to understand their reactions to other people and, perhaps, to operate more effectively. In addition, it is often helpful to point out to group members that other people have the same basic needs; for, if they understand what other people are trying to do, they may be more tolerant of other people's behavior. Since everyone has these needs, everyone tries to get the same thing from other people, even though each may use different adaptive patterns for achieving his ends. To illustrate such a mechanism:

It generally is felt that if an individual has an excessively strong negative reaction to another individual in the setting of a work group, the individual who is irritated fears deep down within himself that he is like the one who annoys him, that he himself has the trait that is so annoying. It is threatening for him to see it in some other individual, and he must immediately deny it and attack it, almost as if he were trying to deny to himself that he is like this.

Awareness of mechanisms of this type may help in understanding what is happening in the group and one's own reaction in the situation.

CONCLUSION

The time seems to have come for the businessman to make use of some of the social scientists' more recent findings on the unconscious, or covert, factors in human interaction. Since the businessman does deal so heavily in interpersonal relations, his skill and success are dependent on his ability to understand interpersonal relations and to deal effectively with them. Thus, it becomes important for him to gain a more basic understanding instead of simply trying out panaceas that aim only at the symptoms of the problems and not at the basic problems themselves. He must understand the vast interpersonal underworld that operates beneath the overt, observable behavior.

As I have already pointed out, current interest in what are called "communications problems" provides an example of the symptomatic approach, for these problems are symptoms of poor interpersonal relations rather than primary causes of operational difficulties. It is an error, therefore, to try to attack the problems of communication by building more effective physical lines of communication, when the trouble really lies in the relation between individuals. The way to attack the basic problem would seem to be to investigate what is going on among the individuals themselves and try to improve those relations.

If it is true that the unconscious factors are so all-important to understanding groups, then we ought to find out exactly how these factors do affect what the businessman is usually primarily interested in—namely, effective operation. In this article I have tried to illustrate the inadequacy of attempting to operate by ignoring interpersonal difficulties and attending to the task only, since in reality the interpersonal factors somehow find their way into the task and directly affect the productivity of the group. No matter how much people try to keep interpersonal problems out by ignoring them, they will turn up in subtle forms such as loss of motivation, tiredness, or the group member's preoccupation with outside tasks; or they may get entangled directly with the solution of the task and have to be worked out in the body of the problem.

I have offered a theoretical framework which may be of some help in understanding the structure of these interpersonal problems in an attempt to aid in the diagnosis of interpersonal behavior. Such a diagnosis may then leave the businessman in a better position to deal with what actually occurs. I have tried to suggest possible lines of solution, but these attempts are offered in a much more speculative manner. Although they are based on rather extensive experience with psychological phenomena, they are only suggestions that the individual businessman must try out and adapt to his own needs.

Marvin D. Dunnette
and John P. Campbell

LABORATORY EDUCATION: IMPACT ON PEOPLE AND ORGANIZATIONS

In recent years, the first author has been asked by a number of firms to play "doctor" to some of their sick organizational units. These assignments were accepted rather reluctantly because the scientific terrain for diagnosing and curing company ills due to dysfunctional behavior is still unfortunately a vast, unmapped wasteland with only a few dirt roads here and there. However, observing inner company workings from the somewhat detached stance of an

From Marvin D. Dunnette, John P. Campbell and Chris Argyris, ' A Symposium: Laboratory Training.' *Industrial Relations* 8 (October, 1968): 1-45. Reprinted by permission. © 1968, Regents of the University of California, Berkeley.

outsider has led to the firm conclusion that it's very easy to get into trouble in business "without really trying." This may seem obvious to the reader, but let us pursue the point a bit further by recounting briefly some of the patterns of human and organizational behavior found in these companies.[1]

A DOCTOR TO ORGANIZATIONS

Competition and crisis. One large, nationally renowned industrial research laboratory comprised of over 100 top flight scientists and engineers encountered rough times. Interviews with key people showed that nearly everyone's morale was low; nearly everyone complained about haphazard decisions, precipitate organizational changes, and constantly changing job assignments; no one seemed to know what the overall goals of the laboratory really were, if, indeed, any existed. The fluidity of the situation was expressed by many in the form of the grim comment: "If you run into my boss, be sure to find out his name and tell me."

Apparently the laboratory had been spoiled by its own success. Only a few years earlier, a select cadre, consisting of an inventor and a dozen applied-development men had scored an innovating and engineering breakthrough to produce an outstanding new product. Sales of the product skyrocketed—so sharply that a whole new industry was created, and competitors moved rapidly and aggressively to penetrate the burgeoning market. With success in the marketplace came rapid expansion. The "group" expanded in about five years' time from just under 20 to nearly 300 professional and supporting personnel.

Unfortunately, the growth seemed to get out of hand. Engineers and scientists were made supervisors and managers without the benefit of either experience or training in the art of supervising and managing. The key man who had stimulated and coalesced the creative forces of his staff of a dozen retained his title of Laboratory Director, but three new levels of supervision were created between him and the people on the bench. For a time, everything went well, but this phase came to a sudden halt when a competitor's product proved suddenly to have greater marketability. Sales suddenly turned drastically downward. The resulting crisis was felt immediately in the laboratory, but it had apparently been organized only to deal with success not crisis. Feelings of anxiety and insecurity, and haphazard threshing about in response to external threat, became prevalent; few of the newly named managers had any clear notion of how to cope with such stress or how to take advantage of the rich intellectual resources of the laboratory personnel.

Being all things to all people. In a second firm, a serious problem grew out of ambiguous and often conflicting role expectations surrounding one of the organizational units. In the eyes of some company officials, the unit was formed

[1] Expenses involved in the preparation of this review were supported in part under U.S. Public Health Service grant, MH08563, National Science Foundation grant, GS1081, and a Graduate Research and Study Grant in the Behavioral Sciences from the General Electric Foundation.

for the sole purpose of servicing present and potential company customers—a kind of consulting service to develop equipment and machinery enabling customers to make optimal use of the company's products. However, in the eyes of an increasing number of other officials (among them, the unit manager's boss), the unit was to be regarded as another profit center in the company—billings for services and equipment should be sufficient to avoid the necessity for subsidies from other company divisions.

The manager of this organizational unit was caught in the middle of these sharply conflicting expectations. Unfortunately, he transmitted the same ambiguous and conflicting expectations to key people in his unit. Most of his subordinates had difficulties understanding either his verbal or written communications, and he seemed entirely unaware of both his impact on other people and of what they were trying to tell him. Because of these problems of perceptual impermeability and distorting, the manager seemed constantly embroiled in destructively belligerent interpersonal exchanges—with key officials throughout the company, with customers, and with his own subordinates.

Loss of people and the beginning of strife. A third unit is the most interesting because it presents a picture of almost total organizational disruption and stress. One of many similar units in a large-scale manufacturing operation, this unit for years had provided manufacturing know-how and managerial talent for most of the firm's other units. During 1964-1967, a number of things occurred to bring about internal difficulties. First, many key people retired from the organization. Second, scores of additional key managers were transferred by the parent company to other units. The unit manager apparently replaced these losses with much less effective supervisors and managers because of lack of available talent, an inadequate supervisory selection system, and a haphazard supervisory training program. Third, manpower shortages at the rank-and-file level and unprecedented consumer demands forced an excessively high rate of overtime (ranging to 60-65 hours a week and extending over a span of three years).

About a year before we began working with this organizational unit, absenteeism at both the supervisory and rank-and-file levels became a severe problem, production quality dropped sharply, and the overall cost of manufacturing rose excessively, exceeding the budgeted cost quotas by tens of thousands of dollars a week. In our interviews with key managers, we found an acute awareness that the plant was "in trouble," combined with an unusual willingness to point to other people or other departments as a major reason for difficulties. Communication among departments had deteriorated into backbiting and finger-pointing; many supervisors used coercive, aggressive, and derogating tactics in fruitless efforts to assure compliance. Many key officials wanted desperately to open up constructive lines of communication directed toward more rational problem-solving and mature methods of conflict resolution, but few knew how such changes could be implemented.

This organization illustrates more closely than either of the other two the pervasive and unfavorable effects of strategies which fail to give sufficient emphasis to the many steps necessary for adequate problem-solving, problem analysis, information synthesis, and cooperative group action, but instead push prematurely toward instant action based mostly on essentially incomplete information or on surface symptoms.

SOLUTION THROUGH EDUCATION?

We have gone into some detail because we believe these three instances of organizational distress illustrate patterns of personal and organizational behavior which are common in industry.[2] Moreover, they illustrate types of behavior and organizational problems specifically in the areas of interpersonal perception, interpersonal interaction, and inter- and intragroup conflict resolution. All these, in turn, are claimed by advocates to be amenable to change through techniques of laboratory education.

By laboratory education we mean those personnel and organizational development and training courses which combine traditional training features—such as lectures, group problem-solving sessions, and role-planning—with T-group or sensitivity training techniques.[3] Laboratory education is being used more and more by industry. No national statistics are available on total volume or frequency of use, but it is clear that consumer demand is high.[4] The National Training Laboratories and the Western Training Laboratories conduct programs for hundreds of industrial managers each year. Many consulting firms now offer such training as a standard part of their bill of fare; many colleges and universities incorporate T-groups into their business, public administration, education, and psychology curricula; and a number of university institutes (e.g., Boston University's Human Relations Center and UCLA's Institute of Industrial Relations) conduct T-groups for business people. Moreover, psychologists working in companies have developed laboratory education programs for internal use by managers, and a substantial number of line managers have been trained to conduct such programs as an ongoing feature of their firms' management development efforts.[5] It is apparent that laboratory education (or a T-group) is now within easy reach of almost any manager.

Our purpose in writing this article has been to report what is known of the behavioral effects (on both people and organizations) of laboratory education. We have approached the task as follows: First, we have examined the difficulties

[2] Our descriptions of these organizational units are really rather stark caricatures of the actual state of events. We departed from reality in order (1) to highlight the major points we wish to make, and (2) more important, to assure anonymity of the units we worked with.

[3] For detailed accounts of the basic T-group method, see descriptions given by S. Klaw, "Two Weeks in a T-Group," *Fortune* 44 (1961): 114-17; A. H. Kuriloff and S. Atkins, "T-Group for a Work Team," *Journal of Applied Behavioral Science* 2 (1966): 63-94; R. Tannenbaum, I. R. Weschler, and F. Massarik, *Leadership and Organization: A Behavioral Science Approach* (New York: McGraw-Hill Book Company; 1961); and I. R. Weschler and J. Reisel, *Inside a Sensitivity Training Group* (Los Angeles: Institute of Industrial Relations, University of California, 1959).

[4] For example, see R. J. House, "T-Group Education and Leadership Effectiveness: A Review of Empirical Literature and a Critical Evaluation," *Personnel Psychology* 20 (1967): 1-32; or the latest *Information Brochure* (1967) describing the 21st Annual Summer Laboratories sponsored by the National Training Laboratories.

[5] Two examples are Dr. Seymour Levy of Pillsbury Mills in Minneapolis and Dr. Joseph McPherson of Dow Chemical Co. in Midland, Mich.

of the organizations described previously in order to discover the major problems of interpersonal behavior common to them and—by extrapolation—to most other troubled organizations. Second, we consider these behavioral problems in the context of what advocates and practitioners of laboratory education claim to be their major behavioral goals. Third, we review and evaluate published research studies which have been done to assess the actual behavioral effects of laboratory education. Finally, we call attention to gaps in our present level of knowledge and offer guidelines for planning future research studies designed to fill the gaps.

ACTION, ATTACK, APATHY, ANOMIE, AND ALIENATION

Most managers in the organizations described above tended to show either apathy or belligerence. Some were consistently apathetic, others consistently belligerent, but most behaved inconsistently, ranging from apathy (withdrawal) to belligerent aggressiveness (attack) from situation to situation. They tended to spend too much time pressing for quick action in response to difficulties. More often than not, they ended up responding inappropriately and nonconstructively to the problems and threats facing them. Why?

We believe two reasons stand out. First, most were so strongly oriented toward accomplishing immediate solutions that they failed to gather data or information about problem causes. They tended to rush in with premature conclusions about causes and remedies (often fixing blame on others) in an attempt to remove opposition (or frustration) rapidly and completely. Needless to say, a few unsuccessful forays of this type would probably result either in further undifferentiated attacks or in discouragement, temporary withdrawal, and apathy. Second, most managers in these units appeared not to trust others sufficiently to deal openly and cooperatively with them in coping with problems. They avoided those confrontations that threatened to reveal opposing viewpoints or lead to open conflict. Most seemed unwilling or unable to cope with others as individuals, to try to know them better, or "to put themselves in the other fellow's shoes."

Thus, the major patterns of individual behavior in these three ailing units involved apathy, overt belligerence, and impatience with analytical procedures for getting to know either problems or people better—symptomatic, in our opinion, of efforts to protect the ego or to save face.

Obviously, these individual behavioral tendencies were related to broader patterns of organizational behavior in these units. Our interviews and questionnaires revealed patterns of poor coordination, inefficient and inaccurate communication, and poorly defined and poorly transmitted organizational objectives. To a degree, these patterns seemed to occur simply because more constructive patterns had never been learned. Coordination, goal definition, and communications in each of the three units suffered for different reasons—extremely rapid growth and poor supervisory assignments in the first, role ambiguity in the second, and loss of key managerial talent in the third. In each of the units, things had been going well just prior to the onset of the "sickness"; unfortunately, proper plans had not been developed nor people readied to respond analytically to crisis situations. Each organization floundered—from the top down. Clear-cut objectives (specific organizational goals, intentions, and actions) were not formulated and could not, therefore, be communicated—even if sound methods for coordination and communication had been available. The tendency to meet threat by fighting or fleeing characterized each organization's behavior as well as that of the individuals making it up, and this yielded finally to a deteriorating downward spiral of threat-induced fear eliciting inappropriate (self-defeating) and precipitate organizational and individual actions, followed by suspicion, alienation, deepening crisis, further nonconstructive counter-actions, and so on.

BEHAVIORAL NEEDS AND THE
GOALS OF LABORATORY EDUCATION

In order to reverse this untoward spiral which might lead ultimately to complete organizational debilitation, new patterns of individual and organizational behavior must be learned and implemented. We suggest that the needs are greatest for teaching people (1) to be more analytical in gathering data about other people and about problem situations, (2) to be less self-centered, less defensive, and more aware of the effects of their own behavior on others, (3) to be more accepting of the necessity for facing up to conflict—in fact, to develop strategies for bringing conflict into the open—in order to be able to work out constructive resolutions, and, (4) to develop both the skills and the motivation to work interpersonally with others for the purpose of learning more about behavior in the work setting and the problems they face in relation to their meeting organizational goals.

Undoubtedly, these areas of needed behavior reeducation are far from unique to the three organizational units we described. In fact, we concur with Argyris that patterns of behavior in these units illustrate what may be expected in *most* organizations in response to such crises as runaway expansion, extreme competitive pressures, excessive losses of key people, or any other internally or externally induced state of organizational threat.[6] There is a widespread need in today's organizations for teaching business managers to be more analytical, more aware of how they affect others, develop better interpersonal skills, and use constructive approaches for resolving conflict.

---

[6] Based on his theories of human and organizational behavior, Argyris argues that most individuals in industry tend to have their needs for growth and maturity frustrated by the demands for dependency made by most organizations. The initial result is employee apathy, but when faced with organizational stress, the apathy may become aggression or withdrawal, which is countered by the organization with further controls and constraints, followed in turn by further employee counteractions. Thus, the vicious cycle of organizational constraints, employee counteractions, further constraints, and so on, is set off. For Argyris's account of his theories and a case study of onset of "sickness" in one organizational unit, see C. Argyris, *Understanding Organizational Behavior* (Homewood, Ill.: Dorsey Press, 1960), and *Integrating the Individual and the Organization* (New York: John Wiley & Sons, Inc., 1964).

Does laboratory education accomplish these goals? Certainly, most of the advocates of the method would argue that it does. For example, the following list—drawn from many sources—is a distillation of the desirable outcomes sought by and advocated, either implicitly or explicitly, by most T-group and/or laboratory education practitioners:

1. Increased self-insight or self-awareness concerning one's own behavior and its meaning in a social context—this refers to the process of learning how others see and interpret one's behavior, as well as insight about one's reasons for behaving in various ways in different interpersonal situations.
2. Increased sensitivity to the behavior of others—this outcome is closely linked to the first. It refers, first, to the development of an increased awareness of the full range of communicative stimuli emitted by other persons (voice inflections, facial expressions, body positions, and other contextual factors, in addition to the actual choice of words); and, second, to developing the ability to infer accurately the emotional or noncognitive bases for interpersonal communications. This goal is very similar to the concept of empathy as it is used by clinical and counseling psychologists; that is, the ability to infer correctly what another person is feeling.
3. Increased awareness and understanding of the types of processes that facilitate or inhibit group functioning and the interactions between different groups—specifically, why do some members participate actively, while others retire to the background? Why do subgroups form and wage war against each other? How and why are pecking orders established? Why do different groups, who actually share the same goals, sometimes create seemingly insoluble conflict situations?
4. Heightened diagnostic skill in social, interpersonal, and intergroup situations—achievement of the first three objectives should provide an individual with a set of concepts to be used in his analysis of conflict situations. Moreover, he should be equipped to work constructively with others to resolve interpersonal and/or intergroup conflict.
5. Increased action skill—the ability to intervene successfully in inter- or intragroup situations in order to increase member satisfactions, effectiveness, or productivity.[7] The major thrust of increased action skill is toward intervention at the *interpersonal* instead of merely the technological level, thereby enhancing the likelihood that coordinated, instead of alienated and disputative efforts will be brought to bear in solving technological problems.
6. Learning how to learn—this refers not simply to an individual's cognitive approach to the world, but instead, and far more importantly, to his ability to analyze continually his own interpersonal behavior in order to help himself and others achieve more effective and satisfying interpersonal relationships.[8]

[7] Although very similar to point 4 this is mentioned separately in M. B. Miles, "Research Notes From Here and There—Human Relations Training: Process and Outcomes," *Journal of Counseling Psychology,* 7 (1960): 301-6.

[8] The sources for the above listing of T-group goals include: C. Argyris, "T-Groups for Organizational Effectiveness," *Harvard Business Review* 42 (1964): 60-74; P. C. Buchanan, "Evaluating the Effectiveness of Laboratory Training in Industry," in *Explorations in Human Relations Training and Research,* 1 (Washington, D.C.: National Training Laboratories, National Education Association, 1965); L. P. Bradford, J. R. Gibb, and K. D. Benne, *T-Group Theory and Laboratory Method* (New York: John Wiley & Sons, Inc.,

Obviously, these outcomes fulfill the organizational needs for behavioral reeducation we listed earlier. It should now be asked: Are these behavioral outcomes really accomplished? If they are, by whom—everyone undergoing such training or just a few? And, if a few, who, and under what conditions? Can sick organizations be "cured" through T-group training and laboratory education? In short, what research evidence can be offered either to support or to question whether this relatively new training strategy accomplishes the aims claimed for it?[9]

ANSWERS ARE HARD TO COME BY

The above questions—easy to pose—are difficult to answer. This is because learning what training accomplishes behaviorially is probably the most difficult and least well-handled area of behavioral science research in industry. Evaluation is poor because training, education, and learning are believed by most people in our society to be inherently good—almost everyone believes that this fundamental truth needs no proof. Moreover, faced with the kinds of organizational needs we have been talking about, what trainer, personnel development expert, or consulting psychologist could afford, or would want, to "fiddle around" designing an elegant experiment to show the world whether or not he actually accomplishes what he set out to? A good physician doesn't withhold his educated guesses during diagnosis, nor does he ignore therapeutic opportunities, simply because all the evidence is not in. Similarly, a "company doctor" must accept responsibility for doing something, and the something will nearly always need to be a promising, but not yet entirely proven method of individual or organizational behavior modification.

We are not condoning this state of affairs. We are just calling attention to it and stating that we understand the reason for it. In doing so, we have been wearing the mantle of the professional—the individual who seeks to deduce from his repertoire of behavioral science knowledge a plan of action for alleviating an organization's ills. Now, however, it is time to slip into the mantle of the scientist and to become more demanding about the research evidence offered in support of the claims made, and hopes possessed, by the professionals. For, without a tough-minded scientist's view, little impetus for better answers will ever be provided and the practices of the professionals will show little or no improvement over the years—eventuating possibly in charlatanism rather than informed or truly expert professionalism.

WHAT NEEDS TO BE DONE?

The *scientific* standards necessary for properly evaluating training experiences are few in number and disarmingly simple, but (for the reasons mentioned

---

1964); E. H. Schein and W. G. Bennis, *Personal and Organizational Changes through Group Methods: The Laboratory Approach* (New York: John Wiley & Sons, Inc., 1965); R. Tannenbaum and others, *op. cit.;* Miles, *op. cit.*

[9] See Appendix A [at the end of this article] for a generalized description of T-group procedure.

above) they are almost never put into practice. First, measures of trainees' status should be obtained *before* and *after* the training experience. Ideally, the measures should sample, as broadly as possible, trainee *behaviors* relevant to the organization's problems and/or to the aims of the training procedures, but attitudinal, perceptual, and other self-report measures may also prove useful. Second, measured changes shown by the trainees between pre- and post-training periods should be compared with changes, if any, occurring in a so-called control group of similar, but untrained persons. Using control groups is the only way to assure that changes observed in the experimental (or trainee) groups are actually the result of training procedures instead of possible artifactual effects—such as the mere passage of time, poor reliability of measures, Hawthorne Effects, or other spurious components. Finally, a third standard necessary for most training evaluation studies stems from the possibility of interaction between the evaluation measures and the behavior of the trainees during the program. For example, if trainees are asked beforehand to answer questions about their supervisory "styles," they may be alerted to look for the "correct answers" during training in order to answer the same questions "more appropriately" (i.e., more in line with the desires of the trainer) when they are asked again after training. One way of estimating the degree of interaction between such measures and the training content is to provide a quasicontrol group which takes part in the training program *without* first completing the measures. Then, comparisons between the two trained groups (experimental and quasicontrol) on the after-measures may give estimates of the relative amounts of change actually due to training or due simply to having been alerted by prior exposure to the measures.

Unfortunately, these three rather simple standards for learning what training accomplishes are actually very difficult to meet, and they have been applied only rarely in studies to evaluate the effects of laboratory education.

THE EVIDENCE

We turn now to a review and evaluation of published research studies done to assess the effects of laboratory education. We have classified the investigations into five groups roughly located at various points along a continuum extending from private (not publicly verifiable), individual perceptions to very broad organizational outcomes. The primary changes measured by studies in each of the groups are: (1) self-reports of changes in the work setting; (2) changes in attitudes, outlooks, perceptions of others, or orientations toward others; (3) changes in self-awareness or interpersonal sensitivity; (4) observed changes in behavior on the job; and (5) changes in organizational outcomes.

The major results shown by studies in each of these areas are summarized below.

SELF-PERCEPTIONS AND SELF-REPORTS

There is an overwhelming amount of anecdotal evidence on the presumed effects of laboratory education. Most, however, involves introspection, free association, or testimonies collected in an uncontrolled and nonsystematic way. Here is a greatly abbreviated excerpt from one such report:

> The leadership laboratory was a marvelous experience. I was in it a month ago, and I am still awestruck. I might be able to give you a glimmer or two about what happened in relaxed conversation, oiled by a martini or two, but a letter is bound to miss, but I'll give it a try anyway. The process is like the dropping of Salome's seven veils. Eventually the group comes to a condition of complete trust, and communications become so acute that they seem metaphysical. Not that the group gets this way without strain. It was fascinating to see how the group came to respect the need for time for an idea to sink in. When an important point was made to a member, the group often fell silent while the point perked, even if it took 30 seconds. The silence wasn't oppressive or embarrassing; it served a purpose. After the last day's session, each group ate at a long table by itself. You never saw such uninhibited, free people. The next morning, my group had a final session and then we walked around the place like a bunch of bananas, we felt so close.[10]

The above account is highly favorable about what happened in the group, but it also is highly subjective, introspective, and nonbehavioral. Because of this, we chose *not* to attempt a review of such reports. As a consequence, we found only two studies using structured or systematic measures for assessing self-report of behavior changes. Neither of the studies used pretraining measures. In both studies, supervisors who had been in intraorganizational laboratory training groups reported (after three to seven months back on the job) changes in the effectiveness of their units or critical job incidents they believed were due to the laboratory training. Buchanan and Brunstetter found that the 224 managers reported relatively more examples of effective changes than a comparison (control) group of 133 untrained managers. Morton and Bass used no control group, but 359 incidents were reported by 97 trainees, and nearly all of them were judged by the authors to be favorable influences relating to improved working relationships.[11]

Obviously, self-reports of the type obtained in these two studies—even though elicited in a systematic way and focused on job behaviors—are subject to a wide variety of biases. The trainees knew that their training was intended to produce certain behavioral effects; thus, they probably tended to note and report many occurrences which would otherwise go unnoticed and unreported. In a sense, one might argue that the trainees had been committed by their company to enumerate instances of the worth or return on the training investment. Thus, self-imposed internalized organizational expectations and response-set biases seem to us an equally viable explanation for the results obtained.

[10] Drawn from a letter from one of the first author's close friends, who prefers to remain anonymous.

[11] R. B. Morton and B. M. Bass, "The Organizational Training Laboratory," *Journal of the American Society of Training Directors* 18 (1964): 2-15; P. C. Buchanan and P. H. Brunstetter, "A Research Approach to Management Development: Part II," *Journal of the American Society of Training Directors* 13 (1959): 18-27.

ATTITUDES, OUTLOOKS, AND ORIENTATIONS

Several studies have examined possible effects of laboratory education on trainees' attitudes and outlooks. Discovering attitudinal effects of laboratory education is important because several of the goals of such training (e.g., better understanding of intergroup processes, improved interpersonal diagnostic skills, increased interest and skill in interpersonal intervention, and stronger drive toward personal learning or improvement) strongly imply the necessity of marked attitudinal changes. Table 1 lists the nine studies we found in this area along with relevant details about measures used, subjects, experimental designs, and results obtained.

We conclude from these studies that there is little firm evidence of any significant change in attitude, outlook, orientation, or view of others as a result of T-group training. This statement is based on the following three observations.

(1). Control groups were not included in five of the nine studies. Because of this, interpretation of the results in terms of T-group training per se is strained, at best. The changes occurring in the trained groups could easily be attributable to the passage of time or to the mere act of taking the same test a second time. Two of the four studies using control groups report no significant differences between the trained and untrained individuals; in the two where differences were obtained (Smith; Schutz and Allen), the nature of the changes is only sketchily described, offering little basis for speculation or further hypothesis formulation.

(2). Eight of the nine studies failed to collect data about possible interaction effects between the evaluation questionnaires or tests and the training program. This is serious when the effort is directed toward evaluating changes via such self-report measures as attitude or orientation inventories because the results from such instruments very often are made available to trainees and actually become a part of the feedback process during training. The result is that trainees, in effect, are either explicitly or implicitly "coached" on the instruments to be used later in evaluating the presumed effects of training. None of the studies we reviewed mention whether or not such strategies were used as part of the training "package," but even if they were not, merely taking the instruments in the pretest session often serves as kind of an alerting mechanism for trainees to alter their responses to the questionnaires when they take them again later.

At least two quasicontrol approaches can be suggested for learning more about the possibility and nature of such instrument-interaction effects. First, a group might take the questionnaires, get feedback on their results, and then retake them after an intervening period of no training. Results would provide an estimate of the possible magnitude of response changes (independent of training content) due to learning more about what the questionnaires are "getting at." Second, an additional trained group might take the evaluation instruments only after training. This is the approach used by Bass in the first study listed in Table 1. If the "after-only" trained group scores like the trained group with both "before" and "after" measures, the possibility of interpreting changes as due only to artifactual interaction effects is greatly lessened.

TABLE 1.

	Nature of measures	Use of measures	Description of subjects	Experimental design	Results
Bass	Subjects finished series of incomplete sentences after seeing film *Twelve Angry Men.*	Before and after two-week T-group training	34 Executives	No control group; two other groups saw film *only* after training to check interaction effects	Subjects became more oriented toward interpersonal relations depicted in the film
Blake and Mouton	Attitudes toward five distinct managerial styles described and "taught" in managerial grid training	Before and after phase I of Managerial Grid training	33 Manager and 23 union representatives	No control group; no check on interaction effects	Managers increased on style depicting maximum concern for both production and people (9, 9). Union men increased emphasis on production (9, 1) and decreased emphasis on people (1, 9)
Baumgartel and Goldstein	Estimates of needs for *affection, inclusion,* and *control* and desires for others to behave with *affection, inclusion* and *control* (FIRO-B); also estimates of one's major values (Allport-Vernon-Lindzey)	Before and after a 15-week college course in Human Relations (including T-groups)	100 Kansas University students; 59 male, 41 female	No control group; no check on interaction effects	Females changed more than males; valued religion less, increased in desire for *control* and decreased in desire for *affection*; definite evidence showing effect of individual differences in nature of changes
Harrison	Descriptions of self and others–scorable in categories of *concreteness* and *tendency toward interference*	Before, three weeks after, and three months after NTL laboratory training	115 Persons from many occupations and institutions	No control group; no check on interaction effects	No effects found for short-term (three-week) follow-up. Modest increase in use of *inferential* concepts for three-month follow-up
Kassarjian	Tendencies toward "Inner" versus "Other" directedness	Before and after college course focused on T-group participation	125 Day school and night school students	Control group of 55 persons similar to those in T-groups; no check on interaction effects	No significant changes or differences between experimental and control groups
Kernan	Questionnaire describing one's orientation toward *consideration* and *initiating structure* (Leadership Opinion Questionnaire)	Before and after three-day laboratory training program	40 Engineering supervisors employed in the same company	Control group of 20 engineering supervisors; no check on interaction effects	No significant changes on either measure for either of the groups

TABLE 1. (cont.)

	Nature of measures	Use of measures	Description of subjects	Experimental design	Results
Oshry and Harrison	Checklist of causes of unresolved work problems and how to deal with them	Before and after two weeks of NTL laboratory training	16 Middle-level managers from various companies	No control group; no check on interaction effects	After training managers viewed their work problems less impersonally and believed they were more directly involved in the problems, but showed no change in the nature of what they would do about problems
Schutz and Allen	Estimates of needs for *affection, inclusion,* and *control* and desires for others to behave with *affection, inclusion,* and *control* (FIRO-B)	Before, after, and six months after a two-week laboratory program of the Western Training Laboratory	71 persons with widely varying backgrounds	Control group of 30 education students at University of California (Berkeley); no check on interaction effects	Correlations between before and after scores were lower for trainees than for control group; lowest correlations between before scores and six-month follow-up; no information given on the nature of the changes
Smith	Estimates of needs for *affection* and *control* and desires for others to behave with *affection* and *control* (4 scales of the FIRO-B)	Before and after T-group training	108 English managers and students (11 T-groups)	Control groups of 44 students in six discussion groups; no check on interaction effects	Disparity between needs and desires from others decreased for trainees, but not for control group members; changes were in direction of less need for *control* and greater need for *affection*

Sources: B. M. Bass, "Reactions to *Twelve Angry Men* as a Measure of Sensitivity Training," *Journal of Applied Psychology,* 46 (1962), 361-64; R. R. Blake and Jane S. Mouton, "Some Effects of Managerial Grid Seminar Training on Union and Management Attitudes Toward Supervision," *Journal of Applied Behavioral Science,* 2 (1966), 387-400; H. Baumgartel and J. W. Goldstein, "Need and Value Shifts in College Training Groups," *Journal of Applied Behavioral Science,* 3 (1967), 87-101; R. Harrison, "Cognitive Change and Participation in a Sensitivity Training Laboratory," *Journal of Consulting Psychology,* 30 (1966) 517-20; H. H. Kassarjian, "Social Character and Sensitivity Training," *Journal of Applied Behavioral Science,* 1 (1965), 430-40; J. P. Kernan, "Laboratory Human Relations Training: It's Effect on the Personality of Supervisory Engineers," *Dissertation Abstracts,* 25 (1964), 665-66; B. I. Oshry and R. Harrison, "Transfer from Here-and-Now to There-and-Then: Changes in Organizational Problem Diagnosis Stemming from T-Group Training," *Journal of Applied Behavioral Science,* 2 (1966), 185-98; W. C. Schutz and V. L. Allen, "The Effects of a T-Group Laboratory on Interpersonal Behavior," *Journal of Applied Behavioral Science,* 2 (1966), 265-86; and P. B. Smith, "Attitude Changes Associated with Training in Human Relations," *British Journal of Social and Clinical Psychology,* 3 (1964), 104-13.

(3). Finally, the actual magnitudes of changes obtained in these studies (even when control groups weren't used and interaction effects weren't checked) are small, and it would be unwise to argue that these minor attitudinal changes indicate, in any substantial way, the accomplishment of the broad behavioral goals and objectives of laboratory education.

Thus, it seems clear that research has not yet demonstrated that T-group training and/or laboratory education has any marked effect on one's "scores" on objective measures of attitude, orientation, outlook, or style.

SELF-AWARENESS AND INTERPERSONAL SENSITIVITY

Our listing of the goals of laboratory education placed self-insight or self-awareness (i.e., the ability to perceive one's self as others see one) and interpersonal sensitivity (i.e., broader awareness of interpersonal stimuli and increased accuracy in inferring others' feelings) in a position central to accomplishing the other goals. In a way, it is unfortunate that the practitioners of T-group or sensitivity training have claimed improved self-awareness and interpersonal sensitivity as goals, for measurement problems in the area of interpersonal perception are among the most difficult the behavioral scientist has ever faced.[12] Still we agree that methodological difficulties, no matter how great, should not deter investigators from considering the area, for we believe that T-group advocates rightly emphasize the crucial role of interpersonal perception in getting to know, and learning to work constructively with, other people.

We located a total of only seven studies related to the effects of laboratory education on self-awareness or interpersonal sensitivity. Of these, only one (Dunnette's) utilized a measurement methodology designed to control the various interpersonal prediction strategies discussed in Appendix B. Table 2 lists the seven studies along with relevant details about measures used, subjects, experimental designs, and results obtained.

Casual examination of this table reveals that most studies failed to use control groups, possible interaction effects between the questionnaires and the training programs were not examined, and (with the exception of the Dunnette study) no precautions were taken to assess the nature of possible differences in the prediction strategies used by subjects in the studies designed to get at possible changes in "interpersonal sensitivity." In terms of self-awareness, the studies by Burke and Bennis and by Gassner, Gold, and Snadowsky deserve special

[12] See Appendix B for a brief discussion of the problem. Recent articles summarizing the difficulties are: M. D. Dunnette, "People Feeling: Joy, More Joy and the Slough of Despond," *Journal of Applied Behavioral Science* (in press), and J. P. Campbell and M. D. Dunnette, "The Effectiveness of T-Group Experience in Managerial Training and Development," *Psychological Bulletin* (in press). Earlier, more technical statements, include L. J. Cronbach, "Processes Affecting Scores on 'Understanding of Others' and 'Assumed Similarity,'" *Psychological Bulletin* 52 (1955): 177-93; and N. L. Gage and L. J. Cronbach, "Conceptual and Methodological Problems in Interpersonal Perception," *Psychological Review* 62 (1955): 411-22.

TABLE 2.

	Nature of measures	Use of measures	Description of subjects	Experimental design	Results
Bass (self-description)	27 Adjectives descriptive of nine different mood factors	Administered five times during 10-day T-group laboratory	30 Supervisors, engineers, and administrators	No control group; check on interaction effects is purpose of the study	Skepticism decreased throughout training; concentration and depression increased and then declined; no significant amount of anxiety expressed at any time
Bennis, et al. (self-awareness)	34 Item inventory of various role behaviors	Before and after semester-long T-group meetings to describe "real" and "ideal" self	12 Business administration students	No control group; no check on interaction effects	No significant changes in discrepancies between real and ideal self-descriptions
Bennis, et al. (sensitivity)	34 Item inventory of various role behaviors	Members "predicted" how other members filled in inventory and discrepancy scores were computed	12 Business administration students	No control group; no check on interaction effects; no control on different strategies	No significant relationships
Burke and Bennis (self-awareness)	19 Bipolar adjectival rating scales	Described (1) each other group member; (2) "How I really am"; (3) "How I would like to be" during first week and during last week	84 Participants in six different NTL groups	No control group; no check on interaction effects	Subjects changed in direction of closer agreement between real self and ideal self ratings and saw themselves more as others saw them
Gassner, Gold, and Snadowsky (self-awareness)	Hill's Index of Adjustment and Values (40-item adjectival checklist)	Before and after training for descriptions of (1) This is characteristic of me; (2) I would like this to be characteristic of me; and (3) Most students would like this to be characteristic of them	3 Experiments; CCNY students; 45-50 in trained groups; 25-30 in control groups	Control groups were used; no check on interaction effects	Subjects changed in direction of less discrepancy between real and ideal selves. However, trained subjects changed no more than control group subjects
Lohman, Zenger, and Weschler (sensitivity)	Gordon Personal Profile (measuring ascendancy, emotional stability, etc.)	Before and after semester-long T-Groups; completed for themselves and for how they felt; trainer filled it in	65 UCLA students	No control group; no check on interaction effects; no control for different strategies	Slight increase in accuracy of students' predictions of trainer's responses but finding is useless because of confounding of different strategies
Gage and Exline (sensitivity)	50-Item questionnaire involving opinions about group processes, leadership styles, etc.	Before and after three-week NTL Laboratory training. Subjects gave own opinions and also predicted for group as a whole	2 Groups of 15 and 18 Persons	No control group; equivalent forms used to control effects of taking inventory twice	No changes in various accuracy and similarity indexes between before and after administrations
Dunnette (sensitivity)	Computer developed "empathy inventories" based on subjects' answers to preference inventory, adjective check-list, and manifest need statements	Before and after six weekly two-hour discussion or T-group sessions	65 University of Minnesota students and trainers; 10 T-groups comprised of 1 trainer and 4 members each; 3 control "discussion" groups of 1 leader and 4 members	Control groups discussed innocuous subjects; no interpersonal discussion; different inventories used before and after training; new methodology employed to control for different prediction strategies	Groups showing highest incidence of interpersonal interaction showed greatest ability to differentiate between persons "best known" and those "least known" at the end of experiment. Control groups and less interactive T-groups showed least ability to differentiate

Sources: B. M. Bass, "Mood Changes During a Management Training Laboratory," *Journal of Applied Psychology*, 46 (1962), 361-64; W. Bennis, R. Burke, H. Cutter, H. Harrington, and Joyce Hoffman, "A Note on Some Problems of Measurement and Prediction in a Training Group," *Group Psychotherapy*, 10 (1957), 328-41; R. L. Burke and W. G. Bennis, "Changes in Perception of Self and Others During Human Relations Training," *Human Relations*, 14 (1961), 165-82; Suzanne Gassner, J. Gold, and A. M. Snadowsky, "Changes in the Phenomenal Field as a Result of Human Relations Training," *Journal of Psychology*, 58 (1964), 33-41; K. Lohman, J. Zenger, and I. R. Weschler, "Some Perceptual Changes During Sensitivity Training," *Journal of Educational Research*, 53 (1959), 28-31; N. L. Gage and R. V. Exline, "Social Perception and Effectiveness in Discussion Groups," *Human Relations*, 6 (1953), 369-81; M. D. Dunnette, "People Feeling: Joy, More Joy and the Slough of Despond," *Journal of Applied Behavioral Science* (in press).

mention. With no control group, Burke and Bennis apparently showed that T-group training has the effect of reducing discrepancies in subjects' descriptions of real and ideal selves. But Bassner, Gold, and Snadowsky obtained the same results for *both* T-group trained and control group subjects, thereby substantially weakening the tenability of any assertions about the *unique* effects of T-group training on the nature of one's self-perception or its relative accuracy.

The study by Dunnette is the only one in this group showing any evidence that T-groups may result in increased interpersonal sensitivity. The methodology was designed to reduce substantially the likelihood of accurate predictions due to stereotypy or assumed similarity strategies. Therefore, accuracy, when it occurred, was much more likely to be the result of truly individualized patterns of interpersonal perception. Moreover, the T-group and control group meetings were recorded and rated according to the quality of interpersonal interaction.[13] Members of the more interactive groups were more accurate in their designations of whom they knew best (as measured by the empathy inventories) than members of the less interactive groups. This is the only direct evidence we know of that the interpersonal interaction of a "good" T-group has the effect of developing greater and more accurate social differentiation among the group's members.

Thus, from this group of studies, we must conclude that evidence in favor of any claims that laboratory education can increase or change interpersonal awareness, "self-insight," or interpersonal sensitivity is very nearly nonexistent. Dunnette's is the only study offering much hope to the practitioners of T-group training, and the conclusions from it must be carefully qualified because the subjects were not industrial employees and no measures of interpersonal sensitivity outside the immediate confines of the T-groups were obtained. As in the other two areas already discussed, we must conclude that much additional research needs to be done; the final answers are still far in the future.

OBSERVED CHANGES IN JOB BEHAVIOR

So far, we have reviewed studies bearing quite directly on whether or not T-groups actually accomplish their stated goals. Now, we move to those studies using more global (and, perhaps, more meaningful) measures of training outcomes. Earlier, we described three "sick" organizational units and characterized the managerial behavior patterns that seemed to be common to them. We also argued that individual behavior change was desirable in at least four broad areas for these organizations to overcome their "sickness" and regain operating effectiveness.[14] Now, we are able to ask about possible evidence in

[13] A system of rating interpersonal interaction called the Hill Interaction Matrix was used to rate the quality of group interchanges. See W. F. Hill, *A Guide to Understanding the Structure and Function of the Hill Interaction Matrix* (Los Angeles: University of Southern California, 1967).

[14] The four areas were to teach managers (1) to be more analytical in their study of people and problems, (2) to be less self-centered and more aware of how they affect others, (3) to face up to and to encourage conflict as an important basis for problem-solving, and, (4) to develop both the skill and desire to work interpersonally with others.

favor of laboratory education's bringing about behavior changes in any or all of these areas.

We located five studies bearing directly on this question.[15] Although carefully designed and conducted, they all suffer from the possibility of bias in the behavior change reports. This is because control groups and job behavior observers were chosen by the trained subjects. Thus, reports of behavior change for trained and nontrained subjects are subject to the contaminating effects of the observers' prior knowledge of the training histories of the persons being described and to whatever selective bias may have affected the trainees' designations of people for inclusion in the control groups. Even so, since these studies did actually focus on independent observations of job behaviors and behavioral changes rather than merely subjects' self-reports or questionnaire responses, they come much closer than other investigations to giving us direct information about possible behavioral effects of laboratory education. Their results constitute the backbone of favorable evidence usually offered by T-group practitioners and advocates.

The central approach used in each of the five investigations was to ask associates of trained and untrained subjects to describe changes they may have observed in the subjects' job behaviors during the previous year (which included the training experience). Efforts were made to match the control group with experimental subjects on such dimensions as type of job, organization (or department), and age. Details on each study and the results obtained are described below:

(1). Miles collected information from and about 34 high school principals who had been through NTL T-group training. Two control groups were used, one a group of 29 principals matched with the trainees, the other a group of 148 principals chosen randomly from a national roster. Observations on job behavior were obtained from an average of five associates for each of the 211 subjects. Pretraining and post-training descriptions were obtained from associates of the trainees and the matched control subjects on the Leader Behavior Description Questionnaire (LBDQ)[16] and the Group Participation Scale (GPS).[17] A check was made on the possibility of interaction between these measures and T-group

---

[15] J. B. Boyd and J. D. Elliss, *Findings of Research into Senior Management Seminars* (Toronto: Hydro-Electric Power Commission of Ontario, 1962); D. R. Bunker, "Individual Applications of Laboratory Training," *Journal of Applied Behavioral Science* 1 (1965): 131-48); M. B. Miles, "Changes During and Following Laboratory Training: A Clinical-Experimental Study," *Journal of Applied Behavioral Science* (1965), 215-42; I. M. Valiquet, *Contribution to the Evaluation of a Management Development Program* (Boston: MIT, 1965); W. J. Underwood, "Evaluation of Laboratory Method Training," *Training Directors Journal* 19 (1965): 34-40.

[16] See R. M. Stogdill and A. E. Coons, *Leader Behavior: Its Description and Measurement,* Business Research Monograph no. 88 (Columbus: Bureau of Business Research, Ohio State University, 1957), for details of the development and use of the LBDQ. The questionnaire measures two major dimensions of leadership behavior: "consideration" and "initiating structure."

[17] See H. B. Pepinsky, L. Siegel, and E. L. Van Alta, "The Criterion in Counseling: A Group Participation Scale," *Journal of Abnormal and Social Psychology* 47 (1952): 415-19, for details of the development and use of GPS. It is a peer nomination device desgined as an aid in evaluating the effects of, or describing the outcomes associated with, counseling.

training content by obtaining only post-training descriptions from half the subjects. Many additional measures were obtained, including ratings of behavior during training, a series of personality descriptions (such as ego strength and flexibility), and various "organizational" measures (such as job tenure, number of teachers supervised, etc).

More behavior changes were observed for trainees (job behavior changes were reported for 30 per cent of them) than for either of the two control groups (10 percent for the matched control group and 12 per cent for the random control group). The nature of the changes were derived from a crude content analysis of the descriptions; they included increased sensitivity to others, increased communication and leadership skill, increased consideration toward others and more relaxed job behavior styles. Surprisingly, however, no significant differences were obtained on any of the structured questionnaires such as the LBDQ or the GPS. The most interesting finding was that job behavior changes were reported most often for those principals who had been perceived by their trainers to profit most from the T-group experience ($r = .55$ between job behavior change and trainer ratings of amount of change during training).

(2). Boyd and Elliss collected information from and about 42 managers selected after taking part in one of three different in-plant T-groups. Two control groups were used: one, 12 managers who had had no training; the other, 10 managers who had been in a standard human relations program. Boyd and Elliss personally interviewed each subject's superior, two of his peers, and two of his subordinates. These observer-associates also sorted a set of 80 statements describing different job behavior changes.

Relatively more observers reported job behavior changes for the T-group trainees (65 percent) than for the conventionally trained control subjects (51 percent) or the untrained control subjects (34 percent). Here again, however, no significant differences were obtained between the three groups when the more structured behavior change descriptions (the set of 80 statements) were examined.

(3). Bunker, in a much larger study, collected information from and about 229 persons (mostly managers or other administrators) who had been in one of six NTL sessions held during 1960 and 1961. One control group was used, consisting of 112 matched subjects whose names were obtained from the trainees in response to a request to "choose a person in a similar organizational position." Questionnaires about observed behavior changes were sent and returned by mail. From five to seven observer-associates completed questionnaires for each subject. Unfortunately, Bunker used no structured questionnaires in his study.

More behavior changes were reported for the trained subjects (at least two observers agreed on changes for 67 percent of the trainees) than for control group subjects (two observers agreed on changes for only 33 percent of the controls). In additional analyses, Bunker developed 15 content categories (on which independent judges showed 90 percent agreement in their classifications) for investigating the nature of the reported behavior changes. Greatest differences between trained and untrained subjects were reported in areas related to more openness, increased interpersonal skills, and better understanding of self and others. Differences in behavior reports for the two groups were small for such things as initiating action, assertiveness, and confidence.

(4). Valiquet's study is similar, on a much smaller scale, to Bunker's. He collected information from and about 34 participants who had taken part in in-plant laboratory training. One control group of 15 untrained subjects was used. Questionnaires were mailed to an average of five observers nominated by the subjects. The content categories developed by Bunker were used in analyzing the results. Results were essentially the same as those reported by Bunker. More changes were reported for trained than for untrained subjects, and the major changes occurred in categories related to openness, interpersonal understanding, and skill in social interaction. Unfortunately, like Bunker, Valiquet relied exclusively on free or open-end responses; no structured questionnaires were used.

(5). Underwood added an interesting twist in collecting information from and about 15 supervisors who had taken 30 hours of in-plant T-group training. He asked observer-associates of the 15 and of a matched control group of 15 untrained subjects to describe not only job behavior changes but also their effects on the subjects' overall job effectiveness. Only one observer was recruited for each subject, and each was asked to keep track of observed changes over a 15-week period rather than relying merely on memory of what may have occurred over the past year. Some change was reported for nine trained subjects and seven untrained subjects; over two-thirds of the total of 36 changes were reported for the nine trained supervisors. Nearly all the changes occurred in areas bearing on personal and interpersonal behavior. Most surprising is the finding that although a large majority (about 70 percent) of the changes in *both* groups were seen as enhancing job effectiveness, the effect was more marked among the *untrained* subjects (80 percent) than among the *trained* subjects (67 percent).

What may be concluded from results of these five investigations? Primarily, we can say that associates of most persons who have received T-group training report observable changes in their (the trainees') behavior back on the job. Whether or not these reported changes are based on actual changes in job behavior is difficult to know because of many possible sources of contamination and bias common to the studies. For example:

(1). Asking the trained subjects to name persons for control groups subjects very likely tipped the hand of the investigators. Trained subjects, knowing they were to be compared in some way with their control mates, might alter their behavior accordingly. Moreover, their selection of possible control persons might be biased in the direction of naming persons who had a history of less effective interpersonal behavior, who had shown fewer recent changes in their job behavior, or both. It is impossible to estimate whether or not these biases occurred or what their relative magnitude may have been. Only Miles, by choosing a random control group in addition to a nominated control group, guarded against such biasing components. It is encouraging, therefore, that his results were similar to those reported by the other researchers.

(2). Many sources of potential bias are related to the subjects' nomination of observers. First, the original designation would be more likely to include friendly co-workers, who would tend to say "good" rather than unfriendly things. Second, subjects—particularly the trained ones—would have the opportunity to "brief" the observers before they responded to the questionnaires. Third, most observers—especially those from the intraorganizational studies—would be aware of which subjects had been through the T-groups and which had not, and such knowledge could easily result in either conscious or unconscious perceptual distortions of "changes" in subjects' behavior. Finally, since several observers were usually chosen for each subject, they would probably have ample opportunity to talk with one another and compare notes before completing and returning their questionnaires. Only Boyd and Elliss, by personally designating the observers ahead of time and by interviewing them instead of depending on questionnaire responses, probably avoided most of these biases.

(3). Judgments about the extent and nature of the behavior changes reported were undoubtedly subject to biases of interpretation, based as they were on analyses of anecdotal responses to open-ended questions. Miles and Boyd and Elliss asked observers to supplement their subjective descriptions with more objective behavior descriptions (such as the LBDQ, the 80-item checklist used by Boyd and Elliss, etc.). Since no differences between trained and untrained subjects were obtained on the objective instruments, it is difficult to know just what factors contributed most to the differences obtained on the subjective material. The probability is great that a major determinant of the differences may be the various biasing sources we have outlined here.

(4). The studies are rendered even more difficult to interpret because all but Underwood relied on retrospective accounts. No observations of job behavior were made before training. Even Underwood used no before measures, but he did ask observers to be alert to and to record instances of behavior change as they occurred rather than relying on their memories and faulty perceptions of possible changes.

(5). Finally, even if it is granted that the reported changes do indeed reflect actual changes in trainees' job behavior, we must note that the changes are restricted almost entirely to the domain of greater openness, better understanding, more consideration, and interpersonal warmth. Few, if any, of the reported changes were in the equally important areas of analytical problem-solving attitudes and skills, encouragement of and increased skill in resolving conflict, or decreased self-centeredness and greater self-awareness. Moreover, none of the studies except Underwood's attempted to estimate the possible effects of any observed changes on overall job effectiveness. Unfortunately, his yielded results opposite to those we should expect.

Based on these observations, we conclude that the evidence of training-produced changes in job behavior, though present, is severely limited by the two major considerations we have mentioned. First, the many sources of bias constitute competing explanations for the results obtained. Second, none of the studies yields any evidence that the changes in job behavior have any favorable effect on actual performance effectiveness. Thus, there is little to support a claim that T-group or laboratory education effects any substantial behavioral change back on the job for any large proportion of trainees. Whatever change does occur seems quite limited in scope and may not contribute in any important way to changes in overall job effectiveness.

CHANGES IN ORGANIZATIONAL OUTCOMES

When a "company doctor" undertakes diagnosis and therapy on a "sick" organization, his ultimate aim must certainly be to turn the functioning of that organization around, to do whatever is necessary to get it on the move again, to restore it to efficient operation. Thus, the ultimate practical payoff for any training or personnel development program is not apt to be changes in trainee attitudes, levels of self-awareness, or even job behavior, but instead, the possibility of a "turnaround" in the overall functioning of the organizational unit. Obviously, this is the broadest, most global level that one may use in undertaking a training evaluation study, and it is rare to find such studies reported. Nonetheless, we have located five (varying *greatly* in quality) which seem to qualify at this level.[18]

The studies by Blansfield and Buchanan are reported so sketchily that they deserve only brief mention. Both involved lengthy laboratory programs within large organizational units. Blansfield's report is devoted exclusively to an anecdotal account of organizational changes presumably due to and reflecting favorably upon the program. Buchanan's report is centered on descriptive material showing changes toward decentralization in decision-making, greater cooperation among work units, and a substantial increase in organizational profits after the organization experienced widespread personnel retrenchment following the 1957 recession.

Blake, Mouton, Barnes, and Greiner presented the first phases of the Management Grid program to all 800 supervisors and managers of a large organizational unit (4,000 employees) of a petroleum corporation.[19] A number of measures were made before and after training and others only after the

[18] See M. G. Blansfield, "Depth Analysis of Organizational Life," *California Management Review,* 5 (1962), 29-42; P. D. Buchanan, *Organizational Development Following Major Retrenchment* (mimeographed report, 1964); R. R. Blake, Jane Mouton, L. B. Barnes, L. E. Greiner, "Breakthrough in Organizational Development," *Harvard Business Review* 42 (1964); 133-55; B. M. Bass, "The Anarchist Movement and the T-Group," *Journal of Applied Behavioral Science* 3 (1967); 211-26; and S. T. White, *Evaluation of an Analytic Trouble Shooting Program: A Preliminary Report* (research memorandum, Kepner-Tregoe and Associates, July 28, 1967), 14 pp.

[19] For a thorough description of the Management Grid program, see R. R. Blake and Jane Mouton, *The Management Grid* (Houston: Gulf Publishing Co., 1964). The program involves several stages. Initially a series of T-group-like (but more heavily instrumented) sessions are used to explore peer relationships and the managerial styles of the participants. An important aim is to change individuals' styles in the direction of so-called 9, 9 management, a style giving heavy emphasis to *both* people and production. Over a year's time, other phases explore authority relationships among management levels, provide practice in resolving intergroup conflict, and offer aids to developing more collaborative problem-solving methods.

program had been completed. The former included organizational outcome indicators such as net profit, controllable operating costs, unit production per employee, and relative success in solving such problems as high maintenance and utility costs, plant safety, and management communication. The information about solving problems was, of course, mostly anecdotal and largely subjective. No comparable organizational unit was used as a control group. During the training program, profits increased substantially and costs decreased. Although a substantial portion of the profit increase was due to economic and other noncontrollable factors and to manpower reduction, the authors estimate that 13 percent (amounting to several million dollars) was due to improved operating procedures and higher productivity per man-hour.

What were these improved operating procedures? According to other indexes, they apparently included such things as more meetings, more efficient use of manpower skills as shown by more job transfers and a higher rate of promotion for young line managers (as opposed to highly tenured staff men), greater success in solving cost, safety, and communication problems, and increased use of the 9, 9 management style (as indicated by post-training responses to attitude measures).

It seems apparent from the report that this organizational unit did indeed accomplish a "turnaround" during the time the supervisors were exposed to the Management Grid program. What is far less apparent is the exact cause of the turnaround. Would *any* total push emphasis pointing up organizational problems, emphasizing the need for more cost consciousness, and calling for greater team effort among the 800 supervisors and managers have worked as well? Or was the specific technology of the T-group-like early phases of the grid program specifically responsible for the changes in organizational outcomes? Might the changes in profits not have occurred without any training at all—merely as a consequence of widespread cost emphasis and extensive manpower reductions? Unfortunately, it is impossible to answer these important questions from the data of this particular investigation.

Both Bass and White used control groups to assess effects of training on organizational outcomes. White's study involved training nonmanagerial employees in a real work setting, whereas Bass's study involved training business students and observing how they did in "running" computer-simulated organizations. Unfortunately, White's research was an evaluation of a variant of the Kepner-Tregoe decision-making program and does not, therefore, relate to T-grouping or laboratory education. Still, the study serves as a model of careful research and deserves mention for that reason, if for no other. The study was conducted on two widely separated production lines—both producing doors—in a large automobile assembly plant. Production measures (readily translatable into dollar costs) were gathered for one month for both lines.[20] During the ensuing three weeks, 31 of the 44 troubleshooters on the experimental line received training in the Kepner-Tregoe Analytic Trouble Shooting program.[21]

[20] Three measures were used: (1) manned downtime, (2) scrap, and (3) off-standard percent (an index of production efficiency).

[21] The program has two main objectives: to develop ability to anticipate and prevent

The 39 troubleshooters on the control line received no training; in fact, they were unaware of the training received by the men on the experimental line. Production measures were gathered again during the month immediately following the training program. Production measures gathered after training were lower (reflecting poorer efficiency) than those gathered before training for *both* lines because preparations were begun during the month for the model change-over. However, the loss in efficiency was negligible for the trained line and substantial for the untrained line.

Bass used the Carnegie Institute of Technology Management Game in an experimental setting to study transfer effects from the T-group setting to a new group.[22] The Carnegie Tech game is extremely complex, simulating the activities of several firms in a multiproduct industry. Several students make up each firm, and they must interact effectively if the company is to prosper. Nine student T-groups (without trainers) met for 15 weeks. At the end of the 15 weeks, three of the groups were divided into thirds and reformed into three new groups, three were split in half and reassembled, and three remained intact. The nine teams then competed with one another in the game. The splintered groups broke even or made a profit; but the intact groups lost an average of 5.37 million dollars over the 15-week trial period, even though the intact groups gave the most positive descriptions of their openness, communication, and cooperation. On the basis of his observations, Bass attributed the lower performance of the intact groups to a general neglect of the control function. Apparently, the members of the intact groups never bothered to check on each other to see if assignments were being completed.

What may we conclude from these studies about the effect of laboratory education on organizational outcomes? Not much, actually. Of the five studies, three were purely descriptive, offering no experimental evidence about possible organizational effects due to the training technology specific to T-groups or laboratory education. It seems safe to say that concurrent T-group training is at least not incompatible with organizational "turnarounds" in profits and overall operating efficiency, but this is a far cry from stating that laboratory education is *the* prescription for an organization's ills. Of the two experimental studies, only one utilized T-group training methodology and that in a simulated rather than real organization setting. The best of the lot (White's study) does yield solid, experimental evidence that a particular training approach, tailor-made to accomplish specific behavioral and organizational outcomes, apparently did so successfully. As such, the study may serve the important function of alerting T-group advocates to the old training dictum that the first step in training

---

trouble from occurring and to find and fix trouble more efficiently when it does occur. The program presents no technical knowledge, but teaches a method of production problem analysis. The program used in this experiment was five days long. Half of each day was spent in the classroom with the instructor, and the other half day was spent practicing the analytic method on actual production problems. The emphasis was entirely on increasing analytical skills and *not* on interpersonal or human relations skills.

[22] See K. J. Cohen and E. Rhenman, "The Role of Management Games in Education and Research," *Management Science* 7 (1961): 131-66, for a description of the Carnegie Tech game.

program development should be a checklist of training needs. Training and development programs might be tailored to accomplish changes in line with such needs, rather than being directed toward the broad and rather amorphous goals (such as increased sensitivity, interpersonal awareness, and social diagnostic skills) usually claimed for their programs by the advocates of laboratory education.

REPRISE, APPRAISAL, AND FORECAST

We have recounted many problems wrought by organizational malaise and reviewed research evidence about individual organizational effects of laboratory education. What may we conclude?

Laboratory education has not been shown to bring about any marked change in one's standing on objective measures of attitudes, values, outlooks, interpersonal perceptions, self-awareness, or interpersonal sensitivity. In spite of these essentially negative results on objective measures, individuals who have been trained by laboratory education methods are more likely to be seen as changing their job behavior than are individuals in similar job settings who have not been trained. These reported changes are in the direction of more openness, better self- and interpersonal understanding, and improved communications and leadership skills. Unfortunately, these behavior reports suffer from many possible sources of bias and must, therefore, be taken with a grain of salt. Moreover, we have practically no evidence about possible effects of laboratory education on individuals' skills in analyzing problem situations, synthesizing information, facing up to and resolving interpersonal conflict, and deriving and implementing solutions to organizational problems. Most research has been restricted to "demonstrating" the so-called human relations effects of T-groups and has given little attention to other equally important areas in the total process of recognizing, diagnosing, and solving problems in an organizational setting. Finally, we do know (from the large-scale study by Blake, Mouton, Barnes, and Greiner) that laboratory education conducted extensively among supervisors can occur concomitantly with a "turnaround" in an organization's overall functioning.

Overall, then, we must recognize that certain "truths" of medical diagnosis and treatment apply equally to the diagnosis and treatment of organizational ills. It is easier to describe symptoms than to identify causal agents. It is easier to prescribe broad spectrum treatments than to specify the exact therapeutic effects of any one. And, cures often occur without any clear indication of which therapeutic agent may have been most effective.

We sincerely hope that this review of research evidence will not be viewed as irrevocably damaging to laboratory education. It is true, unfortunately, that few if any individual or organizational behavioral outcomes can be specified as due strictly to laboratory education. But this is not unusual. The same can be said for most present training procedures in industry.

Primarily then, our review has brought out weaknesses and gaps in the research related to the effects of laboratory education. We believe that research in the area of interpersonal behavior is too important to suffer a demise based on results from the studies done so far. We hope, therefore, that we have provided impetus for an expanded rather than a diminished emphasis on the behavioral effects of laboratory education.

We need to know the behavioral prescriptions—according to different individuals and different organizational situations—that may be attached to laboratory education and T-group training. We need to know the causal agents underlying the symptoms of organizational ill health described earlier. We need, in particular, to know not only the effects on interpersonal skills but also the cognitive, analytical, and information-processing effects of laboratory education. All this must be studied with more sophisticated measures of interpersonal perception and problem solving procedures, more frequent use of control groups, greater attention to possible interaction effects between measures and training content, application of behavioral observations and reports before as well as after training, and increased care to assure the absence of biasing factors in behavioral observations.

We predict that industrial practice is about to witness a revolution in training and training evaluation research. Excellent research investigations will become the rule rather than the exception. Fifteen years from now, we expect that a review article should be able to outline specific behavioral outcomes to be expected from different learners after exposure to particular training programs in response to carefully diagnosed organizational needs. Manpower development in the firm of the future will be centered on no single method or technique. Instead, industrial education will make flexible use of many approaches—carefully researched, programmed, and sequenced to instill in *all* learners the desired repertoire of knowledges, attitudes, and job and interpersonal skills.

APPENDIX A: GROUP TRAINING APPROACHES

Procedures used in laboratory education differ, and no "typical" pattern can accurately describe what goes on in all settings. (For first-hand accounts of actual T-group experiences, see sources listed in footnote 3.) To describe a T-group in very general terms: the focal point is usually a small (10-15 people), unstructured group. There is no agenda, and no activities or topics are planned ahead of time. A professional (called a trainer or educator) is nearly always present, but he rejects a leadership role. Members are to discuss what goes on in the group—behavior, impressions formed, feelings elicited, reasons for these, and so on. In the language of T-group practitioners, the focus is on the "here-and-now," a focus designed to avoid fruitless discussions of past history and behavioral self-reports not subject to direct examination by the group members. Emphasis on the "here-and-now" is intended to reduce the significance of any status symbols (e.g., company position, level of education, family background, etc.) possessed by the members.

Often, the trainer begins by merely stating that the purpose of the group is to improve each member's understanding of his own and others' behavior. He then falls silent and refuses further guidance. The vacuum is very often filled by feelings of frustration, expressions of hostility, and eventual attempts by some members to impose an organized, usually hierarchical (leaders, committees, etc.), structure on the group. Such attempts to assume leadership roles are usually resented by other members, and they may begin to consider why the self-appointed leader tried to force his will on the group. Such behavior soon generalizes and other members and other behaviors become a basis for discussion so that every participant soon has an opportunity to learn more about his own and others' behavior and its implications for his ability to handle different types of personal interactions successfully.

Two conditions are generally believed to be crucial for behavioral reeducation to occur in the group situation. First, an atmosphere of interpersonal support or "psychological safety" must be generated. That is, each member must believe that the group's purpose is productive and good rather than destructive or bad. No matter what a member does or what he reveals about himself, the group must act in a supportive and nonevaluative manner. This atmosphere of support is obviously crucial; otherwise, members will not feel safe in exposing their feelings, dropping their defenses, or trying out new ways of interacting. Second, for behavioral reeducation to occur, articulate and meaningful feedback must take place. Each member must receive information about his impact on others in the group and feedback about the accuracy of the impressions and feelings he derives from the behavior of the others. The role of the trainer is of great importance, for it is up to him more than anyone else to assure that the members develop "here-and-now" behavior patterns of *both* openness and trust. The trainer thus serves mostly as a behavior model. He absorbs initial feelings of hostility and personal attacks without becoming defensive, provides behaviorally oriented rather than personally oriented feedback, expresses his own feelings openly and honestly, and is strongly supportive of similar expressions from other group members.

The T-group focus is used in varying degrees by different managerial laboratory education approaches. For example, in "instrumented" group training, the behavior model for group members is provided by a series of questionnaires requiring them to rate themselves and each other on how supportive they are, how freely they express feelings, and how skillfully they give feedback. These ratings, along with reading assignments, examinations, and other instruments form grist for the mill during the early phases of the widely used Management Grid program (see R. R. Blake and Jane S. Mouton, "The Instrumented Training Laboratory," in I. R. Weschler and E. H. Schein, editors, *Issues in Human Relations Training* [Washington, D.C.: National Training Laboratories, National Education Association, 1962], or Blake and Mouton, *The Management Grid* [Houston: Gulf, 1964]).

In contrast to these approaches is the widely known and utilized approach advocated by C. H. Kepner and B. B Tregoe (see their "Developing Decision

Makers," *Harvard Business Review* 38 [1960] : 115-24). Their problem-solving training program makes no intended use of T-group methodology, but it places heavy emphasis on improving the analytical and information synthesis phases of the problem-solving process. Here, the group members become deeply involved in solving a series of simulated problems involving many aspects of manufacturing, pricing, inventory control, and marketing. The problem-solving sessions (essentially, sohpisticated role-playing exercises) are intertwined with reading assignments and lectures emphasizing the importance of problem analysis and hypothetical testing *before* taking action in meeting organizational problems.

APPENDIX B:
MEASURING INTERPERSONAL SENSITIVITY

The difficulties involved in measuring the elusive phenomenon called "interpersonal sensitivity" will become apparent to the reader if he considers some of the possible strategies an individual might use to discern accurately what others are feeling. First, a person may have an accurate awareness of the modal feelings of various subgroups in our society (e.g., all women, all college graduates, all engineers, etc.). In other words, he may know what the typical response may be for the majority of persons in a subgroup. His strategy then becomes one of predicting that each member of a subgroup is like the majority of persons in the group; to discern a given person's feelings, he must know what "category" he belongs in and what the feelings of "people-in-general" in that category are. To the extent that he does actually possess accurate subgroup stereotypes, he will, of course, be right more often than he will be wrong. But, he will also be wrong a substantial portion of the time. It is a sad commentary, but it nonetheless is true that interpersonal sensitivity might be greatly enhanced if T-groups did nothing more than help the trainees learn to form *accurate* stereotypes; however, we believe that most T-group practitioners would be greatly distressed if we charged them with doing only this.

A second strategy, which also yields accurate predictions of others' feelings, is the "assumed similarity" strategy. Here, an effective and accurate interpersonal perceiver might be "sensitive" in the sense that he can accurately identify the subset of persons whose reactions and feelings are similar to his own. Then, simply by studying his own feelings and attributing them to others, he can accomplish the desirable goal of "knowing others" in his environment. Of course, he also runs grave risks of guessing wrong as he seeks to identify those who are like him. In this case, of course, the successful T-group will be one that manages to make people more similar to one another in their feelings or which successfully teaches people to be able to recognize more accurately those persons who really are similar to them. Here the T-group would be training people to be more alike and presumably more conforming, a charge which also should engender some degree of distress among T-group practitioners. Most T-groups, we believe, hope that they are training people to overcome stereotyped expectations, tendencies toward projection, and the like; their meta-goal is to train people to get to know each new individual as an individual and to be able to make accurate predictions *for him.*

The major point of this discussion of interpersonal prediction strategies is to emphasize the elusive and complex nature of interpersonal sensitivity. There is no *one* strategy, no *one* "sensitivity"; instead, there seem to be many, varying greatly in the levels of interpersonal sophistication necessary for applying them. The nature of the sensitivities developed may differ greatly from person to person and from program to program. Unless the various components and strategies involved in interpersonal sensitivity are taken into account during the design of measuring instruments and during the design and implementation of research investigations, little new knowledge concerning T-group training effects or the likelihood of transferring skills back to the work setting will accrue. So far (as can be seen from our discussion in the text of this article), most investigators have been ignorant of the serious measurement and design problems inherent in this area.

Chris Argyris

ISSUES IN EVALUATING LABORATORY EDUCATION

In order to evaluate whether or not the Dunnette and Campbell paper achieves its purposes, a distinction should be made between research whose aim is scientific understanding and research whose aim is to evaluate systematically social action activities like laboratory education and T-groups.[1] The primary objective of the former type of research is the creation of valid knowledge. Its basic rules are to maximize rigor and elegant explanations regardless of the time and cost. In the field of laboratory education and T-groups, examples of basic research would include understanding the nature of interpersonal relationships or the nature of groups or the interrelationships between the two.

Research to evaluate the effectiveness of laboratory education and T-groups must take into account the purposes for which they are designed. Dunnette and Campbell clearly state certain objectives of T-groups and quite properly ask, Do

From Marvin D. Dunnette, John P. Campbell and Chris Argyris, "A Symposium: Laboratory Training," *Industrial Relations* 8 (October, 1968): 1-45. Reprinted by permission. © 1968, Regents of the University of California, Berkeley.

[1] I wish to thank Fritz Steele and Douglas Hall for their helpful comments on this paper.

T-groups accomplish these objects? Research, if it is to be of help in answering this question *includes, but goes beyond,* the rules used to gain knowledge for the sake of knowledge.

The question, Do T-groups work? really asks much more than what new knowledge has been added. The question really asks, Do T-groups work (1) in nonexperimental settings, (2) with people who are performing nonexperimental roles, (3) at a cost (material or human) that is manageable by the client system, and (4) at an expenditure of time that is reasonable (e.g., change that takes more time, costs more money, etc., than the organization has is not very effective). These questions go beyond the scope of scientific understanding. The big difference is that effectiveness of the product is not measured simply by its adherence to the rules of rigor and elegance; it is measured by the skill with which rigor, elegance, cost, usefulness, and producibility are optimized or "satisficed."

One of the major limitations of the Dunnette and Campbell review is that it attempts to evaluate T-groups by the rules of scientific understanding. For example, they state that "scientific standards for properly evaluating training experiences are few in number and disarmingly simple." The rules that they define are the rules for scientific understanding. What they fail to point out are the *limits* these rules have when one attempts to generalize in the nonexperimental world. Recently even the so-called hard-headed experimentalists have begun to acknowledge the difficulty of understanding the "real" world by the use of traditional rigorous research methods.[2]

This omission leads Dunnette and Campbell to accept some evidence for effectiveness which is not acceptable, to overlook other evidence that is relevant, and to impute goals and motives to training and organizational development people which are not necessarily valid (and about which they present no systematic data). To take the last point first, it may not be accurate to state that these men resist evaluation because they believe all training is good and that it requires no evaluation. "Crying organizational needs" are not the only reason why organizational development people are sometimes loath to "fiddle around" designing an elegant experiment. Thoughtful practitioners may resist the elegant experiment because they have found (by contracting out research to behavioral scientists) that the more elegant the experiment research, in terms of the principles Dunnette and Campbell suggest, the less they really know about the effectiveness of the laboratory program, the more money they may be accused of wasting, and the higher the probability that the research team either alienated itself from the clients or used such "objective" measures that the clients, who filled out the appropriate questionnaires, have little trust in the results.

For example, several companies that attempted to sponsor rigorous research regarding their group programs found that the operational measures designed by the researchers were not rigorous enough. What is the meaning of results about group cohesiveness, they ask, if the operational definition of cohesiveness is the

---

[2] For a review of such research, see Chris Argyris, "Some Unintended Consequences of Rigorous Research." *Psychological Bulletin* (in press).

number of times people say "we" versus "I"? In the practitioners' experience the pronoun "we" may be most frequently used by executives precisely when the group is least cohesive in order to cover up the lack of cohesion. What is the relevance of interaction counts that identify who contacted whom and who initiated action, and then fail to identify the content because "rigorous measures were not available." It is ironic, but, I believe, true that maybe the clients may be more demanding of the research design than are the researchers who follow the "simple" rules of scientific inquiry.

RESEARCH CONDITIONS SIMILAR TO FORMAL ORGANIZATIONS

Let us explore more carefully the requirements of rigorous research. The research strategy that Dunnette and Campbell describe as "simple" can be shown to place subjects in situations that are similar to the conditions at the lower ends of the pyramidal hierarchy in organizations. For example, top management (researcher) defines the workers' (subject's) role as rationally and clearly as possible (to minimize error) and as simply as possible (to minimize having to draw upon a select population, thereby reducing the generalizability of the research findings); provides as little information as possible beyond the tasks (thereby minimizing the time perspective of the subject); and defines the inducements for participating. If the rigorous criteria defined in most texts on research method were carried out, they would tend to create a world for the subjects in which their behavior is defined, controlled, evaluated, manipulated, and reported to a degree that is comparable to the behavior of workers in the most mechanized assembly-line conditions.[3] Mechanistic organizations and rigorous research activities tend to have the same underlying characteristics. Rigorous research, in this sense, is mechanistic research.

People being studied under these conditions may react by withdrawal (physical or psychological), hostility (overt or covert), an increasing emphasis on monetary rewards for having to participate, and finally banding together to fight the noxious agent—in this case—the researcher.[4] And if their hostility is great enough they may attack the superiors in the organization who invited the researcher into the system. They may do so partially because they perceive the superiors as responsible. They may even use the opportunity to express some pent-up feelings toward these superiors. Could it not be that some training, personnel, or organizational development people are well aware that they might get into trouble if they invite researchers in and this is why they tend to resist research? Furthermore, may they not be well aware how many researchers tend to be blind to their negative impact on people in organizations?[5]

Fearing that researchers will tend to create difficulties within their

---

[3] Ibid.
[4] Ibid.
[5] L. L. Ferguson, "Social Scientists in the Plant," *Harvard Business Review* 42 (May-June, 1964): 133-43, and Carl I. Hovland, "Two New Social Science Research Units in Industrial Settings," *American Psychologist* 16 (1961): 87-91.

organization, some practitioners charge that "now is not the time because there is some sort of a crisis" and/or take the position that education is such a good thing that it does not require research! These types of reactions may have been encouraged by the researchers because they have traditionally maintained that in the interests of rigor, the researcher should remain separated from the setting that he is studying.

Some practitioners do take on the role of the "organizational doctor" and focus more on helping than they do on research. However, there are many thoughtful practitioners who would be glad to include research if they could find ways to minimize the very real problems that they foresee if they use the mechanistic research model that is recommended by Dunnette and Campbell. Behavioral scientists have to realize that practitioners are being asked to permit research activity which is so mechanistic that it increases the chances of creating new organizational crises.[6] As Dunnette and Campbell point out, in a system already full of crisis, it would be the height of inhumanity for an organizational development expert to conduct research that would add to the human tension. An excellent example of this problem is related to the use of control groups.

THE USE OF CONTROL GROUPS

Dunnette and Campbell correctly emphasize the importance of control groups. They are very critical of the lack of such controls in much of the research that they reviewed. They admonish the researchers for not being rigorous enough. However, they apparently fail to consider the possibility that some of the studies do not include control groups because the researchers realized that to attempt such a step would be meaningless. For example, how would one define rigorously a control group in studies of top management organic or "family" groups going through change experiences? What comparable organization could one use that would control for all the variables except the ones being manipulated? Also, can a particular president—and the relationships that he has with his vice presidents and they with each other—be rigorously matched with a control group?

The difficulties are also immense when stranger groups are being studied. If one has 100 people attending a laboratory, could one ask a subgroup to sit around and do innocuous things in order that a control group be established? Could one ask two subgroups to remain longer so that one could go through a laboratory and then do nothing for one week and the other do nothing for one week and then go through a laboratory? Even if they agree, how about the feelings that are generated by people who know they are "playing games" and that their management is unaware of it (for if they were, they might have selected different men to attend the laboratory or they might have different expectations which they could unintentionally communicate to the individual before he attended the laboratory—or they might never have sent them)?

---

[6] Some practitioners also tend to resist the more organic research methods.

One reply to these questions is to say that control groups are best used in an experimental setting. However, this solution has some difficulties related to the rigorous definition of an activity for the control group that is truly neutral. For example, Dunnette used control groups that discussed innocuous subjects. There was no interpersonal discussion. A question that remains unanswered by Dunnette, however is—may not people (especially students who, as pointed out above, may be tired of being manipulated for the researcher's pusposes) develop strong feelings about themselves and each other for sitting around and discussing innocuous subjects? What happens if the researcher also imposes a rule that there should not be any discussion of feelings and interpersonal relations? If feelings build up, how are they dissipated? What effects might these feelings have on the behavior and the reports of the control group? Perhaps control group members learn much about themselves as they introspect about their willingness to submit to discussing innocuous things and being, or acting as if they were, involved. If they are not permitted to discuss the emotionality of performing innocuous activities, could they not also hide their learning—or as a minimum, their feelings—in their behavior or the instruments they fill out? Could it be that control groups per se do not necessarily provide more understanding and clarity? Indeed, could they provide a false sense of security if they are not examined very carefully? I do not know the answers to these questions. All I am suggesting is that scientific rigor requires that they be faced.

Speaking of rigor, there is another limitation to much of the research that the authors reviewed. One has no idea of the operational definition of a T-group. A T-group in most cases is treated as a black box. For example, Dunnette used as staff some individuals who had much experience and some who had little. Does this mean that the subjects go through comparable experiences? Probably not, Dunnette might reply, this is why measures were taken to show that the more people discussed emotions effectively the more they gained empathy. There was, Dunnette would point out, differential learning. But, why was there this differential? Dunnette would reply because they focused on emotions. But do we know this with the certainty that is implied? What was the impact of the style of the staff leaders? Could their warmth have been a potent variable? Truax, for example, has shown that in psychotherapy groups where emotions are discussed the style of the therapist (in terms of warmth, acceptance, etc.) is crucial.[7] Could this also be true of laboratories?

These questions are not limited to the Dunnette study. Almost all studies suffer from the same limitation. However, it was Dunnette and Campbell who imply that Dunnette's study provides us with results in which we should feel the greatest confidence.

A third issue related to control groups is the possibility that individual interpersonal competence may increase simply through the passage of time. Merely remaining in an organizational setting may increase an individual's interpersonal competence or it may increase just because he attended a laboratory program,

---

[7] Charles B. Truax, "Some Implications of Behavior Therapy for Psychotherapy," *Journal of Counseling Psychology* 13 (1966): 160-70.

regardless of whether he participates (i.e., one's very presence in an educational setting may change one's behavior).

Organizational theory and research has something to say about the probability that behavior could become more competent (in terms of T-group criteria) over time without education. For example, research suggests that the *natural* thrust of management systems populated by individuals who hold "pyramidal values" is to manifest relatively low interpersonal competence and to generate norms that support low interpersonal competence. The theory and research would lead to the prediction that, over time, the natural tendency is *not* to change behavior in the direction of increasing interpersonal competence. In three different studies, it has been found that the behavior of executives does not tend to become more effective over time even though the executives can identify the costs of relatively low interpersonal competence to themselves and to the organization.[8] The qualitative and quantitative data suggest that they cannot alter their behavior toward increasing interpersonal competence even though they may wish to do so—and even after they were told how to do it and what behavior to change.

This is not surprising to the practitioner of laboratory education. Indeed, laboratory education was invented when it was realized that awareness of the necessity for change, belief in the validity of the change, and a strong motivation to change will *not* be sufficient to bring about behavioral changes.

Research also illuminates the second distinction. For example, it was found that the quantitative patterns of interpersonal competence of 113 executives who had attended an executive program for one week (which included T-groups and education on interpersonal relations) were not significantly different from patterns generated by comparable executives who had been studied in their home settings. This study also showed that some members of the experimental groups learned more and some learned less. Moreover, three weeks later when these individuals were mixed into new groups the interpersonal competence scores significantly decreased. Yet the executives were still attending the executive program.[9]

The theory from which this study was designed would predict these results. It maintains that through the processes of socialization and education individuals become programmed or inculcated with the pyramidal values which in turn lead toward interpersonal incompetence.

THE PROBLEM OF TRUST

As has been already pointed out, one of the hallmarks of rigorous research is strict control over the variables. In physical science research, where this model originated, the major factor that could confound the results was the researcher. He could read the dials incorrectly; he could unintentionally forget or overlook a

[8] Chris Argyris, *Organization and Innovation* (Homewood, Ill.: Irwin, 1965); "Interpersonal Barriers to Decision-Making," *Harvard Business Review* 44 (March-April, 1966): 84-97; and *Interpersonal Competence and Organizational Effectiveness* (Homewood, Ill.: Dorsey Press, 1962).

[9] Chris Argyris, "Explorations in Interpersonal Competence II," *Journal of Applied Behavioral Science*, 1 (July-September, 1965): 255-69.

critical step, etc. The researchers quite properly learned never to trust themselves. They went to great pains to make explicit all the controls they created to prevent contamination of their behavior.

In behavioral science research the problem of contamination is compounded by the fact that the subject is a human being who can react to the research in ways that could contaminate the results. The behavioral science researchers attacked this problem by doing to the subjects what they did to themselves. They established a new galaxy of controls and with that step they communicated louder than words how deeply they *had* to mistrust the subjects. The word *had* is underlined to point out that the researcher mistrusts the subject, not because he dislikes or hates the subject, but because he is required, as a minimum, to assume that the subject can distort data without realizing it. There is research (if it is needed to make the point) to show that human beings resent being mistrusted (partially because they know the mistrust may be valid). The resentment may easily distort the data given to the researcher. This problem is especially acute at universities. One of the country's leading psychologists made a study of 600 undergraduates. He reported the results: students so strongly resented being subjects in most of the research that he would question seriously any experimental research conducted in the university with paid or unpaid subjects. A colleague who is a senior experimental social psychologist has become so dismayed with the problem of "naive" student subjects that he is trying to find locations outside the university in which to conduct research.[10]

The truth about involvement of subjects is that they are always going to be involved. The ideal wished by some researchers, of a naive uninformed subject who will not contaminate the date, may not be realistic. A state of "naivete" *is* involvement. Anyone who has worked in the field knows that subjects from organizations deplore and resent being manipulated for the sake of an experiment, even if they realize intellectually that it is in their best interest.

The question therefore is not if there is subject involvement. There will always be subject involvement, no matter how hard the researcher tries to eliminate it, because the very acts of trying to minimize it may intrigue the subject. The real question is how to create research settings where the individual does not feel the need to distort his behavior and hence produce invalid data.

The answer lies in exploring ways to involve the subjects in the experiment so that they have an influence in its design and a stake in the results. Some researchers have found that through such involvement they get less subject distortion *or* if there is distortion the subject owns up to it more quickly *or* is more willing to accept some secrecy because *he* has participated in defining what will be kept secret from himself.

The mistrust of subjects runs deep with some behavioral scientists who believe that the experimental approach is the primary approach to rigor. Unfortunately this mistrust may also reduce researcher effectiveness. One large corporation appointed a blue-ribbon committee of behavioral scientists. They, in turn. developed a list of nearly 400 behavioral scientists which they narrowed down to 40. In all but a few cases, the committee was quite certain that the men were

[10] Argyris, "Some Unintended Consequencess . . .."

competent researchers, but could not recommend them in the field, because of the interpersonal difficulties it was expected their behavior would create.

In the field settings, the behavioral scientists' underlying mistrust shows through when they are negotiating to conduct a field experiment. They become easily irritated if the potential subjects ask to influence the research. They make secrecy and subject manipulation requirements in a matter-of-fact manner which angers potential subjects. The anger comes less from the fact that the researchers may wish to deceive and manipulate and more from how comfortable they are in making the request and how much glee they manifest in describing the experimental and control manipulations.

Subjects in the field especially resent research relationships where they have to be controlled by or be dependent on others, where they have a short time perspective, and where they are highly constrained in the scope of the participation. The major cause of the resentment is that they have been living with these conditions in their own organizations. It is ironic for them to hear that they may be helped to gain knowledge about how to make their work more effective by submitting, through research, to the same conditions that they wish to overcome! Thus, the researcher has created a bind for himself. The controls that he has developed (to which he gladly adheres) may be resented by the subject and, if so, therein lie some causes of data distortion.

The researcher does not resent the controls he has created because he understands their importance *and* if they work he will gain. To put this in the form of a generalization: the more control an individual has over factors that influence his behavior and the more these factors can lead to rewards that he values, the higher the probability that he will accept limitations ("scientific controls") on his behavior. This generalization, self-evident as it may be, has rarely been applied in research strategy. For example, how can the subject be helped to see the need for controls over his behavior? How can the research he designed so that its successful execution is personally rewarding to the client?

One way to begin to meet these requirements is to design the research in such a way that it fulfills some important needs for the subject. For example, the research can be used partially to solve problems important to him. Such research has many difficulties which will have to be overcome. Some of these may not be overcome completely. However, the costs of conducting helpful research and giving the subject some significant control over the research process may be less than the costs of conducting research for scientific understanding whose requirements will tend to be fought by people just as they fight formal organizations. The latter results in the researcher receiving distorted information. It also results, over time, in increasing hostility toward behavioral science research which, in a free society, can lead to the suppression of mechanistic research. This trend has already begun and partially accounts for the hostility toward research (and psychological tests) on the grounds of "invasion of privacy."

A few examples of subject mistrust may help to illustrate the point. Dunnette and Campbell are concerned with the biases of self-reports. Would not the trainees report more changes than actually occurred in order to feel better about themselves and to please their company? This is an important question and should be systematically studied. Some data do exist. Zand, Steele, and Zalkind found, in a study of scientists and engineers, that the self-reports on such variables as trust and openness went *down* after the laboratory experience. Some increased their self-ratings six months later, but many of these were still below the original scores.[11] Blake and Mouton recently presented evidence on what they call self-deception. For example, 1,800 managers from the United States, Britain, and Japan rated themselves after a grid laboratory significantly lower on 9,9 leadership (the Blake-Mouton ideal leadership style) and significantly higher on 9,1 and 1,9 styles (which are seen as much less effective styles of leadership).[12] On the final day of the seminar, 1,115 managers described themselves as *more* self-deceptive than they did at the beginning. A similar increase in criticalness about one's own work group was also reported.[13]

We must be careful to emphasize that these results are related to participants who have gone through different kinds of laboratory education. The results are not related to participants who have gone through more mechanistic learning experiences, where they may be graded by outsiders on the basis of unilaterally established examinations, the results of which may importantly affect the future of the individual.

Secondly, will individuals tend to be biased in their self-reports in order to please the company? There is some experimental data to show that many line managers are by no means sold on laboratory education. In many cases people may feel they will please line management by writing critical reports.[14]

The mistrust-control problem also arises in respect to the interaction effects between the evaluation questionnaires or tests and the training program. Dunnette and Campbell point out in their article that merely filling out questionnaires in the pretest session "often serves as kind of an alerting mechanism for trainees to alter their responses to the questionnaires." Again, it would be important to test this generalization in a laboratory context where people are coming to learn and where

---

[11] Dale E. Zand, Fred J. Steele, Sheldon S. Zalkind, "The Impact of an Organizational Development Program on Perceptions of Interpersonal, Groups and Organization Functioning," *Journal of Applied Behavioral Science* (in press).

[12] Robert R. Blake and Jane Srygley Mouton, *Corporate Excellence Through Grid Organization Development* (Houston, Texas: Gulf, 1968), p. 52.

[13] Ibid., pp. 54, 96 ff.

[14] A study of written reports to management by 160 executives who attended laboratory programs showed that reactions fell into four different categories (see Argyris, "Explorations . . . ."):

   a. Some executives returned highly critical reports which helped kill (temporarily and in some cases permanently) the use of laboratory education within the firm.
   b. Some executives were so critical that it whetted the appetite of the top management to send more executives. As one president put it, "He was angry and mad. I wondered how he got so involved in one week when he has never been so involved in anything related to people for years."
   c. Some returned so enthusiastic that they were not completely believed.
   d. Some organizations sent representatives to different types of laboratories. A Blake-grid laboratory is very different from most NTL laboratories. The varying reactions from executive who attended different types of sessions helped management decide which kind of program was best for what kind of executive.

it is in their interest to be aware of the possible alerting mechanism and not be influenced by it. In a study conducted by Bolman, but perhaps not available to Dunnette and Campbell, one group took the evaluation instruments only after the training.[15] The "after-only" group results were like the group with both "before" and "after" measures.

A final example of the issue of mistrust is related to Dunnette and Campbell's implication that managers are not as capable as researchers of making accurate evaluations of changes in the behavior of their colleagues who have gone to laboratories. I would like to see a rigorous study made on this issue. In my experience "rigorous" research has its own blind spots; managers have theirs. However, if the choice is between a questionnaire evaluation of change taken at one or two points in time versus a manager's personal evaluation, I am not sure if the manager's evaluation would not be more accurate. He sees the individual all the time, under many different conditions, and can obtain performance data.

Speaking of the preferences of line managers, I am reminded that one of the hallmarks of scientific understanding is the definition of hypotheses in such a way that they can be confirmed or disconfirmed. From a manager's point of view he may be more interested in making a self-fulfilling hypothesis. For example, we may find that change toward increasing openness and trust accounts for only 5 percent of the nonrandom variance. A scientific conclusion would be that trust and openness were not very powerful. The manager might want to learn how he can increase the powerfulness of trust and openness. For example, it may be that if a person who returns from a laboratory knows that there are five people watching to see if he has increased in openness and trust, he may feel more inclined to experiment with new behavior. One may argue that such a change has little to do with the effectiveness of a laboratory. The added change would be due to the fact that the person knew he was observed. This is not necessarily the case. For example, if the individual were told *before* he entered the laboratory that he would be observed when he returned home, he might be more highly motivated to learn during the laboratory. If he and others were more highly motivated, they could in turn influence the effectiveness of the group. Also, as the data described above suggest, going through a successful laboratory may help make people more aware of their own blindness and capacity for self-deception.

Could not the Dunnette and Campbell bias, if accepted uncritically, inhibit the development of research designs that could generate important data about the effectiveness or lack of effectiveness of laboratory education?

THE ROLE OF THE RESEARCH CRITIC

Watson recently published a book that describes clearly the degree of competitiveness that may exist among scientists.[16] The Watson group, for example, enjoyed hiding data from, or pointing out errors to, their fellow

[15] Lee Bolman, "Laboratory Education in a University Executive Program," Graduate School of Industrial Administration, Carnegie-Mellon University, Pittsburgh, Pennsylvania.

[16] James D. Watson, *The Double Helix* (New York: Atheneum Publishers, 1968).

scientists so that they would not be able to solve the problems before the Watson group did.

The Dunnette and Campbell paper gives this reviewer the same impression of competitiveness. The entire inquiry is stated in global win-lose terms. Are T-groups effective or ineffective, instead of under what conditions are T-groups more and less effective or how can T-groups be made more effective? What is the current state of research on T-groups, instead of how are T-groups assessed most effectively at this point in time? (Perhaps T-groups are much more effective or much less effective than our present research technology permits us to conclude.) Are T-groups effective or ineffective, instead of: given different types of T-groups, what consequences can be established regarding individual learning and group development? Another contribution to the tone of win-lose dynamics is the exclusion of Rubin's study.[17] He found that T-groups help individuals increase their self-acceptance and that this can lead to a decrease in prejudice. Also, Bunker and Knowles' recent study, which shows differential learning in two- and three-week laboratories (with the latter being more effective), is very relevant; this reviewer told one of the authors of its availability in prepublication form.[18] The same is true for the Bolman study mentioned earlier.

More important is the lack of discussion of the limits of the rigorous research methods which they recommend. The interaction effects of the measuring instrument with the training that Dunnette and Campbell correctly indentify, can be expanded to include the interaction effects of the researcher, of using control groups, of using "objective" questionnaires, of using different types of trainers, etc. The end result is the impression that only T-groups need to be made more effective; research methodology is already perfect.

What is the reaction of a reader identified with T-groups when he notes important studies omitted, questions phrased in global yes-no, win-lose dynamics, the inadequacies of recommended research methods not discussed, and practitioners as well as professionals in the field backhandedly condemned as "understandably" too busy fighting crises to be concerned about research?

One reaction is to point out the omissions or perceived distortions of the authors. Unfortunately, in doing this there is the risk that the reply bcomes equally competitive and that less energy is utilized in discussing the more subtle distinctions that need to be explored. For example, cannot some readers infer that rigorous research methods are almost impossible to develop usefully in field settings? I, of course, would deny that this is my intention, just as Dunnette and Campbell deny they are anti-T-group.

More importantly, what might be the impact of such a dialogue on younger researchers and on the practitioners? Could not a researcher well trained in

---

[17] Irwin Rubin, "Increasing Self-Acceptance: A Means of Reducing Prejudice," *Journal of Personality and Social Psychologyy*, 5 (February, 1967): 233-38, and "The Reduction of Prejudice Through Laboratory Training," *Journal of Applied Behavioral Science, 3 (1967): 29-50.*

[18] Douglas R. Bunker and Eric S. Knowles, "Comparison of Behavioral Changes Resulting from Human Relations Training Laboratories of Different Length," *Journal of Applied Behavioral Science* 3 (1967): 505-24.

mechanistic rigorous research methods and seeking approval from his teachers, conclude that rigorous field research about T-groups is almost impossible, thereby inhibiting precisely the research Dunnette, Campbell, and I wish to promote? Could not the practitioner become impatient with the "in fighting" and reject help from either side?

These questions are not as extreme as they might seem. Take the researcher as an example. Not too long ago it was fashionable to describe all research based on interviews as not very systematic because the interview was subject to error. Dunnette added to this fad by stating that research conducted with interviews could never add systematically to basic theory. The unintended consequence of this pronouncement was to keep many younger researchers away from using interviews, instead of attracting them to find new ways to make the interview more rigorous. Also, it gave the questionnaire a new and added status. It became a more objective instrument because people didn't face an interviewer who gave off all sorts of nonverbal cues that could influence the answers.

The trouble with these developments was that they helped prevent important research on the impact of questionnaires on individuals. It may be, for example, that the act of completing a questionnaire is more similar to participating in a mechanistic organization then the act of being interviewed. The interview may be subject to the influence of nonverbal cues, but this may be equally true for the questionnaire.

Dunnette and Campbell illustrated this bias when they described the personal letter of a friend as subjective and emotional. This letter could not, in their opinion, become the basis for an evaluation. However, the same individual, in the same emotional state, if asked to fill out a questionnaire, will presumably give more objective answers. The questionnaire will presumably serve to constrain his emotionality and control his subjectiviy. But will it? There is no rigorous (to use their standards) research to support this assumption.

There is much experience to suggest the opposite. T-groups are excellent settings in which to see the problem clearly. As we have pointed out, mechanistic research values the same qualities as do mechanistic organizations. T-groups value more organic conditions (e.g., more interdependence than dependence, more autonomy than submissiveness, etc.). Just imagine a respondent who has gone through the deeply emotional experience of questioning his assumptions—that "strong" leadership, "passive but loyal followers," and a "mechanistic organization" are the most effective way to organize human activity—suddenly being asked to complete a questionnaire which epitomizes these questions (much more than does an interview). The internal anger may be great and in a laboratory setting it is expressed more openly than in other settings. Laboratory staff tend to question the validity of questionnaire research (if handled mechanistically) because, like the professor of social psychology, they have experienced dramatic examples of subject hostility toward research. And such resistance is *not* because the individuals are antiintellectual or antirigorous. It is because the research places them in precisely the same psychological condition that they have come to question.

Finally, competitiveness may also lead to unintentional stretching of the facts. Dunnette, for example, quoted research that questioned the validity of interview responses.[19] A careful inspection of these studies shows that they were related to interviews in public opinion polls, marketing polls, and hiring of employees. Isn't it logical to assume if someone cuts in on your daily life to ask information that will be of much value to him and of little value to you that you may try to find the easiest way out? Was it rigorous for Dunnette to have translated these findings to *all* interviews, especially to those where employees have the expectation that the study may significantly influence their lives? Recently, I might add, there has been a reexamination of the interview. Even in settings of relatively mechanistic research, interviews may be as valid—and for some kinds of data more valid—than questionnaires.[20]

THE ADVOCATES' PERCEPTIONS OF LABORATORY METHOD

Dunnette and Campbell state that the advocates of laboratory education argue that laboratory education accomplishes such goals as (1) increased self-insight and self-awareness, (2) increased sensitivity to the behavior of others, and (3) increased awareness and understanding of the types of processes that facilitate or inhibit group functioning.

This is not quite accurate. The advocate of laboratory education states that learning is possible in terms of these goals *if* the individual wants to learn, *if* he is in a T-group that "orbits," *if* the rest of the laboratory experience is successful. Laboratory education can accomplish nothing by itself, anymore than Minnesota or Yale can promise a student that he will learn while attending a university.

If the advocates of laboratory education have agreed on anything regarding probable payoffs of the first laboratory experience, is that it gives the individual an appreciation of the difficulties in behaving competently[21] and helps him set a realistic level of aspiration as to what he can learn.[22] These "promises" are much more modest than the ones the authors define. Moreover, if taken seriously, the criteria might be designed somewhat differently. For example, as was cited above, the experience of most educators is that individuals tend to

[19] M. D. Dunnette, "Personnel Management," *Annual Review of Psychology* 13 (1962): 285-314.

[20] Clayton P. Alderfer, "Convergent and Discriminant Validation of Satisfaction and Desire Measures by Interviews and Questionnaires," *Journal of Applied Psychology* 51 (December, 1967): 509-20, and R. R. Sears, "Comparison of Interviews with Questionnaires for Measuring Mother's Attitudes Toward Sex and Aggression," *Journal of Personality and Social Psychology* 1 (1965): 37-44.

[21] Edgar Schein and Warren Bennis, *Personal and Organizational Change Through Group Methods* (New York: John Wiley & Sons, Inc., 1965).

[22] Roger Harrison, "Cognitive Models for Interpersonal and Group Behavior; A theoretical Framework for Research," *Explorations in Human Relations Training and Research,* 2 (New York: National Training Laboratories, 1965).

rate themselves lower on trust and openness after a laboratory than before. If one simply looked at the scores it would seem that the individual had not learned or indeed had become worse. However, interviews with the laboratory participants would reveal that many learned how inaccurate they were about their capacity to trust and be open. How many of the no-change results that are reported represent actual learning? The probability is quite high that people fill out questionnaires with higher standards after the laboratory; they are more willing to be honest about their limits, partially since they now realize how many others are as incompetent as they. To my knowledge, none of the instruments used in any of the studies provided the respondent with an opportunity to note whether a lower score or the same score actually meant that he had learned much at the laboratory.

ARE THE RESULTS TRANSFERABLE?

The authors state that another criterion to judge the effectiveness of laboratory education is to see if it makes a difference in the back-home situation. They fail to point out that the advocates are extremely cautious about a successful laboratory experience having a positive impact on the individual's back-home behavior. For example, the values of organizations and the laboratory are by no means consonant. The former tends to reward conformity, closedness, defensiveness, focus on stability, external commitment, and mistrust. The latter focusses on individuality, openness, owning up to feelings, risk-taking, internal commitment, and trust. As has been suggested, one would *not* expect very much transfer of learning to the back-home situation. One would expect more change in terms of the ability to listen accurately, to perceive interpersonal complexity more clearly, to be more tolerant of individual differences, and to understand the pressures of groups more effectively.

Behavioral changes in the back-home situation may be greater when the individual has gone through a laboratory experience with his entire work group. When he returns he is able to find support for his new behavior. Also, change should have a higher probability of occurring if the individual (and his work group) have enough organizational power to institute the changes that they wish to make. It is true, therefore, that—at best—few back-home changes have been measured. However, advocates of laboratory education are quite aware of the back-home situation. Indeed, with stranger groups we are very careful to warn them about going back home and trying, by themselves, to make significant changes in their behavior, or trying to strive for changes in the behavior of others.[23]

[23] For an annotated review of the literature that is more comprehensive than Dunnette and Campbell's, see Lewis E. Durham, Jack L. Gibb, and Eric S. Knowles (eds.) "A Bibliography of Research," *Explorations in Human Relations Training and Research*, 5 (New York: Institute of Applied Behavioral Science, 1957).

Marvin D. Dunnette
and John P. Campbell

A RESPONSE TO ARGYRIS

The principal thrusts of Argyris's comments are the following:

1. The worth of the laboratory method for individual and organizational development should not be judged on a "win-lose," "yes-no" set of ground rules.
2. Generally speaking, the scientific method is not appropriate for studying the behavioral effects of educational efforts such as laboratory training and does not yield useful information.
3. Scientific behavioral research is modeled after Theory X and is dehumanizing for the people whose behavior is under study.
4. With certain exceptions, behavioral scientists are interpersonally incompetent.
5. Dunnette and Campbell are guilty of withholding information, msinterpreting research, and otherwise slanting their review.

We shall comment briefly on each of the foregoing points.

First, we agree fully that the worth of any training method should not be judged on a "win-lose," "yes-no" dichotomy. Even the most unsophisticated of individuals must realize that effectiveness is not a dichotomous variable and the relative effectiveness of any training method for changing behavior must be judged on many dimensions, not just one. Our organization of studies around the different types of criteria (measures of effectiveness) that researchers have used was an attempt to recognize this "many-faceted" nature of a training program's effectiveness. We also agree that the expected effects of any training or development method used in an organizational setting must be balanced against its expected costs. This is why we would hope that the increasing use of any educational or therapeutic procedure would signal opportunities for more and better research designed to learn about the behavioral effects of the procedure instead of closing down the research enterprise as Argyris suggests.

Concomitant with asking what the effects of the laboratory experience are, we must also ask how these effects are moderated or influenced by such things

From Marvin D. Dunnette, John P. Campbell and Chris Argyris, "A Symposium: Laboratory Training" *Industrial Relations* 8 (October 1968): 1-45. Reprinted by permission. ©1968, Regents of the University of California Berkeley.

as individual differences among participants, the environment in which the training takes place, the specific elements in the laboratory program, and the organizational situation from which the participants are drawn. These are complex questions, but the laboratory method deals with a complex domain of behavior and it deserves a pluralistic approach. It was the purpose of our review to portray what is known and what isn't known and to suggest where research might best proceed in the future.

Consideration of costs versus expected effects brings us to the second point. It is the task of the researcher to obtain information on training effects that is as valuable, straightforward, and *free of ambiguity* as possible. We submit that this is the principal goal of *scientific* investigation and that the prime goal is *not* simply the achievement of rigor and elegant explanation for their own sakes. Argyris correctly points out that the aim of scientific investigation is the creation of *valid knowledge*. This is also precisely what management of an organization needs if it is to determine whether or not any given development activity is worth the costs involved.

To illustrate his dichotomy between basic scientific research and some alternative (which remains unspecified), Argyris points to understanding the nature of interpersonal relationships and the nature of groups as examples of *basic* research problems. We agree, although his examples are a bit too global. However, what of questions such as: How does the T-group experience affect certain attitudes? What is the duration of such effects? What effect does laboratory education have on subsequent behavior in problem-solving groups? How is this modified by the type of group and type of problem? How does T-group training affect superior-subordinate relationships? For what kinds of managers? Under what sort of reward system? For what type of organizational climate? We submit that these are all questions that require *controlled, objective* study. Yet, the questions range from basic to applied and are not exclusively the province of either the "basic" or the "applied" researcher. What they do have in common is that they require relevant, nonambiguous information, and we see no other means for obtaining such information than through careful, systematic, and controlled scientific research. Although arguing strongly against such methodology, Argyris fails to specify what strategies he proposes for "evaluating systematically social action activities like laboratory education and T groups." Generalization beyond the experimental setting is the principal reason for designing research studies with the characteristics we described. Research with no controls or without systematic and objective measures cannot be generalized beyond the setting in which the data were gathered.

Third, we believe it is unfortunate that Argyris seeks to demean the scientific approach with such adjectives as mechanistic, pyramidal, programmed, distrustful, hostility-inducing, and unrealistic. He has apparently confused the concepts of controlled experimentation, objective behavior observation, and valid measurement with the notion that the scientist is somehow primarily intent on controlling individuals' (subjects') lives. Carefully designed research conducted to yield firm knowledge about the behavioral effects of a development program need *never* connote any presumed or actual control over any part of the lives of persons participating in the program. It is just as likely that an overzealous practitioner may prescribe laboratory education inappropriately as it is that a researcher may develop an inappropriate or misguided experimental design for studying human behavior. In our opinion, the probability for serious consequences is greater in the former than in the latter case.

An example of an excellent T-group experiment is the one reported recently by Rubin.[1] He hypothesized that persons high in self-acceptance would show lower ethnic prejudice than persons low in self-acceptance, and that a T-group experience, by increasing participants' levels of self-acceptance, would reduce their ethnic prejudice. To test these hypotheses, he carried out a study which was indeed elegant, rigorous, objective, and controlled, but which was *not* mechanistic, pyramidal, distrustful, unrealistic, or hostility-inducing. Two weeks before a sensitivity training program, he obtained responses (by mail) to questionnaires designed to measure self-acceptance and ethnic prejudice from 14 of 50 intended participants. The entire group of 50 filled in the questionnaires on arrival, just before the first training group session, and again on the next to last day of the two-week program. Using this simple, careful (and easy) design, Rubin accomplished two of the three scientific standards for evaluating a training experience that we presented in our article: (1) He measured self-acceptance and ethnic prejudice before and after training, and (2) he provided a control group by administering the questionnaires to the 14 participants at the beginning and at the end of a two-week period of nontraining. His results showed no change, on the average, for the control group members during the two-week span prior to the T-group experience, but substantial average changes toward increased self-acceptance and decreased ethnic prejudice for participants over the two weeks of T-group training.

We believe that Rubin's experiment provides not only "scientific understanding" but also the "systematic evaluation of social action activities like laboratory education and T-groups" that Argyris calls for in his first sentence. We see Rubin's study as an example of the kind of rigorous research that can be undertaken *without* controlling the lives of participants, *without* reducing them to puppets on strings being coldly manipulated by behavioral scientists, and *without* engendering apathy, hostility, or resistance among participants.

Relative to the fourth point, we cannot accept Argyris's view of social scientists as being cold, calculating, inhuman creatures who really shouldn't be allowed out in the real world. We actually know a great many who seem to function quite well. We think we detected an implication in Argyris's remarks

---

[1] Irwin Rubin, "Increased Self-Acceptance: A Means of Reducing Prejudice," *Journal of Personality and Social Psychology,* 5 (1967): 233-39. Rubin's study is one of the three brought to our attention by Argyris; we can only hope that the reader will believe that we failed to include these studies in our review because we were unaware of them, *not* because we deliberately excluded them, as charged by Argyris.

that social scientists may be divided into either "good guys" or "bad guys" and that the "good guys" are the ones usually identified with laboratory education.

In our opinion, Rubin's experiment is just one illustration of the kind of good research that can dispel Argyris's illusion of the careful scientist as a manipulative and "wrongly motivated" person. Were such a dreadful illusion to gain widespread credence, it could serve only to constrain rather than to broaden opportunities for learning more about the behavioral effects of laboratory education.

Finally, we must comment briefly on some of the more personal aspects of Argyris's discussion.

We deny emphatically that we ignored certain studies for the sake of biasing our review. Missing the Rubin article was a serious oversight, but it was unintentional; and although we did get prepublication copies of the Bunker and Knowles[2] and the Zand, Steele, and Zalkind[3] papers, they came to us too late to be included in our paper. The Bunker and Knowles paper is a reanalysis of Bunker's original data[4] and the Zand study yielded equivocal results.

In no sense were we arguing for the virtues of questionnaires over interviews as a means for collecting data. The interview is a valuable technique, and we are certain that it will be developed to an even greater degree of usefulness in the future. Dunnette's *Annual Review* chapter was severely misinterpreted.[5]

In conclusion, we would like to comment that Argyris's view of laboratory education as a development method seems much more pessimistic and negative than ours. He appears to hold only limited hope for transfer of learning back to the organizational situation so that job behavior may be changed in some fashion. He says practitioners make no such promises. The picture is made even more bleak by his apparent unwillingness to subject the possibility of transfer effects to systematic study. We need to know what it is in the training situation or in the organization that facilitates or inhibits the transfer of specified behaviors. For example, Schein and Bennis[6] suggest a number of very meaningful hypotheses that deserve investigation. Unfortunately, as Argyris points out, few facts are now available. In our view, the T-group experience is an interesting and important subject for research; considerably more effort should be expended in that direction, instead of saying it can't and shouldn't be done.

[2] D. R. Bunker and E. S. Knowles, "Comparison of Behavioral Changes Resulting from Human Relations Training Laboratories of Different Lengths," *Journal of Applied Behavioral Science* 3 (1967): 505-24.
[3] D. E. Zand, F. I. Steele, and S. S. Zalkind, "The Impact of an Organizational Development Program on Perceptions of Interpersonal, Group, and Organization Functioning," *Journal of Applied Behavioral Science* (in press).
[4] D. R. Bunker, "Individual Applications of Laboratory Training," *Journal of Applied Behavioral Science,* 1 (1965): 131-48.
[5] M. D. Dunnette, "Personnel Management," *Annual Review of Psychology* 13 (1962): 285-314.
[6] E. Schein and W. Bennis, *Personal and Organizational Change Through Group Methods* (New York: John Wiley & Sons, Inc., 1965).

Chris Argyris

A REJOINDER TO
DUNNETTE AND CAMPBELL

(1). I agree that the goal of research is to obtain information that is free from ambiguity. My position, supported by nearly a dozen scientists, is that research activities have built-in unintended consquences that *increase* ambiguity. To identify many research methods as mechanistic and hostility-inducing is not to demean science; it is to face reality and save science. I have heard Dunnette advise executives that behavioral scientists are not antiorganization when they identify its negative impact on individuals. Dunnette and Campbell may wish to follow this advice when their "god" is found wanting.

(2). The Rubin study is significantly different from Dunnette's in that Rubin studied an actual field situation and designed his research so that it could be a learning experience for the subjects.

(3). Dunnette and Campbell claim that many experimentalists are not interpersonally incompetent because they know some who seem to function well. It is ironic that when they defend their position, they use the same kind of anecdotal evidence that they condemn T-group practitioners for using.

(4). I am not unwilling to subject the possibility of transfer effects to systematic study. As Dunnette knows very well, I have published two, and have directed two other, such studies.

May I close with some advice to all of us, ". . . we have to discriminate between the weight to be given to scientific opinion in the selection of its methods, and its trustworthiness in formulating judgments of the understanding. The slightest scrutiny of the history of natural science shows that current scientific opinion is nearly infallible in the former case, and is invariably wrong in the latter case. The man with a method good for purposes of his dominant interests, is a pathological case in respect to his wider judgment on the coordination of this method with a more complete experience."[1]

From Marvin D. Dunnette, John P. Campbell and Chris Argyris, "A Symposium: Laboratory Training,. *Industrial Relations* 8 (October, 1968): 1-45. Reprinted by permission. © 1968, Regents of the University of California, Berkeley.

[1] A. N. Whitehead, *The Function of Reason* (New York: Beacon, 1929), p. 11.

Walter R. Nord

GROUPS AND ORGANIZATIONS:
SOME CONCLUDING THOUGHTS

The preceding selections demonstrate that groups have powerful effects on individuals and hence on organizations. The management of groups is an increasingly important part of the management of organizations. Rather than seeking to fight groups, as previous theorists did, current management scholars stress the utilization of groups. In fact, Likert (1967) has viewed management as a highly group-centered process. He has argued that groups of people are required for the performance of many tasks and that these task groups, superimposed on organizational charts, should be the vehicles for coordination and decision making. Likert and many other behavioral scientists see the effective utilization of groups as a necessary condition for organizational success.

The group-centered view of management runs counter to cultural bias in favor of the individual. Furthermore, the lack of group leadership and problem-solving skills in our society has generated negative attitudes toward groups as decision-making instruments. Fortunately, knowledge about the nature of group decisions, the behavior of groups, and strategies for the effective use of groups has been expanded by recent research.

THE QUALITY OF GROUP DECISIONS

The issue of group v individual decisions is very complex, and the evidence is mixed. Kelley and Thibaut (1969) reviewed the literature in depth and formulated several hypotheses. They stressed that their conclusions should not be viewed as established facts, since often the amount of supporting data was small and outweighed conflicting evidence by only a small margin.

First, Kelley and Thibaut suggested that the success of groups in solving a problem depends on the characteristics of the problem undertaken. In general, both very difficult and very easy problems are better handled by individuals; but, for problems of moderate difficulty, groups are more effective.

Second, Kelley and Thibaut noted that group discussions usually generate pressures toward uniformity. Numerous studies have shown that individuals can be influenced by group pressure to make inaccurate judgments. However, whether pressures towards conformity in a decision-making group are, on balance, dysfunctional can not be discerned from those results. Successful pressures for uniformity may be useful if they are exerted by the most competent group members on each decision. Thus, while group decisons tend to be more uniform than those of aggregated individual decisions, the consequences on effectiveness will vary from group to group and from decision to decision.

Third, groups tend to be slower than individuals. Kelly and Thibaut observed that most often groups require more time to solve a problem than individuals. However, even when groups are faster, the total output/man hour is apt to be considerably less for groups than for individuals.

Fourth, groups suffer from the fact that *inter*personal coordination tends to be more difficult to accomplish than is *intra*personal coordination. While this statement is clearly true for physical or motor tasks, Kelly and Thibaut noted that it is also true for such complex mental tasks as designing crossword puzzles.

Fifth, groups need to develop organization, and this takes time. In other words, over a period of time groups tend to become relatively more effective.

Sixth, a number of studies have confirmed the finding that groups tend to make decisions involving more risk than do individuals.[1] This finding has interesting implications for organizations. Kelley and Thibaut suggested that the dynamics of this shift toward more risk taking may be the result of a diffusion of responsibility and a "rhetorical advantage" inherent in the English language, favoring those who advocate the more risky position.

Finally, there is the question of how individual member motivation is influenced by group conditions. Much evidence indicates that under a wide variety of conditions participation in decision making increases a member's understanding of the decision and commitment to it. The group decision may then be more likely to result in appropriate action than the decision made by experts[2] not personally responsible for implementation.

Like so many issues in organizational behavior, the relevant question is not an "either-or" one; rather the issue is better seen as: Which method of decision-making is more or less useful for particular purposes under a certain set of circumstances? A variety of factors which influence the effectiveness of group decision making, including the environment, the nature of the task, the people, and the organization have been investigated. From the organization's viewpoint, the question can only be treated in systems terms rather than absolute terms. Attempts at group decision making may be ineffective for a variety of reasons. In some cases group decision efforts may fail because the formal leader is not able or willing to accept group decisions for psychological reasons. Both task and social-emotional factors play central roles in effective organizational decisions.

---

[1] The "risky-shift" phenomenon is coming under attack. For example, Belovicz and Finch (1971) suggested that the shift may be limited to one particular type of measuring instrument.

[2] Certainly the degree of expertise is a limiting condition. A minimum level of competence is required on the part of at least some of the group members if the group is to make effective decisions.

GROUP DYNAMICS AND SUCCESS

Effective management of modern organizations demands attention to both task and emotional needs. Certainly, the growing use of T-groups, teambuilding, and related training experiences is oriented in this direction. Such special training can enhance both the objective quality of decisions and the psychological involvement of group members in the decision, the organization, and the group itself. Effective groups are apt to be those whose members are able to recognize and control the social forces which affect its dynamics, so that these forces work to increase rather than inhibit task performance. In other words, effective groups require both leaders and members who are aware of the psychological processes in a group and who are able to deal with them to satisfy both emotional and task needs. A growing body of literature demonstrates that many groups are not able to function well because they are not able to deal with important social-emotional variables. Argyris (1964) provided a case in point. He noted,

> For example, in some situations . . . mathematicians and engineers dealing with highly technical issues developed strong emotional attachments to these issues. During discussions held to resolve technical, rational issues, the emotional involvements tended to block understanding. Since the men did not tend to deal with emotions their inhibiting effects were never explored. On the contrary, they were covered up by the use of technical, rational arguments. Since these arguments were attempts by people to defend themselves or attack others, there was a tendency for the rationality of the arguments to be weak. This, in turn, troubled the receiver of the argument, who tended to attack obvious rational flaws immediately. The attack tended to increase the degree of threat experienced by the first person and he became even more defensive . . . (pp. 106-7).

Improved capabilities to manage the social-psychological processes of groups are needed. The Rosenberg model presented earlier and Schein's (1969) and Walton's (1969) informative books are helpful for the development of these skills.

Groups which support individuality. Much modern writing on groups has seen them as functional, necessary, inevitable, and costly to individual growth. While it is recognized that social approval and peer relations are important for the stability and identity of individuals, both advocates and critics of groups emphasize that approval of one's peers, often being contingent on conformity to group norms, requires one to sacrifice the expression of individuality. Benne (1961), however, explored the possibility that groups could be developed to reward nonconformity and innovation.

He argued that the pressures for conformity need not suppress individuality. Citing his own experiences in sensitivity training groups, he proposed that under some circumstances interpersonal relationships enhance individuality and freedom. For example, an environment can be created to help members move beyond the traditional mode of stereotyping each other and work toward developing a perception of each other guided by the assumption of a multiplicity of personalities. Under such conditions, people can explore and examine the social and psychological forces which often seem so powerful that they can control our behavior, although we remain unaware of them. Benne leaves us with the provocative challenge to provide ways of using authority and peer-group relations to promote individual freedom and growth as well as group and organizational goals. The establishment of groups and organizations which support individual growth requires an understanding of group processes. Additional insights can be acquired through an exploration of the topic of leadership, to which we now turn.

BIBLIOGRAPHY

Argyris, C. *Integrating the Individual and the Organization.* New York: John Wiley & Sons, 1964.

Belovicz, M., and Finch, F. "A critical analysis for the 'risky shift' phenomenon." *Organizational Behavior and Human Performance 6,* 1971, 150-68.

Benne, K. D. "The Use of Fraternity." *Daedalus: Journal of the American Academy of Arts and Sciences,* 1961. pp. 233-46.

Kelley, H. H., and Thibaut, J. W. "Group Problem Solving." In G. Lindzey and E. Aronson, eds., *The Handbook of Social Psychology.* 2nd ed. vol. 4. Reading, Mass.: Addison-Wesley, 1969. pp. 1-101.

Likert, R. *The Human Organization: Its Management and Value.* New York: McGraw-Hill Book Company, 1967.

Schein, E. H. *Process Consultation: Its Role in Organizational Development.* Reading, Mass.: Addison-Wesley, 1969.

Walton, R. E. *Interpersonal Peacemaking: Confrontations and Third-Party Consultation.* Reading, Mass.: Addison-Wesley. 1969.

CHAPTER *13*

Leadership

Although systematic investigations of leadership are relatively new, Gross (1964) pointed out that since ancient times writers of all persuasions have sought to advise leaders of better methods to conduct affairs. Particularly influential in the past were such writers as Confucious, Plato, Aristotle, contributors to the Bible, and Machiavelli, who collectively admonished leaders to be wise, bold, good, willing to compromise, unscrupulous and well-advised. More recently, advice has been contributed by representatives of various schools of thought about formal organizations—the "scientific management," classical, and human-relations schools. Currently psychologists, sociologists, political scientists, and business academicians and practitioners all contribute theories, principles, and even "cookbooks" for leadership.

Their advice has found an eager audience. As we mentioned earlier, many practicing managers expect communication and motivation to resolve organizational problems. Perhaps an equally large number expect to find the panacea in leadership. This state of buyer readiness and the willingness of writers to supply ready answers have combined to generate a number of fads in management. Strategies which succeeded under one set of circumstances have been applied uncritically to other situations for which they were less well suited. Costly failures have resulted. Recently, substantial controversy and more critical thinking have developed about both the role of leadership and the desired type of leadership for organizations.

F. W. Taylor and the classical theorists provide a convenient starting point for the study of advice to modern organizational leaders. We have already mentioned that these writers tended to focus advice on the design of tasks and the structuring of organizations, assuming relatively passive responses by lower-level participants[1] After publication of the Hawthorne studies, lower-level people could no longer be viewed as passive, but attention was still given to leadership. Since then, managers have been increasingly encouraged to consider the effect of leadership strategies on the organization as a social-psychological system.

1. The writing of Mary Parker Follett was a major exception to this view in the classical literature.

SOME LEADERSHIP ISSUES

What is leadership?

Although there is no general agreement on the precise meaning of the term, Gibb (1969) offered a definition which encompasses many of the ideas put forth by others. He refers to leadership as the influence of one person on another. Since this influence is often felt by several people, we could say that leaders are those members of a group who most significantly influence the group. If influence is the mark of a leader, then formal authority over a group is neither necessary nor sufficient for leadership. The formal head of a group is not a leader if he does not significantly influence the other members, and the actual leader need not occupy a position of formal authority.[2] Also, it is clear that leadership is not just a social position or a set of personality traits; it is a form of social interaction.

Leadership style

How should a leader behave? This frequently asked question has received a variety of answers, generally falling into two categories and suggesting a false dichotomy; a manager should be concerned either with structure or with human relations. For many practitioners and consultants the search for the "one best way" of leadership continues; leader behavior is seen as either good or bad in relation to some particular set of assumptions or theories, the validity of which is often questionable.

A leadership study conducted in the late 1930s by Lewin and his colleagues and reported by Lippitt and White (1958) served to direct attention to "democratic" leadership as a viable management strategy. This experiment investigated the effects of authoritarian, democratic, and laissez-faire leadership on the functioning of children's groups. The most important findings were those concerning differences between the authoritarian and democratic groups. In comparison with democratic leadership, authoritarian leadership produced groups which tended to be more submissive and dependent on the leader, to be characterized by more aggressive and domineering relationships among the group members, to have less group unity, to engage in less work-minded conversation, to be less constructive in work activity in the absence of the leader, and to become more disrupted by frustrating situations. This study, generally taken to show the superiority of democratic leadership over authoritarian leadership, has stimulated much research and is important in the history of the controversy highlighted by the selections by Dubin in this section and Maier and Gomberg in part IV. Much of this controversy concerns the design and interpretation of research, but hidden in the debates are important value issues as well.

Dictatorial or authoritarian political systems are often perceived by Americans as a threat to their values and way of life. One response to this threat

---

2. As French and Raven noted in an earlier selection, there are at least five bases of power, of which formal or legitimate authority is only one.

is to see democratic leadership as good and authoritarian leadership as bad, without recognizing that authoritarian leadership within an organization may be quite unrelated to authoritarian political systems. The issue is also influenced by questions of strength and rights. Often a democratic leader may be labeled weak or a move toward more participation by lower-level participants may be seen as a challenge to the legitimate rights of managers. Certainly, the terms "democratic" and "authoritarian" have surplus meaning when applied to management styles.

The issue of authoritarian *v* democratic leadership is beginning to fade, and an awareness is growing that leadership is a relative phenomenon. Many variables interact to influence what will be a successful leadership pattern in any particular situation. In fact, in many cases the style of leadership may lead to little or no difference in performance.

The contribution of leadership to performance

No one has precisely measured how important leadership is for the accomplishment of group and organizational goals. While much conflict in the published literature exists over the style of leadership, considerably less can be found over the more basic issue— whether differences in leadership style are very important. To some degree this controversy is implicit in differences in what theorists take as problematic in their work. For example, Katz and Kahn (1966) pointed out that some people, such as McGregor and Likert, view leadership as the primary determinant of organizational performance. On the other hand, March and Simon's (1958) highly regarded book on organizations contains no mention of leadership in either the table of contents or the index.

The issue of the importance of leadership style has also been treated more directly. Homans (1965) argued that behavior of the first-line supervisor may have relatively little effect on the productivity of the work group; he noted that technology and work methods are far more important factors. Nevertheless, the behavior of top management may be of great importance. Thus, the magnitude of the effect of leadership styles varies throughout the organizational hierarchy. Perrow (1970) labeled the idea that leadership is the answer to organizational problems an "important prejudice." He argued that, while leadership may be an influential variable, it is certainly not the most significant and in fact may be viewed as dependent rather than an independent variable. Dubin, in the selection which follows, maintains that the magnitude of the effects of different leadership styles is a function of the type of technology. Although these arguments do not appear to have had a significant effect on the emphasis given to leadership, the question of the importance of leadership may deserve as much attention as the age-old search for leadership traits.

Personality v situational factors

In spite of a great deal of research, few if any personality traits have been shown to be consistently related to leadership. Gibb (1969a) made several important observations about the role of personality traits in leadership. First, some traits have been found more consistently among leaders than among nonleaders. However, these traits are neither necessary nor sufficient conditions for leadership; rather their contribution to leadership is influenced by how well they meet the needs of the group in a particular situation. To quote Gibb,

> The traits of leadership are any or all of these personality traits which, in *any particular situation,* enable an individual to (1) contribute significantly to group locomotion in the direction of a recognized goal and (2) be perceived as doing so by fellow group members. Second, there is abundant evidence that member personalities do make a difference to group performance, and there is every reason to believe that they do affect that aspect of the group's behavior to which the leadership concept applies (p. 227).

While no traits can be viewed as universal determinants of leadership, many studies have shown that such characteristics as dominance, intelligence, self-confidence, and empathy or interpersonal sensitivity often contribute to leadership.

Gibb (1969a) noted four possible explanations for the relatively limited relationship that has been found between personality and leadership. First, the existing devices for personality measurements are inadequate. Second, since leadership itself is a complex pattern of roles, characterized by much inconsistency, no specific traits are consistently required. Third, since the groups whose leadership has been studied have differed widely from each other, some of the effects of personality which may occur in more similar groups may have been concealed. Finally, situational factors may be so powerful as to override personality variables. These last two explanations suggest that leadership must be viewed in the context of a particular group of people at a particular time. The needs of group members may be central in the determination of what type of individual behavior will influence the group.

Leaders—people who meet group needs

In sharp contrast to the view that leaders are people who control the group is the position that leaders are people who function to serve the needs of the group and its members. According to the latter idea, a leader is dependent on the group for his influence. Only if the members perceive that their needs will be met if they follow or are influenced by a particular person will that person be influential. This idea is often called the functional view of leadership.

The functional approach supports the notion that groups are formed and maintained as a means of meeting the needs of their members. Leaders are just group members who are especially helpful in meeting certain needs important to the group. Considerable research is consistent with this view.

One early study, by Merei (1949), demonstrated that groups can limit the power of "leaders" who do not meet the needs and expectations of members. For this research children who were rated by teachers as being leaders were separated from the rest of their peers. The remaining children were divided into groups and allowed to play together for several periods. Then one leader was introduced into each of these groups, and the leader's influence on the group was observed. The results showed that a group which had a tradition of playing together was stronger than the leader. Leaders from the normal situation generally were not able to influence the new groups unless they took into account the group norms and practices which had developed. This study is important because it showed that leadership is influenced by group norms and group values. Again, leadership is not a set of traits but is an interaction of people under certain conditions. Previous group history is one relevant condition.

Other support for the functional view of leadership comes from Hamblin's (1958) study on the effect of a crisis upon leadership. Hamblin observed groups engaged in a complex task. After having learned the rules, some of the groups were exposed to a crisis situation; the rules under which the task could be performed were radically changed. During the crisis leadership in the group was effected in two ways. The group members were far more willing to follow a strong leader, and leaders who did not respond rapidly and decisively to the crisis were rejected and replaced by others.

Perhaps the clearest demonstration of the functional nature of leadership has come from Bales (1958), who specified classes of behavior which appeared to be necessary for satisfactory group performance. Members who provided this behavior to the group tended to be influential. In observing discussion groups, which had no formal leader, Bales discovered that he could classify the behavior of influential group members into 12 categories, which could then be grouped into three characteristics: "activity," "task ability," and "likeability." Different leaders exhibited contrasting combinations of the categories. In Bales' view an individual whose behavior strongly shows all three characteristics corresponds to the traditional leader, the "great man". An individual who demonstrates a great deal of activity and task ability may be termed a task specialist. An individual who is active but is most concerned with social-emotional matters is generally ranked high on likeability and is called a social specialist. The task and social specialists each seem to display behaviors which satisfy a set of needs felt by group members—desires to get the job accomplished and to manage social tensions and feelings. The "great man," of course, is able to meet both sets of needs. Since the "great man" is relatively rare, there are often two or more leaders in a group.

The functional nature of the leadership role is demonstrated by changes in the group's preference for various types of leadership behavior. For example, early in the history of a task group, members tend to be interested in getting on with the job; accordingly, they support and approve the behavior of the task specialist. Later, however, interpersonal tensions often appear, and the behavior of the social specialist becomes more desired and approved. In general, groups appear to have two sets of needs, and individuals whose behavior functions to satisfy them tend to become leaders.

Considerable research supports this two-factor view. For example, the work of Fleishman, which is treated in detail by Dubin, distinguished between "initiation of structure" (task orientation and "consideration" (social-emotional orientation). Similarly, *The Managerial Grid* developed by Blake and Mouton

(1964) was composed of the dimensions of "concern for production" and "concern for people." A great deal of current management training and thinking rests on an assumption of the dual nature of group needs and hence leadership.

A corollary of this two-factor view of leadership and groups is the idea that, if groups do have these two sets of needs, then successful groups are apt to be those which satisfy both sets. Tensions arising from any unresolved needs are apt to interfere with the group's progress toward satisfaction of its other needs. For example, unresolved hostility in a group can prevent rational discussions of tasks.

TOWARD A RESOLUTION OF THE ISSUES

The work cited documents the trend toward seeing leadership as closely related to group behavior and individual needs. The dominant view of leadership in organizational behavior appears to emphasize social and psychological factors far more than structural and task factors. This trend contrasts sharply with the "scientific" and classical management positions. The emphasis given to a concern for people in the writings of Likert and McGregor is now widely shared in the thoughts of both students and practitioners of management. McMurry (1958)[3] and others, however, have argued that this concern for people has been oversold in the quest for more "democratic" leadership.

The selections which follow center on the effects on performance of different styles of leadership. The first selection, by Dubin, reviews and evaluates the literature on democratic or group-centered leadership. He presents the major findings of important research but challenges their relevance for many supervisory jobs. In many cases variability in output is almost exclusively a function of technological factors rather than of human motivation. Dubin's article is followed by a selection prepared by the editor which reconsiders the issues raised by Dubin and others and provides a bridge to the concluding part of the book, where participative leadership as a management strategy is further considered.

REFERENCES

Bales, R. F. "Task Roles and Social Roles in Problem-Solving Groups." In E. E. Maccoby, T. M. Newcomb, and E. L. Hartley, eds., *Readings in Social Psychology.* 3rd ed. New York: Holt, Rinehart & Winston, 1958. pp. 437-47.

Blake, R. R., and Mouton, J. S. *The Managerial Grid.* Houston: Gulf Publishing Co., 1964.

Gibb, C. A. *Leadership.* Baltimore: Penguin Books, Inc., 1969.

—— "Leadership." In G. Lindzey, and E. Aronson, eds., *The Handbook of Social Psychology.* 2nd vol. 4. Reading, Mass.: Addison-Wesley, 1969a. pp. 205-82.

3. McMurry's argument is treated more fully in the introduction to Part IV.

Gross, B. *The Managing of Organizations.* vol. 1. New York: The Free Press, 1964.

Hamblin, R. L. "Leadership and Crisis." *Sociometry* 21 (1958): 322-35.

Homans, G. C. "Effort, Supervision, and Productivity." In R. Dubin, G. C. Homans, F. C. Mann, and D. C. Miller, eds., *Leadership and Productivity.* San Francisco: Chandler Publishing Co., 1965. pp. 51-67.

Katz, D., and Kahn, R. L. *The Social Psychology of Organizations.* New York: John Wiley & Sons, 1966.

Likert, R. *The Human Organization: Its Management and Value.* New York: McGraw-Hill Book Company, 1967.

Lippitt, R., and White, R. K. "An Experimental Study of Leadership and Group Life." In E. E. Maccoby, T. M. Newcomb, and E. L. Hartley, eds., *Readings in Social Psychology.* 3rd ed. New York: Holt, Rinehart & Winston, 1958. pp. 496-511.

March, J. G. and Simon, H. A. *Organizations.* New York: John Wiley & Sons, 1958.

McMurry, R. N. "The Case for Benevolent Autocracy." *Harvard Business Review* 36(1958): 82-90.

Merei, F. "Group Leadership and Institutionalization." *Human Relations* 2 (1949): 23-39.

Perrow, C. *Organizational Analysis: A Sociological View.* Belmont, Ca.: Wadsworth Publishing Co., Inc., 1970.

Robert Dubin

SUPERVISION AND PRODUCTIVITY: EMPIRICAL FINDINGS AND THEORETICAL CONSIDERATIONS

TECHNOLOGY, SUPERVISION AND PRODUCTIVITY

The most notable consequence of advances in technology . . . is the man-hour productivity increases with transfer of labor operations from men to machines. In the United States, for example, over-all man-hour productivity has risen about three percent per year, at least since World War I, and probably had increased at an even higher annual rate from the turn of the century until then. Increases in man-hour productivity have been largely the consequence of the efficiency built into machines, a major fact to keep in mind when considering productivity and the influences that bear upon it.

Technology and Management Structure

Only recently has there been reborn an interest in the core feature of the modern industrial world—the technologies upon which it is grounded. Social scientists and management theorists have been preoccupied for several decades with "human problems" and human relations in work organizations. A recent analysis could discover fewer than three dozen research studies in the American, British, French, and German literature empirically dealing with social aspects of the man-machine relationship.[1] This paucity is a harsh commentary on the neglect of technology during the current preoccupation with the psyche of man in industry.

The idea that special technologies have associated with them variations in the structure and function of management is a recent notion that has challenged traditional managerial thinking. Research by Joan Woodward[2] on British

From Robert Dubin "Supervision and Productivity: Empirical Findings and Theoretical Considerations". In Robert Dubin, George Homans, Floyd C. Mann, Robert Miller, *Leadership in productivity: Some Facts of Industrial Life* pp. 10-50. Reprinted by permission of Chandler Publishing Company,©1965.

[1] See the study by Martin Meissner, "Behavioral Adaptations to Industrial Technology" (unpublished Ph.D. dissertation, Dept. of Sociology, University of Oregon, 1963).

[2] Joan Woodward, *Management and Technology* (London: Her Majesty's Stationery Office, 1958).

industry has emphasized the importance of technology in structuring management. Woodward's small monograph, *Management and Technology,* has precipitated lively controversy since its publication in 1958.

Woodward classified approximately 100 English firms according to a simple feature of the technology characterizing their production. She distinguished (1) those firms that produced goods in small batches or in units, from (2) the large-batch and mass-production firms and both of these from (3) companies employing continuous-process production. Among the 24 small-batch and unit-production firms, she found that the median number of levels of management authority was only 3, with a range from 2 to 4... Among the 31 mass-production firms, the median number of levels of management authority was 4; the range was from 3 to 8 or more, with 13 of the 31 firms having 5 or more levels of authority as contrasted with none among the unit-production firms. In the 25 companies employing continuous-process technologies, the median number of levels of management was 6, with but 2 firms having only 4 levels of authority; the rest had 5 or more, and 10 had 7 or more.

Thus, on the simple feature of levels of authority in the firm, it became clear that the production technology was a determinant of managerial structure. Technology made a difference in the structure of management in spite of a high level of communication between and among the managerial groups in Great Britain, and certainly in the South East Essex area where the study was made. Furthermore, British management practice has been strongly influenced by British management theorists, particularly Lyndall Urwick, which could result in great similarities in the structure of management in spite of technological differences among the companies. The fact that there is such marked technological impact on the structure of management leads one to believe that the technology of an industry is an essential influence structuring management and also, at least by inference, the functions and character of supervision.

A closer look at the system of supervision in terms of span of control and ratio of managers and supervisors to workers likewise reveals the technological factor dominant. Woodward found that for the unit-production companies, the median span of control (number of persons controlled) by first-line supervision was between 21 and 30. The median span rose to between 41 and 50 in mass-production industries. In process-production companies, however, the median span of control of first-line supervisors was lowest, between 11 and 20 workers. Furthermore, the distribution of companies according to their span of control, for each type of technology, was characteristically different...

Turning to the ratio of managers and supervisors to other personnel, the impact of technology is also significant... The ratio of managers and supervisory staff to other personnel is lowest in unit-production and highest in continuous-process industries, with mass-production industries falling in between. The differences are very sharp. In continuous-process production the ratio of managers and supervisors to other personnel is between 1 to 7 and 1 to 8, whereas in unit production the ratio ranges from 1 to 24 to as low as 1 to 49. In mass production, the ratio ranges from 1 to 14 through 1 to 18. It should be noted that the ratio of management personnel to workers is little affected by size of firm for mass-production and continuous-process technologies. With a unit-production technology there are more workers per supervisor for firms with about 1000 employees than for either smaller or larger firms, but regardless of company size, fewer managers and supervisors are required for unit-production technologies than for mass-production or continuous-process technologies. The simple measure of the ratio of managers and supervisors to other personnel is clearly related to the technology employed in the industry and is relatively little influenced by the size of the firm.

Technology and Responsibility

Some implications of the impact of technology on the location of responsibility for production are interesting to examine. In continuous-process industries like oil and gas manufacture, the high ratio of managers and supervisors to other personnel is probably a consequence of: (1) the potentiality of an error causing substantial loss in the process should it go on unattended and unnoticed, and (2) the resultant concentration in the ranks of managers and supervisors of inspection and control functions with respect to the technological process. Thus, with high-speed and continuous-process technologies the direct control of technology itself is transferred from operatives to management. (A similar transfer is characteristic of data-processing operations, where control of machines becomes critical, especially in programming the machines, and many of the control and surveillance functions in monitoring quality and quantity of output are transferred from worker level to management.)

As technology in the future tends toward continuous-process manufacture, there will be a shift of control of product quality and quantity from workers to supervisory and managerial personnel. The supervisor will become more immediately involved in the control of output than he is at present. The manager of the machine in continuous-process technologies is no longer primarily the supervisor of people but rather the supervisor of the technology.

On the other hand, in unit production where the time dimension for the production of the unit of output is relatively long, and where the individual is likely to be involved in the production of substantial subassemblies or of the entire product, the control of actual output and quality can be maintained at the worker-operator level. Relatively high levels of skills may be required at the worker level, skills including not only the technical performance of work operations, but also some knowledge about correction of operating errors, inspection, and control. Where the control functions reside in the hands of the worker, the need for supervision is reduced. Woodward's study confirms the consequence, which is a low ratio of managers and supervisors to workers.

The analog to worker-centered responsibility is to be found in the industrial research laboratory, where typically there is unit production (the individual research project), and where there is "colleague authority" in Marcson's sense.[3] Colleague authority means reference to peers rather than to research managers of problems requiring decision. Much is made in the supervision of research

---

[3] Simon Marcson, op. cit. [*The Scientist in American Industry* (Princeton: Industrial Relations Section, Princeton University, 1958]

activities of the need for maximizing colleague authority and the individual scientist's control of quantity and quality of production. The fact is, however, as Woodward's data show, that the opportunity for fixing production responsibility at the worker level exists alike in manual operations and in scientific and intellectual operations, providing the manual operations involve *unit- production technologies.*[4] The supervisory problems of maintaining quantity and quality of output are the same for highly technical people in research and development activities and for workers in unit-production industrial operations.

Technology and Managerial Costs

There are several secondary productivity consequences of variations in supervisory staffing in relation to technology. The simple per worker costs of supervision are considerably less in unit production than in continuous-process production, with mass production midway position between these two. Insofar as management is counted as an indirect cost of production, unit-production systems save money, all other things being equal.

Commitment to the organization on the part of workers and the skill necessary to make the commitment effective in high-quality work vary with the nature of technology. In continuous-process production, commitment may be minimal since supervisors and managers assume the burden of being sure the technological processes are performed adequately. Commitment must presumably be much higher in unit production, since those same responsibilities devolve directly on the worker.

Considerable "cost" may be impressed into the production process if inappropriate supervisory styles are applied under given technological conditions. If close supervision is used in unit production, it may fail or be inefficient. "Democratic" supervision in continuous-process production may prove extremely costly where errors are made in the process operations.

Another way of looking at one of the consequences of the impact of technology on supervision is to note that unit-production technologies have the most "flat" managerial structure and also the fewest managers and supervisors in relation to other personnel. Thus, the total number of managers and the complexity of the managerial structure are both minimal in unit production. On the other extreme, in process production, the number of authority levels in management is highest and the ratio of managers and supervisors to other personnel is also highest. In going from unit production to continuous-process production (mass production lying between unit and continuous production) there is a shift toward the total management component in staffing the enterprise, with more levels of managers and more managers per worker. Management of managers and supervisors, as distinct from management of workers, becomes a critical problem in continuous-process industries. In the area

---

[4] A recent popular article by Vance Packard described two instances where worker-centered responsibility was effective, and in both cases a unit-production technology was employed. See "A Chance for Everyone to Grow," *Reader's Digest* 83: (November 1963) 114-18.

of managing managers we have minimal knowledge and a great deal of speculation.[5]

There is a high probability that it will become increasingly difficult to view the costs of management as "overhead" or "indirect" in continuous-process technologies because so much of the total manpower investment will be in the managerial component. Managers carry relatively high unit prices. The sheer size of the managerial payroll will surely have an impact on production-cost analyses and may bring the development of new ideas regarding the costliness of managers in production.

In passing, mention may be made of other organizational variables that affect complexity of managerial structure. Organizational centralization and decentralization and the structures that flow from them also produce variations in supervisory practices. The technological variable is not the only one that affects managerial practices, and, either directly or indirectly, the productivity of workers.

SUPERVISORS AND GROUP ATMOSPHERES

The question put at the beginning of this chapter implies: What atmospheres created by supervisors affect productivity of their subordinates?

This problem has been approached polemically and with relatively inadequate research. It is useful to begin with a statement of one view of the supervisor's role in creating a working-group atmosphere.

Maier[6] observed: "We are entering a period in work relations where mental cruelty is becoming an appropriate charge in a grievance committee meeting as it is in the divorce court."[7] Specifically, self-determination of behavior is more acceptable than determination by others: "It is apparent that a person accepts his own decisions more often than he does another's. Group decisions are more readily accepted, but may sacrifice quality."[8] Nevertheless: "When production is a matter of coordination of group activity, it can be increased by stimulating the group to decide on a goal. In such cases the goal set should be unanimously approved... Group decision thus becomes an extremely important factor in determining the performance of a team of workers.[9]

Maier's thinking starts with the mental well-being or psychic comfort of the worker and concludes that somehow or other this is positively related to production. The argument is a very tenuous one and it may be accurate. However, the evidence is meager and when marshaled gives weak support to the conclusion. Participation in decisions about own behavior does not necessarily lead to maximizing own behavior to achieve organizational objectives, with a payoff in mental comfort. Even the evidence of the quality of group decisions

---

[5] One of the early students of this problem was Melville Dalton. See his "Managing the Managers," *Human Organization* 14 (1955) 4-10.

[6] Norman R. F. Maier, *Psychology in Industry* 2nd ed. (Boston: Houghton Mifflin Company, 1955).

[7] Ibid., p. 137.

[8] Ibid., p. 141.

[9] Ibid., pp. 151-52.

calls into serious doubt the effectiveness of groups in making production decisions. For example, the original work by Taylor[10] made clear that even in the number of ideas produced in group discourse while "brainstorming" the group output was measurably less than individual output under similar circumstances.

Drucker[11] has pointed out that the trend in modern industrial work emphasizes individual jobs as well as group or team jobs. He noted that many maintenance jobs are individual jobs and that these will increase in number with increasing automation of industry. Furthermore, many sales jobs are individual jobs, and these will also increase in number as secondary economic activity provides an increasing proportion of employment opportunities. An important corrective to current emphasis on the "groupness" of industrial work is to realize that there are now and will probably be an increasing proportion of all jobs which will *not* be performed in groups but will be performed individually and outside of group contexts. For individual jobs, the group theory of motivation simply will not apply and new studies will be necessary to find out how the lone worker can be moved to a high level of productivity and sustained there as a member of a modern work organization. This area is one of present ignorance among industrial psychologists and sociologists as well as among management practitioners.

Superior-Subordinate Interaction

A more analytical reading of the group-dynamics literature was presented by Arensberg and Tootel, who drew the following conclusions:

> But the Mayoites seem to have misread their own data. Reanalysis shows that their "teamwork" and "informal organization" are less multifactorial results, or even steady states, than emergent results of prior and continuous managerial and flow-of-work changes. The process took the form of this definite order of development: (1) an increase of managerial initiative, (2) followed by an increase of inter-worker communication, (3) followed by an increase of redressive up-the-line action of the worker upon foreman or spokesman, (4) which resulted in further changes of rewarding sorts in managerial actions, (5) changing individual attitudes, (6) reaching expression as group attitudes or morale (the "norms" of Homans), (7) which won informal sanction by the workers on one another, (8) and stimulated further releases of individual output and productivity.[12]

Arensberg and Tootel go on to state: "It is worthwhile reiterating the discovery of the 'interactionists' that this process, and the gain in productivity it brings about, seems to have *very delicate and narrow limits.*[13] Their summary is worthy of note:

[10] D. W. Taylor, P. C. Berry, and C. H. Block, "Does Group Participation When Using Brainstorming Facilitate or Inhibit Creative Thinking." *Administrative Science Quarterly* 3:(1958) 23-47.

[11] Peter Drucker, *The Practice of Management* (New York: Harper and Bros., 1951).

[12] Conrad M. Arensberg and Geoffrey Tootel, "Plant Sociology: Real Discoveries and New Problems," in Mirra Komarovsky (ed.) *Common Frontiers in the Social Sciences* (Glencoe: Free Press, 1957), p. 316.

[13] Ibid.

Indeed, present evidence suggests that the release of productivity is not so much limited by human capacity or by "diminishing returns" of maximization, as older efficiency doctrines have it, as it is dependent upon some "feedback" between worker initiative and managerial facilitation. The next advance in our understanding will come when we work out the empirical characteristics of this process.[14]

At a later point in their paper, Arensberg and Tootel conclude with:

... the finding that the process of the social release of productivity, in the empirical studies so far made, is not a matter of offering rewards alone ... We must remember that a plant is not only a place of performance tests and output scores. It is a power situation where a lesser-powered group is performing a test imposed and surveyed by a higher. Even if the management with consummate skill were to use all the goals of its employees there is both theoretical and empirical reason to doubt that the human "contented cows" stay contented under continuous driving. A "strain" is likely to develop.

... If, however, for any reason the cumulative process of change ... which we are discussing, gets under way, a different outcome may ensue. In that case, such a process might move the relevant social system comprising the two groups *toward* some "fusion" so that a common system of shared values might develop about the performance in question.[15]

The statement starts with "the release of productivity" and ends with a "common system of shared values." These are two different things. It still remains to be proved that the shared values are always or ever goals apropos of productivity. This distinction has been recognized by Bakke in his discussion of the "fusion process."[16]

Shared Goals

Perhaps the best single piece of empirical evidence bearing on the issue of a shared goal as the stimulus to high-level group effort is found in the celebrated "Robbers Cave Experiment."[17] Two groups of boys in a boy's camp achieved fusion in the solution of a common problem, after they had been deliberately placed in antagonism to each other, only when they realized that the continuous flow of behavior in each group depended on overcoming this mutual problem. The groups were driven into each other's arms and into cooperation by the need jointly to solve a problem bigger than each could handle separately. Thus, fusion was achieved between two antagonistic groups in overcoming a common obstacle.

It is worth emphasizing that there is a difference between (1) maintaining steady states in a social system and (2) the reaction of the social system to

[14] Ibid., p. 317.

[15] Ibid., p. 332.

[16] E. Wight Bakke, *The Fusion Process* (New Haven: Yale Labor and Management Center, 1953).

[17] Muzafer Sherif, *Intergroup Conflict and Cooperation: The Robbers Cave Experiment* (Norman, Okla.: University Book Exchange, 1961).

blockages or obstacles against the normal flow of activities. Empirical evidence does indicate that "fusion" can develop among diverse groups in overcoming obstacles that they face in common. Such evidence appears in Sherif's studies and in the earlier studies of Kurt Lewin, who examined the problems of group decision to achieve eating-habit changes under wartime shortages of food.[18] Sociologists have long called attention to the fact that national unity and social cohesion are usually the products either of acute crises in the social system or of attack from outside. In wars and other major social crises, many intrasocietal differences are set aside in favor of overcoming the obstacles confronting the society as a whole. Fires, floods, and other disasters in industrial establishments automatically override differences between union and management as they work together to overcome the obstacle and restore the plant to productive effectiveness. In a mine disaster, a union and its members, normally struggling against management, may temporarily set aside antagonisms in the common concern to save the men trapped underground. All these instances bear on the fact that "fusion" of groups with different goals can be achieved when they are simultaneously confronted with a common obstacle that halts the normal flow of behavior in the groups.

The maintenance of a steady state like high productivity, and the accompanying values necessary to sustain it, has not been shown to be the product of the "fusion" of diverse goals and values of the groups involved. Even the neglected and important research of Blake and Mouton[19] has dealt only with problem solving but not with steady-state maintenance.

It is not the purpose here to assert that maintenance of a steady state of high output is impossible, or that it may not be the product of a "fusion" of diverse group values. There is, however, no present empirical evidence to show that the fusion of group values is what sustains steady states in social systems. It is time to devote attention to actual measurement and analysis of this connection.

Supervisor as Environment For Workers

One of the direct consequences of Woodward's work was a study by Thurley and Hamblin[20] of five English firms. The purpose of the study was to focus attention on supervisory behaviors that could be directly associated with technological feature of the work. A number of the findings are highly significant for understanding the functions of direct supervision but are beyond the subject matter of this chapter. One technical factor affecting what the supervisor does on his job was the variability of the operations supervised. Supervisors devoted much attention to meeting schedules and to planning

[18] Kurt Lewin, *Field Theory in Social Science* (Dorwin Cartwright, ed.) (New York: Harper and Bros., 1951).
[19] Some of which is summarized in Robert R. Blake and Jane S. Mouton, "Competition, Communication, and Conformity," and "Conformity, Resistance and Conversion," both in I. A. Berg and B. M. Bass (eds.), *Conformity and Deviation* (New York: Harper & Row, Publishers 1961).
[20] K. E. Thurley and A. C. Hamblin, *The Supervisor and His Job* (London: Her Majesty's Stationery Office, 1963). Comments are based on a prepublication copy of this study.

sequences of operations as well as to overcoming blockages against continuity of product rather than producers. The supervisors also spent significant amounts of time checking machinery—in one department of an electronics company this activity reached 16 percent of the supervisors' total working time. Dealing with contingencies was another major consumer of supervisors' attention and time.

What is important here is to note that the supervisor is constantly caught up with duties focusing on plans, schedules, machines, and overcoming contingencies that interfere with meeting output expectations. In short, supervisors are supervising technical processes and machines, meeting output standards, and maintaining quality controls. People are relatively incidental and instrumental to these preoccupations, the more so as the technology approaches continuous-flow operations.

Workers, too, perceive this operating system and probably in terms not unlike those of the supervisor. Worker expectations of supervisors are molded just as much as are the behaviors of supervisors by the technical and organizational environment.

Structuring of the supervisor's work responds to technical and organizational imperatives, as will appear in the studies of Fleishman, and consideration for the worker as individual decreases as the technology becomes more complicated and the production schedule demands higher rates of continuous output.

MULTIPLE GOALS OF SUPERVISION

Supervisors are not solely oriented toward building and maintaining the productive level of those supervised. Indeed, as theorists like Maier have indicated, the mental health or psychic well-being of workers may be a coordinate goal of the efforts of supervision, along with productivity. Beside the notion of psychic well-being can be set those of morale, of loyalty, of commitment to organization, as other goals toward which supervisory practices may be directed. These all relate to the connection between employee and organization. In addition, there is an extremely large body of studies and theory dealing with such goals of supervision as maintenance of safety, reduction of employee turnover, minimization of employee grievances, reduction of scrap and other losses, quality control, and plant and equipment maintenance.

It is notable that in pursuit of this incomplete list of goals toward which supervisory behaviors are directed a vast range of activities is to be found, many of which are independent of each other. The supervisor's jobs are many and varied, and it should not be at all surprising to find numerous empirical situations in which the supervisor is little, if at all, concerned with people or with productivity. Certainly, under circumstances of complete machine pacing, for example, the variability in productivity that can be attributed to supervisory practices is probably extremely small.

Morale, feelings of well-being, attitudes toward the company, acceptance or nonacceptance of supervisors, cohesiveness of the work group, employee turnover, or grievance incidence rates are in and of themselves important subjects for study and analysis. Because, however, the major test applied by operating management to any innovations in supervisory practices is the influence these may have on productivity, the authors of studies relating supervisory practices to other outcomes often gratuitously conclude that their results support the belief that productivity will also be positively affected. It is important to keep in mind that the various goals toward which supervisory practices are directed are not necessarily interrelated.

Worker Morale as A Goal

A number of studies of supervisory behavior concern its influence on morale of workers. Almost invariably the author will conclude that if the supervisor's behavior can raise morale, then there are probably associated increases in productivity. The study may clearly demonstrate that morale does vary according to the behaviors of supervisors, but the conclusion that morale change in turn influences productivity remains unsupported. Indeed, Dubin[21] has pointed out that high morale in a work group may be the basis for successful sabotage of management's productivity goals, and Seashore[22] has shown that high-cohesion work groups may deviate from production norms on *both* the high and the low sides. Since Seashore's data also show that high-cohesion work groups tend to be high-morale groups, his findings support Dubin's conclusion.

As part of the Yale study of automobile assembly-line workers, Turner[23] showed that the attitudes of workers toward the job itself and toward their own foremen were independent. In particular, Turner found that if the job was of primary importance to the workers, then the foreman and his behaviors made relatively little difference in their orientation toward the organization. "It was as if the nature of the job and the nature of supervision, as perceived by workers, were almost separate influences on workers' over-all attitudes."[24]

Kahn, one of the principal investigators in the Michigan researches, concluded the survey of the Michigan studies of supervisors and workers as follows: "None of the major indices of satisfaction (job, supervision, company, etc.) proved either to relate to productivity or to mediate significantly between productivity and such independent variables as role differentiation, delegation, or employee orientation."[25]

Turning directly to evidence on morale, Kahn stated the following:

> This research, . . . did not provide positive evidence on the matter of morale in relation of productivity. . . . Indices of worker satisfaction were developed by means of factor analysis, which showed four well-defined dimensions of satisfaction: satisfaction with supervision, with the job itself, with the company as a whole, and with the extrinsic rewards of money, mobility, etc. None of these indices was significantly related to productivity.

[21] Robert Dubin, *The World of Work* (Englewood Cliffs, N. J.: Prentice-Hall Inc., 1958), especially Chapter 12.

[22] Stanley E. Seashore, *Group Cohesiveness in the Industrial Work Group* (Ann Arbor: Institute for Social Research, University of Michigan, 1954).

[23] Arthur N. Turner, "Foreman, Job, and Company," *Human Relations,* 10 (1957) 99-112.

[24] Ibid., p. 111

[25] Robert L. Kahn, "The Prediction of Productivity," *Journal of Social Issues* 12 (1956) 41-49, 44.

In line with a statement already made in this chapter, Kahn stated: "The notion that supervision (among other things) determines satisfaction, which in turn determines productivity, has been considerably discredited in our eyes.[26]

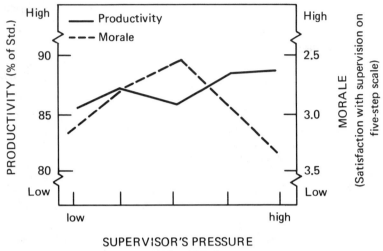

FIGURE 1. The Relation of Productivity and Morale to Supervisor's Pressure for Production. (Redrawn from Rensis Likert, "Developing Patterns in Management," cited in footnote 27.)

Likert[27] has presented some other Michigan data which show that productivity increases with supervisor's pressure for more output (Figure 1). Morale also increases up to about the mid range of supervisory pressure for output, after which it declines, just as sharply as it increased. Thus, even the data used by one of the strongest exponents of worker autonomy shows that pressure *does* produce more productivity and even increases morale through a portion of the range of increasing supervisory pressure. This observation suggests that social systems respond to leadership pressures in "putting the heat on" and holding subordinates to high expectations. In an organized production situation, workers expect to be asked to produce and be held to reasonable levels of output. Furthermore, if the supervisory pressure is not excessive workers' morale goes up with increasing pressure!

Worker Autonomy as A Goal

Management literature is replete with a theme that worker autonomy is a viable goal for supervisory practices. Generally the worker autonomy sought is one best described as the condition wherein workers require little supervision. Sometimes autonomy is specified as the condition requiring minimum "close

[26] Ibid., from pp. 46 and 47.
[27] Rensis Likert, "Developing Patterns in Management," in American Management Association, *Strengthening Management for the New Technology* (New York: The Association, 1955).

supervision.'' The definition of autonomy is almost always in the supervisor-worker context. On its face, worker autonomy should be an acceptable condition for many workers, and it is obviously an aid to supervisors since it reduces their burden.

Kahn,[28] in summarizing the human-relations research program at the University of Michigan, showed that in the studies of clerical and railroad workers the high-productivity groups were supervised in a general fashion rather than in a close or detailed one. This demonstration was the beginning of the repeated emphasis in the Michigan studies, castigating close and detailed supervision and pleading for worker autonomy as one of the important requisites for high output. The idea has persisted to the present and is given renewed emphasis by Likert.[29] But the study of British industry by Argyle, Gardner, and Ciofi[30] did not demonstrate autonomy as a central variable in productivity. These data have never been incorporated into the thinking of the Michigan group.

Perhaps these disparate findings can be reconciled by noting that both railroad and clerical workers, the samples from which the Michigan group drew its conclusions, are involved in unit- or batch-production systems. Woodward's studies of technology and management show that the ratio of supervisors to workers is very low in such systems. A correlate of this low ratio, one noted earlier, is that the responsibility of individual workers may be maximal in such systems. A further correlate is that workers in unit-production technologies will produce most when given only general supervision. This relation is to be attributed to the technology rather than to a general principle that all work situations demand maximum autonomy for workers.

The study by Argyle, Gardner, and Ciofi was based on 90 foremen in eight British factories manufacturing electric motors and switchgear. These factories would all probably be classified as employing large-batch or quasi-mass production, with basic technological features different from those in the routine clerical work in a large insurance company and in the railroad gangs studied by the Michigan group. The British study revealed that the only dimension of supervisory behavior which bore a significant relationship to measured output of the departments supervised was punitive or nonpunitive correction by the foreman of worker mistakes and errors. When general supervision was combined with nonpunitive behavior and democractic relations with employees, these three dimensions of supervisor behavior were positively and significantly correlated with output, but together they accounted only for 18 percent of the variance in output.

Likert reproduced the results of one of his earliest studies in *New Patterns of*

[28] Robert L. Kahn, op. cit. in note 25.

[29] In his widely acclaimed book, *New Patterns of Management* (New York: McGraw-Hill Book Company, 1961).

[30] Michael Argyle, Godfrey Gardner, and Frank Ciofi, "The Measurement of Supervisory Methods," *Human Relations* 10 (1957): 295-313. and by the same authors, "Supervisory Methods Related to Productivity, Absenteeism, and Labour Turnover," *Human Relations* 11 (1958): 23-40.

Management[31] in which he compared the difference between superior and mediocre life-insurance agencies. The data show that an attitude of cooperation with his sales agents by the agency manager was found more often among managers of agencies judged superior in performance. The descriptions of the managers were based on agents' evaluations. Furthermore, these same successful managers gave considerably more autonomy to their agents than the less successful managers.

It is not surprising, in view of these results secured when he made one of his first studies of managerial behavior, that Likert would conclude that considerate, nondirective leadership characteristics symbolize modern industrial statesmanship. However, it is obvious that selling life insurance is a classical unit-production process, a one-customer-one-sale situation. Each sale is a unit by itself, typically taking place away from the office and therefore removed from the point of supervision. It would seem evident that the technology associated with selling life insurance would make autonomy of sales agents an important condition of success.

Evidence is by no means conclusive in support of the contention that worker autonomy is essential for high individual productivity. Indeed, when worker autonomy (of which general supervision instead of close supervision is the foreman facet) is combined with two other dimensions of supervisory behavior found significant in combination in the English factories, the combination still accounts for less than one-fifth of the variance in productivity. Further, there is reason to believe that worker autonomy may be relevant to batch- or unit-production technologies, but probably not to mass-production technologies and almost certainly not to continuous-process technologies.

Consideration For Workers as A Goal

Another popular goal of supervision is to develop considerate treatment of subordinates. This supervisory stance may be characterized as being employee-centered. The presumption underlying a belief in employee-centered supervision is that considerate treatment will be repaid by devoted effort and possibly higher output.

Kahn reviewed the study of two groups of employees in a large business office, the Prudential study.[32] One group was given employee-centered supervision and the other was given just the opposite. Both groups showed a significant increase in productivity. The employee-centered supervision produced an increase in favorable employee attitudes toward supervisors and the company, while the authoritarian-led group showed a marked decrease in employee satisfaction. This classic study, often cited in support of the employee-centered supervision ethic, provides data to show that employee-centeredness is *not* the critical factor that determines individual productivity. If anything, the most direct conclusion from this study is that productivity can either be forced or be encouraged with about the same outcomes with respect to output. Obviously, it is other outcomes that distinguish the two methods of supervision.

[31] Rensis Likert, op. cit. in note 27.
[32] Robert L. Kahn, op. cit. in note 25.

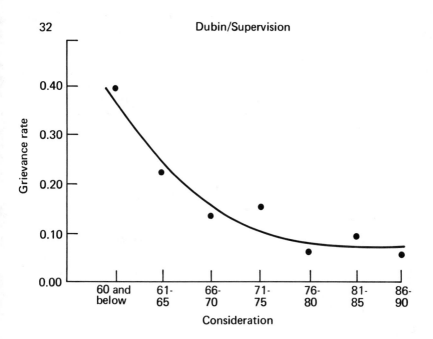

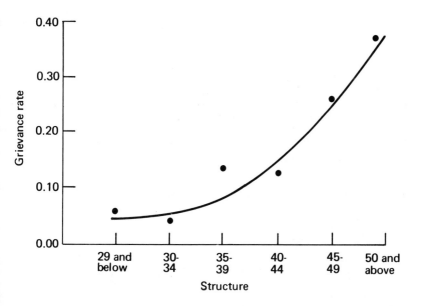

FIGURE 2 (portion). See legend on page 526.

Kahn further reported on the heavy-industry study among 20,000 workers engaged in the manufacture of tractors and earthmoving equipment:

> Like the earlier studies, the research in the tractor factory showed that the foremen with the best production records were the ones who were most skilled at and most concerned with meeting employee needs for information, support, assistance, but they were no less concerned with production . . . The foremen with the best production records, in short, were both production-centered and employee-centered.

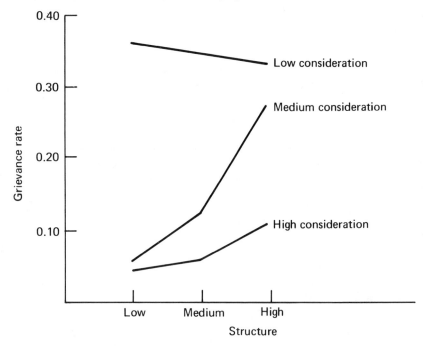

FIGURE 2. Leadership Behavior and Grievances. (Redrawn from E. A. Fleishman and E. F. Harris, "Patterns of Leadership Behavior Related to Employee Grievances and Turnover," cited in footnote 34.)

It is especially desirable to pay attention to one of Kahn's major conclusions:

> It thus appeared that the continuum of supervisory behavior which placed employee-centeredness at one end and production-centeredness at the other was less in accord with the facts than a four-fold classification of supervisors which would include two additional types—the supervisor who combined employee and production orientation and the supervisor who gave neither of these emphases to his role.[33]

In the Fleishman, Harris study[34] of 57 foremen in a motortruck manufacturing plant, it was found that as the degree of consideration shown

---

[33] Ibid., pp. 44 and 45.
[34] E. A. Fleishman and E. F. Harris, "Patterns of Leadership Behavior Related to Employee Grievances and Turnover," *Personnel Psychology* 15 (1962): 45-53.

most markedly if medium consideration is shown toward employees and structuring goes from low to high.

The structuring of the work relationship as measured on a scale of structuring behaviors by the foremen shows a curve in the opposite direction. The more structure imposed upon work by the supervisor the higher the grievance rate. The most marked increase in the grievance rate occurs only after the mid point in the structuring behavior of the foreman is reached.

However, when the two factors of consideration and structure are combined and related to the grievance rate, a very interesting fact emerges. When low consideration for employees is consistent, then the more structuring the behavior of the foreman the *lower* is the grievance rate. On the other hand, when high consideration for employees is shown consistently by the foreman, then the more the structuring the higher is the grievance rate. The grievance rate goes up toward subordinates increased the grievance rate decreased (Fig. 2). This decrease is not a straight-line relationship but is a curvilinear one. The greatest amount of decrease in the grievance rate comes as consideration increases from the lowest levels to near the mid point of consideration.

Employee-turnover rates have a pattern almost exactly like those of grievances when related to foreman consideration and structuring of the work situation. It is again notable that the curvilinear relationships show that the major rate of change in employee turnover occurs at the low end of the consideration scale, with a moderate degree of consideration materially reducing the turnover rate, and with further increase in consideration having no further influence in reducing turnover. Similarly, an increase in structure up to about the mid point produces no increase in turnover, but beyond the mid point it makes for a marked increase in turnover.

This study provides good evidence of the consequences of supervisory behavior for turnover and grievances; but again, it should be emphasized, neither of these have been demonstrated to be directly related to productivity. Multiple goals of supervision are illustrated here and it is demonstrated quite adequately that differences in supervisory practices will produce measurable differences in turnover and grievance behaviors of employees.

Attention is especially directed to the curvilinear relationships. To know that some structuring of work for subordinates does not induce high grievance rates among them and that they begin to grieve in material amounts only when supervisory structuring of work behavior becomes marked is quite different from thinking that the more structuring the more grievances, or the less structuring of work the fewer grievances. Yet, most of the precepts of management and supervision are couched in linear terms.

The related study by Fleishman, Harris, and Burtt[35] revealed that ". . . there was a clear-cut tendency for the divisions that were under the pressure of time to have foremen who were most inclined toward initiating structure and vice versa. There was also a very marked tendency for the foremen in the most demanding

[35] E. A. Fleishman, E. F. Harris and R. D. Burtt, *Leadership and Supervision in Industry* (Columbus: Ohio State University Press, 1955).

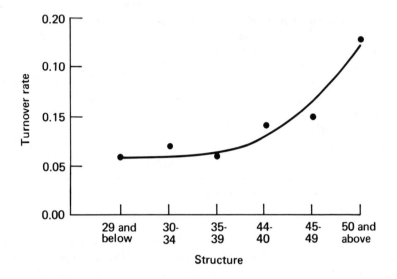

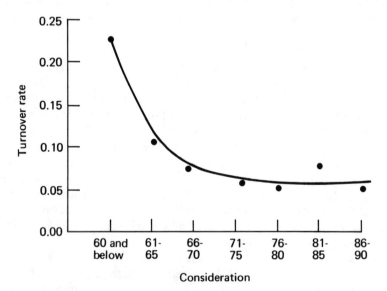

FIGURE 3. Leadership Behavior and Turnover Rates. (Redrawn from E. A. Fleishman and E. F. Harris, "Patterns of Leadership Behavior Related to Employee Grievances and Turnover," cited in footnote 34.)

divisions to operate with the least consideration."[36] This is a study of the motor-truck manufacturing plant of International Harvester Company, a unit-production technology in the final assembly line but one accompanied by mass production technologies in the parts departments and in some subassembly departments. Thus, the authors' emphasis on time pressures leading to more structuring and less consideration might well give way to emphasis on the character of the technology in which little worker autonomy is needed to get the work out, hence the prevalence of supervisory structuring of work for subordinates.

The authors add: "The results go on to show that the more efficient foremen, as rated by the boss, are inclined to show more initiation Structure and less Consideration. This appears to be a function of the demandingness of the time schedule."[37]

The theme that technology affects supervisory behaviors appeared in this early study by Fleishman, Harris, and Burtt. However, neither they nor subsequent analysts recognized what Woodward later discovered. The following quotation explains:

> Results indicate that there appears to be a difference between production and nonproduction departments in the requisite kinds of leadership. [This is one way of stating the difference in this sample between mass-production and unit- or batch-production technologies in Woodward's terms.] In the nonproduction departments, the foremen who are rated most proficient by their own supervisors apparently motivate their work groups to get the job done by creating a friendly atmosphere and by considerate behavior with a minimum of emphasis on work methods, standards, and structuring of activities. [In production departments foremen play a difficult role. Their] considerate behavior is very good from the morale standpoint, but not so good for proficiency as judged by the foreman's own boss.[38]

In the Fleishman and Peters study[39] of the effectiveness of middle managers in a continuous-production operation, soap and detergent manufacture, 39 managers in the ranks between line foremen and plant managers were studied. The major conclusions are: (1) "there is an absence of relationship between leadership attitudes and rated effectiveness," and (2) "no particular combination of Structure and Consideration attitudes was predictive of effectiveness ratings."[40] Here the managers' efficiency was rated by their own superiors.

Thus, for production workers in unit and small-batch technologies, the factors of high consideration and low structure do have a bearing on rated departmental efficiency and foreman proficiency, if not on output. In mass production, efficiency and effectiveness are positively related to low consideration by the foreman and much structuring of the work situation by

[36] Ibid., p. 99.
[37] Ibid., p. 99.
[38] Ibid., p. 103-4.
[39] E. A. Fleishman and D. R. Peters, "Interpersonal Values, Leadership Attitudes and Managerial 'Success'," *Personnel Psychology* 15 (1962): 127-43.
[40] Ibid., p. 136.

him. In managing middle managers, neither consideration nor structuring relates to rated efficiency of performance.

Sensitivity To Workers as A Goal

A firmly established notion stemming from the group dynamics tradition has been that supervisors who are sensitive to the needs of their subordinates have an important requisite for being effective leaders. The insensitive supervisor is presumably an ineffective leader. The idea that "sensitivity" is an essential ingredient of supervisory practice has even been incorporated into a formal training program called "sensitivity training."[41]

In a study by Nagle[42] a questionnaire was administered to supervisors to measure their sensitivity, and six plant executives rated departments as to their productivity. Then these data on 14 departments composed of office workers in a large industrial organization were correlated. It was found that there was a correlation of .82 between supervisor sensitivity and rated productivity of the department.

The meaning of "sensitivity" is variously interpreted. According to Fiedler,[43] sensitivity means the ability to discriminate clearly among subordinates on the basis of their characteristics. Thus Cleven and Fiedler,[44] in their study of steel-mill open hearth supervisors, took note of discrimination as exercised by pit foremen and melters, the supervisors most directly involved in open-hearth operations. They found that those whose crews had good production records discriminated more sharply between the most- and the least-liked coworkers; those whose crew production records were below average discriminated less sharply.

This meaning of sensitivity, sensitivity to the differences among subordinates and the ability to use this information effectively to supervise them, may be the factor which accounts for the high correlation that Nagle found between supervisor's sensitivity and the attributed productivity of his group. The Cleven and Fiedler results were obtained in a batch-production situation and the Nagle results in a unit-production technology (office work). These are similar technologies and demand high worker autonomy. The results of the two studies may legitimately be put together to support the opinion that in such a technology sensitivity to the individual characteristics of the worker is one of the supervisor traits which is successful in getting a high level of productivity from workers. That is, the supervisor may well give different kinds of autonomy to individual workers in accord with their special personalities and other characteristics. The more successful supervisor may be the one best able to

---

[41] See the description of "sensitivity training" in Robert Tannenbaum, Fred Massarik, and Irving Weschler, *Leadership and Organization* (New York: McGraw-Hill Book Company 1961).

[42] B. F. Nagle, "Productivity, Employee Attitude, and Supervisor Sensitivity," *Personnel Psychology* 7 (1954):219-33.

[43] Fred E. Fiedler, *Leadership Attitudes and Group Effectiveness* (Urbana: University of Illinois Press, 1958) summarizes the several studies made by Fiedler in this area.

[44] W. A. Cleven and Fred E. Fiedler, "Interpersonal Perceptions of Open Hearth Foremen and Steel Production," *Journal of Applied Psychology* 40 (1956):312-14.

perceive these individual characteristics (discriminate them, in Fiedler's terms) in order to tailor his own actions to the individual's unique qualities.

Worker Participation as A Goal

A particularly important study in the analysis of supervisory practices was that by French and Coch,[45] in which the effects of employee participation in a decision affecting them were measured. It was concluded that those who participated in decisions regarding work changes ultimatly reached somewhat higher levels of output than a comparable group of workers who were told to change their methods of work. This study has been the cornerstone of theory concluding that worker participation is desirable for efficiency reasons and improvement of output levels.

Wickert[46] studied employee turnover and feelings of ego involvement in the day-to-day operations of telephone operators and female service representatives in the Michigan Bell Telephone Company. About 700 women were studied. The principal finding was that those who stayed with the company had a greater feeling of involvement in the day-to-day operations of the company than those who left. Specifically, those who stayed tended to say (1) they had a chance to make decisions on the job, and (2) they felt they were making an important individual contribution to the success of the company. It will be noted that telephone operators and service representatives are all involved in unit production, since they each have to depend upon someone initiating a call or a service request before they go into action. Under these circumstances of technology a material degree of autonomy is probably essential in maintaining levels of output. A chance to make decisions on the job and contribute to company success are measures of participation. It might be concluded, however, that these aspects of participation in work are mediated by the need for autonomy that comes from the technology employed.

In Rice's study of the Indian weaving shed,[47] a comparison was made of production before and after a change in the organization of the work. The individual workers in the experimental weaving groups revised the production process from what had previously been a confused and relatively unstructured one. The data demonstrate that the subsequent steady state of output was markedly and significantly higher after the workers reorganized the work themselves. Furthermore, the rate of cloth damage in the weaving mill was lower than before reorganization of production.

Several comments need to be made about this study. The self-organizing productive groups increased their efficiency by about 18 percent if we take the before-reorganization figures as the base. This improvement tends to give the impression, as Rice suggests, that the self-organization of work is one means for

[45] Lester Coch and John R. P. French, Jr., "Overcoming Resistance to Change," *Human Relations* 1 (1948):512-32.
[46] F. R. Wickert, "Turnover and Employee's Feelings of Ego-Involvement," *Personnel Psychology* 4 (1951):185-97.
[47] A. K. Rice, "Productivity and Social Organization in an Indian Weaving Shed," *Human Relations* 6 (1953):297-329.

increasing efficiency considerably. But a disturbing feature of this situation also must be taken into account. The original structuring of the work situation, which continued to obtain in the nonexperimental groups in the same company, was one in which there were confused task and worker relationships, and no perceptible internal work-group structure. Thus the base from which change was measured in this study may be an instance of industrial "anarchy," or near anarchy, in which the designs of the production processes themselves were scarcely adequate.

Under these circumstances, any attention to the *organization* of work, whether management-initiated or worker-initiated, undoubtedly would have produced significant increases in productivity. Weaving, being a continuous-process production technology over short time spans, would require high structure for adequate performance. In the light of Fleishman's results it seems probable that structuring itself is what may have improved productivity in the Indian weaving shed, not worker participation. It may not, therefore, be desirable or warranted to draw the conclusion that high autonomy and participation in decisions by the Indian weavers are what really produced higher output.

Likert, in an early paper,[48] made the point that

> Available research findings indicate, therefore, that when . . . the amount of participation used is less than or very much greater than expected, an unfavorable reaction is likely to be evoked. Substantially greater amounts of participation than expected appear to exceed the skill of the subordinate to cope with it and produce a negative reaction because of the threatening nature of the situation to the subordinate. The available theory and research findings suggest that the best results obtain when the amount of participation used is somewhat greater than expected by the subordinate, but still within their capacity to respond to it effectively.

Likert had made this point as early as 1952, but it is a point that is rarely given attention by those who urge participative management as the be-all and end-all of supervisory practice.

Likert clearly argued for an optimal rather than a maximal level of participation of subordinates in decision making relative to their own destinies. That is, there is a curvilinear relation between worker participation and such consequences as output. This relation recalls Fleishman's studies of initiating structure and consideration which relate in a curvilinear fashion to turnover and absenteeism. That is to say, over part of the range of consideration and initiating structure for subordinates there is no material change in their reactions, but beyond a critical point their reactions become prompt and decisive.

The general conclusion that emerges is that employee participation is probably not linearly related but rather curvilinearly related to aspects of working behavior. Likert has pointed out that his own researches have indicated that supervisory behavior in excess of normal expectations will not be favorably accepted by subordinates. This disfavor may be particularly likely if the

---

[48] Rensis Likert, "Effective Supervision: An Adaptive and Relative Process," op. cit., p. 329.

supervisor invites participation beyond the subordinate's normal level of acceptance. This conclusion recalls Barnard's "zone of indifference," in which reactions of the subordinate become significant only if the supervisor exceeds the tolerance limits customarily adopted by the subordinate.[49]

Rewarding Workers as A Goal

One of the important functions of supervisors is that of rewarding subordinates. In modern industrial firms the immediate supervisor has relatively little connection with monetary rewards, except perhaps to recommend promotions and pay increases. There remains, however, a range of nonfinancial rewards that each supervisor can monitor in influencing his subordinates. Surprisingly little research has been directed at finding out what effects such rewards have.

In the interesting study by Zaleznik, Christensen, and Roethlisberger,[50] 50 industrial workers were analyzed to determine the influences of social factors on productivity. Among the major findings was the fact that individuals with high status and high status congruence (agreement between self-conception and other's perception that they are properly placed in a social system) tended to produce at the normal or expected levels of output more than they tended to deviate from "on-line" output. On the other hand, of individuals with low status and low status congruence twice as many were deviant in output as were "on-line."

In analyzing status by itself it was found that the high-status people were average in productivity and "on-line" more than they deviated, while the low-status people deviated more than they were "on-line" in output. However, when status congruence was examined by itself the relationship turned out to be nonsignificant between that and level of productivity.

The study showed that when both management and the peer group rewarded the workers, more of them produced "on-line" than were deviant by a ratio of eight to three. Similarly when management did not reward the worker but the group did, more produced "on-line" by the ratio of six to three. However, when management rewarded the individual and the group did not, or when neither rewarded, then the preponderance was deviancy by the individual from the "on-line" expectations of output. When management alone rewarded the worker, he tended to produce below norm. When neither rewarded the worker, however, he tended to produce above average.

Another way of examining the influences of the social factors on productivity is to look at the character of group membership and its impact on productivity. Those who were regular members of a group tended to produce in the ratio of 14 at the expected average to six "off-line." Those who were perceived by the group as being deviant individuals were predominantly "off-line" in output in the ratio of ten to three who were "on-line," while isolates from the group

[49] Chester I. Barnard, *The Functions of the Executive* (Cambridge, Mass.: Harvard University Press, 1938).

[50] Abe Zaleznik, Charles R. Christensen, and Fritz J. Roethlisberger, *The Motivation, Productivity, and Satisfaction of Workers* (Cambridge, Mass.: Harvard University Press, 1958).

tended to produce "off-line" in the ratio of nine to three who were "on-line." Thus, being a deviant or isolate from the work group meant that the individual would not produce at the expected norm of output. It is interesting to note that those who were deviants from the work group tended to produce higher than the norm, while those who were isolates from the work group tended to produce below standard.

These results, suggestive as they are, must be approached cautiously since the numbers on which they are based are small, there being only 45 workers in the total sample for whom full data were available. The conclusions can be treated as suggesting the following speculations.

It seems that individual productivity is influenced by (1) the location of an individual in a social group, (2) the status accorded to him by those in his social environment, and (3) the sources of social rewards coming to him. The smallness of the sample precludes any cross tabulations to isolate the impact of rewards vs. social position when these are considered simultaneously.

What seems especially notable is that individual productivity varies with social factors in the work situation that may not be within the influence range of the supervisor. Indeed, strange as it may seem, insofar as supervisors manipulate nonfinancial rewards without parallel rewards coming from the peer work group, the worker response may be output lower than the norm! This finding is significant for reinforcement theorists in the realm of industrial incentives. Complicating the reinforcement theorist's problem even further is the finding that nonreward produces output higher than normal! Maybe if we really want high productivity, the social payoffs with which we reward industrial workers should be withheld!

The study just analyzed calls attention to the importance of the working peer group as a source of reward and reinforcement of individual behavior. This importance turns attention to the characteristics of peer groups. Among those features studied that bear on productivity is peer-group cohesivesness.

Seashore's study[51] of group cohesiveness in the industrial work group showed (Fig. 4) that among low-productivity groups, worker-perceived pressure for productivity decreased as the group cohesiveness increased. When the condition of maximum group cohesiveness was approached the perceived degree of pressure for productivity went up markedly. This tendency contrasted with that in groups of high productivity, which perceived a declining degree of pressure for productivity as group cohesiveness increased.

For the low-productivity group, management pressure for productivity was perceived only if the group was highly cohesive. Thus, one of the consequences of cohesiveness in low-productivity groups is to provide the opportunity for supportive rebellion against management. This conclusion is further supported by the general summing up by Seashore: "High cohesive groups differ more frequently and in greater amount than low cohesive groups from the plant norms of productivity. These deviations are toward both high and lower productivity."[52]

[51] Stanley E. Seashore, op. cit.
[52] Ibid., p. 98.

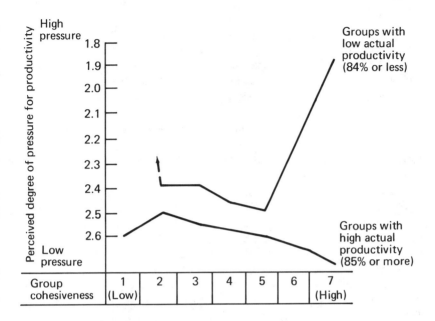

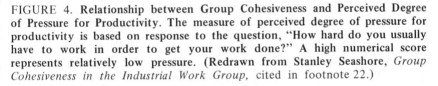

FIGURE 4. Relationship between Group Cohesiveness and Perceived Degree of Pressure for Productivity. The measure of perceived degree of pressure for productivity is based on response to the question, "How hard do you usually have to work in order to get your work done?" A high numerical score represents relatively low pressure. (Redrawn from Stanley Seashore, *Group Cohesiveness in the Industrial Work Group,* cited in footnote 22.)

CONCLUSION

Supervision does make some difference in productivity. Supervisory practices also affect other aspects of work. The details of these conclusions depart significantly from current views, and are both unique and surprising.

(1). Supervisory behavior affects the productivity of individuals by being appropriate to the work setting. One key to describing the characteristics of work settings is to know the nature of the technologies employed. The descriptive task has just begun but the results are promising. By drawing simple distinctions between unit- and mass-production technologies, and viewing continuous production as another type of technology, supervisory styles are found appropriate to each technological type. The more a production process resembles a unit or batch technology, the greater is the probability that worker autonomy and its supervisory counterpart—general rather than close supervision—will be appropriate. The more a technology resembles a continuous-production system the more appropriate will close supervision be.

(2). This first proposition leads directly to the second. There is no "one best" method of supervision. As in all human systems, there is variability in the systems of supervision of industrial and commercial work. Several styles of supervision are effective, but they are individually successful only in relation to appropriate work settings. Variety in supervisory behaviors may no longer be considered a challenge to choose the "one best" for all settings, but rather as a challenge to understand where each does or does not work.

(3). As far as empirical data take us, it seems clear that the influence of supervisory behaviors on productivity is small. The studies are few in number, however, and not adquately designed to measure magnitude of influence of supervision on productivity.

(4). Supervision of industrial and commercial work has many functions. The variety of areas in which supervisors act is the consequence of their having numerous functional contributions to make. For a given situation supervision may have relatively little to do with individual productivity, and yet supervisors, because they perform many other functions, may retain importance in work organizations. Executives must therefore constantly face the difficult problem of organizational design and the choice of operating goals for supervisors. If, for example, top management wants workers to be happy this goal may be attained by appropriate supervisory behaviors.

(5). The goals of supervision and the behaviors of supervisors are independent of each other in one sense and linked in another. A variety of goals may be assigned to supervisors, and those selected do not appear to be limited or determined by any features of organizational structure or process. Thus, consideration of workers may be emphasized in unit production, in mass production, or in process production if top management chooses consideration as a goal. Supervisory practices in each technological system will be different although directed toward the same goal. It is in this sense that the goals of supervision and the behaviors of supervisors are independent of each other.

On the other hand, goals and behaviors are linked through technology since behaviors necessary to achieve a particular goal must be appropriate to the operating situation. For example, consideration of workers in unit-production technologies may exhibit itself by providing workers with maximum opportunities to pace their own work, while in continuous-production technologies the same consideration may be most appropriately expressed as detailed concern with safety or physical comfort of the worker.

(6). It is now possible to take a sophisticated view of the impact of supervision on working behaviors. Most analysts up to this time have assumed that whatever the linkage, it tended to be a linear one. That is, a unit change in a particular supervisory behavior was assumed to produce a corresponding change in worker response throughout the range of supervisory action. This view is simply false. Many behaviors have thresholds above which the behavior is responded to by others, but below which the behaviors produce little or no effect. Thresholds were revealed, for example, in the relationship between supervisory consideration and worker responses in terms of grievances and absenteeism. This phenomenon was also discovered in the relation between opportunity to participate in decisions and worker responses to the opportunity.

(7). A supervisory practice in the low range may have one effect on worker response, but in the high range may produce exactly the opposite effect. This disparity was exhibited in the consequence of supervisory pressure for worker morale. At least in some demonstrable instances the relationship between supervisory behavior and worker response is nonlinear and may even be parabolic. Evidence supports the contention that if a little bit of a supervisory behavior may be good, a lot may be very bad indeed. This optimization notion is sometimes overlooked in the theory and practice of personnel administration.

(8). An important technological trend is making for a fundamental shift in industry from the management of people to the management of things. The detailed study of continuous-process manufacture showed the highest ratio of managers to other workers for any type of technology. It has been inferred that this high ratio reflects the need for supervisor surveillance of high-speed production processes to insure that product runs are error-free, since large numbers of defects can be produced by the time the process is halted to correct an error. As supervisors supervise machines more and people less, they will become increasingly responsible for production. Supervisory controls will not be controls on speed of output, since output will be machine or process-paced. The supervisors will be largely concerned with controlling quality, and the operating contingencies that influence the go-no-go performance of the production process.

(9). Knowledge of leadership and supervision as they affect working behavior is almost exclusively the result of studying American industrial practices. A few important English studies have been cited here, and additional studies dealing with other national economics are scattered through the literature.[53] Culture does make a difference in supervisory practices. It follows, then, that caution is necessary in applying present knowledge to cultural settings different from those in which the knowledge was gained. Generalizations may work universally, but then again they may not. We have no *a priori* reason for guessing which of these two outcomes will obtain.

(10). All the studies of human relations and supervision tell little about how much productivity is affected by individual supervisory practices. Only one study attempted to tease out the answer to this question and it suggested that not more than one-fifth of the variance in productivity can be accounted for by a combination of three supervisory practices. The Western Electric and other researches showed that fellow workers influence the individual's output. Advances in technology produce steady increases in man-hour productivity. There has never been a proper analysis of variance to assay that relative importance of simultaneous factors effecting individual output. It is certainly time to turn empirical attention to just this kind of problem.

---

[53] I cite just two studies conducted in Scandinavian countries which have been scarcely noticed by American scholars although both are significant contributions. K. Raino, *Leadership Qualities: A Theoretical Inquiry and an Experimental Study of Foremen* (Helsinki: Annales Academiae Scientiarum Fennicae, Series B, vol. 95.1, 1955); Uno Remitz, *Professional Satisfaction among Swedish Bank Employees* (Copenhagen: Munksgaard, 1960).

Walter R. Nord

LEADERSHIP:
A CURRENT PERSPECTIVE

Current models of leadership contrast sharply with those of the classical management era, which were drawn from the administrative structures of the Roman Catholic Church and military organizations. The classical models stressed authority, discipline, and control and looked upon leadership as determined by organizational position, which one attained through ability. Most modern theorists, on the other hand, hold a subordinate-centered view, stressing the interdependence of leader and group and defining leadership as a form of interaction between the two. Considerable evidence has been accumulated that, in most organizations, attention of a group leader or head to social-emotional needs often pays dividends in organizational effectiveness. It has recently been suggested that the advocates of a subordinate-centered approach have overstated their case. A new synthesis now seems to be developing.

Interactionist View of Leadership

We have seen throughout this book that most organizational phenomena are the product of multiple, interacting forces. Perhaps no topic reflects this multivariate perspective more plainly than that of leadership. Gibb (1969) has provided a clear statement of the interactionist view of leadership. He stressed that groups are vehicles for satisfying the needs of individuals. As group members interact, a structure emerges from individuals' expectations about the behavior of others. While all groups develop some type of role differentiation, particular roles develop as a product of the needs experienced in the group. The needs are influenced by the task, the size of the group, and a host of other variables. Personality traits, abilities, and skills of members influence how each will be perceived by other members and thus play a part in the development and performance of roles within the group. Leadership, then, is one aspect of the more general process of role differentiation; like any other type of role differentiation, leadership is a function of the dynamic interaction of personal attributes and variables in the social system. As Gibb says,

> Both leadership structure and individual leader behavior are determined in large part by the nature of the organization in which they occur. Leadership structure is relative, also, to the population characteristics of

*This article was prepared especially for this volume.

the group, or, in other words, to the attitudes and needs of the followers. Leadership inevitably embodies many of the qualities of the followers and the relation between the two may often be so close that it is difficult to determine who influences whom and to what extent. For this reason, it is possible for leadership to be nominal only (p. 271).

With this interactionist view in mind, one can more easily understand both the advocates and critics of democratic-participative leadership.

DEMOCRATIC LEADERSHIP RECONSIDERED

Currently an important group of organizational behaviorists relies heavily on the idea of involving organizational participants in the decision-making process in order to win their commitment to organizational goals. A great deal of research has supported the view that the democratic approach to leadership can produce positive changes in organizational performance. However, Dubin and others have suggested that this research has been too narrowly conceived.

In the preceding selection Dubin suggested that the research which has found participative leadership to be far superior has been confined to studies of batch-type operations. Democratic management may be most valuable for the unprogrammed tasks characteristic of many managerial, research and craft jobs. A logical implication is that democratic leadership may have fewer benefits in divisions, departments, organizational levels or organizations in which the operations are less variable.

Mann (1965) showed that organizational level is an important determinant of the demands placed on a supervisor. The mix of supervisory skills required at lower levels is likely to be weighted in favor of technical rather than administrative competence; at intermediate levels the technical skills are less necessary and the administrative more so. Top management positions require even more administrative ability but relatively little technical proficiency. Competence in a third area, human relations, is important throughout the organization but probably more essential at lower levels, where motivation is likely to be a greater problem.

Additional support for Mann's ideas has come from Nealey and Fiedler (1968), who concluded that the skills required of second-level managers are often quite different from those needed at the first level. They reviewed research which used as indices of a supervisor's effectiveness the satisfaction of his subordinates and the rating of his performance by his superior. At the first or lowest level of supervision, most successful supervisors scored high on both consideration and initiating structure. Successful second-level supervisors, on the other hand, scored high on consideration but low in initiating structure. Successful first-level supervisors tended to have low Least Preferred Co-worker (LPC)[1] scores, whereas successful second level supervisors tended to have high

---

[1] The LPC is a device developed by Fiedler to measure the degree to which a person describes his least-preferred co-worker in positive terms. A high LPC indicates an underlying motive to obtain good relations with others in the group, and a low LPC indicates a leader who seeks rewards from accomplishing tasks.

ones. These differences may be, at least in part, a reflection of the different needs and charactersitics of the people reporting directly to first- and second-level supervisors.

Mann (1965) suggested that different stages of organizational growth also affect the type of leadership required. Lippitt and Schmidt (1967) provided further exploration of this idea. They viewed the development of organizations as progressing through the stages of birth, youth, and maturity. At each stage an organization faces different critical concerns and key issues. At birth, organizations are concerned with creation and survival and must decide what to risk and what to sacrifice. During youth—when organizations are concerned with gaining stability, reputation, and pride—the critical activities are organizing, reviewing, and evaluating. At maturity, organizations are concerned with achieving uniqueness and adaptability and contributing to society, so they must decide whether and how to change and share. The central concerns at each stage require different skills and temperaments. The human-relations skills appear to assume their greatest importance in the mature phase, since many people may feel threatened by change. In contrast, technical and administrative skills are more important at the earlier stages than later.

Leadership and Organizational Climate

We have suggested that a variety of organizational factors dictate which leadership style will be most appropriate. However, the actual behavior of a leader will also be influenced by the manner in which he himself is supervised.

Correlation between the behavior of a supervisor and that exhibited by his boss was reported by Fleishman (1953). Men who worked for considerate bosses were reported to be more considerate toward their subordinates than were men working under less considerate bosses. A similar chain of effect was shown for initiation of structure. Furthermore, the success of supervisory training programs was also influenced. Foremen who had taken part in human-relations training programs tended to continue practicing what they had learned only if their supervisors maintained a supportive climate. Foremen whose supervisors scored low in consideration tended to revert to former patterns of behavior. Clearly, supervision and supervisory training cannot be divorced from the organizational system in which the participants function.

Similarly, Sykes (1962) reported that supervisors who had been trained in a program emphasizing human relations and group participation became very frustrated when their organization refused to adapt to their new, human relations view. The top executives seemed unwilling to practice themselves what they had encouraged their subordinates to learn. As a result, a group that had been highly successful from the organization's point of view before training became highly dissatisfied, and a large percentage of these men left the organization. Prior to the training program there had been almost no turnover within this group.

Nealey and Fiedler (1968) suggested that second-level leadership in an organization can have an even more important effect on the productivity of the group than first-level leadership. They summarized several studies which found a higher correlation between the performance of a group and the leadership style of managers two levels above the group than between group performance and leadership style of the group's immediate supervisor. Nealey and Fiedler suggested that the second-level superior can make his influence felt through direct contacts with the group and through various administrative programs.

Additional evidence suggests that the degree of influence which subordinates perceive their supervisor to have with his superiors may be a determinant of the effectiveness of a given leadership style. For example, Pelz (1952) found that when subordinates perceived their supervisor as powerful in the organizational hierarchy, his "going to bat" for them and siding with them in disputes with management tended to be associated with supervisory effectiveness. On the other hand, supervisors who followed these same practices but were not perceived as having power in the hierarchy received negative reactions from their subordinates. Pelz concluded that "social closeness" and "siding with" employees only raises employee satisfaction if the supervisor has enough influence to produce actual benefits for this group.

A similar argument about the consequences of an individual's power position for leadership was made by Fiedler (1965), who proposed that the state of leader-member relations, the type of group tasks, and the power position of the leader all interact to determine which of two leadership styles will have a higher probability of success. He characterized one style as controlling, structuring, or active and the second as permissive, passive and considerate. In Table 1, cells marked CAS indicate those conditions under which controlling, active, structuring leadership is most apt to be effective, and those marked PPC indicate those conditions which favor a permissive, passive, considerate style.

TABLE 1. **Summary of Fiedler's Work on the Relationship Between Effective Leadership Style and Situational Factors**

	Leader-Member Relations			
	Good		*Poor*	
Leader Power Position	*Task Structured*	*Task Unstructured*	*Task Structured*	*Task Unstructured*
Strong	CAS	CAS	PPC	PPC
Weak	CAS	PPC	PPC	CAS

Although Fiedler's data are more suggestive than conclusive, he provides a useful model for relating effective leadership styles to organizational conditions.

In summary, the importance of organizational climate for leadership has been amply demonstrated. In addition, most of the recent writers pay particular attention to the role of task and organizational structure. Since Dubin has so comprehensively shown the role of technology in organizational leadership, little more need be added here. What remains is to spell out for management the implications of our knowledge of leadership. For this purpose, an extremely perceptive paper by Tannenbaum and Schmidt (1958) is very helpful.

An Integrative View of Leadership Behavior:
Tannenbaum and Schmidt's View

Tannenbaum and Schmidt assumed that boss-centered leadership and subordinate-centered leadership are merely opposite ends of a continuum. Leadership is not simply "theory X" or "theory Y" but rather may be exercised in a variety of ways ranging between two extremes. The alternatives open to a manager include making a decision and announcing it, to selling his decision, presenting his ideas and inviting questions, presenting a tentative decision subject to change, presenting the problem, getting suggestions and then making his own decision, and defining the limits and requesting the group to make a decision within the prescribed limits. A further possibility, not mentioned by Tannenbaum and Schmidt, is that of asking the group to make a decision and define its own limits. Of course, a manager varies his behavior along this continuum from one situation to another. Tannenbaum and Schmidt examined some of the factors that determine which alternative will seem to be most appropriate. One group of factors relate to the manager himself, another to the other members of the group, and a third to the situation at hand. The manager chooses not just any leadership style but one consistent with his own personality—his values, his confidence in his subordinates, his leadership inclinations, and his feelings of security in the situation. The wise leader also bases his choice on his subordinates' individual needs for independence, their tolerance for ambiguity, their willingness to accept responsibility, their interest and expertise in the problem, their understanding of organizational goals, and their experience in decision making. Among the situational factors to be considered Tannenbaum and Schmidt included the degree of time pressure, the type of problem, the ability of the group to work together, and the type of organization.

A successful manager, then, is one who is aware of the situation, the people he is dealing with, himself, and the dynamic interaction of these factors. An understanding of these relationships is important, but it is useful only to the degree that it influences behavior. This point is best summarized by Tannenbaum and Schmidt themselves:

> Thus, the successful manager of men can be primarily characterized neither as a strong leader nor as a permissive one. Rather, he is one who maintains a high batting average in accurately assessing the forces that determine what his most appropriate behavior at any given time should be and in actually being able to behave accordingly. Being both insightful and flexible, he is less likely to see the problems of leadership as a dilemma (p. 101).

A NEW ROLE FOR LEADERS IN ORGANIZATIONS

Increasingly, many leaders appear to be required to stimulate, facilitate, and utilize group resources rather than to plan, direct and control. The resources of group members are more relevant for a problem than those of the formal leader.

The advice of the classical theorists, so widely accepted in our society, provides inadequate guidelines for meeting these new demands.

A major problem for leadership in the future may well be a conflict between the cultural definition of a leader and the actual requirements of many leadership roles. For example, leaders are commonly thought to be the most competent, the strongest, the most aggressive, and the most intelligent people in a group. As tasks of managers increasingly require the coordination of the efforts of experts, a person with the foregoing characteristics is apt to be less successful than in the past. In many cases, the leader may best act as a facilitator of intragroup communication and an agent who helps the group use its own resources. Directing and controlling produce dependence on the director and inhibit the communication needed for the group to best use its own resources. The work of Maier (1967) has made these general points well.[2]

Maier argued that in many situations the leader contributes most to a group task not by presenting his ideas but by enhancing the group's ability to generate its own ideas. In this case the leadership function is one of clarifying, supporting novel ideas which might otherwise be rejected prematurely, reflecting, and helping to integrate. Such a leader must be aware of group dynamics and skillful in helping the group to move in constructive directions. In many ways, leadership behavior of management and professional groups should resemble the behavior of a facilitator more than that of a director.

In general, different organizational situations require different leadership behavior. A successful leader is aware of the wide spectrum of relevant variables and is able to help the group to achieve organizational goals. Organizational leadership is as complex as organizations themselves.

REFERENCES

Fielder, F. E. "Engineer the Job to Fit the Manager." *Harvard Business Review* 43 (1965): 115-22.

Fleishman, E. A. "Leadership Climate, Human Relations Training, and Supervisory Behavior." *Personnel Psychology* 6 (1953): 205-22.

Gibb, C. A. "Leadership." In G. Lindzey and E. Aronson, eds., *The Handbook of Social Psychology.* 2nd ed. vol. 4. Reading, Mass.: Addison-Wesley, 1969. pp. 205-82.

Lippitt, G. L., and Schmidt, W. H. "Crises in a Developing Organization." *Harvard Business Review* 45 (1967):102-12.

Maier, N. R. F. Assets and Liabilities in Group Problem Solving: The Need for an Integrative Function." *Psychological Review* 74 (1967): 239-49.

Mann, F. C. "Toward an Understanding of the Leadership Role in Formal Organization." In R. Dubin, G. C. Homans, F. C. Mann, and D. C. Miller, *Leadership and Productivity.* San Francisco: Chandler Publishing Co., 1965. pp. 68-103.

Nealey, S. M., and Fiedler, F. E. "Leadership Functions of Middle Managers." *Psychological Bulletin* 70 (1968):313-29.

[2] Some of Maier's ideas are presented in the first selection in Part IV.

Pelz, D. C. "Influence: A Key to Effective Leadership in the First-Line Supervisor." *Personnel* 29 (1952):209-17.

Sykes, A. J. M. "The Effect of a Supervisory Training Course in Changing Supervisors' Perceptions and Expectations of the Role of Management." *Human Relations* 15 (1962):227-43.

Tannenbaum, R., and Schmidt, W. H. "How to Choose a Leadership Pattern." *Harvard Business Review* 36 (1958):95-101.

part 4

TOWARD
SOME ANSWERS?

The first three sections explored some of the controversies in the basic foundation areas of psychology, sociology, and social psychology. In general, the controversy seems even greater when the knowledge is applied to organizations. Despite conflict, the existing concepts have been shown to have practical relevance now and great potential for the future. That this potential has gone unrealized may be the result of a futile hope for across-the-board answers to management problems, a hope which has eclipsed the more realistic idea of situational relativity in the minds of many people. In this final section, our theme of concepts and controversy is applied to some of the more popular strategies for contemporary management: participative management, management by objectives, "theory Y," and the emerging systems approach. The theoretical merits of these and other, closely related approaches have already been debated; our emphasis at this point is on the practice of these strategies.

Given the controversy in the foundation areas, less than perfect agreement on strategies is to be expected. The selections on participative management and management by objectives focus on the reasons for this lack of consensus. The final selection and the editor's concluding note attempt to show how various approaches to management and to organizational behavior itself may be synthesized for the development of a more useful applied behavioral science.

PARTICIPATIVE MANAGEMENT

As noted earlier, effective leadership styles depend on many variables, including the work group, supervisor personality, the organization, and the work flow. The Maier-Gomberg controversy which follows adds the dimensions of training and value questions to the participative issue. Maier focuses on means of developing and practicing democratic supervision to yield high-quality decisions and performance. While his article predates many of the others reprinted in this volume, his arguments are still a good summary of his important views on leadership. In fact, Maier's (1967) more recent review paper contains many of his earlier arguments about leadership and group decision making.

In the more recent paper he argued that a leader can serve an important facilitating function in a group without contributing any substantive ideas. In this view, the leader's role is to aid interaction and communication among group members. According to Maier the leader is analogous to the nerve ring in a starfish, which receives, relays, and integrates information and responses. In other words, he helps decisions get made rather than to make decisions. This later article differs from his earlier arguments mainly in the additional support provided by valuable research on leadership conducted by Maier and his colleagues in the intervening 20 years.

While Maier's arguments are still relevant to organizational behavior today, so are the counterarguments raised by Gomberg, who is the only trade-unionist whose work is reprinted in this book. At the time Gomberg made his reply to Maier, he was director of the Management Engineering Department of the International Ladies Garmet Worker's Union. From Gomberg's perspective what Maier and the other participative theorists propose is better described as manipulation than democracy.

The Maier-Gomberg controversy of 1949, reprinted in this section, dealt with issues which are still alive today. For example, the more recent exchanges between Gomberg and Bennis (1966) and Gomberg and Marrow (1966) involve the same points. The Gomberg-Bennis-Marrow controversy centered around the famous Harwood experiments conducted by Coch and French (1948), a cornerstone study of the introduction of change through participative techniques. Gomberg was involved with the Harwood Corporation on the union side. He argued that what the researchers termed "worker participation" was perceived by the group of workers as insidious control. More generally, while Gomberg acknowledged the merits of the Lewinian value structure, he argued that its proponents (Bennis and others) failed to provide a strategy for implementation which would enable the manager to fulfill his primary objective of getting the job done profitably. To do so, he must make decisions and exercise power in ways which will be pleasing to some people and frustrating to others. Gomberg questioned whether participative methods would permit the necessary decisions to be made and carried out.

Gomberg was unhappy with the democratic approach for other reasons, too. He questioned the morality of attempts to use quasi-psychotherapeutic techniques for industrial purposes. He also charged that the human relations approach had confused democracy with decentralization. For Gomberg, decentralization was not a technique of democracy but a means of maintaining central control while allowing relatively unimportant decisions to be handled on the periphery. In addition, Gomberg suggested that so-called democratic management may be just an attempt to break up groups of workers. Finally, Gomberg speculated that the successes of participative management might have been based on fear, on the part of relatively powerless workers, about the consequences of failure to go along with the new techniques.

The advocates of democratic management, of course, take serious issue with Gomberg. Bennis, in his reply, noted that he favored democracy mainly because he felt it to be efficient under many conditions. In addition, he questioned Gomberg's understanding of the Harwood experiments. In a later exchange (Gomberg and Marrow, 1966), Marrow, president of the Harwood Company and an important social scientist, joined the debate. Marrow took issue with Gomberg's charge that participative management was not apt to be consistent with organizational needs by pointing to Harwood's strong competitive position. He also countered Gomberg's argument that participative management produced worker hostility toward management by pointing to Harwood's good relationships with employees. In his final reply, Gomberg (1966) questioned whether Harwood's management was in fact democratic. He cited a statement by French, one of the original Harwood researchers, to the effect that management at Harwood laid out and followed a policy of fairness and openness. This approach, according to Gomberg, differed little from the General Electric's policy of Boulwarism, in which management offered what it believed would be a fair settlement for a union contract and stuck with it. The one difference between the two according to Gomberg, was that Boulware did not call his approach democratic or participative management.

In place of democracy, Gomberg advocated benevolent autocracy. In this argument, he is not alone. McMurry (1958) made a strong argument for number of modern organizations. McMurry argued that the characteristics of subordinates and leaders in organizations, as well as the characteristics of organizations themselves, are much more consistent with some type of autocracy.

In order to help people know where they stand and what is expected of them and to focus on goals for individual performance and growth, McMurry would institute conferences to review employee performance. Such conferences, in McMurry's view, are to be instructive, not critical or admonitory. Also, McMurry would introduce surveys of employees' opinions on a regular basis to find out where problems exist and how to deal with them. This is a technique of Likert (1967) himself. In a sense, McMurry has taken an in-between view, recognizing the important role of power and the effect power has on people in the organizations and, at the same time, the desirability and practicality of at least some elements of the democratic or participative approach to management.

McMurry maintained that people want and require considerable direction from above in modern organizations. If this is true, his choice of autocracy over democracy would seem appropriate. However, it may be that autocratic practices in the past have brought about the conditions which McMurry sees as necessitating autocratic practices in the present. The democratic theorists would argue that this cycle may be broken by management styles which encourage more participation of all organizational members in decisions which affect their work.

In this respect their ideas appear to represent an advance beyond those of

McMurry and Gomberg; at the same time, however, the democratic theorists may be faulted for having given inadequate attention to power as a variable, despite its importance in organizations. They seem to have been more concerned with power equalization than with the study of power itself. It is certainly laudable to note that power has dysfunctional consequences and to strive to eliminate them, but it is not possible to do so by neglecting the subject of power in both research and therapies. While many will not agree with the view of Gomberg, McMurry, and others, their ideas are important because they focus on an important organizational variable which has been sidestepped in the writings of many current organizational behaviorists.

MANAGEMENT BY OBJECTIVES

A second modern strategy for applying the findings of behavioral science is management by objectives. The popularity of this approach can be partially explained by its demonstrated success. However, its positive reception may be due to its consistency with both a hierarchical view of organizations and with entrepreneurial values demanding that individuals be given autonomy to work and rewards commensurate with their achievements. Drucker (1954) is generally credited with coining the phrase "management by objectives." McGregor (1960) drew on Drucker to develop a means of implementing his theory Y approach. More recently, Odiorne (1965) dealt at length with the implementation of management by objectives in systems terms.

Those who manage by objectives work jointly with their subordinates to identify organizational and individual goals, to define responsibility for each manager by specifying expected results, to measure actual results, and to utilize them as a means of assessing and improving individual performance. Recently, a research report by the National Industrial Conference Board (1968) suggested that management by objectives should be considered as management *with* objectives, because management by objectives is only one of many strategies which can be followed simultaneously. It is not a total system of management. Rather, it is a technique to supplement others. Further, the NICB report noted that management by objectives is not a standardized technique. Instead, the introduction, evolution, and form of the objectives programs vary among companies.

The strategy also has had mixed results. Most companies which have adopted it have reported both benefits and problems, the benefits generally outweighing the problems. Common benefits included better management performance, more complete planning, better control (since the objectives and plans themselves are the major tools of control), improved subordinate-superior relationships, and better development of managerial abilities. Common problems included the relatively long time period required for supervisors to learn to manage by objectives, an overemphasis on the objectives alone (which means a failure to tend to other important problems), confusion and difficulty resulting from attempts to use management by objectives as a tool for appraisal, and problems in changing administrative procedures to support rather than conflict with the objectives program.

Generally, management by objectives has been well received by both theorists and practicing managers. In many ways this acceptance is due to its success as well as its consistency with the prevailing assumptions and values of the culture in which it evolved. The procedure is oriented toward reward for results, toward individual freedom and variation, toward measurement, and toward reevaluation and readjustment. It is also consistent with the notions of organizational

However, Levinson (1970) has attacked the approach as being much more consistent with hierarchy than with effective management of people. While not rejecting management by objectives as a technique, Levinson argued that its current implementation is more consistent with the methods of Frederick Taylor and industrial engineering than with the true integration of individual and organizational purposes. According to Levinson, characteristically top management sets the corporate goals, and the individual manager is limited to choosing which of those goals to pursue and helping to select the statistics which his superiors will use to evaluate his work. In essence then, management by objectives is " . . . based on a short-term, egocentrically oriented perspective and an underlying reward-punishment psychology (p. 128)." It treats a person differently from a rat in a maze only in allowing him to select " . . . his own bait from a limited range of choices (p. 128)." A subordinate's personal objectives are seldom taken into account, since top-level executives assume that they alone have the prerogative to determine objectives, provide rewards and targets, and drive people who work for the organization. Under such conditions individual managers come to view appraisal as a hostile, destructive act and find it difficult to give constructive criticism. Levinson concluded that executives can improve management by objectives by exploring its underlying psychological assumptions, by utilizing group appraisal, and by considering the personal goals of the individual ahead of organizational goals. Unless these changes are made, Levinson considers the technique, as currently practiced, to be self-defeating in the long run.

The reading by Tosi and Carroll presents evidence related to Levinson's argument. They, too, demonstrate the need for more research on the implementation and consequences of management by objectives.

TOWARD SOME RESOLUTION

The third article in this section, by Morse and Lorsch, in many ways summarizes the major points developed in this book. Theory Y often provides a useful orientation for management toward human behavior, but it is more sound in some situations than others. The same is true of Theory X or perhaps any general orientation. What matters most is that one's management orientation, whatever its nature, should be chosen deliberately, not assumed a priori.

The final article in this section is the editor's assessment of the state of knowledge of organizational behavior and implications for the development of managers. The article is designed to help integrate the material and to suggest some of the paths that students of organizational behavior may find rewarding. Every section of this book stresses the effect of the interaction of multiple variables on the behavior or organizational participants. Organizational behavior must be both multi- and interdisciplinary. While this last selection does not give firm answers, it suggests that people must be prepared to seek answers and to deal realistically with highly complex human situations. Thus, it is more a paper on a strategy for obtaining answers than on answers themselves.

REFERENCES

Coch, L., and French, J.R.P. "Overcoming Resistance to Change." *Human Relations* 1 (1948): 512-32.

Drucker, P. *The Practice of Management.* New York: Harper & Row, Publishers, 1954.

Gomberg, W. "Democratic Management—Gomberg Replies." *Trans-action* 3 (1966): 48.

Gomberg, W., and Bennis, W. G. "The Trouble with Democratic Management, and a Reply:When Democracy Works." *Trans-action* 3 (1966): 30-36.

Gomberg, W., and Marrow, A. "Democratic Management—The Debate Continues." *Trans-action* 3 (1966): 35-37, 56.

Levinson, H. "Management by Whose Objectives?" *Harvard Business Review* 48 (1970): 125-34.

Likert, R. *The Human Organization.* New York: McGraw-Hill Book Company, 1967.

McGregor, D. *The Human Side of Enterprise.* New York: McGraw-Hill Book Company, 1960.

McMurry, R. N. "The Case for Benevolent Autocracy." *Harvard Business Review* 36 (1958): 82-90.

Maier, N. R. F. "Assets and Liabilities in Group Problem Solving: The Need for an Integrative Function." *Psychological Review* 74 (1967): 239-49.

Managing by—and with-Objectives. Personnel Policy Study No. 212. New York: National Industrial Conference Board, Inc., 1968.

Odiorne, G. S. *Management by Objectives.* New York: Pitman Publishing Corp., 1965.

Tannenbaum, R., and Schmidt, W. H. "How to Choose a Leadership Pattern." *Harvard Business Review* 36 (1958): 95-101.

Norman R. F. Maier

IMPROVING SUPERVISION THROUGH TRAINING

NEW CONCEPTS IN SUPERVISION

For the past five years I have been working with four large industries in an attempt to improve supervision. The program centers on what has been called democratic leadership in management.[1] The basic feature of democratic leadership is to shift the responsibility for decisions from the leader to the group. In making this shift, one changes the leadership from the autocratic type to the democratic type.

This change in the placement of responsibility for solutions gives rise to some questions. If, for example, a group solves problems, how is one to decide which of the solutions suggested represents the group? One method is to use a majority vote. When this is done, the group is divided into a majority and a minority and as a consequence one may develop two or more opposed subgroups. Another method[2] is to attempt to obtain a hundred per cent agreement in the group. In order to accomplish a full meeting of minds, free discussion is essential and the leader develops a new leadership role. His effectiveness becomes primarily one of being able to conduct a problem-solving conference. It is this type of leadership that seems essential if the group is to remain unified and constructive. To achieve this effect, the leader must develop skills in sensitivity and permissiveness. At the same time, he must not permit himself to become a passive leader, but must be able to exert controls. Permissiveness and controls seem somewhat contradictory activities, and the interpretation of these becomes one of the important problems in training and an important area of investigation.

From Norman R. F. Maier, "Improving Supervision Through Training" and Discussion in *Psychology of Labor-Management Relations,* Proceedings of Industrial Relations Research Association, Denver, Colorado, (Sept., 1949). Edited by Arthur Kornhauser. Reprinted by permission.

[1] A. Bavelas, "Morale and the Training of Leaders," Chapter 8 in *Civilian Morale* (edited by G. Watson), Reynal and Hitchcock, 1942. A. Bavelas; "An Analysis of a Work Situation Preliminary to Leadership Training," *Journal of Educational Sociology* 17 (1944): 426-30. L. P. Bradford and R. Lippitt, "Building a Democratic Work Group," *Personnel* 22 (1945): 2-13. N. R. F. Maier, "A Human Relations Program for Supervision," *Industrial and Labor Relations Review* (1946): 443-64.

[2] K. Lewin, "The Dynamics of Group Action," *Educational Leadership* (1944): 195-200. K. Lewin, *Resolving Social Conflicts,* Harper and Brothers, 1948. K. Lewin, R. Lippitt and R. K. White, "Patterns of Aggressive Behavior in Experimentally Created Social Climates," *Journal of Social Psychology* 10 (1939): 271-301.

For the present, it seems clear that some of the controls are as follows:

(1). Problems presented must fall within the leader's area of freedom. At each level of supervision there are problems that a supervisor may decide himself. It is these problems that he can share with the group that reports to him if the group members have interest. Thus, decisions cannot violate company practices or policies (unless the supervisor involved is at the policy-making level) nor can they violate working agreements since problems involving these factors do not ordinarily fall within the supervisor's area of freedom.[3] Frequently, the "how to do a job" rather than the "what job to do" is the problem that can be solved.

(2). Presenting the subject for discussion in such a manner that it is a problem rather than a criticism of the group or an individual in the group. Whether or not a group becomes defensive or interested in solving a problem depends in considerable measure on the way it is presented. Just how important the manner of presentation is we do not know, but it is clear from case studies that the incidence of defensive reactions can be traced to the supervisor's statement of the problem. On one occasion the supervisor stated as his problem the fact that certain members of the group failed to close file drawers. Immediately the group requested new files which would operate more smoothly. Considering the condition of the files this appeared to be a defensive reaction.

(3). Serving in the role of an expert. The supervisor frequently has much background and information which is of value in solving a problem. Instead of using this information as a way to discredit solutions and thereby gain an advantage over group members, he can give the group the benefit of his experience by presenting them with the information at his disposal.[4] For example, he can point out how much space the group will have in the new office location and ask them to help plan the office arrangement. If he withheld this information and the group planned an office arrangement which required too much space, he would be in the position of having to reject certain solutions. Soon his position would be one opposed to that of the group. If all relevant facts are given at the outset the problem becomes more interesting because it is more difficult.

(4). Reducing hostility by permitting free expression. In permitting the expression of hostile reactions one reduces frustration and encourages motivated behavior. My own research in this field indicates that frustration and motivation are opposed processes.[5] By reducing frustration, one reinstates problem solving behavior. Rogers'[6] work also supports this contention.

(5). Encouraging all members to participate in the discussion. This technique causes members of a group to interact. In interacting, the members learn their

---

[3] N. R. F. Maier, "A Human Relations Program for Supervision," *Industrial and Labor Relations Review* 1 (1946): 443-64.

[4] Ibid.

[5] N. R. F. Maier, *Frustration: The Study of Behavior Without a Goal* (New York: McGraw-Hill Co., 1949).

[6] C. R. Rogers, *Counseling and Psychotherapy* (Boston: Houghton Mifflin Company, 1942).

areas of disagreement, they learn about group fairness, and they learn that each cannot have things his particular way. It is in free discussion that social pressure can operate. Social pressure is always present in social behavior. The leader uses social pressure for constructive purposes by seeing to it that all feel free to participate. Certain dominant individuals must become aware of their role as listeners and certain reticent individuals must learn that they owe it to the group to speak their minds. The leader can play an important part in bringing about these awarenesses.

(6). Protecting the minority. The leader can do much to relieve hostility and to bring deviants back into the group by showing special consideration to minority positions. Frequently, a few persons refuse to go along with the group because they feel excluded. If the leader gives this group of individuals special attention, demonstrating a desire to have them in the group and giving their opinions the most favorable interpretation possible, they can be made to feel that they have not been excluded from the group.

(7). Making the group responsible for agreeing on a solution. A group may attempt to escape the responsibility of working as a group and continue to disagree. In practice this is much more rare than is usually anticipated. When it occurs, however, the supervisor can bring this responsibility to awareness. He can point out that a new problem has arisen, which is, "How can we get together on a solution?" Since the objective is to obtain a meeting of minds, the problem cannot be settled by taking a vote and following the majority. Thus, when full agreement is the objective, the leader becomes reluctant to split the group and holds out for keeping the group intact. This makes the leader and group members more permissive. It also forces each person to realize his responsibility as a group member. Social pressure operates in a constructive manner and one hears such remarks as, "Oh, Bill, why don't you give the idea a try?" "Come on, Jim, don't be so damn selfish." In such instances the group, not the supervisor, is applying pressure.

(8). Keeping the discussion on the subject. Whether or not progress is experienced in group discussion depends, to some extent, on whether or not extraneous matters are discussed. The responsibility of keeping a discussion problem-centered belongs to the leader. However, this can easily lead to regimentation. Enough leeway should be permitted to avoid introducing into the discussion an atmosphere of pressure or strictness. Further, the supervisor must be careful not to judge whether something is irrelevant. He might ask the person whether his ideas are tied in with the problem; if the person feels they are not, he can ask whether the issue raised should be discussed at a future time. Thus again, a balance must be struck between a rigid and fully controlled discussion and one that is loose and disorganized.

It is apparent that the types of control discussed above are different from those used by an autocratic leader, and yet it can be seen that they are techniques which are psychologically sound in their effectiveness.

The techniques of sensitivity and permissiveness likewise deviate from those ordinarily used by an autocratic supervisor. These may be listed as follows:

(1). Sensitivity to feelings rather than to words or logic. The supervisor must be trained to realize that the reasons a man gives for being for or against something frequently are irrelevant rationalizations. A man doesn't like something and it is the dislike that is a fact that must be accepted with understanding. Often the objections to something are fears but the words expressed are criticisms. To require proof or evidence in such instances merely increases insecurity. The fact of fear must be accepted and respected. Fears can best be overcome by permitting them to be expressed and recognized for what they are.[7] Thus, the supervisor must react to the feeling tones and not to the words. This sensitivity to feelings must be developed through training.

(2). Permissiveness must be developed. A permissive supervisor is not on the defensive; he has no "face-saving" reactions and he is primarily concerned with the way the group members feel. Basically he believes that the group members, through free discussion, can integrate their various interests better than he can. He believes that a group is more able to solve its problem than an outsider. As a consequence, the permissive supervisor becomes an active listener. The function of permissiveness in group discussions is fundamentally the same as in non-directive counseling.[8]

(3). Reflecting the feelings expressed. As in counseling,[9] the technique of reflecting feelings demonstrates permissiveness; it encourages discussion and it brings feelings out in the open where they can be freely examined and explored. It is an aid to insight in that only through the explorations of ideas and feelings can new relationships be discovered. It is desirable for the supervisor to use a blackboard for this purpose. By means of writing opinions on the board he shows acceptance and permits further exploration since he now can ask, "Are there other ideas on this matter?"

Further exploration is one of the best ways of having poor ideas rejected. The supervisor must learn not to discredit poor ideas. If he puts a poor idea on the board and then requests other ideas or reactions he can get poor ideas rejected without acting as a censor or critic.

(4). The use of exploratory questions. Problem solving can be enhanced in a group by the use of analytical questions. Such questions as, "How could that be done?", "Would that plan be useful under emergency conditions?", help explore issues further and bring out additional details. Care must be exercised so that the questions asked do not discredit, degrade, or indicate an objection to the idea.

(5). Summarizing ideas and solutions. The value of summaries from time to time is to see to it that all members are properly understanding the issues. Summarizing also serves as a means for holding interest in that it permits progress to be experienced.

The techniques of listening and reflecting are in direct contrast to the techniques of selling employees on a solution. Frequently supervisors confuse the idea of giving up autocratic techniques with the adopting of skill in selling

---

[7] Ibid.
[8] Ibid.
[9] Ibid.

ideas to employees. As a consequence they employ sales techniques and believe they are using the democratic technique. Such supervisors are more difficult to train than many autocratic supervisors because the latter are not confused in their distinctions.

SOME TRAINING PROBLEMS

It is apparent that the training problems involved in the institution of the type of program described are very large. The supervisor must undergo a great deal of change and, as we know, a change is frequently met with resistance. At the present time, we know that the democratic technique is one of the best change techniques we have. It is, therefore, desirable to use it as a means for obtaining acceptance of the democratic concepts themselves. In this respect I disagree with Lewin[10] who has expressed the opinion that autocratic methods may be necessary to achieve democracy.

The change required, in this instance, is a fundamental one and actually amounts to a personality change. The supervisor must not only view employees differently, but he must also view himself and his position in a new light. The change in attitude toward employees is not as difficult to obtain as the change in attitude toward one's self or one's position. This is evidenced by the fact that one can obtain the ready acceptance of higher management for the program when they view it as a program for supervisors beneath themselves, but when the program is given for them to practice they seek ways to demonstrate that the program is not adapted to their positions. Likewise, lower levels of supervision react by wanting to know why their boss doesn't practice democratic leadership. Thus, generally, the program can be accepted as applying to others before one can see it as applying to himself. This observation leads to two basic requirements in training.

(1). Higher management must practice the democratic method so that those below can experience it first hand and also to supply the motivation that higher management's support may give.

In one training unit, which included three levels of supervision, we had succeeded in motivating the first-line supervisors to try the group decision technique. These attempts were successful in that the men reacted favorably and the results were good. Some weeks later, however, interest declined and further illustrations of its use were not forthcoming. Personal interviews with first-line supervisors revealed that they, as a group, had rebelled because the men to whom they reported had failed to practice the group method with them.

(2). Role-taking procedures[11] and discussions, using problems supplied by the group, must be used to create the experience that the method applied to the group members' problems. Such experiences can then be extended by having group decisions in which all agree to try the method in the following week.

[10] K. Lewin, *Resolving Social Conflicts* (New York: Harper Row, Publishers, 1948).
[11] A. Bavelas, "An Analysis of a Work Situation Preliminary to Leadership Training," *Journal of Educational Sociology* 17 (1944): 426-30. L. P. Bradford and R. Lippitt, "Building a Democratic Work Group," *Personnel* 22 (1945): 2-13.

In the previous case, in which the first-line supervisors rebelled, this step was missing for the higher levels of supervision. The role-taking and group decision phases were applied to the first-line supervisors and higher levels merely gave their consent and support.

The value of role-taking and discussion as change agents for attitudes is most difficult for management to accept. Industry has been sold on visual aids and sees role-taking and discussion procedures as time consumers. Unless one experiences their value personally they are not convincing. Since higher management frequently judges the program on intellectual grounds, they are not easily convinced. Even when such individuals consent to observe these procedures, this observation is given limited time; usually just enough to arouse hostility because the observers experience a threat to their own attitudes. Hostility passes when roles are played a number of times and then one can be satisfied that a major step has been taken. However, this added time often cannot be obtained.

It has been my experience that attempts to cut the program invariably are in the reduction of role-taking and discussion time. In one industry, the abbreviation of the training time is now being corrected by a follow-up program consisting largely of role-taking and discussion procedures.

I have indicated that attitude change, which is akin to personality change, is a basic training problem. This does not mean that the usual training problems are not also present. Some of these may be evaluated in passing.

(1). It is apparent that effective training must be preceded by a *need*. At the present time this is not a difficult problem. If supervisors are asked on what phase of the job they feel they most need help, there is almost complete agreement that help in the area of dealing with people is most needed.

(2). Knowledge about psychology is important. Such subjects as individual differences, frustration, attitudes, motivation, fatigue, and counseling are of vital interest to supervisors and can, in part, be taught by the lecture method. For this type of training, time is readily made available. These subjects have a value in encouraging an analysis of human relations problems and permit the use of the discussion method.

(3). Skills must supplement this knowledge. In order to develop skills, practice on the job, interviews with trainees, and role playing are needed. When the basic attitude change is accomplished, the opportunity for developing skills is no longer difficut to obtain.

(4). Certain aptitudes must be present in the trainees. However, we have not found these requirements very great. Although persons with above average intelligence absorb the knowledge content more readily than others, their attitudes are not more easily changed. We have also seen very autocratic personalities change attitudes more readily than the friendly type of paternalist. It is desirable to investigate this problem in detail since it is quite possible that the traits which make for good supervision, when a company does not train its supervisors in democratic methods, may be quite different from the traits that are essential to good democratic supervision. It seems that some men are autocratic merely because they have not given attention to human relations, but when they see these relationships as problems they develop a real interest. Thus, men with engineering training can become interested in psychological problems when scientific concepts are incorporated in the training.

THE RISK TECHNIQUE
IN GROUP DISCUSSION

For some time now we have been using a technique which seems highly effective for reducing fears. It amounts to the nondirective counseling method applied to groups and is based on the assumption that our fears are not the opposite of our goals. Thus, the fear of a union shop does not necessarily reflect a desire for an open shop. Rather, the avoidance of the one alternative leaves the person in the open shop camp. Sometimes it is only because the union wants the union shop that suspicion is aroused. Likewise, the union may fear to lose its gains, and management's opposition to the union shop arouses fear. Analysis of the fears reveals a different problem from that shown by an analysis of the motives.

Likewise, the fear of the group decision technique is not the same as a desire for autocratic methods. Thus, the problem in training is not a matter of demonstrating that the democratic method is superior to the autocratic, but rather the problem is one of removing the fear of a change. To reduce fears, one must release expression and this is the crux of the risk technique.

After a conference training group has been presented with a description of the difference between autocratic, laissez-faire, and democratic techniques by reporting the children experiments of Lewin, Lippitt, and White,[1][2] the group is asked, "What are some of the risks that management would take if supervisors practiced democratic leadership on the job?"

Each risk that is presented is recorded on the blackboard. Frequently, the risk is reworded by the discussion leader to point up the issue. This procedure is similar to the "reflecting feelings" technique in nondirective counseling. A little discussion follows to determine the amount of support and the degree of feeling that the statement written on the board represents a risk. The leader uses his office to support the reasonableness of the risk in case the rest of the group opposes it. By this method, the group soon feels free to express risks and the leader ceases to be an individual who is trying to sell them something. Group members also can recognize unreasonableness in each other.

A group of 18 to 28 usually finds 13 to 22 risks with a mean of 18. The risks include statements indicating that production will fall, quality will decline, the union will oppose the method, morale will drop, supervisors will lose prestige, the union will get control, the decisions will be selfish, planning will be inefficient, time will be wasted, etc.

At regular intervals in a 12-week program (one day per week), the list of risks is reexamined and, whenever there is unanimous agreement that a risk no longer applies, it is removed from the list. This procedure allows social pressure to

[1][2] K. Lewin, R. Lippitt and R. K. White, "Patterns of Aggressive Behavior in Experimentally Created Social Climates," *Journal of Social Psychology* 10 (1939): 271-301.

operate. The group members interact with each other and the leader finds himself in the position of having to protect minority individuals who still have fears. Of importance is the fact that the risks gradually are removed. Even the discussion on individual differences, during which the democratic method is not mentioned, is followed by a reduction in the list of risks. The discussion on counseling, which occurs last, usually serves to have the last items removed. When all are not removed, it is because one or two persons still wish to retain one or two risks.

It is also of interest to observe that presenting the group with a knowledge of the controls (given at the outset) which logically overcome certain risks, has little effect on the fears. Even the report of cases which show that the method works on the job fails to influence the risks to an appreciable degree, but a personal success with the method causes that individual's risks to decrease.

The technique of removing risks causes the group values to come to the fore so that the trainer no longer is in a position of defending the program. Rather, the support for the program comes from the group membership who soon assume the responsibility for reducing the list of risks. Frequently, it is claimed that they initially did not understand what was meant by a risk. With changed attitudes, many of the risks begin to appear ridiculous. An analysis of the risks throws added light on the problem.

We have compared the risks submitted by 10 top and intermediate management groups with those submitted by 39 groups of college students taking similar training on the campus. It was assumed that management and student personnel differed primarily in business experience. If the risks submitted are judgments supported by experience, then the risks should be different in the two groups since management personnel have had much more experience in supervisory problems than students.

This analysis revealed that (1) the number of risks, (2) the type of risks, and (3) the order in which they occurred in the list, were surprisingly similar. Only one difference, which is not statistically significant, seems worthy of mention, namely that the student groups seem somewhat more distrustful of workmen.

We conclude, from this failure to obtain a difference, that the fears are not based on business experience but are emotional objections. These objections are then rationalized to point up some undesirable consequence. Both management and student personnel can use logic, so that the risks constitute deductions of all of the things that might be different if a change is introduced. Students, however, felt their risks were incomplete and that they would be able to think of more and better ones after they had business experience. Thus, experience tended to give confidence in opinions but it did not aid in furnishing opinions.

It was also found that if risks are requested after certain controls and industrial experiences with the method are presented to a group, the content of the list of risks is not altered. However, less support is given to those risks which are answered by the added content, but this is offset by the fact that more support is given to other risks.

THE QUALITY OF GROUP DECISION

Although it may be conceded that objections to the democratic type of supervision are largely attitudes based upon fears, there is one type of objection that may have a factual basis. This is the doubt that may be raised as to the quality of group decisions. There is little question but that group decision makes for better acceptance than decisions imposed by the leader. However, high group acceptance of poor quality decisions may not always be as desirable as less acceptance and better quality.

The relative importance of acceptance and quality, of course, will vary with the type of problem. If the problem is merely one of determining who will work on Sunday, the actual solution is unimportant, but an acceptance by the group that the person chosen is a fair choice is of great importance.

On one occasion, two out of three girls were needed for Sunday work. All three had dates and none wished to work. Obviously, any solution that the supervisor would present would meet with objections. He put the problem to the girls. The discussion revealed that one girl had a date with girls and all agreed this was not a real date. She therefore agreed it was logical for her to work. Of the two remaining girls, one had a date with the man she was engaged to, while the other had a date with a new man. All of the girls agreed that an engaged girl could alter her date, so it was agreed that the girl with a new conquest had priority. She was excused from Sunday work despite the fact that she had least seniority and had worked less often on Sundays.

In other instances, the group may expect to improve the quality of decisions because they are near to the job. Thus, they know why men violate safety practices, which individuals are spoiling a job, why they stop for coffee the first thing after leaving the company garage, etc. These sources of information can be tapped to improve solutions and at the same time supply acceptance and motivation.

On one occasion a supervisor of a repair crew had a group discussion and asked the crew for ideas on how the job could be improved. The discussion revealed that the crew thought that the company procedure on difficult repairs was all wrong. The plan used was that when a repair man failed to do a satisfactory repair job, a more skilled man was sent out on the job. The men said they had no way of learning about their mistakes by this method. The group's solution was that, in case of a customer's report of a failure on a repair, the foreman should accompany the man who first visited the job, and together they should locate the difficulty. This method, the men thought, would supply added work interest in that the men would be able to follow up on their work; it would give added training; and it would prevent the foreman from passing unfair judgments on their work.

The group's solution was put into practice and within six months the number of "repeat" repairs fell to one-fourth of the original figure. Thus, a nearness to the job supplied essential information for a good solution.

However, there still remain problems whose solutions have the quality of inventiveness or elegance. Suppose the supervisor or an expert knows a better way to do the job. Must he abandon a good idea if the group cannot discover this superior solution? Watson[13] and Shaw[14] found that group thinking is better than individual thinking, but this is true only when no outstanding creative individual is involved. What happens when the leader has an elegant solution that the group members cannot discover?

In order to test this possibility we selected an industrial problem, one solution of which had the quality of elegance.

The problem chosen was a subassembly job in which seven men worked on a production line. The separate operations were given as requiring like aptitudes. One man in the group, however, was a slow worker and was described as a bottleneck. Because of him, production was low. The question raised was how to increase the group's production. In the actual presentation all relevant details were supplied and Fig. 1 was used to describe the situation.

"Parasol" Assembly Problem

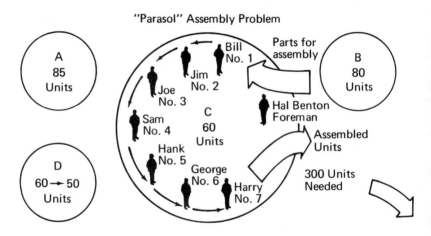

FIGURE 1. Each circle represents a group of men working on a subassembly job. Seven men work in a circle and assemble a piece of equipment. The production of each group is shown in the diagram.

The foreman in group C has a problem. Work piles up in Joe's position so that production is slowed down. The company needs more production and both groups C and D are falling behind. Each group has a foreman, but the foremen do not have the authority to exchange men. How can the foreman of group C best solve his problem? The foreman of group D attempted to solve his problem and as a result his production fell from 60 to 50 units.

[13] G. R. Watson, "Do Groups Think More Efficiently than Individuals?" *Journal of Abnormal and Social Psychology* 23 (1928) 328-36.

[14] M. E. Shaw, "A Comparison of Individuals and Small Groups in the National Solution of Complex Problems," *American Journal of Psychology* 44 (1932): 491-504.

The solution regarded as elegant was periodically to rotate the position of the men so that the work of the slow man would be spread to all positions. Logically, this solution should make the pace of the line equal to that of the average of the group's ability and motivation.

Twenty small groups (of five to seven) of college students, and 40 students working as individuals, all failed to present the elegant solution as the method to use. Almost all of the solutions were directed toward removing the bottleneck. This preliminary experiment demonstrated that the elegant solution was not obvious.

Further, it was found that when the instructor presented the groups with the elegant solution it was not accepted by more than half of the persons and very few of those accepting it regarded the solution as superior to others suggested.

The problem was now changed in two basic ways: (1) Roles were assigned so that each person in a discussion group could be given a position in the production line and a definite attitude to portray. (2) A person was put in charge of the group and was asked to play the part of the foreman and to reach a decision that all of the workers would agree to. This person was specifically trained or instructed. The following experimental conditions were then used.

Condition 1. A total of 31 individuals was asked to work on the problem as individuals and come up with a recommendation such as an expert might evolve.

Condition 2. A total of 42 individuals was given the roles and each was told that these roles would give him an idea of the kind of men he had to deal with. Each person was asked to recommend a solution as in Condition 1.

Condition 3. A total of 29 groups of persons was given the roles to play and a person untrained in guiding group thinking was asked to be the supervisor. He was asked to hold a discussion and obtain a unanimous group decision from his workers.

Condition 4. A total of 17 groups was given the roles as in Condition 3, but the leader was trained in democratic leadership as well as in how (a) to influence the direction of thinking, (b) to ask questions which lead out of blind alleys, and (c) to keep the group trying out new ideas. These added instructions were based upon the author's studies on how to improve reasoning performance. He also knew the elegant solution, but was instructed never to supply it or any part of it. He was merely to stimulate the group. The writer, as well as instructors, played these leadership roles.

The results obtained from these 4 conditions are shown in Table 1, which divides the solutions presented into seven types.

It will be seen that only in Condition 4 does the elegant solution occur with any degree of frequency (73.5 percent). Thus far, we cannot say to what extent the leader's knowledge of the solution contributed and to what extent his skill contributed to the results. The fact remains, however, that in the preliminary experiments the leader was unable to sell the solution to the groups.

It is also important to note that the next best solution, that of finding some way of giving the less capable workers less work to do, was progressively more often presented as we go from Condition 1 to Condition 2 to Condition 3, in which this solution was presented 25.8 percent, 54.8 percent and 72.4 percent of the time, respectively. Thus, a knowledge of the roles was better than no knowledge of the roles. When actual people played these roles there was even more recognition of individual differences than when these roles were not played. The attack on Joe, the slow worker, was primarily confined to Condition 1. Joe was the bottleneck and the problem became one of removing the bottleneck. When real people were made a part of the situation by introducing roles, the inadequacy of this solution became apparent. The removal of Joe would create bad morale and become a threat to the next slowest worker.

TABLE 1. Relative Frequency of Each Type of Solution

Conditions for Solving	Individual (Without Roles) Percent	Individual (With Roles) Percent	Group (Untrained Leader) Percent	Group (Trained Leader) Percent
Number of cases	31	42	29	17
A. Elegant solution	0.0	2.3	3.4	73.5
B. Give less capable less to do	25.8	54.8	72.4	17.7
C. Change Joe's make-up	4.8	0.0	0.0	0.0
D. Promote Joe to foreman	4.8	4.7	1.7	0.0
E. Get rid of Joe	50.0	9.5	3.4	0.0
F. George mentioned in solution	0.0	17.5	3.4	0.0
G. Solutions violating stated conditions	14.5	10.7	15.5	8.8
Total	99.9	99.9	99.8	100.0

The last two conditions in which groups were used may also be compared on the basis of the acceptance of the decision reached. Since unanimous decisions were desired we shall consider the frequency with which this condition was obtained. For this comparison we have divided the trained leaders into two groups, those led by the author, who it was supposed was most highly trained, and those led by instructors, who followed the author's instructions.

These results are shown in Table 2. This table shows that complete acceptance was obtained most frequently under the conditions which also led to the elegant solution. Thus, the quality of the group decision did not have to be sacrificed for the sake of acceptance. As a matter of fact, acceptance and decision quality went together as leadership skill was increased.

TABLE 2. Acceptance of Solution Under Different Leaders

Type of Leader	Number of Groups Listed	Percent Unanimous Agreement Was Obtained
Untrained	29	62.1
Instructed	11	72.7
Most highly trained	6	100.0

Discussions following the solution indicated that no one suspected that the leader had a solution in mind. All groups felt that the solution was supplied by the membership.

These experiments show that a leader who has creative ideas need not sacrifice them in order to obtain acceptance. Rather he can use his leadership skill to lead a discussion which will result in a creative solution, one that groups as well as individuals fail to achieve without this leadership. If he lacks a creative idea himself, he can still achieve acceptance and have a solution that is at least as good as one he could obtain by working alone. Thus, if his own ideas are fair and have objective excellence, he can stimulate creative thought. If, however, he attempts to take advantage of a group or impose his ideas on them, then the group will throw obstacles in his path. Supervisors so inclined are not ready for democratic supervision.

SUMMARY AND CONCLUSIONS

In this paper, I have attempted to point out that the problems in human relations training are primarily problems in attitude change. Attitude changes which involve attitudes toward one's self and one's fellow man amount to altering personality. If training methods are to accomplish this type of change, they must approach the techniques of therapy rather than the techniques of disseminating information.

Primary concern was given the problem of training supervisory attitudes and skills for democratic leadership in management. By this technique, each supervisor, regardless of his level in the organization, would solve problems which involve group attitudes by a type of conference procedure. The main objective of the conference would be to resolve differences and reach a solution which represents a full meeting of minds. This type of leadership introduces new types of controls which are consistent with a permissive and open-minded type of social behavior. These new leadership controls are briefly described.

Special consideration was given to a "risk technique" which adapts nondirective counseling principles to conference procedures. Work along this line has revealed that fears are a major action-barrier to the democratic type of supervision.

One serious question concerning the use of the democratic technique was raised for detailed consideration. Assuming that it is an excellent technique for obtaining acceptance of the group which participates, what can be said about the quality of decisions obtained by the method? Experiments bearing on this question were reported briefly. The results clearly indicate that the skilled leader need not sacrifice the quality of solutions in order to obtain a solution that has acceptance. Rather, if he has the proper skill, he can actually raise the problem-solving ability of the group to a creative level and have increased satisfaction. With lesser skill he can still obtain good solutions and a high degree of acceptance.

William Gomberg

COMMENTS ON PAPER
BY MAIER

Mr. Maier in his paper is recommending a technique to factory managers which has been used by progressive educators ever since John Dewey wrote his first tracts on education.

However, there seems to be a confusion here between the trappings of democracy and its inner substance. Maier is quite aware of this. He states that the main purpose of his technique is to deal with the how of the job rather than with whether or not the job is to be done at all.

Now the essence of democracy is the diffusion of power among contending groups so that they must reach agreement in order to function. The trappings of democracy granted at the sufferance of a despot and removable at his whim represent a very transparent façade for the real thing. Maier's technique, no matter how well intentioned or sincerely offered, must of necessity degenerate into a manipulative technique. You are not asking or consulting people about what to do. You are maneuvering them so that they do what you want, but more efficiently. Perhaps such techniques are indispensable to the operation of a business enterprise. It is an open question whether or not an individual business enterprise can operate along any other but authoritarian lines. If it must, then Maier has something to offer, but this should not be confused with democracy.

Perhaps I can best illustrate what I mean by citing the example given by Maier. You will recall that he describes a situation where a supervisor needed two of three girls for Sunday work. All three girls had dates, one with girls, the second with her regular boy friend, and the third with a boy of whom she hoped to make a new conquest. The supervisor called all the workers together to determine "democratically" which two of the girls should be compelled to come in on Sunday. After deliberation, the group decided that the girl who could keep her date was the girl seeking the new conquest.

If that factory were organized, the problem would be handled by asking the girls whether they would be willing to work on Sunday in the first place. There would be no implied assumption that the girls' dates after working hours were any less important than the employer's production problem. If the girls are not willing to work after regular working hours, the employer is expected to seek a

From Norman R. F. Maier, "Improving Supervision Through Training" and Discussion in *Psychology of Labor-Management Relations,* Proceedings of Industrial Relations Research Association, Denver, Colorado, (Sept., 1949). Edited by Arthur Kornhauser. Reprinted by permission.

different solution to his production problem. This makes the difference between real democracy, where power is distributed between the employer and the working force, and play-acting democracy, where all problems are solved on the basis of the satisfaction of the employer's achievement of his objectives. Thomas Jefferson once observed that the continuation of democracy did not lie in the idyllic cooing of the lion and the lamb. It rested in the mutual suspicion and distrust of equal contending groups, neither of whom would permit the other absolute power. They would function together by compromise.

I do not mean to imply that there is no room for the industrial psychologist in the democratic scheme of things. Not at all. However, the psychologists must make up their minds within which system of values they are going to practice their techniques. Psychology can be considered among the social sciences. It is anxious to receive support, and some business spokesmen in rather unabashed terms have made clear under what set of circumstances the social scientists may expect to receive business support. They want operating techniques which will promote their own private concept of good industrial relations, that is, the relationship between the good shepherd and his sheep.

Frankly, I am suspicious of any technique which purports to eliminate all industrial conflict. What we have to know is how to handle these conflicts without rending the social fabric of the country.

GENERAL DISCUSSION

Morris S. Viteles: Labor's interest in short-run gains, which Mr. Gomberg emphasizes, must not be permitted to obscure the basic importance of long-run economic improvement. The long-term approach offers more fundamental security than does the short-term. Quotations like those in my paper from a management spokesman and from Stalin regarding the need for increasing material prosperity indicate agreement on this point. Management is not blameless; it does restrict production, but its view is more elastic and more aware of the long-run role of increased production and the effective use of human resources. Our concern must be with total human satisfactions.

William Gomberg: Union labor is *not* opposed to high production, but we want first things first. The basic economic problems of industry come before such things as the techniques of psychological selection. Plant shutdowns and unemployment are management's method for restricting production. Management's interest is in costs, not in best production. Prices and production are controlled by management in the interest of profits. If labor is to go along with moves to increase job efficiency, first give us unrestricted and continuous production by management.

Dr. Tiffin assumes that job evaluation is the sole determinant of wage structure. This assumption when applied has proved disastrous. Job evaluations deal with job *content*. But the relative content of jobs is only one factor in determining wages. The union wants job content to be part of wage determination, but only a part. For example, traditional wage relations in the industry must also be taken into account. Any psychologist ought to understand that these traditions and customs are an integral part of the factory's social environment. It is difficult to understand what useful purpose is served by upsetting these relationships which both parties accept as equitable. Professor Viteles observes in some writings on job evaluation in 1941 that the maximum range of capacity between the least intelligent and the most intelligent never exceed three to one. This suggests that if income is to be distributed according to what jobs are worth, nobody should be making more than three times what anybody else is making. Given $200 to distribute between two people according to their relative worth, one would receive no more than $150 to the other's $50. We all know, however, that it would not take too much effort on the part of the $150 man to get away all of the $50 from the other person. One of the tools used to get part or all of this $50 away would be long talks about the great responsibilities which fall upon the shoulders of the $150 man. If job evaluation experts keep insisting that their techniques are the only guide to the relative worth of jobs, then they ought to be careful lest the labor movement apply their philosophy to the whole range of incomes, from top to bottom—not only within the working group.

Norman R. F. Maier: Mr. Gomberg objects that the procedure I described permits management to have its way, and he quotes my reference to the need for limiting employees' discussion to the "how" rather than the "what." My point was that men could not solve all of the "what to do" problems because this would permit them to change the industry. Each level of management has its specific problems, and the procedures I described should be used at each level.

That democratic group decision techniques can be manipulative has certainly to be considered. I felt that the requirement of 100 percent agreement on a solution should protect men from a scheming management and for this reason I placed emphasis on it.

Why should the union criticize participation when it frequently demands more of a say-so itself? Do the union leaders want participation for the men or for the union? Whom do the leaders represent?

William Gomberg: Professor Maier indicts his procedure when he asks: "Do the leaders want participation for the men or for the union?" It has been precisely our point of view that management finds many of these so-called democratic techniques attractive because they hope thereby, though fruitlessly, to drive a wedge between the union and its members. To put it crudely, it sounds very much like streamlined union busting.

Francis D. Tyson (from the floor): I am moved to make a few comments on Professor Tiffin's presentation on job evaluation. The question I wish to raise has to do with aim and method in the social sciences and in contemporary psychology. Is there not a real danger of overemphasis on techniques and of unwarranted satisfaction with what is merely taxonomic analysis in narrow areas of study?

Economics has been, at its best, a discipline of human evaluation, although it must be admitted that 150 years of intellectual endeavor in Britain, Germany and the United States have resulted in all too scant agreement. We are, today, badly in need of aid from a scientific psychology, with special regard to problems of motivation and the determination of group behavior. Are not some of the representatives of the new science of psychology in danger of getting bogged down in mere taxonomy, or classification of facts, as was so long the case in economics? Does such unfocused approach reflect a certain naivete? May I call attention to the practical hazard, for instance, of limiting your contribution to the substitution of a new psychological "jargon" in job evaluation, to compete with that developed by the engineers, who initiated job study decades ago? Why not start by formulating psychology's distinctive objectives?

There is surely no need to begin anew as if nothing had yet been done in the field of job study. On job evaluation, for instance, with all praise for the technical effectiveness of Professor Tiffin's work, would it not be wiser to practice division of labor, recognizing that a major part of the work in this field is primarily that of the engineers, a task early preempted by them. The engineering divisions of some of our big companies in Pittsburgh—for example, Carnegie-Illinois, Westinghouse, and Alcoa—have been making definitive job studies ever since World War I. They have long used representative committees with good effect, even, as so widely in Steel, to resolve job inequities and arrange effective wage and salary classification systems. Are we not "carrying coals to Newcastle"?

The true role of the psychologist, as he assays the task of human evaluation, and the study of men at work, should be to measure the interaction of human interests and abilities with industry's work requirements. You need not concentrate, at this late date, on mere improvements of the procedures devised by engineering managment. The American Management Association and Society for the Advancement of Management are fully competent to serve that end in industry, where such work must be done, rather than in the university.

"Why and to what end," rather than merely "how," is the true concern of the social scientist. A vast and still uncharted opportunity calls for the humanizing and socializing of the essential work of the engineers and technicians of industry. We need not seek full identity with their techniques or limit our approach to the narrower problems already recognized by them. Our job may best begin with critical review of such work, looking to its redirection—for instance, to the joint use of job study by organized labor, as well as by management alone. Industrial economists may be further along in grasping the larger problems engendered by industrialism, having passed through the period of taxonomic study and mere concern with method, and having knocked their heads against stone walls for too long! Economists now ask the cooperative aid of psychologists, as of other social scientists, in the study of really significant problems of value, for the more rational guidance of our complex and confused economy.

* * *

Henry L. Tosi
and Stephen J. Carroll

MANAGERIAL REACTION
TO MANAGEMENT
BY OBJECTIVES

Interest in the "management by objectives" approach has been growing steadily since it was popularized in the fifties by Drucker and McGregor.[1] Odiorne describes the process as one in which

> . . . the superior and the subordinate managers of an organization jointly define its common goals, define each individual's major areas of responsibility in terms of the results expected of him and use these measures as guides for operating the unit and assessing the contribution of each of its members.[2]

While the major discussion of benefits of this approach tends to center around the possibility of more objective performance evaluation, other values may accrue. If goals are set and understood by the subordinate, frustration and anxiety resulting from ambiguity surrounding job expectations may be reduced. Higher levels of performance may be achieved. If the goals are progressively more difficult from period to period, and the participation of the subordinate leads to increased levels of ego-involvement in their attainment, higher levels of motivation may obtain.

For the most part, "management by objectives" has been implemented on the

From Henry L. Tosi and Stephen J. Carroll "Managerial Reaction to Management by Objectives," *Academy of Management Journal* 11, (December, 1968): 415-26. Reprinted by permission.

[1] Peter Drucker, *The Practice of Management* (New York: Harper and Row, Publishers, 1954) and Douglas McGregor, "An Uneasy Look at Performance Appraisal," *Harvard Business Review* (May-June, 1957). As an indication of the growing interest, see for example Charles L. Hughes, *Goal Setting* (New York: AMA, 1966); Raymond F. Valentine, *Performance Objectives for Managers* (New York: AMA, 1966); J. D. Batten, *Beyond Management by Objectives* (New York: AMA, 1966); Earnest C. Miller, *Objectives and Standards of Performance in Financial Management* (New York: AMA, 1968); Nathaniel Stewart, *Strategies of Managing for Results* (Englewood Cliffs, N.J.: Prentice-Hall, Inc., 1966); George Odiorne, *Management by Objectives* (New York: Pitman, 1965). Textbooks include George Strauss and Leonard R. Sayles, *Personnel* (Englewood Cliffs, N.J.: Prentice-Hall, Inc., 1967); Wendall French, *The Personnel Management Process* (Boston: Houghton Mifflin Company); Paul Pigors and Charles A. Myers, *Personnel Administration* (New York: McGraw-Hill Book Company. 1965).

[2] Odiorne.

basis of its apparent theoretical practicability and advantages. There has been only limited research examining its effects. One set of studies was conducted by Raia.[3] A large firm implemented "Goal Setting and Self Control," a variant of management by objectives. By the end of the first program year productivity had increased, managers were more aware of the firm's goals, and specific goals had been set in more areas than had been the previous experience. Prior to the program, productivity was decreasing at the rate of 4 percent per month. After the program was instituted, the trend reversed and was increasing at 3 percent per month. Raia concluded that:

> A contribution of the program in the area of performance appraisal has been quite significant. There was unanimous agreement among the line managers in the department, particularly plant managers, the Goals and Controls had simplified the evaluation of the individual's performance. The statement by the manager who, while being interviewed, remarked that he was now judged by his job performance and not "by the way I comb my hair," is quite meaningful.

Among the other advantages cited were better planning of resource utilization, pinpointing of problem areas, and improved communications and mutual understanding.

A follow-up study of the same program sheds additional light on the Goal Setting Program.[4] This study generally supports the findings of the first. The level of goal attainment increased, there were continuing increases in productivity and improved managerial planning and control. Some managers, however, felt the program was "easy to beat." There seemed to be an overemphasis on production or measureable goals. Some of the participants reevaluated their initial feeling about appraisal and felt that the program did not provide adequate incentives to improve performance. The managers asked, "What does it mean to the individual when he fails to meet certain goals?" They were not able to link the goal setting program to the organization's reward system.

The study by Meyer, Kay, and French examined the effect of a Work Planning and Review Program.[5] The basic features of this program are very similar to management by objectives.

> In WPR discussion, the managerial subordinates do not deal in generalities. They consider specific objectively defined work goals and establish the yardstick for measuring performance. These goals stem, of course, from broader departmental objectives and are defined in relation to the individual's position in the departments.

Managers using this system were compared to those operating under the traditional performance appraisal method used in the company studied. Those

---

[3] Anthony P. Raia, "Goal Setting and Self Control," *Journal of Management Studies II,* 1 (Feb., 1965): 34-53 and "A Second Look at Goals and Controls," *California Management Review* (Summer, 1966), pp. 49-58.
[4] Raia, "A Second Look . . . ."
[5] Herbert H. Meyer, Emanuel Kay, and John R. P. French, Jr., "Split Roles in Performance Appraisal," *Harvard Business Review* 43 (Jan.-Feb., 1965): 123-29.

managers operating under the old appraisal method did not change in the areas measured.

The WPR group, by contrast, expressed significantly more favorable attitudes on almost all questionnaire items. Specifically, their attitudes changed in a favorable direction over the year that they participated in the new WPR program with regard to:

1. Amount of help the manager was giving them in improving performance on the job and the degree to which the manager was receptive to new ideas;
2. The ability of the manager to plan;
3. The extent to which the managers made use of their abilities and experience;
4. The degree to which they felt the goals they were shooting for were what they *should be;*
5. The extent to which they received help from the manager in planning for future job opportunities;
6. The value of the performance discussions they had with their managers.

In addition to changes in attitudes, the authors concluded that the members of the WPR group were much more likely to have taken specific actions to improve performance than those who were continuing to operate within a traditional performance appraisal approach.

Mendleson found that while there was no significant relationship between the *extent* of goal setting within a superior-subordinate pair of managers and the superior's *ratings of his subordinate's present performance,* there was, on the other hand, a positive relationship between *goal setting and the superior's rating of his subordinate's promotability.*[6]

The research evidence points to three general conclusions. First, changes in performance and attitude, which seem positive and desirable, appear to be associated with management by objectives. Secondly, some signals of caution must be noted. Last, the number of researches in this topic is limited.

THE CURRENT STUDY

The management by objectives program studied here was implemented in a large manufacturing firm. The company produces both industrial and consumer products. It is a large national concern with sales, manufacturing, and distribution locations dispersed throughout the United States.

The *work planning and review* program (WPR is the program designation by the company) was instituted at the initiative and the authority of a new vice president of personnel. He found, on joining the company, that the appraisal system was essentially based on "personality traits and characteristics." The Personnel Department began developing manuals and procedures necessary for the change to an objectives-oriented appraisal system. These were prepared and

---

[6] Jack L. Mendleson, "Managerial Goal Setting: An Exploration Into Meaning and Measurement" (unpublished dissertation, Michigan State University, 1967).

distributed. Meetings were held with the top management group in the company to discuss the use and rationale underlying the objectives approach. They were instructed to implement it in their own units. Needless to say, the degree of implementation and management support varied within different departments. Essentially, the purposes of the program are to motivate managers and improve individual job performance. Goals were to be set in two areas, performance and self-improvement. The performance goals were described in the instruction manual as those

> things to be accomplished, changes to be made, and standards of performance to be met. This is a plan of action for the year. *Be Specific.* Indicate how each item is to be accomplished. Show priorities, when each item is to begin and when it is to be completed. Indicate specific amounts, dates or quality. Don't try to include everything; just the important things.

A self-improvement plan was also to be devised. Managers were instructed to

> select a few, preferably not more than three or four, items for personal improvement—ways to expand your knowledge or improve your effectiveness. *Be Specific.*

This study basically reports the results of in-depth interview with 48 managers at all levels ranging from vice president to foremen. Some additional data, in the form of supporting correlation coefficients, have been included from the more extensive questionnaire survey of managers in the company. Table 1 shows the distribution of managers at various organizational levels who participated in the interview phase of the study.

TABLE 1.

Vice President	6
Director	12
Middle Management	20
Lower Management	10
Total	48

The mail questionnaire was distributed to 150 managers in the company. Of the 120 responses, there were at least 98, and in some cases slightly more, usable replies for calculating the correlation coefficient.

FINDINGS

The study is one phase of a more complete examination of the program. This phase deals with four general areas. First we were concerned with the manager's perceptions of the underlying rationale, problems, and advantages associated with an objectives approach. From this naturally follows a set of suggested changes to improve the approach.

Philosophy, Rationale, and Purpose of the Program

During the interview, each manager was asked the following question: "What are the purposes of the program as you see them? What is the rationale for this approach? Table 2 below presents a summary of the responses.

TABLE 2. **Philosophy and Rationale of the Objectives Approach**

RATIONALE	n^*	%
1. To Link Evaluation to Performance	17	35.4
2. Aid Manager in Planning	12	25.0
3. Motivate Managers	11	22.9
4. To Increase Boss/Subordinate Interaction & Feedback	11	22.9
5. Development of Management Potential	8	16.6
6. Link Company Objectives to Department Objectives	8	16.6
7. Managers Know What Their Job Is	6	12.5
8. Give Management Information About What's Going On at Lower Levels	4	8.3
9. Management Club to Pressure Performance	3	6.25
10. No Mention	7	14.5

n=48 Managers
*The totals are more than 48 since a respondent may have cited more than one advantage.

Those purposes cited most frequently tend to parallel those stated in the company manuals. The largest percentage (35 percent) felt that an objectives program was intended to link the evaluation of an individual to his actual performance rather than to personality or to other personal characteristics. About 25 percent considered the approach as useful as a planning aid. Increased feedback and the positive motivational effect of the objectives approach were mentioned by 22 percent of the respondents.

The magnitude, or rather lack of it, of the percentages suggests little general agreement among managers about the underlying philosophy and rationale of the program. Only one item, "the attempt to relate evaluation to performance," was noted by more than 30 percent of the respondents. It could be that those items which were cited most frequently, i.e., evaluation, feedback, planning, and motivation, may well be the respondents' verbalization of the content of the organization policy. There seemed to be no central item or set of items around which the responses clustered. Perhaps the attempts to introduce and initiate the program did not substantially affect the attitudes and knowledge of the managers about the program.

Advantages

The managers interviewed were asked the advantages of the objectives program. They reported advantages as indicated below in Table 3. By far the major advantage was that one was more likely to "know what is expected of him by his boss." Over 58 percent of the managers noted this advantage. One marketing executive said:

Now we can focus our evaluation on what people do, rather than what they are. This is the best thing we have for evaluating the performance of our men. And it has a substantial motivational effect. These goals set up a challenge for them. I have seen changes in men's work habits after I began to use this approach. I have been able to watch improvements occur in some of my men.

TABLE 3. Advantages of Management By Objectives

ADVANTAGE	*n**	*%*
1. I Know What is Expected of Me	28	58.6
2. It Forces Planning and Setting Target Dates	20	41.6
3. It Forces Boss/Subordinate Feedback & Communication	15	31.2
4. Increases Awareness of Company Goals	9	18.7
5. Documented Goals Relating Evaluation to Performance	8	16.6
6. Focus on Self-Improvement	7	14.5
7. I Know Where I Stand	6	12.5
8. Coordinates Activity toward Company Objectives	6	12.5
9. Subtle Pressure and Motivation to Perform Better	5	10.4
10. Improves Performance if Used	4	8.3
11. Only a General Help	3	6.2
12. No Advantages Mentioned	5	10.4

n=48

*The total responses are more than 48 since a manager may have noted more than one advantage.

An engineer felt that

... while I did not have much to say in what the final determination of my goals were, at least I knew what my boss wanted and I knew what to do. I think this motivated me to work harder, or at least to work on those things that I knew were important to him. I also knew whether or not I achieved targets set for me.

The next item cited most frequently (41 percent) was that the program forced more planning, specification of projects, and setting target dates. As one of the managers indicated:

There is a kind of discipline involved in this program. I had to sit down and think about what I am going to be doing next year. I need to spell out what kind of resources are required and when I expect a particular project to be accomplished. This is a great help to me in determining what priorities should exist. Of course, it is an advantage to have these priorities verified by your boss.

Several managers (31.2 percent) felt that it forced bosses to interact with their subordinates, providing more communication and feedback. One of the respondents, who had recently joined the firm, thought it to be

... a fantastic idea to have a voice along with your boss in setting individual goals. Not only do you get a chance to put your two cents worth in but it gives your boss the benefit of the individual's thinking. I thought it was a psychological lift. I like the fact that they ask me what I thought my goal levels should be. I think the chance to sit down with your boss is important.

Another manager said:

I like the fact that I sit down with my boss to set these objectives. Every time I sit down and talk with him, I can't help but learn more about what he expects of me. Anything that does that is a help.

The advantages cited are fairly consistent with those one would have expected and those found earlier by Raia.[7] The most frequently cited advantages he noted were (1) planning, (2) pinpointing problem areas, (3) objective performance measures, and (4) improved communications. Meyer, Kay, and French similarly found better planning, improved appraisal, and a greater acceptance of the goals set as some of the positive effects. It seems reasonable to conclude that objectives oriented programs increase certainty about job requirements, result in a more comfortable feeling about the kind of criteria used in evaluation, and create a situation which ostensibly forces superiors to communicate with subordinates.

Problems Encountered

A number of managers (37.5 percent) indicated no problems with the objectives approach. The major problem, cited by 43 percent of the managers, was compliance with the formal procedural requirements, the process of completing forms, updating changes, and providing other information to the personnel unit. Raia also found this a major irritant and dubbed it the "paperwork problem."[8]

Some (20.8 percent) felt that the objectives approach was not used to its full potential in the organization. One of the respondents said:

I am not sure that many managers know how to use and develop objectives and goals. Everyone seems to think in terms of "target dates." Some jobs just don't lend themselves to that kind of goal. We need to recognize that different kinds of goals and objectives might be required for different functions, different jobs, and maybe even different managerial levels. Yet if you look at these review sheets all the goals look the same—a project designation and a target date. And besides, the self-improvement goals really seem to just be an appendage and not an integral part of the process.

In general, with the exception of the problems cited above, the problem and disadvantages cited tend to be fairly well distributed across the range of items listed in Table 4.

[7] Raia, "Goal Setting . . . ."
[8] Raia, "Goal Setting . . . ."

TABLE 4. Problems and Disadvantages Associated with Management by Objectives

PROBLEM	n^*	%
Excessive Formal Requirements	21	43.7
Not Used to Full Potential	10	20.8
Need to Consider Different Goals for Different Jobs and Levels	7	14.5
Never Get Good Feedback	7	14.5
I Was Never Really Involved in the Program	7	14.5
It is Undesirable to Commit Oneself to Goals Formally	5	10.5
Lack of Information About Personal Characteristics	2	4.2
No Real Problems	18	37.5

n=48
*More than one response from each subject was possible.

Additional insight into the problem areas was obtained by asking the subjects "How would you improve the program?" Table 5 lists the suggestions and the percentage of executives reporting them.

TABLE 5. Suggestions for Improving the Objectives Program

SUGGESTIONS	n^*	%
1. Insure Review and Feedback	24	50.0
2. Develop a Way to Update Goals so that Changes Can be Noted	20	41.6
3. Use by Top Management so that *Their* Goals are Known at Lower Levels	19	39.5
4. Include "Personal" Evaluations in Addition to Goals	16	33.3
5. Top Management Support for the Program	15	31.2
6. Increase the Understanding of the Program and How to Set Goals	12	24.9
7. Include "Normal Job Requirements"	10	20.8
8. Due Dates of Program are Incompatible with Unit Planning and Control Cycles	7	14.5
9. Insure "Real" Participation and Involvement in Goal Setting	5	10.4
10. Others	11	22.9

n=48
*More than one response from each manager was possible.

The major responses to this question point to a lack of top management support, use, and reinforcement. This is, of course, a reiteration of item 2 in Table 4 above—the program was "not used to full potential." Note that in Table 5, with the exception of item 2, the major suggestions focus on the manner in which the program is implemented by superiors. Obviously, the respondent's perception of how his boss uses the MBO process has an impact on the manner in which the subordinate uses and reacts to it.

If we turn to the mail questionnaire, we begin to get some additional light shed upon specific managerial behavior associated with the subordinates' satisfaction with the objectives process. The responses to items on the mail questionnaire indicate that the individual's satisfaction with the WPR program is highly correlated with items describing conditions dealing with goal clarity, feedback, and management support for the program. The frequency of feedback is importantly related to satisfaction with Work Planning and Review. The items below are those which were significantly correlated with *Satisfaction with Work Planning and Review.*[9]

FREQUENCY OF FEEDBACK

How often were you given feedback on progress toward performance goals?	.42
How often were you given feedback on progress toward self-improvement?	.29
The kind of feedback you get from your boss about performance.	-.22

The questionnaire responses also illustrate the importance of specific *managerial support* for WPR. The items below describe supervisory behavior directed toward the program.

SUPPORT FOR THE PROGRAM

How much interest do you think the company has in the program?	.34
How much interest do you think your boss has in the program?	.46
How much time does your boss devote to WPR?	.44
How concerned do you feel your boss would be if you failed to achieve the goals established for your job to a significant degree?	-.29

Although other factors, such as the type of job and level of management, may affect the precision with which targets and goals may be described, the perceptions of managers about how clearly goals have been spelled out and can be measured may also be a function of the manner in which the boss uses the program. The following items show the relationship between *satisfaction with WPR* and items describing *goal characteristics.*

GOAL CLARITY AND IMPORTANCE

What was the level of difficulty of your self-improvement goals?	*.29*
The extent to which performance goals met the most pressing needs of the department and the company.	*.21 (x*
How clearly were performance goals stated with respect to expected results.	*.44*
The extent to which the relative importance of performance goals was pointed out to you.	*.33*
The difficulty the boss has in measuring your performance.	*-.26*

There is an important point (Table 5, Item 2) which should not be overlooked. Over 40 percent of the managers indicated that after their goals had been set, their time had been preempted by higher levels of management and they were placed to work on another project. In most cases, this change was not noted formally on the Review Forms. While most agreed that their immediate superior took this into consideration in evaluation, some expressed concern that if their boss left and a new man came in, "he would find that I did not achieve

---

[9] The correlation coefficients reported were calculated from an n of at least 98 and all are significant at the .01 level except the one marked (xx) which is at the .05 level. Negative correlations should be reversed in sign. They appear because responses were reversed in the questionnaire.

any of the objectives on the form, and consequently, my performance might be evaluated lower than it is." Several expressed a degree of anxiety and threat because they had to commit themselves to goals on paper which may well change due to demands upon them over which they have little control.

CONCLUSIONS

Perhaps the most notable limitation in the management-by-objectives literature has been a consistent avoidance of a discussion of its problems. Its proponents have been essentially positive, stressing the advantages as an appraisal technique and a motivational tool. Goal-oriented systems do not eliminate all the problems that might have been attributable to "trait oriented" appraisal systems. Our findings, especially the negative implications, are similar to those found elsewhere.[10] Problems of appraisal and motivation do not fade into the sunset when this method is used. If anything, the demands are more rigorous and problems probably magnified when members' expectations about feedback and appraisal are raised and not met. It seems to us that the apologists for these methods have long avoided subjecting them to the same scrutiny applied to the "old" techniques. Yet the unanticipated consequences seem to be of sufficient magnitude that they must be taken into account. Management by objectives is not the sovereign remedy that some seem to suggest. The implications of its use, especially the problems of implementation, need to be evaluated more completely. These have been discussed elsewhere.[11] To move toward an objectives-oriented system probably constitutes a fundamental change in the managerial orientation and style which may well require an alteration of the general organization climate. We believe the data from this study point to some major areas which require attention.

Use By Managers

Satisfaction with WPR is positively related to subordinate's perceptions of boss (r=.46) and company (r=.34) interest in the program and how much time the boss spends on it (r=.44). This, we believe is strong evidence of the link between managerial support and the degree to which the program is accepted by an individual. It is only when all levels of management reinforce the use of the program by subordinates by *using the system themselves* that benefits can obtain. One manager said, "I have never been asked by my boss whether or not I used the system. I don't know whether he really cares about it." Obviously the fundamental requirement of executive support *and use* is critical before any substantial benefits can occur. One manager said:

> We ought to go at this full blast or not at all. I haven't had to answer to my boss to the fact that I haven't set objectives yet this year. We need

---

[10] Raia, "Goal Setting . . . ."
[11] Henry L. Tosi, "Management Development and Management by Objectives: An Interrelationship," *Management of Personnel Quarterly* 4 no. 2 (Summer, 1965).

some indication that management is really behind us. I can't really be sure. I think the program is beneficial.

The Formulation of Goals

Greater attention must be given to introducing not only the philosophy, but the mechanics of goal setting. The importance of the goal itself is significant. From the questionnaire, it was found that managers who were satisfied with WPR felt that the goal represented the unit's most pressing needs (r=.21), that the importance of the goals was made clear to him (r=.33), that the goals were clearly stated (r=.44), and the boss had less difficulty in measuring his performance with some objective criteria (r=.26). Managers must either intuitively be able to set goals or learn how to set them properly to get the full benefits of the objective approach.

Provide Feedback

Now more than ever, the managers want feedback. They seem to recognize the attempt to link performance with evaluation (see Table 2, #1), and believe it to be of benefit to "know what is expected" (Table 3, #1), yet only a few mention feedback as an advantage. Just 12 percent felt that they "knew where they stood" (see Table 3, #7), and the major suggestion for improvement, noted by the majority, was to "insure feedback" (Table 5, #1). This is also reflected by the comment that the "program was not used to its full potential" (Table 4, #2). This was also reflected in the responses to the mail questionnaire. Those who were more satisfied with WPR also reported relatively frequent feedback about progress toward performance goals (r=.42) and self-improvement goals (r=.29) and the objectivity of the feedback (r=.22). This suggests a failure to effectively use the whole program cycle. There was apparently some "work planning" and it seems that it was positively valued by the respondents. Yet this developed expectancies for performance "review," which apparently did not occur to their satisfaction. Benefits did not accrue, which might have, had the planning and review cycle been completed.

Program Maintenance Over Time

There may be a tendency for these objective-oriented systems to have only a short-range impact. The enthusiasm in the early stages seems to fade into disenchantment in later periods. For instance, Raia detected the beginnings of managerial dissatisfaction in his follow-up study. He noted a tendency to revert to production goals, more easily measured. Questions were raised of the value and meaning of the Goals and Controls Program. Some managers sensed a lack of top management support, lack of incentive, and a tendency to play "the reporting game."

Similar indications were found in this study. One manager maintained that:

... everyone was interested in this a year ago. This year, it just fell between the chairs. No one picked it up, except personnel. My boss never asked me about it, I haven't set my objectives yet.

Another suggested that he could

... not guess what would happen if goals were missed. I don't know anyone who has ever gotten any "negative" feedback. I don't believe everyone in the company met all their goals. What good is it if we don't know how well we did.

Enthusiasm and support wane. The novelty wears thin and the need to cope with the difficulties of an objectives approach may force managers toward the path of least resistance, compliance with the minimum formal requirements, use of unimaginative goals, and only surface support. The program must be kept viable and relevant. This is supported by the respondents to the mail survey. Those satisfied with the program were those, who for one reason or the other, found that WPR was applicable to their job (r=.66) and was helpful to them in the performance of their duties (r=.52).

Recognize the Constraints of Participation

Relevance may be increased by participation. If so, then managers must be cognizant that "mutual goal setting" may require a reallocation of influence in setting goals. The subordinate has to be given the opportunity to participate. The superior must be willing to relinquish some influence. If this redistribution does not occur, participation will not work. *Participation is power redistribution,* and power means some control over the work environment. For instance, those managers in the questionnaire study who were satisfied with WPR also felt they had control over the means to achieving their performance goals (r=.36).

SUMMARY

These problems cited above tend to be the practical limitations of the objectives approach. To obtain benefits, the necessary condition is to use it. Constant review is needed to insure that the program fills a legitimate need in the organization, a need which operating managers sense exists. There is a kind of motion and effort economy that tends to drive unimportant, unnecessary, and most importantly, unrequired activities from a manager's list of priorities. The objectives approach cannot be sold in books, meetings, or theory. It can only be sold in practice.

John'J. Morse
and Jay W. Lorsch

BEYOND THEORY Y

During the past 30 years, managers have been bombarded with two competing approaches to the problems of human administration and organization. The first, usually called the classical school of organization, emphasizes the need for well-established lines of authority, clearly defined jobs, and authority equal to responsibility. The second, often called the participative approach, focuses on the desirability of involving organization members in decision making so that they will be more highly motivated.

Douglas McGregor, through his well-known "Theory X and Theory Y," drew a distinction between the assumptions about human motivation which underlie these two approaches, to this effect:

Theory X assumes that people dislike work and must be coerced, controlled, and directed toward organizational goals. Furthermore, most people prefer to be treated this way, so they can avoid responsibility.

Theory Y—the integration of goals—emphasizes the average person's intrinsic interest in his work, his desire to be self-directing and to seek responsibility, and his capacity to be creative in solving business problems.

It is McGregor's conclusion, of course, that the latter approach to organization is the more desirable one for managers to follow.[1]

McGregor's position causes confusion for the managers who try to choose between these two conflicting approaches. The classical organizational approach that McGregor associated with Theory X does work well in some situations, although, as McGregor himself pointed out, there are also some situations where it does not work effectively. At the same time, the approach based on Theory Y, while it has produced good results in some situations, does not always do so. That is, each approach is effective in some cases but not in others. Why is this? How can managers resolve the confusion?

A NEW APPROACH

Recent work by a number of students of management and organization may help to answer such questions.[2] These studies indicate that there is not one best

John J. Morse and Jay W. Lorsch, "Beyond Theory Y," *Harvard Business Review* 48 (May-June, 1970): 61-68.© by President and Fellows of Harvard College; all rights reserved. Reprinted by permission.

[1] Douglas McGregor, *The Human Side of Enterprise* (New York; McGraw-Hill Book Company, Inc., 1960), pp. 34-35 and pp. 47-48.
[2] See for example Paul R. Lawrence and Jay W. Lorsch, *Organization and Environment*

organizational approach; rather, the best approach depends on the nature of the work to be done. Enterprises with highly predictable tasks perform better with organizations characterized by the highly formalized procedures and management hierarchies of the classical approach. With highly uncertain tasks that require more extensive problem solving, on the other hand, organizations that are less formalized and emphasize self-control and member participation in decision making are more effective. In essence, according to these newer studies, managers must design and develop organizations so that the organizational characteristics *fit* the nature of the task to be done.

While the conclusions of this newer approach will make sense to most experienced managers and can alleviate much of the confusion about which approach to choose, there are still two important questions unanswered:

1. How does the more formalized and controlling organization affect the motivation of organization members? (McGregor's most telling criticism of the classical approach was that it did not unleash the potential in an enterprise's human resources.)
2. Equally important, does a less formalized organization always provide a high level of motivation for its members? (This is the implication many managers have drawn from McGregor's work.)

We have recently been involved in a study that provides surprising answers to these questions and, when taken together with other recent work, suggests a new set of basic assumptions which move beyond Theory Y into what we call "Contingency Theory: the fit between task, organization, and people." These theoretical assumptions emphasize that the appropriate pattern of organization is *contingent* on the nature of the work to be done and on the particular needs of the people involved. We should emphasize that we have labeled these assumptions as a step beyond Theory Y because of McGregor's own recognition that the Theory Y assumptions would probably be supplanted by new knowledge within a short time.[3]

THE STUDY DESIGN

Our study was conducted in four organizational units. Two of these performed the relatively certain task of manufacturing standardized containers on high-speed, automated production lines. The other two performed the relatively uncertain work of research and development in communications technology. Each pair of units performing the same kind of task were in the same large company, and each pair had previously been evaluated by that company's management as containing one highly effective unit and a less effective one. The study design is summarized in Exhibit 1.

(Boston: Harvard Business School, Division of Research, 1967); Joan Woodward, *Industrial Organization: Theory & Practice* (New York: Oxford University Press, Inc., 1965); Tom Burns and G.M. Stalker, *The Management of Innovation* (London: Tavistock Publications, 1961); Harold J. Leavitt, "Unhuman Organizations," HBR July-August 1962, p. 90.
[3] McGregor, op. cit., P. 245.

Characteristics	Company I (predictable manufacturing task)	Company II (unpredictable R&D task)
Effective performer	Akron containers plant	Stockton research lab
Less effective performer	Hartford containers plant	Carmel research lab

Exhibit 1. Study design in "fit" of organizational characteristics

The objective was to explore more fully how the fit between organization and task was related to successful performance. That is, does a good fit between organizational characteristics and task requirements increase the motivation of individuals and hence produce more effective individual and organizational performance?

An especially useful approach to answering this question is to recognize that an individual has a strong need to master the world around him, including the task that he faces as a member of a work organization.[4] The accumulated feelings of satisfaction that come from successfully mastering one's environment can be called a "sense of competence." We saw this sense of competence in performing a particular task as helpful in understanding how a fit between task and organizational characteristics could motivate people toward successful performance.

Organizational dimensions

Because the four study sites had already been evaluated by the respective corporate managers as high and low performers of tasks, we expected that such differences in performance would be a preliminary clue to differences in the "fit" of the organizational characteristics to the job to be done. But, first, we had to define what kinds of organizational characteristics would determine how appropriate the organization was to the particular task.

We grouped these organizational characteristics into two sets of factors:

1. Formal characteristics, which could be used to judge the fit between the kind of task being worked on and the formal practices of the organization.
2. Climate characteristics, or the subjective perceptions and orientations that had developed among the individuals about their organizational setting. (These too must fit the task to be performed if the organization is to be effective.)

We measured these attributes through questionnaires and interviews with about 40 managers in each unit to determine the appropriateness of the organization to the kind of task being performed. We also measured the feelings of competence of the people in the organizations so that we could link the appropriateness of the organizational attributes with a sense of competence.

MAJOR FINDINGS

The principal findings of the survey are best highlighted by contrasting the highly successful Akron plant and the high-performing Stockton laboratory.

---

[4] See Robert W. White, "Ego and Reality in Psychoanalytic Theory," *Psychological Issues* 3, No. 3 (New York: International Universities Press, 1963).

Because each performed very different tasks (the former a relatively certain manufacturing task and the latter a relatively uncertain research task), we expected, as brought out earlier, that there would have to be major differences between them in organizational characteristics if they were to perform effectively. And this is what we did find. But we also found that each of these effective units had a better fit with its particular task than did its less effective counterpart.

While our major purpose in this article is to explore how the fit between task and organizational characteristics is related to motivation, we first want to explore more fully the organizational characteristics of these units, so the reader will better understand what we mean by a fit between task and organization and how it can lead to more effective behavior. To do this, we shall place the major emphasis on the contrast between the high-performing units (the Akron plant and Stockton laboratory), but we shall also compare each of these with its less effective mate (the Hartford plant and Carmel laboratory respectively).

Formal characteristics

Beginning with differences in formal characteristics, we found that both the Akron and Stockton organizations fit their respective tasks much better than did their less successful counterparts. In the predictable manufacturing task environment, Akron had a pattern of formal relationships and duties that was highly structured and precisely defined. Stockton, with its unpredictable research task, had a low degree of structure and much less precision of definition (see Exhibit 2).

Characteristics	Akron	Stockton
1. Pattern of formal relationships and duties as signified by organization charts and job manuals	Highly structured, precisely defined	Low degree of structure, less well defined
2. Pattern of formal rules, procedures, control, and measurement systems	Pervasive, specific, uniform, comprehensive	Minimal, loose, flexible
3. Time dimensions incorporated in formal practices	Short-term	Long-term
4. Goal dimensions incorporated in formal practices	Manufacturing	Scientific

Exhibit 2. Differences in formal characteristics in high-performing organizations

Akron's pattern of formal rules, procedures, and control systems was so specific and comprehensive that it prompted one manager to remark: "We've got rules here for everything from how much powder to use in cleaning the toilet bowls to how to cart a dead body out of the plant."

In contrast, Stockton's formal rules were so minimal, loose, and flexible that one scientist, when asked whether he felt the rules ought to be tightened, said: "If a man puts a nut on a screw all day long, you may need more rules and a job definition for him. But we're not novices here. We're professionals and not the kind who need close supervision. People around here *do* produce, and produce under relaxed conditions. Why tamper with success?"

These differences in formal organizational characteristics were well suited to the differences in tasks of the two organizations. Thus:

Akron's highly structured formal practices fit its predictable task because behavior had to be rigidly defined and controlled around the automated, high-speed production line. There was really only one way to accomplish the plant's very routine and programmable job; managers defined it precisely and insisted (through the plant's formal practices) that each man do what was expected of him.

On the other hand, Stockton's highly unstructured formal practices made just as much sense because the required activities in the laboratory simply could not be rigidly defined in advance. With such an unpredictable, fast-changing task as communications technology research, there were numerous approaches to getting the job done well. As a consequence, Stockton managers used a less structured pattern of formal practices that left the scientists in the lab free to respond to the changing task situation.

Akron's formal practices were very much geared to *short-term* and *manufacturing* concerns as its task demanded. For example, formal production reports and operating review sessions were daily occurrences, consistent with the fact that the through-put time for their products was typically only a few hours.

By contrast, Stockton's formal practices were geared to *long-term* and *scientific* concerns, as its task demanded. Formal reports and reviews were made only quarterly, reflecting the fact that research often does not come to fruition for three to five years.

At the two less effective sites (i.e., the Hartford plant and the Carmel laboratory), the formal organizational characteristics did not fit their respective tasks nearly as well. For example, Hartford's formal practices were much less structured and controlling than were Akron's, while Carmel's were more restraining and restricting than were Stockton's. A scientist in Carmel commented:

"There's something here that keeps you from being scientific. It's hard to put your finger on, but I guess I'd call it 'Mickey Mouse.' There are rules and things here that get in your way regarding doing your job as a researcher."

Climate characteristics

As with formal practices, the climate in both high-performing Akron and Stockton suited the respective tasks much better than did the climates at the less successful Hartford and Carmel sites.

Perception of structure: The people in the Akron plant perceived a great deal of structure, with their behavior tightly controlled and defined. One manager in the plant said:

"We can't let the lines run unattended. We lose money whenever they do. So we make sure each man knows his job, knows when he can take a break, knows how to handle a change in shifts, etc. It's all spelled out clearly for him the day he comes to work here."

In contrast, the scientists in the Stockton laboratory perceived very little structure, with their behavior only minimally controlled. Such perceptions encouraged the individualistic and creative behavior that the uncertain, rapidly changing research task needed. Scientists in the less successful Carmel laboratory perceived much more structure in their organization and voiced the feeling that this was "getting in their way" and making it difficult to do effective research.

Distribution of influence: The Akron plant and the Stockton laboratory also differed substantially in how influence was distributed and on the character of superior-subordinate and colleague relations. Akron personnel felt that they had much less influence over decisions in their plant than Stockton's scientists did in their laboratory. The task at Akron had already been clearly defined and that definition had, in a sense, been incorporated into the automated production flow itself. Therefore, there was less need for individuals to have a say in decisions concerning the work process.

Moreover, in Akron, influence was perceived to be concentrated in the upper levels of the formal structure (a hierarchical or "top-heavy" distribution), while in Stockton influence was perceived to be more evenly spread out among more levels of the formal structure (an egalitarian distribution).

Akron's members perceived themselves to have a low degree of freedom vis-à-vis superiors both in choosing the jobs they work on and in handling these jobs on their own. They also described the type of supervision in the plant as being relatively directive. Stockton's scientists, on the other hand, felt that they had a great deal of freedom vis-à-vis their superiors both in choosing the tasks and projects, and in handling them in the way that they wanted to. They described supervision in the laboratory as being very participatory.

It is interesting to note that the less successful Carmel laboratory had more of its decisions made at the top. Because of this, there was a definite feeling by the scientists that their particular expertise was not being effectively used in choosing projects.

Relations with others: The people at Akron perceived a great deal of similarity among themselves in background, prior work experiences, and approaches for tackling job-related problems. They also perceived the degree of coordination of effort among colleagues to be very high. Because Akron's task was so precisely defined and the behavior of its members so rigidly controlled around the automated lines, it is easy to see that this pattern also made sense.

By contrast, Stockton's scientists perceived not only a great many differences among themselves, especially in education and background, but also that the coordination of effort among colleagues was relatively low. This was appropriate for a laboratory in which a great variety of disciplines and skills were present and individual projects were important to solve technological problems.

Time orientation: As we would expect, Akron's individuals were highly oriented toward a relatively short time span and manufacturing goals. They responded to quick feedback concerning the quality and service that the plant was providing. This was essential, given the nature of their task.

Stockton's researchers were highly oriented toward a longer time span and scientific goals. These orientations meant that they were willing to wait for long-term feedback from a research project that might take years to complete. A scientist in Stockton said:

> "We're not the kind of people here who need a pat on the back every day. We can wait for months if necessary before we get feedback from colleagues and the profession. I've been working on one project now for three months and I'm still not sure where it's going to take me. I can live with that, though."

This is precisely the kind of behavior and attitude that spells success on this kind of task.

Managerial style: Finally, the individuals in both Akron and Stockton perceived their chief executive to have a "managerial style" that expressed more of a concern for the task than for people or relationships, but this seemed to fit both tasks.

In Akron, the technology of the task was so dominant that top managerial behavior which was not focused primarily on the task might have reduced the effectiveness of performance. On the other hand, although Stockton's research task called for more individualistic problem-solving behavior, that sort of behavior could have become segmented and uncoordinated, unless the top executive in the lab focused the group's attention on the overall research task. Given the individualistic bent of the scientists, this was an important force in achieving unity of effort.

All these differences in climate characteristics in the two high performers are summarized in Exhibit 3.

As with formal attributes, the less effective Hartford and Carmel sites had organization climates that showed a perceptibly lower degree of fit with their respective tasks. For example, the Hartford plant had an egalitarian distribution of influence, perceptions of a low degree of structure, and a more participatory type of supervision. The Carmel laboratory had a somewhat top-heavy distribution of influence, perceptions of high structure, and a more directive type of supervision.

COMPETENCE MOTIVATION

Because of the difference in organizational characteristics at Akron and Stockton, the two sites were strikingly different places in which to work. But these organizations had two very important things in common. First, each organization fit very well the requirements of its task. Second, although the

Characteristics	Akron	Stockton
1. Structural orientation	Perceptions of tightly controlled behavior and a high degree of structure	Perceptions of a low degree of structure
2. Distribution of influence	Perceptions of low total influence, concentrated at upper levels in the organization	Perceptions of high total influence, more evenly spread out among all levels
3. Character of superior-subordinate relations	Low freedom vis-à-vis superiors to choose and handle jobs, directive type of supervision	High freedom vis-à-vis superiors to choose and handle projects, participatory type of supervision
4. Character of colleague relations	Perceptions of many similarities among colleagues, high degree of coordination of colleague effort	Perceptions of many differences among colleagues, relatively low degree of coordination of colleague effort
5. Time orientation	Short-term	Long-term
6. Goal orientation	Manufacturing	Scientific
7. Top executive's "managerial style"	More concerned with task than people	More concerned with task than people

Exhibit 3. Differences in "climate" characteristics in high-performing organizations

587

behavior in the two organizations was different, the result in both cases was effective task performance.

Since, as we indicated earlier, our primary concern in this study was to link the fit between organization and task with individual motivation to perform effectively, we devised a two-part test to measure the sense of competence motivation of the individuals at both sites. Thus:

The *first* part asked a participant to write creative and imaginative stories in response to six ambiguous pictures.

The *second* asked him to write a creative and imaginative story about what he would be doing, thinking, and feeling "tomorrow" on his job. This is called a "projective" test because it is assumed that the respondent projects into his stories his own attitudes, thoughts, feelings, needs, and wants, all of which can be measured from the stories.[5]

The results indicated that the individuals in Akron and Stockton showed significantly more feelings of competence than did their counterparts in the lower-fit Hartford and Carmel organizations.[6] We found that the organization-task fit is simultaneously linked to and interdependent with both individual motivation and effective unit performance. (This interdependency is illustrated in Exhibit 4.)

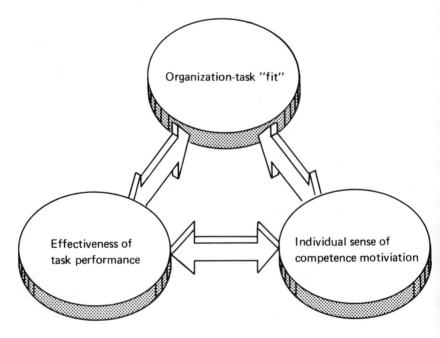

Exhibit 4. Basic contingent relationships

[5] For a more detailed description of this survey, see John J. Morse, *Internal Organizational Patterning and Sense of Competence Motivation* (Boston: Harvard Business School, unpublished doctoral dissertation, 1969).

[6] Differences between the two container plants are significant at .001 and between the research laboratories at .01 (one-tailed probability).

Putting the conclusions in this form raises the question of cause and effect. Does effective unit performance result from the task-organization fit or from higher motivation, or perhaps from both? Does higher sense of competence motivation result from effective unit performance or from fit? Our answer to these questions is that we do not think there are any single cause-and-effect relationships, but that these factors are mutually interrelated. This has important implications for management theory and practice.

CONTINGENCY THEORY

Returning to McGregor's Theory X and Theory Y assumptions, we can now question the validity of some of his conclusions. While Theory Y might help to explain the findings in the two laboratories, we clearly need something other than Theory X or Y assumptions to explain the findings in the plants. For example, the managers at Akron worked in a formalized organization setting with relatively little participation in decision making, and yet they were highly motivated. According to Theory X, people would work hard in such a setting only because they were coerced to do so. According to Theory Y, they should have been involved in decision making and been self-directed to feel so motivated. Nothing in our data indicates that either set of assumptions was valid at Akron.

Conversely, the managers at Hartford, the low-performing plant, were in a less formalized organization with more participation in decision making, and yet they were not as highly motivated like the Akron managers. The Theory Y assumptions would suggest that they should have been more motivated.

A way out of such paradoxes is to state a new set of assumptions, the Contingency Theory, that seems to explain the findings at all four sites:

1. Human beings bring varying patterns of needs and motives into the work organization, but one central need is to achieve a sense of competence.
2. The sense of competence motive, while it exists in all human beings, may be fulfilled in different ways by different people depending on how this need interacts with the strengths of the individuals' other needs—such as those for power, independence, structure, achievement, and affiliation.
3. Competence motivation is most likely to be fulfilled when there is a fit between task and organization.
4. Sense of competence continues to motivate even when a competence goal is achieved; once one goal is reached, a new, higher one is set.

While the central thrust of these points is clear from the preceding discussion of the study, some elaboration can be made. First, the idea that different people have different needs is well understood by psychologists. However, all too often, managers assume that all people have similar needs. Lest we be accused of the same error, we are saying only that all people have a need to feel competent; in this *one* way they are similar. But in many other dimensions of personality, individuals differ, and these differences will determine how a particular person achieves a sense of competence.

Thus, for example, the people in the Akron plant seemed to be very different from those in the Stockton laboratory in their underlying attitudes toward uncertainty, authority, and relationships with their peers. And because they had different need patterns along these dimensions, both groups were highly motivated by achieving competence from quite different activities and settings. While there is a need to further investigate how people who work in different settings differ in their psychological makeup, one important implication of the Contingency Theory is that we must not only seek a fit between organization and task, but also between task and people and between people and organization.

A further point which requires elaboration is that one's sense of competence never really comes to rest. Rather, the real satisfaction of this need is in the successful performance itself, with no diminishing of the motivation as one goal is reached. Since feelings of competence are thus reinforced by successful performance, they can be a more consistent and reliable motivator than salary and benefits.

Implications for managers

The major managerial implication of the Contingency Theory seems to rest in the task-organization-people fit. Although this interrelationship is complex, the best possibility for managerial action probably is in tailoring the organization to fit the task and the people. If such a fit is achieved, both effective unit performance and a higher sense of competence motivation seem to result.

Managers can start this process by considering how certain the task is, how frequently feedback about task performance is available, and what goals are implicit in the task. The answers to these questions will guide their decisions about the design of the management hierarchy, the specificity of job assignments, and the utilization of rewards and control procedures. Selective use of training programs and a general emphasis on appropriate management styles will move them toward a task-organization fit.

The problem of achieving a fit among task, organization, and people is something we know less about. As we have already suggested, we need further investigation of what personality characteristics fit various tasks and organizations. Even with our limited knowledge, however, there are indications that people will gradually gravitate into organizations that fit their particular personalities. Managers can help this process by becoming more aware of what psychological needs seem to best fit the tasks available and the organizational setting, and by trying to shape personnel selection criteria to take account of these needs.

In arguing for an approach which emphasizes the fit among task, organization, and people, we are putting to rest the question of which organizational approach—the classical or the participative—is best. In its place we are raising a new question: What organizational approach is most appropriate given the task and the people involved?

For many enterprises, given the new needs of younger employees for more autonomy, and the rapid rates of social and technological change, it may well be that the more participative approach is the most appropriate. But there will still be many situations in which the more controlled and formalized organization is desirable. Such an organization need not be coercive or punitive. If it makes sense to the individuals involved, given their needs and their jobs, they will find it rewarding and motivating.

CONCLUDING NOTE

The reader will recognize that the complexity we have described is not of our own making. The basic deficiency with earlier approaches is that they did not recognize the variability in tasks and people which produces this complexity. The strength of the contingency approach we have outlined is that it begins to provide a way of thinking about this complexity, rather than ignoring it. While our knowledge in this area is still growing, we are certain that any adequate theory of motivation and organization will have to take account of the contingent relationship between task, organization, and people.

Walter R. Nord

SOME PARTING THOUGHTS

The preceding paper by Morse and Lorsch indicated the direction that organizational behavior is apt to take in the future. As the controversy in this book has demonstrated, effective management of human resources requires a systems approach, a consideration of individual elements and their relationships and interdependencies. In this concluding note, several possible steps for the development of such an approach will be considered.

The traditional approach of students of management has been to focus on one set of variables—be it technology, structure, individual behavior, group behavior, or even organizational environment—and to attempt to hold constant all other variables. Such an approach will continue to have only limited success, because it neglects the true dynamics of organizations. Advocates of multidimensional approaches or systems views have often made an equally serious error by proposing that, since everything in the system is interrelated, it must all be dealt with at once. Meaningful research and guidelines for action then become impossible to develop, since so many variables are involved.

The approach suggested here assumes that the systems people are correct in saying that everything is interrelated. At the same time, it contends that some things are more interdependent than others and that some things have more powerful effects than others. This view demands a search not for variables which have merely statistically significant effects but for those which have the most powerful effects. Such a guideline permits the development of a body of knowledge based on scientifically rigorous research, conducted within a holistic framework and centered on variables which have important practical effects. It is from this systems perspective that applied behavioral science may be most productive.[1]

The application of systems thinking to organizations is not new. Some early sociologists such as Saint Simon, Comte, and Durkheim were systems oriented. In the area of organizational theory, Mary Parker Follett in 1933 (1949) noted,

> You will understand that I am simplifying when I speak of A, B, C and D adjusting themselves to one another. They are, of course, at the same time adjusting themselves to every other factor in the situation. Or it would be more accurate to say that all the factors in the situation are going through this process of reciprocal relating . . . . I am trying to express a total which shall include all the actors in a situation not as an additional total but as a relational total—a total where each part has been permeated by every other part (p. 79).

Although organizations have long been seen as complex systems, this awareness has not found its way into management action. Even the most systems-oriented people, when confronted by a problem, tend to engage in limited search behavior, to make present decisions similar to past decisions, and to focus on a relatively limited set of variables. Furthermore, people find it difficult to act in accordance with systems considerations. More than an increased cognitive appreciation of systems is needed. Successful management requires affective and behavioral changes as well; specific possible changes are discussed in the remainder of this concluding note.

NEEDED COGNITIVE CHANGES

The cognitive needs may be viewed in three parts. First, the student of management must acquire an awareness and understanding of the individual concepts or elements themselves. It is on this level that the individual readings in this book may be more useful. While topics have been separated for analytical purposes, they are actually overlapping and interwoven. Each provides a way of thinking about some elements of the system. However, as the relatedness of these separate topics reveals, an understanding of the individual elements is not

[1] Relatively recent books edited by Buckley (1968) and Emery (1969) are excellent sources for the student of organizational behavior who wishes to develop further a systems perspective.

adequate. It is at this point in our reasoning that the structure of this book becomes important. Many conflicting findings are due to effects of variables other than the ones taken as problematic. Therefore, the second cognitive need is that people be trained to think in terms of interrelationships rather than mere cause and effect. In many ways, our language, logic, and organization of knowledge by discipline rather than by problem predispose modes of thought which are not readily adapted to the idea of interrelatedness. Such books as those mentioned in footnote 1 by Emery and Buckley may be very helpful in suggesting new ways of thinking for the behavioral scientist.

Research methods. The third set of cognitive needs involves research methods. Gradually, rigorous research on complex systems is becoming more feasible. The current approaches and issues involved in organizational research were well summarized in March's (1965) *Handbook of Organizations.* The three chapters by Scott, Weick, and Cohen and Cyert all dealt with approaches to the study of organizational systems. Most researchers who have sought to study organizations as systems have done some type of field study, and the field methods discussed by Scott were generally systems oriented. However, the other two chapters presented additional means to conduct research in systems terms. Weick suggested that laboratory experimentation could incorporate many of the appropriate properties of organizational systems. He argued convincingly that, for a wide variety of problems, the control permitted by laboratory methods could be exercised without a sacrifice of the data's relevance to natural organizations. He contented that an important correspondence between laboratory situations and actual organizations can often be maintained, because, organizational problems have many extraneous and superfluous details. Weick seems to be suggesting that organizations are indeed systems but that, since some things are not highly interrelated with others, many elements can be studied without consideration of the states of the other variables. Obviously, some elements can be studied in the laboratory more realistically than others. Finally, the chapter by Cohen and Cyert suggested organizational simulation as a research approach to organizational systems. In many ways computer simulation may provide a valuable tool by which students of management may analyze the micro-components of organizations to obtain implications for the dynamics of the system as a whole.

The work of Campbell and Stanley (1963) and of Webb, Campbell, Schwartz, and Sechrest (1966) has provided two additional ways of thinking about systems research. Campbell and Stanley outlined various designs for carrying out research in naturalistic settings with some of the rigor of the experimental method. These designs, ranging from weaker, quasi-experimental to very well-controlled, point to the possibility of highly controlled research on systems. A fine example of the potential of such thinking was provided by Rosen's (1969) study of leadership. Rosen collected premeasures on a variety of dimensions of supervision and of group preferences and performance. He then experimentally studied the relationship between different leadership styles and group composition by reassigning the supervisors. Rosen's work demonstrated that such research is possible, though costly in terms of time and effort. He also found that the process by which the particular experimental changes were introduced had important effects. He concluded from the results of such an experiment within an on-going social system that the search for causal relationships among organizational variables may not be very promising. Rather, some type of systems equilibrium model, which searches for both equilibrium-disturbing and equilibrium-restoring variables, might be more fruitful. Nevertheless, his work and that of Campbell and Stanley demonstrate the possibilities of precise research in on-going systems.

The work of Webb et al. presented some creative ways in which to obtain data in on-going social situations. Data collected from archives, erosion and accretion methods, and simple observations all seem to have substantial potential for organizational research.[2] Since organizations are relatively permanent social systems and keep a substantial body of records quite amenable to research, the analyst will find many sources of data already developed and waiting to be discovered; he may need to generate few himself. The work of Webb et al. provided some interesting guides for discovery of sources.

It can be seen from the foregoing that cognitive tools for systems thinking are being developed. There is a growing body of concepts and ideas about the separate aspects of organizational behavior. Furthermore, greater attention is being devoted to the development of systems perspectives. Finally, research methods exist which permit attention to complex relationships without the sacrifice of too much control. Thus, on the cognitive level, the field of organizational behavior is becoming better equipped to deal with organizations as systems. How can individual managers translate their new awareness into action?

FEELING AND RESPONDING IN SYSTEMS TERMS

Lawrence and Lorsch (1969) argued that man is limited, in his rational capacities, to attending to about seven variables at a time. They promoted the concept of "bounded rationality" to warn the reader that they were unable to treat all the interdependencies of organizational systems at one time. They seemed to be taking a reasonable approach for exploration and perhaps even consultation. However, complex organizations may require managers to act on the basis of more than the seven variables he can process cognitively. Acting in systems terms requires more than man can do cognitively. Fortunately, man has an affective side, which processes additional information rapidly and usefully.

One of the purposes of this book has been to create affective as well as cognitive change. New feelings about organizations and human behavior are needed if an ability to operate in systems terms is to be taught. Until recently, education in organizational behavior and other subjects has tended to be almost exclusively cognitive. In addition, education is often oriented toward providing

---

[2] The suggestion of Webb et al. of employing hidden hardware is also a possibility, although it introduces certain ethical, legal, and practical problems.

answers to problems defined on only one or a very few dimensions. The focus on controversy in this book has deliberately attempted to discomfort those who are tempted to approach the field in such a simplistic manner, by highlighting the complexity of human behavior in organizations. Hopefully, the reader is uncomfortable when he hears of a simple theoretical model which purports to solve organizational problems.

In addition to questioning a strictly cognitive approach, the focus on controversy may be an aid to the development of an intuitive feeling about systems. While social science has recognized the value of a dialectical approach to knowledge, the role of dialectics in the applied area has not been thoroughly developed—with good reason. Since applied scientists are often interested in solving short-run problems, relatively closed bodies of knowledge and approaches tend to develop. In fields of study which are applications oriented, approaches which encourage "open" systems thinking, a dialectical framework may be most useful.

The preceding paragraph should not be taken to indicate a position against a problem-centered approach. In fact, since real problems inevitably are open ended, focusing on problems rather than on theories or individual concepts is an important means by which people can begin to think in systems terms. Often people are trained in a certain body of knowledge and attempt to fit the world into that orientation. Such approaches inhibit the development of means which would enable people to collect valid data about reality and act on the basis of those data rather than on a priori theory. A valuable supplement to and/or substitute for the traditional disciplinary approach to teaching applied sciences may well be problem-centered teaching. Such teaching must, however, stress the differences among problems, rather than merely foster a search for generalized solutions.

In many applied areas the case method has served this purpose. However, since case writers are human, cases are often constructed and taught by individuals who have a particular view of the world, which is limited in terms of the variables which are stressed in both the case writeup and the analysis. The data are often collected and organized through the casewriter's eyes; consequently the student is not required to search actively for data in a complex world. Especially in the behavioral area, cases and experiences in which the student is an active participant may provide the best vehicle for teaching organizational behavior. Written cases cannot induce the feelings of an on-going situation nearly as adequately as more direct experiences. The use of internship programs, where actual experience and academic training are combined may prove to be most beneficial,[3] although administrative problems may be difficult to overcome. More easily developed methods may include the use of classrooms and schools themselves as actual cases in organizational dynamics. More traditional role playing and newer types of simulations and T-groups may be

---

[3] An article by Livingston (1971), "Myth of the Well-Educated Manager" questions whether important managerial skills can be acquired in the normal classroom. How much exposure to organizations and managing people is needed to maximally benefit from management training?

useful. All types of experiences in other subject areas can facilitate the learning of orgnaizational behavior if time and encouragement are provided to focus on issues of possible relevance.

In addition, Vaill (1969) has outlined a valuable supplement to the case method. He developed a data bank containing information required for analysis of a case. The data were not structured in the normal manner of a case but rather were stored in a computer. Each piece of information could be purchased at a price calculated to represent the cost of collecting such data. The students could buy information up to the limits of a budget, which was not large enough to permit purchase of all the data. Vaill noted this approach made students more aware of the utility of planning, of theories or models as guides, of the need to determine the relevance of data, and of the variety of ways to diagnose a social system.

A systems view may require a reconsideration of the process by which people are taught to think. Management of organizations in the future will require an ability to deal with the many variables which comprise the organizational climate. Litwin and Stringer (1968) suggested some teaching techniques to help students to acquire this ability. Since organizational climates are composed of many stimuli which operate simultaneously, Litwin and Stringer proposed the use of technology which simulates these climatic conditions. Their solutions included multimedia, intermedia, and mixed-media approaches, which expose people simultaneously to several types of media. Intermedia technology, as described by Litwin and Stringer employs eight automatic slide projectors, three film projectors, and stereo sound under programmed control. They argued that, since lectures, discussions and film tend to create or present only discrete or sequential stimuli, they are consistent with outdated views of environments which emphasize specific or discrete qualities of stimuli. However, these older technologies are not adequate for teaching responses to situations in which the total configuration of the environment is central. New technologies which communicate along many channels at the same time may produce an emotional involvement and a realistic simulation of environments, which other teaching methods can not.

In addition to new technologies, it would seem that other eductional changes are necessary. In fact, the whole process of education, especially in applied areas, may need to be reexamined. Educational systems have been highly concerned with content while neglecting process. McLuhan's ideas as applied by Postman and Weingartner's (1969) argument merits repeating: it is the process of education, rather than the content, which produces the most learning. While the emphasis on process often is taken to mean the exclusion of content, the choice is not really "either - or." Rather, the question is one of developing a process which supports the desired learning outcomes. If modern organizations are going to demand that people have an awareness and feel for systems, clearly the process by which people are taught must parallel these needs. Particularly in the field of organizational behavior, the process of teaching must be consistent with the view of the world and the responses that are the end of the teaching.[4]

---

[4] A curious state exists in many classes in organizational behavior: Professors preach the

Postman and Weingartner's goal of making students into "open systems," which are capable of making competent responses to rapidly changing environments coincide with the needs of modern organizations as seen by Bennis and others. The approach coming to be known as organizational development (OD) may provide a means of instruction and change in which the desired complementarity of process and content exists.

ORGANIZATIONAL DEVELOPMENT: THE WAY FOR THE FUTURE?[5]

Increasingly, many of the better business schools of the country are becoming involved in OD. Although this approach is still in its infancy, some important themes can be discerned. While OD has its roots in sensitivity or laboratory training, the current practitioners are moving far beyond these basic beginnings. For example, the recent Addison-Wesley series in OD reflects the development of an action-oriented systems approach. In one of the overview volumes of this series, Bennis (1969) described OD as

... an educational strategy employing the widest possible means of experience-based behavior in order to achieve more and better organizational choices in a highly turbulent world (p. 17).

OD focuses on the organization's environment, population characteristics, work values, tasks and goals, organizational structure, and individual motivation as interdependent elements. More important than the mere recognition of the interdependence of the elements is the development of means to change organizational systems. Specialized external consultants and internal change agents are being trained in techniques of diagnosis and therapy to help organizations manage their own effectiveness and health, in a planned manner, through the application of knowledge from the behavioral sciences. True, the techniques of change employed in this area are still as much art as science. Nevertheless, ways are being found to increase the ability of organizational participants to collaborate in pursuit of organizational goals. The OD approach, seeks to improve an organization's abilities to coordinate its interdependent elements, and reduce unanticipated dysfunctional consequences which occur in attempts to coordinate effort. The aim is the development of a process by the system itself which allows it to meet its own needs.

OD is systems oriented, yet shares many important cultural values, such as an individual worth. In fact, individual growth is both a basic means and partial end of OD. Organizational development and individual growth are viewed as mutually supporting outcomes.

A salient characteristic of the OD approach is the attention it gives to the feelings of social scientists themselves as well as the feelings of participants in

---

importance of trusting subordinates. However, the professors seem unable to trust their students.

[5] I owe much of my knowledge and enthusiasm for this approach to Sam Culbert and Robert Tannenbaum of UCLA.

social systems. Clearly, attention to feelings and personal growth are a vital element in applied sciences because they are not value free. The problems studied, the data collected, and the conclusions drawn all reflect the feelings and the psychological needs of the scientist. The decisions managers make as to which conclusions are useful are similarly influenced by personal needs. Since intellectual and affective changes are interdependent, any science has an important affective component. Butterfield (1957), one of the leading scholars of the history of science, has noted that the great discoveries in science have been related to changes in the feelings of people. Writing about the development of science between 1300 and 1800, Butterfield commented

It would appear that the most fundamental changes in outlook, the most remarkable turns in the current intellectual fashion may be referable in the last resort to an alteration of men's feelings for things, an alteration at once so subtle and so generally pervasive that it cannot be attributed to any particular writers or any influence of academic thought as such . . . Subtle changes like this—the result not of any book but of the new texture of experience in a new age—are apparent behind the story of the scientific revolution, a revolution which some have tried to explain by a change in man's feelings for matter itself (p. 130).

Perhaps the great discoveries in organizational behavior await similar changes in men's feelings about organizations. It is the editor's hope that, after exploring the issues raised in this book, the reader feels differently about organizations and that these new feelings will be helpful in the application of knowledge to manage organizations.

REFERENCES

Bennis, W. G. *Organizational Development: Its Nature, Origins, and Prospects.* Reading, Mass.: Addison-Wesley, 1969.

Buckley, W., ed., *Modern Systems Research for the Behavioral Scientist.* Chicago: Aldine Publishing Company, 1969.

Butterfield, H. *The Origins of Modern Science 1300-1800.* rev. ed. New York: The Free Press, 1957.

Campbell, D. T., and Stanley, J. C. "Experimental and Quasi-Experimental Designs for Research." In N. L. Gage, ed., *Handbook of Research on Teaching.* Chicago: Rand McNally & Co., 1963. pp. 171-246.

Emery, F. E. *Systems Thinking.* Middlesex, England: Penguin, 1969.

Foliett, M. P. *Freedom and Co-ordination.* L. Urwick, ed. London: Management Publications Trust, 1949.

Lawrence, P., and Lorsch, J. *Developing Organizations: Diagnosis and Action.* Reading, Mass.: Addison-Wesley, 1969.

Litwin, G. H., and Stringer, R. A. *Motivation and Organizational Climate.* Boston: Harvard University Graduate School of Business, 1968.

Livingston, J. S. Myth of the Well-Educated Manager. *Harvard Business Review* 49, (Jan.-Feb., 1971), 79-89.

March, J. G., ed., *Handbook of Organizations.* Chicago: Rand McNally & Co., 1965.

Postman, N., and Weingartner, C. *Teaching as a Subversive Activity*. New York: The Delacorte Press, 1969.

Rosen, N. A. *Leadership Change and Work-Group Dynamics: An Experiment*. Ithaca, N.Y.: Cornell University Press, 1969.

Vaill, P.B. "An Approach to Social Systems Diagnosis: The Data Bank." Paper presented at the meeting of the American Psychological Association, Sept., 1969.

Webb, E. J., Campbell, D. T., Schwartz, R. D., and Sechrest, L. *Unobtrusive Measures: Nonreactive Research in the Social Sciences*. Chicago: Rand McNally & Co., 1966.